M000158360

LECTURES
on the
PHILOSOPHY
of
RELIGION

Lectures on the Philosophy of Religion
One-Volume Edition: The Lectures of 1827

Hegel's *Lectures on the Philosophy of Religion* represent the final and in some ways the decisive element of his entire philosophical system. In Peter C. Hodgson's masterly three-volume edition, being reissued in the Hegel Lectures Series, from which this volume is extracted, the structural integrity of the lectures—delivered in 1821, 1824, 1827, and 1831—is established for the first time in an English critical edition based on a complete re-editing of the German sources by Walter Jaeschke. This one-volume edition presents the full text and footnotes of the 1827 lectures, making the work available in a convenient form for study.

Of the lectures that can be fully reconstructed, those of 1827 are the clearest, most mature, and most accessible to nonspecialists. In them, readers will find Hegel engaged in lively debates and important refinements of his treatment of the concept of religion, the Oriental religions and Judaism, Christology, the Trinity, the God-world relationship, and many other topics.

This edition contains an editorial introduction, critical annotations on the text and tables, bibliography, and glossary from the complete edition. The English translation has been prepared by a team of eminent Hegel scholars: Robert F. Brown, Peter C. Hodgson, and J. Michael Stewart, with the assistance of H. S. Harris.

GEORG WILHELM FRIEDRICH HEGEL

LECTURES ON THE PHILOSOPHY OF RELIGION

ONE-VOLUME EDITION

THE LECTURES OF 1827

Edited by

PETER C. HODGSON

Translated by

R. F. BROWN, P. C. HODGSON, and J. M. STEWART
with the assistance of
H. S. HARRIS

CLARENDON PRESS · OXFORD

OXFORD

UNIVERSITY PRESS

Great Clarendon Street, Oxford OX2 6DP
Oxford University Press is a department of the University of Oxford.
It furthers the University's objective of excellence in research, scholarship,
and education by publishing worldwide in

Oxford New York

Auckland Cape Town Dar es Salaam Hong Kong Karachi
Kuala Lumpur Madrid Melbourne Mexico City Nairobi
New Delhi Shanghai Taipei Toronto

With offces in

Argentina Austria Brazil Chile Czech Republic France Greece
Guatemala Hungary Italy Japan Poland Portugal Singapore
South Korea Switzerland Thailand Turkey Ukraine Vietnam

Oxford is a registered trade mark of Oxford University Press
in the UK and in certain other countries

Published in the United States
by Oxford University Press Inc., New York

This book is an abridgment of the 3-volume edition published first by the
University of California Press (1984, 1985, 1987) and then by
Oxford University Press (2007), which is a translation of *Vorlesungen über die
Philosophie der Religion*, edited by Walter Jaeschke (*G. W. F. Hegel Vorlesungen:
Ausgewählte Nachschriften und Manuskripte*, vols. 3–5),
copyright © 1983, 1984, 1985 by Felix Meiner Verlag GmbH, Hamburg

The English edition has been prepared with financial support from the Program
for Translations of the National Endowment for the Humanities, the Fritz
Thyssen Stiftung of Cologne, and the Vanderbilt University Research Council

© Peter C. Hodgson 2006

The moral rights of the author have been asserted
Database right Oxford University Press (maker)

First published by Oxford University Press 2006

British Library Cataloguing in Publication Data

Data available

Library of Congress Cataloguing in Publication Data

Data available

Prelims typeset by SPI Publisher Services, Pondicherry, India
Printed in Great Britain
on acid-free paper by
Biddles Ltd., King's Lynn

ISBN 0–19–928352–4   978–0–19–928352–1

1 3 5 7 9 10 8 6 4 2

CONTENTS

APPENDIXES

PREFACE

This one-volume abridged edition of Hegel's *Lectures on the Philosophy of Religion* is intended for student and classroom use as well as for a wider readership. It reprints, from the three-volume critical edition (originally published by the University of California Press, now reissued by Oxford), the complete text of Hegel's lectures delivered in 1827. Of the three series of lectures on philosophy of religion that presently can be reconstructed, those of 1827 are the latest, the most clearly organized, and the most accessible to nonspecialists. Here for the first time a complete version of Hegel's lectures on this topic is made available in a single volume and in a form corresponding to Hegel's original presentation.

The editor wishes to express his appreciation to Walter Jaeschke, editor of the new German edition, to the cotranslators, Robert F. Brown and J. M. Stewart, for their assistance in preparing this volume, and to the Translations Program of the National Endowment for the Humanities for its continued support. The primary translation responsibility for the 1827 text has been that of Brown, while Stewart has done much of the work on the footnotes and checked the whole, as has H. S. Harris. The editor has prepared a new introduction for this edition.

ABBREVIATIONS, SIGNS, AND SYMBOLS

SIGNS AND SYMBOLS

[. . .]   = Editorial insertions in the text.

⌐ . . . ⌐   = Passages in the main text that correspond to footnoted variant readings. These symbols are used only in the case of textual variants, which offer a different version of the designated passage, usually from a different source, not textual additions, which occur at the point marked by the note number in the main text. Normally the variant is placed in the notes at the end of the parallel in the main text; exceptions are noted.

¹ ² ³ etc.   = Footnotes containing (a) textual variants, additions, and deletions; (b) special materials from *W* and *L*, both variant readings and additions; (c) editorial annotations. The type of note is designated by an initial italicized editorial phrase in each instance. Notes are at the bottoms of the pages and are numbered consecutively through each text unit.

[*Ed.*]   = Editorial annotations in the footnotes; materials following this symbol are editorial.

62 | = Page numbers of the German edition, on the outer margins with page breaks marked by vertical slash in text. The German edition is *Vorlesungen über die Philosophie der Religion*. Edited by Walter Jaeschke. Hamburg, 1983–1985. The page numbers for the *Introduction* and *The Concept of Religion* are from

Part 1, *Einleitung, Der Begriff der Religion*; for *Determinate Religion*, from Part 2, *Bestimmte Religion*; for *The Consummate Religion*, from Part 3, *Die vollendete Religion*. (These are published as vols. 3–5 of *G. W. F. Hegel Vorlesungen: Ausgewählte Nachschriften und Manuskripte.*)

PUBLISHED SOURCES

W W$_1$ W$_2$ = *Werke.* Complete edition edited by an Association of Friends. Vols. 11–12 contain *Vorlesungen über die Philosophie der Religion.* 1st ed., edited by Philipp Marheineke (Berlin, 1832) (W$_1$); 2d ed., edited by Philipp Marheineke and Bruno Bauer (Berlin, 1840) (W$_2$). When no subscript is used, the reference is to both editions.

L = *Vorlesungen über die Philosophie der Religion.* Edited by Georg Lasson. 2 vols. in 4 parts. Leipzig, 1925–1929 (reprint, Hamburg, 1966).

UNPUBLISHED SOURCES

Ms. = Hegel's lecture manuscript of 1821
G = Griesheim transcript of the 1824 lectures
An = Anonymous transcript of the 1827 lectures
B = Boerner transcript of the 1827 lectures
Hu = Hube transcript of the 1827 lectures

SPECIAL MATERIALS IN W AND L

These are given in parentheses and identify the no-longer-extant sources of the variant readings and additions making up the special materials found in W and L.

(MiscP)   = Miscellaneous papers in Hegel's own hand
(1827?)   = Unverified transcripts of the 1827 lectures
(1831)   = Transcripts of the 1831 lectures
(HgG)   = Notes by Hegel in the copy of G used by W_1 and W_2
(Ed)   = Editorial passages in W_1 and W_2
(Var)   = Variant readings in W or L

FREQUENTLY CITED WORKS
BY HEGEL

Werke = *Werke.* Complete edition edited by an Association of Friends. 18 vols. Berlin, 1832 ff. Some volumes issued in second editions.

GW = *Gesammelte Werke.* Edited by the Academy of Sciences of Rhineland–Westphalia in association with the Deutsche Forschungsgemeinschaft. 40 vols. projected. Hamburg, 1968 ff.

Berliner Schriften = *Berliner Schriften 1818–1831.* Edited by J. Hoffmeister. Hamburg, 1956.

Encyclopedia (1817, 1830) = *Encyclopedia of the Philosophical Sciences.* Translated from the 3d German ed., with additions based on student transcripts and lecture manuscripts, by W. Wallace and A. V. Miller. 3 vols. Oxford, 1892 (reprint 1975), 1970, 1971. *Enzyklopädie der philosophischen Wissenschaften im Grundrisse.* 1st ed. Heidelberg, 1817: forthcoming in *GW*, vol. 13. 3d ed., Berlin, 1830: *Werke,* vols. 6–7 (containing additions based on student transcripts and lecture manuscripts); forthcoming in *GW*, vol. 19. 6th ed., based on the 3d ed. without additions, edited by F. Nicolin and O. Pöggeler, Hamburg, 1959. Citations given by section numbers in the 1817 or 1830 editions.

History of = *Lectures on the History of Philosophy.*
Philosophy   Translated from the 2d German ed. (1840)
by E. S. Haldane and F. H. Simson. 3 vols.
London, 1892. *Vorlesungen über die Geschichte der Philosophie.* Edited by C. L.
Michelet. 1st ed., Berlin, 1833: *Werke,*
vols. 13–15. Because of variations between
the two German editions, the English translation often does not correspond exactly to
the cited German texts. A new German edition is being prepared by P. Garniron and
W. Jaeschke, and a corresponding English
translation by R. F. Brown and J. M.
Stewart.

Phenomenology = *Phenomenology of Spirit.* Translated by
of Spirit   A. V. Miller. Oxford, 1977. *Phänomeno-
logie des Geistes.* Bamberg and Würzburg,
1807. *GW,* vol. 9 (edited by W. Bonsiepen
and R. Heede).

Philosophy of = *Lectures on the Philosophy of World
World History   History.*
Sibree ed. = *The Philosophy of History.* Translated
from the 2d German ed. (1840) by J. Sibree. Revised edition. New York, 1900.

Nisbet ed. = *Lectures on the Philosophy of World
History: Introduction: Reason in History.*
Translated from vol. 1 of *Vorlesungen über
die Philosophie der Weltgeschichte* (ed.
Hoffmeister) by H. B. Nisbet, with an introduction by Duncan Forbes. Cambridge,
1975.

*Vorlesungen über die Philosophie der Welt-
geschichte.*
Hoffmeister ed. = Vol. 1, *Die Vernunft in der Geschichte.* Edited by Johannes Hoffmeister. Hamburg,
1955.

Lasson ed. = Vol. 2, *Die orientalische Welt*. Vol. 3, *Die griechische und die römische Welt*. Vol. 4, *Die germanische Welt*. Edited by Georg Lasson. 2d ed. Hamburg, 1923. Vols. 1–4 are paginated cumulatively. Since vols. 2–4 have not been translated, corresponding references from the Sibree translation of the 1840 ed. are cited when possible.

Science of Logic = *Science of Logic*. Translated by A. V. Miller. London, 1969. *Wissenschaft der Logik*. Vol. 1, *Die objektive Logik*. Nuremberg, 1812–13. *GW*, vol. 11 (edited by F. Hogemann and W. Jaeschke). Vol. 2, *Die subjektive Logik*. Nuremberg, 1816. *GW*, vol. 12 (edited by F. Hogemann and W. Jaeschke). 2d ed. of vol. 1, Book 1, *Die Lehre vom Sein*. Berlin, 1832. Forthcoming in *GW*, vol. 20 (edited by F. Hogemann and W. Jaeschke). The English translation uses the 2d ed. of vol. 1, Book 1, hence there is not an exact correspondence between it and *GW*, vol. 11, Book 1.

(Frequently cited works by other authors are included in the Bibliography of Sources at the back of the volume.)

INTRODUCTION

1. Hegel's Four Series of Lectures on the Philosophy of Religion

From the beginning of his academic career at the University of Jena in 1801, Hegel lectured frequently on a broad range of topics—philosophical encyclopedia, logic and metaphysics, the philosophies of nature, art, and world history, anthropology and psychology, natural law and political science, and the history of philosophy. But it was only after some twenty years, in the summer semester of 1821 at the University of Berlin, that Hegel lectured for the first time on the philosophy of religion—lectures that he was to repeat on three occasions, in 1824, 1827, and 1831, but which he himself never published.

Hegel's delay in addressing the topic of religion was not a sign of lack of interest. On the contrary, there was no topic in which he had a deeper and more abiding concern, as evidenced from his days as a theological student in Tübingen through the years spent in Jena and Nuremberg. As headmaster at the Gymnasium in Nuremberg he gave religious instruction to the students, but when he returned in 1816 to a university post at Heidelberg, which he held until 1818, he did not lecture either on philosophy of religion or on theology, nor did he during the first years in Berlin.

Philosophy of religion was in fact a relatively novel topic at the beginning of the nineteenth century. Insofar as philosophy dealt with God, it was customarily in the form of rational theology, as a special branch of metaphysics. What led Hegel to address himself to this new discipline was very likely the impending publication of a major work in dogmatics by his colleague and rival on the theological faculty in Berlin, Friedrich Schleiermacher. Hegel had reason to believe that he would have serious reservations about Schleiermacher's theological position and its implications for the projected union between the Lutheran and Reformed Churches of Prussia. Hegel's decision to lecture on the philosophy of religion was evidently taken rather quickly, and the lecture manuscript was hurriedly composed just before and during the course of the lectures. After the first volume of Schleiermacher's *Glaubenslehre* had appeared in June 1821, Hegel indicated his negative attitude toward it both in private correspondence and in a forthright preface he wrote to a work by H. W. F. Hinrichs published in 1822.[1]

According to faculty records as well as the lecture manuscript itself, Hegel's first series of lectures on the philosophy of religion lasted from 30 April to 25 August 1821—four hours per week for seventeen weeks—and had 49 auditors. The 1824 series lasted from 26 April to 26 August, and the number in the class rose to 63. By 1827, when the course lasted from 7 May to 10 August, Hegel was lecturing to 119 students, which made this one of his best-attended series of lectures. The last offering was in the summer of 1831, completed less than three months before Hegel's unexpected death at the age of 61 on 14 November 1831. Hegel by no means simply repeated the lectures on subsequent occasions. To the contrary, he revised them so drastically that he was able to use his original lecture manuscript only to a limited extent in 1824 (primarily on the basis of extensive marginal additions and revisions) and scarcely at all in 1827 and 1831. Each new series of lectures was based on a revised auditor's transcription of the preceding series as well as on additional miscellaneous papers, but especially in the later years much of the actual presentation must have been extemporaneous. The changes were so extensive that it would not be unfair to say that the only constant factor remained the main division into three

1. For details see Richard Crouter, "Hegel and Schleiermacher at Berlin: A Many-sided Debate," *Journal of the American Academy of Religion* 48 (March 1980): 19–43; Walter Jaeschke, "Paralipomena Hegeliana zur Wirkungsgeschichte Schleiermachers," in *Internationaler Schleiermacher-Kongress Berlin 1984*, ed. Kurt-Victor Selge, Schleiermacher-Archiv, vol. 1 (Berlin and New York, 1985), pp. 1157–1169; and the Editorial Introduction to the unabridged ed., Vol. 1:2–4.

parts, the *Concept of Religion, Determinate Religion,* and *Consummate Religion.*

What accounts for changes of this magnitude? Four factors may be distinguished. There was, in the first place, an attempt to work out more adequately the science of philosophy of religion. As we have indicated, this was a novel discipline at the beginning of the nineteenth century. Although Hegel had had a long, abiding, and deep interest in religion, he faced for the first time in 1821 the task of adumbrating in a systematic way the philosophical treatment of religion; and philosophy of religion was the last of the major disciplines for which he achieved a comprehensive framework of interpretation. Hence there was much more fluidity in his lectures on this subject than in those on others from the Berlin period. Although Hegel's basic philosophical conception of *religion* did not radically change during this eleven-year period, his conception of the *philosophy of religion* underwent significant revisions in both structure and content. This accounts in large measure for the important changes in the structure of Part I of the lectures, which treat the *Concept of Religion.*

In the second place, there was a continual assimilation of new materials and an enrichment and variation in the content of the lectures. This was especially the case in Part II, *Determinate Religion,* where Hegel treated the non-Christian religions, and where his analyses of primitive religion, the Asian religions, and Judaism in particular were shaped and refined by new literature and new insights.

In the third place, there was the influence of concurrent lectures on other disciplines. The philosophy-of-religion lectures were always delivered in the summer semester conjointly with those on logic and metaphysics, and the fact that Hegel was addressing the two topics simultaneously reinforced the substantive connection between them and helped to account for the increasingly logical structure assumed by the lectures on religion. Likewise, the lectures on the history of philosophy helped to shape Hegel's treatment of the *Concept of Religion* (especially the relation between religion and philosophy); those on the philosophy of world history and art contributed to the enrichment of Part II; while lectures on the proofs of the existence of God helped to refine his analysis of the proofs in the 1827 and 1831 philosophy-of-religion lectures.

Finally, and for our purposes most important, Hegel was increasingly engaged in disputes with contemporary theology and with criticisms of his own work. Thus each of the lecture series had a distinctive polemical or argumentative frame of reference, and these intellectual *Sitze im Leben* more than anything else shaped the nuances and themes that Hegel chose to highlight in his successive presentations. We shall discuss this matter specifically in Sec. 3 below. For the moment we simply note that previous editions of the lectures, because they conflated the sources into a single, editorially constructed text, inevitably obscured the differences that alone could provide a valid basis for interpretative judgments of Hegel's argument in specific contexts.

In the absence of an adequate text, there has been no firm basis on which to refute two faulty interpretations of the evident shifts in Hegel's treatment of religion during the Berlin period which became and have remained popular. The first was an attempt to discern either a leftward or a rightward drift to his thought, depending upon which passages were quoted out of context from the editions produced by Marheineke and Bauer (in 1832 and 1840). However, left- and right-wing interpretations of religion would have been alien to Hegel's central intention of overcoming unproductive antitheses between tradition and criticism, faith and knowledge, revelation and reason, finite and infinite, theism and atheism. In the second place, it has sometimes been said (on the basis of Lasson's edition of the 1920s [see Sec. 2 below]) that an initially "immature" conception of religion in the original manuscript was worked out with greater "maturity" in later years; or, conversely, that initially fresh and creative insights gave way to an increasing "scholasticism of the concept" during Hegel's latter days in Berlin. While, as we shall argue below, the later lectures undoubtedly presented the material with greater clarity, precision, and structural maturity, it is misleading to suggest that the original manuscript was philosophically "immature"—or that Hegel's creative powers were exhausted by it. We hope that the new edition, which separates and reconstructs the four series of lectures on the basis of a complete reediting of the sources, will lay these and other misconceptions to rest.

The new edition has at the same time the disadvantage of assuming quite massive proportions just because no textual material has been omitted and each of the first three lectures has been reconstructed as completely as possible. From the point of view of classroom and student use, the three large volumes of this edition are impractical, and a paperback version of the same would still be quite expensive. Yet any attempt at an editorial abridgment of the text would have reintroduced many of the old problems. Why not, then, allow *Hegel* to provide the shorter version needed for a one-volume edition by selecting one of his four lecture series and reproducing it in full? Once it became clear that this was the best of the available options, the choice fell between the 1824 and 1827 lectures. The lecture manuscript of 1821 is for a variety of reasons not suitable for such purposes. The text of the 1831 lectures cannot be reconstructed from the presently available sources (only an outline is attainable from Strauss's excerpts [see Sec. 2 below]). Our text for 1824 is more secure than that of 1827 since it is based directly on an extant and highly reliable source. Moreover, the 1824 lectures play a crucial and fascinating mediating role between Hegel's first attempts in the manuscript of 1821 and the later lectures. But in 1824, Hegel had not yet attained the clarity and precision of expression that he did later, and only the third of the three main parts of the lectures, the *Consummate Religion,* achieved definitive structural resolution at this time. Without question the 1827 text is more accessible to nonspecialists than the other lectures, and it was substantially revised in 1831 only in the second part, *Determinate Religion.* Our 1827 text also has the advantage of brevity in relation to 1824 (the summer semester was some three weeks shorter), and it is more readable. Once it was evident that the 1827 lectures could in fact be successfully reconstructed from the presently available sources (see Sec. 2 below), they became the text of choice for the one-volume edition.

A distinct disadvantage of this procedure, of course, is that Hegel's development during the eleven years of his Berlin lectures cannot be traced, and the wealth of material from 1821 and 1824 which is not repeated in 1827 cannot be obtained from the present edition. (However, most of the *Werke* passages attributable to the 1831 lectures are footnoted in relation to corresponding 1827 text, and these passages are retained in the abridgment. Concerning the *Werke* see below, Sec. 2.) The unabridged edition remains available for those who have need of it. From it we have reproduced at the back of this volume the tables providing comparative analyses of the structure of the texts for each of the four lecture series. Some references to this comparison are given in the footnotes to the 1827 text, and these will prove intelligible to readers of this volume who consult the tables. The text and footnotes for 1827 in the one-volume edition are identical with those in the unabridged edition, except that cross-references in the footnotes to other lectures have been revised or deleted.

We also reproduce from the unabridged edition the Bibliography of Sources for Hegel's Philosophy of Religion and the German-English Glossary. The Bibliography lists a large number of works upon which Hegel drew for these lectures, the majority of which were used primarily or exclusively for *Determinate Religion*.[2] An analysis of these sources indicates that Hegel had an astonishing mastery of the available literature on the history of world religions.[3] The Glossary contains a selection of frequently used and/or technical Hegelian terms, especially those posing problems in translation.[4] The index serves partially as an English-German glossary.

2. The 1827 lectures contain references to many but not to all of the works listed in the Bibliography; we have, however, reproduced the latter in unabridged form for this edition. The Bibliography provides complete data on the works cited, often in short form, in the editorial footnotes; similar information on frequently cited works by Hegel is given at the beginning of the volume.

3. For such an analysis, see the unabridged ed., Vol. 2:3–12.

4. For a discussion of the translation principles guiding this edition, see the unabridged ed., Vol. 1:52–58, and Vol. 3:3, 8–9. Briefly: to achieve uniformity in the translation of key terms, we have worked from a common glossary, which was gradually elaborated as the project advanced; we have attempted not to sacrifice precision for the sake of fluency and have discovered that the more precisely Hegel's thought is rendered, the more intelligible it generally becomes; we have also attempted to preserve a sense of the spoken word and of Hegel's oral style; we have used a "down" style and have avoided capitalizing Hegel's technical terminology;

2. Sources and Editions of the Philosophy-of-Religion Lectures[5]

The sources may be divided into three groups: (a) papers in Hegel's own handwriting, used for preparation of the lectures; (b) student transcripts or notebooks of the lectures as delivered; (c) previous editions, which preserve sources that otherwise are no longer available.

Hegel's own lecture manuscript (*Ms.*), composed during the spring and summer of 1821, is the primary document in the first category. It was deposited in the Royal Library of Berlin and is now located in the Staatsbibliothek Preussischer Kulturbesitz (West Berlin), where it has survived intact. The manuscript contains extensive marginal passages consisting of revisions and additions to the original text; these together with Hegel's obscure handwriting and his frequent abbreviations (both of words and of sentences) render the decipherment of this text exceedingly difficult. A second handwritten source, one that unfortunately is no longer in existence, was made up of a large collection of miscellaneous drafts and notes, varying in their degree of completion, which were used primarily in relation to the post-1821 lectures. The original editors drew upon these miscellaneous papers for the second *Werke* edition of 1840 (discussed below); such passages can be identified by text-critical means and are footnoted in relation to corresponding or similar passages in our text of the 1824 and 1827 lectures (abbreviated *MiscP*).

The second major source consists of auditors' transcripts or notebooks (*Nachschriften*) of the lectures as delivered. Hegel's slow and repetitious style of delivery made it possible to take virtually verbatim notes. Frequently students worked together, combining

---

we have used generic terms for human beings whenever appropriate but have refrained from attempting to make Hegel's references to God sex-inclusive. As to the translation of specific terms, it should be noted in particular that *Sein* is translated as "being," *Seiende* as "actual being" (God) or "subsisting being" (finite entities), *seiend* as "having being" or "subsisting," and *Dasein* as "existence" or "determinate being," and that when the verb *sein* is predicated of God, we have generally translated as "is" rather than "exists" in order to avoid the misimpression that God "exists" in the manner of worldly objects.

5. For a detailed discussion, see the unabridged ed., Vol. 1:8–33.

their notes into a carefully rewritten fair copy. Altogether, twenty-one transcripts of the philosophy-of-religion lectures are known to have existed (some as verbatim notes, others as fair copies, and yet others as freely edited and rewritten). Of these, eight have survived to the present—five for the 1824 lectures and three for 1827. One of the lost transcripts of the 1821 lectures, made by Leopold von Henning, was extensively used in the preparation of the second edition of the *Werke,* and passages from it can be identified and footnoted in relation to the lecture manuscript. The four transcripts of the 1831 lectures used by the *Werke* editors have also been lost, but again these passages can be recovered and footnoted in relation to our 1827 text. David Friedrich Strauss's forty-nine pages of excerpts from an unidentified transcript of the 1831 lectures were recently rediscovered and are printed as an appendix to our unabridged edition.

Finally, the three previous published editions of the lectures take on the character of a source for original materials that have since been lost. The first edition was brought out by Philipp Marheineke within a year of Hegel's death, in 1832, as volumes 11 and 12 of the *Werke* (W_1), a posthumous edition of Hegel's complete works published by an Association of Friends of the Deceased. Marheineke relied primarily on a few of the best auditors' transcripts of the 1824, 1827, and 1831 lectures, and his edition achieved a greater degree of homogeneity than the later ones, although an abundance of material was omitted (especially from Hegel's own hand). In response to criticisms of these omissions as well as apparent ambiguities in the text, a second edition (W_2) was prepared by Bruno Bauer but published under Marheineke's name in 1840. Now extensive use was made of Hegel's own handwritten materials—the lecture manuscript of 1821 and the miscellaneous papers—as well as of Henning's transcript of the first lecture series and of additional transcripts for the later lectures. By attempting to insert materials from the quite differently conceived 1821 lectures into the structural fabric of the later lectures, Bauer introduced marked tensions that disrupt Hegel's train of thought and often make it appear to be illogical, inconsistent, and, worst of all, ambivalent—the very problem that the new edition was intended to overcome. Nevertheless, W_2 is much richer in content than W_1, and it is our most valuable source for original materials that have now been lost—especially the Henning transcript and the miscellaneous papers. Both W_1 and W_2 serve as sources for the lost 1831 transcripts, and they both provide confirmation and supplementation of the 1827 text as reconstructed from Lasson.

Georg Lasson (L) attempted to produce the first critical edition of the philosophy-of-religion lectures in 1925–1929. He distinguished Hegel's lecture manuscript, printing it in special type and using it as the structural basis for the entire work—a plan that had disastrous consequences for Parts I and II of the lectures. He combined the transcripts of the 1824 and 1827 lectures into an editorially constructed train of thought, fragmenting the materials to a much greater degree than the *Werke* and providing only a brief and unreliable apparatus for their identification. The main loss of original source materials occurred before Lasson set to work—Henning's transcript of the 1821 lectures, the miscellaneous papers, and all of the transcripts of the 1827 and 1831 lectures used by the *Werke* editors. But Lasson was fortunate enough to have discovered two new transcripts for 1827, comparable in quality to those used by the earlier editors. The principal loss that has occurred since Lasson is precisely the transcripts he used for 1827, which cannot be replaced by those presently available to us.

Thus for our edition of the 1827 lectures, Lasson takes on the character of a source, although 1827 text could be extracted from his editorial conflation only by a painstaking process of source criticism. Lasson's two 1827 sources were discovered in the Stadtbibliothek of Königsberg (and were later destroyed in the bombing of 1945). One of these was an anonymous fair copy, the other a verbatim transcript made by Johann Eduard Erdmann. Lasson's 1827 text agrees to an astonishing extent with that of the *Werke*—so much so, in fact, that there are good reasons for suspecting that his anonymous fair copy is identical with the Meyer transcript used in the preparation of both editions of the *Werke*. If so, there must have been two copies of Meyer, since the copy used by W_1 included notes in Hegel's hand made in preparation for the 1831 lectures, whereas the copy available to Lasson lacked such notes.

In recent years three additional transcripts of the 1827 lectures have been discovered—another anonymous now in private possession (abbreviated *An*), a verbatim transcript by Ignacy Boerner located in Warsaw (*B*), and a fair copy, stylistically awkward but rich in content, by Joseph Hube, in Cracow (*Hu*). None of these is remotely comparable to the 1827 text contained in W or L, and thus they cannot be used as the basis of a new edition. But they serve an exceedingly valuable function in terms of identifying and verifying the 1827 text that we have extracted from L. As we have said, L frequently conflated his 1824 and 1827 sources. But since we possess all the 1824 sources available to L, the 1824 text could be subtracted and the remainder should be 1827 material. This material could then be checked, properly ordered, and when necessary corrected or supplemented by *An, B,* and *Hu*. Passages for which there is no support in the extant sources have been removed from the main text of L to the footnotes. Other passages have been added to the main text from our sources at points where L omitted material in order to avoid repetitions between 1824 and 1827 text, or where in the process of combining the 1824 and 1827 series L found 1827 material that seemed to resist integration. At still other points, L's text has been corrected when one or another of the extant sources offers a more plausible reading. Thus our 1827 text is not simply a reproduction of L but an edited version based on the presently available original materials. The resulting text reads smoothly and cohesively, and we believe it can be used with confidence as a reliable indication of the content of the 1827 lectures.

The *Werke* was not used as the basis for reconstructing the 1827 text because the editors of W, unlike L, also had available to them source material from 1831 as well as the miscellaneous papers. Very likely some of this material was conflated with 1827 text, and it could not be positively identified (in the way that 1824 material conflated by L with 1827 could be) since the originals have been lost. However, our reconstructed 1827 text from L has been compared from beginning to end with W_1 and W_2, and any significant divergences other than mere variant readings are indicated in the footnotes.[6]

Passages in the main text which correspond to footnoted variant readings (whether from W or L or from one of the extant sources) are marked by tildes (˜ . . . ˜), while footnoted additions occur at the point in the main text marked by the note number. Section headings are the responsibility of the German and English editors, although their wording derives in part from suggestions contained in the transcripts. It is unlikely that Hegel himself dictated headings, but the 1827 lectures, unlike those of 1824, are structured in a rigorously systematic fashion, and there can be no doubt about their actual course. Further confirmation is provided by the dates found in the margins of B and, in a few cases, also of Hu; these have been reproduced in our footnotes.

3. The Structure, Context, and Distinctive Themes of the Lectures in Brief

The categorial scheme of Hegel's logic serves as the "deep structure" out of which his interpretation of various domains of human experience and thought is generated. In this respect, Alan White (following Klaus Hartmann) is correct in stating that Hegel's logic is a *transcendental ontology*.[7] "To say that [it] is *ontological* is to say that it is a doctrine of categories rather than of supersensible entities; . . . to say that it is *transcendental* is to say that it presents conditions of possibility of experience, and that the conditions are discovered through philosophical reflection." But it is a *Hegelian* as opposed to a Kantian transcendental ontology, for it grounds

---

6. Because we have reconstructed the 1827 text and provide in the footnotes recoverable passages from the 1831 lectures, our one-volume edition approximates in certain respects the first edition of the *Werke*. This is not inappropriate since W_1 is the most structurally coherent of all the previous editions, being based primarily on transcripts of Hegel's later lectures. W_1 does, however, conflate 1824 materials with those from 1827 and 1831, and in Part II of the lectures, *Determinate Religion*, it follows the twofold division of 1824 rather than the triadic structure of 1827 or 1831.

7. Alan White, *Absolute Knowledge: Hegel and the Problem of Metaphysics* (Athens, Ohio, 1983), pp. 3–6.

more than empirical, sense-based knowledge. It makes the claim to ground both theoretical knowledge (reflection upon the conditions of possibility for sensible knowledge) and practical knowledge (reflection upon the conditions of possibility for ethical action), and it attempts to interrelate the theoretical and the practical in ways that Kant failed to do. It is reflection *upon* reflection, for which Hegel used the term "speculative" in order to distinguish his thought from the merely "reflective" philosophy of Kant and other Enlightenment thinkers. Speculative philosophy also grounds aesthetic, religious, and historical experience. In grounding religious experience, it does not produce a theology in the traditional, "metaphysical" sense of the study of supersensible entities. It is a "postmetaphysical" theology if metaphysics is taken to mean "onto-theo-logy."[8] Hegel's God is not a supersensible entity, a "supreme being," but rather the *ultimate* condition of possibility for the *totality* of experience and for religious experience in particular, the experience of the "religious relationship" of finite and infinite. In this sense, the philosophical first principle and the theological first principle are one and the same: God = absolute idea. But to say that Hegel's God is not a supersensible entity is not to say that God is not actual (*wirklich*). God *is* actual, "absolute actuality" (*absolute Wirklichkeit*), "actual being in and for itself" (*das Anundfürsichseiende*)—but only in and through worldly reality, not as a separated, supersensible entity. Apart from the world, God's actuality remains abstract, unrealized; in and through the world, of which God is the ideal condition of possibility, God becomes concrete, living, true actuality—or absolute *spirit*. The implications of all of this for theology are enormously complex and cannot be pursued further here.

The logical deep structure is grounded in the dialectic of the syllogism, which is the basic movement of thought itself.[9] The three

8. See Martin Heidegger, "The Onto-theo-logical Constitution of Metaphysics," in *Identity and Difference,* trans. Joan Stambaugh (New York, 1969), pp. 42–74. Heidegger, however, does not regard Hegel as having moved decisively beyond onto-theo-logy; rather he is said to bring the Western metaphysical tradition to its culmination by disclosing its internal aporias.

9. See Hegel, *Encyclopedia,* §§ 181–192; *Science of Logic,* pp. 664–704 (*GW* 12:90–126).

moments, or figures, of any syllogism, according to Hegel, are: (1) universality (*Allgemeinheit*), that is, the universal substance or principle of a statement; (2) particularity (*Besonderheit*), the particular quality or determinate modification of the universal in the case at hand; (3) individuality or singularity (*Einzelheit*), the subject about which the statement makes a new predication. For example, in the syllogism

All human beings are mortal
Socrates is human
Therefore, Socrates is mortal

human beings = the universal substance (U), mortality = the particular quality (P), and Socrates = the individual subject (I). In this form of the syllogism, U is the middle or mediating term, but all syllogisms can be varied so that P and I in turn assume the middle position. In Hegel's basic philosophical ordering, P assumes the middle position so that the sequence is U-P-I.[10] Now this syllogistic structure is mirrored in every aspect of Hegel's philosophical system: in the system as a whole (logical idea, nature, spirit); in the science of logic (being [immediacy], essence [reflection], concept [subjectivity]) and its subdivisions; in the dialectics of consciousness (immediacy, differentiation, return; or identity, cleavage, reunification); in the doctrine of the Trinity (Father, Son, Spirit); and in the philosophies of nature, spirit, right, art, religion, and world history. The threefold division of the philosophy of religion reflects this logical structure (*Concept of Religion, Determinate Religion,* and *Consummate Religion*), as do the subdivisions of each of these main parts. The table found in the Appendix on p. 492 illustrates some of these correlations. For the subdivisions of the three parts of the philosophy of religion, the table gives only the final or mature version (although in the case of Part II, *Determinate Religion,* there is no final resolution and both 1827 and 1831 versions are indicated).

10. For a fuller discussion, see the editor's chapter on Hegel in *Nineteenth Century Religious Thought in the West,* ed. Ninian Smart et al., vol. 1 (Cambridge, 1985), pp. 81–86.

It must be stressed, however, that Hegel's interpretations of the various domains of human experience, while generated out of his logical deep structure, are by no means simply read off from that structure. Rather, experience as it actually presents itself in the realms of history, art, religion, ethics, politics, anthropology and psychology, and so on, is determinative of the way in which the deep structure concretely appears—and it appears in a bewildering variety of forms, shapes, variations. The logic functions as a hermeneutical key or paradigm for reading and interpreting experience, but it is a key that must be used experimentally, in the manner of a heuristic device. The *Werke* edition presented Hegel's lectures on the various *Realwissenschaften* as part of a completed, consistent, unitary system, but we now know that Hegel approached these lectures in an innovative spirit, unwilling ever simply to repeat what he had said before. On no subject was this truer than that of religion. From our new edition of *Determinate Religion* it is evident for example that, far from imposing an abstract, preconceived, a priori schema on the history of religions, Hegel approached this topic as an experimental field in which a variety of interpretative arrangements should be tried out. His evident willingness to incorporate new data and experiment with new schemas suggests that for him speculative philosophy as a whole involved a kind of "conceptual play" with the deep structure in order to arrive at new insights, to grasp connections, differences, types, trends, directions, to understand more fully the inexhaustible wealth of what presents itself. He certainly was not offering empirical descriptions but rather imaginative constructions intended to evoke disclosures of the "truth" of the world in which human beings dwell.

For this purpose the medium of oral lectures was ideally suited. Duncan Forbes claims, in his introduction to the *Lectures on the Philosophy of World History*,[11] that Hegel's philosophy "is best approached in the spirit of Plato's, as something that is in danger of being destroyed or distorted if it is written down." Forbes points out that Hegel in fact was extremely reluctant to publish and that if one views the *Encyclopedia of the Philosophical Sciences* and the

---

11. Hegel, *Lectures on the Philosophy of World History,* Nisbet ed., pp. xiii–xiv.

Outline of the Philosophy of Right as Hegel viewed them, namely as compendia for courses of lectures, then he published only two books in the proper sense, the *Phenomenology of Spirit* and the *Science of Logic*. These are of course among the greatest books of philosophical literature, but to give them a definitive priority over Hegel's spoken lectures (with which he was almost exclusively occupied during the last decade of his career) is to treat his philosophy as a closed book, whereas it was an attempt to "think life," dialectically yet concretely, holistically yet with shrewd insight into detail. The only way to appreciate this kind of thinking, says Forbes, is to "watch it at work." One watches it at work on the podium. Once it ceases to be thinking and becomes thought, once it stops speaking and is reduced to an editorial amalgam, it ceases to be a living process and becomes a system. The primacy of speaking on Hegel's part did not entail any sort of romantic attachment to his own subjectivity or intentionality; rather it permitted the process of *thinking* to remain open, fluid, and continuous. Jacques Derrida's insight is a shrewd one, that Hegel was "the last philosopher of the book and the first thinker of writing"—a "primary writing" that includes both speaking and writing in the ordinary sense and is not bound by the covers of a book.[12]

We offer now a brief description of the context and distinctive themes of each of Hegel's four lecture courses on the philosophy of religion, both to illustrate the fluidity of which we have just spoken and to provide a framework for the ensuing analysis of the text of the 1827 lectures in Sec. 4. The tables in the Appendix giving a comparative analysis of the structure of Hegel's Introduction and of the three main parts of the lectures (below, pp. 494–501) will be of help for the following discussion. The detailed analyses of the text contained in the Editorial Introductions to the three volumes of the unabridged edition should be consulted for more complete information.

1. *The Manuscript.* While Hegel's decision to lecture on philosophy of religion was apparently occasioned by concern over

12. Jacques Derrida, *Of Grammatology*, trans. G. C. Spivak (Baltimore, 1976), p. 26; cf. pp. 7, 44, 46, 56.

Schleiermacher's forthcoming *Glaubenslehre,* there are no substantive references to this work in the *Ms.* since Schleiermacher's first volume did not actually appear until Hegel was well into his lectures. Hegel found himself facing the same basic theological problems that concerned Schleiermacher, but his proposed resolution of them took quite a different tack. In the *Ms. Introduction,* Hegel stresses the profound conflict in the modern world between the sacred and the secular, religion and science. The prevailing theological tendencies of the Enlightenment and its aftermath—rationalism and supernaturalism, deism and Pietism—have in Hegel's view been unable to heal the conflict. In defending itself against the onslaughts of science and criticism, theology has given up all content in religion, all cognitive claims, retreating into the realm of the noncognitive, feeling, intuition, piety, faith (Hegel has in mind at this time primarily Kant and Jacobi). The primary polemic of the *Ms.* is aimed against the unproductive alternative of rationalism versus Pietism, and the purpose of the philosophy of religion is to show that God can be known cognitively.

Part I, the *Concept of Religion,* does not, however, address this agenda directly. In the *Ms.* the *Concept* has as its two main objectives the provision of a preliminary description of religion, including a derivation of its concept from its appearance in the various forms of religion; and a scientific demonstration of the necessity of the religious standpoint, a "proof" of religion (not of God). The preliminary description shows religion to be a matter of a *relationship* between human consciousness, the subjective side, and God, the objective side. In authentic religious experience there occurs an "elevation" or "passing over" from the subjective side to the objective. The demonstration of religion is properly not to be in terms of its *external* necessity (the function or utility of religion in society) but rather in terms of its *internal* necessity, showing how and why finite consciousness raises itself to religion through an inward teleology. This is the task of the "phenomenology of spirit," which precedes the philosophy of religion in the philosophical system. To these two main points Hegel appends a concluding section on the relationship of religion to art and philosophy, an agenda inherited

16

from the *Phenomenology of Spirit* and the *Encyclopedia of the Philosophical Sciences.*

In Part II, *Determinate Religion,* the concept of religion is to be "grasped in its determinate aspects," aspects that constitute the "forms of consciousness of the absolute idea." This suggests that the whole of Part II is intended as a phenomenology of religion, that is, of the various forms of consciousness assumed by the absolute idea as it emerges and advances through the history of religions. This phenomenology is carried out through the application of two sets of analytic categories—one internal to the religions, the other relating them externally. The internal set identifies three "moments" of a religion: its abstract concept of divinity, the ways in which God is known representationally in the texts and symbols of the religion, and the practical relationship in which communion with the deity is established; or, in brief, a religion's metaphysical concept, its concrete representation, and its cultus. The external analysis arranges *Determinate Religion* into a triad corresponding to the fundamental moments of logic, namely, being, essence, and concept. But in the case of the religions, these categories are applied in the mode of determinateness and finitude; hence the operative triad is one of prereflective immediacy or undifferentiated substance (the Oriental religions of nature), differentiation in the form of particularity (Jewish religion) and necessity (Greek), and external purposiveness (Roman religion). The first section, on immediate or nature religion, is quite brief in the *Ms.* Hegel does not treat the religion of magic (primitive religion) at all, nor does he discuss the Oriental religions separately. By contrast he devotes an extensive discussion to Roman religion, which represents the apotheosis of finitude and thus prepares the transition from all the finite religions to the Christian religion.

When he arrived at Part III, the *Consummate or Revelatory Religion,* Hegel was on familiar ground, which he had worked through previously for the *Phenomenology of Spirit,* Chap. VII.C (*Die offenbare Religion*), and the *Encyclopedia of the Philosophical Sciences,* Part III.3.B (*Die geoffenbarte Religion*). In the *Ms.* he titled Part III *Die vollendete oder offenbare Religion.* Neither here

17

nor in any of the subsequent lectures did he use the title *Die absolute Religion,* which was an editorial invention, although in the text of the lectures he does refer to Christianity as "the absolute religion" along with other, more commonly used, designations. In the *Ms.,* Hegel's treatment of the Christian religion is structured into two triads, one within the other. The outer triad employs the analytic framework already applied to each of the determinate religions in Part II, namely, the distinction between abstract concept, concrete representation, and cultus. The inner triad sets forth the concrete representation of God that is found in the Christian religion: (a) the idea of God in and for itself (the immanent Trinity); (b) the idea in diremption or differentiation (creation and preservation of the natural world); (c) the appearance of the idea in finite spirit (the history of estrangement, redemption, and reconciliation). A peculiarity of this arrangement was that the figure of the "Son" occupies the third moment of the triad rather than the second, while the "Spirit" becomes a kind of appendage, treated under the third section of the outer triad, "Community, Cultus." This difficulty was not resolved until the next course of lectures.

2. *The Lectures of 1824.* The polemic against rationalism and Pietism now was heightened and took on more specific targets. Rationalism has led on the one hand to a preoccupation with merely historical investigations of what was once believed, and hence Hegel attacks theological "historicism" (theologians are like "countinghouse clerks" who keep the accounts of other people's wealth but have no assets of their own). Rationalism has led on the other hand to the view that reason is limited to objects of sense experience and that therefore God cannot be known cognitively (Kantianism); here we find a preoccupation with the investigation of the cognitive faculty before engaging in acts of cognition. Pietism reinforces this with the view that the proper domain of religion is the realm of faith and feeling (Jacobi, Fries, Schleiermacher). But investigation of the cognitive faculty, Hegel argues, is already an act of cognition (the only way to learn to swim is to go into the water).

Once we investigate cognition, we are already engaged with the proper subject matter of theology and religion, God, for "God is essentially rational, is rationality that is alive and, as spirit, is in and for itself." Religion is now shown to be not merely the consciousness *of* God but also *God's* self-consciousness, absolute spirit's self-knowing, mediated in and through our finite consciousness. Religion is not the affair of the single human being but the highest determination of the absolute idea itself. The religious relationship, the relationship of consciousness and God, of finite and infinite spirit, is constituted by the self-mediation of the infinite rather than the self-projection of the finite. This is the speculative insight, and Hegel develops it over against the reflective philosophy of subjectivity (Kant, Fichte, Jacobi) and especially against the "empirical," experiential approach of Schleiermacher, which can never arrive at what is distinctively religious, namely, the *relationship* of finite and infinite spirit. It can never get off the ground, so to speak, can never escape the gravity of subjectivity. In the 1824 lectures Hegel's polemic against Schleiermacher is at its height, and there is a great deal of stress on the objectivity and absoluteness of content of the Christian religion. But God is not an alien object to consciousness, an incomprehensible beyond. Rather, consciousness finds itself in finding God; God, the infinite, overreaches and encompasses the finite.

The 1824 *Concept of Religion* is dominated by a lengthy critique of the "empirical" approach to religion, aimed at Schleiermacher, Jacobi, and the Kantians. With this Hegel contrasts the "speculative" approach. Religion finally is not merely an empirical, experiential reality based on immediate self-consciousness but is a speculative reality because it is a "mirroring" (*speculum*) of the absolute precisely in the religious relationship to the absolute, precisely in the feeling and consciousness of the absolute. Here for the first time Hegel is able to work out the speculative insight to which we have alluded—hints of which are already present in the *Ms.*—into a speculative definition of religion. This definition provides the basis for an adequate exposition of the *concept* of religion. If the speculative concept of religion is absolute spirit in its self-mediation, then we can expect that religion will reflect the development or self-realization of absolute spirit in the three moments of its sub-

stantial self-unity, its self-differentiation, and its self-consumma-
tion, or return to self. The moments of the life of the eternal *God*
are definitive of the moments of *religion*: the abstract concept of
God (God as abstract, universal, self-identical substance), religious
consciousness as the knowledge of God (the "theoretical" religious
relationship), and religious cultus (the "practical" religious relationship, participation in the being of God). By the time Hegel had
worked all of this out, it was too late in the semester to structure
Part I of the philosophy of religion in such a fashion; that would
have to wait until 1827.

Part II of the 1824 lectures is reorganized and greatly expanded
in scope and content by comparison with the *Ms.* The most obvious external difference is that *Determinate Religion* is divided
into two main sections rather than three. Hegel started with a threefold schema in mind, similar to that of the *Ms.,* but altered it in
the course of lecturing. Jewish, Greek, and Roman religion are all
included in the second main section ("The Religions of Spiritual
Individuality"), distinguished according to different ways in which
divine purpose actualizes itself in relation to finite spirit (as particular, plural, or universal). Determinate religion is no longer made
up of an inner triad (the religions of nature, finite spirit, and external purposiveness) but forms the first two parts of a larger triad
(nature religion, the religions of spiritual individuality, consummate
religion) that culminates in Christianity. But this "culmination"
does not occur as a progressive advance since finite religion ends
in degeneracy and death, in a return to the primitive at a more
developed stage of culture. The whole dialectical structure resists
any monolithic, linear theory of progress. In the first main section
("Immediate Religion or Nature Religion"), Hegel introduces for
the first time what he calls the "religion of magic," in which he describes primarily the religious practices of Africans and Eskimos as
well as the ancient religion of the Zhou dynasty in China. Following
this, he provides much more extensive as well as separate treatments
of Buddhism, Hinduism, Persian religion, and Egyptian religion.
During the intervening years since 1821, he has assimilated much
of the available literature on primitive and Eastern religions, and
the topic is clearly one of growing fascination for him. At the same

time he has begun to modify in significant ways his interpretation of Judaism. Only the approach to Greek and Roman religion remains relatively unchanged since the *Ms.*

In Part III the 1824 lectures introduce some important structural adjustments. Hegel drops entirely the analytic scheme of "abstract concept," "concrete representation," and "community, cultus," which did not work well for the Christian religion; and he converts the inner triad of the *Ms.* into genuinely trinitarian moments, identified as three "elements" of the self-development of the idea of God: (a) the idea of God in and for itself (the immanent Trinity, symbolized by the figure "Father"), (b) representation and appearance (creation, fall, and reconciliation, the work of the "Son"), (c) the community of faith (its origin, subsistence, and worldly realization, the work of the "Spirit"). Thereby Hegel's mature treatment of the consummate religion has been attained, and it will not be altered significantly at the structural level in the later lectures. Distinctive theological nuances continue to appear, however, in each of the lecture series. This is especially the case with respect to questions of historical positivity, christology, and eschatology.

3. *The Lectures of 1827.* With the lapse of three more years the ground had shifted rather dramatically. The battle with Schleiermacher was no longer so hot and fresh, and a new theological challenge was appearing on the scene, potentially a more bitter rival to speculative philosophy than rationalism and the theology of feeling had been, namely, the combination of Neopietism and Oriental studies in the writings of F. A. G. Tholuck.[13] On the one hand, Tholuck and the other Pietists began attacking Hegel's alleged "pantheism" and "atheism" with increasing boldness; they did so by labeling him a "Spinozist." On the other hand, they were suspi-

---

13. Tholuck, the leading theologian of the Halle faculty and an immensely popular and influential figure at the time, attacked Hegel indirectly in two works: *Die Lehre von der Sünde und vom Versöhner,* 2d ed. (Hamburg, 1825), and *Die speculative Trinitätslehre des späteren Orients* (Berlin, 1826). A few years later there appeared an anonymous work, *Ueber die Hegelsche Lehre, oder: Absolutes Wissen und moderner Pantheismus* (Leipzig, 1829).

cious of anything "speculative" in theology, above all the doctrine of the Trinity. Tholuck traced trinitarian speculation to Greek, Islamic, and Oriental sources and regarded the Trinity as mere "decorative timbering" (*Fachwerk*), whereas in Hegel's view it was "the fundamental characteristic of the Christian religion." Hegel responded to these attacks in several ways. In Part I of the 1827 lectures he refuted at length the charge of pantheism, arguing that those who make such charges are unable to distinguish the "actual" from the empirical or to grasp the dialectic of identity and difference. He highlighted the trinitarian structure of the Christian religion, establishing a closer connection between logic and the philosophy of religion. He drew together the previously dispersed proofs of the existence of God into an extended discussion at the end of Part I, thus coping at least indirectly with the charge of atheism. And at the beginning of Part III he introduced a new section on "the positivity and spirituality" of the Christian religion, partly as a way of responding to the criticism that speculative philosophy does not take finite, "positive" historical reality seriously but simply identifies the world with God. Whereas in 1824 he had been attacking historicism, now he was defending historicality.

We shall discuss these and other matters in more detail in the analysis of the 1827 text found in the next section. Here we shall merely mention a few of the distinctive structural features of the third course of lectures as compared with the first two. The *Concept of Religion* is now divided into three sections, which correspond to the three moments of the self-explication of the idea of God as adumbrated at the end of the 1824 *Concept*. These moments are: (a) the concept of God (which is shown to include not only abstract substance but also concrete subjectivity, hence any literal pantheism is simply an absurdity); (b) the knowledge of God (the various forms of religious consciousness, culminating in a treatment of the proofs of God's existence under the theme of "religious knowledge as elevation to God" [14]); (c) the cultus (which involves both a sen-

---

14. In all the other lectures, the proofs are taken up in relation to the God-concept of specific religions: the cosmological and teleological proofs in relation to one or more of the determinate religions, the ontological proof in relation to the Christian religion.

sible enjoyment and a higher, mystical enjoyment of God). By 1827 the mature form of Part I of the lectures has been established. In Part II, *Determinate Religion,* 1827 returns to a threefold division reminiscent of the *Ms.,* but the basis of the division is no longer the logical categories of being, essence, and concept, for the use of which Hegel was unable to provide a convincing justification in 1821. Rather the basis is the interplay of nature and spirit. The three stages are: religion as the unity of the spiritual and the natural (nature religion), the elevation of the spiritual above the natural (Jewish and Greek religion), and the religion in which purposiveness is not yet spiritual (the religion of expediency, which can also be called the religion of fate or destiny because it is devoid of spirit). Of the several detailed changes in 1827 the most notable is the reversal of the order in which the Greek and Jewish religions are treated, the reasons for which will be examined below. Finally, in Part III, the *Consummate Religion,* the structural differences between 1824 and 1827 are quite minor, but the theological emphases diverge because the polemical ground has shifted. The shift is most noticeable in Hegel's approach to christology.[15]

4. *The Lectures of 1831.* The last lectures remained within the trajectory established in 1827. The self-mediation of the triune God has become the centerpiece: the God who distinguishes himself from himself and is an object for himself, while at the same time remaining identical with himself, knows himself in a consciousness that is distinct from him; therefore finite consciousness is itself a moment in the divine process. This mediation is both internal and external, both within the divine life and at the same time constitutive of worldly actuality. While the worldly mediation is given special stress in 1831, as part of Hegel's continuing rejection of pantheistic, distinctionless identity, it is balanced by his insistence that the condition of possibility for God's self-realization in and through world process is his ideal self-relatedness. The ground of the difference between God and world is (to borrow Whiteheadian termi-

---

15. See Peter C. Hodgson, "Hegel's Christology: Shifting Nuances in the Berlin Lectures," *Journal of the American Academy of Religion* 53 (1985): 23–40.

nology) their "primordial" and "consequent" identity. The 1831 lectures combined a transcendent theology of the Trinity with an immanent theology of the world. They were grounded in a post-metaphysical theo-logic but issued in a project of world-transformation. Right-wing and left-wing impulses were held together in the center by a powerful vision of the God-world nexus. In this respect they were representative of Hegel's religious thought at its best and clearest, and it is unfortunate that they survive only in Strauss's excerpted version and in fragments recoverable from the *Werke*. But perhaps their fragmented condition is symptomatic of the fragmentation that Hegel's religious thought was soon to undergo. Perhaps too the context of these last lectures was Hegel's premonition of a warring conflict about to erupt among his own students and followers. The danger was no longer to be found primarily among the Kantian rationalists, or in Schleiermacher's theology of feeling, or from Tholuck and the Neopietists, but within the Hegelian school itself.

Parts I and III of the 1831 lectures followed the arrangement and content of 1827 quite closely. While Hegel continued to introduce interesting theological modulations, the only structural changes of significance were the addition of a new section on the relationship of religion to the state at the end of Part I and the restoration of the ontological proof to Part III (both these sections were preserved in full by the *Werke* and are printed as appendixes to Volumes 1 and 3 of our unabridged edition).

All the major innovations occurred in Part II. It is clear that Hegel was not yet satisfied with his treatment of *Determinate Religion,* and he was continuing to assimilate new materials. The threefold division from 1821 and 1827 is retained, but it is no longer based on the dialectic of being, essence, and concept, or on the interplay of nature and spirit. Rather the operative triad is that of immediacy, rupture, and reconciliation, categories that are not so much logical as they are descriptive of the general life of the concept and of the dialectic of consciousness—a dialectic that is taken into the divine life and becomes genuinely trinitarian in the Christian religion. In the first stage, that of natural religion, a relationship of immediacy exists between consciousness and its object. Hegel now includes here only magic, which is not yet properly religious. Religion emerges with the inward cleavage or rupture of consciousness, in such wise that consciousness is aware of the gulf between its own transitory being and God as absolute power. This cleavage permits an elevation of the spiritual above the natural, and Hegel now locates the beginning of this process at a much earlier point than he did in 1827. The "Oriental religions of substance"— Chinese religion, Hinduism, Buddhism—are now all located in the second stage rather than the first. This must be viewed as a significant upgrading of these religions in Hegel's phenomenology of the stages of religious consciousness.

The third stage entails the overcoming of the cleavage through a reconciliation of consciousness and its object at a higher, mediated level, where freedom becomes actual for the first time. This occurs in three phases. The first phase is a transitional one in which, in reaction against the confusion of the natural and the spiritual in the preceding stage, subjectivity seeks to establish itself in its unity and universality. Hegel here discusses the religion of the good (Persian and Jewish), the religion of anguish (Phoenician), and the religion of ferment (Egyptian). In the second phase the subject knows itself to be free in relation to the divine object. This is the religion of freedom proper, or Greek religion. But since the subject has not yet passed through the infinite antithesis of good and evil, and since the gods are not yet infinite spirit, the reconciliation that occurs at this stage is not complete. Nor is it completed by Roman religion, which issues instead in infinite unhappiness, anguish, and servitude—the birth pangs of the religion of true freedom and true reconciliation.

New and unresolved problems were introduced by the location of Judaism between Persian religion and the purely mythological religion of the "phoenix" and by the inclusion of Roman religion under the category of "freedom." In fact, all of Hegel's attempts to subsume the history of religions under a single, encompassing philosophical conceptuality, which was supposed to establish genetic, developmental connections and a hierarchy of religions, ultimately failed. What he accomplished in his successive attempts, as Walter Jaeschke suggests,[16] was less a unified *history* of religion than a *typology* and *geography* of religions, which is very likely all that *can* be accomplished and is closer to the truth than a strict logical construction.

4. Analysis of the Text of the 1827 Lectures[17]

In order to focus our analysis upon the three main parts of the lectures, we omit any detailed discussion of Hegel's introduction to the 1827 course. Some of the themes of the introduction have already been alluded to in our depiction of the distinctive polemical context of the 1827 lectures, and editorial footnotes will help to guide readers through this material, which is generally quite accessible. We offer only the following observations at this point: (a) The prefatory remarks at the beginning of the introduction, in which Hegel describes in general what religion is about, are repeated without much change from the earlier lectures. They cannot be reconstructed from either *W* or *L*, and we have had to rely on the awkward German of the Polish student Hube, whose notebook is the only presently available source for Hegel's opening remarks in 1827; the best version of these remarks remains that of the *Ms.* (unabridged ed., Vol. 1:83–86). (b) The first section is new in 1827, having been worked out in detail in one of the miscellaneous papers (n. 6), and is concerned to show that philosophy and religion have one and the same object, namely, "the eternal truth, God and

16. Walter Jaeschke, *Die Vernunft in der Religion: Studien zur Grundlegung der Religionsphilosophie Hegels* (Stuttgart–Bad Cannstatt, 1986), pp. 274–295, esp. 288–295.

17. This analysis is based on corresponding sections of the Editorial Introductions to the three volumes of the unabridged edition. The treatment of Hegel's introduction and of Part I has been revised rather extensively. Readers will be helped by referring to the tables in the Appendix that provide a comparative analysis of the several parts of the text (below, pp. 494–501). Section numbers and headings are the work of the editors and are not attributable to Hegel himself, although frequently wording in the text suggests the formulations used for headings. Reference will be made to the more detailed discussion of specific matters in the editorial footnotes so as to avoid repetition between the introduction and the notes. These references are cited not by page numbers but by note numbers, which run consecutively through each text unit. By using the running heads, readers can readily identify the appropriate text units.

nothing but God and the explication of God." (c) The next section, "The Relationship of the Science of Religion to the Needs of Our Time," is the longest of the 1827 introduction, and, as we suggest in n. 11, it is a potpourri of themes taken over and highlighted from the corresponding sections of the 1824 lectures. The polemical situation has shifted, and Hegel is no longer concerned simply with Kantian rationalism and Schleiermacherian piety but also with the emergent Neopietist attacks on "trinitarian speculation" and "Spinozistic pantheism," to which we have referred above. In response Hegel affirms the necessity of both doctrinal tradition and philosophical speculation. (d) The concluding "Survey of Our Subject" is longer and more detailed than in the earlier lectures. The systematic structure of the subject is now clearly in view for Hegel, and he lays it out with precision.

a. The Concept of Religion

Hegel begins in 1827 at a point corresponding to the third and last section of the 1824 lectures, that is, with an exposition of the realization of the concept of religion in its three moments—the "abstract" concept of God, the knowledge of God (the "theoretical" religious relationship), and the cultus (the "practical" relationship)—which correspond to the moments of the self-explication of the idea of God itself (n. 6). All preliminaries have been dispensed with other than a brief discussion of the problem of securing a beginning. In scientific knowledge everything should be proved, that is, shown to follow with necessity from something antecedent. At the "beginning" of philosophy we are in the presence of sheer immediacy. But with philosophy of religion we are not beginning philosophy afresh; indeed, philosophy of religion is the *final* science within the philosophical system and thus presupposes all the other philosophical disciplines, starting from a premise that already has been established, namely, that religion is a "necessary" human activity.

The Concept of God

The content of this activity is that "God is the absolute truth" and that "religion alone is the absolutely true knowledge." This content appears to be the result of the whole of philosophy. The three branches of philosophy—logic, nature, and spirit—lead to God as their final result. But since this "result" is the absolute truth, it cannot be merely a result; it must also be a presupposition, the first as well as the last, that which results from itself. As such, God is what is "enclosed within itself" (*das in sich Verschlossene*), the universal that is "concrete and full within itself" and "maintains itself as the absolutely enduring foundation." God is the absolute substance. If we cling to this declaration undialectically, then surely we are guilty of Spinozism or pantheism (n. 11). "But the fact that God is *substance* does not exclude *subjectivity*." Indeed, substance is an attribute of God's absolute being-with-self and abiding-with-self that we call *spirit, absolute spirit*. When we speak of substance, "the universal is not yet grasped as internally concrete"; only when it is so grasped is it spirit. God is not sheer, undifferentiated substance, not a "mere soil" out of which distinctions subsequently grow, but an "abiding unity" in which all distinctions remain enclosed (on the implications of this for trinitarian reflection, see n. 16). We have this content, this God, not primarily in the mode of feeling, willing, imagining, and so on, but in the mode of *thought*. "Thought is alone the soil for this content, is the activity of the universal—the universal in its activity and efficacy." "Animals have feelings, but only feelings. Human beings think, and they alone have religion." Thus religion has its "inmost seat" in thought, though doubtless it can also be felt, believed, imagined, represented, and practiced.

This is the abstract concept of God that emerges from speculative philosophy, and Hegel spells it out for the first time in the 1827 lectures. Some people, he adds, want to designate this idea of God as "pantheism," and the philosophy associated with it as an "identity-philosophy" (a term used by Schelling to characterize his main writings of 1801–1804). Hegel encountered the charge of pantheism directed against his own philosophy for the first time in the mid-1820s (n. 20), and he took the occasion of this new section of the 1827 *Concept* to refute it. If "pantheism" means literally everything is God—this paper, this snuffbox (n. 149), this table—then no serious philosophy has ever maintained that! Authentic

28

pantheism (whether Spinozistic or Oriental) identifies God with the *essence,* the *universal power,* that is in all things, not with things as such. Since this essence is what, philosophically speaking, is actual, the world in the strict sense has no "actuality," although it does of course "exist." The tendency of Spinoza's philosophy is toward acosmism rather than atheism (nn. 27, 28), since above all it is the actuality of God that is affirmed by this philosophy rather than the actuality of the world. Those who accuse Spinoza (and Hegel) of "atheism" merely prove that they are unable to liberate themselves from finitude, since for them the "actual" must be the empirical.

As to the term "identity-philosophy," the crucial point, which the term merely serves to obscure, is whether this identity—or, better, unity—is defined as abstract substance or as concrete spirit. "The whole of philosophy is nothing else but a study of the definition of *unity*; and likewise the philosophy of religion is just a succession of unities, where the unity always [abides] but is continually becoming more determinate."

The Knowledge of God: Faith, Feeling, Representation, Thought

The second section, "The Knowledge of God," is quite lengthy. Into it Hegel incorporates and systematically arranges a large body of material treating the various forms of religious consciousness—immediate knowledge (faith), feeling, representation, thought—inherited primarily from the first section of the 1824 lectures. The theme of religious knowledge corresponds to the second moment of the divine life, namely differentiation or distinction, which is the precondition of relationship. We can view the relationship from the point of view of both God and consciousness. The God who is known and represented in the world is a concrete, differentiated, self-manifesting subject, not merely an abstract, self-identical, universal substance. From the point of view of consciousness we may distinguish a number of different forms of religious knowledge, which are "partly psychological" in character. The discussion here bears a number of resemblances to the first part of the section on "psychology" in the *Encyclopedia of the Philosophical Sciences*

(§§ 445–468), where Hegel provides a psychology of "theoretical mind," or what we would call "epistemology."

In the 1827 text Hegel sets forth an internally integrated religious epistemology in which each of four elements is essential and each is related to the others (see nn. 49, 75). The first element is that of *immediate knowledge*—the immediate certainty that God *is,* and indeed that God is "this universality having being in and for itself [*diese an und für sich seiende Allgemeinheit*], outside me and independent of me, not merely having being for me." Certainty (*Gewissheit*) is the immediate relation of this content and myself. The first and most basic form of this certainty is that of *faith* (*Glaube*), which is not to be placed in opposition to knowledge (*Wissen*) but is a form of knowledge. Hegel does not frequently use the term "faith," probably because of his polemic against Jacobi and Schleiermacher. But he introduces it here in place of the term used in his general epistemology, "intuition" (*Anschauung*). The reason is that the certainty faith possesses of its object, God, cannot be based on any sort of immediate sensible intuition since God is not an object of sense experience. Nor does faith possess insight into the *necessity* of its content, which would be "intellectual" intuition. In neither the Kantian (sensible) nor speculative (intellectual) senses does the word "intuition" properly identify that form of immediate knowledge which is distinctively religious. For the latter the word "faith" is the most appropriate, despite its misleading interpretations: it is not based on external authority but on the witness of the Spirit, and it is not merely a subjective emotion but a mode of knowing an objective (albeit nonostensive) content.

The second element, *feeling* (*Gefühl*), designates the subjective aspect of the immediate certainty, namely, its connection with our own determinate, particular existence. We have at once the feeling of a content (e.g., a hard object) and the feeling of ourselves (the feeling "hardness"). Feeling is presently in vogue, says Hegel, because when we feel something, "we are personally and subjectively involved" in it, giving validity to ourselves as well as to the thing felt. "What one has in one's heart belongs to the being of one's personality, to one's inmost being." Thus it is quite appropriate that we should be expected not only to know God, right, duty, and

30

the like, but to have these things in our feeling; religion is a matter of the heart as well as of the head. We thus become identified with what we believe, and we act accordingly.

But there are severe limitations to feeling. As such, it is indeterminate, neither good nor evil, neither true nor false. "Every content is capable of being in feeling: religion, right, ethics, crime, passions." Because of its subjective involvement, feeling has no capacity for making *judgments* with respect to the validity of its contents. Thus the feelings of the heart must be purified and cultivated, and this involves precisely *thought*. When we think, "consciousness has made its entrance, and [with it] a parting or division that was not yet in feeling. . . . Consciousness is the ejection of the content out of feeling; it is a kind of liberation." Moreover, contents such as God, right, and duty do not belong to feeling in the sense of having been produced by it; they are determinations of the "rational will" and hence products of thought. They may be and in fact are also in feeling, but in an "inadequate mode"; "thought is the soil in which this content [God] is both apprehended and engendered alike." [18]

Before reaching thought, however, we encounter the form of knowledge known as *representation* (*Vorstellung*). If feeling concerns the subjective aspect, then representation attends to the objective aspect, the content, of whatever it is that we are immediately certain about, but it does not yet penetrate this content rationally

18. It is clear that feeling occupies quite a different place in Hegel's religious epistemology than it does in Schleiermacher's. For Schleiermacher, religious feeling, the feeling of utter dependence, the consciousness of being related to the ultimate whence and whither of existence, is the precognitive condition of possibility for cognizing anything in the world whatsoever, functioning rather like Husserl's natural attitude, or *Urglaube*. It is closer to what Hegel calls "immediate knowledge" or "faith," except that it also includes insight into the necessity of its content and thus approximates intellectual intuition. It is a mode of apprehension independent of knowing and doing, yet the ground of both, whereas for Hegel it is a (limited) form of knowledge. Neither Hegel nor Schleiermacher adequately understood the position of the other, nor did they appreciate how they could make use of the same or similar terms quite differently; hence their mutual polemics were often misdirected. Hegel's discussion of feeling in 1827 is much less polemical than it was in 1824, when there were a number of pointed allusions to Schleiermacher (see unabridged ed., Vol. 1:268 n. 20, 279 n. 37).

or cognitively (n. 75). Religion is certainly a matter of both feeling and representation, and the question arises which one we should begin with. The question can be answered in two ways. Since feeling is indeterminate and can contain any possible content, it is correct to say that it is prior. But feeling itself cannot serve as the justifying criterion for its content; it cannot determine that something is true just because it is in feeling. Hence when it comes to the matter of truth, representation is prior. Indeed, we know that religious instruction begins with representation. "By means of doctrine and teaching the feelings become aroused and purified; they are cultivated and brought into the heart."

Representation has two basic forms, or configurations: sensible and nonsensible. The sensible forms we call "images" (*Bilder*), for which the principal content or mode is taken from immediate, sensible intuition. But what the image signifies is not merely an immediate, sensible object. Rather it has a double signification, "first the immediate and then what is meant by it, its inner meaning." Thus the image is something symbolic, allegorical, metaphorical, mythical (Hegel does not further distinguish and define these figurative forms here). When, for example, we say that "God has begotten a son," we know quite well that this is not meant in the literal sense but rather that it signifies "a different relationship, which is something like this one." Not only what is manifestly figurative (*bildlich*) belongs to representation in its sensible aspect but also things that are to be taken as historically real (*Geschichtliches*). To be sure, many narratives having the appearance of history, especially religious narratives, are purely mythical, such as stories about Jupiter; but there are other narratives that are supposed to be, and in fact are, history in the proper sense, such as the story of Jesus. But this story is really "twofold": it is both an outward history, the ordinary story of a human being, and a divine history, a divine happening, deed, action. "This absolute divine action is the inward, the genuine, the substantial dimension of this history," and in that sense the history is representational.

Included also under representation are nonsensible configurations (*nichtsinnliche Gestaltungen*), which do not depend on sensible images or figures, although they may originally have derived from them. These have to do with spiritual (*geistige*) contents, activities, relationships. For example, if we say, "God created the world," then the terms "God" and "world" are functioning as non-sensible representations, and the reference is not to an empirical activity. God, after all, is the universal that is determined within itself in manifold ways, but in this representational statement we have God on the one side and the world on the other. Similarly, the world is an endlessly manifold complex, but when we say "world" we have it in the simple mode of representation. Although these and other terms—indeed, the whole vocabulary of religion and theology—proceed from thought and have their "seat and soil" in thought, they are representational in form, since they exist alongside each other as independent entities, linked by conjunctions; they are not yet inwardly analyzed and conceptually mediated in such a way that their distinctions and connections are seen to be essential.

The section on *thought* (*Denken*) is quite long, and we are presently discussing only the first two parts of it, which are concerned with the relationship of thought and representation and the question whether religious knowledge is immediate or mediated (Sec. B.4.a,b). With respect to the first of these, the primary point is that representation apprehends its various contents (sensible and spiritual) in their determinate *isolation,* whereas thought seeks for *relationships* and *universality.* "Thought dissolves this form of the simple, in which the content is found in representation, in such a way that distinct determinations within this simple reality are grasped and exhibited so that it is known as something *inwardly manifold.*" Thought does this by raising representational configurations to conceptual form. A "concept" (*Begriff*) precisely grasps-or holds-together (*be-greifen*) those elements that remain disparate in the simple placing-before (*vor-stellen*) the mind of various sensible or nonsensible images. Conceptual thinking for the most part does not invent new terms but makes use of the materials furnished by representation. What it does is to develop arguments and hypotheses that elucidate the unity—indeed, the necessary unity—of representational features. In this fashion it arrives at "conviction" (*Überzeugung*), which is certainty in the form of thought. Although

Hegel does not say so explicitly, it seems evident that thought continues to be fructified by the imagistic materials thrown up by representation; without representation there could be no thought, and a dialectic between representation and thought is constantly taking place.

While for conceptual thought itself there is nothing immediate but only and essentially mediation, religious knowledge is epistemically mixed and (like knowledge in general) is therefore both immediate and mediated. This is illustrated by a number of examples. Religious knowledge is on the one hand mediated: we are educated within a religion and receive doctrinal instruction, positive religion is based on revelation external to the individual, and so on. But on the other hand "neither positive revelation nor education can bring about religion in such a way that religion would be effected from outside, something mechanically produced and placed within human beings." Mediated knowledge rather brings about a "stimulation" (*Erregung*), a "recollection" (*Erinnerung*), of something that we originally bear within ourselves, immediately. "Religion, right, ethics, and everything spiritual in human being is merely aroused [*erregt*]. We are implicitly spirit, for the truth lies within us and the spiritual content within us must be brought into consciousness." This has important implications for the later discussion of the "positivity" and "spirituality" of the Christian religion, which is one of the distinctive concerns of the 1827 lectures.

Proofs of the Existence of God

The third and final subsection of "Thought," while headed "Religious Knowledge as Elevation to God" (Sec. B.4.c), actually is concerned with the proofs of the existence of God (see n. 109). Hegel's transition to this topic is rather complex. At the beginning of the discussion of "immediate and mediated" knowledge, he says that "mediated knowledge emerges more nearly in the form of the so-called proofs of God's existence." Knowledge of God entails a mediation between myself and an object other than myself, God. The mediation between two terms in a syllogism is provided by the third term, which has the character of a proof. Thus the knowledge of God takes the form of the proofs of God's existence. Moreover, the mediation contained in this knowledge is religion itself, for religion is an act of mediation: it is not simply a reference to an object but inwardly a movement, a passing over or an elevation to God. The passage is of a twofold sort: from finite to infinite being, and from subjective to objective infinitude. The first of these passages corresponds to the cosmological and teleological proofs, the second to the ontological proof. The proofs, then, are the concrete forms that the knowledge of God assumes in the various religions.

In all the other lecture series, Hegel treated the proofs in relation to the concepts of God that appeared in specific religions: the cosmological proofs in relation to the religions of nature and to Jewish and Greek religion, the teleological proof in relation to Roman religion, and the ontological proof in relation to the Christian religion. Only in the 1827 lectures did he gather all of the proofs into one section toward the end of the *Concept of Religion*. This may simply be the consequence of Hegel's continued experimentation with the structure of the lectures. Or it may be an attempt to give the proofs a greater impact in response to the charge of atheism directed against his philosophy, or even to ward off the threat of atheism in the modern secular-bourgeois world. Hegel seems to have been concerned with the question of the reality-status of God during his last years in Berlin; he gave separate lectures on the proofs of the existence of God in the summer of 1829 and was preparing them for publication when he died in 1831. (The 1827 version of the proofs in the philosophy-of-religion lectures may have served as a first sketch of the separate 1829 lectures.) Before discussing the proofs individually, he now addresses two significant questions: the distortion present in most of the proofs, and the authentic form of the proofs. This material is new in 1827, and it does seem intended to salvage the proofs from the general discredit into which they had fallen.

Two sorts of distortion are present in the attempt to "prove" God's "existence." The first is the suggestion that God can be said to "exist," for "existence" (*Dasein*) refers to determinate, finite being, whereas God's being is in no way limited (n. 111). It would be better to say, "God and his being, his actuality or objectivity," and the purpose of the proofs would be to show the connection or coherence (*Zusammenhang*) between God and being (*Sein*), that is, between the concept of God and the being (or actuality, objectivity) of God. The second distortion is the notion that it is possible to "prove" or demonstrate God's being from finite being, for this would be to make God a result or a consequence, dependent upon the being of the finite, whereas God is precisely the nonderivative, is "utterly actual being in and for itself." But religion remains an "elevation" to God even after this form of demonstration has been stripped away. The Kantian critique of the demonstrative form of the proofs cannot be considered to have demolished religious knowledge and activity as such. It is only that "elevation" to God does not properly entail a "demonstration" of the infinite from the finite on the basis of a self-projection of the finite.

This brings us to the authentic form of the proofs. Hegel's point, put concisely, is that the religious elevation to the infinite, which is engendered by our awareness of finitude and contingency, is not based upon an "affirmation" of the finite, its self-extension or projection into infinitude, for that would result in the "spurious infinite" (a merely extended finite); rather it is based on the *negation* of the finite, its self-canceling or sublation. The finite thus becomes aware of the infinite not as one "aspect" of a relationship but as the whole, that which overreaches both finite and infinite, includes negation within itself, and thus alone truly is. What is "affirmative" or active is not the finite but the infinite. The religious relationship and hence the proofs are based not on an autonomous self-elevation of finite spirit but, speculatively expressed, on the return of infinite and absolute spirit to itself in and through the self-negation of finite spirit (see n. 132).

Hegel's discussion of the specific proofs (see n. 133) simply illustrates and confirms these two points. He starts with the *cosmological proof,* which is an attempt to argue from the contingency of the world to absolutely necessary essence. But this is not a valid argument, since something that is necessary can scarcely be demonstrated from something that is contingent. Absolute necessity cannot be conditioned by or dependent on anything outside itself. The authentic form of this proof would be to start with the process of mediation intrinsic to absolute necessity, and to comprehend contingent things as moments or stages in the process, posited by the absolute precisely as contingent, as negative, as not having being in and for themselves. But this is the ontological proof, not the cosmological proof. Hegel makes this point more clearly in the 1824 lectures, where he also establishes that there are three basic forms of the cosmological proof, related to specific religions: the argument from finite to infinite (the religions of nature), the argument from the many to the one (Jewish religion), and the argument from contingency to necessity (Greek religion).[19]

The *teleological proof* is based upon the experience of purposiveness (*Zweckmässigkeit*). In the form in which we usually encounter this proof (e.g., in Roman religion), it is a matter of *external* purposiveness: given the apparently marvelous harmony between externally related things in the world, a third rationally ordering principle must be posited, which arranges specific means for specific ends. This proof has God involved in quite trivial and unworthy pursuits, such as providing cork trees in order to have stoppers for bottles, or mice for cats to feed upon. Kant, in his critique of external purposiveness, introduced the "important concept" of *inner* purposiveness, according to which every living thing is a telos that has its means implicit within it. From this finite organic life the proof leads to an absolute organic life, to a universal purposiveness, hence to a world-soul or *Nous*—not because the latter is required to account for finite arrangements and purposes but because of the negation of the particularity of finite organic life. This "physico-theological" proof, however, arrives only at a definition of God as "soul" or "power," not as "spirit," and in that respect it remains deficient.[20]

19. See our analysis in the Editorial Introduction to Vol. 2 of the unabridged ed., pp. 31–32, 46–47.

20. See our analysis of the teleological proof as presented in the 1824 lectures, unabridged ed., Vol. 2:47–48. In the 1831 lectures Hegel associated Greek as well as Roman religion with this proof (Vol. 2:83). It is noteworthy that Hegel never assessed Kant's proof based on *moral* teleology or "ethicotheology," which in Kant's view was the only valid proof, namely, that God (as guarantor of the kingdom of ends) is a necessary postulate of action in accord with moral ends. Already in the 1790s Hegel was convinced of the failure of the moral interpretation of religion; consequently, moral teleology and its accompanying doctrine of postulates were in his view completely unpersuasive. (I am indebted to W. Jaeschke for this observation.)

Valid elements are contained in both the cosmological and the teleological proofs, but they find their correction and fulfillment in the *ontological proof*. This proof passes over, not from (finite) being to God, but from God to being, that is, from the concept of God to the being or reality of God. The insight into this proof, the only genuine proof, was attained only in the Christian era, and indeed not until the twelfth century, by Anselm of Canterbury. The problem with Anselm's argument from "perfection"—a problem clearly exposed by Kant—was that it *presupposed* the very unity of concept (thought) and being (reality) that must be demonstrated. Hegel attempted to respond to the Kantian critique with a post-Kantian version of the ontological proof, one based on his own logic. His first efforts at this in 1824 were halting; 1827 went considerably further; but the 1831 lectures presented the clearest argument.[21] The true concept is not a mere abstract representation of consciousness (e.g., the "idea" of a hundred dollars). The true concept is alive and active; it mediates itself with itself; it is the movement or process of self-objectifying by which its subjectivity is sublated—just as, when human beings realize their drives or purposes, what was at first only ideal becomes something real. The concept "makes itself reality and thus becomes the truth, the unity of subject and object" (1831). This logical truth is most fully manifest in the Christian religion, which is the religion of incarnation: God takes on finite, worldly, determinate being (*Dasein*) in and through the process of self-diremption and self-return by which God becomes absolute spirit. In this sense it is not, after all, inappropriate to speak of the *Dasein Gottes*. The proof of this sort of divine existence does not involve some illicit logical trick (existence as something "plucked" from the concept of the most perfect); it is rather provided by God's self-involvement in world-process. God, who is utterly actual being (*das Seiende*), takes on worldly, determinate, "existential" being (*Dasein*). The religious "elevation" to God presupposes this divine descent.

21. See our analysis in the unabridged ed., Vol. 3:48–50. The *Werke* provides a full text of the ontological proof in the 1831 lectures; it is translated in our Vol. 3:351–358.

The Cultus

The concluding section, "The Cultus," is much abbreviated from the 1824 version (n. 169), but it is more clearly organized and presented. In the case of the knowledge of God, the theoretical religious relationship, I am immersed in my object and know nothing of myself. But the true situation is the *relationship* of myself and this object; I must *know myself* as filled by it. What accomplishes this unity is *action,* the activity of the cultus, which is accordingly the practical religious relationship. Cultus is "the including, within my own self, of myself with God, the knowing of myself within God and of God within me." This is accomplished through the act of "enjoyment," "partaking," or "communion" (*Genuss,* n. 174), which is the definitive cultic act. It does not *bring about* the reconciliation of God and humanity but presupposes it, participates in it as something already implicitly and explicitly accomplished by the grace of God.

Hegel distinguishes three basic forms of the cultus. The first is *devotion* (*Andacht*), which is "not the mere faith that God is, but is present when the faith becomes vivid, when the subject prays and is occupied with this content not merely in objective fashion but becomes immersed therein." Then there are two external cultic forms, the *sacraments* (reconciliation brought into feeling, into present sensible consciousness) and *sacrifice* (the negation involved in elevation sensibly accomplished). The third and highest form is *repentance,* whereby one not only renounces external things but also offers one's heart or inmost self to God. When purity of heart is properly "cultivated," it issues in *ethical life,* which is "the most genuine cultus," but only to the extent that consciousness of God remains bound up with it. Thus social and political ethics represent an extension and "realization" of the religious cultus—a point that Hegel elaborates only at the very end of the lectures, in his treatment of the Christian cultus.[22]

---

22. In 1831, Hegel added a section on "The Relationship of Religion to the State" at the end of Part I, immediately following "The Cultus." See unabridged ed., Vol. 1:451–460.

b. Determinate Religion

The substance of Hegel's interpretation of the determinate religions was established in the 1824 lectures, as a consequence of assimilating a great quantity of new primary and secondary source material, of penetrating it speculatively, and of devoting a larger proportion of time to this topic. The 1827 lectures built upon and refined the attainments of 1824. Although he was working from an edited copy of the Griesheim transcript of 1824, Hegel did not simply repeat the earlier lectures; as always, he was seeking new formulations and experimenting with new interpretative proposals. In many respects the argument of the 1827 lectures was presented with greater clarity and simplicity and with more concrete references to religious practices. Because 1824 and 1827 are so closely related in Part II, we will discuss this relationship at a number of points below, in order to bring out distinctive features of 1827.

The introductory summary of the three stages of determinate religion is inherited from 1824, which initially projected a threefold division as well. Already the summary anticipates certain changes that are more fully developed in 1831 (see n. 2), but it does not anticipate the reversal in the order in which Greek and Jewish religion are actually treated in 1827 (see nn. 18, 347). The three stages are: religion as the unity of the spiritual and the natural (nature religion), the elevation of the spiritual above the natural (Jewish and Greek religion), and the religion in which purposiveness is not yet spiritual (the religion of expediency, which can also be called the religion of fate or destiny because it is devoid of spirit).

Immediate Religion, or Nature Religion

The discussion of the "original condition" of humanity expands the 1824 version by introducing an exegesis of the biblical story of the fall of humanity. In order to support his argument that the original condition was not a state of innocence and innate wisdom (which he believed to be the point of view of Schelling and Schlegel, n. 22) but rather one of barbarism and savagery, Hegel appeals to the "profound" story in Genesis, which shows that the cleavage or rupture of consciousness occurred at the very beginning of human history. It is by means of this cleavage that the knowledge of both good and evil first arose, a knowledge that is the condition of possibility for human freedom and maturation. "That is the genuine idea in contrast with the mere image of paradise, or this stupefied innocence devoid of consciousness and will." Hegel repeats this interpretation of the fall in Part III, which is the only context in which it is found in the *Ms.* and 1824. Since such repetition is unusual for him, he may initially not have intended to do so. In 1831 the discussion of the fall was transferred from Part III to Part II, but there it was treated in relation to Jewish religion rather than in relation to the so-called original condition.

Nature religion, says Hegel, is not religion in which natural, physical objects are taken to be God and revered as God. Rather it is the spiritual that is the object of nature religion as well, but "the spiritual [recognized] first in its immediate and natural mode," which takes the form of particular, sensibly existing, immediately present human beings. Such human beings exercise *power* over nature by virtue of special gifts (e.g., shamans or magicians) or roles (priests, emperors), and they are to be venerated and feared, as also are the spirits of the dead and the powers of fetishes and animals. This is the religion of magic, and the several stages of nature religion are distinguished, according to Hegel's introductory summary, on the basis of how "spirit is to be purified of this externality and naturalness, this sensible immediacy, and be shown as spirit in thought." The next stage after the religion of magic is one in which consciousness withdraws from this immediate externality, enters into itself and concentrates itself internally, "so that this inwardness is the essential, higher, powerful and ruling factor." This is the religion of "being-within-self," or Buddhism. In the third stage, consciousness discovers itself to be outside as well as inside this abstract self-contained being, and the latter disintegrates "into endlessly many powers, configurations, and universal moments, which stand in connection with the self-contained essentiality, and which are more or less imaginative forms of this essentiality": the religion of phantasy, or Hinduism. Finally, the fourth stage is "the incipient severance or objectification of what is known as the highest." This has two shapes, in the first of which objectified substance still has the abstract, natural form of "light"

(Persian religion), while in the second the concept of the subjectivity of the substantial begins to come to expression (Egyptian religion). The 1827 phenomenology of the stages of nature religion differs from that found in 1824 in that the definitive objectification of the divine appears to occur much later, at the point of Persian rather than of Buddhist religion. Yet Buddhism is now clearly recognized to be a distinct stage and not simply the highest form of the religion of magic.

The Religion of Magic

In 1824 Hegel combined a phenomenology of stages of primitive religious consciousness with specific examples of the religion of magic in the first two subsections of "The Religion of Magic." In 1827 he separated these two elements, placing the phenomenology in the subsection we have titled "The Concept of Magic" and the discussion of specific historical practices in the subsection titled "Less Developed Religions of Magic" (n. 52). The examples of the religion of magic presented in the second subsection are identical with those in the 1824 materials, namely the religious practices of the Eskimos and of certain African tribes, and they are drawn from the same few missionary and travel sources (nn. 78, 82, 87, 91). Yet the analysis presented in "The Concept of Magic" differs considerably in content from that found in 1824. Magic involves a more or less *direct* power over nature and is to be distinguished from the kind of *indirect* power exercised by higher culture on the basis of stepping back from an immediate relationship to the natural world, understanding it scientifically in terms of physical laws and measuring and controlling it through technical instruments. Gone from the 1827 treatment is the description of stages of the "formal objectification of the divine object," which in 1824 located the beginnings of an indirect relationship to nature already at an early stage. Rather, according to 1827, all the "less developed" forms of magic involve a direct use of power in one form or another. From this is distinguished only a "more developed" form of magic—the religion of ancient China, which in 1824 was identified with the fourth and final phase of formal objectification.

The State Religion of the Chinese Empire and the Dao

This religion is still magic, according to 1827, but it is a *developed* religion of magic. Despite this classification, Hegel's treatment in 1827 has advanced considerably beyond that found in 1824—has advanced, in fact, to the point where it is difficult to argue that we really are still at the stage of magic. At the outset Hegel distinguishes three phases of Chinese religion: the oldest is the state religion of the Chinese empire, which is the religion of heaven; the second is the religion of the Dao, or of reason; the third is Chinese Buddhism, introduced in the first century A.D. The present subsection is concerned with the first two of these religions.

As to the first, which is the ancient religion of the Zhou dynasty (n. 96), Hegel now recognizes, on the basis of closer study of the Jesuit *Mémoires concernant les Chinois* (1776–1814) as well as volume 6 of the *Allgemeine Historie der Reisen* (1750), that what we find is not simply emperor worship but a higher religious symbol, that of heaven or Tian, which represents the power of nature but displays moral characteristics as well. It designates "wholly indeterminate and abstract universality." Because of the abstractness of Tian, it is still the emperor who is sovereign on earth. Only the emperor is connected with Tian, and only he rules over everything earthly, including the natural powers and the departed spirits. Tian itself is empty; everything concrete derives from the emperor and his direct control: hence in Hegel's view this is still a religion of magic. Following these references to Tian, Hegel returns to the rites surrounding the establishment of a new dynasty, including the role of the Shen, to which he devoted exclusive attention in 1824.

Hegel's discussion of the religion of the Dao ("reason" or "the way") is based on the Jesuit *Mémoires,* Gaubil's French translation of the Shu-jing (1770), and Abel-Rémusat's *Mémoire sur la vie et les opinions de Lao-Tseu* (1823). According to these sources, the Daoist sect arose in the twelfth century—a view not supported by modern scholarship (see n. 115). Hegel believes that it is a sect of masters and teachers, withdrawn from the state religion, who lived in the mountains, devoted to the study of the way and to religious exercises. Because it represents a return of consciousness to itself and the demand for the inward mediation of substantial power, Daoism constitutes a transition to the next stage of nature religion, that of being-within-self. In Daoism itself, however, the symbols remain abstractly rational ciphers—exhibiting a triadic structure, to be sure—so that vitality, consciousness, and spirituality remain attached to the immediate human being, the emperor. In this respect we are still at the stage of magic, despite the reforms introduced by Lao-zi and Confucius.

The Religion of Being-Within-Self: Buddhism

Hegel now considers Buddhism as a distinct phase of nature religion, not as the highest form of the religion of magic (n. 138), and his portrayal is more fully developed, although it is not based on new sources; rather the sources available in 1824 are utilized more fully. These consisted primarily of reports by English travelers to the Far East, together with de Mailla's *Histoire générale de la Chine* (1777–1785). Hegel's sources were most explicit about Burmese and Tibetan Lamaism, but he did not understand the difference between it and Buddhism, nor was he familiar with the main schools of Buddhism. The view prevalent in his day placed the life of Buddha around 1000 B.C.E., and this early dating probably led Hegel to assume that Buddhism was an older religion than Hinduism. Moreover, he seems to have confused the dates of Siddhartha Gautama with the introduction of Buddhism into China, which Hegel calls the religion of Fo after the Chinese name for Buddha. He assumes, therefore, that Buddhism/Lamaism existed well before the life of Gautama, who was one of several Buddhas.

According to Hegel, Buddhism is the first religion that grasps the genuine objectivity of universal substance, comprehends it as independent, as having being-within-self (*Insichsein*). In the 1827 lectures he is more specific than before about the fact that the Buddhists conceive this ultimate reality as "nothing" or "not-being" (n. 145). This, he says, is "the absolute foundation, the indeterminate, the negated being of everything particular"; "only the nothing has genuine autonomy, while in contrast all other actuality has none." The goal of human existence is the state of negation in this nothing, which the Buddhists call nirvana—a state of eternal tranquillity, of cessation, of indifference, of purity, of freedom from worldly miseries. It may seem strange to think of God as nothing, but in fact an important dimension of the truth about God is thereby expressed. For it means that God is nothing determinate; just this absence of determinacy constitutes his infinity. When we say that God is infinite, we mean that he is the negation of everything particular. Thus to say that God is nothing does not mean that he is not, but rather that God is "the empty" and that "this emptiness is God."

This sympathetic attempt to grasp the meaning of Buddhist nirvana—although couched in Western ontological categories—brings Hegel to a defense of Oriental pantheism over against the attacks on pantheism to which the 1827 lectures respond at a number of points (n. 138). For Oriental consciousness the main theme is the independence and unity of the universal, whereas for Western consciousness it is the individuality of things, especially of human beings. But there is an essential truth in the Oriental intuition of the universal—not the spurious claim that "all is God" (which would be an apotheosis of finite things) but rather the truth that "the All is God," "the All that remains utterly one" and thus is the *negativity* of finite things (n. 167). The "pan" of pantheism is to be taken as universality, not as totality. This is the essential truth that was grasped by Spinoza, despite the "babblers" who accuse him of atheism.

The limitation in the Oriental (and presumably also in the Spinozistic) view is that God is not merely substance, the absolutely one substance; he is also subject, the one infinite subject. Oriental consciousness recognized this only indirectly and imperfectly, by claiming that the one substance also exists in immediate sensible presence in empirical human beings. Hence we find the—to us "shocking"—view that a particular Buddha or Dalai Lama simply *is* God, indeed that the subjectivity and shapes of the one substance are multiple, since there are several lamas and many Buddhas. The "rational aspect" of such a view is that precisely thereby subjectivity and substance are mediated, though in a defective shape. The defectiveness is heightened for Hegel by the accounts of the Tibetan lamas provided by English travelers, especially Turner's version (n. 188) of how a new lama was discovered in a still-nursing child when the previous one suddenly died of smallpox.

The Hindu Religion

Hegel offers a negative assessment of Hinduism in all the lectures. Most of the secondary sources available to him were prejudiced or ill informed, reflecting the attitudes of the British East India Company, even though he also drew on less prejudiced articles published in *Asiatic Researches* and had apparently studied fairly carefully the Code of Manu available in the *Institutes of Hindu Law* (1794) as well as portions of the Mahābhārata and the Bhagavad-Gītā. In addition we know that Hegel was suspicious of the romantic attachment to India that had been prevalent in Germany during his own formative years, as expressed especially by Friedrich Schlegel's *Ueber die Sprache und Weisheit der Indier* (1808). It is evident that his general assessment of Hinduism, which he found confirmed in the English reports, was intended as a deliberate corrective to what he took to be uncritical enthusiasm in German intellectual circles.

The one universal substance, which the Buddhists call nothingness and the Hindus call Brahman, is now particularized in a multiplicity of finite, personified natural powers, which are not images produced by a "beautiful imagination" (*schöne Phantasie*) but are merely "fanciful" or "fantastic" (*phantastisch*). The 1827 lectures are characterized by several comparisons between Hindu and Greek religion (always unfavorable to the former), which may reflect the fact that in 1824 Hegel argued that the two represent corresponding stages of natural and spiritual religion, respectively. Perhaps Hegel dropped his earlier designation "phantasy" for Hinduism (n. 192) partly with the view in mind that Greek religion represents the true, the higher *Phantasie*. As in the earlier lectures, Hegel provides a detailed account of the three figures of the Trimurti—Brahmā (the active, generative father), Vishnu (manifestation, appearance, incarnation), and Shiva (mutability, creation and destruction)—a triad that really remains external to the undifferentiated substance of Brahman. He also describes the austere practices or yogic discipline through which union with Brahman is achieved, as well as the

46

privileged caste of Brāhmans, and the elements of immolation, superstition, lack of ethical life, unruliness, and formlessness, which he found so unattractive.

The section ends with a "Transition to the Next Stage," which is new in 1827. In the next stage, which is that of Persian and Egyptian religion, the Buddhist-Hindu distinction between the abstract universal and immediate subjects reverts to a concrete, implicitly spiritual unity; and there occurs a separation of empirical self-consciousness from absolute self-consciousness, "so that here God attains proper objectivity for the first time." God no longer subsists "in an empirical, human mode" but becomes "truly and intrinsically objective," is "essentially object," "altogether in opposition to human beings." These strong claims suggest that Hegel is beginning to perceive a sharper distinction between the Far Eastern and Near Eastern religions; and as a matter of fact, in the 1831 lectures they are treated in separate stages. Persian and Egyptian religion, together with Judaism, are viewed in 1831 as the first of the religions of freedom, by contrast with the cleavage of consciousness present in the religions of China and India. Anticipations of the 1831 reorganization are clearly evident in the 1827 discussion of "the religions of transition."

The Religion of Light: Persian Religion

The next stage after the Hindu dichotomization of unitary substance and multiple powers is the "resumption" of being-in-and-for-self into itself; just because the true content has independence and objectivity, it is "the good," from which all things proceed. Negativity, however, is not included within the good; it remains external to it. Hegel attends more specifically to this "Oriental dualism" in 1827 than in 1824, comparing it with recent philosophical trends of which he is critical. The endless conflict between good and evil suggests the Kantian-Fichtean notion that the good can be realized only in an infinite progression (n. 277); and the dualism between good and evil anticipates the contemporary reemphasis of the gulf between finite and infinite: the separated, autonomous finitude of modern rationalism is precisely what is evil (see n. 278). The reason for the dualism is that the good, the ulti-

47

mate, is still conceived in naturalistic terms. In nature, relationships remain external and sensible; hence, if good is symbolized as light, its opposite is darkness, which remains external to it. But if spirit is the basis of the relationships, they are mediated internally.

Hegel's knowledge of the religion of ancient Persia (Zoroastrianism) was based primarily on his own study of the Zend-Avesta in the translation by Kleuker (1776–1783) from the French edition of Anquetil du Perron and of a few secondary sources (see nn. 269, 284). The Persians, or Parsees, revere light, not in the form of a physical object, the sun, but as denoting the good, the universal essence, which pervades everything as does light. Light (or "primal fire" as distinguished from "material fire") assumes human shape in the figure of Ormazd, whose kingdom is the kingdom of light. This universal light is the "ideal" that is present in all things— human spirits both living and departed, animals, rivers, mountains, trees. For Parsees who live in the kingdom of the light, life as a whole is their cultus: their religious law is to do good, live purely, be and act like light. Unlike Hinduism, this is a life-affirming, life-enhancing religion. To this general depiction of Parseeism, common to the 1824 and 1827 lectures, the latter add a discussion of the Mithra cult (nn. 287, 288) and of the organization of the Persian state as compared with the kingdom of light (n. 286).

Yet another "Transition to the Next Stage" is included at this point. The transition in question is that of the resumption of the multiple into concrete unity, a unity that includes subjectivity within itself. In Persian religion this resumption remains truncated because it is external and natural; and the two sides, the substantive and the subjective, are still unmediated. The next step is that subjectivity should unify within itself the opposed elements; indeed, subjectivity is precisely a process of such unification. The negative moment, construed as natural, is death; and if there is to be a true reconciliation, death is something that God himself must undergo. Thus we come upon a religion in which God dies and rises again to life. The negation of death is really posited in God, which is a fundamental difference from the many transient incarnations of Hindu mythology; yet it remains a natural negation, not a spiritually self-imposed negation, as found in the Christian Trinity. In

1827 this transition is set forth as a theoretical moment in the process of religious cognition; in 1831 Hegel finds a historical instance of it in the so-called religion of anguish (Syrian or Phoenician religion), a religion in which "for the first time we have the dying of God as internal to God himself."

Egyptian Religion

As compared with 1824, the 1827 lectures provide a much more extensive discussion of the actual materials of Egyptian religion, even though Hegel is still relying primarily on reports of the classical historians who had visited Egypt, notably Herodotus and Plutarch, and on modern interpreters of these sources. During the 1820s new information became available as a result of the decipherment of the hieroglyphic system in 1824 and archaeological expeditions, but Hegel made little use of it.

The principal figure of Egyptian religion is Osiris, to whom is opposed Typhon, the principle of negation and opposition. But the opposition does not remain external to Osiris; it enters into him, and consequently Osiris dies but is perpetually restored, serving as lord of the dead as well as of the living. Behind the Osiris myth is a grasping for the first time of the universal substance as subjectivity. But subjectivity is still known only in the mode of representation, and it is represented in both natural and human form. What we find in Egyptian religion is a curious passing back and forth between these forms in terms of the relationship between signifier and signified. Clearly, natural objects are now regarded as representational symbols of the universal, subjective essence; they refer not to themselves but to something other than themselves. Thus we have the sun, the Nile, the change of seasons: these all represent a "cycle turning back upon itself," which is what subjectivity essentially is. On the one hand, Osiris signifies the sun; but on the other hand, the sun signifies Osiris. One is the inner element, the other the signifier by which the inner discloses itself outwardly. As we have said, the roles can reverse. "But what in fact is the inner is Osiris, subjectivity as such"; this is the direction in which Egyptian religion is moving.

Egyptian culture exhibited a tremendous impulse to express and construct outwardly this inner element. This is what gave rise to art for the first time. The testimony of the ancient historians is confirmed by the archaeological remains: the Egyptians engaged in an immense artistic labor from which there was no cessation; "the toiling spirit did not rest from making its representation visible to itself." What they produced, however, was not pure and fine art (*schöne Kunst*) but only the craving for fine art. This craving "involves the struggle of meaning with material," the striving "to place the stamp of inner spirit on outer configuration." But in Egyptian art the two remain separate and to some degree opposed. The artistic figure (*Gestalt*) "is not yet spiritualized to clarity; what is sensible and natural has not yet been completely transfigured into the spiritual." In fact, the tendency is for the spiritual to remain *buried* within the sensible. In a striking image Hegel says that "the pyramid is a self-sufficient crystal, in which a dead man is preserved; but in the work of art, which is reaching out for beauty, the externality of the configuration is imbued with the inner soul, with the beauty of what is within" (n. 340).

This, finally, accounts for the *enigmatic* character of Egyptian religion. The inner, spiritual meaning has not yet achieved outward clarity of expression. This is how Hegel interprets the inscription related to the goddess Neith in Sais: "No mortal has yet lifted my veil" (see n. 345). The Greeks, however, lifted the veil.

The Elevation of the Spiritual above the Natural

If the religion of nature involves the natural unity of the spiritual and the natural, then the next stage of determinate religion entails the elevation of the spiritual above the natural; this is the religion of the Greeks and the Jews (see n. 347). The universal characteristic of this second stage, says Hegel, is that of "free subjectivity." Subjectivity has now attained mastery over nature and finitude. The subject now is *spirit,* and spirit is subjective; that is, it is free spirit, spirit that is for itself. The natural and the finite are only a *sign* of spirit, only instrumental to its manifestation.

What accounts for the reversal in the order in which the two religions dealt with in this section are treated, so that now Greek religion is considered first and Jewish religion second?[23] It seems to be based primarily on the different ways in which the "elevation" occurs in the two religions. For Greek religion the natural element is taken up and transfigured in free subjectivity, but it is not purified of its externality and sensibility, so that this religion is still tinged by finitude: the gods are represented by the sensibly beautiful human shape, and they are many. For Jewish religion the sensible element is left behind; it is ruled and negated by the one God who is infinite subjectivity and subsists without shape, only for thought, the God who is sublimely free spirit in relation to the natural world. Judaism, then, is the more purely spiritual religion. At the beginning of the section on Jewish religion, Hegel states that in this distinction lies "the necessity of the elevation of the religion of beauty into the religion of sublimity," namely, "that the particular spiritual powers, the ethical powers, should be embraced within a spiritual unity."

In the two earlier lectures, those of 1821 and 1824, the relationship between Jewish and Greek religion was regarded as mutually complementary rather than as progressive; Hegel never referred to the "elevation" of one into the other. This is evident from the organization of the *Ms.*, in which the representational and cultic forms of the two religions are subordinated to an inclusive scheme, even though the portrayal of Jewish religion is considerably less attractive there than the portrayal of Greek. The dialectical structure of the 1824 lectures resists, as previously mentioned, a linear or progressive development among the determinate religions. That Hegel should now speak of the "elevation" of the religion of beauty into the religion of sublimity seems to follow in part from his continuing and increasingly favorable reassessment of Judaism, but it may also be related to the polemical context of the 1827 lectures, namely, Hegel's defense against the charge of pantheism and atheism. Here he clearly aligns himself with Jewish monotheism.

23. A correlative advantage of the new arrangement is that it permits a transition directly from Egyptian to Greek Religion, which suits Hegel's interpretation quite conveniently. This advantage is preserved in 1831 by placing Jewish religion ahead of Egyptian rather than after Greek. This may have been a contributory factor to the reorganization.

But this "advance" from Greek to Jewish religion is not undialectical even in 1827. Judaism may not be tinged by finitude, but neither is finitude transfigured and overreached by infinitude in it. Moreover, the one universal God of Judaism is believed to be the God of a particular people. At the beginning of the section on Roman religion, Hegel refers to the "one-sidedness" of both Greek and Jewish religion, and this in fact seems closer to his actual view. It is only from particular perspectives that one appears "higher" than the other. From the point of view of the idea of God, monotheism, and spiritual unity and subjectivity, Judaism is higher. But from the point of view of the idea of the mediation of divinity and humanity (i.e., the incarnation) as well as of free ethical institutions, Greek religion is higher. Their respective one-sidednesses are finally overcome, not in Roman religion, which proves to be an abortive and retrograde, arbitrary and expedient, unification of the religions, but in the Christian religion (although Roman religion plays a necessary transitional role). Perhaps one element in Hegel's 1827 "reversal" is his conviction that the unity and spirituality of the God of Israel is the necessary foundation of true and consummate religion: therefore Christianity must arise among the Jewish people. Hegel knew this already in 1821, but his assessment of Judaism in the earlier lectures did not bear it out.

The Religion of Beauty, or Greek Religion

In 1827 the presentation of Greek religion is oriented to a different central question, and as a consequence the organization of the material differs somewhat; but the actual content of the treatment is quite similar to 1824, and no additional sources are utilized.[24] Whereas in 1824 Hegel was concerned to show how in Greek re-

24. Hegel had more resources at his disposal for the study of Greek religion than of any other. He was thoroughly familiar with, and frequently referred to, the classical authors: the pre-Socratic philosophers (Anaxagoras, Parmenides, Xenophanes), Plato and Aristotle, the poets (Homer, Hesiod, Pindar), the tragedians (Aeschylus, Euripides, Sophocles), the historians (Thucydides, Herodotus, Diodorus Siculus, Pausanias, Xenophon). Among modern authors, by far the most important was G. F. Creuzer, whose *Symbolik und Mythologie der alten Völker, besonders der Griechen* (2d ed., 1819–1821) contained a wealth of information; but there were a number of others as well, to whom reference is made in the footnotes.

ligion divinity determines or "particularizes" itself, making itself available to and infusing the world of human spirit, in 1827 the central concern is with the elevation of the spiritual above the natural.

The substantial foundation of Greek religion is that of the rationality and freedom of spirit, which results in the formation of an "ethical life" (*Sittlichkeit*). Consequently the Greek divinities must be essentially ethical/spiritual powers. At the same time these divinities have been shaped out of the old gods of the primitive Greek nature religion. Thus the "war with the Titans" is the essence of Greek religion. Hegel elaborates on this at some length, showing how the natural element is subordinated but not totally vanquished and that what we continue to find is a "mingling" of the natural with the spiritual in the Greek gods; thus Zeus is not only the natural firmament generally but also the father of gods and humans and especially the political god, the god of the state. Both the oracles and the mysteries are carryovers from the old religion. The first mode of giving oracles is by mere natural sounds; later the oracle is given in human tones but not in clear speech.

Two other aspects of the divine content—the relationship of the gods to necessity above and contingent singularization below—are taken over directly from the 1824 lectures. On the one hand, the universal power of necessity hovers above the gods. This power is devoid of purpose and subjectivity, it is incomprehensible and abstract; and hence these two sides of divinity remain unmediated. On the other hand, there is a purely contingent singularization of the divine content, based not on the principle of particularization but on contingent natural aspects (such as the procreative, generative element in nature) or on the involvement of the gods in human affairs.

The discussion of the "shape" or configuration in which the gods appear differs somewhat in 1827. Because we are still only at the initial stage of freedom and rationality, the ethical gods must appear in an external, sensible shape. "Phantasy" (*Phantasie*) is the means of giving representational status to the divine. Phantasy, says Hegel, is the activity of shaping external or immediate being in such a way that "the external being is no longer independent but is downgraded into being just a sign of the indwelling spirit." We have seen phantasy at work in more primitive forms in Hindu and Egyptian religion. What distinguishes the Greeks is their recognition that the human figure is the only way in which spirit can be adequately represented in natural, sensible shape. "That is why the Greeks represented the gods as human beings." They were right in doing so, and they did so with consummate artistry, both plastic and poetic. The only problem is that the gods thus made are still finite. "This finitude of content is why they originate in a finite manner as human products. At this stage the divine is grasped neither by pure thinking nor in pure spirit." Hegel does not go on to compare the human shape of the gods in Greek religion with the Christian idea of incarnation, as he does in 1824 and more specifically in 1831.

In the section on the Greek cultus, Hegel addresses two issues primarily. Cultus in general involves a consciousness or feeling of unity with the divine. The Greeks take this to an extreme in the sense that human beings have an essentially *affirmative* relationship to their gods. Finitude for them does not *negate* itself in the religious relationship but extends itself to infinitude; hence the "substantial element that is revered as God is at the same time the proper essentiality of the human being." For example, Pallas Athena is not merely the goddess of the city but the living, actual spirit of the Athenian people. Thus cheerfulness, serenity, and freedom characterize this cultus. In worshiping the gods, "human beings celebrate their own honor."

But another element is introduced through the relationship to necessity, as expressed in the tragedies. It is recognized that the divine also shares in the lot of finitude, which is limitation and death. The ethical powers come into collision in virtue of their one-sidedness, and the heroes, who have committed themselves to realization of one or another such power, perish as an unavoidable consequence. Because "the higher element does not emerge as the infinitely spiritual power" but is necessity or fate (*Anankē*), there remains an "unhealed sorrow" in Greek religion, and of a higher reconciliation only intimations can occur because it is a matter merely of external purification (rather than of inner conversion) and of the balancing of ineluctable one-sidednesses.

The Religion of Sublimity, or Jewish Religion

Quite apart from the reversal of the order in which Greek and Jewish religion are treated, and the argument for the necessity of "the elevation of the religion of beauty into the religion of sublimity," the 1827 lectures carry further the favorable reassessment of Judaism begun in 1824. Gone are all earlier references to the "fear of the Lord" that is "the beginning of wisdom" and to the "execrations" of Leviticus; Job is mentioned only briefly, and the critique of Judaism is muted. Almost the entire section is given over to a careful analysis of the Jewish idea of God and to various aspects of the relationship of God and world. This material is already present in 1824, but it is reworked, expanded, and presented more clearly. Hegel's interpretation is based almost entirely on his own reading of the Hebrew scriptures (primarily the Pentateuch, Job, the Psalms, Second and Third Isaiah) and, to a lesser extent, a few commentaries.

The great contribution of Israel to the history of religion is its comprehension of the "spiritually subjective unity" of God. This subjective unity is not mere substance but is absolute power, wisdom, and purpose, for which reason it is "holy," it merits the name "God" for the first time. It is in fact "infinite subjectivity," which is the highest philosophical concept; as such, God subsists without sensible shape, only for thought ("thinking is the essential soil for this object").

But this one God does not remain in self-enclosed, abstract identity with himself. Rather, God's wisdom contains the process of "divine particularization" (a description reserved to Greek religion in 1824), that is, divine self-determining, dividing, creating. This process is not yet posited *within* God concretely but remains abstract and external; it is not yet an immanent Trinity. But the act of creation is a highly important, in fact definitive, determination of the Jewish God. God *is* the creator of the world. This has implications both for the world and for God. First, the world does

55

not emanate from God, as in Hindu and Greek cosmogonies, but is created *ex nihilo*. This means that the subjectivity of the One remains what is absolutely first and is not superseded by what has gone forth. Second, God's relations to the world—the more specific moments of divine wisdom, which are goodness and justice—are definitive of God's own being, so that we do in fact *know* God in knowing his relations. The categories of goodness and justice are now defined more fully. As good, God releases and sets free from himself the created world; only what is genuinely free can do this, can let its determinations go as free, can release them to "go their separate ways," which is the totality of the finite world. As just, God maintains the world in relation to himself, does not abandon it to radical autonomy, specifies its purpose. Third, the world is rendered profane, prosaic; nature is divested of divinity, and there is no cheap identity of finite and infinite. The manifestation of God in the world takes on the character of sublimity, which is its genuine form, or of miracle, which is specious. Finally, God's purpose is made manifest in the natural and human worlds. This purpose is simply that the whole earth and all peoples should proclaim the glory of God. This glorification of God is the "inner aspect" of all human ethical activity. Without it, moral righteousness counts as nothing; with it, one may be confident of the fulfillment of one's worldly existence. This is what underlies the "remarkable" faith of the Jewish people; it is the theme of the Old Testament as a whole but especially of the Book of Job. It is not finally a human quality but a dimension of the holiness of God.

At the end of this notably sympathetic phenomenology of the Jewish representation of God, Hegel mentions briefly certain "limitations." These are principally three: the self-determining wisdom of God is not yet an inward self-development (the idea of God as "what is eternally self-developing within itself" is found only in the manifest or revelatory religion); despite the implicit universalism, the God of Judaism remains a national God, the God of a limited national family rather than of the whole human family; and the divine purposes are abstract because they are simply commandments given by God as something prescribed and immutable, rather than purposes worked out in the conflict and dialectic of historical/

ethical life. These limitations appear in the Jewish cultus, about which there is virtually no discussion in the 1827 lectures—whether because Hegel did not wish to emphasize the limitations, or because he was short of time, or because Lasson's text and the available transcripts are incomplete at this point, we do not know.

The Religion of Expediency, or Roman Religion

The treatment of Roman religion in 1827 is quite similar to that of 1824; both of these versions are much briefer than the corresponding section of the *Ms.* and are dependent on it. Hegel's interpretation of Roman religion remained more constant through the eleven-year period of his lectures than that of any other religion. He was thoroughly familiar with the Roman authors and alluded to them frequently, but among secondary sources relied mainly on Karl Philipp Moritz's *Anthousa; oder, Roms Alterthümer* (1791), although he was in fundamental disagreement with it. He worked out his own interpretation in great detail in the *Ms.* and in the later lectures simply summarized the essential points. Only the transitions are different.

What is still lacking, according to the 1827 version, is a divine purposiveness that is at once holy, universal, and concrete. The Greeks achieved concreteness in the ethical content of their gods, but they lacked holiness and sacrificed universality to multiplicity. The God of Israel was one and holy but was claimed as the God of a particular people, whose laws were abstract. Roman religion, says Hegel, is a *relative* totality, in which the Greek and Jewish religions "indeed lose their one-sidedness, but the two principles perish conjointly, each by means of assimilation into its opposite; still, it is this very homogeneity that interests us in them. The religion of beauty loses the concrete individuality of its gods and hence also their ethical, independent content; the gods are reduced to means. The religion of sublimity loses the orientation toward the One, the eternal, the transcendent." The universal purposiveness of the Romans is flawed because it is external, empirical, finite, utilitarian. Religion, when reduced to a means to extrinsic, worldly ends, is finally destroyed. Roman religion is the religion to end all religion—a fact symbolized by collecting the gods of all the religions

57

into a single pantheon, where they are subjected to Jupiter Capitolinus and cancel out one another, a veritable *Götterdämmerung*.

Hegel stresses once again, in opposition to Moritz's view, that the Greek and Roman gods are essentially quite different. Greek religion, as we have seen, is serene and cheerful and does not take its gods too seriously. Roman religion, by contrast, is deadly serious and utterly utilitarian. Its gods serve both public and private purposes. The public or state purpose is Roman world dominion; the private and civic purposes relate to every aspect of economic and social activity (raising grain, baking bread, feeding livestock, minting coins, fever, plague, sanitation, leisure, trouble and care, etc.). These gods have no true meaning of their own; they are "lifeless imitations" of the Greek gods, "machinery devoid of sense."

As to the cultus, "the Romans worship the gods because they need them and when they need them, especially in times of particular exigency. For the Romans such need is the general theogony from which the gods arise." This can be seen in the innumerable religious festivals honoring specific deities. The Romans also effectively worship death, which is to be seen in their plays, contests, and spectacles. Here they enact their conviction that individuals must totally serve the interest of the state, and the highest *virtus* is to die in combat. "This cold-blooded murder was a delight to their eyes; in it they beheld the nullity of human individuality, the worthlessness of the individual. . . . It was the spectacle of the hollow, empty destiny that relates to human beings as a contingency, as blind caprice." By contrast the Romans also insisted on abstract personal rights, but these were limited to property rights and did not include higher ethical rights. The Romans attained only a purely abstract subjectivity.

The transition from this state of affairs to Christianity is difficult to reconstruct from the conclusion of the 1827 *Determinate Religion* in the form in which we have it. The 1831 variant contained in n. 544 suggests that this destruction of the sublimity and beauty, the holiness and ethical quality, the faithfulness and serene happiness of religion "produced this monstrous misery and a universal sorrow, a sorrow that served to prepare the birth pangs of the religion of truth." Hegel may have had something like that in mind in 1827. Our text says only that when the moments that subsist in contradiction and in a spiritless way in Roman religion are unified, then we shall have advanced to the "next and final stage of religion." Presumably these moments are the authentic moments of the religions of beauty and sublimity as well as the heritage of the religions of nature—moments that have been "homogenized" in Roman religion, not truly unified.

c. The Consummate Religion

Introduction

The brief opening section goes back to the Ms. and offers a similar "definition" of Christianity, namely, that in it the concept of religion has become "objective to itself." "Religion, in accord with its general concept, is the consciousness of God as such, consciousness of absolute essence." Initially, in the finite or determinate religions, the two elements of this relationship, human consciousness on the one hand and absolute or divine essence on the other, remain juxtaposed and externally related in such a way that consciousness knows God only as an otherworldly "supreme being" and God is not self-mediated through consciousness; both remain abstract, finite entities. When, however, the concept of religion becomes "objective to itself," this opposition is recognized to be false. For consciousness comes *to itself* in knowing God, and this knowledge is at the same time God's *self*-knowledge, by which absolute essence becomes true, infinite, absolute *spirit*. The truth is the whole, consciousness and God together; and the religion in which this truth is made manifest is the consummate religion, the religion of spirit *for* spirit, or the religion of *infinite* spirit.

But Christianity is not only a spiritual religion; it is also a positive religion. As we have seen, by 1827 Hegel was no longer preoccupied with the need to attack theological subjectivism and historicism, to which part of the 1824 introduction to *The Consummate Religion* was devoted; rather he was facing the Neopietist charge of "pantheism" brought against his own work. One aspect of this charge was that speculative philosophy does not take finite, "positive," historical reality seriously but instead simply identifies the world with God. Hegel is essentially responding to this charge in the new and lengthy introductory section on "the positivity and spirituality" of the Christian religion (see n. 6).

It is now necessary to say that the absolute religion is both *revelatory* and *revealed*: that is, not only is the absolute truth made open and manifest in it but also this truth has come to humanity from without, in positive, historical fashion. This is true not just of religion but of everything with spiritual or rational content— ethics, laws, scientific discoveries, and so on. "Everything that is *for* consciousness is *objective* to consciousness. Everything must come to us from outside." But the validity or truth of the content is not constituted by positivity as such but by its conformity to what is rational or conceptual. "The spiritual . . . cannot be directly verified by the unspiritual, the sensible." Thus we find already in religion itself a critique of proofs based on miracles, and we are led to the insight that the only true verification is by means of spiritual witness. Hegel understands the witness of the *Holy* Spirit to occur in and through the witness of *our* spirit to spiritual truth (see n. 16). This can occur in diverse ways, ranging from a kind of preconscious "resonance" to the good and the true, to the conceptual system of philosophy. But "it is not required that for all of humanity the truth be brought forth in a philosophical way." For some people, indeed for most, belief on the basis of authority and testimonies still has a place.

The Bible is for Christians the fundamental basis that strikes a chord within them; but, although many people lead pious lives just by holding to it, we must move beyond it to thought, that is, to theology. Indeed, this is unavoidable once attempts are made to interpret the *meaning* of the words of the Bible. Presuppositions are brought in that are not in the Bible itself. Present-day presuppositions such as that humanity is good by nature or that God cannot be known make it exceedingly difficult to interpret the Bible, and it is necessary to work through these presuppositions critically and conceptually: that is the task of philosophy. Similarly, the fundamental doctrines of Christianity have by and large disappeared from present-day dogmatics because of its presuppositions, and it is now philosophy that is orthodox, maintaining and preserving the basic truths of Christianity. Hegel ends this second section with the well-known statement that "we" shall not set to work in "merely historical" (*historisch*) fashion but rather shall proceed "conceptually" or "scientifically" (n. 41). Thus, while attending to historical starting points and historical details, these must finally be "put aside" in the speculative redescription of the truth of this religion.

The third introductory section, "Survey of Previous Developments," is also new in 1827. It is based on a logical grasp of the dialectics of the relation of finite and infinite, which yields the insight that the "elevation" of the finite to the infinite is at the same time the return of the infinite to itself (n. 44). Hegel's treatment begins with the concept of religion, then advances to the realization or actualization of the concept as "idea." The idea first appears in the form of immediacy, or the *natural religions* (n. 49), a second phase of which involves the withdrawal-into-self of spirit from its submersion in the natural (Buddhism, Hinduism, n. 50). The second main stage in the development of religion is *spiritual religion*, for which the natural is not an independent content but only the appearance of something inward. This inwardness is for Greek religion the beautiful human form and soul, and for Jewish religion the one spiritual, personal God ("who first merits for us the name of God") (see nn. 52, 55). Finally, there is the *religion of purposiveness*, or Roman religion (n. 56), which represents a phase distinct from spiritual religion, and indeed does not understand the gods as spiritual subjectivities but rather as abstractions instrumental to the well-being of the state.

Before completing this section, Hegel offers an argument for the transition to the consummate religion based on the logic of the concept: the concept becomes spirit only insofar as it has traversed the finite forms of religion, has achieved determinacy through the circuit of self-diremption and self-return. The absolute *idea* is the implicit unity of concept and reality (objectivity); it comes to be *spirit* when this unity has been realized. At this point Hegel is incorporating elements of the ontological proof, which establishes the identity of concept and objectivity, thinking and being, in terms of the self-mediation of the concept. As we have seen, in the 1827 lectures the ontological proof has been transferred to Part I along with the other proofs. But traces of it are still discernible in the old location.

The final section of the Introduction, "Division of the Subject," provides a summary of the three main sections into which the discussion of the consummate religion is divided. These sections correspond to three "elements," or moments, in the self-development of the idea of God. They can be explicated in terms of the categories of consciousness, in which case we have "three ways by which the subject is related to God," namely (1) thought or thinking, (2) sensible intuition and representation, (3) sensibility and subjectivity. But they can also be explicated in terms of the objective categories of logic, to which spatiotemporal representations have been attached by the Christian doctrine of the Trinity. Thus we arrive at the following schema: (1) universality—the absolute, eternal idea in and for itself, God in his eternity before the creation of the world and outside the world; (2) particularity: God creates the world of nature and finite spirit, first positing the separation, then reconciling what is alien to himself; (3) singularity: through this process of reconciliation, God is the Holy Spirit, the Spirit present in its community. Hegel concludes by insisting that these are not "external distinctions" produced by us; "rather they are the activity, the developed vitality, of absolute spirit itself." Christianity (we might say) is the consummate religion because the very structure of its belief in God corresponds to the object of that belief, the divine life itself.

The First Element: The Idea of God In and For Itself

Well into this section Hegel offers an inclusive definition of the triune God in speculative categories: "God in his eternal universality is the one who distinguishes himself, determines himself, posits an other to himself, and likewise sublates the distinction, thereby remaining present to himself, and is spirit only through this process of being brought forth" (pp. 426–427). We can express this in the mode of sensibility by saying that "God is love," for "love is a distinguishing of two, who nevertheless are absolutely not distinguished for each other." Thus God as love "is this distinguishing and the nullity of the distinction, a play of distinctions in which there is nothing serious, distinction precisely as sublated, i.e., the simple, eternal idea" (n. 71). This obviously has reference to the immanent Trinity; the economic or worldly Trinity, God's relation to otherness *ad extra,* involves (we might say) a play of distinctions that is "deadly serious"—to the extremity of death on the cross, which is the death of God.

Much of this section is devoted to the argument that the speculative idea of God cannot be grasped by the categories of sense experience or of the understanding, for neither is able to grasp the speculative truth of *identity in difference.* For the understanding, God is either an abstract, undifferentiated monad or a sum of distinct and mutually contradictory predicates that express God's relation to himself or to the world. For sensible consideration and the understanding, the Trinity remains an impenetrable μυστήριον, as does life itself, with its alternation of distinction, contradiction, and annulment. The situation is not eased by the fact that "because religion is the truth for everyone," the content of the divine idea appears in forms accessible to sense experience and understanding, namely, the symbols of the trinitarian "persons." The understanding is baffled by the seeming contradiction that there is one God, yet three divine persons—even though personality, too, has this dialectic of identity and difference within itself ("the truth of personality is found precisely in winning it back through this immersion . . . in the other").

The conclusion of the section is taken up by a discussion of anticipations of the triad as the true category in earlier religions and philosophies (Hinduism, Pythagoreanism, Platonism, Alexandrian Judaism, Gnosticism). The main thing to know is that "these fermentations of an idea" (n. 105), "wild as they are, are rational." Jacob Boehme knew this because he recognized that the Trinity is the universal foundation of everything, and he perceived traces of it "in everything and everywhere," even though his way of representing this was "rather wild and fanciful." Hegel's own agenda, especially in the 1827 lectures, might be understood as that of demonstrating traces of the Trinity in everything by showing the rational, dialectical structure of all reality. Thus the idea of the triune God is not an impenetrable mystery or mere theological "decoration," as was being suggested by recent attacks on the Trinity to which Hegel was at pains to respond.[25]

The Second Element: Representation, Appearance

God is "represented" or "appears" in the world under the modalities of both "differentiation" and "reconciliation," and it is these that provide the basis for the two main sections into which the Second Element of the idea of God is divided. Each of these is further divided into a number of steps or subsections.

Subsection (a) of "Differentiation" is concerned with differentiation within the divine life and in the world; this is an important section since it sets forth as clearly as found anywhere Hegel's views on creation and the relationship of God and world. The first sort of differentiation is basically a matter of the inner-trinitarian dialectic: "the act of differentiation is only a movement, a play of love with itself, which does not arrive at the seriousness of other-being, of separation and rupture." In this state it is still only an abstract distinction, lacking realization and reality. But it belongs to the absolute *freedom* of the divine idea that "in its act of determining and dividing, it *releases* the other to exist as a free and independent being. The other, released as something free and independent, is *the world* as such." In other words, because otherness is already a moment within the divine idea, the idea is free to allow this its own *other* also to obtain "the determinacy of other-*being,* of an actual entity," without losing itself or giving itself up. It can give freedom and independent existence to the other without losing its own freedom: "It is only for the being that is free that freedom *is.*" This independence, however, is not autonomy: the truth of the world is its *ideality,* not its reality; it is something posited or created and has being, so to speak, only for an instant. Its destiny is to sublate this separation and estrangement from God and return to its origin. Hence the second element as a whole is "the process of the world in love by which it passes over from fall and separation into reconciliation."

The analysis of the creation and fall of humanity, of good and

25. See Hegel's *Introduction,* n. 17.

evil, and of knowledge and estrangement in the next three subsections is also one of Hegel's clearest discussions of the subject. The subsection on "natural humanity" (b) focuses on the ambiguity in the statements that humanity is good or evil "by nature." Humanity is *implicitly* good because created in the divine image; but the human vocation is not to remain in the condition of implicitness. If it does, if it chooses to do so, to exist according to nature, then it is evil; but likewise, passing beyond the natural state is what first constitutes the cleavage, which in turn introduces evil. The story of the "fall" (c) is discussed next, for the reasons indicated in n. 138. Hegel's concern is not so much to highlight the "contradictions" in the story, as it was in the earlier lectures, as to extract the conceptual truth hidden in its representational form—the truth about the involvement of the whole of humanity in evil, about knowledge or cognition as what is distinctively human, issuing in both good and evil, about labor as a necessary consequence of knowledge, and about immortality as something possessed by humanity not in virtue of its natural life but only through the activity of thinking.

The linkage between knowledge, estrangement, and evil is a complex and important matter in Hegel's thought. Cognitive knowledge (*Erkenntnis*) entails an act of judgment or primal division (*Ur-teil*); it thus issues in separation, cleavage, rupture into two (*Ent-zwei-ung*) (n. 141). This cleavage or estrangement (*Entfremdung*)—the words are quite similar, n. 138—is not, strictly speaking, in itself evil but rather is the inherent condition of finite spirit just because it is consciousness and cognizes, but finitely, that is, is unable finally to overcome the divisions posited by its acts of knowing. It is the *precondition* or *occasion* of evil, however, since evil entails the conscious or deliberate actualization of the state of separation, the choice to live in isolation from the depths of spirit, to cut oneself off from both the universal and the particular, to gratify immediate desires, to exist "according to nature" (*nach der Natur*). Yet self-rupture or self-estrangement gives rise not only to evil but also to the need for reconciliation, which may be seen when estrangement is associated with the anguish (*Schmerz*) of Jewish religion and the misery or unhappiness (*Unglück*) of Hellenistic-Roman culture.

This is a matter emphasized in a special way by the 1827 lectures in the concluding subsection (d) of "Differentiation," which accordingly has a transitional character. Anguish arises from the awareness of the seemingly unbridgeable gulf between the infinite and the finite, the good God and evil humanity, whereas misery expresses the awareness of the inability of human beings to find true happiness in finite and worldly ends. When the awareness of estrangement and evil had intensified to the extreme degree—or "when the time had fully come"—there arose a recognition of the need for a reconciliation that is universal, divine, and infinite.

Sec. 2, "Reconciliation," takes up the definitive occurrence of reconciliation, for which the soil has been prepared by the preceding history of religions. In the first subsection (a), Hegel addresses the question how the idea of reconciliation can appear and why it must appear in a single historical individual. The *condition of possibility* for reconciliation is that the antithesis between divinity and humanity is already implicitly sublated. Because other-being or difference is already present within the divine idea (indeed, is what makes it *spirit*), "the other-being, the finitude, the weakness, the frailty of human nature is not to do any harm to that divine unity which forms the substance of reconciliation."

The *necessity* of a divinely mediated reconciliation has already been considered at some length: the subject is aware of the incongruity, of the *need* for reconciliation, but cannot bring it about on its own account. The necessity that reconciliation should appear in a single historical individual is grounded in the fact that it must be brought forth not merely in a form suitable to philosophical speculation but in one accessible to the whole of humanity, namely, the form of *sensible certainty*. Therefore, "God *had* to appear in the world in the flesh"—not just flesh as such, which would be an abstraction, but the flesh of *singular* human being. However, *many* or even *several* single incarnations will not do, because what is involved here is something that stands *over against* immediate, subjective consciousness in its condition of need. "The unity in question must appear for others as a singular human being *set apart*; it is not present in the others but only in *one* from whom all the others are excluded." This one is the human being who is what humanity implicitly is (*das Ansich,* n. 172), humanity in itself as such (*der Mensch an sich,* n. 171); there can be only one such ultimate. For this one the church has used the "monstrous compound," the "God-man."

In addition to the questions of possibility and necessity, that of *actuality* must also be addressed: "*Who was* this one individual?" (subsection b). Hegel initially makes a quite sharp distinction between a "nonreligious" and a "religious" perspective. The nonreligious perspective views Christ as an ordinary human being in accord with his external circumstances; it views him as a Socrates, a teacher of humanity, a martyr to the truth. Yet it must be said that as Hegel proceeds to expound the nonreligious perspective, the distinction between it and the religious perspective becomes blurred. Although Christ is born and has needs like all other human beings, he does not share the corruption and evil inclinations of others or pursue worldly affairs. "Rather he lives only for the truth, only for its proclamation." He *is,* his identity is in, his teaching. Hegel's presentation of the teaching must go back to the *Ms.,* since it is fuller than in 1824, and similar themes are identified: the kingdom of God as the symbol for the constitution of a new world, a new consciousness of the reconciliation of humanity with God; the polemical, indeed "revolutionary" attitude toward all of the established worldly orders; and the connection of the person of the teacher with the teaching. Christ speaks not merely as a teacher but as a prophet, that is, as one who expresses the demand *immediately* from God and by whom God himself speaks it and confirms it. The one who says this is essentially human, but his is an essential humanity in which essential divinity is present. "It is the Son of Man who speaks thus, in whom this expression, this activity of what subsists in and for itself, is essentially the work of God—not as something suprahuman that appears in the shape of an external revelation, but rather as [God's] working in a human being, so that the divine presence is essentially identical with this human being." If this much can be said from the nonreligious perspective—and Hegel insists that this is all that is involved so far—then the "nonreligious" history of Christ does seem to offer a kind of attestation to the truth of the religious perspective, the spiritual witness that God is definitively and reconcilingly present in this individual. On the one hand, Hegel is guarding against reliance on historical proofs, in accord with the predominant emphasis of the 1824 lectures; but on the other hand, he is holding on to the religious and philosophical significance of this particular history in its specificity and detail, thus harking back to a leitmotiv of the *Ms*.

The death of Christ can also be viewed from the nonreligious perspective: he died as a martyr to the truth, who sealed the truth of his teaching by the manner of his death (see the end of subsection b and n. 196). But his death also inaugurates the transition into the religious sphere, and this is the topic taken up in subsection c. "Comprehended spiritually," the death of Christ "becomes the means of salvation, the focal point of reconciliation." The "Lutheran" statement, "God himself is dead," represents a spiritual interpretation, because it means that everything human, fragile, and finite is a moment of the divine, that "God himself is involved in this," and that what is happening is a "stripping away" of the human element, an entrance into glory.

When the history of the life and death of Christ obtains a spiritual interpretation, there begins "the history of the resurrection and ascension of Christ to the right hand of God." Since the community of faith also begins at this point, we must assume that the history of the resurrection and the history of the community are in some sense coterminous, although Hegel does not elaborate. The community is founded on the consciousness and certainty of divine-human unity and divine reconciliation. For it, Christ's history is a "divine history," "the eternal history, the eternal movement, which God himself is." To say that "Christ has died for all" is to understand this not as an individual act but as a moment in the divine history, the moment in which other-being and separation are sublated.

The Third Element: Community, Spirit

The third element is briefer in the 1827 lectures than in 1824 and 1821; only two lectures remained before the end of the semester (n. 212). In Sec. 1, on the "origin of the community," after stating, as he has in earlier lectures, that the community of faith is the Spirit of God "as existing and realizing itself," Hegel introduces a new theme, namely, that the community "begins with the fact that the truth is at hand"—the truth that God is a triune God (the recurring affirmation of which is, as we have seen, a leitmotiv of the 1827 lectures). Faith is the inward, subjective appropriation of this truth, the truth that reconciliation is accomplished with certainty by the self-mediation of the triune God. The difficulty residing in the fact that faith is initially the act of single individuals is overcome by taking finite subjectivity up into the infinite subjectivity of the absolute (or Holy) Spirit, which is no longer isolated and singular. Individual human subjects are, as it were, "essentialized" in the transfigured intersubjectivity of the spiritual community.[26]

The community as *realized* or *subsisting* (Sec. 2) is the *church*, which is the "institution whereby [its] subjects come to the truth." The foremost of its institutions is *doctrine*, which is now something presupposed, fixed, taught as universally valid and authoritative. The church is essentially a teaching church. No longer is a person elevated to the absolute by the outpouring of the Holy Spirit; rather he or she is instructed by the appropriate authorities, and this instruction must be assimilated in a process of education and cultivation. The individual partakes of the truth of reconciliation qua individual through the rite of *baptism*; one's transgressions are wiped out through the practice of *repentance* or *penitence*; and believers appropriate God's presence in the sacrament of *Holy Communion*. Notably, no mention is made of the preaching of the Word. Hegel certainly does seem to stress the sacramental character of the church in a way that is not customary among Protestants; and his silence with respect to the sermon (as at least a distinctive

26. The language here is not exactly Hegel's, but the content is. What Hegel says is that individual subjects still do not exist in a way appropriate to their "inward, substantial essentiality" and that in reconciliation, finitude is reduced to an "inessential" state. The language of "essentialization" comes from F. W. J. Schelling and has been adopted by Paul Tillich, who also employs the expression "spiritual community." See Tillich, *Systematic Theology,* vol. 3 (Chicago, 1963), pp. 149 ff., 400 ff. Similarly, in the 1831 lectures Hegel says that in the life of the community the "privatism" of individuals is "consumed" (n. 258).

form of "instruction") may reflect a suspicion of Protestant moralism as well as a low regard for the abilities of the Protestant clergy.[27]

Sec. 3, the "realization of the spirituality of the community" in universal actuality, is built upon the corresponding section in 1824, but its structure is worked out in a more rigorously logical form, and the contents are unusually suggestive (Hegel's final lecture [n. 242] was tightly packed!). Reconciliation must be actualized not only in the individual heart and in the church but also in the world in the form of rational freedom. The "community" should not remain simply ecclesiastical, nor will it simply pass away; rather it is to become a world-historical community. Three moments of this realization may be distinguished, which are not only logical types but also historical stages (albeit highly selective).

(a) The first is *real*, or reconciliation in *life*, worldly realization as such. This moment, in turn, is composed of three stages: that of immediacy or renunciation of the world, inner religiousness (primitive Christianity); that in which religiosity and worldliness remain external to each other, and the church has dominion over the world yet takes worldliness into itself (the medieval Catholic church); and that in which religion and world are reconciled in the "ethical realm" (n. 249), where the principle of freedom has penetrated into ethical life and its institutions of family, civil society, and state (the modern secular-bourgeois world).

(b) The second moment of realization is *ideal*, or reconciliation in *thought*. In the modern world this takes two forms (see n. 261). The first is that of the philosophy of the *Enlightenment*. Since its principle is one of abstract identity, it is directed not merely against externality but also against everything that is concrete—including the idea of the triune God. Since nothing concrete can be known of God, God is not known at all, and the Enlightenment ends with the "servitude of spirit in the absolute region of freedom." The other form is that of *Pietism*—"an inward weaving of spirit within

27. At the end of the 1821 *Ms.*, Hegel says that the gospel as preached tòday is like salt that has lost its savor, and he is quite critical of the clergy, who have abandoned their teaching responsibility. See unabridged ed., Vol. 3:160–161. On Hegel's early attitude toward sermons, see H. S. Harris, *Hegel's Development: Toward the Sunlight 1770–1801* (Oxford, 1972), pp. 129n, 163, 165.

itself," the pious life of feeling, which acknowledges no objective truth and which is "turned polemically against the philosophy that wants cognition." It was from this quarter that Hegel found himself attacked for his "pantheism" and speculative trinitarianism, and this attack served as the polemical context for the whole of the 1827 lectures. Thus it is not surprising that in 1827 he substituted a counterattack on Neopietism ("subjectivity devoid of content") for the treatment of Islamic religion that stood in this place in 1824.[28]

(c) The third and final moment is the *ideal-real*: subjectivity develops beyond itself in accord with the necessity of the content, which is objective. This is the standpoint of *speculative philosophy*, according to which "the content takes refuge in the concept and obtains its justification by thinking" (see n. 262). Here we find the true mediation of content and concept, of reality and thought, of the real and the ideal. Such a philosophical mediation is the justification of religion by showing how the content of religion accords with reason. Philosophy "is to this extent theology" because it presents the reconciliation of God with himself and with the otherness of nature and finite spirit—the "peace of God" that does *not* "surpass all reason" (n. 266) but is what reason is all about.

28. In the 1824 lectures Hegel contrasted the antireligious ideology of Enlightenment rationalism with the fanatic religiosity of Islam, both of which he thought were abstract and undialectical ways of thinking, although diametrically opposed, and both of which posed present-day challenges to Christianity. See unabridged ed., Vol. 3:35, 242–244. This is one of Hegel's few references to Islam in the lectures; it lacked a place in Hegel's schema of determinate religions and appeared only as a contemporary rival to Christianity.

INTRODUCTION

THE LECTURES OF 1827

Preface[1]

What we must take into consideration is first the relation of the philosophy of religion to philosophy as a whole, and second the relationship of the science of religion to the needs of our time.

The object is religion. This is the loftiest object that can occupy human beings; it is the absolute object. It is the region of eternal truth and eternal virtue, the region where all the riddles of thought, all contradictions, and all the sorrows of the heart should show themselves to be resolved, and the region of the eternal peace through which the human being is truly human. All the endless

---

1. [Ed.] None of the extant manuscripts has an initial heading. One might suppose, on the basis of the summary statement in the opening sentence, that the first topic to be considered, beginning immediately in the next paragraph, is "the relation of the philosophy of religion to philosophy as a whole." But this summary is misleading since the first topic Hegel considers—and only after what we are calling the "Preface"—is rather different (see n. 5). The summary of the first of the two points to be considered actually reflects the 1824 lectures, which indicates that Hegel used the Griesheim transcript of 1824 when he lectured in 1827, changing the content of the latter lectures as he proceeded. The first long paragraph ("The object is religion . . . our intent to consider") is based on the opening remarks in the Ms., which Hegel repeated in 1824 and 1827. In order to identify this common material we are using the heading "Preface," although it is not an expression used by Hegel himself. The 1827 "Preface" cannot be reconstructed from either W or L since both of them tightly interweave materials from 1821, 1824, and 1827 in an editorial version of Hegel's opening remarks. Our text at this point is based on the transcript of the Polish student Hube, whose German left something to be desired. His staccato sentences, rapid shifts of images, and grammatical infelicities have been smoothed out a bit, but the style is not characteristic of Hegel and the contents are abbreviated.

intricacies of human activity and pleasures arise from the determination of human being as implicitly spirit. Everything that people value and esteem, everything on which they think to base their pride and glory, all of this finds its ultimate focal point in religion, in the thought or consciousness of God and in the feeling of God. God is the beginning and end of all things. God is the sacred center, which animates and inspires all things. Religion possesses its object within itself—and that object is God, for religion is the relation of human consciousness to God. The object of religion *is* simply through itself and on its own account; it is the absolutely final end in and for itself, the absolutely free being. Here our concern about the final end can have no other final end than this object itself. Only in this context do all other aims experience their settlement. In its concern with this object, spirit frees itself from all finitude. ˜This concern is the true liberation of the human being and is freedom itself, true consciousness of the truth.˜[2] Everything [else] drops into the | past. Finite life seems like a desert. Religion is the consciousness of freedom and truth. If our concern with it is a feeling then it is bliss, and if an activity then it has to manifest God's glory and majesty. This concept of religion is universal. Religion holds this position for all peoples and persons. Everywhere this concern is regarded as the sabbath of life. Truly in this region of the spirit flow the waters of forgetfulness from which the soul drinks.[3] All the griefs of this bank and shoal[4] of life vanish away in this aether, whether in the feeling of devotion or of hope. All of it drops into the past. In religion all cares pass away, for in it one finds oneself fortunate. All harshness of fate passes into a dream. Everything earthly dissolves into light and love, not a remote but an actually present liveliness, certainty, and enjoyment. Even if [the bliss of] religion

62

2. *Thus Hu with An;* W₁ *reads:* In its concern with this object, spirit unburdens itself of all finitude. This concern leads to satisfaction and liberation. W₂ *(Var/1831?) reads:* In the region in which spirit concerns itself with this aim it unburdens itself of all finitude and gains ultimate satisfaction and liberation; for here spirit no longer relates itself to something other and limited, but to the unlimited and the infinite instead. This is an infinite relationship, a relationship of freedom and no longer one of dependence.
3. [*Ed.*] The mythical underworld river *Lēthē*, the personification of oblivion.
4. [*Ed.*] Cf. Shakespeare, *Macbeth*, act 1, sc. 7.

is put off into the future, it is still radiant in life here and now, or in the actuality within which this image is effective and substantial. Such is the universal content of religion among human beings; this content it is our intent to consider.

1. Comparison of Philosophy and Religion with Regard to Their Object[5]

[6]But it should be noted straightaway that the proposal to "consider" it involves a relationship to it that is already twisted out of shape. For when | we speak of "consideration" and "object" we are distinguishing the two as freestanding, mutually independent, 63

---

5. [*Ed.*] In this section Hegel does not consider "the relation of philosophy of religion to philosophy as a whole," as he suggests in his initial summary statement (see n. 1), but rather offers a comparison of philosophy and religion with regard to their object (hence our editorial section heading). Hegel makes two basic points: that the object or content of philosophy and religion is one and the same, and that the connection between philosophy and religion has already been established in the tradition. While this section may be considered to be new, it draws on materials from earlier lectures, including parts of the *Ms. Introduction* and Sec. A of *The Concept of Religion* in the *Ms.*

6. *Similar in* W$_1$; W$_2$ *(MiscP) reads (parallel in main text follows):* Since we remarked earlier that philosophy makes religion the object of its consideration, and since this consideration now seems to have the aspect of something distinct from its object, it looks as if we are still standing in the relationship where both sides are independent of one another and remain separate. In assuming this observational relationship, we would be stepping outside of the region of devotion and enjoyment that religion is; the object and the [act of] consideration as the movement of thought would then be as distinct as (for example) the spatial figures in mathematics are distinct from the spirit that considers them. But this is only the relationship as it appears to begin with, when cognition is still severed from the religious side and is *finite* cognition. If we look more closely, however, it is evident that in fact the content, need, and interest of philosophy is something it has in common with religion.

The object of religion, like that of philosophy, is the eternal truth in its very objectivity, God and nothing but God and the explication of God. Philosophy is not worldly wisdom but cognition of the nonworldly; not cognition of external mass or of empirical existence and life, but cognition of what is eternal, of what God is and what flows from God's nature: for this nature must reveal and develop itself. Hence philosophy is only explicating *itself* when it explicates religion, and when it explicates itself it is explicating religion. Since it is the concern with eternal truth, which is in and for itself, and indeed since it is the occupation of thinking spirit (not of [individual] caprice and of particular interest) with this object, philosophy is the same activity as religion. In its philosophizing, spirit immerses itself just as vitally in this object, and relinquishes its particularity in the same way. For it

fixed sides that are mutually opposed. For example, space is the object of geometry, but the spatial figures that it considers are distinct from the considering spirit, for they are only its "object." So if we say now that philosophy ought to consider religion, then these two are likewise set in a relationship of distinction in which they stand in opposition to one another. But on the contrary it must be said that the content of philosophy, its need and interest, is wholly in common with that of religion. The object of religion, like that of philosophy, is the eternal truth, God and nothing but God and the explication of God. Philosophy is only explicating *itself* when

---

penetrates its object just as the religious consciousness does, which also has nothing of its own but only wants to immerse itself in this content.

Thus religion and philosophy coincide in one. In fact philosophy is itself the service of God; it *is* religion, because it involves the same renunciation of subjective fancies and opinions in its concern with God. Thus philosophy is identical with religion, and the distinction [between them] is that philosophy exists in a way peculiar to itself, distinguished from the mode we are accustomed to call "religion" as such. What they have in common is that they are both religion; what distinguishes them consists only in the type and mode of religion [that each is]. They differ in the peculiar character of their concern with God. But this is where the difficulties lie, which seem so great that for philosophy ever to be one with religion counts as an impossibility. The apprehensive attitude of theology toward philosophy and the [mutually] hostile stance of religion and philosophy arise from this. In the perspective of this hostile stance (as theology construes it), it seems that philosophy works to corrupt the content of religion, destroying and profaning it, and that the concern of philosophy with God is completely different from that of religion. This is the old antipathy and contradiction that we already see among the Greeks; for even among the Athenians, that free and democratic people, books were burned and Socrates was condemned to death. But now this antipathy is held to be an acknowledged fact, and more so than the just-asserted unity of religion and philosophy.

Old as this antipathy is, however, the linkage of philosophy with religion is just as ancient. Already for the Neopythagoreans and Neoplatonists, still situated within the pagan world, the folk deities were not deities of phantasy but had become deities of thought. Afterward this linkage found a place in the work of the most eminent church fathers, who adopted an essentially conceptual approach in their religiosity, by setting out from the assumption that theology is religion together with a thinking, comprehending consciousness. The Christian church owes to their philosophical instruction the first beginnings of a content of Christian doctrine.

This uniting of religion with philosophy was carried through even more fully in the Middle Ages. So far were they from believing that conceptual knowing might be injurious to faith that it was regarded as essential to the further development of faith itself. These great men—Anselm, Abelard, etc.—developed the definitions of the faith still further on the basis of philosophy.

it explicates religion, and when it explicates itself it is explicating religion. For the *thinking* spirit is what penetrates this object, the truth; it is thinking that enjoys the truth and purifies the subjective consciousness. Thus religion and philosophy coincide in one. In fact philosophy is itself | the service of God,[7] as is religion. But each of 64 them, religion as well as philosophy, is the service of God in a way peculiar to it (about which more needs to be said). They differ in the peculiar character of their concern with God. This is where the difficulties lie that impede philosophy's grasp of religion; and it often appears impossible for the two of them to be united. The apprehensive attitude of religion toward philosophy and the hostile stance of each toward the other arise from this. It seems, as the theologians frequently suggest, that philosophy works to corrupt the content of religion, destroying and profaning it. This old antipathy stands before our eyes as something admitted and acknowledged, more generally acknowledged than their unity. The time seems to have arrived, however, when philosophy can deal with religion more impartially on the one hand, and more fruitfully and auspiciously on the other.

This linkage between them is nothing new. It already obtained among the more eminent of the church fathers,[8] who had steeped themselves particularly in Neopythagorean, Neoplatonic, and Neoaristotelian philosophy. | For one thing, they themselves first 65 passed over to Christianity from philosophy; and for another, they applied that philosophical profundity of spirit to the teachings of Christianity. The church owes to their philosophical instruction the first beginnings of Christian doctrine, the development of a *dogmatics*. (Of course it is often said to be a pity that Christianity ever required a determinate content and a dogmatics. We shall have to say more later about the relationship [of the dogmatic content] to religious sensibility, to the purely intensive element in devotion.)

7. [*Ed.*] *Gottesdienst*, "worship," literally "service of God."
8. [*Ed.*] Hegel is presumably thinking in particular of Tertullian, Clement of Alexandria, and Origen, even though in the sense of orthodox dogmatics the latter two do not count as church fathers, or do so only in a qualified way. Perhaps he is also thinking of Augustine. Nowhere can more exact information about the church fathers be obtained from his work.

We can see the same linkage between theology and philosophy in the Middle Ages, too. Scholastic philosophy is identical with theology; theology is philosophy, and philosophy is theology. So far were they from believing that thinking, conceptual knowing, might be injurious to theology that it was regarded as necessary, as essential to theology itself. These great men—Anselm, Abelard, etc.—built up theology out of philosophy." Thus Anselm said: *cum ad fidem perveneris, negligentiae mihi esse videtur non intellegere quod credis.*[9] [10] |

66

2. The Relationship of the Science of Religion to the Needs of Our Time[11]

"Although it follows upon a period when the antipathy became

---

9. [Ed.] "When you have achieved faith, it seems to me to be negligence not to understand what you believe." This is an abbreviated quotation from memory, taken from Anselm's *Cur Deus Homo*, chap. 2: *Sicut rectus ordo exigit ut profunda Christianae fidei credamus, priusquam ea praesumamus ratione discutere, ita negligentia mihi videtur, si, postquam confirmati sumus in fide, non studemus quod credimus intellegere* (Migne *Patrologia Latina* 158.362b.) "As the right order requires us to believe the deep things of Christian faith before we undertake to discuss them by reason; so to my mind it appears a neglect if, after we are established in the faith, we do not seek to understand what we believe" (translation by S. N. Deane, *St. Anselm: Basic Writings* [LaSalle, Ill., 1962], p. 179). While Hegel was familiar with the major works of Anselm—the *Cur Deus Homo*, the *Monologion*, and the *Proslogion*—and considered this eleventh-century theologian to be a seminal figure in the history of speculative thought about God, he probably knew Abelard only from the accounts in the histories of philosophy by Jacob Brucker, Dietrich Tiedemann, and Wilhelm Gottlieb Tennemann, to which he refers in commenting on Abelard in his *Lectures on the History of Philosophy*.

10. W_2 *(MiscP) adds:* In constructing its world for itself over against religion, cognition would have made only a finite content its own. But in that it has developed itself further, i.e. into the true philosophy, it has the same content as religion.

But if in a preliminary way we now seek out the distinction between religion and philosophy as it comes to prominence within this unity of content, we find it to be as follows.

11. [Ed.] This heading, suggested by the summary statement in the opening paragraph (see n. 1), designates the longest section in the 1827 *Introduction*. It is not clearly organized and appears to be something of a grab bag of themes taken over and highlighted from the 1824 *Introduction*. For example, the first topic, the reduced doctrinal content of present-day theology, is a modification of the critique of historical theology in Sec. 2 of the 1824 lectures. The second topic, in which Hegel argues that the knowledge of God, while based on immediate experience,

once more a presupposition,[12] the present day seems again to be more propitious for the linkage of philosophy and theology. In support of this view two circumstances must be underlined. The first concerns the content, the second the form.‾[13] With reference

---

also has cognitive content, further develops the critique of the theology of reason and the theology of feeling found in the same section of the 1824 *Introduction*. The argument that there can be no investigation of the cognitive faculty in advance of cognition draws upon one of the "preliminary questions" in Sec. 4 of 1824, namely, that there is no epistemological prolegomenon to philosophy that is not already speculative in character. Only the summary description of speculative method— which achieves a unification of opposites in which the element of difference is not extinguished but sublated—appears to be new. It is clear that in 1827 Hegel's conflict with the philosophical and theological views of the time becomes the dominant theme of the *Introduction*. However, this polemic does not spill over into *The Concept of Religion* as it does in 1824, so it may well be that Hegel determined in 1827 to concentrate the polemic in the *Introduction*, allowing *The Concept of Religion* to be organized according to the moments of the self-explication of the concept of God, quite apart from partisan considerations. Some material from Sec. A of the *Ms. Concept* is also included here—material of an introductory character no longer appropriate to the 1827 *Concept*.

12. [*Ed.*] A reference possibly to the confessionalism of the Lutheran Reformation with its attack on Scholastic thought, and certainly to the eighteenth-century Enlightenment philosophies that sharpened the distinction between natural and revealed (positive) religion in a manner critical of the latter.

13. W_2 *(MiscP) reads:* Thus in accordance with all its base ramifications, the contemporary view unconcerned with knowledge of God does not hesitate, in the blind arrogance that is peculiar to it, to turn against philosophy. Yet philosophy is the liberation of spirit from that disgraceful abasement; and philosophy has drawn religion forth once more out of the level of profoundest suffering that it was forced to undergo from that standpoint. The very theologians who are still at home only in that state of vanity have dared to complain against philosophy for its destructive tendency, theologians who [themselves] no longer possess any of the content that is subject to possible destruction. In order to repulse these objections, which are not only unfounded but even more frivolous and unprincipled, we need only to look briefly to the way in which the theologians have rather done everything [they could] to dissolve the determinate character of religion. They have (1) thrust the dogmas into the background or declared them to be unimportant, or have (2) considered the dogmas only as alien definitions by other people and as mere phenomena from a history that is long gone. When we have reflected thus upon this aspect of the content, and have seen how philosophy reinstates it and renders it secure from the depredations of theology, then we shall (3) reflect upon the form of that standpoint, and shall see here how that orientation, which in its form is antagonistic to philosophy, is so ignorant about itself that it does not even know in what way it contains implicitly within itself the very principle of philosophy.

to the *content*, the reproach has usually been brought against philosophy that by it the content of the doctrine of the revealed, positive religion is suppressed, that through it Christianity is destroyed. Only a so-called natural religion[14] and theology has been admitted in philosophy, i.e., a content that the natural light of reason could supply regarding God; but it was invariably considered as standing opposed to Christianity. At present this reproach that philosophy is destructive of dogma has been removed, and in fact the theology of our time, i.e. of the last thirty to fifty years, has on its own part effected this removal.

In recent theology very few of the dogmas of the earlier system
67 of ecclesiastical confessions have survived or at least | retained the importance previously attributed to them, and others have not been set in their place. ˉOne could easily arrive at the viewˉ[15] that a widespread, nearly universal indifference toward the doctrines of faith formerly regarded as essential has entered into the general religiousness of the public. For though Christ as reconciler and savior is still constantly made the focus of faith, nevertheless what formerly was called in orthodox dogmatics the work of salvation has taken on a significance so strongly psychological and so very prosaic that only the semblance of the ancient doctrine of the church remains. In lieu of the former dogmas we now behold in Christ merely "great energy of character and constancy of conviction, for the sake of which Christ deemed his life of no account."[16] This is now the universal object of faith. Thus Christ is dragged down to the level of human affairs, not to the level of the commonplace but still to that of the human, into the sphere of a mode of action of which pagans such as Socrates have also been capable. And so, although Christ has remained the focal point of faith for many

14. [*Ed.*] The idea of a "natural religion," as contrasted with revealed religion, is common throughout the Enlightenment. See in particular Herbert of Cherbury (with whose thought Hegel would not have been familiar), Leibniz, Wolff, and Hume. The idea of a "natural light of reason," however, may be traced back to Bacon, Thomas Aquinas, and Cicero.

15. W_2 *(Var) reads (similar in W_1):* One can easily convince oneself [of this] by considering what now actually passes for the dogmas of the church

16. [*Ed.*] This quotation cannot be identified in its present form. Hegel may have conflated passages with which he was familiar from rationalistic exegesis and dogmatics in a fashion such as this.

people who are religious and also more profound in outlook, it must still seem that the most weighty doctrines have lost much of their interest, faith in the Trinity for example, or the miracles in the Old and New Testaments, etc.[17]

If a large part of the educated public, even many theologians, had to declare with hand on heart whether they hold those doctrines of faith to be indispensable for eternal blessedness, or whether not believing | in them would have eternal damnation as its conse-   68 quence, there can surely be no doubt what the answer would be.[18] "Eternal damnation" and "eternal blessedness" are themselves phrases that may not be used in so-called polite company; such expressions count as ἄρρητα.[19] Even though one does not disavow them, one still would be embarrassed to have to declare oneself about them.[20] And if one has read the books of dogmatics, of

17. W₂ *(1831) adds (similar in* W₁*):* The divinity of Christ, i.e., the dogmatic element proper to the Christian religion, is set aside or reduced to something universal only. Indeed this did not only happen in the Enlightenment, but it happens also in the work of more pious theologians. Both parties agree that the Trinity may have entered Christian doctrine from the Alexandrian school, or from the Neoplatonists. But although it must be conceded that the church fathers studied Greek philosophy, it is still primarily immaterial where that doctrine came from. The question is solely whether it is true in and for itself. That point, however, is not investigated, and yet that doctrine is the fundamental characteristic of the Christian religion.

[*Ed.*] From the allusion to "more pious theologians," as well as from the Preface to the 2d ed. of the *Encyclopedia* (1827), we can assume that Hegel here has especially in mind F. A. G. Tholuck, whose *Die speculative Trinitätslehre des späteren Orients* was published in 1826. Tholuck was convinced that the doctrine of the triad was widespread in Islamic thought and in late Greek philosophy, and that the Christian doctrine of the Trinity is closely linked with Neoplatonism. In his *Die Lehre von der Sünde und vom Versöhner,* 2d ed. (Hamburg, 1825), Tholuck argues that, while the speculative idea of the Trinity may be "decorative timbering" (*Fachwerk*), it can never be the foundation of the house of faith (pp. 219–220). Hegel responds to this view critically in his letter to Tholuck of 3 July 1826 (*Briefe 4/ 2*:60–61).

18. [*Ed.*] The neglect of the doctrine of the Trinity is traceable to deism, the neologians (W. A. Teller, J. G. Töllner), and Schleiermacher.

19. [*Ed.*] Literally, "inexpressible." W adds as an explanatory comment: "such things as one is averse to [or dreads] expressing."

20. W *(1831) has* express *in place of* declare *and adds:* In the doctrinal theologies of these theologians we shall find that the dogmas have become very lean and shriveled up, though there may, to be sure, be a great flurry of words.

edification and sermons of our day, in which the basic doctrines of Christianity ought to be expounded or at any rate taken as fundamental, and one were obliged to pass judgment on whether in the greater part of current theological literature those doctrines are expressed in an orthodox sense and without ambiguity or escape hatches, then again there is no question what the answer would be. ⌐If now theology no longer places such importance on the positive doctrines of Christianity, or for that matter if through their interpretation these doctrines are enveloped in such a fog, then one impediment to the philosophical comprehension of dogmas drops away, which used to arise from the fact that philosophy was considered to be an opponent of the teachings of the church. If those doctrines have declined so sharply in their interest, then philosophy can operate without constraint in regard to them.⌐[21]

The most important sign that these positive dogmas have lost much of their importance is that in the main these doctrines are treated *historically.* [22]As far as this historical procedure | is concerned, it deals with thoughts and representations that were had, introduced, and fought over by others, with convictions that belong to others, with histories that do not take place within our spirit, do not engage the needs of our spirit. What is of interest is rather how these things have come about in the case of others, the contingent way in which they were formed.[23] The absolute way in which

69

21. W *(1831) reads:* It seems that, in accord with the general education of most of them, the theologians themselves endow the principal doctrines of positive Christianity with the importance that was formerly ascribed to them (when they were even valued as principal doctrines) only after they have been enveloped in a fog of vagueness. Now if philosophy ever did count as the opponent of church doctrine, it can be an opponent no longer; for the doctrines whose ruin philosophy seemed to threaten are no longer valid in the universal conviction. So when it considers those dogmas in a conceptual manner, a great deal of the danger for philosophy from this quarter should therefore have been set aside, and philosophy can operate without constraint in regard to the dogmas that have declined so sharply in interest for the theologians themselves.

22. *Precedes in L (1827?):* This theology, which adopts only a historical attitude with respect to the cognition of God, and which is indeed a cornucopia of cognitions but only of an external sort, clings tightly to merely historical perspectives and piles up a mass of content as external information.

23. *L (1827?) adds:* The subject is there dealing not with its own commitments to believe, with a cognition that should belong to it and be for its own benefit, but

these doctrines were formed—out of the depths of spirit—is forgotten, and so their necessity and truth is forgotten, too, and the question what one holds as one's own conviction meets with astonishment. The historical procedure is very busy with these doctrines, though not with their content but rather with the external features of the controversies about them, with the passions that have attached themselves to them, etc. ˉFor this reasonˉ[24] philosophy no longer has to face the reproach that it devalues the dogmas. Instead it suffers the reproach of containing within itself too much of the teachings of the church, ˉmore than the generally prevailing theology of our time.ˉ[25] |

ˉThe other circumstance that seems to favor the renewed linkage of theology and philosophy concerns the *form*. Here indeed it is a question of the conviction of the ageˉ[26] that God is revealed immediately in the consciousness of human beings, that religion

70

---

with a cognition of the opinions and views of others, not with the thing itself; the thing itself would benefit anyone concerned with it. W_2 *(Var) reads:* formed and appeared; and the question what one holds as one's own conviction meets with astonishment. W_1 *(Var) reads:* formed and appeared.

24. *W (1831) reads:* Here theology has by its own act been set in a sufficiently abject position. W_1 *(1831) adds further:* For this reason philosophy seems to be in little danger when it is reproached for treating the Christian dogmas in a thoughtful way, or indeed for opposing the church doctrines themselves. If there are now only a few dogmas, or if these dogmas are now only a matter of history, then philosophy could no longer be opposed to them, and then

25. W_1 *(1831) reads:* It is also quite correct that philosophy contains infinitely more than the more recent superficial theology. The latter is wholly built upon just that reflection for which philosophy will not grant any validity, and it reduces the positive doctrines to a minimum. The reinstatement of the authentic doctrine of the church must emanate from philosophy, for philosophy is what guides that vacuous reflective activity back to its ground, that is, philosophy is that in which it goes to the ground [i.e. perishes]. The one circumstance that can be called propitious for the philosophical consideration of religion concerned the content.

26. *Similar in* W_1; W_2 *(MiscP) reads:* Because of the emptiness of the standpoint we are considering, it might seem that we have only referred to the reproaches that it raises up against philosophy, in order to declare expressly that our own aim, which we, by contrast,`shall not relinquish, is to do the opposite of what that standpoint holds to be ultimate—namely, to have cognition of God. Yet it still has in its form an implicit aspect in which it must actually hold a rational interest for us; and under this aspect the more recent stance of theology is even more propitious for philosophy. For bound up with the fact that all objective determinateness has collapsed into the inwardness of subjectivity, there is precisely the conviction

amounts just to this point, that the human being *knows God immediately*. This immediate knowing is called "religion," but also "reason" and "faith," too, though faith in a sense different from that of the church. ¯All conviction *that* God is, and regarding *what* God is, rests, so it is surmised, upon this immediate revealedness in the human being, upon this faith.[27] This general representation is now an established preconception.¯[28] It implies that the highest or religious content discloses itself to the human being in the spirit itself, that spirit manifests itself in spirit, *in this my own spirit,* that faith has its root in the inner self or in what is most my own, that my inmost core is inseparable from it. This is the general principle,

27. [*Ed.*] While Hegel may also have Schleiermacher in mind at this point, in his view it was primarily Jacobi who laid the theoretical foundation for the theology of immediacy with the claim that all human knowledge derives from an attitude of immediate certainty that he called "faith." In a letter to Moses Mendelssohn, Jacobi wrote: "We have all been born into faith and must remain in faith, just as we have all been born into society and must remain in society. *Totum parte prius esse necesse est.* How can we strive for certainty if we are not already acquainted with it, and how can we be acquainted with it otherwise than by means of something that we already acknowledge with certainty? This leads to the concept of an immediate certainty that not only requires no grounds but utterly excludes every ground, and is purely and simply the representation itself harmonizing with the represented thing. Conviction based on grounds is a certainty at second hand. . . . If every truth-claim that does not spring from rational grounds is faith, then conviction based on rational grounds must itself come from faith and receive its force from faith alone" (Jacobi, *Briefe über Spinoza,* pp. 215–217 [*Werke* 4/1:210–211]). Jacobi's views are summed up in the epigram: "The element in which all human cognition and agency takes place is faith" (*ibid.,* p. 228 [p. 223]). See also his *David Hume,* pp. 24 ff. (*Werke* 2:145 ff.). On Hegel's criticism of these views, see his *Encyclopedia* (1830), § 63 remark.

28. *Thus L; similar in An; Hu reads:* This contention is completely familiar and requires no further discussion. *Follows in L (1827?):* Later we shall discuss more precisely how it came about. For the present we take it in its direct sense, without any polemical orientation against philosophy, as the contention that the consciousness of God is immediately present in [human] spirit along with its consciousness of itself. W_1 *(Var) reads:* All conviction . . . in the human being. This contention in the direct sense, aside from the fact that it has given itself a polemical orientation against philosophy (we will deal with that later), requires no proof, no corroboration. W_2 *(Var) reads:* Regarded now from this standpoint, all knowledge, all conviction and piety, rests upon the fact that in [human] spirit as such the consciousness of God is immediately present along with its consciousness of itself. (a) This contention in the direct sense, aside from the fact that it has given itself a polemical orientation against philosophy, is valid as such and requires no proof, no corroboration.

the way in which religious faith is defined in recent times as immediate intuition, as knowledge within me | that absolutely does   71
not come from without. Its effect is utterly to remove all external
authority, all alien confirmation. What is to be valid for me must
have its confirmation in my own spirit. The impetus can certainly
come from without, but the external origin is unimportant. *That* I
believe is due to *the witness of my own spirit.*

Now this being-present or manifesting of that content is the
simple principle of philosophical cognition itself: namely, that our
consciousness has immediate knowledge of God, that we have an
absolutely certain knowledge of God's being. Not only does philosophy not repudiate this proposition, but it forms a basic determination within philosophy itself. In this way it is to be regarded
as a gain, as a kind of good fortune, that basic principles of philosophy itself are active as general preconceptions in the universal
[i.e. popular] mode of representation, so that the philosophical
principle can more easily gain general assent among educated
people.[29]

[30][However, in the first place,] in regard to this immediate knowledge it is noteworthy that the principle does not stand still at this
simple determinacy, this naive content. It does not express itself
merely affirmatively. Instead the naive knowledge proceeds polemically against cognition and is especially directed against the cognition or conceptual comprehension of God. What it demands is
not merely that one should believe, should know immediately. What
it maintains is not simply that consciousness of God is conjoined
with self-consciousness, but rather that the relationship to God is
only and exclusively an immediate one. The immediacy of the connectedness is taken as precluding the alternative determination of

29. *Thus also* W₁; W₂ *(MiscP) adds:* In this general disposition of the spirit of
the age, not only has philosophy therefore secured an outwardly favorable position
(it has no dealings with what is external, least of all where philosophy and occupation
with it exist as a state institution), but it is inwardly favored if its principle already
lives of its own accord as an assumption in the spirit [of the people] and in their
hearts. For philosophy has this principle in common with contemporary culture:
that reason is the locus of spirit in which God reveals himself to human beings.

30. *In B's margin:* 8 May 1827

[*Ed.*] See below, n. 49.

mediation, and because it is a mediated knowledge philosophy is disparaged on the grounds that it is only a finite knowledge of the finite. |

72

More precisely, the *immediacy* of this knowledge is supposed to reside above all in the fact that one knows *that* God is, *not what* God is. The expansion, the content, the fulfillment of the representation of God is thus negated. But what we call "cognition" involves knowing not only *that* an object is but *also what* it is; and knowing what it is, not just in a general way or having a certain acquaintance with it, some certitude about it, but knowing what its determinations are, what its content is, so that our knowing is a fulfilled and verified knowledge in which we are aware of the necessary connectedness of these determinations.

It is claimed that God cannot be cognized at all, but that we are only aware that God *is*; this we [supposedly] *found* in our consciousness.[31] If we first set aside the polemical orientation of this claim and consider only just what is involved in the assertion of immediate knowledge, ˉit is this: that on the one hand it is our spirit itself that bears witness to this content, that the content does not come from without or only through instruction. On the contrary, our convicton about it rests on the assent of our own spirit, on our consciousness, that spirit finds this content within itself.ˉ[32] On the other hand, consciousness also relates itself to this content, so that this consciousness and this content, God, are inseparable. In fact it is *this connection* in general, this knowledge of God and the inseparability of consciousness from this content, that we call *religion in general*. But at the same time the implication in this assertion of immediate knowledge is that we ought to stop short with the consideration of religion as such—more precisely, with the consideration of this connection with God. There is to be no progressing to the cognitive knowledge of God, to the divine content

31. [*Ed.*] This standpoint is found in the contemporary philosophy originating from Jacobi; see esp. his *Briefe über Spinoza*, pp. 426–427 (*Werke* 4/2:155).

32. W₁ *(1831) reads:* [it is] a self-limitation, which, with respect to its origin, is even acknowledged by philosophy, but then also resolved and exhibited in its one-sidedness and untruth by philosophy.

as this content would be divinely, or essentially, in God himself. In this sense it is further declared that we can know only our relation to God, not what God himself is. "Only our relation" falls within what is meant by religion generally.[33] That is why it is that nowadays we merely hear religion talked about but find no investigations into God's nature or what God might be within himself, | how God's   73 nature must be defined. God as such is not made the object [of inquiry] himself; God is not before us as an object of cognition, and knowledge does not spread out within this sphere. ˉOnly our relation to God, or religion as such, is an object [of inquiry] for us. Our discussion concerns religion as such and does not, or at least not very much, concern God. Expositions of God's nature have become ever fewer. What is said is only that human beings ought to have religion. The connection religion has with philosophy and the state is discussed, but not God.ˉ[34]

But if we elucidate what is implied in the thesis of immediate knowledge, what is immediately declared by it, then God himself is expressed in relation to consciousness in such a way that this relation is something inseparable or that we must consider both sides together, ˉand this is the essential object of our consideration.ˉ[35] ˉThis is itself the philosophical idea, and is not opposed to

33. [Ed.] Here Hegel draws the consequences of the contemporary assertion of the noncognizability of God as found in Kant and Jacobi. Perhaps he has specifically in mind Schleiermacher's view that the divine attributes do not denote "something special in God, but only something special in the manner in which we relate our feeling of absolute dependence to God." Der christliche Glaube, 1st ed., § 64; in the 2d ed., § 50, the concluding clause is revised to read: ". . . in which the feeling of utter dependence is to be related to him."

34. Similar in W₁; W₂ (Var) reads: and does not display differentiated determinations within it [i.e. in God as object of cognition], so that it is itself grasped as the relationship of these determinations and as relationship within its own self. God is not before us as object of cognition, but only our connection with God, our relationship to him. And while expositions of God's nature have become ever fewer, it is now demanded only that human beings ought to have religion or ought to abide in religion, and there is not supposed to be any advance to a divine content.

35. Thus B; L (1827?) adds (similar in W): We can, to be sure, distinguish subjective consciousness on the one hand, and God as object, God [viewed] objectively, on the other. This is an essential distinction in the entire doctrine of religion. But at the same time it is said that there is an unbreakable, essential relation between the two, and this is the important thing, not what one opines or fancies about God.

the philosophical concept.‾[36] According to the philosophical concept God is *spirit,* concrete; and if we inquire more precisely what spirit is, it turns out that the basic concept of spirit is the one whose development constitutes the entire doctrine of religion. If we ask | our consciousness for a provisional account of what spirit is, the answer is that spirit is a self-manifesting, a being for spirit. *Spirit is for spirit* and of course not merely in an external, contingent manner. Instead it *is* spirit only insofar as it is *for* spirit. This is what constitutes the concept of spirit itself. Or, to put the point more theologically, God's spirit is [present] essentially in his community; God *is* spirit only insofar as God is in his *community.*[37]

Because the inseparable unity of consciousness with God is affirmed in what immediate knowledge contains, this inseparability therefore contains what is implied in the *concept of spirit:* [namely,] that spirit is for spirit itself, that the treatment cannot be one-sided or merely treatment of the subject according to its finitude, i.e., according to its contingent life; instead it [must be] considered under the aspect in which it has the infinite absolute content as its object. When the subject is considered by itself (the subjective individual as such) it is considered in its finite knowing, its knowledge of the finite. By the same token it is also maintained regarding the other side of the relation that God is not to be considered in isolation, for that is not possible. One knows of God only in connection with consciousness.[38]

‾‾What has been stated are the basic characteristics that we can regard as immediate impressions and unmediated convictions of

36. *Thus B; W₂ (Var) reads:* Now what this contention contains as its real kernel is the philosophical idea itself, except that it is held by immediate knowledge within a limitation that is resolved and exhibited in its one-sidedness and untruth by philosophy. *W₁ (Var) reads:* If we set in relief what this contention contains, [we see] it is the philosophical idea itself.

37. *W₂ (MiscP) adds:* It is said that the world or the sensible universe must have onlookers and must be for spirit. And so God, too, must be for spirit all the more.

38. *W₂ (1831) adds (similar in W₁):* and thus the unity and inseparability of the two determinations, i.e., of knowledge of God and of self-consciousness, itself presupposes what is expressed in identity, and the dreaded identity is contained right in this unity and inseparability.

the age | relating expressly to religion, to knowledge of God.[39]   75
Therefore only what are basic elements or fundamental concepts
of philosophy of religion can be linked up with this foundation.
This also provides us with an external justification[40] for forging
a path to our science without having to be polemical toward the
views that supposedly stand in the way of philosophy. Certainly
these contentions do oppose themselves to philosophical cognition,[41] for there is no limit to that lack of awareness about the
knowledge of God which is opposed to philosophy. But exactly
those contentions, which for this reason maintain that they are
contradicting philosophy, that they are contesting it and are most
sharply opposed to it—if we look at their content, the determinate
view they express, then we see that in themselves they exhibit agreement with that which they assail.

The result of the study of philosophy is that those walls of division, which are supposed to separate absolutely, become transparent; or that when we get to the bottom of things we discover

39. L (1827?) adds (similar in W₁): I have taken them straightforwardly according to what they contain, and have left to one side their opposition from the
standpoint of philosophical cognition. We are still only in the introduction.

40. W₁ (Var) reads: Through this agreement with respect to the elements, to
which attention has been drawn, an external justification is first of all provided in
regard to our discussion

41. Similar in W₁; W₂ (MiscP) reads: In fact we thus see the basic concept of
philosophy present as a universal element within the culture of the age. And it is
also evident here how philosophy does not stand above its age in the form of
something completely different from the general determinateness of the age. Instead
one spirit pervades actuality and philosophical thought, except that the latter is the
true self-understanding of the actual. In other words, there is but one movement by
which the age and philosophy themselves are borne along, the difference being simply
that the determinateness of the age still appears to be present contingently, it still
lacks justification, and so it can even yet stand in an unreconciled, hostile antithesis
to that genuine and essential content, whereas philosophy, as justification of the
principle, is also the universal peacemaking and reconciliation. Just as the Lutheran
Reformation led the faith back to the primary centuries, the principle of immediate
knowledge has led Christian cognition back to the primary elements. But if this
reduction also causes the evaporation of the essential content at first, then it is
philosophy that cognizes this principle of immediate knowledge itself as a content,
and leads it on as such to its true unfolding within itself.

absolute agreement where we thought there was the most extreme antithesis.[42]

More specifically, these contemporary impressions are polemical against the amplification of the inherent content. We are to believe in God, but in general are not to know what God is, are not to have any determinate knowledge of | God. The possession of determinate knowledge is what is meant by "cognition." On this basis theology as such has been reduced to a minimum of dogma. Its content has become extremely sparse although much talking, scholarship, and argumentation go on. This tendency is principally directed against the mode of amplification called dogmatics. We can compare this shift in attitude to what was done for the purpose of the Reformation. Then the amplification of the system of hierarchy was contested, and the leading of Christianity back to the simplicity of the first Christian era was offered as the defining goal. Similarly, it is basically characteristic of the modern period that the doctrines of the Protestant church have been brought back to a minimum. But despite theology's reduction of its knowledge to a minimum it still needs to know many things of different sorts, such as the ethical order and human relationships. Moreover, its subject matter is becoming more extensive; the learning displayed in its manifold historical eloquence is highly accomplished.[43] Thus one is engaged not with one's own cognition but with cognition of other people's representations. We can compare this bustling about of theology with the work of the countinghouse clerk or cashier, because all the active bustle is concerned with the alien truths of others.[44] It will become

42. *Thus also* W$_2$; W$_1$ *(1831) adds:* One must know only what is here the essential category of thought. Faith is also a knowledge, but an immediate knowledge. Thus the antithesis reduces to the abstract determinations of immediacy and mediation, which we have to refer to only in logic where these categories of thought are considered according to their truth.

43. *L (1827?) adds:* But because this proliferating content is not developed from the concept, does not and is not supposed to come about according to the concept, or according to cognition, it takes place arbitrarily, according to argumentation, which is opposed to rational cognition.

44. *W (1831) adds the following, after giving the 1824 version of this analogy:* Theology of this kind does not find itself any longer in the domain of thought at all; it does not any longer deal with infinite thought in and for itself, but deals with

plain in our treatment of the science of religion that it is the peculiar concern of reason to form itself into an all-embracing intellectual realm. The main thing about this intellectual formation is that it occurs *rationally,* according to the necessity of the subject matter, of the content itself, not according to caprice and chance. | 77

¯Because it has thus contracted exclusively into the knowledge *that* God is, theology has extended its object to embrace ethical life and morality; and because this extension itself is not supposed to occur via cognition, it takes place *arbitrarily,* rather than according to necessity.¯[45] This argumentative thinking makes some assumption or other, and proceeds according to the relationships of the understanding [employed in the kind] of reflection that we have developed within us through our education, without any criticism of these relationships. That approach is gaining ground in this science [theology]. In contrast, development by means of the concept admits of no contingency. That is just why it is so fervently denounced, because it chains us down to proceeding according to the necessity of the thing rather than according to fancies and opinions.

That argumentative method involves assumptions, which themselves can in turn be called in question. Yet the argumentative theology of the Christian church pretends nevertheless to possess a firm footing, asserting, "For us the firm footing is the Bible, it is the words of the Bible." But against this one can quote the essential sense of the text, "the letter kills,"[46] etc. One does not take the words [of the Bible] as they stand, because what is understood by the biblical "word" is not words or letters as such but the spirit with which they are grasped. For we know historically that quite

---

it only as a finite fact, as opinion, representation, and the like. History occupies itself with truths that used to be truths, i.e., for others, and not with truths such as would be the possession of those who concern themselves with them.

45. W_1 *(1831) reads:* Although theology has severely reduced its actual knowledge of God to a minimum, it still needs to know many things of different sorts, such as the ethical order and human relationships. Moreover, its range and subject matter is becoming more extensive. But because, in the case of this proliferating content, this does not and is not supposed to come about according to the concept, according to cognition, it takes place arbitrarily, according to argumentation, which is opposed to rational cognition.

46. [*Ed.*] See 2 Cor. 3:6. "The written code kills, but the Spirit gives life."

opposite dogmas have been derived from these words, that the most contrasting viewpoints have been elicited from the letter of the text because the spirit did not grasp it. In these instances appeal was to the letter, but the genuine ground is the spirit.

The words of the Bible constitute an unsystematic account; they are Christianity as it appeared in the beginning. It is *spirit* that grasps the content, that spells it out.[47] How it is done depends on how spirit | is disposed, on whether it is the right and true spirit that grasps the words. This true spirit can only be the one that proceeds within itself according to necessity, not according to assumptions. This spirit that interprets must legitimate itself on its own account, and its proper legitimation is the subject matter itself, the content, that which the concept substantiates.

Hence the authority of the canonical faith of the church has been in part degraded, in part removed. The *symbolum* or *regula fidei* itself is no longer regarded as something totally binding but instead as something that has to be interpreted and explained from the Bible. But the interpretation depends on the spirit that explains. The absolute footing is just the concept. To the contrary, by means of exegesis such basic doctrines of Christianity have been partly set aside and partly explained in quite lukewarm fashion. Dogmas such as those of the Trinity and the miracles have been put in the shadows by theology itself.[48] Their justification and true affirmation can occur only by means of the cognizing spirit, and for this reason much more of dogmatics has been preserved in philosophy than in dogmatics or in theology itself as such.

[49]We should note in the second place the consequence of imposing

78

47. W (1831) *adds after an interpolation from the 1824 lectures:* Whether the Bible has been made the foundation more for honor's sake alone or in fact with utter seriousness, still the nature of the interpretative explanation involves the fact that thought plays a part in it. Thought explicitly contains definitions, principles, and assumptions, which then make their own claims felt in the activity of interpreting.

48. [*Ed.*] See above, nn. 17, 18.

49. *In B's margin:* 10 May 1827

[*Ed.*] If the following comments on investigating the cognitive faculty itself are "in the second place," then presumably what is first, in the discussion of the form of religious thought, is the preceding analysis of the immediate knowledge of God culminating in the remarks on its assumptions in relation to biblical authority (see above, n. 30). Both points are marked by a date notation in the margin of *B*.

upon philosophy, in particular upon philosophy of religion, the demand that before we embark upon cognitive knowing we must investigate the nature of the cognitive faculty itself; only this investigation of the instrument would show for certain whether we can rightfully try for cognition of God. We wanted just to proceed to the thing itself without turning to further preliminaries. But this question lies so close to our concern that it must be attended to. It seems to be a fair demand that one should test one's powers and examine one's instrument before setting to work.[50] But plausible as this demand may appear, it proves to be no less unjustified and empty. With such analogies it is often the case that forms that suit one context do not suit another. How should reason be investigated? Doubtless rationally. Therefore this investigation is itself a rational cognizing. For the | investigaton of cognition there is no way open 79 save that of cognition. We are supposed to cognize reason, and what we want to do is still supposed to be a rational cognizing. So we are imposing a requirement that annuls itself. This is the same demand as the one in the familiar anecdote in which a Scholastic declares that he won't go into the water until he has learned to swim.[51]

50. [*Ed.*] Hegel's thought is fundamentally at odds with a procedure that grants to epistemology, whether of the Cartesian, the empiricist, or the critical variety, a prior and privileged position within the philosophical enterprise. Cf. his critique of this procedure in the opening paragraphs of the Introduction to the *Phenomenology of Spirit*, where his principal targets (as in this passage) are the critical philosophies of Kant and Reinhold.

51. [*Ed.*] This anecdote is contained in a collection of witticisms written in Greek, known as φιλογέλως ("Friend of Laughter"), collected by Hierocles of Alexandria and Philagrios the Grammarian in late antiquity. See *Philogelos der Lachfreund: Von Hierokles und Philagrios,* ed. A. Thierfelder (Munich, 1968), p. 28: § 2. "A Scholastic who wanted to swim was nearly drowned. He swore never again to go into the water until he had learned to swim." In the 1824 *Introduction* Hegel alludes to the same anecdote, but, according to G, uses the term *Gascogner* ("Gascon") instead of *Scholastikus,* thus appearing to convert it into an ethnic joke about Frenchmen from Gascony, reputedly noted for their boasting. However, such a change makes little sense, and since only G gives this version he probably simply misunderstood Hegel or reconstructed the anecdote later from memory incorrectly. Hegel also used the anecdote in his *Lectures on the History of Philosophy;* a student notebook of 1825–26 gives the Greek form σχολαστιχός, as does the 2d ed. of these lectures in the *Werke* (see *History of Philosophy* 3:428), while the 1st ed. simply reads: "a man who wanted to swim" (*Werke* 15:555).

Besides, in philosophy of religion we have as our object God himself, *absolute reason*.[52] Since we know God [who is] absolute reason, and investigate this reason, we cognize it, we behave cognitively. Absolute spirit is knowledge, the determinate rational knowledge of its own self. Therefore when we occupy ourselves with this object it is immediately the case that we are dealing with and investigating rational cognition, and this cognition is itself rational conceptual inquiry and knowledge. So the [critical] requirement proves to be completely empty. Our *scientific cognition is itself the required investigation* of cognitive knowing.

The second circumstance[53] requiring discussion at this point is the following observation. We should recall here what we said by way of introduction, that on the whole religion is the highest or ultimate sphere of human consciousness, whether as feeling, volition, representation, knowledge, or cognition. It is the absolute result, the region into which the human being passes over as that of absolute truth. In order to meet this universal definition, consciousness must already have elevated itself into this sphere transcending the finite generally, transcending finite existence, conditions, purposes, and interests—in particular, transcending all finite thoughts and finite relationships of every sort. In order to be within the sphere of religion one must have set aside these things, forgotten them. In contrast with these basic specifications, however, it very frequently happens when philosophy in general and philosophizing about God in particular are criticized, that finite thoughts, relationships of limitedness, and categories and forms of the finite are introduced in the service of this discourse. Opposition that draws upon such finite forms is directed against philosophy generally and especially against the highest kind, the philosophy of

80 religion | in particular. Belonging to such finite forms is the immediacy of knowing or the "fact of consciousness." Examples of

---

52. L (1827?) adds: God is essentially rational, a rationality that, as spirit, is in and for itself.

53. [Ed.] The ensuing paragraphs challenge a simplistic application of the Kantian categories of finitude to the religious object. Perhaps this makes them the "second circumstance" in the passage on investigating the cognitive faculty, the first being the more general discussion of the preceding two paragraphs.

such categories include the antitheses of finite and infinite and of subject and object, abstract forms that are no longer in place in that absolute abundance of content that religion is.[54] They must of course occur in our science, for they are moments of the essential relationship that lies at the basis of religion. But the main thing is that their nature must have been investigated and cognized long beforehand. If we are dealing with religion scientifically, this primarily logical cognition must lie behind us. We must long since have finished with such categories.[55] The usual practice, however, is to base oneself on them in order to oppose the concept, the idea, rational cognition. These categories are employed entirely uncritically, in a wholly artless fashion, just as if Kant's *Critique of Pure Reason* were nonexistent, a book that put them to the test and arrived in its own way at the result that they can serve only for the cognition of phenomena and not of the truth.[56] In religion, however, one is not dealing with phenomena but with the absolute content.[57] How totally improper, indeed tasteless, it is that categories of this kind are adduced against philosophy, as if one could say something novel to philosophy or to any educated person in this way, as if anyone who has not totally neglected his education would not know that the finite is not the infinite, that subject is different from object, immediacy different from mediation. Yet this sort of cleverness is brought forward triumphantly and without a blush, as if here one has made a discovery.

¯That these forms¯[58] are different everyone knows; but that these

54. *L (1827?) adds (similar in W):* In the spirit (or in the disposition that has to do with religion) determinations wholly other than such meager ones as finitude and the like are present, and yet what is supposed to be important in religion is subjected by argumentative [criticism] to determinations of this kind.

55. [*Ed.*] Hegel refers here to his criticism of the categories of the understanding in his *Science of Logic.*

56. [*Ed.*] See Kant, *Critique of Pure Reason,* B 269, B 571, B 611.

57. *W₂ MiscP/Var?) adds:* But the Kantian philosophy seems in the view of that argumentative thinking to have come into existence only so that we might operate all the more unabashedly with those categories.

58. *Similar in* W₁; W₂ *(MiscP/Var?) reads:* Here we merely note the fact that such determinations as finite and infinite, subject and object (and this always constitutes the foundation of that clever and cheeky chatter)

determinations are still at the same time inseparable is another
81 matter. | There is reluctance to ascribe to the concept this power,
though it can be encountered even in physical phenomena. We know
that in the magnet the south pole is quite distinct from the north
pole, and yet they are inseparable. We also say of two things, for
example, that they are as different as heaven and earth. It is correct
that these two are plainly different, but they are inseparable. We
cannot point out earth apart from the heavens, and vice versa.
Immediate and mediated knowledge are *distinct* from one another,
and yet only a very modest investigation is needed in order to see
that they are *inseparable*. Hence, before one is ready to proceed to
philosophy of religion, one must be done with such one-sided forms.
From these considerations it can easily be seen how difficult it is
for a philosopher to engage in discussion with those who oppose
philosophy of religion in this fashion; for they display too great an
ignorance and are totally unfamiliar with the forms and categories
in which they launch their attack and deliver their verdict upon
philosophy. Being unfamiliar with the inner spirit of the concepts,
they bluntly declare that immediacy is surely something different
from mediation. They utter such platitudes as something novel, but
in so doing they also assert that immediate knowledge exists in
isolation, on its own account, wholly unaffected, without having
reflected upon these subjects, without having paid attention to their
outer nature or inner spirit to see how these determinations are
82 present in them.[59] This kind of opposition to philosophy has | the

59. *Thus also* W$_1$; W$_2$ *(MiscP) adds:* Actuality is not accessible to them, but
alien and unknown. The gossip that they direct in hostility against philosophy is
therefore school chatter, which saddles itself with empty categories that have no
content; whereas we in the company of philosophy are not in the so-called "school"
but in the world of actuality, and we do not find in the wealth of its determinations
a yoke in which we might be confined, but we move freely within them. And then
those who contest and disparage philosophy are even incapable of comprehending
a philosophical proposition through their finite thought. Just when they perhaps
repeat its very words they have distorted it, for they have not comprehended its
infinity but have dragged in their finite relationships instead. Philosophy is so patient
and painstaking that it carefully investigates its opponent's position. Admittedly that
is necessary according to its concept, and it is only satisfying the internal impulse
of its concept when it cognizes both itself and what is opposed to it (*verum index
sui et falsi* ["truth is the touchstone of itself and of the false": Spinoza, *Opera* 4:124,

tedious consequence that in order to show people that their contentions are self-contradictory one must first go back to the alphabet
of philosophy itself. But the thinking spirit must be beyond such
forms of reflection. It must be acquainted with their nature, with
the true relationship that obtains within them, namely the infinite
relationship, in which their finitude is sublated.

Only slight experience is needed to see that where there is immediate knowledge there is also mediated knowledge, and vice
versa. Immediate knowledge, like mediated knowledge, is by itself
completely one-sided. *The true* is their unity, *an immediate knowledge that likewise mediates,* a mediated knowledge that is at the
same time internally simple, or is immediate reference to itself. That
one-sidedness makes these determinations finite. Inasmuch as it is
sublated through such a connection, it is a relationship of infinity.
It is the same with object and subject. In a subject that is internally
objective the one-sidedness disappears; the difference emphatically
does not disappear, for it belongs to the pulse of its vitality, to the
impetus, motion, and restlessness of spiritual as well as of natural
life. Here is a unification in which the difference is not extinguished,
but all the same it is sublated.[60] |

83

320]). However, it should be able to expect as *quid pro quo* that the antithesis will
now also desist from its hostility and cognize philosophy's essence peaceably. That,
however, does not ensue, and the magnanimity of wanting to acknowledge its opponent and heap coals of fire on his head is of no avail to philosophy, for the
opponent will not keep quiet, but is persistent. But when we see that the antithesis
dissipates like an apparition and dissolves into a mist, then our only wish for the
contest is to render an account of ourselves and of conceptual thought, and not
simply to gain the verdict over the other side. And to convince the opposition fully,
[or to have] this personal influence upon it, is impossible because it remains within
its limited categories.

60. *L (1827?) adds:* However, the argumentative method of the finite understanding that was mentioned has not elevated itself to such concepts. It uses them
in a crude, coarse fashion without thinking them through. *W₂ (MiscP) adds instead:*
Since in the following discussion we are beginning with religion, with the supreme
and the ultimate, we must now be able to assume that the futility of those relationships has long been overcome. But at the same time, because we did not com-
mence with the beginning of science but expressly considered religion, we must have
regard also, within religion itself, for the sort of relationships of the understanding
that ordinarily come under consideration above all in connection with religion.

3. Survey of the Treatment of Our Subject[61]

˜After making these remarks, if we wish to get closer to our object itself, all that still remains by way of introduction is to give an outline of its articulation, to provide in the most general way a conspectus or a survey of our science and of how it is internally divided, so that we may be historically informed about it.˜[62]

There can be but *one method* in all science, in all knowledge. Method is just the self-explicating concept—nothing else—and the concept is one only. Here too, therefore, the *first moment* is, as always, the *concept*. The *second moment* is the *determinateness of the concept,* the concept in its determinate forms. These forms are necessarily involved in the concept itself. In a philosophical mode of treatment it is not the case that the universal element, or the concept, is set forth at the beginning as though merely for the sake of its prestige. In the way in which they are prefixed to the single sciences, however, concepts such as nature, right,[63] and the like are general definitions that are placed at the beginning, although one

61. [*Ed.*] This heading is adopted from *An,* which reads literally: "Conspectus of the Treatment of Our Object." The paragraphs preceding the detailed survey of the three parts of the philosophy of religion offer a speculative description of the moments of the concept of religion in the process of its self-explication and self-manifestation—the moments of pure conceptuality (universality), self-determination (differentiation, particularity), and self-reunification (reestablishment, consummation, subjectivity), which serve as the logical, rational basis for the actual historical appearance of the religions and the division of the subject into three parts. These paragraphs seem to be an expansion of the brief survey at the end of the *Introduction* in the 1821 *Ms.,* which also is couched in the speculative terminology of the *Logic.* The 1827 lectures then add a detailed division and survey, which is lacking in the *Ms.* Having been through the lectures on two previous occasions Hegel now, in 1827, had a clear idea of what would actually follow.

62. *Similar in* W_1; W_2 *(Ed?) reads:* With this reference to the discussion itself that is to follow we now directly provide the general survey or division of our science.

63. [*Ed.*] From the three basic philosophical sciences of Hegel's *Encyclopedia* (logic, philosophy of nature, philosophy of spirit), others can be distinguished, such as the "science of right" (*Rechtswissenschaft*). *Recht* is occasionally translated below as "law," although in Hegel's own *Philosophy of Right* the concern is not principally with law in the juridical sense but with the broader foundations of civil society and the state. In this derogatory sentence, however, Hegel is not referring to his own work but to the individual sciences as set forth by others.

is embarrassed by them because nothing depends on them. What really matters instead is the detailed content, chapter by chapter. A so-called concept of this kind has no further influence on this subsequent content. It indicates roughly the field where the investigator is, and in which the issues are located, so that content from another domain may not be introduced [inadvertently]. But the content— e.g., magnetism or electricity—is what counts as the subject matter, whereas the prefixed concept is [only] the formal aspect.[64]

The concept constitutes the beginning in philosophical treatment, too. But here it is the substance of the thing, like the seed from which the whole tree unfolds. The seed contains all of its characteristics, the entire nature of the tree: the type of its sap, the pattern of its branches, etc. However, these are not preformed, so that if one took a microscope one would see the twigs and leaves in miniature, but they are instead enveloped in a | spiritual manner. Similarly the concept contains the entire nature of the object, and cognition is nothing but the development of the concept, the development of what is contained in the concept but has not yet emerged into existence, is not yet explicated, not yet displayed.

Therefore the *first moment* is the *concept of religion* or religion in general, and the *second* is our consideration of *determinate religion*. And we do not derive the determinateness from outside, but rather it is the free concept that impels itself to its own determinateness. It is not the same in this case as when one treats right or law empirically, for example. The determinate details of the history of law do not follow from the concept, but we derive them from another source. There we first define in general what "right" designates; but the determinate legal systems such as the Roman and the German have to be taken from experience. Here, on the contrary, the determinateness has to result from the concept itself. The determinate concept of religion, then, is religion in its finitude, finite religion, something one-sided constituted in opposition to other religions as one particular type set against another.

84

---

64. *Thus, also* W$_1$; W$_2$ *(MiscP/Var?) adds:* But in such a mode of consideration the prefixed concept, for instance right, can also become a mere name for the most abstract and most contingent content.

For that reason we consider in the *third place* the concept as it comes forth to itself out of its determinateness, out of its finitude, as it reestablishes itself out of its own finitude, its own confinement. This *reestablished concept* is the infinite, true concept, the *absolute idea* or the *true religion*. These are therefore the three divisions in general, expressed in abstract terms.

Religion in its concept is not yet the true religion. The concept is true within itself, to be sure; but it also belongs to its truth that it should realize itself, as it belongs to the soul that it should have embodied itself. To begin with, this realization is a determination of the concept; but the absolute realization is when this determination is adequate to the concept. This adequate concept-determination is the absolute idea, the true concept. This progression is the development of the concept, and initially this development is the experience, cognition, and knowledge of what religion is.[65] |

85

The concept that we have here before us is now *spirit itself* without qualification. It is spirit itself that is this development and that is active in this way. Spirit, if it is thought immediately, simply, and at rest, is no spirit; for spirit's essential [character] is *to be altogether active*. More exactly, it is the activity of *self-manifesting*. Spirit that does not manifest or reveal itself is something dead. "Manifesting" signifies "becoming for an other." As "becoming for an other" it enters into antithesis, into distinction in general, and thus it is a *finitizing* of spirit. Something that is *for an other* is, in this abstract determination, precisely something finite. It has an other over against itself, it has its terminus in this other, its boundary. Thus spirit that manifests itself, determines itself, enters into existence, gives itself finitude, is the second moment. But the third is its manifesting of itself according to its concept, taking its former, initial manifestation back into itself, sublating it, coming to its own

65. *Similar in* W_1; *L (1827?) adds:* The stages that we accordingly have to traverse are: first, the concept of religion; second, religion in its determinate existence; third, the infinite, absolute religion. As concept, religion is still without determinate being [*Dasein*]. In determinate being it is incommensurate with its concept. In the absolute religion concept and determinate being correspond for the first time and for that reason become the idea of religion.

self, becoming and being *explicitly* the way it is implicitly. [66]This is the rhythm or the pure eternal life of spirit itself. If there were not this movement, then it would be something dead. Spirit is the having of itself as object. Therein consists its manifestation, in its being the relationship of objectivity, its being something finite.[67] The third moment is that it is *object to itself*, is reconciled with itself in the object, has arrived at freedom, for freedom is being present to itself.[68]

[69]The division, as we are setting it out beforehand, | whose various parts and content we now propose to specify in more detail, is[70] only historical. But it is adopted for the simple reason that it is also necessary according to the concept.

86

66. *Precedes in* W₂ *(1831) (similar in* W₁*):* According to the moments of the concept, the presentation and development of religion will therefore occur in three divisions. We will consider the concept of religion: first in general; then in its particularity as self-dividing and self-differentiating concept, which is the aspect of primal division [*Ur-teil*, i.e. judgment], of limitation and difference, and of finitude; third, the concept that closes with itself, the syllogism or the return of the concept to itself, out of its determinateness in which it is unequal to itself, so that it comes to equality with its form and supersedes its limitedness.

67. *Thus also* W₁; W₂ *(Var) reads:* but above all it is a relationship of objectivity, and in this relationship it is finite.

68. *Thus also* W₁; W₂ *(MiscP) adds:* This rhythm, in which the whole of our science and the entire development of the concept is in motion, also recurs, however, in each of the three indicated moments, for each of them in its determinateness is the totality implicitly, until the totality is posited as such in the final moment. Hence, although the concept appears first in the form of universality, then in the form of particularity, and finally in the form of singularity, or if the entire movement of our science is such that the concept becomes the judgment and consummates itself in the syllogism, the same development of moments arises in every sphere of this movement. The only qualification is that in the first sphere the development is held together in the determinateness of universality, whereas in the second sphere, that of particularity, it allows the moments to appear independently, and only in the sphere of singularity does it return to the actual syllogism that mediates itself in the totality of the determinations.

69. *Precedes in* W *(1831):* Thus this division is the movement, nature, and activity of spirit itself that we, so to speak, simply witness. It is necessary through the concept, but the necessity of the progression has to exhibit, explicate, and prove itself only in the development itself.

70. *L adds:* therefore

[*Ed.*] The "therefore" makes sense only in the context of the preceding passage from W, which is also included in L.

I. The Concept of Religion[71]

As we have already stated, we shall consider in the first part the concept of religion. In the simple concept of religion what appears as content, or as the determination of the content, is solely the universal. Determinacy, or particularity as such, is not yet present. Hence the basic definition, or the character, of this first part of the philosophy of religion is that of *universality*.

In its concept religion is the relation of the subject, of the subjective consciousness, to God, who is spirit. In its concept regarded speculatively it is therefore spirit conscious of its own essence, conscious of its own self. Spirit is conscious, and that of which it is conscious is the true, essential spirit. True spirit is *its* essence, not the essence of an other. To this extent religion is forthwith explicitly *idea,* and the concept of religion is the concept of this idea. The idea is the truth, the reality of the concept in such a way that this reality is identical with the concept, or is determined simply and solely through the concept. If we call the concept "spirit," then the reality of the concept is consciousness. Spirit as concept, universal spirit, realizes itself in the consciousness that is itself spiritual, the consciousness for which alone spirit can be. |

87

Religion is therefore *spirit that realizes itself in consciousness.* Every realization, however, is a relationship in which two aspects must be considered: the elevation of the human being to God, the consciousness that itself is conscious of God, of spirit; and the spirit that realizes itself in consciousness. These two aspects are connected with one another. This is the first moment in the idea, their connection, that in which the two sides are identical. This does not mean the commonality, however, or the superficial universality in which we liken several things to one another, but rather the inner unity of the two. So this *first moment* of the idea is the *substantial unity,* the universal in and for itself, the purely spiritual without further determination. Universality is the foundation. Only with determinate religion do we have determinate content.

The *second moment* to this initial universal one is precisely what

71. *In B's margin:* 11 May 1827
[*Ed.*] The heading is in B.

is called "relationship," the going apart of this unity. Here we have subjective consciousness, for which this universal in and for itself exists, and which relates itself to it. This can be called "elevation of the human being to God," because the human being and God are related [to each other] *as distinct*. Precisely what is called religion first makes its appearance here. We have to consider this relation according to its particular determinations. The first of these is feeling; and certainty in general, or faith, is classed under it. The second determination is representation. The third is thought, the form of thinking. We shall have to inquire more closely at this point to what extent religion is a matter of feeling. The form of representation is next for consideration after that, and the form of thought is third. Under this last determination we will most especially speak of religion.

Whenever we philosophize about religion, we are engaging in religious thinking. ¯From this religious thinking in general we have to distinguish the type of religious thinking that we have to deal with here as a characteristic of the abstract concept of religion, and that is a thoughtful activity of the understanding.¯72 This thoughtful understanding will show itself to be what used to be called "proofs for the existence of God." We will consider here the significance of this "proving." Today the "proofs" have fallen into neglect or into contempt | because it is supposed that we are beyond all that. But 88 for the very reason that they were authoritative for more than a thousand years[73] they deserve to be considered more closely. Even if we discover that they have deficiencies, we shall see at any rate what is genuine in the procedure they express, namely that they in fact display the process of the elevation of the human being to God, except that the form of understanding obscures it. We shall show what they lack in order to be the form of reason. Thus we need to consider the form of reason in contrast with that of the understanding, and to see what is wanting in the latter in order to express

72. W₁ *(Var) reads (similar in An, B):* In this religious thinking we have in particular to deal at first only with what is a thoughtful activity of the understanding.

73. [*Ed.*] Hegel appears to have in mind here the form that the proofs for the existence of God assumed in the ancient world—e.g., in Xenophon, Plato, Cicero, Augustine, and Boethius.

this process, which takes place in every human spirit. If one thinks on God, one's spirit contains the very moments that are expressed in this procedure.

Religion is for everyone. ˉIt is notˉ[74] philosophy, which is not for everyone. Religion is the manner or mode by which all human beings become conscious of truth for themselves. Here we must consider the modes of consciousness, especially feeling and representation, and then also thoughtful understanding. The concept of religion has to be considered in this universal mode in which the truth comes to human beings; and therefore the second moment in our consideration is the relationship of the subject [to God] as the feeling, representing, thinking subject.

ˉThe *third moment* in this first part isˉ[75] the sublating of this antithesis of the subject and God, of the separation, this remoteness of the subject from God. Its effect is that as a human being one feels and knows God *internally,* in one's own subjectivity, that as this subject one elevates oneself to God, gives oneself the certainty, the pleasure, and the joyfulness of having God in one's heart, of *being united with God,* "being received by God into grace" as it is phrased in theological parlance. This is the *cultus.*[76] The simple form of the cultus, namely the inner cultus, | is devotion in general. But what is best known within devotion is the mystical attitude, the *unio mystica.*[77]

89

---

74. W₁ *(Var) reads:* Not so

75. *Thus B; L (1827?) reads (similar in* W₁*):* If we have recognized spirit in general, the absolute unity, as the first moment, and as the second the relationship of the subject to the object, to God (not yet to a determinate God, to a God with determinate content, and similarly not yet [having] determinate sensations, determinate representations, determinate thoughts, but merely feeling, representation and thinking in general), then the third is

76. *L (1827?) adds (similar in* W₁*):* To gain for oneself this certain apprehension that God accepts human beings, and receives them into grace, is not only a matter of relationship or of knowledge, but is also a deed, an action.

77. W₁ *(1831) adds in conjunction with a passage from 1824:* The highest concept is the knowledge of spirit. Absolute spirit knows itself; this knowledge is distinguished from it and is therewith the distinct knowing that finite spirit is. In finite knowing, absolute spirit knows itself, and, vice versa, finite spirit knows its essence as absolute spirit. This is the universal concept of religion in general. We have then to consider the forms in which religion in general occurs, as feeling, as

II. Determinate Religion[78]

Determinateness must issue from the concept. The concept as such is what is still enveloped, and the determinations or moments are contained within it but not yet spread out.[79] God, the concept, judges or divides [*urteilt*]; that is, God determines. Only now within this category of determination | do we have existing religion— 90
religion that at the same time *exists determinately*.

We have already noted above that spirit is in principle not immediate—it is not [found] in the mode of immediacy. It is living, is active, is what it makes of itself. The living thing *is* this *activity*. Stone or metal is immediate, it is complete and remains just as it is. But anything alive is already this activity of mediation with itself.

---

representation, and especially as faith, which is the form in which this knowledge by spirit of itself occurs. Finally there is the cultus or the community. In the cultus the formal consciousness frees itself from the rest of its consciousness and becomes consciousness of its essence; the cultus consists in the consciousness that God knows himself in the human being and the human being knows itself in God. As knowing itself in God, the subject, within its inmost self, is the subject in its genuineness. That is the basis of its life as a whole. Its life also then applies itself outwardly, for the subject has a worldly life that possesses that true consciousness as its substantial ground; i.e., the way in which the subject determines its goals in its worldly life depends upon the substantial consciousness of its own truth. This is the aspect under which religion reflects itself in worldliness. This is therefore the knowledge of the world, and to that extent philosophy has been called "worldly wisdom" (though it is, above all, knowledge of absolute spirit). In this way religion also ventures out into the world. The morality and political constitution of the people must have the same character as its religion; for morality and the political constitution are governed wholly by whether a people has only grasped a limited representation of freedom of spirit, or has attained to the true consciousness of freedom. In an appendix to this first part I will say something more about this connection of religion and the political constitution.

[*Ed.*] This allusion to the treatment of the relationship of religion and the state can be viewed as an additional indication that this passage belongs to the 1831 lectures, since only in that year did Hegel fully take up this theme.

78. *B reads:* II. The Second Part or Determinate Religion

79. *L (1827?) adds (similar in W):* [They] have not yet received the legitimation of their distinction. This distinction is the judgment or primal division [*Urteil*], the category of determinateness, the second [sphere] in general. The concept, or merely inner subjectivity, determines itself to objective existence; for only through being its own result is it the concept for itself explicitly. With respect to absolute spirit this point is presented as follows:

The plant is not yet complete when the bud is present, for this meager existence of the bud is just its abstract initial existence. [To exist] it must develop, must first bring itself forth. And finally the plant recapitulates its unfolded self in the seed—this its beginning is also its final product.[80] In the case of the plant there are two sorts of individual. The seed corn, which is the beginning, is something other than what is the completion of its life, into which this unfolding ripens. It is the same for living things generally, for the fruit is something other than the initial seed. But because it is altogether alive, spirit is just like this. At first it is only implicitly, or is in its concept; then it enters into existence, unfolding itself, bringing itself forth, becoming mature, and bringing forth what it is in itself, the concept of its own self, so that what is implicit, its concept, may now be explicit. The child is not yet a rational human being, for it has merely a capacity, is to begin with merely implicit reason, implicit spirit. Only through its formation and development does it first become spirit, for spirit is only genuine spirit insofar as it is the final stage.[81]

Therefore the concept in general is only the first moment. The second is its *activity of self-determining,* of entering into existence, of being for an other, of bringing its moments into mutual distinction and spreading itself out. These distinctions are nothing else but the determinations that the concept itself inwardly contains. In respect to the concept of religion, to the activity of the religious 91 spirit, this self-determining yields the determinate or ethnic | religions.[82] The different forms or determinations of religion, as mo-

80. *L (1827?) adds (similar in* W*):* In the same way the animal goes through its cycle to beget another animal; and the human being, too, is first a child and, qua natural being, goes through the same cycle.

81. *W (1831) adds:* This is also called self-determination, entering into existence, being for an other, bringing its moments into mutual distinction, and spreading itself out. These distinctions are nothing else but the determinations that the concept itself contains within itself.

82. *L (1827?) adds:* The religious spirit has stages in the formation of the consciousness of its absolute essence. At every stage its consciousness is determinate consciousness of itself, the path whereby spirit is educated; it is consciousness regarding the determinate aspects of its concept even though it is not absolute consciousness of the concept in the totality of its determinations.

ments of the concept, are on the one hand moments of religion in general, or of the consummate religion. They are states or determinations of content in the experience and the consciousness of the concept. On the other hand, however, they take shape by developing on their own account in time and historically. Insofar as it is determinate and has not yet traversed the circuit of its determinations, with the result that it is finite religion and exists as finite, religion is *historical* and is a *particular shape* of religion. By indicating, in the series of stages, the principal moments in the development of religion, how these stages also exist in a historical manner, I will in effect be furnishing a single sequence of configurations, or a history of religion.

III. Absolute Religion[83]

⌐Here spirit,⌐[84] being in and for itself, no longer has singular forms or determinations of itself before it in its developed state, and knows itself no more as finite spirit, as spirit in some sort of determinateness or limitedness. Instead it has overcome those limitations and is explicitly what it is implicitly. Spirit's knowing of itself as it is implicitly is the *being-in-and-for-self* of spirit, the consummate, absolute religion in which it is manifest what spirit is, what God is; and this religion is the Christian religion. That spirit must run its course in religion as in all else is necessary in spirit's concept. It *is* spirit only by virtue of the fact that it is for itself as the negation of all finite forms, as this absolute ideality.

I have representations and intuitions, which constitute a specific content: this house, etc. They are my intuitions and represent themselves to me. But I | could not represent them to myself if I had not   92
grasped this content within myself. This entire content must be

---

83. *B reads:* III

84. *Similar in* W₁; W₂ *(MiscP) reads:* The manifestation or development and the determining do not proceed to infinity and do not cease contingently. The genuine progression consists rather in the fact that this reflection of the concept into self terminates itself when it actually returns into itself. Thus the very appearance is infinite appearance, the content is in conformity with the concept of spirit, and the appearance is such as the spirit is in and for itself. The concept of religion has itself become objective for itself in religion. Spirit,

posited within me in a simple and ideal way. Ideality means that this being [that is] external [to me] (i.e., its spatiality, temporality, materiality, and mutual externality) is sublated. Inasmuch as I know this being, its contents are not represented things, being outside one another; rather they are within me in a simple manner. Though a tree has many parts, it nevertheless is merely simple in my representation. Spirit is knowledge. For it to be knowledge, the content of what it knows must have attained this ideal form, it must have been negated in this manner. What constitutes spirit must have come into its own in such a way. Spirit must have been educated, must have traversed this circuit. These forms, distinctions, determinations, and finitudes must have been, in order for it to make them its own and to negate them, in order for what it is in itself to have emerged out of it and stood as object over against it, yet at the same time be its own.

This is the path and the goal by which spirit has attained its proper concept, the concept of itself, and has arrived at what it is in itself. And it only arrives at it in this way, the way that has been indicated in its abstract moments.[85] The Christian religion appeared when the time had come.[86] This time is not a contingent time, a discretionary or whimsical choice, but is rather grounded in an essential, eternal decree of God. That is, it is a time determined in the eternal reason and wisdom of God, not one determined in a contingent fashion. Rather it is the concept of the matter, the divine concept, the concept of God's own self.

This is the preliminary presentation of the plan of the content that we wish to consider.

85. W (1831) adds: The revealed religion is the revelatory or manifest religion because God has become wholly manifest in it. Here everything is commensurate with the concept; there is no longer anything secret in God. Here the consciousness of the developed concept of spirit exists, the consciousness of being reconciled not in beauty, or in gaiety, but in spirit.

86. [Ed.] See Mark 1:15, Gal. 4:4, Eph. 1:10.

PART I
THE CONCEPT OF RELIGION

THE LECTURES OF 1827

The question with which we have to begin is: "How are we to secure a beginning?" For it is of course at least a formal requirement of all scientific knowledge, and especially of philosophy, that nothing should occur in it that has not yet been proved. At the beginning, however, we have not yet proved [anything] ¯and we cannot yet appeal to anything antecedent.¯¹ In the superficial sense "proving" means that a content, proposition, or concept is shown to result from something prior to it. In that way we cognize its necessity. But when we are supposed to make a beginning, we do not yet have before us any result, anything mediated or posited through something else. At the beginning we are in the presence of the immediate. The other sciences have an easy time of it in their own way. In geometry, for example, we begin with the proposition: "There is a space, a point, a line, etc." There is no talk of proving, for the fact is directly conceded. In philosophy we are not allowed to make a beginning with the phrase "there is" or "there are"; for that would be the immediate.

²In the present case, however, we are not beginning philosophy afresh. The science of religion is one science within philosophy; indeed it is the *final* one. In that respect it presupposes the other philosophical disciplines and is therefore a result. In its philosophical aspect we are already dealing with a result of premises that lie

---

1. *Thus Hu; An reads:* but we do presuppose something.
2. *Precedes in L (1827?) (similar in W₂):* With regard to philosophy as a whole there may be a difficulty here. Logic elucidates how such a difficulty is met.

266

behind us. We have only to begin from religion, and to make sure that this standpoint of religion has been proved and that we can advert from it to our own consciousness; ˉthe truth will become evident in the progression itself.ˉ³ The original content, the foundation of the philosophy of religion, is a result, namely a lemma | or subsidiary proposition to the effect that the content with which we begin is genuine content. ⁴In regard to this initial content, however, we can also appeal to the general consciousness and in that way take hold of a starting point that is ˉgenerally validˉ⁵ at least empirically. Whatever is to be valid in science must be something proved; [whereas] something conceded is what is presupposed in a subjective way, so that the beginning can be made from it.

A. THE CONCEPT OF GOD⁶

The beginning of religion, more precisely its content, is the concept of religion itself, that God is the absolute truth, the truth of all things, and subjectively that religion alone is the absolutely true

---

3. *Thus Hu; L (Var) reads:* and that, too, ought then to occur here.
4. *In B's margin:* 14 May 1827
5. *Thus L; B reads:* correct
6. [*Ed.*] After the preceding brief introductory remarks on the problem of securing a beginning, in which there are only faint echoes of the earlier discussion (in 1824 and especially 1821) of the need to prove the necessity of the religious standpoint (a matter briefly pursued further at the beginning of Sec. A), the 1827 lectures move immediately to an exposition of the moments of the concept of religion, which correspond to the moments of the self-explication of the concept of God as absolute idea. Since the speculative definition of religion as the self-consciousness of absolute spirit had been arrived at in 1824, in 1827 it was only necessary to spell out the logical aspects of this definition, dispensing with all preliminary matters or absorbing their contents into the speculatively structured treatment. The three moments of the concept of religion correspond to the logical moments of the concept qua concept, as is evident from the syllogism: the moments of universality, particularity, and individuality or subjectivity (cf. *Encyclopedia* [1830] §§ 183–189; *Science of Logic*, pp. 600–622, 666–681 [*GW* 12:32–52, 92–106]). In terms of religion these three yield the abstract concept of God, religious consciousness or the knowledge of God (the theoretical religious relationship), and the cultus (the practical relationship). This heading, like all those in the 1827 *Concept*, is editorial.

knowledge. For us who have religion, what God is, is something well-known, a content that can be presupposed in subjective consciousness. Scientifically regarded, the expression "God" is, to begin with, a general, abstract name that has not yet received any genuine import, for only the philosophy of religion is the scientific development and cognition of what God is. Only through it do we come to a cognitive awareness of what God is, for otherwise we would have no need at all for philosophy of religion. ˉIt is said to develop this awareness in us for the first time.ˉ7

ˉˉOur starting point (namely, that what we generally call "God", or God in an indeterminate sense, is the truth of all things) is the result of the whole of philosophy. According to our division of it, philosophy considers first the logical domain, or pure thinking ˉin its development, and then | nature.ˉ8 The third division is spirit, which as finite spirit stands in connection with nature and elevates itself to absolute spirit. The course of philosophy leads to the point that the final result of all this is God. This highest point is then the proof that God is, or in other words that this universal, which is in and for itself, embracing and containing absolutely everything, is that through which alone everything is and has subsistence—that this universal is the truth. This *One* is the result of philosophy. We make our beginning straightaway from this result of philosophy.

This may give the distorted impression that God, so represented, becomes a *result*. But anyone acquainted with philosophical method knows that "result" has here the meaning of "being the absolute truth." This implies that just because what appears as result is the absolute truth, it ceases to be something resulting—that this very attitude, whereby what results derived from an other, is thus sublated or abolished. The proposition, "God is the absolutely true," means just as much that God is not the result, but rather that,

267

7. *Thus An; L (Var) reads (similar in W):* God is this representation that is so familiar to us, but a representation that is not yet developed and cognized scientifically.

8. *Thus Hu; L (Var) reads (similar in W₁):* which resolves itself upon nature, resolves itself to exist externally, as nature.

inasmuch as it is the last thing, what is absolutely true is just as much the first. But it is only the true insofar as it is not just the beginning but also the end or result, insofar as it results from itself. ˜In this sense the result of philosophy is here the beginning.˜⁹

At this point you have only my assurance that this is the result of philosophy.˜˜¹⁰ With respect to this assurance, however, we can appeal to the religious consciousness. Religious consciousness has the conviction that God is really the midpoint, the absolutely true, that from which everything proceeds and into which everything returns, that upon which everything is dependent and apart from which nothing other than it has absolute, true independence. This then is the content of the beginning.

At the same time we must notice here that, however full one's heart may be with this representation, the beginning remains scientifically abstract. In the scientific domain we are not dealing with what is in feeling, but exclusively with what is outside it—and indeed is set forth for thought—as an object for consciousness, more explicitly for the thinking consciousness, in such a way that 268   it has attained the form of thought. | To give this fullness [of content] the form of thought or of the concept is the business of our science.

Because this beginning (as the initial content) is still abstract, this universality has, so to speak, a subjective status, as if the universal were universal in this way only for the beginning and would not remain in this universality. But the beginning of the content is to be grasped in such a way that, in all the further developments of the content, inasmuch as the universal itself will show itself to be something absolutely concrete, rich, and full of content, we never step outside this universality. The consequence is that the universality, which under one aspect we leave behind (according to its

9. *Thus Hu; L (Var) reads (similar in W₁):* This has also been asserted quite generally about the concept of spirit.

10. *Similar in W₁; W₂ (MiscP) reads:* With [i.e. because of] the indication of this self-justifying development within our science, we take it [only] as an assurance, to begin with, that the result of philosophy is that God is the absolutely true, the universal in and for itself, that which comprehends and contains everything and bestows subsistence on everything.

form) because it proceeds to a determinate development, to a richness of content, to greater concreteness, nevertheless maintains itself as the absolutely enduring foundation and is not simply a subjective beginning. At the beginning, God is for us inasmuch as God is the universal; in relation to the development, God is what is enclosed within itself [*das in sich Verschlossene*] or is in absolute unity with itself. If we say, "God is the [self-]enclosed," we are of course speaking with reference to a development that we anticipate. But in its reference to God himself, or to the content itself, this enclosedness (as we have labeled God's universality) is not to be grasped as an abstract universality outside which, and over against which, the particular might still be independent. "God is the enclosed." The particular seems in this definition to be distinct from this universal, but the latter is to be grasped in such a way that the development does not step forth out of the universality. Thus it is to be grasped as the absolutely full, replete universality. [To say that] God is this universal that is concrete and full within itself is [to say] that God is only *one* and not in antithesis to many [other] deities. Instead there is only the One, who is God.

The things and developments of the natural and spiritual world constitute manifold configurations, and endlessly multiform existence; they have a being differentiated in rank, force, intensity, and content. The being of all these things is not of an independent sort, however, but is quite simply something upheld and maintained, not genuine independence. If we ascribe a being to particular things, it is only a borrowed being, only the semblance of a being, not the absolutely independent being that God is.

God in his universality, this universal in which there is no limitation, finitude, or particularity, is the absolute subsistence and is so alone. Whatever subsists has its root and subsistence | only in 269 this One. If we grasp this initial content in this way, we can express it thus: "God is the absolute substance, the only true actuality." All else that is actual is not actual on its own account, has no subsistence on its own account; the uniquely absolute actuality is God alone. Thus God is the absolute substance. I will speak at once about how this substance is related to subjectivity.

117

God is the absolute substance. If we cling to this declaration in its abstract form, then it is certainly Spinozism or pantheism.[11] But the fact that God is *substance* does not exclude *subjectivity,* for substance as such is not yet at all distinguished from subjectivity. That God is substance is part of the presupposition we have made that God is *spirit, absolute spirit,* eternally simple spirit, being essentially present to itself. Then this ideality or subjectivity of spirit, which is the perspicuity or ideality of every particular, is likewise this very universality, this pure relation to itself, the absolute being-

11. [*Ed.*] The relation of Spinozism to pantheism and the viability of these doctrines were hotly-debated issues in the *Aufklärung* and German idealism. The controversy began when the prominent eighteenth-century critic and dramatist Lessing showed sympathies with Spinoza's thought in his own rationalistic essays on philosophical and theological topics. F. H. Jacobi wrote to Moses Mendelssohn in 1783 that he had heard Lessing confess to being a Spinozist just before his death (see below, n. 31). In his *Morgenstünden* or lectures on God's existence (1785), Mendelssohn rebutted Jacobi's probably inaccurate charge and tried to draw some distinctions regarding pantheism and the teachings of Spinoza and of Lessing. The problem is complicated by the fact that the term "pantheism" appears in English deism some time after Spinoza's death, and the propriety of applying it and its associations retrospectively to Spinoza is open to question. Jacobi replied immediately to Mendelssohn in a series of letters *Concerning the Doctrine of Spinoza* (1785), and the debate continued with a further published exchange between them the following year. Herder joined the fray from the literary side with his *God, Some Conversations* (1787), a dialogue presenting a Spinozistic philosophy of nature in sympathetic fashion. Jacobi remained the central figure in the "pantheism controversy" because of the argument of his *Briefe* that Spinozism is the only consistently logical system and that it is equivalent to pantheism, atheism, and fatalism. (On the interpretation of Spinozism as atheism, see below, n. 28. On the charge of fatalism, see Christian Wolff, *Theologia naturalis,* Pars posterior, § 709; and Jacobi, *Werke* 4/1:55, 59 ff., 71, 223.) Jacobi intended by his critique to discredit rationalistic philosophy in order to make room for his own "faith philosophy," a type of fideism grounded in feeling and partly based on Hamann's thought. For the philosophers of German idealism Jacobi's treatment of these issues seemed a grotesque caricature that they sometimes attacked and sometimes ridiculed. Schelling presented Spinozism appreciatively in his *Letters on Dogmatism and Criticism* (1795), which nevertheless supported Fichte's moral idealism as an equally coherent, and to Schelling preferable, rational philosophy. Hegel criticized Jacobi's "faith philosophy" in his essay, *Faith and Knowledge* (1802). Schelling made careful distinctions regarding pantheism and the God-world relation (obviously with Jacobi's polemic in mind) in his *Of Human Freedom* (1809), and brutally parodied Jacobi's attempt at an irrational "leap of faith," in an essay published in 1812 (Schelling, *Werke* 8:19–136). Hegel surely has this long-standing controversy in mind when he makes conceptual distinctions regarding pantheism and Spinozism here and elsewhere in these lectures.

with-self and abiding-with-self; it is absolute substance. At the same time, when we say "substance" there is then the distinction that that universal is not yet grasped as internally concrete. Only when grasped as concrete is it spirit; but even in its determination as internally concrete it remains this unity with itself, this one actuality that we have just now denominated as substance. A further determination is that the substantiality or unity of absolute actuality with itself is only the foundation, only one moment in the definition of God as spirit.[12] The determination, the concrete being, the unity of differentiated determinations, only arises when we proceed further. It presupposes a one and an other, though at the beginning we do not yet have differentiated determinations, a one and an other. At the beginning we have before us only the one, not the other. If we are concerned with the other, we have already gone further. So if we speak of the beginning, we have this one actuality as a relating of itself to itself and not to an other; | we do not yet   270
have an advance, not yet concrete being. Therefore even the content exists in the form of substantiality. Even when we say "God" and "spirit," they are empty, indeterminate words or representations. It all depends on what has entered into consciousness. What enters into consciousness in the beginning is the simple, the abstract. In this initial simplicity we have God as substance, but we do not stop at that point.

This is the form of the content at the beginning, and this content remains the foundation. All through the development God does not step outside his unity with himself. In God's creating of the world, as tradition has it, no new principle makes an appearance, nor is something evil established, something other that would be autonomous or independent. God remains only this One; the one true actuality, the one principle, abides throughout all particularity.

12. L (1827?) adds (similar in W): Thus substance is only one determination in what we affirm about God. This statement is preliminary, in order to prevent misconceptions. The disparagement of philosophy arises especially from this quarter. It is said that philosophy must be Spinozism if it is to be consistent, and that consequently it is atheism and fatalism. What is implied in this content of the beginning is that we only have this abundance or this concrete being before us insofar as it is still wholly universal.

We express this beginning thus, as a content within us, an object for us. *We* have this object, and so the immediate question is: Who then are "we" who have the content within us? When we say "we," "I," or "spirit," that is itself something very concrete, something manifold: I am intuiting, I see, I hear, etc. I am all of that—the feeling, intuition, sight, and hearing. Therefore the more exact meaning of our question is: Under which of those determinations is this content for our awareness? Is it representation, will, phantasy, or feeling? What is the place in which this content or this object is at home? What is the soil for this content? If we recall the usual answers, then [they are that] God is within us as believing, feeling, representing, and knowing beings. Later on[13] we shall have to consider rather more closely these forms, capacities, and aspects of ourselves (namely feeling, representation, and faith), especially in connection with the very point under discussion here. But [at the moment] we are not casting about for just any sort of answer, and are not guided by experiences or observations to the effect that we have God in feeling, etc. To begin with, we keep to what we have before us—this One or universal, this abundance, which is the transparent aether remaining unchangeably itself.

If we take up this One that we have before us, and ask for which of our spiritual capacities or activities this One, this utterly universal being, *is*, then we can name, as the soil in which this content can be at home, only the activity or mode of our spirit that corresponds to it. If we now ask ourselves what we call this aspect of our consciousness | for which the universal on the whole is, whether it be determined abstractly or concretely within itself, then the answer is *thought*. For thought is alone the soil for this content, is the activity of the universal—the universal in its activity and efficacy. Or, if we speak of it as the apprehending of the universal, then it is always thought for which the universal is. The product of thought or what is engendered by means of thought is something universal, a universal content. The form—that within us which apprehends the universal—is for that very reason thought. As we said, this universal—which can be produced by thought and is for thought—

13. [*Ed.*] See below, pp. 135 ff.

can be wholly abstract. Then it is the immeasurable, the infinite, the sublating of all limits and all particularity, and this *negative* universal likewise has its seat only in thought.

It is a universal and ancient preconception that human beings are thinking beings, and that by thinking and thinking alone they distinguish themselves from the beasts. Animals have feelings, but only feelings. Human beings think, and they alone have religion. From this it is to be concluded that religion has its inmost seat in thought. No doubt it can subsequently be felt, ¯as we shall show later in our discussion.¯[14]

We also express this process thus: When human beings think of God, they elevate themselves above the sensible, the external, the singular. We say that it is an elevation to the pure, to that which is at one with itself. This elevation is a transcending of the sensible, of mere feeling, a journey into the pure region; and this region of the universal is thought. This is the content of the beginning, and in the subjective mode it is the soil for this content.[15] |

272

What we have before us is this single absolute. We cannot yet call this content or this determination "religion," for to the latter there belongs subjective spirit, consciousness. Thought is of course the locus of this universal, but, to begin with, this locus is absorbed in the One, the eternal, this actual being in-and-for-itself. In this genuine, absolute determination, although it is not yet developed or consummated, God remains absolute substance and does so

14. *Thus B; L (Var) reads:* but it is a faulty objection that religion and the like should be [only] a feeling, as if the content that is in one form belonged essentially to that form alone.

    [*Ed.*] See below, pp. 138 ff.

15. *L (1827?) adds (similar in W):* The content is this absolutely undivided and continuous being, an abiding with self, the universal, and thought is the mode for which this universal is.

    We have called God the universal, and there is for thought a distinction between itself and the universal, which we initially called God. This distinction belongs in the first instance to our reflection and is by no means contained explicitly in the content as yet. It is the faith of religion and the result of philosophy that God is the one true actuality and that there is no other actuality at all. From this standpoint an actuality that we call thinking has as yet no proper place. *In W₂ (Var) the final sentence reads:* In this one actuality and pure clarity, the actuality and distinction that we call thinking has as yet no place.

through all of the development. For this universal is the foundation, the beginning point, the point of departure, though at the same time it is simply the abiding unity and not a mere soil out of which the distinctions grow. Instead all distinctions remain enclosed within this universal.[16] It is also not an inert, abstract universal, however, but rather the absolute womb or the infinite fountainhead out of which everything emerges, into which everything returns, and in which it is eternally maintained. This basic determination is therefore the definition of God as substance.[17]

Some people have wanted to designate this representation of the philosophical idea that we make for ourselves—namely, that God is this actual being, this abiding with self, the one truth, the absolute actuality—by the term *pantheism,* and the philosophy [associated with it] as *identity-philosophy.*[18] Identity-philosophy is also said to be more precisely pantheism, for here everything is identity, or unity with self. This can be entirely superficial, and when speculative philosophy is said to be an identity system, "identity" is being taken in the abstract sense of the understanding. Rather than "pantheism" it could more accurately be called "the representation of substantiality," because in it God is defined above all only as substance. The absolute subject (the spirit) also remains substance, although it is defined not only as substance | but also inwardly as subject. Those who say that speculative philosophy amounts to pantheism

273

16. [*Ed.*] Thus in the Christian religion we arrive at the insight that this absolute substance is also internally self-differentiated: it is the immanent Trinity. God is not *sheer* substance, an undifferentiated monad, but rather an "abiding unity." In going out from himself and entering into determinacy, God actually never leaves himself, for the distinctions are already present within God.

17. W_2 *and L add (MiscP):* The universal therefore never steps forth out of this aether of equality with itself and of presence to itself. As this universal, God can never come to the point of being in fact along with an other whose subsistence is more than a [*L reads:* more a] play of illusion. Compared with this pure unity and clear transparency, matter is nothing impenetrable, and spirit or the I does not have the rigidity to possess true substantiality on its own account.

18. [*Ed.*] Schelling gave the name "identity-philosophy" to his main writings of 1801–1804. In the *Darstellung meines Systems der Philosophie* of 1801 (*Werke* 4:105–212), he elucidated his notion of the absolute identity as the prius and ground of the real and ideal realms (nature and spirit).

usually know nothing of this distinction; as always, they overlook what matters most.[19]

We need to make more explicit some of the characteristics of the pantheism that pious people usually reproach in philosophy.[20] "Pantheism" in the proper sense means that everything, the whole, the universe, this complex of everything existing, these infinitely many individual things—that all this is God. And the accusation made against philosophy is that it maintains that everything is God, "everything" meaning here this infinite multiplicity of individual things—not the universality that has being in and for itself but the individual things in their empirical existence, as they exist immediately but not in their universality. If one says, "God is everything, is this paper," and so on, then that is pantheism. When I say "genus," that is also a universality, of course, though quite a different one from when I say "totality." The genus is the universal only as the inclusion of all individual existences. Actual being, what lies at the foundation—the proper content is all individual things, [so it is said].

Now it is a wholly false contention that pantheism of this sort is effectively present in any ˉphilosophyˉ[21] whatsoever. It has never occurred to anyone to say that everything, all individual things collectively, in their individuality and contingency, are God—for example, that paper or this table is God. No one has ever held that. Still less has this been maintained in any philosophy. We will become acquainted with Oriental pantheism or genuine Spinozism later, in [treating] Oriental religion. Spinozism itself as such, and Oriental

19. *Thus also* W₁; W₂ *(Var) adds:* and they disparage philosophy in that they make something false out of it.

20. [*Ed.*] Explicit attacks on Hegel's "pantheism" began to appear in the mid-1820s. See F. A. G. Tholuck, *Die Lehre von der Sünde und vom Versöhner,* 2d ed. (Hamburg, 1825), p. 231; and Anonymous [Hülsemann], *Ueber die Hegelsche Lehre, oder: Absolutes Wissen und moderner Pantheismus* (Leipzig, 1829). The proximity in time to the Preface to the 2d ed. of the *Encyclopedia* (1827), as well as the mention of "pious people," makes it certain that Hegel is here aiming especially at the theologian Tholuck. In addition to the work mentioned above, see Tholuck's *Blüthensammlung aus der Morgenländischen Mystik nebst einer Einleitung über Mystik überhaupt und Morgenländische insbesondere* (Berlin, 1825), pp. 33, 37.

21. *Thus B, Hu, An; L and W read:* religion

pantheism, too, comprise the view that the divine in all things is only the universal aspect of their content, the *essence* of things, but in such a way that it is also represented as the *determinate* essence of things. For example, the Orientals state that Krishna, Vishnu, and Brahmā say regarding themselves: "I am the luster or brilliance in metals, the Ganges among rivers, the life in the living, the understanding in those who have understanding."[22] For in saying, "I am the luster in | metal, etc.," one has thereby already superseded [the contention] that everything (metal, river, understanding) is God. Each of these (the one with understanding, the rivers, the metals) is something existing immediately. Krishna is not metal but the luster in metals. The luster is not the metal itself but the universal or substantial [aspect], separated out from the individual [aspect] but no longer the πᾶν or the all as the sum of individual [things]. Therefore what is expressed here is no longer what [the critics] call pantheism, for what is designated is the *essence* within such individual things. Many other features belong to individual things, such as spatiality and temporality; but here the focus is only upon the imperishable element in this individuality.[23]

274

The usual representation of pantheism derives from the practice of focusing on the abstract unity rather than the spiritual unity, and from entirely forgetting that—in a religious representation in which only the substance or the One has the value of genuine actuality—individual things, in this very contrast with the One, have disappeared and no actuality is ascribed to them. Instead one retains this actuality of individual things. Against this the Eleatics[24] said, "There is only the One," and expressly added, "and nothing is not at all." Everything finite would be limitation or negation of

22. [*Ed.*] These words are spoken by the Hindu god Krishna, an avatar of Vishnu. Hegel conflates parts of three verses from the *Bhagavad-Gita* (10.36, 31, 22). The Sanskrit of Hegel's "luster or brilliance in metals" is rendered in exceedingly diverse ways by modern translators.

23. *L (1827?) adds (similar in W):* But if we say, "Everything is God and God is everything," then individuality is being taken according to all of its limitations, its finitude and transitoriness. The "life of the living" within this sphere of life is the unlimited, the universal.

24. [*Ed.*] Hegel refers to a statement of Parmenides (Fragment 6), transmitted by Simplicius (*in Phys.* 117.4): "That which can be spoken and thought needs must be; for it is possible for it, but not for nothing, to be" (G. S. Kirk and J. E. Raven, *The Presocratic Philosophers* [Cambridge, 1957], p. 270).

the One (*omnis determinatio est negatio*[25]), but they say, "nothing, limitation, finitude, the limit and the limited, simply are not." Thus, stopping short at this kind of philosophical definition[26] means that no actuality at all is ascribed to individual things, and that Spinozism is *acosmism*[27] rather [than pantheism]. Spinozism has also been reproached as *atheism*;[28] however, in Spinozism this world or this "all" simply *is not* [*ist gar nicht*]. Certainly the "all" appears, one speaks of its determinate being [*Dasein*], and our life is a being within this existence [*Existenz*]. In the philosophical sense, however, the world has in this view no actuality at all: it simply *is not*.[29] But | the accusers of Spinozism are unable to liberate themselves from 275 the finite; hence they declare that for Spinozism everything is God, because it is precisely the aggregate of finitudes (the world) that has there disappeared. [30]If one employs the expression "all is one"[31] and [claims] therefore that unity is the truth of multiplicity, then

25. [*Ed.*] This expression ("all determination is negation") goes back to Spinoza. See his letter No. 50 (to Jareg Jellis) in *Chief Works* 2:369–370.

26. *L (Var) adds:* such as that of the Eleatics or of Spinozism

27. [*Ed.*] Hegel may have first encountered the interpretation of Spinoza's system as "acosmism" rather than as "pantheism" or "atheism" in Salomon Maimon's *Lebensgeschichte* (Berlin, 1792), or in C. T. de Murr's *Adnotationes* on Spinoza's *Tractatus Theologico-Politicus* (The Hague, 1802). This interpretation assumes that for Spinoza finite things are absorbed into the infinite and that therefore his system is one of "cosmotheism." Hegel accepted this interpretation in contrast with Jacobi, who contended that there really is no difference between acosmism (or cosmotheism) and atheism (Jacobi, *Werke* 4/1:xxxiv–xxxv). For Hegel's view of Spinozism as acosmism, see his *History of Philosophy* 3:276, 280–282 (*Werke* 15:404, 408), and the *Encyclopedia* (1830), § 50 remark and § 573 remark.

28. [*Ed.*] The interpretation of Spinozism as atheism is found, among other places, in Wolff, *Theologia naturalis*, Pars posterior, § 716. But above all it was Jacobi who advanced the charge, "Spinozism is atheism" (*Briefe über Spinoza*, p. 223 [*Werke* 4/1:216, cf. pp. xxxvi–xxxvii]). On Hegel's criticism that "the accusers of Spinozism are unable to liberate themselves from the finite" and that "hence they declare that for Spinozism everything is God," see unabridged ed., Vol. 1:254, incl. n. 184.

29. *L (1827?) adds:* No actuality is ascribed to "the all," to these finitudes. There are finitudes, and about them it is said that they simply *are not*.

30. *Precedes in L (1827?):* There has never been a pantheism of the sort they have in mind.

31. [*Ed.*] Hegel alludes to the alleged deathbed confession of Lessing, as reported by Jacobi: "The orthodox conceptions of the deity are no longer for me; I cannot take pleasure in them. Ἕν καὶ Πᾶν ["One and All"]! I know no other" (Jacobi, *Briefe über Spinoza*, pp. 22, 23, 62 [*Werke* 4/1:54, 55, 89]).

the "all" simply is no longer. The multiplicity vanishes, for it has its truth in the unity. But those critics cannot master the "being-vanished" of the many, or the negativity of the finite that is implied in it.

Furthermore there is the general accusation that Spinozism has the following consequence. If everything is one in the way this philosophy asserts, then it asserts with it that good is one with evil, that there is no distinction between good and evil, and therewith all religion is annulled. In this connection it is entirely correct that if "everything" actually were God, then God would be sublated. But here it is all the finite that is sublated instead. It is said that in Spinozism the distinction of good and evil has no intrinsic validity, that morality is annulled, and so it is a matter of indifference whether one is good or evil. That is no less superficial a consequence. For they indeed say that this would be an inevitable inference from this philosophy, but for charitable reasons they were not willing to draw this conclusion. It can in fact be conceded that the distinction of good and evil is sublated implicitly, that is, sublated in God as the sole true actuality. In God there is no evil. [However,] the distinction between good and evil exists only if God is also evil. But it will not be conceded that evil is something affirmative and that this affirmative element is in God. God is good and good alone. The distinction of good and evil is not present in this One, in this substance, for it first makes its entrance along with distinction in general.

[32]The distinction of good and evil makes its entrance together with the distinction of God from the world, in particular from human beings. With regard to the distinction of God and humanity, the basic determination in Spinozism is that human beings must have God alone as their goal. | For the distinction, i.e., for human beings, the law is the love of God,[33] that they be directed solely toward this love and not grant validity to their distinction or wish

276

32. *Precedes in L (1827?) (similar in W):* God is the One, abiding absolutely as present to self. There is no distinction within substance.

33. [Ed.] Hegel refers to Spinoza's *Ethics*, Part V, Prop. 36: "The intellectual love of the mind toward God is that very love of God whereby God loves himself, not insofar as he is infinite, but insofar as he can be explained through the essence of the human mind regarded under the form of eternity; in other words, the intel-

to persist in it, but have their orientation toward God alone. This is the most sublime morality, that evil is what is null, and human beings ought not to let this distinction, this nullity, be valid within themselves nor make it valid at all. We can will to persist in this distinction, can push it to the point of opposition to God, the universal in and for itself. In so doing we are evil. But we can also deem our distinction to be null and void, and can posit our essential being solely in God and in our orientation toward God. In so doing we are good.[34] This distinction is not [applicable] within God as such, within God under this definition as substance. But for human beings there is this distinction, since distinctiveness in general enters with human existence, and more specifically the distinction between good and evil.

In regard to the polemic [of the theologians] against philosophy generally, there is an unfortunate circumstance: on the one hand philosophy must become polemical, and on the other hand the objections are so shallow that philosophical instruction must begin from the primary elements. A further superficiality that is employed in the polemic against philosophy is that philosophy is said to be an identity-system. It is entirely correct that substance is this identity with itself—and so is spirit.[35] But to speak of identity-philosophy is to stick with abstract identity, or unity in general, and to neglect the point on which alone everything hinges, namely the inherent determination of this unity, whether it is defined as substance or as spirit. The whole of philosophy is nothing else but a ˉstudyˉ[36] of the definition of *unity;* and likewise the philosophy of religion is just a succession of unities, where the unity always [abides] but is

---

lectual love of the mind toward God is part of the infinite love wherewith God loves himself" (*Chief Works* 2:264 f.). Cf. the corollary and note that follow in Spinoza's text.

34. *L (1827?) adds (first sentence similar in W):* Thus the distinctiveness of good and evil certainly enters into Spinozism. God and the human being confront one another, and indeed do so with the specification that evil is to be deemed null and void. Therefore it is so far from being the case that morality, ethics, and the distinction between good and evil are absent from this standpoint that, on the contrary, this distinction here stands entirely in its place.

35. *Thus also* W₁; *W₂ (Var) adds:* Identity or unity with self is, in the end, everything.

36. *Thus B, An, W; L (Var) reads:* system

277 continually becoming more determinate. We can | make the one-sidedness of the polemic clear with an example drawn from nature. In the physical domain there are a lot of unities, such as water, into which earth is introduced. That is a unity, too, although a mixture. When I have a base and an acid, and a salt or a crystal forms from them, I also have water there. Similarly, it is present in muscle fibers and the like, although it is not visible. In this case the unity of the water with this material is again one that is quite differently determined from the unity that results if I mix water and earth. In all these things the unity of water with other substances is there, although the determinations of this unity are different in each case. If we now omit this particular determination upon which everything depends and cling to the unity abstractly, we are finally reduced to applying the poorest category, that of mixture, to all these higher configurations, to crystals, plants, living organisms, etc. The main thing is the distinction of these determinations of unity. Thus the unity of God is always unity, too, though everything turns quite strictly upon the manner in which this unity is defined. It is just this definition, however, that is overlooked by such a superficial apprehension, namely the apprehension on which everything depends.

B. THE KNOWLEDGE OF GOD[37]

The first [moment] in the concept of religion is this divine universality, spirit wholly in its indeterminate universality for which there is positively no distinction. ˉThe second [moment] after this

---

37. *In B's margin:* 17 May 1827

[*Ed.*] B's notation is actually adjacent to the beginning of the second sentence below. The heading is editorial, although *An* writes: "Starting from ourselves, how do we arrive at the knowledge of God?" Into this section, which treats the various forms of the knowledge of God or of religious consciousness—namely, immediate knowledge, faith, feeling, representation, thought—Hegel incorporates much of the material from Secs. A and B.1 of the 1824 lectures, and from Secs. B and D of the 1821 *Ms.* This previously dispersed material now finds its logically appropriate place in the second moment of the concept of God, the moment of particularity or differentiation, the moment of relationship. Under the theme of "Religious Knowledge as Elevation to God" (a subcategory of "Thought"), Hegel also gathers together his treatment of the proofs of the existence of God, previously dispersed across Parts II and III and considered in conjunction with specific religions. (See below, n. 109.)

absolute foundation is distinction in general, and only with distinction does religion as such begin. |

This *distinction* is a spiritual distinction, it is consciousness. In general the spiritual, universal relationship is the knowledge of this absolute content, of this foundation. This is not the place to analyze the cognition of this absolute judgment [or primal division]. The concept judges, that is, the concept or the universal passes over into primal division, diremption, separation. Because it is one of the logical determinations and these are presupposed,[38] we can express it here as a fact that this absolute universality proceeds to the internal distinction of itself, it proceeds to the primal division or to the point of positing itself as determinateness.

Thus we arrive at the standpoint for which God (in this general indeterminateness) is object of consciousness. Here for the first time we have two [elements], God and the consciousness for which God is. Because we have these two, in representation we can start just as readily from one as from the other.¯[39]

¯Suppose that we take *God* as our point of departure.¯[40] Then God or spirit is this judgment [or primal division]; expressed concretely, this is the creation of the world and of the subjective spirit for which God is object. Spirit is an absolute manifesting. Its manifesting is a positing of determination and a being for an other. "Manifesting" means "creating an other," and indeed the creating of subjective spirit for which the absolute is. The making or creation of the world is God's self-manifesting, self-revealing. In a further and later definition we will have this manifestation in the higher form that what God creates God himself is, that in general it does not have the determinateness of an other, that God is manifestation of his own self, that God is for himself—the other (which has the

38. [*Ed.*] See *Science of Logic*, pp. 623 ff. (*GW* 12:53 ff.).

39. *Similar in* W₁; W₂ (*MiscP*) *reads:* But upon this absolute foundation—we still express it primarily as fact—there now also arises distinction in general, which, as spiritual distinction, is consciousness; only with it does religion as such begin. In that the absolute universality proceeds to judgment [or primal division], i.e., proceeds to posit itself as determinateness, and in that God *is* as spirit for spirit, we thus arrive at the standpoint for which God is object of consciousness, and the initially universal and distinct thought has entered into relationship.

40. *Thus Hu;* L (*1827?*) *reads (similar in* W₁): We can say that the judgment [or primal division] proceeds absolutely from God.

empty semblance of [being] an other but is immediately reconciled), the Son of God or human being according to the divine image.[41] Here for the first time we have consciousness, the subjectively knowing spirit for which God is object.[42]

From this it follows that God can be known or cognized, for it is God's nature to reveal himself, to be manifest. Those who say that God is not revelatory[43] do not speak from the [standpoint of the] Christian | religion at any rate, for the Christian religion is called the revealed religion. Its content is that God is revealed to human beings, that they know what God is. Previously they did not know this; but in the Christian religion there is no longer any secret—a mystery certainly, but not in the sense that it is not known.[44] For consciousness at the level of understanding or for sensible cognition it is a secret, whereas for reason it is something manifest. When the name of God is taken seriously, it is already the case for Plato and Aristotle[45] that God is not jealous to the point of not communicating himself. Among the Athenians the

279

41. *L, W₁ add (1827?):* Adam Kadmon.
[*Ed.*] As the ontologically primordial human being of ancient and medieval Jewish mysticism and later heterodox Christian theosophy (including Jacob Boehme, whose works Hegel knew), Adam Kadmon is the first spiritual configuration to emanate from the divine light.

42. *L (1827?) adds (first sentence similar in W₁):* God *is* in being revelatory for spirit, and the self-revealing is at the same time the begetting of spirit. Creation means nothing other than that God reveals himself.

43. *W₁ (1827?) adds:* that we can know nothing of God

44. *L (1827?) adds (similar in W₁):* (All Athenians knew the Eleusinian mysteries.) A mystery is something profound, and later among the Neoplatonic philosophers it is the speculative element that expresses the immediate God.
[*Ed.*] Cf. Hegel, *History of Philosophy* 2:448 (*Werke* 15:72; cf. 91n.): "However, μυστήριον has not to the Alexandrians the meaning that it has to us, for to them it indicates speculative philosophy generally." Hegel sees such a connection of mystery and speculation for Proclus in particular. Here he is probably thinking as well of the existential unity for Proclus of faith in the mysteries and philosophical speculation. Cf. Marinus, *De vita Procli;* and Proclus, *Theologia Platonis,* the Introduction and especially the trinitarian teaching of Book 3, chaps. 9–14.

45. [*Ed.*] On the absence of jealousy on the part of divinity, see Plato *Phaedrus* 247a and *Timaeus* 29d–e, and Aristotle *Metaphysics* A 982b–983a. None of these passages, however, speaks of the divine as actively communicating itself to human beings (except for the *Timaeus,* in the specific sense of an ontological communication).

death penalty was exacted if one did not allow another person to light his lamp from one's own, for one lost nothing by doing so. In the same way God loses nothing when he communicates himself.[46] Therefore this knowledge on the part of the subject is a relationship that issues from God; and, as issuing from God, it is the absolute judgment that God *is as* spirit *for* spirit. Spirit is essentially a being for spirit, and spirit *is spirit* only insofar as it is *for spirit*. This is how we can represent to ourselves the relationship of consciousness to its content, when we take spirit as our point of departure.[47] |

280

46. *L, W₁ add (1827?):* God reveals himself, or gives himself to cognition.

47. *In W₁ there follows an interpolation from 1831 that, in the amplified form given below, is also contained in W₂:* In the doctrine of God we have God before us as object quite simply on his own account. It is true that the relation of God to human beings is then appended. Whereas this relation did not appear to belong essentially to the doctrine [i.e.; to God as object for himself] according to the usual representation in former times, modern theology by contrast treats of religion more than of God. All it requires is that human beings should have religion: that is the main thing, and it is even regarded as a matter of indifference whether or not they know anything of God. Or else it holds that this [knowledge] is only something wholly subjective, and that we have no proper knowledge of what God is. In the Middle Ages, on the other hand, God's essence was given more consideration and definition. We have to acknowledge the truth implicit in the [modern practice] of not considering God in isolation from the subjective spirit. But we do so not for the reason that God is something unknown, but only because God is essentially *spirit*, is [God] as *knowing* [spirit]. Thus there is a relation of spirit to spirit. This *relationship* of spirit to spirit lies at the basis of religion.

If we were now to be excused from beginning with the proof that God is, we still would have to prove that *religion* exists and that it is *necessary*, for philosophy does not have its object as something given.

We could indeed say that that proof is not needed, by appealing to the fact that all peoples have religion. But that is only taken for granted, and in general we do not get around [the issue] particularly well with the expression "all." For there are also peoples of whom it can scarcely be said that they have religion; their highest [being], what they in some way worship, is the sun, the moon, or whatever else is striking to them in sensible nature. There is also the phenomenon of a cultural extreme where the being of God has been denied altogether, and where it is likewise denied that religion is the most genuine expression of spirit. Indeed it has been seriously contended by this extreme that, by instilling religion in human beings, priests are only deceivers, since their intention in so doing was only to make people subservient to them.

[*Ed.*] The accusation of priestly deception occurs above all in the French Enlightenment. See, e.g., Boulanger (= d'Holbach), *Le christianisme dévoilé; ou,*

On the other hand, if we take the *human being* as our point of departure, in that we presuppose the subject and begin from ourselves because our immediate initial knowledge is knowledge of ourselves, and if we ask how we arrive at this | distinction or at the knowledge of an object and, to be more exact in this case, at

281

Examen des principes et des effets de la religion chrétienne (London, 1756), esp. chap. 15; and *Théologie portative; ou, Dictionnaire abrégé de la religion chrétienne, par l'abbé Bernier* (London, 1768), esp. entries "Sacerdote" and "Sacrilège." Hegel's acquaintance with these writings is not verified. He did at least know this accusation from Lessing's publication, *Aus den Papieren des Ungenannten* [Reimarus], Fragment 5: *Über die Auferstehungsgeschichte* (Lessing, *Sämtliche Schriften* 12:397–428, esp. 402).

Follows additionally in W₁ *(1831):* Consequently it is by no means superfluous to exhibit the necessity of religion, and it can rightly be demanded in a scientific consideration. But we must excuse ourselves from this exhibition when we consider the means through which alone it can take place. Philosophy of religion constitutes one part of the whole of philosophy. The parts of philosophy are the links of a chain or the parts of a circle. They are developed within this context, and their necessity is presented within it. The necessity of religion must therefore follow from the whole content, so that religion stands within it as result and is to that extent mediated. This demonstration lies already behind us, for it is present in philosophy, this relationship has already been noted. When something is a result, it is mediated through another. When we have carried out the proof that God is, then God is represented as a result; this appears as nonsensical, for it is God's very nature not to be a result. It is this way with religion, too, for it is substantial knowledge; likewise this implies that religion ought not to be a result, but rather the foundation. But the more precise sense of this "being-mediated" does need to be provided here.

The procedure through which the genuineness and necessity of religion is demonstrated is briefly the following. We begin from intuitions of nature, and we know first about the sensible realm; that is natural consciousness. But spirit presents itself as the truth of nature: it is shown that nature returns into its ground, which is spirit in general. Nature is cognized as a rational system: the final peak of its rationality is that nature itself exhibits the existence of reason. The law of the vitality of things is what activates nature. But this law is only in the inner being of things; in space and time it exists only in an external manner, for nature knows nothing of the law. Spirit or the true exists in nature in an existence not conformable to itself. The genuine existence of that which is in itself is spirit; thus spirit goes forth out of nature and shows that it is the truth (i.e., the foundation) and the highest [moment] within nature. At first, spirit stands in relationship to nature as to something external, and in this mode it is finite consciousness; it knows the finite and stands over against nature as an other—for, to begin with, spirit exists as finite spirit. But the finite has no truth and passes away; finite spirit returns into its ground, for as finite it is conceived in contradiction with itself. Spirit is free; to be [present] in what is external is contradictory to its nature, for it is itself the freeing of itself from what is null

132

the knowledge of God,[48] then in general the answer has already been given: "It is precisely because we are thinking beings." God is the absolutely universal in-and-for-itself, and thought makes the universal in-and-for-itself into its object. This is the simple answer that contains within itself much that we are to consider later on.

1. Immediate Knowledge[49]

At this point we are at the standpoint of the *consciousness* of God and hence for the first time at the standpoint of religion in general. We have now to consider this consciousness or this standpoint more closely. We begin at once by taking up the content of this relationship and describing the way in which we find it before us and what its particular forms are. These forms are partly psychological in character and fall on the side of the finite spirit. We have to take them up here inasmuch as we are dealing with religion as a wholly concrete content of science. |

282

As we said, the universal is, to begin with, the consciousness of God. It is not just consciousness but, more precisely, it is certainty,

---

and the elevating of itself to itself (i.e., to itself in its genuineness)—and this elevation is the emergence of religion. This process, which is exhibited in its necessity, has, as its final result, religion as the freedom of spirit in its true essence. True consciousness is solely the consciousness of spirit in its freedom. In this necessary process lies the proof that religion is something genuine, and the same process immediately brings forth the concept of religion. Thus religion is given through what precedes it in science, and is therefore cognized as necessary.

48. *W₁ (1827?) adds:* or how this primal division is to be grasped, starting from our side.

49. [*Ed.*] Hegel begins his description of the forms of religious knowledge with an analysis of "immediate knowledge" or "faith"—the certainty that God *is* independently of my awareness of him. He does not begin with "intuition" (*Anschauung*), as in Sec. D of the 1821 *Ms.*, because faith is something other than sensible intuition; we do not have immediate sense-experience of God, although our consciousness of God may be given expression in sensible, artistic form, as in the religion of art, in which case it takes on the form of intuition. On the other hand, faith is something less than what might be called "intellectual intuition" or the speculative "insight" into the necessity of this content (God), which comes only with mediated knowledge or cognition. Hegel also distinguishes between faith as such (the immediate certainty that God is) and its *forms* or *modalities*, namely feeling and representation, which are taken up in the following two sections. These various distinctions become clear in the course of the discussion.

too. First among its more specific aspects (and bearing upon the *subjective* side) is *faith*—i.e., certainty inasmuch as it is *feeling* and exists in feeling. Second, there is the *objective* side, the mode of the content. But the form in which God initially is for us is the mode of *representation,* and the final aspect is the form of *thought* as such.

First of all we have the consciousness of God in general, namely the fact that God is object for us, that we have representations of God. What we are conscious of, however, is not only that we have this object as our representation but also that it is not merely representation, that it *is.* This is *certainty* of God, *immediate knowledge.*

The fact that something is an object in consciousness or a representation means that this content is within me, is my own. I can have representations of wholly imaginary or fictitious objects. In this case the content is only mine, it is only in representation, and I simultaneously know that it *is not.* In dreams I am also consciousness and have objects, although [apart from me] they are not.[50]

However, we take the consciousness of God to be the consciousness that God also *is*—not merely [as] my own or [as] a subject within me, but [as] independent of me and of my acts of representing and knowing. God is in and for himself: that is implied in this content itself. God is this universality having being in and for itself, outside me and independent of me, not merely having being for me. This [feature] is present in every intuition, in every consciousness, and indeed these two different determinations are combined within it [consciousness]: I have this content, it is within me; but it also is on its own account. That is *certainty in general.* God is distinct from me, is independent, absolutely in-and-for-himself, and, vis-à-vis myself, this actual being that is in-and-for-itself is at the same time my own, is in my I or self. Even as this content is independent, it is also inseparably within me.

Certainty is the immediate relation of the content and myself. If

---

50. *L (1827?) adds:* What constitutes the general character of representation is the fact that something is an object of my consciousness.

I wish to express this relation forcefully, then I say, "I know this as certainly as [I know that] I myself am." The certainty of this external being | and the certainty of myself are both one and the same certainty.[51] This oneness of certainty is the inseparability of the content that is distinct from me;[52] it is the inseparability of the two aspects that are distinguished from one another, and this undivided unity is within the certainty. Thus both an independent being, an actual being in-and-for-itself, and I as the one who knows of it, are contained within this consciousness of God. I am certain that it is; there is this one certainty, this immediate relation.

It is possible to stop with these abstract definitions; it is even asserted that we must stop with this certainty. But as a rule people straightaway make the following distinction. Something can be *certain*, but it is a different question whether it is *true*. We set certainty in opposition to truth, for in that something is certain it is not yet true.[53]

For the time being we stick with the topic of certainty. Its universal aspect is this primal division between God and the knowing subject. Certainty is the undivided unity of these two together.

The first particular form of this certainty is that of *faith*. Faith properly has an antithesis within itself, but one that is more or less indeterminate. Faith is set in opposition to knowledge, [but] this is a vacuous antithesis because what I believe, I also know—it is a content in my consciousness. Knowledge is the universal, whereas belief is only a part of knowledge. If I believe in God, then God is in my consciousness, and I also know that God is. But by "knowledge" we ordinarily mean a mediated knowledge that cognizes and demonstrates, and that is something else again. Still, knowledge in general cannot be placed in opposition to faith in this way.

More precisely stated, a certainty is termed "faith" partly inasmuch as it is not immediate sensible certainty and partly inasmuch

51. W₂ (1827?) *adds:* and I would annul my own being and not know of myself were I to annul that being.

52. W₂ (1827?) *adds:* and my own self;

53. [*Ed.*] In another philosopher one might have expected: "not necessarily true." However, since cognition of truth is for Hegel a function of mediated knowledge, to which we have not yet come, his "not yet" is likely intentional.

as this knowledge is also not a knowledge of the necessity of this content. In one respect immediate certainty is said to be *knowledge*. I do not need to believe what I see before me, for I know it. I do not believe that a sky is above me; I see it. On the other hand, when I have rational insight into the necessity of a thing, | then, too, I do not say "I believe." For example, it is assumed that one does not accept the Pythagorean theorem on authority but rather has gained insight into its demonstration for oneself. Thus faith [being neither of these] is a certainty that one possesses apart from immediate sensible intuition, apart from this sensible immediacy, and equally without having insight into the necessity of the content. In recent times faith has also been taken wholly in the sense of "certainty," in a sheer antithesis to insight into the necessity of a content. Jacobi[54] in particular introduced this meaning. He says that we only believe we have bodies; we don't know it. Here knowledge has the narrower meaning of "awareness of necessity." ⁻Jacobi says specifically that it is merely a belief that I see this. My intuiting and feeling, and all such sensible knowledge, is wholly immediate, unmediated—there is no ground for it.⁻[55] Here belief in general has the meaning of "immediate certainty."

The expression "faith," however, is used chiefly for the certainty that there is a God; and it is indeed used inasmuch as we do not have insight into the necessity of this content. And to that extent we say that "faith" is something subjective, as opposed to which the knowledge of necessity is termed objective. [56]For this reason, too, we speak of "faith in God"—according to ordinary linguistic usage—because we have no immediate sensible intuition of God.

54. [*Ed.*] See above, 1827 *Intro.*, n. 27.

55. *Thus L, similar in W; An reads:* Jacobi says I merely believe that paper lies before me. I look there and so I see it, but I do not see the necessity.

[*Ed.*] In the form given by *An*, this citation is not identifiable in Jacobi's writings. When Hegel said (according to *L*) "it is merely a belief that I see this," he may have picked up or pointed to a sheet of paper. According to the *Lectures on the History of Philosophy,* Hegel introduced a reference to paper—"paper lies here"—into a quotation from Jacobi's *Briefe über Spinoza* that makes no mention of paper (see Hegel, *Werke* 15:545 [not in the Eng. trans.]; Jacobi, *Werke* 4/1:211).

56. *Precedes L (1827?) (similar in W):* We *believe* in God because we do not have insight into the necessity of this content, namely *that* God is and *what* God is.

But we do believe in God, and to that extent we have the certainty that God is. Of course we also speak here of the "*grounds* of faith." But that surely is not to be taken literally. When I have grounds, that is to say, objective and proper grounds, then the thing is proved for me. But again the grounds themselves can be of a subjective nature, whereupon I let my knowledge pass for a proven knowledge and say "I believe."[57] The main ground, the one ground for | faith   285
in God is *authority,* the fact that others—those who matter to me, those whom I revere and in whom I have confidence that they know what is true—believe it, that they are in possession of this knowledge. Belief rests upon testimony and so has a ground. But the absolutely proper ground of belief, the absolute testimony to the content of a religion, is the witness of the spirit[58] and not miracle or external, historical verification. [59]The genuine content of a religion has for its verification the witness of one's own spirit, [the witness] that this content conforms to the nature of my spirit and satisfies the needs of my spirit. My spirit knows itself, it knows its essence—that, too, is an immediate knowledge, it is the absolute verification of the eternally true, the simple and true definition of this certainty that is called faith.

This certainty (and faith with it) enters into an antithesis with thought, and with truth in general; but it is only later[60] that we have to discuss this antithesis. First we want to deal with the next two forms that emerge in the company of this certainty, namely feeling and representation. Feeling comes under consideration more in a subjective regard, whereas representation concerns more the objective mode of the content, i.e., how it is an object of consciousness for us—the determination of objectivity.[61]

---

57. *Similar in* W$_1$; *follows in* W$_2$ *(MiscP/Ed?) as transition to the section on feeling:* The first, simplest, and still most abstract form of this subjective grounding is this, that in the beginning of the I the being of the object is also contained. This grounding and this appearing of the object is given as the first and immediate grounding and appearing in feeling.

58. [*Ed.*] Cf. Rom. 8:16.

59. *In B's margin:* 18 May 1827

60. [*Ed.*] See below, pp. 155 ff.

61. *L (1827?) adds:* To begin with, we have only to describe these two forms, and in doing so to indicate their limitedness and imperfection.

2. Feeling[62]

As far as the *form* of feeling is concerned, we ask first what it means to say, "I have that in my feeling" or "I have a feeling of something," e.g., of sensible or even of moral objects. We will find that possession in feeling is nothing else but the fact that a content is *my own*, and indeed is my own as this particular individual—the fact that it belongs to me and is for me, that I have and know it in its determinateness and that at the same time I know myself in this determinateness. It is the feeling of a content and | the feeling of oneself—both at once. The content is in such a way that my particularity is at the same time bound up with it.

286

Any content can be in feeling, just as it can be in thought generally. In feeling, however, we at no time have the content or the thing as such (for example, law or right) alone before us. Instead we know the thing in its connection with ourselves, and thereby we take pleasure in ourselves, i.e., in our own fulfillment with the thing. Feeling is for this reason such a popular theme, because when we feel [something] we are personally and subjectively involved, too, according to our particularity and personal character. In feeling we give validity to ourselves at the same time as to the thing we feel. [63]A [person of] "character" who has a firm purpose, and pursues this purpose throughout an entire life, can be very dispassionate about it. Such a person has only the thing, has only this purpose. "Warmth of feeling," on the other hand, signifies that at the same time I am fully with the thing in all my particularity, and that is an anthropological aspect. The particularity of our own person is its corporeality so that feeling pertains also to this corporeal side. With [aroused] feelings the blood becomes agitated and we become warm around the heart. That is the character of feeling. The whole complex of feeling is what we call "heart" or "emotional temper" [*Gemüt*].

62. [*Ed.*] Cf. below, n. 75.
63. *Precedes in L (1827?):* In our thinking we forget ourselves and possess the objective content [in thought] rather than our own self-consciousness. But along with thinking we can also have feeling, and then we concurrently involve ourselves with the content and bind ourselves to it, so that our particularity is there, too. We speak of warmth of feeling for the thing; this is not "interest" in the general sense.

It is required not only that we know God, right, and the like, that we have consciousness of and are convinced about them, but also that these things should be in our feeling, in our hearts. This is a just requirement; it signifies that these interests ought to be essentially our own—that we, as subjects, are supposed to have identified ourselves with such content. ⁻A human being who has the right in his heart is one who is identified with the spirit. In the same way the phrase "religion of the heart"⁻⁶⁴ expresses this iden-tification of the | content with the subjectivity and personality of 287 the individual. It is also part of "acting upon principles" not only that one knows the principles but also that they are in one's heart. There can also be bound up with bare conviction the fact that other inclinations exert force against it. But if the conviction is in the heart, then the agent acts upon it; one has this disposition and acts in accordance with what (in this dispositional manner) one *is*. What one has in one's heart belongs to the being of one's personality, to one's inmost being. So far as I am moral, honest, or religious, then duty, law, or religion is identified with me; my actuality is in them and they are in my actuality; they constitute my being, for that is the way I am.

We cannot say of feeling that it is good or not good, that it is correct and genuine on the one hand, or false or spurious on the other. This indeterminateness is feeling [per se]. Where there is feeling, our attention is drawn at once to the *determinateness* of the feeling, to what kind of feeling it is: feeling of fear or anxiety, base feelings, etc. This determinateness is what appears as its con-tent. To the extent that we have a representation of this determi-nateness and are ourselves conscious of it, we have therefore an object that also appears at the same time in a subjective mode, as an object of feeling. In the case of outwardly sensible feeling its

64. *Thus B, similar in Hu; L (Var) reads:* As something actual, as this one, I should be determined thus throughout. This determinateness should be peculiar to my character, it should constitute the general mode of my actuality, and it is therefore essential that every genuine content should be in feeling, or in the heart. What we carry in the heart in this way is our disposition: that is how we are. For instance, to one human being right is custom and usage, and it is part of the being of this person. Feeling as a whole

determinateness is the content—for example, when we feel something hard, the determinateness of the feeling is therefore a hardness. But we also say about this hardness that there is a hard object present. The hardness therefore [both] is subjective and exists as an object. We reduplicate the feeling. ˥We swiftly pass over from it to consciousness,˥[65] and we say at the level of consciousness that there is a hard object that has this effect upon us that we call feeling. Before we have felt it, we do not know that it is a hard object. Only after the [experience of] feeling do we assume that it is constituted thus and so.

But then we also have other feelings: feeling of self, feeling of God, feeling of right and of ethics. Here the very determinateness of the feeling *is* the content. God, or the right, is equally something subjective and something objective, | i.e., something having being in-and-for-itself, independently—in this case as the external object. When I know God in this way, and know the right, and have religious feeling, then I know this content; I know this content within myself and myself within this content. I am this content, [for] I know the unification of myself with it, and in that knowledge I at the same time have knowledge of my own particular person. [I know] that I have assimilated this content to myself and myself to it, the content that is nevertheless in and for itself—such as right, the ethical realm, and the like. When I know God and the right, then consciousness has made its entrance, and [with it] a parting or division that was not yet in feeling. In vision we not only know ourselves, but we place the object outside us and withdraw ourselves. Consciousness is the ejection of the content out of feeling; it is a kind of liberation.

If we dwell on the fact that in feeling the content is identified with us, what transpires is that we have the representation of feeling as the *source* of this content, of religious and honest feeling as the source of faith and of the knowledge of God, right, and ethical life. At the same time we represent the fact that the content is in our heart as the confirmation and justification for the claim that it is

65. *Thus An; L (Var) reads:* We make this conversion instantly in the case of the sensible content that we have in our subjective feeling, for we assume the presence of an external object that corresponds to that content,

the genuine content. "We find it in our heart"—that is the point it is important to consider, because in recent times it has been declared that we must consult the human heart in order to learn what is just and ethical. The opinion is that we discover within our hearts what God is. The heart is alleged to be the source, the root, and the justifying [factor] for this content. How are we to evaluate this opinion? ˉIs this religion of feeling the true religion? Is it feeling that justifies our acting in this way or that?ˉ66 | 289

I can even grant that for me the heart is the seed, root, and source of this content, though that is not saying very much. Calling it the source amounts to saying the heart is the initial mode in which such content appears to the subject. In the first instance the human being perhaps has religious feeling, but perhaps not. To that extent the heart has, to be sure, the significance of the seed. But, just as in the case of a single vegetable seed that is the first mode of existence of a plant, feeling is also this enveloped mode. The seed with which the life of the plant begins is the first [phase] only in the empirical mode, or only in appearance; for it is just as much a product or result, the final [phase]. It is therefore a wholly relative moment of origin (as we have already seen in the case of immediate knowledge). The enveloped being of the tree's nature, this simple seed, is the product or result of the entire developed life of this tree. And in feeling, too, the entire genuine content is within our subjective actuality in this enveloped fashion. But it is something else entirely [to say] this content as such is supposed to belong to feeling as such—ˉfor example, contents such as God, right, and duty.ˉ67 God

66. *Thus An; similar in B, Hu; L (Var) reads:* Thus the religion of feeling is in fact the genuine one. The heart is what justifies faith in this content, and action according to its specifications. *In W₂ (MiscP), two paragraphs earlier:* Indeed, it is so far from the case that we can find God solely and truly in feeling, that we must already be acquainted with this content from elsewhere if we are to be able to find it in feeling. And if it means that we have no cognition of God, and can know nothing of God, how then are we to say that God is in feeling? We must first have searched elsewhere within consciousness according to specifications of the content that is distinguished from the I; for we can identify the feeling as religious only insofar as we rediscover in it just these specifications of the content.

67. *Thus An; L (Var) reads (similar in W₁):* The most we can say is that contents such as God, the human being's relationship to God, right, duty, etc., are brought before representation [in the way they are] determined by feeling. *W₂ (Var) adds:* A content such as

is a content that is universal in and for itself; and in the same way the definitions of right and duty are a determination of the *rational will*.[68] As will, I exist in my freedom, in my universality itself, in the universality of my self-determination; and if my will is rational, then [self-]determination is a determining in general, something universal, a determining according to the pure concept. Rational will is sharply distinct from contingent willing or willing according to contingent impulses and inclinations, for it determines itself in accord with its concept, and the concept or substance of the will is pure freedom. All rational determinations of the will are developments of freedom, and the developments that issue from it are duties and are thereby rational. Determination by means of, and in accordance with, the pure concept is the constituent element that belongs to rationality. | Therefore it belongs just as essentially to thought.[69] Even in the case of God we have already drawn attention to the fact that this is a content that belongs to thought, for thought is the soil in which this content is both apprehended and engendered alike.

290

[70]Now insofar as it is the nature of this content to be only in thought in its authentic mode, it follows that the way in which it is in feeling is an inadequate mode. The fundamental determination of feeling is the specificity or particularity of my own subjectivity. As subject, as both intelligent and willing subject, I may be convinced with such fixity that other, particular grounds avail nothing against this fixity of my conviction, or that indeed they are not present at all. If I am ethical will, then I have this very determination within me. I am it, without my conviction or my will being conjoined with a consciousness of the particularity of my person. But all the same, this content belongs to my actuality also, and then what we say is that "I have it in my heart," for this *is* "my heart." In other words, the content is within my own self-certainty, in my intellect

68. *L, W add (1827?):* I am will and not only desire, [for] I do not just have inclination. The I is the universal.

69. *L (1827?) adds (similar in W):* Will is rational only insofar as it is thinking. It is an erroneous representation that will and intellect are two different compartments within spirit, and that will could be rational and ethical without thought.

70. *In B's margin:* 21 May 1827

and will as such, or else the consciousness of the particularity of my person is conjoined with it. In this latter case it is in feeling.

Is then something true or legitimate because it is in my feeling? Is feeling the verification, or must the content be just, true, or ethical in and for itself? These days we often find the former contention advanced.[71] We have means enough in our consciousness for evaluating this contention. In our consciousness we know very well that, in order to know that a content is of the right kind, we must look about for grounds of decision other than those of feeling. For it is true that every content is capable of being in feeling: religion, right, ethics, crime, passions. Each content has a place in feeling. |

291

If feeling is the justifying element, then the distinction between good and evil comes to naught, for evil with all its shadings and qualifications is in feeling just as much as the good. Everything evil, all crime, base passions, hatred and wrath, it all has its root in feeling.[72] The murderer feels that he must do what he does. Everything vile is the expression of [some] feeling. In the Bible it says that wicked thoughts of blasphemy and the like proceed from the heart.[73] Undoubtedly the divine or the religious is in feeling, too, but evil has its own distinctive seat in the heart. This natural particularity, the heart, is its home. But that the human being's own particularity, egotism, and selfhood as such should be legitimated is not what is good or ethical. On the contrary, that is evil. ˉThe contentˉ[74] must be true in and for itself if the feeling is to count as

71. L (1827?) adds: We have a feeling of God, a feeling of our dependence, and a feeling of right, too. The feeling of right is on that account a just feeling, and this content or higher element is something true just because we have this feeling. On this view the feeling is made into the criterion of what is true and ethical.

72. L (1827?) adds: The evil person, for whom at this moment this determinate purpose or this interest transcends all other determinations, is, by his feeling, lifted beyond all that is upright and ethical. It is the same way with opinion. One person opines and feels this, another that; one and the same person now this, now that.

73. [Ed.] Cf. Matt. 15:19.

74. L (1827?) reads: The element of selfhood is the subjective element that we call heart in general. It must, of course, be the case with respect to the good also that the content belongs to me myself, that I have my own self within it. But that is only the form for a content that comes from elsewhere. Its distinguishing or proper feature is the very fact that feeling is a form, and that what matters is the content of the feeling; this

true. For that reason it is also said that one's feelings or one's heart must be purified and cultivated; natural feelings cannot be the proper impulses to action. What this says is precisely that what is genuine is not the content of the heart as such, but instead what ought to be the heart's *goal* and *interest*—this content and these determinations should become and be what is genuinely true. But what the genuinely true is we first learn through representation and thought.

3. Representation[75]

The form of feeling is the subjective aspect, the certainty of God. The form of representation concerns the objective aspect, the content of the certainty. The obvious question is: "What is this content?" The content is God. For human beings God *is* primarily in the form of representation. | ˉ[Representation is]ˉ[76] a consciousness of something that one has before oneself as something objective.

The fact that the religious content is present primarily in the form of representation is connected with what I said earlier,[77] that religion is the consciousness of absolute truth in the way that it occurs for all human beings. Thus it is found primarily in the form of representation. ˉPhilosophy has the same content, the truth; [it is] the spirit of the world generally and not the particular spirit.

292

---

75. [*Ed.*] Both religious feeling (*Gefühl*) and religious representation (*Vorstellung*) are forms or modes of expression of the immediate certainty that God *is*. Feeling describes the subjective aspect of this certainty, namely, its connection with our own determinate, particular existence. But feeling as such can make no judgments with respect to the *content* of whatever it is that we feel. This is a matter of consciousness, in the form first of representation but ultimately of thought (*Denken*). Representation, or nonsensible intuition (see n. 76), attends consciously to the *objectivity* of what is in feeling, but it does not yet penetrate this content rationally or cognitively. It continues to view it imagistically or reflectively, in terms of the finite categories of the understanding (*Verstand*). While all these forms of the religious relationship—faith, feeling, representation, etc.—are knowledge (*Wissen*) in the broad sense, the knowledge of God does not reach its goal until it becomes thought (*Denken*) or cognition (*Erkenntnis*) in the strict sense.

76. L (1827?) *reads:* For "representation" we may also use the term "intuition." Thereby we are not speaking of sensible intuition; it is only that, in using the word "intuition," one always denotes

77. [*Ed.*] See above, 1827 *Intro.*, p. 106.

Philosophy does nothing but transform our representation into concepts. The content remains always the same. The true is not for the single spirit but for the world spirit. But for the latter, representation and concept are *one*. The difficult thing is to separate out from a content what pertains only to representation. In its paring away of what pertains to representation, philosophy is reproached for removing the content, too. | This transformation is therefore held to   293
be a destruction. These are the moments that are to be considered more closely. But first we are to consider the characteristics possessed by representation.⁻⁷⁸

In the first place, sensible forms or configurations belong to representation. We can distinguish them by the fact that we call them *images* [*Bilder*]. Those sensible forms for which the principal content or the principal mode of representation is taken from immediate intuition can in general be termed images. We are directly conscious that they are only images but that they have a significance distinct from that which the image as such primitively expresses—that the image is something symbolic or allegorical and that we

78. *Thus An with Hu; W₁ (Var) reads (cf. n. 88):* Here then it is quite important in principle to be acquainted with the distinction between representation [on one side] and thought and concept [on the other]—and to know what is peculiar to representation. Philosophy is the transformation of what is found in the form of representation into the form of the concept. The content [of each] is the same and should be the same, i.e., the truth. What is true is [true] for the spirit of the world generally, for the human spirit. This content, this substantial element, cannot be one thing for spirit in its representing and another thing in its conceptualizing [activity].

But insofar as human being thinks, and finds the need to think essential, the same content that is found at first in the form of representation gets elevated into the form of thought. That is where the difficulty comes of separating, in a content, what is content as such, or thought, from what pertains to the representation as such.

The reproaches that are directed against philosophy boil down to this: that philosophy strips off the forms that pertain to representation. Ordinary thinking has no awareness of this distinction; because truth for it is conjoined with these determinations, it supposes that the content has been removed altogether. This is the general point. But it can also be the case that a philosophy has a content different from the religious content of a particular religion; this recasting or translation is usually taken to be a total alteration or destruction.

We have to consider these moments more closely—i.e., what pertains to philosophy and what pertains to the mode of representation as such.

have before us something twofold, first the immediate and then what is meant by it, its inner meaning. The latter is to be distinguished from the former, which is the external aspect. Thus there are many forms in religion about which we know that they are only metaphors. For example, if we say that God has begotten a son, we know quite well that this is only an image; representation provides us with "son" and "begetter" from a familiar relationship, which, as we well know, is not meant in its immediacy, but is supposed to signify a different relationship, which is something like this one. This sensible relationship has right within itself something corresponding for the most part to what is properly meant with regard to God.[79]

So there are many representations that derive from immediate sensible intuition as well as from inner intuition. Thus we soon know that talk of God's wrath is not to be taken in the literal sense, that it is merely an analogy, a simile, an image. The same holds true for emotions of repentence, vengeance, and the like on God's part. Moreover, we also find developed allegories, for instance the stories of Prometheus, who instructs human beings, and of Pandora's box[80]—these, too, are images having a nonliteral meaning. Thus we hear of a tree of the knowledge [*Erkenntnis*] of good and evil.[81] When the story arrives at the eating of the fruit, it begins to become dubious whether this tree should be taken as something 294 historical, as a properly historical tree, | and the eating as historical, too; for all talk of a tree of knowledge is so contrary [to ordinary experience] that it very soon leads to the insight that this is not a

79. *Thus also* W₂; W₁ *(1831/Var?) adds:* But one who relies entirely on sense sticks with his representation and gives little thought to it, and the present-day theologies of feeling and understanding, for their part, also know how to make nothing of it; they either discard the thought-content along with the image, or they hold fast the image and let go the thought.

80. [*Ed.*] The myth of Pandora's box is first given by Hesiod, *Erga* 79–105 and *Theogony* 570–590. But Hegel is not referring directly to Hesiod's version, since he speaks also of Prometheus as the instructor of human beings—an expansion of the Prometheus myth that is not found in Hesiod but for the first time in the literature of the fourth century B.C.

81. [*Ed.*] Cf. Gen. 2:9, 16–17.

matter of any sensible fruit, and that the tree is not to be taken literally.[82]

However, it is not merely things that are manifestly figurative that belong to the mode of representation in its sensible aspect, but also things that are to be taken as historical. Something can be expounded in a historical mode and yet we do not take that to be its serious sense; we certainly do attend to the story with our imagination, but we do not ask whether it is meant seriously. We enjoy the narratives of Jupiter and the other deities, but we do not in the main inquire further about what Homer reports of them to us, we do not take it in the way we do some other historical report. Still, there is also something historical that is a divine history—a story, indeed, that is supposed to be history in the proper sense, namely the story of Jesus. This story does not merely count as a myth, in the mode of images. Instead it involves sensible occurrences; the ⁻nativity, passion and death⁻[83] of Christ count as something completely historical. Of course it therefore exists for representation and in the mode of representation, but it also has another, intrinsic aspect. The story of Jesus is something twofold, a divine history. Not only [is there] this outward history, which should only be taken as the ordinary story of a human being, but also it has the divine as its content: a divine happening, a divine deed, an absolutely divine action. This absolute divine action is the inward, the genuine, the substantial dimension of this history, and this is just what is the object of reason. Just as a myth has a meaning or an allegory within it, so there is this twofold character generally in every story. Undoubtedly there are myths in which the outward appearance is the predominant feature. But ordinarily a myth contains an allegory, as in the case of Plato.

Generally speaking, every history contains this external sequence of occurrences and actions; but they are occurrences with respect to a | human being, a spirit. What is more, the history of a state is the action, deed, and fate of a universal spirit, the spirit of a people.   295

82. *Thus also* W$_2$; W$_1$ *(Var) adds:* This is the mode of representation, of the figurative.
83. *Thus An; Hu reads:* birth, death, passion, and resurrection

Histories of this kind already have a universal feature within them, implicitly and explicitly. If we take this superficially, we can say that from every history a moral may be extracted. The moral encapsulates at least the essential ethical powers that have contributed to the action and have brought about the event, and they are the inner or substantial element. So history certainly has this aspect of segmentation, of singularity, of extreme outward individuation; and yet the universal laws and powers of ethical life are also recognizable within it. These universal powers, however, do not exist for representation as such; for representation, history exists in the mode in which it presents itself as story, or the way in which it exists in appearance. But all the same, even for those whose thoughts and concepts have not yet attained any determinate formation, that inner power is contained in a history of this kind. They feel it, and have ˉan obscureˉ[84] consciousness of those powers. Thus the historical as such is what exists for representation, and on the other hand there are images. For ordinary consciousness, for consciousness in its ordinary formation, religion exists essentially in these modes, as a content that primarily presents itself in sensible form, as a series of actions and sensible determinations that follow one another in time and then occur side by side in space. The content is empirical, concrete, and manifold, its combination residing partly in spatial contiguity and partly in temporal succession. But at the same time this content has an inner aspect—there is spirit within it that acts upon spirit. To the spirit that is in the content the subjective spirit bears witness—initially through a dim recognition lacking the development for consciousness of this spirit that is in the content.

In the second place, however, nonsensible configurations also belong to representation. The spiritual content as it is represented in its simple mode—an action, activity, or relationship in simple form—is of this kind. For instance, the creation of the world is a representation. God himself is this [sort of] representation. God,

---

84. *Thus W; L reads:* a thinking *Hu reads:* although obscurely, a

after all, is the universal that is determined within itself in manifold ways. In the form of representation, however, God is in this simple manner in which we have God on one side | and the world on the other. Again, the world is internally this endlessly manifold complex, or the complex of this endlessly manifold finite reality. But when we say "world," we have it in the simple mode of representation. Now we say "the world is created," and designate thereby a kind of activity completely different from an empirical activity.[85]

Every spiritual content and all relationships generally—of whatever sort they may be (sovereign, court of judgment, etc.)—are representations; spirit itself is a representation. Though they do indeed proceed from thought and have their seat and soil in thought, they are all still representations on account of their form. For they are determinations that are related simply to themselves, that are in the form of independence. In saying, "God is all-wise, wholly good, righteous," we have fixed determinations of content, each of which is simple and independent alongside the others. The means for combining the representations are [the words] "and" and "also." On the other hand determinations such as "all-wise" and the like are concepts, too. But to the extent that they are not yet analyzed internally and their distinctions are not yet posited in the way in which they relate to one another, they belong to [the realm of] representation.[86] What we say is, "something happens," "change occurs," or "if it is this, it is also that, and then it is in this way." Thus these determinations have, to begin with, the contingency that

85. L (1827?) adds (similar in W): If we employ the expression "activity from which the world arises," it is indeed an abstraction, though one that is tailored to representation and still not a concept; for the coherence of the two sides is not posited in the form of necessity. Instead it is either expressed according to the analogy of natural life and events, or designated as the sort of coherence that is supposed on its own account to be wholly one of a kind and inconceivable.

86. L (1827?) adds (similar in W): Thus, insofar as it is not something figurative, sensible, or historical, but rather something spiritual, something thought, the content of the representing activity is taken in its abstract, simple *relation to itself*. Insofar as such content contains manifold determinations within itself in any case, the connection of this manifoldness is taken in a merely external fashion by representation, and therefore only an external identity is posited.

297   gets stripped away from them only in the form of the concept.[87] |

Because the form of feeling stands over against that of representation, and because feeling concerns the form of subjective faith whereas representation on the contrary concerns the objective aspect or the content, there arises here, too, a relationship of representation to feeling. Representation concerns the objective side of the content, whereas feeling concerns the manner in which the content exists within our specific being, or within the specificity of consciousness. It is true that religion is a matter of feeling, but it is also just as much a matter of representation. Thus the question can directly arise: "Should we begin from representation, and are religious feelings awakened and determined through it, or should we begin on the other hand from religious feeling, and do religious representations proceed from it?"

If we begin from feeling, making it the first or original factor, then we say that religious representations derive from feeling. From one point of view that is entirely correct, for the feelings contain this enveloped subjectivity. But feeling is, on its own account, so indeterminate that everything possible can be within it, and, as we have seen, feeling cannot be the justifying [criterion] for the content.

---

87. L (1827?) adds (similar in W₂, though in a different sequence): The essential content stands fast by itself in the form of the *simple universality* in which it is enveloped. Its passing over through itself into another, or its identity with the other, is lacking, for it is only identical with itself. The single items lack the bond of necessity and the unity of their distinction. Hence as soon as representation makes a start at grasping an essential connection, it also lets it stand in the form of contingency, and does not advance to its genuine in-itself and to its eternal, self-permeating unity. For example, the thought of providence is in representation in this way, and it draws the movements of history together and grounds them in God's eternal decree. But this very connection is straightaway transferred into a sphere in which it is supposed to be incomprehensible and inscrutable for us. Therefore the thought of the universal does not become determinate within itself, and is no sooner expressed than it is instantly sublated again. *Precedes in* W₂ (MiscP): Or if the representation contains relationships that are already closer to thought—for example, that God created the world—the relationship is nevertheless grasped by it in the form of contingency and externality. Thus in the representation of the creation, God remains by himself on one side and the world on the other. *Follows instead in* W₁ (Ed?): These determinations are clearly and explicitly considered, to the extent that we pass over to a higher level and first of all take up together and compare the two sides considered previously.

In its objectivity the content appears first as representation; this is the more objective mode in which it is present within consciousness. In this connection we do not have to discuss the relationship of subject and object exhaustively. We need only to recall here in a general fashion | something that in one way we know very well, namely that whatever I hold as true, whatever ought to be valid for me, must also be in my feeling, must belong to my being and character. The highest peak of subjectivity is the certainty that I have about something. This certainty is found in feeling, although it can also be in another form. But feeling is still nothing justificatory, for everything possible is capable of being in feeling. If what is in feeling were true just for that reason, then everything would have to be true: Egyptian veneration of [the sacred bull] Apis, Hindu veneration of the cow, and so on.

In contrast, representation already contains more of the objective—that which constitutes the contents or determinacy of feeling. This content is what matters, for it must justify itself on its own account. That it should legitimate itself, or offer itself to cognition as true, therefore falls more on the side of representation.

Regarding the necessity of representation and the path through representation into the heart, we know that religious instruction begins with representation. By means of doctrine and teaching the feelings become aroused and purified; they are cultivated and brought into the heart. But this bringing of feelings into the heart essentially has the other aspect also that its original determinacy lies in the nature of spirit itself. It is still another question whether the deteminacy lies implicit in one's essence, or whether one knows from it what one essentially is. Representation is necessary for it to come to feeling and to consciousness, for it to emerge into consciousness and be felt. Instruction and teaching belong to this [process of] representation, and religious formation everywhere begins from this point.

4. Thought

What now holds our closer interest is *thinking*—the stage at which what is properly objective comes under consideration. We have an immediate certainty of God; we have faith in him and feeling and representations of him. But we also have this certainty in thought, and here we call it "conviction." Conviction involves grounds, and these grounds essentially exist only in thought. |

299

a. The Relationship of Thought and Representation

We have therefore still to consider the form of thought from the side [of representation], and first of all to give an account of how thought differentiates itself from the form of representation.

As we last said above, representing holds all sensible and spiritual content in the mode in which it is taken as isolated in its determinacy. Under the sensible content we have sky, earth, stars, color, and the like, and with respect to God we have wisdom, benevolence, etc. But the general form of thought is *universality,* and universality even played a role in representation, for that has the form of universality within it, too. We take the expression "thinking" in this respect, insofar as thinking is reflective or still more is comprehending—not merely thought in a general sense, but rather insofar as it is first reflection and then concept.

The first point, therefore, is that thought dissolves this form of the simple, in which the content is found in representation, ⌐in such a way that⌐[88] distinct determinations within this simple reality are grasped and exhibited so that it is known as something *inwardly manifold.* To inquire after the concept of a thing is to inquire after the relationship of the distinct determinations within the thing itself. We have an instance of this as soon as we ask, "What is that?" Blue, for example, is a sensible representation. If we ask, "What is blue?" it is first set before our eyes so that we may obtain the intuition. The intuition is then already contained within the representation. However, with that question we also want to know

---

88. *Thus L, similar in* W_1; W_2 *(MiscP) reads (cf. n. 78):* and that is the very reproach that is usually directed at philosophy, when one says that it does not allow the form of representation to subsist, but instead alters it or strips away the content. And because for ordinary consciousness the truth is conjoined to that form, one supposes that when the form is changed the content and the subject matter are lost, and one declares that the recasting is a destruction. When philosophy transposes what is in the form of representation into the form of the concept, there does certainly emerge the difficulty of separating, in a content, what is content as such or thought from what belongs to representation as such. But to dissolve the simple reality of the representation principally means only [that]

the concept, to know blue in its relationship to itself, in its distinct determinations, and in their unity. Thus according to Goethe's | 300 theory blue is a unity of light and darkness, and that in such a way that the darkness is the ground and the cause of opacity while the light is an illuminating element, a medium through which we see this darkness.[89] The sky is dark and dim whereas the atmosphere is bright; through this bright medium we see the blue darkness. That is the concept of blue. The representation of blue is quite simply blue; the concept of blue is first of all a representation of distinct determinations [and afterwards] a unity of them.

If we now ask, "What is God?" or "What is justice?" we still have these representations at first in the form of simplicity. But when we think them, different determinations should be given of which the unity, their sum so to speak or more exactly their identity, constitutes the object. The determinations of this unity exhaust the object. But if we say that God is just, omnipotent, wise, and gracious, we can go on in this way without ceasing. The Orientals say that God has an infinite number of names, that is, of characteristics; what God is cannot be exhaustively expressed. If we are therefore supposed to grasp God's concept, then distinct determinations have to be given and this multitude of characteristics has to be reduced to a restricted set, so that the object may be completely exhausted by means of this restricted set of distinct characteristics and their unity.

[90]In representation, however, the distinct characteristics stand on their own account; they might either belong to a whole or be placed outside one another. In thought the simple character is resolved into distinct determinations, or else those determinations that lie outside one another are compared in such a way that what comes to consciousness is the contradiction of the very factors that are at

89. [Ed.] This theory, presented in his *Zur Farbenlehre* (Tübingen, 1810), pp. 57–59, is one product of Goethe's speculative studies in natural science. See Goethe, *Theory of Colours*, trans. Charles Lock Eastlake (1840; reprint, Cambridge, Mass., 1970), §§ 151, 155.

90. *Precedes in L (1827?) (similar in W):* Insofar as something is thought, it is put in relation to an other. The object is known inwardly as a relation of distinct elements to one another, or as a relation of itself to an other that we know externally to it.

the same time supposed to constitute a unity. If they are mutually contradictory, it does not seem that they could belong to *one* content. The consciousness of this contradiction and its resolution belongs to thought. When we say that God is both gracious and just, we require no deliberation to come to the conclusion that benevolence contradicts justice. It is the same when we say that God is 301 | omnipotent and wise, the power in the face of which everything disappears or does not exist—this negation of everything determinate is a contradiction of the wisdom that wills something determinate, the wisdom that has a goal and is the limitation of the indeterminacy that omnipotence is. It is this way with many things. In representation everything has its place peacefully alongside everything else: the human being is free and also dependent; there is good in the world and there is evil as well. In thought, on the contrary, these things are drawn into mutual connection, and thus contradiction becomes visible.

The precise category that enters in along with thought is *necessity*. In representation there is a space. Thought demands to know the necessity of it. In representation there is [the content] "God is." Thought requires to know why it is necessary that God is. This necessity lies in the fact that in thought the object is taken not as having being, not just in its simple determinacy, its pure relation to itself, but essentially in relation to an other, so that it is essentially a relation of distinct elements. We call something "necessary" when, if one [element] exists, the other is thereby posited. The first only exists determinately insofar as the second exists, and vice versa. For representation the finite is "what is." But for thought the finite is at once just that sort of thing which does not exist on its own account, but instead requires something else for its own being and exists by means of an other. For thought generally, and more precisely for comprehension, there is nothing immediate. Immediacy is the principal category of representation, where the content is known in its simple relation to itself. For thought there is nothing immediate but only the sort of thing in which mediation is essential.[91]

---

91. *L (1827?) adds (similar in W):* Such are the abstract, universal characteristics, the abstract distinction between religious representing and thinking.

b. The Relationship of Immediate and Mediated Knowledge

If we relate this [distinction] to our field [of interest], then all the forms that we have [considered thus far] belong to the side of representation. The more precise question with reference to our object here is whether knowledge of God, i.e., religion, is | an immediate or a mediated knowledge. Mediated knowledge emerges more nearly in the form of the so-called proofs for God's existence [*Dasein*]. 302

God is. ⌐We spoke of this statement in connection with immediate knowledge.¬[92] But because we have now passed over to the determination of thought and so to that of necessity, a knowledge of necessity or of mediation enters in, a knowledge that requires mediation in any case, and includes it. This knowledge comes in as opposed to immediate knowledge, faith, feeling, and the like. ⌐Thus it is in this respect that we have to address this issue.¬[93]

It is a very widespread view or tenet that knowledge of God is found only in an immediate mode; the question about this seems in contemporary culture to be the most interesting one. We say that it is so, that it is a fact of our consciousness,[94] that religion or the knowledge of God is only faith. Mediated knowledge is ruled out; it corrupts the certainty and security of faith as well as its content.[95]

We may remark here in advance that thought, i.e., concrete thought, is a mediated knowledge. Mediated knowledge is knowl-

92. *Thus B; L (1827?) reads (similar in* W₁*):* Until now we have spoken of this statement (which we took at first as fact) only as of a form of the knowledge of God, which we have so far only described [by saying]: religion is knowlege of God and knowledge that God is.

93. *Thus B;* W₂ *(Var) reads:* and it is to be considered initially in terms of this antithesis.

94. *L (1827?) adds (similar in* W*):* We have a representation of God and in addition the certainty that the representation is not just within us subjectively but also exists. It is said

[*Ed.*] The reference to "facts (*Tatsachen*) of consciousness" is found initially in Fichte; see his *Versuch einer Kritik aller Offenbarung*, 2d ed. (Königsberg, 1793), p. 15 (*Gesamtausgabe* 1:140). But since Fichte later criticized the mere appeal to such facts, it is possible that Hegel's criticism is directed not against Fichte but rather against similar phrases in Jacobi (see *Briefe über Spinoza*, pp. 426–427 [*Werke* 4/2:155]) and his disciples. See esp. F. Köppen, *Ueber Offenbarung, in Beziehung auf Kantische und Fichtische Philosophie*, 2d ed. (Lübeck and Leipzig, 1802), pp. 17, 115 ff.

95. *L (1827?) adds (similar in* W*):* Here we have the antithesis of immediate and mediated knowledge.

edge of necessity regarding the content. But immediacy and mediation of knowledge, the one as well as the other, are both equally one-sided abstractions. We do not here assume or hold the opinion that correctness or truth should be attributed to either of them by itself in isolation. We shall see subsequently that true thought or comprehension unites both of them within itself and does not exclude either. To mediated knowledge belongs conclusion from one 303 thing to another, dependence, conditionality of one | determination upon another, i.e., the form of reflection. Immediate knowledge removes all distinctions, these modes of coherence, and has just one simple thing, just one coherence, namely the subjective form or the knowing [itself], and so the determinacy of the "it is." It is therefore the coherence of myself with being. To the extent that I assuredly know that God is, the knowledge is my own being, is the coherence of myself with this content. As certainly as I am, so certainly God is, too.[96]

In considering immediate knowledge in a more explicit and specific way, we do not want to begin with speculative considerations; at first we only want to take up the issue itself in an *empirical* fashion. That means we must place ourselves at the standpoint of immediate knowledge. ˉImmediate knowledge is empirical knowledge.ˉ[97] I find the representation of God within myself; that is an empirical [datum]. The standpoint requires that one should not go beyond this empirical knowledge, for only what is found within consciousness is supposed to have validity. I should not inquire why the knowledge of God is found within me. I do not ask why I find it or in what way it is necessary, for that would lead [me] to cognition. And the assertion is that cognition is the very evil that has to be kept at a distance. What accordingly presents itself is the empirical question of whether there is an immediate knowledge.

We deny that there is because, as we have already shown, there

96. L (1827?) *adds (similar in W):* My being and the being of God are *one* nexus, and being is the connection. This being is something simple and at the same time something twofold. In immediate knowledge this nexus is wholly simple, for all modes of relationship are wiped out.

97. W *(Var) reads:* In general this is what we call empirical knowledge: that I know just this, that it is an actual fact of consciousness.

is no mediated or immediate knowledge in isolation. [98]The object is mediated knowledge, to which the knowledge of necessity belongs. What is necessary has a cause; it must be, and there is essentially something other as well through which it exists. Inasmuch as this other exists, the first itself exists; here we have a nexus of distinct things. Now the mediation can be merely finite and can be grasped in a merely finite manner. The effect, for example, is taken to be something that is on one side, and the cause as something that is on the other. | The finite is something that is dependent upon something else.[99] In contrast, the higher mediation, the mediation of the concept or of reason, is the concept's mediation with itself. This cohering of two things belongs to the mediation of reason; it is a coherence such that the one [term] exists only insofar as the other exists.

Now when we claim to have immediacy of knowledge, mediation is excluded. Whatever else immediacy involves, this is the first thing to be said. We speak of an "immediate existence." But even though we empirically relate ourselves [to the world] only in external fashion, there is still nothing at all that is immediate. There is nothing to which only the determination of immediacy is applicable to the exclusion of mediation; instead what is immediate is likewise mediated, and immediacy itself is essentially mediated. It is the nature of finite existences to be mediated. It is the nature of every thing, of every individual, to be mediated. Every thing such as a star or an animal is created or generated, it exists. If we say of a human being that he is a father, then the son is mediated and the father appears as the immediate; but in that he is begetter, he himself is also something begotten. In the same way every living thing, in that it is a begetter, is defined as something originative and immediate; but nevertheless it is itself something begotten and therefore mediated.

98. *In B's margin:* 25 May 1827

99. *L (1827?) adds (similar in W):* and does not exist in and for itself; something else pertains to its existence. Human beings are physically dependent and so have need of external nature, of external objects. We posit these things through ourselves, though they appear to have being independently of us, and we can prolong our lives only so long as they exist and are utilizable.

Immediacy means being in general; being, or this abstract relation to self, is immediate to the extent that we remove relationship. But if we posit being as one side of a relationship, then it is something mediated. Thus the cause is cause only to the extent that it has an effect, and therefore the cause is mediated, too. Hence when we define an existence as such, which is one of the sides within a relationship, as the effect, then what is relationless, namely the cause, is recognized as the sort of thing that is mediated. Everything that is immediate is also mediated. This is a most paltry and trivial insight, had by everyone—that everything which exists *is*, to be sure, but only is as something mediated (first of all the finite, for we are not yet speaking of mediation with self). But it *is mediated*, is relative, is essentially a relationship; some other is necessary to its being, | to its immediacy. To that extent it is mediated. The logical is the dialectical—where being, considered as such on its own account, turns out to be the untrue, even turns out to be nothing; and the next determination, the truth of being, is becoming. Becoming is a simple representation relating itself to itself, something wholly immediate, although it contains within itself the two determinations, being and nonbeing. What becomes already is, although in another sense it is not but only comes to be for the first time. Thus becoming is mediated, although it is also immediate insofar as it is a simple thought. Only book-learning wrestles with immediacy. It is an inferior understanding which believes that there, in immediacy, one has something independent as opposed to something mediated.

It is the same with immediate knowledge, a particular mode or type of immediacy. For there is no immediate knowledge. We distinguish an immediate knowledge from a mediated knowledge. Immediate knowledge is knowledge in which we do not have any consciousness of mediation; but mediated it is. We have feeling, and that seems to be immediate; we have intuition, and it appears under the form of immediacy.[100] If we consider an intuition, then

---

100. L (1827?) adds (similar in W): But if we are dealing with thought-determinations, then we must not stop at this point in the way it initially occurs to us; we must rather ask whether in fact this is the case.

first I am the knowing or intuiting, and second I know an other, an object—⌐I have knowledge only by means of the object.⌐[101] I am mediated in sensation, and only through the object, through the determinacy of my sensing.[102] Knowing is quite simple; but I must know *something,* for if I am only knowing, then I know nothing at all. Similarly, I must see *something,* for if I am pure vision, then I see nothing at all. Therefore the universal or knowing, a subjective element, belongs together, in the second place, with an object, something determinate. There is a subjective element and a content in all knowledge. It is essentially a relation | of distinct things to one   306 another, and this essentially contains a mediation. With immediate knowledge, therefore, it is the case that there is no such thing. If someone tells us that immediate knowledge is the true knowledge, then we must first see what this brings to mind—and it is evident that immediate knowledge is an empty abstraction, pure knowing.[103]

But it is more specifically the case in regard to religious knowledge that it is essentially a mediated knowledge. In whatever possible religion we may find ourselves, we know that we have been educated within this religion and have received instruction in it. This instruction and education provide me with a knowledge that is mediated through doctrine. Moreover, if we speak of positive religion, then the religion is revealed, and indeed revealed in a manner that is external to the individual. So faith in this religion is essentially mediated through revelation. In rejecting mediation, therefore, one manifestly rejects along with it whatever the revealed element is in a positive religion[104]—one rejects instruction, educa-

101. *Thus B, similar in Hu; L (1827?) reads (similar in W):* or, if it is taken not as something objective but as something subjective instead, a determinateness.

102. *L (1827?) adds (similar in W):* There is always a content present to which two aspects belong.

103. *L (1827?) adds (similar in W):* This pure knowing can be termed immediate, for it is simple. But if knowledge is actual, then both knower and known are present, and hence relationship and mediation, too. But it is not permissible to consider knowledge as real and genuine just because it is mediated; knowledge that is *only* mediated is likewise an empty abstraction.

104. [*Ed.*] This stress on the importance of the "positive" (historically mediated) dimension of religion is characteristic of the 1827 lectures. It is introduced again at the beginning of Part III.

tion, etc.[105] We can, to be sure, draw this distinction here and consider revelation or education as an external condition by means of which religion can indeed be implanted within me, but which I have transcended if I have faith. In that case the education is behind me, just as the revelation is also a thing of the past for us. Religion exists only within self-consciousness; outside that it exists nowhere. We might now discuss how far it is justifiable to abstract from such mediation. Even if we regard the mediation as a thing of the past, the kind of determinations we have just now called external conditions must still always belong to the actuality of religion nonetheless, and hence they are essential and not contingent.

307 But if we now look back to the other, inward, aspect and abstract from, or forget, the fact that faith or conviction is something mediated, | we are in the position of considering the inward aspect by itself. The assertion of immediate knowledge bears especially upon this point. "We know God immediately; this knowledge is a revelation within us." That is an important principle to which we must essentially hold fast. It implies that ˉneither positive revelation nor education canˉ[106] bring about religion in such a way that religion would be something effected from outside, something mechanically produced and placed within human beings. Knowledge of religion is certainly necessary, for that mediation belongs to it. It must not be considered as something mechanical, however, but as a *stimulation [Erregung]* instead. Plato's ancient saying is apropos here: that we learn nothing, but only recollect something that we originally bear within ourselves.[107] Taken in an external and nonphilosophical way, this means that we recollect a content that we have known in a previous state [i.e., before this present life began]. That

105. L (1827?) adds (similar in W): These circumstances of doctrine and revelation are not contingent or accidental, but essential. They do, of course, concern an external relationship, but not one that is unimportant just for the reason that it is external.

106. *Thus B; L reads:* positive revelation alone cannot *Hu reads:* neither revelation nor education can *An reads:* instruction cannot *W (Var) reads:* positive revelation cannot thus

107. [Ed.] See Plato *Meno* 81c–d.

is its mythical presentation. But its implication is that religion, right, ethics, and everything spiritual in human beings, is merely aroused [*erregt*]. We are implicitly spirit, for the truth lies within us and the spiritual content within us must be brought into consciousness.

Spirit bears witness to spirit. This witness is spirit's own inner nature. It involves the important specification that religion is not mechanically introduced into human beings but lies within them, in their reason and freedom generally. When we abstract from the condition of being aroused, and consider what this knowledge is and how this religious feeling and self-revelation in the spirit is constituted, then, like all knowledge, it is immediacy, to be sure; but it is an immediacy that equally well contains mediation within itself. The immediacy of knowledge by no means excludes mediation.

As an example we can further cite the fact that something can seem wholly immediate, yet be the result of mediation. What we actually know we have immediately before us—say a mathematical result. It was arrived at by many intermediate steps, though it finally appears as something that one knows immediately. It is the same with drawing or with performing music, each being a result of practice or something mediated | by an endless number of actions. 308 This is true of every skill and so on.[108] But when we consider *religious* knowledge more specifically, then it is indeed an immediate knowledge. When I represent God to myself, then I have God immediately before me. Yet mediation is also contained in this simple, immediate relation. First, I am the knower, and second, there is an object, which is God. My knowing God is in general a relationship, and therefore is something mediated. I am a knower and a religious believer only through the mediation of this content, through this object. We cannot point to anything at all that does not contain mediation within itself.

---

108. *L (1827?) adds:* Thus immediate knowledge proves to be a result. This is a simple psychological consideration that we do not remember in the context of that view.

c. Religious Knowledge as Elevation to God[109]

If we thus consider religious knowledge more closely, it proves to be not only this simple connection of myself with my object, but is something inwardly much more concrete instead. This total simplicity, this knowledge of God, is inwardly a movement; more precisely, it is an *elevation to God*. We express religion essentially as an elevation, a passing over from one content to another. It is the finite content from which we pass over to God, from which we relate ourselves to the absolute, infinite content and pass over to it.

The characteristic nature of mediating is what is determinately expressed in the passing over. This passage is of a double kind. First it is a passing over from finite things, from the things of the world or from the finitude of consciousness and from this finitude in general that we call "we"—or, as this particular subject, "I"—to the infinite, to this infinite being more precisely defined as God. The other kind of passing over has abstract aspects that relate ˉto a more profound and more abstract antithesis.ˉ[110] Here the one aspect is defined as God or the infinite in general as it is known by us (therefore as a subjective content), and the other aspect, to which

309   we pass over, | is determinacy as something objective in principle

---

109. [*Ed.*] If the *being* of God is what is at stake in the various forms of the *knowledge* of God, and if the task of thought, as the highest form of knowledge, is to demonstrate the *necessity* of what is known in the mode of immediacy and representation at earlier stages, then it is not surprising that the primary task of thought with reference to God is to demonstrate the necessity of God's "existence" (*Dasein*), although in the strict sense, from Hegel's point of view, God cannot be said to "exist" (see below, n. 111). Such demonstration constitutes the cognitive dimension of the "elevation to God," which Hegel characterizes in 1821 as intrinsic to the religious relationship when viewed speculatively. Religion is no mere passive receptivity but an active passing over to the infinite, a passage that occurs above all by means of thought.

This section is exceptionally long because Hegel gathers into it his version of the proofs, which in the earlier lectures were considered in relation to the concept of God in the specific religions—the cosmological proof being implicit in the religions of nature, beauty, and sublimity; the teleological proof, in the religion of purposiveness; and the ontological proof, in the revelatory religion. This gathering has the advantage of logical, speculative precision, but it loses the phenomenological matrix in which the proofs were first considered.

110. *Thus L, W; Hu reads:* to more profound and more abstract laws.

or as actual being. In the former passage the common element is *being,* for this content common to both sides is posited as finite and infinite [respectively]. We can represent being to ourselves as a straight line that is determined on one side as finite. The passage occurs from this side to the other or infinite side. Being remains common to both sides. The passing over is simply the fact that the finite disappears. In the second passage the common element is the *infinite,* which is posited in the form of the subjective and the objective. These are the forms that were formerly called the *proofs of God's existence.*[111]

[112]Knowledge of God is in principle mediation, because here there

111. [*Ed.*] That is, the cosmological and teleological proofs in the first case, and the ontological proof in the second. Here and elsewhere in this section, in deference to the tradition, Hegel uses the expression *Dasein Gottes,* although in the strict sense God cannot be said to "exist" or have "determinate being." (The literal sense of *Dasein* is "there-being"; in the *Logic,* pp. 109 ff. [*GW* 11:59 ff.], Hegel defines it as "determinate being" [*bestimmtes Sein*]. Our translation of *Dasein* as "existence" blurs whatever distinction Hegel may have intended between it and the term foreign to German, *Existenz,* which he also sometimes uses.) God "is" *(ist),* he "has being" *(seiend)* in and for himself, absolutely, or is utterly "actual being" (*das Seiende*); but only finite being "exists" (*existiert*) or has being in a determinate, limited, worldly sense (*Dasein*). When the tradition speaks of the "existence of God" (*Dasein Gottes*), it does so representationally or figuratively; but conceptually it is more appropriate to speak of the "being of God" (*Sein Gottes*), and the distortion of speaking of God's "existence" must be removed from the proofs if they are to be grasped rationally. (See the third paragraph below and n. 132 below.) God as the universal does, to be sure, have existence (*Existenz*), says Hegel (see below, p. 181), but we normally understand this representationally as finite existence (i.e., as *Dasein*), whereas we must be clear that God's *Existenz* is infinite and that therefore he is *subject* but not something *subjective.* (Here the distinction between *Existenz* and *Dasein* is important.) It is another matter, though, if one wishes to argue that concrete, determinate existence *also* belongs to or is included within the concept of the absolute: in order to be itself, the absolute becomes something other than itself, positing an actual finite world in which it determines and particularizes itself and from which it returns to itself "spiritualized" or "existentialized," as it were, because it encompasses finitude within itself (although as negated, sublated). In this sense reference to the "existence" (*Dasein*) of God may not be entirely inappropriate, but it is properly grasped only from the point of view of the religion of incarnation, the Christian religion, and is an aspect of the ontological proof, which is associated with this religion (see below, pp. 184 ff.).

112. *In B's margin: 28 May 1827 Precedes in L (1827?) (similar in W):* The relationship of knowing God has therefore now to be considered within itself. Knowing is relationship, and is mediated within itself either through another or inwardly.

163

obtains a relation between myself and an object, God, who is something other than I am. Where a relation of distinct things is present, and one of them is essentially related to the other, the relation is called mediation. One is this and the other is something else, so that they are distinct from one another; they are not immediately identical, not one and the same. God and I are distinct from one another. If both were one, then there would be an immediate self-relation, one without mediation and without relation, i.e., a unity without distinction. In that the two are distinct, each one is not what the other is. But if they are nevertheless connected, or have identity at the same time in their distinctiveness, then this identity itself is distinct from their distinct being; it is something different from both of them because otherwise they would not be distinct.[113]

The mediation accordingly is in a third [term] over against these two distinct sides, and is itself a third that brings them together and in which they are mediated and are identical. Here we have the familiar relationship of the syllogism, in which there are two distinct [terms] and a unity in which both of them are posited as one through a third. Hence it is not only obvious but inherent in the matter itself that, whenever we speak of knowing God, | our discourse at once takes the form of a *syllogism*.[114] For this reason the form of the knowledge of God occurs more specifically in the form of the *proofs of God's existence*. The knowledge of God is presented in this way as a mediated knowledge, for what is abstractly just One is what is unmediated. The proofs present the knowledge of God because this knowledge contains mediation within itself, and the mediation is religion itself, or the knowledge of God;[115] and this mediated knowledge, the explication of the proofs of God's existence, is the explication of religion itself.

113. *L (1827?) adds (similar in W):* Both are distinct, for their unity is not they themselves. That in which they are one is that in which they are not distinct. But they are distinct. Therefore their unity is distinct from their distinctness.

114. *W (Var) adds:* Both are distinct, and there is a unity in which both are posited in one through a third [term]: that is the syllogism. Hence we have to discuss more precisely the nature of the knowledge of God, which is mediated essentially within itself.

115. *An adds:* the cultus being [for now] excluded from it;

Still, this form of proof does, to be sure, involve some distortion, and it is in order to exhibit this distortion that this knowledge is itself looked at as a series of proofs. This distortion has been the target of [philosophical] criticism; but the one-sided moment of the form that this knowledge has does not bring the whole matter to naught. On the contrary, our task is to restore the proofs of God's existence to a position of honor by stripping away that distortion. When we hear the expression "proofs of God's existence," it brings in straightaway the possibility that some distortion is involved in it. There is talk of God and his "existence" [Dasein]; "existence" is determinate, finite being—and Existenz, too, is used in a determinate sense. But God's being is in no way a limited being. It would be better to say, "God and his being, his actuality or objectivity." The demonstration has the aim of showing us the coherence between the two determinations [God and being] because they are distinct, not because they are immediately one. Everything is immediate in its relation to itself, God as God, being as being. What is demonstrated is that these initially distinct things also cohere together and are identical—though they do not have an abstract identity, which would be sameness and hence immediacy.

To show coherence means in general to prove. The coherence can be of different kinds, and the proof leaves this difference undefined. For instance, there is a coherence that is *wholly external* or mechanical. We see that a roof is necessary to the walls, because the house has this characteristic protection against weather and the like. The purpose is | what links the walls with the roof, and we 311 can therefore say it is proved that a house must have a roof. This is no doubt [logically] coherent, but we are aware at the same time that the coherence of the walls with the roof does not affect the being of these objects. Or again, the fact that wood and tile make up a roof does not concern their being, and is for them a merely external nexus.[116] But there are also [types of] coherence that are *involved in the thing* or the content itself. This is the case, for

116. *Follows in W (Var):* What is involved here in "proving" is the showing of a coherence between determinations of a kind for which the nexus itself is external.

instance, with geometrical figures. "The three angles in a triangle add up to two right angles."[117] That is a necessity of the thing itself, whereas beams and stones are what they are even without being joined together. In the triangle the connection is not of the kind where the coherence is external; in this case, rather the one [term] cannot be without the other, for the second is directly posited along with the first. But the proof that we give for this, or the kind of insight [we have] into this necessity, is distinct from the coherence that the determinations have within the thing itself. The procedure that we follow in demonstration is not a process of the thing itself— it is something other than what is involved in the nature of the thing. We draw auxiliary lines. But it would not occur to anyone to say that, in order to have three angles equal in magnitude to two right angles, a triangle should adopt the procedure of extending one of its sides, and that only by that means would it arrive at this determination. That, by contrast, is the path of our insight; the mediation through which we pass and the mediation in the thing itself are separate from one another. Construction and proof serve only as an aid to our subjective cognition; they do not constitute the objective mode by which the thing attained this relationship through mediation. It is indeed a subjective necessity, but not the coherence or mediation within the object itself.

With regard to the knowledge of God, to the internal coherence of God's determinations and the coherence of our knowledge of God and of God's determinations, this type of demonstration is

312 directly unsatisfactory | on its own account. In this procedure of subjective necessity we start from certain initial definitions that are already familiar to us. There are assumptions or initial conditions, for example that the triangle or the right angle is given. Definite [logical] connections are presupposed, and we then show in proofs of this kind that if there is one determination then the other is, too. That is, we make the result dependent on given specifications al-

117. *Thus Hu, similar in An; L (1827?) adds (similar in W):* In the case of the right triangle there is also present the determinate relationship of the square on the hypotenuse to the squares on the shorter sides.

ready present. What we arrive at is represented as something dependent upon assumptions.[118]

In the application of this model [*Vorstellung*] of demonstration to the formulation [*Vorstellung*] of proofs of God's existence, what appears at once is the inappropriateness of wishing to exhibit a coherence of this kind in the case of God. This appears particularly in the first procedure, which we called the elevation of the finite to God, so that (if we embrace the process within the form of the proof) we have a relationship in which the finite is the foundation from which the being of God is demonstrated. In this [logical] nexus the being of God appears as a consequence, as dependent upon the being of the finite. This is the distortion, that this progression that we call "proving" is unsuited to what we represent to ourselves under [the name] "God"—for God is, of course, precisely the non-derivative, he is utterly actual being in and for itself. But if we now suppose that, by pointing this out, we have shown this procedure as a whole is vacuous, then this, too, is a one-sided view—and one that directly contradicts the universal consciousness of humankind. For what this nexus contains when we strip away that *form* of demonstration is the elevation to God, and the proofs are nothing more than a description of the self-elevation to God. It is because of the Kantian critique of reason that these proofs of God's existence have been discarded, consigned so to speak to the rubbish heap.[119]

[120]Human beings consider the world and, because they are thinking and rational beings (since they find no satisfaction in the contingency of things), they elevate themselves from the finite to absolute necessity. | They say that, because the finite is something contingent, 313 there must be something necessary in and for itself which is the

---

118. L (1827?) adds (similar in W): As sheer demonstration for understanding, the geometrical proof is undoubtedly the most perfect example. It is the demonstration for understanding that is carried through most consistently, so that one thing is in fact exhibited as dependent upon an other.

119. [Ed.] See Kant, *Critique of Pure Reason*, B 611–658.

120. *Precedes In L (1827?):* We will take into account later what is false and what is omitted in this description.

ground of this contingency.[121] Human beings will always go through this concrete procedure so long as they have religion, and will conclude that, because there are in the world living things, each of which organizes itself internally for the sake of its vitality as such and is this sort of harmony of its different parts, and because all these living things in like manner need external objects, such as air and the like, which are independent of them and which, without being posited by them, harmonize with them in their turn—because of this, some inner ground of these harmonies must be present. There is this one harmony in and for itself; this presupposes an activity through which it has been produced, a being that acts purposively. ¯This universal procedure is involved in the present demonstration of God's existence; it is not upset by criticism of this demonstration, for it is necessary.¯[122]

[123]Against the proofs of God's existence it is also said that they do not lead to inner and strong conviction.[124] The proofs leave us cold, for we are dealing with objective content and can see well enough that if this is the case, then so is that, but the insight remains something external only. This is a deficiency only for subjective cognition, since what also comes into prominence is the fact that in the proof we have a cognition concerning something external. But when this procedure is said to be too objective and to produce only a cold conviction (whereas conviction must be in the heart), then the deficiency is expressed from the opposite side. What is

121. *L, W₁ add (Var):* This is the course of human reason, or of the human spirit. *W₂ (Var) adds further:* and this proof of the existence of God is nothing but the description of this elevation to the infinite.

122. *Thus Hu, similar in An; L (Var) reads (similar in W):* This is what we call "admiring the wisdom of God in nature," or this marvel of the living organism and the harmony of external objects with it. Human beings raise themselves up from this harmony to the consciousness of God. We are mistaken when we suppose that, because their form is attacked, the proofs of God's existence have become antiquated with respect to their content. But the content is, of course, not presented in its purity. *W adds:* We can even draw attention to this deficiency.

123. *In B's margin:* 29 May 1827

124. *[Ed.]* Hegel apparently alludes here not to a specific work but to a complaint about the proofs heard fairly commonly at his time. See, e.g., F. Köppen, *Ueber Offenbarung, in Beziehung auf Kantische und Fichtische Philosophie,* 2d ed. (Lübeck and Leipzig, 1802), pp. 52–53, 139.

more precisely involved in this reproach is the demand that this procedure of demonstration should rather be *our own elevation,* that our spirit or heart ought to elevate itself, that we | ought not   314 merely to behave as if we were considering a nexus of external determinations. No, the feeling and believing spirit, the spirit as a whole, ought to be elevated. Spiritual movement, the movement of our own selves and our will, ought to be there in the demonstration, too—and this is what we are missing when we say that it is an external nexus of determinations. This is the deficient feature.

There are two determinations present, which are conjoined— namely, God in general or the indeterminate representation of God, and being. These two are to be united—being is to be exhibited as the being of God, and God is to be exhibited as having being. Inasmuch as there are two determinations, so that a progression occurs, we can therefore begin from being and pass over to God, or begin from God and pass over to being. Because this procedure has been characterized as elevation, the immediate beginning is pure being, and the result is the union of both determinations as the knowledge that *God is.* When we consider this first procedure, which we have called elevation, then the form of the proof of God's existence contains the proposition: Because there is something finite, there must also (on that account) be something infinite and not bounded by an other, or an absolutely necessary essence. The finite is what is not inwardly its own ground, it is what is contingent; there must therefore be something that is not in turn grounded in an other.[125]

Human beings certainly follow this procedure within their own spirit; it exhibits itself more precisely as the following mediation. We have a consciousness of the world as an aggregate of endlessly many contingent phenomena, of many singular objects that deter- mine themselves for us as finite. When our consciousness or our thought is enveloped in the form of feeling or of devotion, then the movement of our spirit is that the finite has for it no truth but is something contingent; it is a being, to be sure, but one that in fact

---

125. [*Ed.*] Hegel orients his presentation of the cosmological proof largely toward Kant's *Critique of Pure Reason,* B 632 f.

is only a nonbeing. This nonbeing of the finite in positive form is inwardly affirmative; this affirmative nonfinite is the infinite, it is absolute being, and to begin with we have only this definition for God. Thus there is here a mediation of finite and infinite. But the essential point is that, in its departure from the finite, the mediation ⁻negates this finite in the elevation, does not allow it to subsist. The finite has a negative determination; the affirmative element is the infinite, absolute being.⁻¹²⁶ |

So if we therefore consider this mediation more precisely in its moments, then distinct determinations are present, which have to be gone through: immediate existence, the existence of mundane things, and God. The point of departure is the finite; the most proximate determination is that the finite is not genuine, it has no genuine being, it is negative.¹²⁷

To begin with, therefore, we have the negative aspect, the negation of the finite, the fact that it is its inner nature to be contradiction, i.e., not to be but rather to destroy itself—it is self-sublation. In its speculative significance and form this proposition is treated in logic.¹²⁸ But we are also convinced of it per se, and can therefore address a challenge to ordinary consciousness: that finite things have the characteristic of perishing—their being is the sort that directly sublates itself. Accordingly we have at first only the negation of the finite. The second [determination] is that this negation of the finite is also affirmative. There is a spurious affirmation that consists in the repetition of the finite, in the fact that it only brings forth again the finite that was there before, with the result that one finite thing posits another, and so on unto the spu-

126. *Thus B with Hu; L (Var) reads:* does not merely negate this finite in the elevation but also allows it to subsist. The finite has indeed no truth, for in it as finite there is essentially negation. The infinite, however, is the affirmative of the finite, it is absolute being.

127. *L (1827?) adds:* The third [determination] is that this negation of the finite is itself affirmation, and is therefore infinite, absolute being.

[*Ed.*] L apparently construes *nächst* to mean "next" rather than "nearest" or "most proximate," as we have done. What L designates as the *third* determination is identical with what is described as the *second* determination in the main text below.

128. [*Ed.*] Cf. *Science of Logic*, esp. pp. 137–138 (GW 11:78–79).

rious infinite. Heraclitus said that everything is changeable, every-thing flows.[129] In this there is only a progression from negation to ceaseless transformation; this affirmation would be an accumula-tion of nongenuine existences in which change would be the ultimate feature. This intermediate form is taken into consideration in logic; here this much can be said, that by it the finite is changed not one whit. For the finite is indeed the sort of thing that changes itself and passes over into an other, although this other is in turn some-thing finite. Another thing becomes another thing; both are there-fore the same. The one is the other, for the one is the finite and the other is the finite. In this way the other coincides with itself; it comes to itself and the negation is superseded. The passing over into an other, or this spurious affirmation, is the spurious progress of the finite; it is simply the tedious repetition of one determination; but the true affirmation is already contained within it. The finite changes itself; it appears as an other, [and so] | other comes to other.   316 What is the case here is that both are the same. The other coincides with itself and in the other comes to itself, to its equality with itself, to its connection with itself. This is the affirmation, this is being. Genuine transition does not consist in change, in perennial alter-ation. Instead *the genuine other of the finite is the infinite,* and this is not bare negation of the finite but is affirmative, is being. That is the quite simple consideration involved here. This affirmative process is the process of our spirit; it brings itself about uncon-sciously within our spirit; but philosophy is having the conscious-ness of it. We bring the same thing to pass when we raise ourselves up to God. Thus the infinite itself is at first something finite or negative. The second [moment] is that it is something affirmative. There is a progression through different determinations, and it is by no means an external one but is rather necessity itself. This necessity is the deed of our spirit.

If we compare this inner mediation with the proofs for God's existence, the distinction is as follows. In the proofs it is argued

129. [*Ed.*] Heraclitus's words are transmitted by Plato and Aristotle. See Plato, *Cratylus* 402a, Aristotle, *De caelo* 298a29 ff., *Metaphysics* 987a33 f. and 1078b14 f. On the "spurious infinite" (*schlechtes Unendliche*), see n. 128.

that, because the finite is, for that reason the infinite is, too. What is expressed here, therefore, is that the finite is; this is the point of departure, the foundation. From this arises the objection against these proofs that they are said to make the finite into the foundation for the being of God. The finite is an abiding point of departure, and in this procedure the being of God is mediated through the being of the finite. In our procedure, on the contrary, the conclusion is rather as follows. In the first place there is indeed the finite. But in the second place, because the finite is not, is not true in itself but is rather the contradiction that sublates itself, for *that* reason the truth of the finite is this affirmative element that is called the infinite. Here there is no relationship or mediation between two elements each of which *is* [abides]; for rather the point of departure sublates itself; there is a mediation that sublates itself, a mediation through the sublation of mediation. The infinite does not constitute merely one aspect. For the understanding there are, in the mediation, two actual beings: on this side there is a world and over yonder there is God, and the knowledge of the world is the foundation of the being of God. But through our treatment the world is relinquished as a genuine being; it is not regarded as something permanent on this side. The sole import of this procedure is that *the infinite alone is;* the finite has no genuine being, whereas God has only genuine being. [130]This is a | distinction that relies upon the most wholly refined abstractions; but they are precisely the most universal categories within our spirit. That is just what makes it important to be cognizant of the distinction, in order not to be mistaken in regard to it.

317

The principal objection to this procedure rests upon the erroneous determination that the finite is and endures. This criticism is also expressed in the following way. There is no passage from the finite to the infinite, no bridge between the two. We are these limited natures [*Wesen*]; hence we cannot with our consciousness get across

---

130. *Precedes in L (1827?):* The first [element], which is our starting point, does not abide but rather relinquishes itself, is sublated. That is the point on which everything turns. The first [element], the starting point, sublates itself.

the abyss, we cannot grasp the infinite.[131] The infinite is just infinite, and we are finite, for our knowledge, feeling, reason, and spirit are limited and persist in their limitedness. But this talk is already contradicted in what has been said. It is undoubtedly correct that we are limited; so we are not talking about the limitedness of nature but about the dependence of reason. However, it is equally correct that this finite element has no truth, and reason is precisely the insight that the finite is only a limit. But inasmuch as we know something as a limit, we are already beyond it. The animal or the stone knows nothing of its limit. In contrast, the I, as knowing or thinking in general, is limited but knows about the limit, and in this very knowledge the limit is only limit, only something negative outside us, and I am beyond it. We must not have such absurd respect in the presence of the infinite. The infinite is the wholly pure abstraction, the initial abstraction of being according to which limit is omitted—a being that relates itself to itself, the universal within which every boundary is ideal, is sublated. Therefore the finite does not endure, and inasmuch as it does not endure, there is also no longer a gulf present between finite and infinite, [they] are no longer two. Because the finite vanishes into a semblance or a shadow, it therefore also admits of no passage to infinity. The starting point is certainly the finite, but spirit does not leave it subsisting. This is the more precise development of what is called knowledge of God. Knowledge of God is this very elevation.[132] | 318

131. [*Ed.*] Hegel here touches on the old problem of the *finitum (non) capax infiniti*, which had become a decisive issue in his time in light of Kant's *Critique of Pure Reason* and Jacobi's insistence on the *non capax* (Jacobi, *Werke* 4/1:56). See also Schelling, *Philosophische Briefe über Dogmatismus und Kriticismus*, (1795), (*Sämtliche Werke* 1/1:308 ff., 314 ff.); and *Abhandlungen zur Erläuterung des Idealismus der Wissenschaftslehre* (1796–1797) (*Sämtliche Werke* 1/1:367–368).

132. [*Ed.*] In the last paragraphs Hegel again touches on a theme found in the 1821 and 1824 lectures, which may be described as a "speculative reversal" in the relationship between the finite and infinite. While the finite is the starting point, it itself does not serve as the ground for passing over to the infinite, which would then appear to be a result. Rather the finite negates or sublates itself, cognizes its own nonbeing in knowing its limits, and thus also knows the infinite as not simply "one aspect" but as the whole, that which overreaches both finite and infinite, includes

[133]At this point we can also make some historical observations. The first of the familiar proofs of the existence of God is the *cosmological*, where the starting point is the contingency of the world. Here the affirmative element is defined not merely as the infinite in general but rather—in direct antithesis to the determination of contingency—as the absolutely necessary or, represented as subject, as the absolutely necessary essence. Hence some even more specific determinations enter in, and these proofs can in principle be multiplied by the dozen; every step of the logical idea can serve this purpose, for instance [the step] from essence to the absolutely necessary essence.[134]

Absolutely necessary essence, taken in the general or abstract sense, is being not as immediate but as reflected into self, as essence. We have defined essence as the nonfinite, as the negation of the negative—¯a negation that we call the infinite.¯[135] So the transition is not made to abstract, arid being but to the being that is negation of the negation. Therein lies the distinction. This being is the dis-

negation within itself, and thus alone truly is. What appears to be the result develops a "counterthrust" and shows itself to be "the first and alone true" (1824 lectures, unabridged ed., Vol. 1:322). Or, as Hegel describes it metaphorically in the 1821 lectures, the progression from finite to infinite is like "a stream flowing in opposite directions" (unabridged ed., Vol. 1:227n.115). It is by means of this insight that Hegel proposes to restore the proofs to a position of honor by divesting them of distortion—the distortion that finitude is the ground from which God's "existence" is demonstrated. The "elevation" to God is not an autonomous self-elevation of finite spirit into what could only be a spurious infinite, but, speculatively expressed, the return of true and infinite spirit, i.e., absolute spirit, to itself.

133. [*Ed.*] From this point to the end of the section, both editions of the *Werke* print the 1827 text as an appendix to the "Lectures on the Proofs of the Existence of God" at the end of volume 2. Hegel gave these lectures in the summer of 1829 and was preparing them for publication when he died in 1831. His treatment of the proofs in the 1827 and 1831 philosophy-of-religion lectures is obviously closely related to the separate series of lectures on this topic—a topic that increasingly occupied him during his last years in Berlin. But there was no justification on the part of the editors of W for taking the philosophy-of-religion material out of its original context.

134. [*Ed.*] An exact account of a transition of this kind, i.e., from essence to the absolutely necessary essence, is not given in the *Science of Logic*. Hegel is probably thinking of the development of essence to absolute necessity (cf. esp. p. 552 [GW 11:391]).

135. *Thus B; L (Var) reads (similar in W):* a negative that we call the finite.

tinction that takes itself back into simplicity. Involved within this essence is the determination of ¯what is distinguished; but it is a determining of what is distinguished as it relates itself to itself, a self-determining. Negation is determination. Negation of determination is itself a determining.¯[136] Where there is no negation, there is also no distinction, no determination. Determination is posited together with the positing of distinction, for without that there would be only affirmation and not negation. So determining in general is involved in absolute being, or in the unity of the essence; it lies within it and is therefore self-determining.[137] Distinction does not come into it from outside, for this unrest lies within it as being itself the negation of the negation. More precisely, it determines itself as *activity*. This self-determination of the essence within itself, namely the positing of the distinction and its sublation in such a way that it is an action, | and that this self-determining remains in simple connection with itself, is inward *necessity*.[138]

319

[139]The *physicotheological* or *teleological* proof is another formulation in which this same mediation is the foundation; i.e., the proof is the same with regard to its formal characteristics, but the content is more extensive. Here, too, there is finite being on one side, though it is not just abstractly defined, or defined only as being, but rather as being that has within it the more substantial determination of being something physically alive. The elaboration of this proof can be made very wide-ranging, because the more detailed determination of the living thing is apprehended to mean that there are purposes within nature and an [overall] arrangement

136. *Thus B with L; W (Var) reads:* the distinction—negation of the negation— but as it relates itself to itself. But such a thing is what we call self-determining. Negation is determination, and negation of the determination is itself a determining, a positing of a distinction; determination is posited right along with it.
    [*Ed.*] See above. n. 25.
137. *W (Var) adds:* Thus it is determined as determination within itself.
138. *L (1827?) adds (similar in W):* Finite being does not remain an other, for there is no gulf between infinite and finite. Finite being is what sublates itself, so that its truth is the infinite, is actual being in and for self. Finite, contingent being is the intrinsically self-negating; but this its negation is equally the affirmative, and this affirmation is the absolutely necessary essence.
139. *In B's margin:* 31 May 1827

that, though suited to those purposes, is not at the same time brought forth by means of them, so that the arrangement comes forth independently on its own account. (In another definition it is also purpose, but in the sense that the [living thing] met with previously shows itself to be compatible with that purpose.)

The physicotheological mode of treatment involves the consideration of merely external purposiveness.[140] Hence it has come into disrepute, and deservedly so; for in that mode we are thinking of finite ends that require means, and the process of specification goes on forever. For example, human beings have needs; they require any number of things for their ¬animal¬[141] life. If we assume that such ends are primary and that means for their satisfaction are available, but that it is God who allows the means for these ends to arise, then any such consideration soon shows itself to be inadequate to what God is and unworthy of God. For to the extent that these ends are divided up and specialized, they become something unimportant on their own account, something for which we have no regard and which we cannot represent to ourselves as direct objects of God's will and wisdom. This attitude of mind, which thus turns into something trivial, is captured in one of Goethe's satirical epigrams, | where the creator is extolled for creating a bottle and also the cork tree in order to have a stopper for it.[142]

With regard to the Kantian philosophy we should observe that in his *Critique of Judgment* Kant led thought back to the important concept (which he himself established) of *inner purposiveness*—i.e.,

320

---

140. [*Ed.*] Cf. Kant's *Critique of Judgment*, §§ 61 ff., for the background of this discussion of purposiveness in nature. See especially §§ 63, 66, and 82 for the distinction (that Hegel draws below) between the inner purposiveness of organic beings and the merely external purposiveness of nature expressed in the notion of utility or expediency. Kant defines "physicotheology" as "the attempt on the part of reason to infer the supreme cause of nature and its attributes from the *ends* of nature—ends which can only be known empirically"; from which he distinguishes "moral theology" or "ethicotheology," which is "the attempt to infer that cause and its attributes from the moral end of rational beings in nature—an end which can be known *a priori*." See *Critique of Judgment*, § 85.

141. *Thus W; L reads:* moral

142. [*Ed.*] See the *Musen-Almanach für das Jahr 1797*, ed. Friedrich Schiller (Tübingen), Epigram no. 202, "Der Teleolog." Cf. Schiller, *Werke: Nationalausgabe*, vol. 1 (Weimar, 1943), p. 311, no. 15.

the concept of *organic life*.[143] This is also Aristotle's[144] concept of nature [according to which] every living thing is a *telos* that has its means implicit within it—i.e., its members and its organization. The operation of these members constitutes the *telos* or purpose, its organic life. This is *nonfinite* purposiveness in which end and means are not external to one another—the end brings forth the means and the means brings forth the end. The principal determination is that of organic life. The world is alive; it contains organic life and the realms of organic life. At the same time the nonliving (inorganic nature, such as sun and stars) exists in an essential relation with the living, with human beings insofar as they are living nature on the one hand, and insofar as they themselves devise particular purposes on the other. This finite purposiveness falls within human [experience].

That is the definition of organic life generally, but [in the form of] extant, worldly organic life. The latter, to be sure, [aims at] being *inward* vitality, *inward* purposiveness; but at the same time it [achieves this] in such a way that every singular living thing and its species is a very narrow sphere, a very limited nature. The proper progression, then, is from this finite organic life to absolute organic life, to universal purposiveness—such that this world is a *cosmos*, i.e., a system in which everything has an essential connection to everything else and nothing is isolated. The cosmos is something internally ordered in which each thing has its place, is embraced within the whole, subsists by means of the whole, and is in the same measure active and effective for the generation and life of the whole. Thus the main thing is the movement away from finite ends toward a universal organic life, toward the one purpose that articulates itself in particular ends—so that this particularization exists within harmony, within a reciprocal and essential relation.

143. [*Ed.*] The discussion in Kant's *Critique of Judgment*, Part II, Critique of Teleological Judgment, concerns the unique reciprocal causality between the parts and the whole that is characteristic of living things, i.e., the evidently purposive structure inherent in organic beings. To keep this feature firmly in view the biologically (though not philosophically) redundant term "organic life" is sometimes used for *Lebendigkeit*, which means literally "vitality" or "liveliness."

144. [*Ed.*] See Aristotle *Physics* 2.8–9, esp. 199a21–32.

God is initially defined as the absolutely necessary essence. As Kant already noted,[145] however, this definition is by no means sufficient for the concept of God. Certainly God alone is absolute necessity; but this definition does not exhaust the concept of God, 321 | and the definition [in terms] of organic life or of one universal life is already as much nobler as it is more profound. Since "life" is essentially something living and subjective, this universal life is also something subjective, a soul, Νοῦς. Soul is thus contained within universal life; it is the determination of the one, all-disposing, governing, and organizing Νοῦς. This is as far as the teleological proof goes initially.

With regard to its formal aspect, we should recall the same point in the case of this proof as we did in that of the preceding one. That is to say, the transition is not in truth concluded in the following manner (as the understanding supposes): Because there are arrangements and purposes of this sort, therefore there is a wisdom coordinating and disposing all things. The transition is simultaneously an elevation that equally includes the negative moment (which is the main thing), specifically that this living thing in its immediacy, and hence these purposes as they exist in their finite organic life, are not the true. Instead their truth is really that one organic life, the one Νοῦς. There are not two distinct forms, for the initial starting point does not persist as the foundation or condition. Instead the untruth or negation of the initial point is contained in the passage away from it, i.e., the negation of the negative or finite aspect in it, of the particularity of life. This negation is negated, for in this elevation finite organic life disappears and, as truth, the object of consciousness is the system, the Νοῦς of the one organic life, the universal soul.

But here again it is the case that the [resulting] definition is still not yet adequate for the concept of God: "God is the one universal activity of life, the disposing soul bringing forth, positing, and or-

---

145. [Ed.] Hegel is probably alluding to Kant's *Critique of Pure Reason*, B 614–615, also B 639. In these passages Kant's interest lies, of course, in the link between the concept of the absolutely necessary being and the concept of the most real being. Cf. also B 660–661. Cf. also Kant's *Critique of Judgment*, §§ 85 ff., 91 n.

ganizing a cosmos."[146] The concept of God contains essentially the determination that God is *spirit*. We can make the transition, then, in such a way that this being [*Wesen*] who governs the world is a cause sundered from the world, is a wise being. But "cause" and "wisdom" are further specifications that strictly do not yet occur at this point; the highest feature that emerges from the determination of finite organic life is just the very universality of organic life, the Noῦς. That is as far as the content involved in the starting point goes.

The third and most essential form of this transition, the one which from this point of view is absolute, has still to be considered. We noted just now | that the content of the transition is organic   322 life; similarly in this third form the content that lies at its foundation is *spirit*. If we wanted to convey the transition in the form of an inference, we would have to say: Because there are finite spirits (i.e., the being that is the starting point here), therefore the absolute, infinite spirit is, and here we arrive at the definition of God as spirit. But this "because" or this solely affirmative relationship in turn contains a deficiency, in that finite spirits would be the foundation and God the consequence of the existence of the finite spirits—and this is the distortion again. The negative aspect of the finite spirits must be negated. For that reason the genuine form is as follows: there are finite spirits. But the finite has no truth, for the truth of finite spirit and its actuality is instead just the absolute spirit. The finite is not genuine being; it is implicitly the dialectic of self-sublating or self-negating, and its negation is affirmation as the infinite, as the universal in and for itself.[147] It is surprising that this transition was not specified in the proofs of God.

146. [*Ed.*] It is not certain whether this formulation of the results of the physicotheology refers to Hegel's own formulation given at the end of the second paragraph above, or to a specific text, and, if so, which one. The idea of an all-disposing Noῦς is found since Anaxagoras, the idea of the world-soul since Plato (e.g., *Laws* 896–899). See Schelling, *Von der Weltseele* (Hamburg, 1798) (*Sämtliche Werke* 1/2:345 ff.). In terms of content, Hegel's criticism of the proof of God in physicotheology corresponds to that given by Kant in the *Critique of Judgment*, § 85, which provides the occasion for his advancing to moral theology.

147. W₂ *(Var) adds:* This is the highest transition, for here the transition is spirit itself.

With reference to this relationship we could take account of what is called *pantheism*. But we have already stated[148] that a pantheism in the strict sense has never been propounded. "Pantheism" means "all is divine," and amounts to the notion that every thing taken singularly is God—this [snuff] box or the pinch of snuff.[149] What is meant by this absurd label is that God is thought of as substance, and the finite is thought of in terms of accidents of the divine substance. I said that finite organic life is not the true; rather, the truth of finite spirit is absolute spirit, so it is this negation of spirit on the one hand, while on the other hand it is absolute spirit. For Spinoza the absolute is substance, and no being is ascribed to the finite; his position is therefore monotheism and acosmism. So strictly is there only God, that there is no world at all; in this [position] the finite has no genuine actuality. Our modern babblers, however, cannot break free from the view that finite things as well as God have actual being, that they are something absolute. But as for *our* transition, we have the finite as our starting point; and it turns out to be something negative, the truth of which is the infinite,

323 | i.e., absolute necessity or, by a more profound definition, absolute vitality, or spirit. In this [their] relation comes about as I have exhibited it, but still without any determination whether absolute spirit in its relationship to the finite has being as *substance* only or as *subject,* and whether finite spirits are effects or accidents of the infinite. This last is certainly a distinction, but it does not deserve so much fuss. The main thing is whether the absolute is defined as substance, or as subject and spirit. ˝Those who speak of pantheism are wanting in the simplest categories of thought.˝[150]

We have set being and God in opposition. Insofar as we begin from being, then according to its initial appearance being is immediately the finite. But inasmuch as there are these determinations,

148. [*Ed.*] See above, p. 123.
149. [*Ed.*] Hegel used snuff. At this point he probably held up his snuffbox and took a pinch.
150. *Thus B; L (Var) reads:* However, that is not yet pertinent here. In our consideration of spirit we will see that subjectivity is an essential feature of spirit.

we are equally well able to begin from God and to pass over to being.[151] When we begin from God, the starting point or God is posited in finite form, of course, because it is not yet posited as identical with being and represented as having being [absolutely]; for a God who *is not* is something finite, and not genuinely God. The finitude of this relation is that it is subjective: God [is here defined] not as *subject* but as something *subjective*. God, this universal in general, does indeed have existence [*Existenz*], but, in terms of our representation, only this finite existence. This is one-sided. We have God or this content as afflicted with the one-sidedness and finitude that is called *representation* of God. It is our interest that representation should strip away this blemish of being merely something represented and subjective, and that the definition for this content should become that of *being*.

We are to consider this second aspect of the mediation as it occurs within the finite form of the understanding as the *ontological* proof. This proof passes over from the concept of God to the being of God. The ancients, i.e., Greek philosophy, did not have this transition; even within the Christian era it was not accomplished for a long time, because it involves the most profound descent of spirit into itself. One of the greatest Scholastic philosophers, the profoundly speculative thinker Anselm of Canterbury, | grasped this 324 representation for the first time in the following way. We have the representation of God. But God is no mere representation, for God *is*.[152] How then are we to accomplish this passage, how are we to gain the insight that God is not merely something subjective within us? Or, how is the determination of being to be mediated with God? For being and God are two different things.

151. *L (1827?) adds (similar in W):* ("We are able"—though we shall see later, in [discussing] the concept of God, that then there is no talk of "being able," for God is absolute necessity.)

152. [*Ed.*] See Anselm's well-known proof in his *Proslogion*, chap. 2: "Well then, Lord, you who give understanding to faith, grant me that I may understand, as much as you see fit, that you exist as we believe you to exist, and that you are what we believe you to be. Now we believe that you are something than which nothing greater can be thought. . . . For it is one thing for an object to exist in the

The Kantian critique has directed itself against this so-called "ontological" proof, too[153]—and, in a manner of speaking, it emerged triumphant in its day. Right up to the present the assessment is that all these proofs for God have been refuted as empty efforts of the understanding. But just as the preceding proofs are elevations to God, or the action of spirit (more precisely the peculiar activity of thinking spirit, which humanity will not renounce), so it is with this proof. In reference to the historical aspect we saw that the ancients did not have this transition. Only when spirit has grown to its highest freedom and subjectivity does it grasp this thought of God as something subjective and arrive at this antithesis of subjectivity and objectivity.

[154]Anselm expressed the mediation in the following way. A feature of the representation of God is that God is absolutely perfect (a very indeterminate expression).[155] We can say that on the whole that is quite correct. But if we hold fast to God only as a representation, then what is merely represented is something deficient and not what is most perfect. For that which is perfect is something that is not merely represented but also *is, actually* is. Therefore,

---

mind, and another thing to understand that an object actually exists. . . . And surely that-than-which-a-greater-cannot-be-thought cannot exist in the mind alone. For if it exists solely in the mind even, it can be thought to exist in reality also, which is greater. If then that-than-which-a-greater-cannot-be-thought exists in the mind alone, this same that-than-which-a-greater-*cannot*-be-thought is that-than-which-a-greater-*can*-be-thought. But this is obviously impossible. Therefore there is absolutely no doubt that something-than-which-a-greater-cannot-be-thought exists both in the mind and in reality." Eng. trans. by M. J. Charlesworth in his *St. Anselm's Proslogion* (Oxford, 1965).

153. [*Ed.*] Cf. *Critique of Pure Reason*, B 620–630. Kant's criticism of course does not bear directly upon the argument in the form in which Anselm presented it.

154. *In B's margin:* 1 June 1827

155. [*Ed.*] In his proof, Anselm does not speak of God as "absolutely perfect" in the way that Hegel here implies. Rather he calls God "that-than-which-a-greater-cannot-be-thought" (see n. 152), or (though not in the context of the proof) "that-which-is-greater-than-can-be-thought" (*Proslogion*, chap. 15). In other places he uses equivalents for "absolutely perfect," such as "supreme good" (*Proslogion*, Preface), but not as premises of the proof. Hegel's criticism of the indeterminacy of Anselm's expression adopts the criticism already advanced by Gaunilo in his *Response*.

because God is that which is perfect, God is not only a representation, for actuality and reality belong to God as well. The Kantian critique objects first to the abstract universal, namely that the concept of God is presupposed, that it is taken as point of departure, and reality (i.e., being and thought) is supposed to be deduced or "plucked" from the concept itself.[156]

In the subsequent and more extensive elaboration of Anselm's thought by understanding, it was said that the concept of God is that God is the quintessence of all reality, the most real essence.[157] Now being is also a reality; so being also belongs to God. The objection to this is | that being is no reality,[158] is not part of the reality, of a concept. The reality of the concept means the concept's determinateness of content; through being, however, nothing is added to the content of the concept. If we have some content and define it, for instance that gold has a certain specific gravity, then this feature is one of its realities. To this accrues further the yellow color and the like, as other realities of the concept. Hence Kant constructed this plausible case. I represent to myself a hundred dollars.[159] The concept or the determinateness of content is the same

325

156. [Ed.] Cf. Kant, Critique of Pure Reason, B 631: "To attempt to extract from a purely arbitrary idea the existence of an object corresponding to it is a quite unnatural procedure and a mere innovation of scholastic subtlety." Hegel's herausgeklaubt ("plucked") and Kant's ausklauben are more colorful expressions, suggesting an even more high-handed procedure than Kemp Smith's "extract," for which there are a number of ordinary German words.

157. [Ed.] A reference to the concept of the ens realissimum; cf. also Kant, Critique of Pure Reason, B 624 ff. Hegel may be using "most real essence" as analogous to "most perfect essence" (ens perfectissimum), which was more predominant in the tradition to which he is referring. See Descartes, Meditations, chap. 3; or Wolff, Theologia naturalis, Pars posterior, § 6. The designation of God as ens realissimum as distinguished from ens perfectissimum is found, among other places, in Baumgarten, Metaphysica, §§ 806, 810.

158. [Ed.] See Kant, Critique of Pure Reason, B 626: "'Being' is obviously not a real predicate; that is, it is not a concept of something which could be added to the concept of a thing. It is merely the positing of a thing, or of certain determinations, as existing in themselves."

159. [Ed.] See Kant, Critique of Pure Reason, B 627: "A hundred real thalers do not contain the least coin more than a hundred possible thalers. For as the latter signify the concept, and the former the object and the positing of the object, should the former contain more than the latter, my concept would not, in that case, express

whether I represent the determinateness to myself or have the money in my pocket. Using the hundred-dollar example we can also restate plausibly the objection to the first Anselmian form of the argument, according to which being is supposed to follow from the concept in general, namely the objection that concept and being are distinct from one another, that each is on its own account, and that being must be introduced from without or from elsewhere because it does not lie within the concept. The concept of a hundred dollars has no bearing whatever on the existence of the money. This is therefore the criticism directed against the ontological proof; it is what has counted as valid until now. Thus the main issue is whether being lies within the concept and may be deduced from it.

To these objections there is the following rejoinder. In ordinary life we do indeed call a representation of a hundred dollars a concept. It is no concept, however, but only a content-determination of my consciousness; an abstract sensible representation such as "blue," or a determinacy of the understanding that is within my head, can of course lack being. This sort of thing, however, is not to be called a concept. We must take the concept as such, we must take the absolute concept in its consummate form or the concept in and for itself, the concept of God—and this concept contains being as a determinacy.

The concept is what is alive, is what mediates itself with itself; one of its determinations is also being. This can be shown very easily in two ways. First, as far as the concept is concerned, it is immediately this universal that determines and particularizes itself—it is this activity of dividing, of particularizing and determining itself, of positing a finitude, negating this its own finitude and being identical with itself through the negation of this finitude. This is the concept as such, the concept of God, the absolute concept;

---

the whole object, and would not therefore be an adequate concept of it. My financial position is, however, affected very differently by a hundred real thalers than it is by the mere concept of them (that is, of their possibility). For the object, as it actually exists, is not analytically contained in my concept, but is added to my concept (which is a determination of my state) synthetically; and yet the conceived hundred thalers are not themselves in the least increased through thus acquiring existence outside my concept."

this is just what God is. As spirit or as love, God is this self-particularizing. God creates the world and produces his Son, posits an other to himself and in this other has himself, | is identical with 326 himself. This is the case in the concept as such, and even more so in the idea: through the negation of the particularizing (for which particularizing the concept itself is equally the positing activity) the concept [comes] to be identical with itself or to relate itself to itself.

If we further inquire what being is—this attribute, determinacy, or reality that we are under such necessity to know as united with the idea of God—then we must reply as follows. "Being is nothing more than the inexpressible or the conceptless; it is not the concrete, which the concept is, but is wholly and only the abstraction of relation to self." Whatever is, is; it relates itself to itself. We can say that it is *immediacy*. Being is the immediate as such, and conversely, the immediate is being and is in relation to self—which means that mediation is negated. This definition of "relation to self" or "immediacy" is now directly explicit in the concept in general, and in the absolute concept or in the concept of God; it is the wholly abstract and most meager definition that God is relation to self. This abstract relation to self lies directly within the concept itself, and logic begins with it. [160]To that extent being is different from the concept, because it is not the entire concept but is only one of its determinations, only this simplicity of the concept (the fact that it is by itself, or is identity with self, relation merely to self). This is the simple insight, that being is within the concept. Thoughtlessness concerning being prevails to the point that it is asserted that being is not within the concept. It is indeed different from the concept, but only as a determination of the concept. Thus this determination is immediately within the concept. "Concept" must not be exchanged for "representation" as we do in ordinary life.

[161]The other {way of proving that the concept of God involves

160. *Precedes in L (1827?):* One must directly have this simple insight.

161. *Precedes in L (1827?) (similar in W):* Being is therefore this determination found within the concept, but different from the concept because the concept is the whole, whereas being is only one determination.

being] would be as follows. We have said that the concept contains this determination in itself; it is *one* of the concept's determinations. But being is also different from the concept because the concept is the totality. Insofar as they differ, mediation also belongs to their union, | for they are not immediately identical. All immediacy is true and actual only insofar as it is inwardly mediation, and, vice versa, all mediation is true only insofar as it is inwardly immediacy or has relation to itself. The concept is different from being, and the difference is of the kind where the concept is what sublates the difference.

327

The concept is this totality, the movement or process of self-objectifying. The concept merely as such, as distinct from being, is something merely subjective; that is a deficiency.[162]

To grasp the movement of the concept as activity is a task that clearly belongs to logic. Still we can at least make it palpable. First we must cease thinking of the concept as such as something that we only have or form within ourselves. The concept is the purpose of an object, the soul of the living thing. What we call soul is the concept, and in spirit and consciousness the concept as such comes to existence as free concept, or in its subjectivity—as distinct from its reality in itself. The sun or an animal only *is* the concept but does not *have* the concept. The concept does not become objective for them. There is not this separation [of being and having] in the sun or in the animal; but in consciousness there is what is called the "I," the existing concept, the concept in its subjective actuality, and I, this concept, am the subjective. But no human being is satisfied with a bare selfhood; the I is *active,* and this activity is a self-objectifying, the giving of actuality and determinate being to oneself. In its further and more concrete determination this activity of the concept (already in the animal and then also in the I or in spirit) is what we call a *drive.* Every satisfaction of a drive is for the I this

162. *L (1827?) adds (similar in W):* The concept is, however, the deepest and the highest thing; it is the nature of every concept to sublate its deficiency, its subjectivity, this difference from being; it is itself the action of bringing itself forth as having being objectively.

process of sublating subjectivity, and thus positing its subjective or inner being as something likewise external, objective, and real; it is the process of bringing forth the unity of what is only subjective with the objective, of stripping away this one-sidedness from both of them. When I have a drive, that is a condition of deficiency, something subjective. The satisfaction of the drive procures for me my feeling of self. If I am merely in a state of longing | or striving, then I am nothing actual. The striving must come into existence. All the action in the world is a sublating of the subjective and a positing of the objective, and so is the production of the unity of both. There is nothing else of which everything is so illustrative as the sublating of the opposite, and the bringing forth of the unity of the subjective and the objective. To posit itself not only subjectively but also objectively, or even neither subjectively nor objectively—that is what the concept is. Hence on the one hand the concept has in itself this impoverished, abstract determination of being. But inasmuch as it is differentiated—and because it is living it must be differentiated—the concept is just what, as living thing, negates the subjective and posits it objectively.

328

This, then, is what ought to be called the critique. Anselm's thought is thus a necessary and true thought according to its content; but, as with the preceding modes of mediation, the form of the deductive proof undoubtedly has a deficiency. It presupposes the pure concept, the concept in and for itself, the concept of God, but it also presupposes that this concept at the same time *is,* that it has being. The unity of concept and being is a presupposition, and the deficiency consists in the very fact that it is a mere presupposition, ˉwhich is not proved but only adopted immediately.ˉ163 If we compare this content with that of faith or immediate knowledge, what faith means is that God is a fact of our consciousness,164 that I have a representation of God and the being of God is bound up with it. What is declared, therefore, is that being, too, is insep-

163. *Thus Hu; W (Var) reads:* —the presupposition that the pure concept, the concept in and for itself, the concept of God, *is,* that it contains being, too.
164. [*Ed.*] See above, n. 94.

187

arably conjoined with the representation of God. In the case of the concept, being is not supposed to be a mere *esse in idea* [being in thought] but also an *esse in re* [being in fact]. It is thus the same content as Anselm's presupposition. To presuppose means to accept something immediately as primary and unproved. It is the same with faith. ¯As the saying goes, "we know it immediately, we believe in it."¯[165] Therefore since Anselm's day we have come no further in any respect. But, as we said, the defective feature is the fact that this is a presupposition and therefore something immediate, and so one does not recognize | the necessity of this unity. The presupposition is now ubiquitous, even in Spinoza, for he defines God or the absolute cause in no other way. He says that substance is that which cannot be thought without existence [*Existenz*], the concept of which includes existence within itself[166]—in other words, that the representation of God is immediately conjoined with the being [of God]. That is what Anselm said and what is said in the faith of the present day.

329

Spinoza says that substance includes being within itself. This inseparability of concept and being is only absolutely the case with God. The finitude of things consists in the fact that the concept (and the definition of the concept) and its being according to its definition are different. The finite is that which does not correspond to its concept, or rather to *the* concept. [167]We say that human beings are mortal. We even express that mortality as the ability of body and soul to separate, for body is finite whereas soul is the concept. Here there is separation, but only inseparability is present in the pure concept. We have said that every drive is an example of the concept that realizes itself. By the drive of spirit or of the living thing we must understand not only the formal aspect, but also

165. *Thus B; W₂ (Var) reads:* If we say "we believe that, we know it immediately," this unity of representation and being is expressed as a presupposition just as much as it is by Anselm.

166. [*Ed.*] See Spinoza, *Ethics,* Part I, Prop. VII (*Chief Works* 2:48).

167. *Precedes in L (1827?) (similar in W):* We have the concept of soul. Its reality or being is corporeality. W₁ *(Var) adds before this sentence:* Moreover, the [following] ordinary rejoinder has been made to Anselm.

188

together with it the content of the drive. The satisfied drive is in any case infinite according to its form; but the drive has a content according to which it is finite and limited, and so it does not correspond to the concept, to the pure concept.[168] |

330

C. THE CULTUS[169]

[170]In the second topic that we have dealt with—the *knowledge of God*—I have God as my object and am engrossed therein; the object alone is before me and is a certainty to me, and to that extent alone I know it. Of course I also know the finite from which I set out; but I have passed over from its negation to the knowledge of the truth, the knowledge of God. I have raised myself into this spiritual domain and set myself upon the spiritual soil that is God or the divine. This relationship is therefore *theoretical*; it still lacks the *practical* element, which comes to expression in the cultus.

168. L (1827?) adds (similar in W): This is the explication of the standpoint of the knowledge of the concept. What we have considered finally is the knowledge or certainty of God in general. Its principal characteristic is as follows. If we know an object, then the object is before us and we are immediately related to it. But this immediacy contains mediation—what we have called elevation to God, in that the human spirit deems the finite to be worthless. By way of this negation the human spirit raises itself up to God and joins itself together with God. This conclusion, "I know that God is," or this simple connection, arose through that negation.

After inserting materials from 1824 and MiscP, L appends a passage that purports to be from the 1827 lectures: The first [moment] that we have dealt with was the realm of religion in general, and the second was the knowledge of God. The third, which we have yet to consider, is that negative moment as it occurs in religion, the moment that we call the cultus.

169. In B's margin: 14 June 1827

[Ed.] The heading is found in B, An. In this section Hegel gathers together material found in Sec. A of the Ms. and Sec. B.3 of the 1824 lectures, giving it a systematic organization not hitherto achieved. The 1824 "Cultus" treats certain preliminary matters—the question of faith and its grounds, the issue of pantheism—and provides a detailed survey of the various developmental forms that cultic practice assumes in the history of religions, but it does not offer an analysis of the religious cultus in its essential forms, as the 1827 lectures do.

170. Precedes in L (1827?): What the cultus is we find already contained in what we have considered in the concept of religion generally.

189

In the theoretical relationship I am immersed in my object and know nothing of myself.[171] But this knowledge, this connection without relationship, is not the whole of what is in fact present. I stand over against the object with which I am filled. That I am and that I have an object is a reflection upon consciousness; I consider my knowledge of the object: thus I am, and the object is. Thus, inasmuch as I have this reflection—I and the object—there are two elements, and these two are different. In intuition or in the theoretical relationship there is only one object with which I am filled; I know nothing of myself. The true, however, is the relationship of myself and this object.

At this point the practical relationship commences, in which I exist on my own account, I stand over against the object, and I now have to bring forth my own union with it. I have not only to know the object, to be filled, but to *know myself* as filled by this object, to know it as within me and likewise myself as within this object that is the truth—and so to know myself in the truth. To bring forth this unity is *action*, or the aspect of the cultus. This parting of subjectivity and objectivity has its proper beginning first in the practical relationship, in the will; | for in the theoretical domain I am filled by the object.[172] Only here, in the will or in the practical domain, do I exist on my own account, am I free, and related to myself as subject; only now do I stand over against the object. To that extent, limitation first begins within the practical domain, not within the theoretical relationship. It is said that there is unlimitedness in will, that only in knowledge am I limited. But the latter can properly be said of will. In willing I exist for myself; other objects stand over against me and so they are my limit. The will has an end and moves toward this end; it is the activity of sublating this finitude, this contradiction, the fact that this object is a limit for me. In the practical determination there is finitude

171. *L (1827?) adds:* The conclusion of the knowledge of God is an immediate relation. It is also this way with more mundane examples. For instance, I know this paper. In this knowing I am filled by the representation of the paper and in this context know nothing of my own self.

172. *L (1827?) adds:* and do not posit myself over against it. To the extent that I know the object, it is and I am not.

because I exist on my own account as will or subject, and there is another object to which I am directed. Insofar as I act, I have the need to assimilate this object to myself, to sublate my finitude in relation to it, to reinstate my feeling of self. In the state of need I am limited, and the lack appears as the fact that for me the object appears as external.

In the practical domain, therefore, we have an other as object. In religion this object is God, whom we know. Inasmuch as human beings look back upon themselves, this object is an other for them, something lying beyond them. In the theoretical domain they do not reflect upon this antithesis; what is there is this immediate unity, immediate knowledge, faith. In the theoretical domain they include themselves with this object; that is how we can express theoretical consciousness according to its result or its conclusion. In the cultus, on the contrary, God is on one side, I am on the other, and the determination is *the including, within my own self, of myself with God,* the knowing of myself within God and of God within me.[173]

The cultus involves giving oneself this supreme, absolute enjoyment.[174] There is feeling within it; I take part in it with my particular, subjective personality, | knowing myself as this individual included   332
in and with God, knowing myself within the truth (and I have my truth only in God), i.e., joining myself as myself in God together with myself.

The presupposition in the cultus is that the reconciliation of God with humanity is implicitly and explicitly consummated, that it is not a matter of first having to bring this reconciliation about absolutely; instead it only needs to be produced for me, the particular person, because I am actual in the practical domain as this single individual. Participation in this reconciliation that is implicitly and explicitly accomplished is the action of the cultus. Universally, this

173. L (1827?) *adds (similar in* W): —this concrete unity. For our consideration, theoretical consciousness, too, is concrete consciousness, but only implicitly so; that it should be concrete for the subject also is precisely the practical relationship.

174. [*Ed.*] *Genuss* is the term Hegel uses to describe the communion with deity that is at the center of all cultic activity. At root is the quite physical image of eating and drinking. It also has the connotation of "enjoyment," "pleasure," "gratification."

reconciliation is accomplished; it is the foundation of all religious consciousness.

We have begun with the solid soil of religion, with this substantiality. Implied in it is [the awareness] that God alone is truth, or in a more developed form that God is gracious, has created human beings, etc. The presupposition is that God alone is true actuality, that insofar as I have actuality I have it only in God; since God alone is actuality, I should have my truth and actuality in God. That is the foundation of the cultus.

[175]Today this aspect of the cultus is more or less pushed to one side and no longer stands forth in all its importance; we talk | only of eliciting faith in God within human beings. But it is something outside of religion [altogether], if one wants to elicit it for the first time.[176] We will have occasion later to enlarge upon different forms of this cultus. ˉIn dogmatic theology the traditional chapter *de*

333

---

175. *Precedes in L (1827?):* It is presupposed either that the reconciliation is accomplished, or that it is implicitly and explicitly present from the outset. Thus among the pagans there is the consciousness of their bliss, the consciousness that divinity is near to them, that the gods are friendly to them.

Precedes in W_2 *(MiscP):* And so, too, if today we have only the perpetual urgency of injecting faith into human beings, and we talk only of eliciting misery within them and therewith the faith that God is, then this is not only not the cultus, but this perpetual wishing just to elicit religion for the first time is [something] outside of religion [altogether]. The cultus, on the other hand, exists within religion; and the knowledge that God is, and is [all of] actuality, is in the cultus the soil to which I have only to assimilate myself. Unhappy the age that must content itself with being forever told only that there may be a God!

Since the cultus, on the contrary, presupposes the being-in-and-for-self of the ultimate goal of the world, but on this presupposition is aligned in opposition to empirical self-consciousness and its particular interests, [W_2 *(1831) continues (similar in* W_1*):*] a world of absolute finitude has not yet set up an absolute infinity over against itself. Thus, among the pagans the consciousness of their bliss prevails, the consciousness that God is near to them as the God of the people and the city, this feeling that the gods are friendly to them and grant them the enjoyment of what is best. If in this way Athena is known by the Athenians as their divine power, they know themselves thus as originally at one with it, and they know the divinity as the spiritual power of their people itself.

176. *L (1827?) adds:* However, the cultus exists only within religion; it is within the cultus itself that God is, and that God is the true actuality, namely this ground. What is elicited by means of the cultus is what was formerly called the *unio mystica*, this feeling, this gratification [*rejoins main text 3d sentence below*]

unione mystica deals with this cultus."[177] As a whole the mystical is everything speculative, or whatever is concealed from the understanding. Feeling—the gratification that I am with God in his grace and that God's spirit is alive within me, the consciousness of my union and reconciliation with God—this is the innermost feature of the cultus.

The first form of the cultus is what is called *devotion* in general. "Devotion is not the mere faith that God is, but is present when the faith becomes vivid, when the subject prays and is occupied with this content not merely in objective fashion but becomes immersed therein; the essential thing here is the fire and heat of devotion. The subject takes part in this way; it is subjectivity that possesses itself therein, that prays, speaks, passes through [and beyond] representations, knows itself and the object itself, and is concerned with its elevation. Devotion is the self-moving spirit, holding to itself in this movement, for this object. This inwardness is devotion in general."[178]

To the cultus belong, in the second place, the external forms through which the feeling of reconciliation is brought forth in an external and sensible manner, | as for instance the fact that in the   334 *sacraments* reconciliation is brought into feeling, into the here and now of present and sensible consciousness; and [further] all the manifold actions embraced under the heading of *sacrifice*. That very negation, about which our insight (in the case of theoretical consciousness) was that the subject rises above the finite and consciousness of the finite, is now consciously accomplished in the cultus, for here the subject is concerned chiefly with itself.

In the ardor and liveliness of devotion there is indeed a removal of representations—this energy and forcefulness of holding oneself

177. *Thus Hu; L (Var) reads:* In dogmatics we had a *unio mystica*. There is [now] a great aversion to the mystical.

178. *Thus L; W₂ (MiscP) reads:* When the subject, in the fire and the heat of devotion, becomes immersed in the object, it does indeed take part itself; the subject is the very one that possesses itself in this devout enterprise, the one that prays there, speaks, passes through [and beyond] representations, is concerned with its own elevation. But in devotion the subject does not maintain itself in its particularity, but only in its movement within the object and only as this self-moving spirit.

firmly and in active manner within the truth, in opposition to the consciousness with its former interests. Negation exists within devotion and even maintains an outward configuration by means of sacrifice. The subject renounces something or negates something in relation to itself. It has possessions and divests itself of them in order to demonstrate that it is in earnest. On the one hand this negation is accomplished in a more intensive fashion only through the sacrificing or burning of something—even through human sacrifice; on the other hand the sensible enjoyment [of the sacrifice], for instance the eating and drinking, is itself the negation of external things. Thus from this negation or from the sacrifice one advances to enjoyment, to consciousness of having posited oneself in unity with God by means of it. The sensible enjoyment is linked directly with what is higher, with consciousness of the linkage with God.

The third and highest form within the cultus is when one lays aside one's own subjectivity—not only practices renunciation in external things such as possessions, but offers one's heart or inmost self to God and senses *remorse* and *repentance* in this inmost self; then one is conscious of one's own immediate natural state (which subsists in the passions and intentions of particularity), so that one dismisses these things, purifies one's heart, and through this purification of one's heart raises oneself up to the realm of the purely spiritual. This experience of nothingness can be a bare condition or single experience, or it can be thoroughly elaborated [in one's life]. If heart and will are earnestly and thoroughly cultivated for the universal and the true, then there is present what appears as *ethical life*. To that extent ethical life is the most genuine cultus.[179] But consciousness of the true, of the divine, of God, must be directly bound up with it.

To this extent philosophy [too] is a continual cultus; it has as its object the true, and the true in its highest shape | as absolute spirit, as God. To know this true not only in its simple form as God, but also to know the rational in God's works—as produced by God and endowed with reason—that is philosophy. It is part of

335

179. [*Ed.*] Hegel expands on this point in the 1831 lectures; see unabridged ed., Vol. 1:451 ff.

knowing the true that one should dismiss one's subjectivity, the subjective fancies of personal vanity, and concern oneself with the true purely in thought, conducting oneself solely in accordance with objective thought. This negation of one's specific subjectivity is an essential and necessary moment.[180] |

336

180. *In* W$_2$, *and also in shorter form in* W$_1$, *the following material from the 1831 lectures, which serves as a transition to the treatment of the cultus, is associated with text from the 1824 lectures:* The "I," this empirical existence [*Existenz*] from which essence is of course still distinct, is that which is without essence.

Subjective consciousness itself, however, is a limited, determinate consciousness: i.e., particular spirit. For this particular spirit, for spirit with determinacy, truth, too, exists only in this determinate mode. The way in which subjective spirit is constituted is also the way in which there is objective truth for it.

Consciousness and knowledge themselves, however, lie within God. There is one content, and inseparable from it is the form that consists in this content being the object of consciousness. With consciousness we are in the domain of *particular spirit*, and faith adapts itself to the developmental stages of the spirit and determines itself to another content. Thus it is quite right to talk already to a child about God, its creator, and thereby the child comes to have a representation of God, of a higher being; this higher being is grasped by consciousness in the early years, although only in a limited way, and a foundation of this kind gradually develops further. The *one spirit* is in principle the substantial foundation; this is the spirit of a people in the way it is determined within the individual periods of world history—the *national spirit*. This national spirit constitutes the *substantial foundation* within the individual, for all of us are born within our own people and belong to its spirit. This spirit is what is substantial in general, and is by nature, as it were, what is identical; it is the absolute ground of faith. By this standard it is determined what counts as truth. In this way the substantial element exists for itself as against the individuals; it is their [sovereign] power in its connection with them as individuals, and within this relationship to them it is their absolute authority. As belonging to the spirit of their people, all individuals are thus born into the faith of their forefathers without either being responsible for it or deserving it, and the faith of their forefathers is something holy for them, and is their authority. This constitutes the ground of faith that is given by historical development.

There arises here the question of how a religion is grounded, i.e., in what way the substantial spirit comes to the consciousness of peoples. This is a historical matter; its beginnings are inconspicuous. Those who know how to express this spirit are the prophets and the poets. Herodotus [*Histories* 2.53] says that Homer and Hesiod made the gods of the Greeks for them. On this view Homer and Hesiod have an authority, but that is only because their declarations were in conformity with the Greek spirit. Still earlier beginnings, which were the first glimmer of the divine, preceded even these poets; for we cannot say that the cultural formation as it appears in Homer had been there from the beginning. Awe in the presence of the

"Stated in a cursory way, religion is our relation to God. We have said that this relation is found in thinking. God is for thought because God is the universal in and for itself. The primal division 337 [or judgment] of this implicit and explicit | universal, or the creation, is self-particularizing, the differentiating of the particular spirit over

---

supersensible expressed itself initially in a manner still unrefined. Fear is the beginning, and in order to banish it and to ingratiate themselves with that supersensible power, people employed magical charms and prayed in hymns. In this way consciousness developed little by little, and the few who (at that stage) know what the divine is, are the patriarchs and the priests; or there can even be a caste or a particular family marked out just for the supervision of teaching and worship. Every individual is accustomed to live within these representations and sensations, and so a spiritual contagion spreads among the people; education plays its part, so that the individuals dwell within the atmosphere of their people. Thus the children, suitably attired and adorned, go along to worship; they share in the rites or have their own role to play in them; in any event they learn the prayers and attend to the representations of the community and of the people, taking their own place within these contexts and accepting them in the same immediate way in which standardized styles of dress and the manners of everyday life are transmitted.

This is natural authority, but its power is greatest in the spiritual realm. However much pride individuals may take in their independence, they cannot fly above this spirit, for it is the substantial, it is their very own spirituality itself.

At first this authority is quite constrained and stands fast immediately in the people, without any prohibition of an opposing position. In that situation the single individuals are neither free nor unfree, for no antithesis of reflection or of subjective thought is present at all. We say "the people believed this"; but they themselves do not call it "believing," insofar as this term implies consciousness of an antithesis [to this faith].

There are, however, different forms of faith and different religions that can come into collision with one another. While this encounter *can* occur upon the soil of representation and reflection, and advocacy may be supported by reasons and proofs for the truth, it can also take the form of one people compelling others to acquiesce in its faith. In the latter case faith becomes a compulsory state authority, both within the inner life of the state itself on the one hand, and in its foreign affairs on the other. This collision has precipitated countless wars. Into this category, for instance, fall the wars of the Muslims, and the religious wars between Catholics and Protestants as well as the Inquisition; and further the battles between the devotees of Shiva and those of Vishnu, among the Indians. Such conflicts are fought for the glory of God, so that God will be acknowledged in consciousness and the truth of the people will meet with recognition. Freedom of faith in general rises up against compulsion of this kind; but this freedom can then also assume more sharply the attitude of standing above the different contents that are asserted as the truth. So, in a formal sense this is what freedom of faith as such is; while *what* is believed should remain irrelevant. This is then the formal requirement of freedom, which looks not to the truth of faith and relates only to subjective freedom; the content

against the absolute spirit. The first relationship that we considered was that of knowledge, the theoretical | relationship. The second 338 is the practical relationship or the knowledge of this elevation (and the elevation is itself knowledge). The third moment is the knowing of this knowing. That is actual religion.⌐[181]

---

may be of whatever stripe one pleases. This is where the distinction arises between the inner self or the locus of conscience in which I am by myself, and the essential content. The inner self is the holy place, the locus of my freedom, which ought to be respected; this is an essential demand that human beings make insofar as the consciousness of freedom is awakened within them. The ground here is no longer the substantial content of faith but its formal aspect.

When we consider the matter in the perspective of abstract thinking, however, freedom of faith appears at once as a contradiction in itself, for in the very act of believing one accepts something given, something already present; whereas freedom demands that this given should be posited or produced by me. But in that requirement of freedom, belief is in fact grasped as my personal faith, as my own most special and inmost certainty. My faith has its source and its locus in this certainty of my self, in my conviction, and I am free on my own account as against others, let the type of my faith itself be what it will; in other words, the definite grounds, reflections, and feelings upon which it is built are irrelevant here. Faith is of course still not free in itself in regard to the content, and it is only thought that seeks to be free with regard to the content, too.

Here then, where freedom relates also to the content, is where the breach between thought and faith arises, the breach that we see already in Greece at the time of Socrates. Thought is a new relation over against faith. The aspect of form comes into relation specifically as opposed to the substantial aspect of truth. This principle is present in the Christian religion from its outset; Christianity does, indeed, begin on the one hand from an external history that is believed; but at the same time this history has the significance of being the explication of God's nature. In accordance with the distinction that arises here at once, Christ is not only a human being who has undergone this fate, but is also the Son of God. So the *explication* of the story of Christ is its more profound aspect; this explication took place in thought and brought forth dogmatics, the church's doctrine. With it goes the requirement of inwardness or of thought. The breach between thought and faith develops further as a result. Thought knows itself to be free not only according to its form but also with regard to its content. Freedom is not, however, without authority in thought; thought has certain principles, which are of course its own and to which it reduces everything, though these principles belong to the development itself. An age has certain principles, and to that extent there is also authority present within it. The ultimate analysis, in which there are no longer any assumed principles, arrives only in the advance to philosophy.

181. *Thus L; Hu reads:* These are the three moments of the concept of religion. *An reads:* Elevation to God is knowledge; knowing of this knowing is for the first time true religion.

PART II
DETERMINATE RELIGION

THE LECTURES OF 1827

Introduction[2]

[3]Here belong the particular religions or determinate religions, religion in its determinateness; for there are determinate, particular, | and   412

    1. *B, Hu, An read:* Religion in its Determinacy

    2. [*Ed.*] The introduction to the 1827 lectures reestablishes the threefold division of *Determinate Religion* inherited from the *Ms.* but modified in 1824 into a twofold structure. The summary provided in the introduction is similar to that found in 1824, which is not surprising since Hegel made use of Griesheim's transcript of the 1824 lectures when lecturing in 1827. In fact, the introduction to the 1824 lectures also anticipated a threefold structure. The 1827 introduction anticipates certain changes that are more fully developed in 1831, e.g., the two senses of "natural religion" as meaning both primitive religion (the religion of immediacy) and rational religion (see n. 8), and the recognition that in the higher of the so-called nature religions (Buddhism, Hinduism, Persian and Egyptian religion) there is already an elevation of thought above merely natural powers, hence an implicit cleavage of consciousness (in 1831 this leads to the treatment of these religions under entirely different categories from that of "nature religion"). With respect to the second main stage, the elevation of the spiritual above the natural, the introduction does not anticipate the reversal of order in which Greek and Jewish religion are in fact treated in 1827 (see below, nn. 18, 347). It suggests, in line with 1824, that the sequence is from particular (Jewish) to plural (Greek) to universal (Roman). Thus it is evident that, just as in 1824, so also in 1827 the initial plan was altered as Hegel proceeded with the detailed treatment. Finally, the distinctiveness of Roman religion from Greek and Jewish is reaffirmed: it cannot be subsumed under the general category of the "religions of spiritual individuality." While providing a transition to Christianity, it does so only in a negative sense: it is universal and purposive but also utterly finite, external, and utilitarian. It is scarcely a religion of freedom and spirit.

    3. *W contains the following introduction to the 1831 lectures:* When we speak of determinate religion, it is implied, in the first place, that religion generally is taken as genus and the determinate religions as species. From one point of view this relationship of genus to species is quite legitimate, as when we pass over from the

universal to the particular in other sciences. But in that case the particular is understood only in an empirical manner; it is a matter of experience that this or that animal, this or that right exists. In philosophical science it is not permissible to proceed in this fashion: the particular cannot just be added to the universal; on the contrary, the universal itself definitely resolves itself into the particular. The concept divides itself; it produces an original determination from out of itself. In all cases of determinateness, determinate being and connectedness with an other are directly posited. What is determinate is for an other, and what is indeterminate is not there at all. That for which religion is, its determinate being, is consciousness. Religion has its reality as consciousness. What is to be understood by the realization of the concept is this: that the content is determined by its being for consciousness and being in a certain way. Our procedure is as follows: We began by considering the concept of religion, what religion implicitly is; that is what it is for us, as we have seen it; it is quite another matter [W_1: how it comes to consciousness. W_2: for it to bring itself to consciousness.] . . . Only in the true religion does what it is in and for itself, what its concept is, become known; for actual religion is concordant with the concept. We now have to consider the course by which genuine religion comes about. Religion is still not *a* religion in its concept either—for it is essentially present as such only in consciousness. This is the sense of what we are here considering, the self-realizing of the concept. How realization occurs has already been indicated in a general way: the concept is, as it were, a potentiality within spirit, it constitutes the innermost truth, but spirit must attain to the knowledge of this truth. Only then does genuine religion become actual. It can be said of all religions that they are religions, [W_1: but if they are still limited W_2: and correspond to the concept of religion; but at the same time, in that they are still limited,] they do not correspond to the concept. And yet they must contain it, or else they would not be religions. But the concept is present in them in different ways. At first they contain it only implicitly. These [W_2: determinate] religions are only particular moments of the concept, and for this very reason they do not correspond to the concept, for it is not actual within them. Thus, while humanity is, of course, implicitly free, Africans and Asiatics are not, because they have not the consciousness of what constitutes the concept of humanity. Religion is now to be considered in its determinacy. The highest that is or can be attained is for the determinacy itself to be the concept; for in that case the barrier is sublated and religious consciousness is not distinguished from the concept—this is the idea, the perfectly realized concept, but we can discuss that only when we reach the concluding division of our subject.

To educe the concept of religion and make it the object of consciousness has been the labor of spirit over thousands of years. The way this labor has been performed is that immediacy or the natural state formed the starting point; and this had then to be overcome. Immediacy is what is natural, but consciousness is elevation above nature. Natural consciousness is sensuous consciousness, just as the natural will is desire, the individual that wills itself in accordance with its natural state and particularity—sensuous knowing and sensuous willing. Religion, however, is the relationship of spirit to spirit, spirit's knowledge of [W_2: spirit in] its truth, not in its immediacy or its natural state. Religion becomes determinate as it advances from the natural state to the concept. Initially the concept is only the inward element, the implicit potential of consciousness, not its expression. Regarding this ambiguity, that the concept originally *is* but that its first existence is not its authentic originality, we shall have something more to say later.

hence finite religions, the *ethnic religions* generally.[4] Up to this point we have spoken generally of God, of consciousness of God and connection with God, of our human knowledge of the divine spirit within ourselves and of ourselves within the divine spirit. [These connections] have been referred to only as indefinite representations, but we want to have them [as definite] in our consciousness. (The third division is the absolute religion, the fulfilled concept of religion, religion worked out in its fullness.) It is in determinate religion that determinations first enter into that universal essence; this is where cognition of God begins. By means of | thoroughgoing determination, 413 the thought of God first comes to be the concept.

Even as the content, God, determines itself, so on the other side the subjective human spirit that has this knowledge determines itself too. The principle by which God is defined for human beings is also the principle for how humanity defines itself inwardly, or for humanity in its own spirit. An inferior god or a nature god has inferior, natural and unfree human beings as its correlates; the pure concept of God or the spiritual God has as its correlate spirit that is free and spiritual, that actually knows God. In determinate religion, spirit is determinate both as absolute spirit or object and as the subjective spirit that has its essence or absoluteness as its object. Here both sides first achieve their determinateness.

[5]In determinate religion as such, in finite religion, | we have 414 before us only subordinate determinations of spirit or of religion;

4. *L (1827?) adds:* (The third division is the absolute religion, the fulfilled concept of religion, religion educed in its fullness.)

5. *W₂ (1831) reads (parallel in main text follows):* Hence the sphere we have to deal with first contains the determinate religion that does not yet emerge from determinacy so far as its content is concerned. A fully achieved freedom is not involved in the activity of emerging from immediacy, but only a process of breaking free, which is still entangled in that from which it is freeing itself.

The first step here is to consider the form of natural, immediate religion. In this first, natural religion, consciousness is still natural, i.e., sensuously desirous consciousness. Hence it is immediate. As yet there is here no inward cleavage of consciousness, for a cleavage of that kind has the characteristic that consciousness distinguishes its sensuous nature from what is essential, so that the natural is known only as mediated through those aspects that are essential. This is where religion can first originate.

In connection with this exaltation to the essential, we have to consider the concept of this exaltation generally. Here the object is defined with certainty, and this *true* object, from which consciousness distinguishes itself, is God. This exaltation is the

we do not yet have the religion of absolute truth. But the progression [of finite religions] is a condition for the arrival of religion at its absolute truth, for spirit's coming to be for spirit, for the relationship of spirit to spirit, a condition for the attainment by spirit itself

415   of its truly infinite determinateness. | These determinate religions

---

same one that occurs in a more abstract way in the proofs of the existence of God. In all of these proofs there is the very same exaltation; it is only the starting point and the nature of this essence that differ. But this elevation to God, however it may be defined, is only the one side. The other is the converse: God, defined thus and so, enters into relation with the subject that has thus elevated itself. At this point then arises the question of how the subject is defined; but this is known just in the way that God is defined.

It is also necessary to adduce the subject's conscious turning toward this essence, and this brings in the aspect of the cultus, the subject's uniting with its essence.

The division [of the subject matter] is therefore as follows.

1. Natural religion is unity of the spiritual and natural, and God is here comprehended in this unity that is still natural. Humanity in its immediacy is just sensuous, natural knowing and natural willing. Insofar as the moment of religion is involved in this, and the moment of elevation is still shut up within the natural state, there is something there that has nonetheless to be regarded as higher than anything merely immediate. This is magic.

2. Second, there is the cleavage of consciousness within itself, so that it knows itself as merely natural and distinguishes the genuine or the essential from this. Within the essential [being] this natural state, this finitude, is of no value and is known to be such. In natural religion spirit still lives in neutrality with nature, but God is now defined as the absolute power and substance, within which the natural will, the subject, is only something transient, an accident, something lacking selfhood, devoid of freedom. The highest merit of humanity here is to know itself as something null.

But initially this elevation of spirit above the natural realm is not yet carried through in a consistent manner. On the contrary, there is still present a fearful inconsistency, as a result of which the different spiritual and natural powers are all mixed up with one another. This still inwardly inconsistent elevation has its historical existence in the three Oriental religions of substance.[a]

3. But the confusion of the natural and the spiritual leads to the struggle of subjectivity, which seeks to establish itself in its unity and universality. This struggle has also had its historical existence in three religions, which form the religions of the transition to the stage of free subjectivity.[b] But since spirit has not yet completely subjected the natural to itself in these stages, any more than in the preceding ones, they constitute, together with the preceding ones, the sphere of

A. Nature Religion.

Set against this is the second stage of determinate religion, at which the elevation of spirit is carried through consistently vis-à-vis the natural realm, i.e.,

B. The Religion of Spiritual Individuality, or Free Subjectivity.[c]

[Ed.] [a]By the "three Oriental religions of substance" Hegel means in the 1831 lectures Chinese religion, Hinduism, and Buddhism/Lamaism. Cf. the 1831 passage

are definite stages[6] of the consciousness and knowledge of spirit. They are necessary conditions for the emergence of the true religion, for the authentic consciousness of spirit. For this reason too, they are extant historically, and I will even draw attention to the historical mode in which they have existed, for we come to know them in these particular forms as historical religions. In the true science, in a science of spirit, in a science whose object is human being, the development of the concept of this concrete object is also its outward history and has existed in actuality. Thus these shapes of religion have also existed successively in time and coexisted in space. We shall now discuss their general classification.‾

Of necessity the *first* form of religion is immediate religion, what we can also call *nature religion*. In the modern period this term "nature religion" or "natural religion" has for some time had a different sense; we have understood it to mean what human beings‾are supposed to be able to cognize‾[7] through their reason, through the natural light of their reason.[8]

---

transmitted by W_2 in n. 49 below. The W_2 and Strauss texts corroborate each other.
ᵇBy the "three religions of transition" Hegel means in the 1831 lectures the religion of the good (Persian and Jewish), the religion of anguish (Phoenician), and the religion of ferment (Egyptian). Here again the materials in W_2 (n. 266) and the Strauss text confirm each other. ᶜThe concluding outline, beginning with the words "But since spirit," has been editorially revised. It confuses the design of the 1831 lectures with that of 1824. According to Strauss, the "religions of transition" are not included under nature religion, which is confined to magic, but follow the "three Oriental religions of substance," forming the beginning of the third stage of *Determinate Religion,* the "religion of freedom." The only lectures in which Hegel refers to the "religions of spiritual individuality" are those of 1824.

6. *In B's margin:* 15 June 1827

7. *W (Var) reads:* can educe and cognize of God

8. [*Ed.*] The concept of the natural light of reason can be traced back through the Enlightenment, Descartes, Francis Bacon, and Thomas Aquinas to Cicero; see his *Tusculanae disputationes* 3.1. The concept of "natural religion" was widespread among thinkers of the Enlightenment, e.g., Leibniz, *Theodicy* (1734), ed. A. Farrar, trans. E. M. Huggard (New Haven, 1952), p. 51 (*Philosophische Schriften,* ed. C. J. Gerhardt, 7 vols. [Berlin, 1875–1890], 6:26–27); and Christian Wolff, *Theologia naturalis,* Pars posterior, 2d ed. (Frankfurt and Leipzig, 1741), p. 497 (§ 512), and *Philosophia moralis,* Pars tertia (Halle, 1751), chap. 9, pp. 731 ff. While Leibniz made natural religion clearly subordinate to revealed religion, Wolff already placed the two on an equal level. Hegel's criticism of the concept of natural religion could have been prompted by Hume's *Dialogues Concerning Natural Religion* (London, 1779), with which he was probably familiar, although this cannot be confirmed.

From that point of view natural religion has been opposed to revealed religion, ˉas the religion delivered by reason.ˉ9 "Natural reason" is an erroneous expression. We do indeed speak of the nature of reason, i.e., its concept; but on the whole "the natural" is understood to mean "the immediate," the sensible generally, the uncultivated. Reason then, by contrast, is the not being [of something, and specifically of human nature] in the way that it immediately is to begin with; spirit is precisely this self-elevation above nature, this self-extrication from the natural; not only is it liberation vis-à-vis the natural but the subjection of the natural to itself, making it fit the measure of, and be obedient to, itself. Because of this ambiguity we should avoid the expression "natural | reason" in this modern meaning. The genuine sense of natural reason is "spirit or reason according to the concept." When reason is taken in this sense, however, as what reason or spirit truly is within itself, then there is no antithesis between it and revealed religion. The latter is revelation of God, revelation of the Spirit. We should nevertheless remark here that spirit according to its concept can indeed be set in opposition to revealed religion; but on the other hand ˉrevealed religion is valid onlyˉ10 for spirit, and spirit can reveal itself only to spirit. What spirit is in its essence, or according to its genuine meaning, cannot be revealed to what is devoid of spirit or devoid of reason; on the contrary, for reception through the Spirit to be possible, the receiver must itself be spirit. "Spirit must bear witness to the Spirit," ˉas it is traditionally expressed in religious terms.ˉ11 All religion is natural in the sense that spirit has to bear witness, i.e., it is in conformity with the concept and addresses spirit.

"Natural religion," as the term has been employed in more recent times, has also referred to mere metaphysical religion, where "metaphysics" has had the sense of ˉ"understandable thought."ˉ12

416

9. W_2 *(Var) reads:* and maintains that only what human beings have in their reason can be authentic for them.

10. *Hu reads:* only revealed religion is valid

11. *Thus Hu; L (1827?) reads:* The witness that spirit bears to spirit is the highest witness; all other kinds of attestation or authorization serve merely as a stimulus for the standpoint of consciousness that we have to consider here. Once spirit has attained to its consciousness of self, it has risen above external attestations of the kind that are directed to its phantasy etc.

12. *W (Var) reads:* understandable thoughts, representations of the understanding.

That is the modern religion of the understanding—or what is called "deism," a result of the Enlightenment, the knowledge of God as an abstraction, ˉthe knowledge that God is the father of all humanity.ˉ[13]

The first [stage] for us is nature religion, i.e., religion defined as the unity of the spiritual and the natural, | where the spirit still is   417 in unity with nature. In being this way, spirit is not yet free, is not yet actual as spirit.[14] This placid unity, this neutrality with nature or mingling of the spiritual with the natural, spirit in its wholly immediate mode, is first of all the human individual. Religion begins in the situation where the human being as singular counts as the highest or absolute power; one takes oneself to be an absolute power and is so regarded by others.

The *second* stage of religion is the *elevation of the spiritual above the natural.* This can occur in two ways: on the one hand *in thought,* namely that God is for thought and only for thought, i.e., "God" can be regarded abstractly; on the other hand, that God is present as a *concrete individuality.* But this individuality does not exist in an immediate or natural manner only, and is not a natural essence at all; for on the contrary, the spiritual is the ruling or dominant aspect, although it still has the natural as its reality or outward shape. It is not yet present as pure spirit[15]—as spiritual individuality. In consequence the natural is subordinated to spirit, and at the same time the individuality is this particularized one. It follows at once that there is a multitude of such particularized individualities, which

13. W_2 *reads:* to which all definitions of God—all belief—are reduced. *L, W (1827?) continue:* This cannot, properly speaking, be called natural religion; it is the final, extreme position of the abstract understanding that results from the Kantian critique.
[*Ed.*] A reference to Kant's criticism of all speculative theology in the *Critique of Pure Reason,* trans. N. Kemp Smith (London, 1930), B 659–732, esp. 703.

14. *L (1827?) adds:* God is everywhere the content; but here it is God in the natural unity of the spiritual and the natural. It is the natural mode that characterizes this form of religion in general. It assumes many different shapes, all of which are called nature religion. In nature religion, so we are told, spirit is still identical with nature, consciousness stands united with nature, and to that extent this religion is the religion of unfreedom.

15. *L (1827?) adds:* That first moment, that first form, is the religion of sublimity, the Jewish religion. The other moment is where the spiritual appears as concretely spiritual

are still burdened with natural existence and a natural config-uration.[16]

⌐The *third* form is the *religion of expediency or purposiveness,*⌐[17] where there is posited in God a purpose, or purposes generally, albeit a rather external purpose and not yet a purpose that is purely spiritual, not yet the absolute purpose. This can also be called the

418 religion of fate or destiny, | because the purpose is not yet a free and purely spiritual purpose. One particular purpose is posited in God, and this purpose is then something without any [absolute] reason as compared with other private purposes, because those purposes might be no less justified than this one, which is only another particular purpose too.

So far as the historical development is concerned, nature religion is the religion of the East. The second form of religion, namely that in which the spiritual elevates itself above the natural, is in one aspect the religion of sublimity (that of the Jews) and in the other aspect the religion of beauty (that of the Greeks).[18]

If we speak here of "the elevation of spirit," this must be defined more precisely, for even within nature religion we will find an elevating of thought above mere natural powers, above the dominion of the natural. But this elevation is carried out inconsistently, and it is just this monstrous and terrible inconsistency, in which the

16. *L (1827?) adds:* —this is the religion of beauty, or Greek religion.

17. *L (1827?) reads:* In its gods, singular spirit wills only its own subjective purpose; it wills itself, not the absolute content. So the religion of expediency is that

18. *W₂ (1831) adds:* In the religion of sublimity, the one God is the lord, and the singular subjects behave as his servants. In the religion of beauty too, the subject has purified itself from its merely immediate knowing and willing; but it has also retained its will and knows itself as *free.* It knows itself as free, moreover, because it has completed the negation of its natural will and, as an ethical, free being, has an affirmative relation to God. But the subject has not yet passed through the consciousness and the antithesis of good and evil. Hence it is still contaminated with naturalness. So even if the religion of beauty forms the stage of reconciliation as contrasted with the sphere of sublimity, this reconciliation is still an unmediated one, because it is not yet mediated through consciousness of the antithesis.

[*Ed.*] In the 1827 lectures Hegel actually treats Greek religion (the religion of beauty) first and Jewish religion (the religion of sublimity) second. See below, n. 347. In 1831 the order of 1821 and 1824 is restored, but Jewish and Greek religion are treated under different categories—consciousness of good and evil, and consciousness of reconciliation and freedom, respectively.

differentiated powers, the natural and the spiritual, are blended together, just this mixture of the spiritual and the natural, that is the content of this stage. The second stage is therefore the consistent elevation into self as against the natural, so that the natural is subordinated: on the one hand, as something entirely mastered (in the religion of sublimity); on the other hand, so that it serves only as the outward shape, appearance, ⁻or manifestation of subjectivity.⁻[19]

The third form, the religion of external purposiveness or expediency, is Roman religion, which we certainly have to distinguish from Greek religion | and which constitutes the transition to absolute   419
religion.[20] It is the religion of external purposiveness—external in that although the purpose is essentially posited, the only extant purposes are limited ones, themselves finite and external. These are the three forms of the determinate religions.

A. IMMEDIATE RELIGION, OR NATURE RELIGION

Introduction[21]

a. The Original Condition

Before we consider religion in its characteristic shape, we need to pay attention to a representation that is customary, which our imagination depicts for us, and which moreover is affirmed and treated as valid. It was the view that the first religion was also the true and excellent one, and that all subsequent religions present only

19. *Thus L; Hu reads:* manifestation, or beauty.
20. *In B's margin:* 18 June 1827
21. [*Ed.*] The introduction to Sec. A of the 1827 lectures retains only the discussion of the "original condition" of humanity as represented in religious mythology. The lengthy treatment of the cosmological proof, which occurs here in 1824, is gone, having been assimilated along with the other proofs into the section on "Religious Knowledge as Elevation to God" in Part I. The generic representation of God in nature religion is also removed from the introduction, which concludes with an outline of the four main forms of nature religion. The four differ from 1824 in that the religion of being-within-self (Buddhism, Lamaism) is no longer considered a subcategory of the religion of magic, and the Persian and Egyptian religions are combined under the category of "the religions of transition."

a degenerate state of this religion. Remains, fragments, and indications have survived from the decline of this religion, and these are the foundation of the subsequent religions; these remains are recognizable, and historical cognition of them holds particular interest for us.[22]

This view is believed to be justified partly in and for itself or a priori, and partly in a historical way, a posteriori. If we pursue the history of religion, science, and cognition right back to its origin, we find there traces of truths and cognitions that indicate a yet higher origin and that have preserved themselves in the later states of religion—traces that we are unable to understand in connection with the determinate religions themselves or even with the scientific culture and information of the nations concerned.

The a priori aspect is just the view that we have already mentioned: that human beings were originally created by God and in God's image [Gen. 1:26–27]; that the first human beings were in conformity with their concept; that in the purity of their concept they were good without evil; and, more specifically, that [they lived] knowingly in this unity with God and nature, so that in this original purity they knew God | as God is; that they behaved in accordance with God's essence and with their own proper essence; that they had not yet stepped forth into duality and were still uncorrupted. And so, because spirit's gaze was not yet clouded and darkened, because humanity had not yet sunk down into the prose of reflection and understanding, which is just what constitutes the divorce between the subject and nature; because they had not yet found themselves thus sundered from nature, or from external things, and did not yet have particular interests that could make them view [nature] practically as a complex of useful things—because of this they beheld the inner being of nature itself, they knew the inner being of nature

420

22. [Ed.] Hegel is alluding especially to the views of F. W. J. Schelling and Friedrich Schlegel. See Schelling's On University Studies (1803), trans. E. S. Morgan (Athens, Ohio, 1966), p. 83 (Sämmtliche Werke 5:287); Schelling's Treatise on "The Deities of Samothrace," trans. R. F. Brown (Missoula, Mont., 1977), p. 25 (Sämmtliche Werke 8:362); and Schlegel's Ueber die Sprache und Weisheit der Indier (Heidelberg, 1808), pp. 198, 205 (Kritische Friedrich-Schlegel-Ausgabe 8:295–297, 303). See also below, n. 42.

and cognized nature truly.[23] ‾Just as they related themselves to the pure God according to their own purity, | so also they related to   421 nature not as to an external thing; instead they saw into the heart of nature as it is; thus they possessed absolute knowledge just as they did the true religion.‾[24] We can form this representation readily for ourselves just by thinking; but, as we have already said, it is also found in the religions of diverse peoples. Most religions begin with a sojourn in paradise, and hence with an original state of human innocence—thus the Greeks have the golden age and the Romans the Saturnian age.[25] This is very much a universal representation

23. [Ed.] Expressions of a mystical unity with nature are found in Albrecht von Haller's poem, "Die Falschheit der menschlichen Tugenden," in Versuch schweizerischer Gedichte, 6th ed. (Göttingen, 1751), no. 6, p. 100; and in Jacob Boehme's De signatura rerum, in Theosophia revelata (1715), pp. 2178–2404, esp. pp. 2180–2181.

24. W (1831) reads: Cognition of nature of the former [i.e., pre-rational] kind is explained as intuiting, which is nothing else but immediate consciousness. If we ask, "What has been intuited?" it is not sensuous nature superficially considered (a kind of intuition that can also be attributed to animals) but the essence of nature. But the essence of nature, as the system of its laws, is nothing but the universal. Nature in its universality, the system of developing organic life, and this development in its authentic form, [W_1: this W_2: not nature in its singularity, in which it exists for sensuous perception or for intuition, but the form of the natural,] is nature as permeated by thought. Thinking, however, is not something immediate; it starts with the given, but rises above [W_1: it W_2: the sensuous manifoldness of what is given]. It negates the form of singularity, forgets what has happened in sensuous form, and produces the universal, the genuine. This is not action of an immediate kind but is the labor of mediation, the emergence from finitude. [W_2: It is of no avail to contemplate the heavens no matter with what pious and innocent faith; what is essential can only be thought.] Hence the assertion that one has a direct sight or vision of things [ein Schauen], an immediate consciousness, proves itself to be worthless as soon as we ask what is to be seen in this way. The knowledge of nature in its truth is a mediated form of knowing, not immediate knowing. And it is the same with willing. The will is good insofar as it wills the good, what is right and ethical. But this is something quite different from the immediate will. The immediate will is the will that does not advance beyond singularity and finitude, that wills the singular as such. The good on the contrary is the universal; in order for the will to attain to the point of willing the good, a mediation is necessary through which it has purified itself from that sort of finite willing. This purification is the education and labor of the mediation, and the mediation cannot be something immediate and primary. The same applies to the cognition of God; God is the center of all truth, the pure truth without any boundary, and in order to attain to him it is even more imperative that human beings should have labored to free themselves from their natural particularity of knowing and willing.

25. [Ed.] See Hesiod, Works and Days 108–119, and Virgil, Eclogues 4, 6.

which even in modern times thought has sought to justify once more by argument alone.

This, then, is what[26] has been understood by "nature religion"—an initial or original revelation, a revelation first impaired by human beings, lost or corrupted by them as they passed over to the evil side through sin, passion, and evil generally. Of course it is easy to recognize that evil, ignorance, passion, selfish inclination, private pursuits, and the will that wishes to determine itself for itself obscure the moment of insight into truth as the knowing and willing of the good. So the question is whether this character [of innocence] is to be viewed as a state, and in fact as the initial, original, and authentic state.

So far as the basic determination in that representation is concerned, it must be acknowledged not only to be correct but also, as a true representation, to be foundational. But we must distinguish the form, i.e., whether in fact this true representation should be characterized as an initial, original, natural, and authentic *state*. The basic determination is nothing else but this, that the human being is no natural essence as such, is no animal, but rather spirit. Insofar as humanity is spirit, it has this universality in itself quite generally, the universality of rationality, the activity of concrete thought | and reason; and it is partly the instinct of reason, and partly its development, to know that reason is universal and that nature is therefore rational. Of course nature is not conscious reason, but it has determination according to purpose within it. Nature is rationally ordered, it was made by a wise creator—and wisdom is purpose, concept, free rationality itself. Thus spirit also knows that God is rational, absolute reason, absolute rational activity, and it has this belief instinctively, it knows that it cognizes God as well as nature, that it must find in God something quite distinct [from itself] but also its own essence too, when it relates itself to these objects in its rational investigation. Spirit believes that in its rational inquiry into God and nature it will recognize itself, the rational.

This is undoubtedly the basic determination [of the story]; but now the question is whether it describes the initial state. As far as

26. *L (1827?) adds:* apart from the metaphysical meaning discussed earlier,

the representation of the lost paradise is concerned, however, we should declare here that the very fact that it is a *lost* paradise shows already that it is not an essential state. The true or the divine does not get lost; it is eternal, and abides in and for itself. So if this unity of humanity with God and nature is represented as the true, then the higher concept shows that this [lost paradise] is not the state of the true.⁻[27] This unity of humanity with itself, with God, and with nature is, in the universal sense or as in-itself, in fact the substantial, essential determination. Humanity is reason, is spirit; in virtue of the capacity of reason, of the fact that humanity is spirit, it is implicitly what is true. But that is only the concept or the in-itself, and when we arrive at the *representation* of what the concept is, or what is in itself, we are quite accustomed to represent it to ourselves as something past or future, not as something inward that is in and of itself. We picture it instead in the mode of immediate, external existence, as an [actual] state.[28] |

423

So, of course, the concept must realize itself; but the realization of the concept, the activities through which it actualizes itself, and the present shapes and appearances of this actualization and of the actuality, have a different look to them than does that which is the simple concept within itself. The unity of which we speak is in fact the concept, or the in-itself, and not an actual state or existence; only the realization of the concept constitutes actual states or existence, and this realization must be quite different from the way that the state of paradise and innocence is depicted.

The human being is essentially spirit, and spirit[29] is essentially this: to be for oneself, to be free, setting oneself over against the

---

27. *Thus An with B and Hu; L (Var) reads:* But as we have said, it is not to be represented as a state, as it is pictured among most peoples that what was original in point of time is the true human state and the one we long for, the loss of which was a misfortune and an occasion for mourning.

28. *W₂ (1831) adds:* So what is involved here is only the form of existence or how the state occurs. The concept is what is inward, the implicit potential, but it has not yet come into existence. So the question arises what stands against our believing that the implicit potential was present in advance as actual existence. And what does stand against it is the nature of spirit. Spirit is only what it makes itself. This bringing forth of what is implicit is the positing of the concept of existence.

29. *W₂ (Var) adds:* is not in immediate fashion, but

natural, withdrawing oneself from immersion in nature, severing oneself from nature and only reconciling oneself with nature for the first time through this severance and on the basis of it; and not only with nature but with one's own essence too, or with one's truth. We make this truth objective to ourselves, set it over against us, sever ourselves from it, and through this severance we reconcile ourselves with it. This oneness brought forth by way of severance is the first spiritual or true oneness, that which comes forth out of reconciliation; it is not the unity of nature. The stone or the plant is immediately in this unity, but in a oneness that is not a unity worthy of spirit, is not spiritual oneness. Spiritual oneness comes forth out of severed being.

A misunderstanding can arise when we call that initial state the state of *innocence*. Then it can seem objectionable to say that human beings must depart from the state of innocence and become guilty. But the state of innocence consists in the fact that nothing is good and nothing | is evil for human beings; it is the state of the animal; ˉparadise (παράδεισος) is in fact initially a zoological garden [*Tiergarten*];[30] it is the state where there is no accountability. An ethical state of humanity begins only with a state of accountability or of capacity for guilt,ˉ[31] and this is now the human state. "Guilt" means in general "holding to account."[32] But guilt in the universal sense means that for which human beings are accountable; to have guilt means to be accountable, that this is one's knowledge and one's will, that one does it as what is right.

424

30. [*Ed.*] See Xenophon, *Anabasis* 1.2.7, where Cyrus is said to have kept wild animals in a large park for hunting. The Hebrew word for "garden" was translated in the Septuagint as παράδεισος, which stems from the Old Persian *pairi daēza*, meaning a park enclosed by a wall. See also Diodorus Siculus, *Bibliotheca historica* 2.10, and Josephus, *Antiquities* 10.226.

31. *Thus An with B and Hu; L (Var) reads, similar in W:* —(paradise = zoological garden)—or of unconsciousness, where humanity is totally ignorant both of good and of evil, and what is willed is not determined either as good or as evil. If there is no knowledge of evil, then there is no knowledge of good either. But the state of guilt, in contrast with this, is the state of accountability,

32. *L (1827?) adds, similar in W:* "Guilt" is usually taken in a pejorative sense. It is usually understood to mean that someone has done something evil. What this says is that humanity *must* become evil.

As a state of existence, that initial natural oneness is in actuality not a state of innocence but the state of savagery, an animal state, a state of [natural] desire or general wildness. The animal in such a state is neither good nor evil; but human beings in the animal state are wild, are evil, are not as they ought to be. Humanity as it is by nature is not what it ought to be; human beings ought to be what they are through spirit, to which end they mold themselves by inner illumination, by knowing and willing what is right and proper. This point, that human beings as they are according to nature are not as they ought to be, has been expressed in the thesis that human beings are by nature evil. When it is represented as original sin [*Erbsünde*], then inheritance [*Erblichkeit*] is a form that exists for representation, a form of popular guise.[33] In this way the primordial state according to the concept hovers before the imagination of [all] peoples, and this primordial state is oneness. But they express this primordiality as either a past or a future state. What is primordial as a state, however, is | savagery, while on the other hand what is primordial in thought is the concept, which realizes itself by releasing itself from the form of its naturalness.

425

We find in the Bible a well-known story [*Vorstellung*] abstractly termed *the fall*. This representation is very profound and is not just a contingent history but the eternal and necessary history of humanity—though it is indeed expressed here in an external and mythical mode. For this reason there are bound to be inconsistencies in this representation. In its vitality the idea can be grasped only by thought and can be presented only by thought; when it is expressed in sensible imagery, then, of necessity, elements that will not fit together must emerge. Therefore the story is not without inconsistencies. But the essential or basic features of the idea are contained in it: namely that, although human beings are implicitly this unity, they depart from this in-itself or leave the natural state behind because they are spirit, so that they must come into distinction, into (primal) division, must come to judgment between what is theirs and what

---

33. *L (1827?) adds, similar in W:* What this implies is that human beings, insofar as they live only according to nature and follow their heart, i.e., what merely springs up spontaneously, their inclinations, ought to regard themselves as not being as they ought to be.

is natural. Only thus do they first know God and the good. When one knows this, one has it as the object of consciousness; and when one has it as the object of consciousness, then, as an individual, one distinguishes oneself from it. So if the idea, that which is in and for itself, is portrayed mythically in the mode of a temporal process, then inconsistency is unavoidable.

The basic features of this representation are as follows [cf. Gen. 3]. The tree of the knowledge of good and evil portrayed in it belongs to the sensible mode; we see that straightaway. Then the story says that human beings let themselves be led astray and ate this fruit, and in this way they came to the knowledge of good and evil. This is called the fall, as if they had come only to the knowledge of evil, and had become only evil; but they came equally to the knowledge of good. The story says that this should not have happened. ˉBut on the one hand it is involved in the concept of spirit that human beings must come to the knowledge of good and evil.ˉ[34]

426 As for what the story | says—that they ought not to have come to this knowledge—this too is involved in the idea, inasmuch as ˉreflection, or the rupture of consciousness, is contained in this knowledge of good and evil. In other words, there is posited here the cleavage that is freedom, the abstraction of freedom. Insofar as human beings exist for themselves (i.e., they are free), good and evil exist for them and they have the choice between the two. This standpoint of formal freedom in which human beings are face-to-face with good and evil and stand above both, are lords of both, isˉ[35] a standpoint that ought not to be—ˉthough not, of course, in the sense that it should not be at all or should not arise. On the contrary, it is necessary for the sake of freedom, else humanity is not free, and is not spirit; rather it is a standpoint that must be sublated, that must

34. W₂ *(Var) reads:* But it is involved in the concept of humanity that it should come to knowledge; in other words, spirit consists in becoming cognitive consciousness. *L (1827?) adds:* However, as already noted, humans know nothing of good if they know nothing of evil. And yet this knowledge is also essential; humans *are* human and rational *only* to the extent that they have this consciousness, this knowledge, of good and evil.

35. W₂ *(Var) reads:* the cleavage and reflection constitute freedom, implying that the human being has a choice between the two sides of the antithesis and stands before us as lord over good and evil; so we have

come to an end with reconciliation, in the union with the good.⁻³⁶ Consciousness grasps the double aspect within itself: on the one hand this cleavage, namely that together with reflection and freedom it contains within itself the bad or evil, that which ought not to be; on the other hand, however, it is likewise the principle or source of healing, of freedom, i.e., it is spirit. It is also clear that both aspects are contained in the story. The one aspect, that the standpoint of cleavage ought not to persist, is implied by the statement that a crime has been committed, something that ought not to be, ought not to endure. ¨It was the serpent who said: "You will be like God."⁻³⁷ The arrogance of freedom is the standpoint that ought not to persist. The other aspect, that the cleavage ought to persist, insofar as it contains the source of its healing, is expressed in the speech of God: "Behold, Adam has become like one of us, knowing good and evil." So what the serpent said was no lie; | on the contrary, even God himself corroborated it. But this verse is usually overlooked, or else nothing is said about it.

427

So we can say that it is the eternal story of human freedom that we do go forth out of this stupor, in which we are in our earliest years, and come to the light of consciousness, or, speaking more precisely altogether, that there is good for us and also evil.³⁸ So far as we apprehend what is actually there in this portrayal, it is the same as what ¨appeared again later in the Christian religion,⁻³⁹ namely that human beings, as spirit, must come to reconciliation.⁴⁰ That is the genuine idea in contrast with the mere image of paradise, or this stupefied innocence devoid of consciousness and will.

36. W₂ (Var) reads: that must be sublated. It is not, however, one that should not make its appearance at all, the truth rather being that this standpoint of cleavage terminates, according to its own nature, in reconciliation.

37. W₂ (Var) reads: Thus it is said that the serpent beguiled humanity with its lies.

38. L (1827?) adds: On the one hand this standpoint also involves cleavage, formal freedom, evil, pride; here human beings have the choice between good and evil, so that it is also necessary for them to emerge from this standpoint, to the extent that it is a standpoint of cleavage.

39. Thus Hu; L, W (Var) read: is in the idea,

40. L (1827?) adds, similar in W: or, to put it superficially, that they must become good, must fulfill their vocation. In order for this to come about, this standpoint of reflective consciousness, or cleavage, is [L, W₁: no less necessary. W₂: no less necessary than the abandonment of it.]

That in that initial state human beings ⌐had the most perfect acquaintance with the good and with nature has certainly been an accepted notion, but it is quite absurd.⌐⁴¹ ⌐I have this brief comment 428 about it. The laws | of nature and the like are discovered only through meditative thinking, and it is only the maturest meditation that arrives at the knowledge that these things are in accord with the idea; this thinking is in utter contrast with immediate knowledge.

As for the historical data that have been appealed to [in support of the claim] that the oldest religions and sciences still contain remains of earlier sciences, it is partly untrue and partly based upon the earlier erroneous historical accounts of the lofty knowledge of the Indians and the Chinese. Since we in Europe have become acquainted with the sources, such notions have shown to be invalid. Thus, for example, Delambre has exposed the false assertions of Bailly[42] regarding Indian astronomical records.⌐⁴³

41. *W (Var) reads:* had the highest knowledge of nature and of God, occupied the highest standpoint of science, is a foolish view, and one which, moreover, [has] been shown to be quite unfounded historically.

42. [*Ed.*] The view that the earliest tangible evidences of scientific knowledge are simply the remains of the science of an earlier, forgotten period was fairly widespread at the end of the eighteenth century. See, e.g., Jean-Sylvain Bailly, *Histoire de l'astronomie ancienne depuis son origine jusqu'à l'établissement de l'école d'Alexandrie,* 2d ed. (Paris, 1781), pp. 106–107. Hegel believed that Bailly's view of the matter—which was shared by Schelling, *Treatise on "The Deities of Samothrace,"* pp. 25, 37 (cf. *Sämmtliche Werke* 8:362, 416–417), although Schelling was here referring to Greek mythology and the Kabbala rather than Chinese and Indian mythology— had been refuted by Jean-Joseph Delambre in his *Histoire de l'astronomie ancienne,* 2 vols. (Paris, 1817), esp. pp. vi, xix, 400.

43. *W (1831) reads:* When Indian literature was first discovered, it was said that the huge chronological numbers point to a very great age of the culture and appear to yield quite new information. Recently, however, we have been compelled to abandon this [implausible] Indian chronology, [W_1: for in a few places the numbers express ratios or orders of magnitude, but are otherwise quite meaningless. W_2: for the numbers express no prosaic conditions whatever as regards years or recollection of the past.] The Indians are also said to possess great astronomical knowledge; they have formulae for calculating the eclipses of the sun and the moon, but they use them in a quite mechanical way, without knowing what is presupposed in them or how to derive the formulae. More recently, however, the astronomical and mathematical knowledge of these peoples has been more closely investigated.[a] A distinctive cultural tradition is acknowledged to be undoubtedly present here, but in these branches of knowledge the level that they reached was still far below that of the Greeks. The astronomical formulae are so needlessly involved that they are far behind the methods of the Greeks,

b. The Forms of Nature Religion

Let us sum up as briefly as possible our discussion of this initial form of religion, or nature religion; knowledge of God in the universal sense belongs to religion generally, and we can assume at least this much, that God is spirit. Hence nature religion contains the spiritual moment directly,[44] so that the spiritual is the highest reality for human beings.

This rules out the view that nature religion is one in which human beings revere natural objects as God. Reverence for natural objects does indeed play a part in it, but in a secondary way. Even in the basest religion the spiritual is, for human beings as such, always nobler than the natural; for instance, the sun is not | nobler than   429
a spiritual being for them. ⌐Hence nature religion is not a religion in which external, physical objects are taken to be God and are revered as God; instead it is a religion in which the noblest element for human beings is what is spiritual, but the spiritual [recognized] first in its immediate and natural mode. The initial and natural mode is the human being, this existing human being. Inasmuch as it is natural, therefore, nature religion has the natural within it, but not sheer external or physical naturalness; it has a spiritual side at the same time, but what is *naturally* spiritual, this human being here present and sensibly facing us.⌐[45] The spiritual element is not the idea of humanity, Adam Kadmon, the primordial human being,[46]

---

let alone our own; genuine science is precisely that which seeks to reduce its problems to the simplest elements. These complicated formulae point, no doubt, to a praiseworthy diligence, to painstaking effort, but more than that is not to be found in them; what they rest on is long-continued observations.

[*Ed.*] ªIn addition to the work by Delambre cited in the preceding note, Hegel could be referring to a number of works on Indian astronomy. See, e.g., *Asiatic Researches,* vols. 8 (J. Bentley), 5 (F. Wilford), 2 (W. Jones).

44. W *(Var) adds:* and therefore essentially,

45. W₂ *(MiscP/Var?) reads:* In its beginnings, or as immediate religion, the religion of nature means this: the spiritual, a human being, even in its natural mode, ranks as what is highest. This religion does not have the merely externally and physically natural element as its object, but the *spiritually* natural, this human being as the one actually facing us.

46. [*Ed.*] The idea of Adam Kadmon as receiving and transmitting the divine primal energy is referred to by August Neander in his *Genetische Entwicklung der vornehmsten gnostischen Systeme* (Berlin, 1818), pp. 88 ff., 102. Hegel drew heavily from this work.

or the Son of God—those are more developed images only present through thinking and for thought. Therefore it is not the thought-image of human beings in their universal essentiality, but rather this particular and natural human being. It is the religion of the spiritual in its externality, naturalness, and immediacy, that is to say, this human being here present, immediately and sensibly facing us. This is another reason why it concerns us to become acquainted with nature religion, in order to make us conscious that God is always a present reality for human beings from time immemorial, and in order to bring us back in this way from the abstract otherworldliness of God.

The way forward from this initial, abstract determination is for spirit to be purified of this externality and naturalness, this sensible immediacy, and to be known as spirit in thought, i.e., that human beings should attain to the representation of spirit as spirit in both their imagination and their thought.[47]

The *first* religion is this, that consciousness of the highest is consciousness of a human being as dominion, power, and lordship over nature. This first religion, if we can call it that, is the religion of

430 *magic.* |

[48] [49] ˜The *second* form, which contains the higher element, is no longer the human being in the immediate, natural state, in immediate

47. *L (1827?) adds:* Such is the definition of the field of nature religion, of which we see different forms; for the sphere of the natural is always the mutual externality of distinct elements.

48. *In B's margin:* 19 June 1827

49. *W₂ (1831) reads (parallel in main text follows):* The way forward from this first form of religion is for spirit to be purified from externality, from sensible immediacy, and attain to the representation of spirit as spirit in both imagination and thought.

The interesting feature in this advance is just the objectifying of spirit, i.e., that spirit becomes purely objective and comes to have the meaning of universal spirit.

II.
The Inward Rupture of Consciousness within Itself

The first step forward is for the consciousness of a substantive power, and the powerlessness of the immediate will, to enter on the scene. Since God is here known as the absolute power, this is not yet the religion of freedom. For although the entry of a substantive power upon the scene of consciousness means that humanity does rise above itself, and although the essential differentation of spirit is accomplished, still, since this power on high is known *as* power and is not yet further determined, the particular is something merely accidental, merely negative and of no account. Everything subsists by means of this power; in other words, it is itself the subsistence of everything, so that the freedom of subsisting-for-self is not yet recognized. This is pantheism.

This power, which is something thought, is not yet known as a thought product or as inwardly spiritual. Since it must now have a spiritual mode of existence but does not yet have the moment of being free on its own account within itself, it once more has the moment of spirituality only in one human being, who is known as this power.

In the elevation of spirit with which we are here concerned, the point of departure is the finite, the contingent, this being defined as the negative, and the universal, self-subsistent essence as that in which and through which this finite is something negative, something posited. Substance, on the contrary, is what is not posited, the self-subsistent, the power in relation to the finite.

Now the consciousness that elevates itself does so as thought, but without having a consciousness regarding this universal thought, without expressing it in the form of thought. And to begin with, the elevation is an upward movement only. The other movement is the converse one, namely, that this necessary element has returned to the finite. In the first movement the finite forgets itself. The second is the relationship of substance to the finite. Since God is determined here only as the substance of the finite and the power over it, he himself is still undetermined. He is not yet known to be inwardly determined on his own account; he is not yet known as spirit.

On this general basis several forms take shape, progressive attempts to grasp substance as self-determining.

1. To begin with (in the religion of China), substance is known as the simple foundation, and so is immediately present in the finite or contingent.

The progress made by consciousness comes from the fact that even though substance is not yet grasped as spirit, spirit is nonetheless the truth implicitly underlying all the phenomena of consciousness and that therefore even at this stage nothing can be lacking of what pertains to the concept of spirit. So here too, substance will determine itself as subject, but the question is how it does this. At this point the determinations of spirit, which are present implicitly, come on the scene in an external mode. Complete determinateness, the culminating point of the shape of being-for-self, of the unity of being-for-self, is now posited externally, in the sense that an actually present human being [*ein präsenter Mensch*] is known as the universal power.

This consciousness is already apparent in the Chinese religion, where the emperor is at all events what wields or actuates the power.

2. In Hinduism substance is no longer known merely as foundation, but as abstract unity, and this abstract unity is also more nearly akin to spirit, since spirit is itself this abstract unity as ego. In raising itself to its inner abstract unity, humanity raises itself here to the unity of substance, identifies itself with it, and thus gives it existence. Some by nature partake in the existence of this unity, while others are capable of rising to it.

Of course, the unity that is here the dominant element does also attempt to unfold itself. The true unfolding, and the negativity that grasps all differences at once, would be spirit, which determines itself inwardly and becomes apparent to itself in its subjectivity. This subjectivity of spirit would give it a content worthy of it, and this

431   self-consciousness, or in subjective desires, but instead the human being as entering into self and concentrating self internally, so that this inwardness | is the essential, higher, powerful and ruling factor. This second form is the human being as *being within self* or *self-contained* [*in sich seiend*].

432   The *third* form is then this, that human consciousness (albeit self-contained and withdrawn into itself) is at the same time outside | this abstraction of being-within-self, that the concrete is not situated in the self-containment as such but is instead a disintegration into endlessly many powers, configurations, and universal moments, which stand in connection with the self-contained essentiality, and which are more or less *imaginative forms of this essentiality.*⁻

    The *fourth* form is the incipient separation from the immediate individual, *incipient severance or objectification of* what is known as *the highest*. This has two shapes. In the first, the simple is set against the concrete in this objectification; but this simple aspect is

---

content would itself have a spiritual nature too. But in the present case the characteristic of naturalness still remains, inasmuch as an advance is made to differentiation and unfolding *only*, and the moments occur in an isolated fashion alongside one another. Thus the unfolding that is necessary in the concept of spirit is here itself devoid of spirit. Hence one is sometimes at a loss to find the spirit unfolded in nature religion. This is the case, for instance, with the image of the incarnation and the triad in Hindu religion. Moments will be found that pertain to spirit, but they are interpreted in such a way that at the same time they do not pertain to it. The characteristics occur in isolated fashion and present themselves as falling to pieces. Thus the triad in Hinduism does not become the Trinity since only absolute spirit has the power over its own moments.

The representation of nature religion evinces major difficulties in this respect; it is everywhere inconsistent, and inwardly contradictory. Thus on the one hand the spiritual, which is essentially free, is posited, while on the other hand it is represented in natural determinacy, in a [state of] singularity, with a content that has hard-and-fast particularity, and that is therefore wholly inappropriate to spirit, since it is only as free spirit that spirit is genuine.

3. In the last form that belongs to this stage, that of the cleavage of consciousness, the concrete embodiment and presence of substance subsists and lives in *one* individual, and the unstable unfolding of the unity that was peculiar to the previous form is sublated at least to the extent that it is nullified and evaporated. This is Lamaism or Buddhism.

Before proceeding to consider more closely the historical existence of this religion, we have [to discuss] the general determinacy of this whole stage and its metaphysical concept. More precisely, we have here to define the concept of elevation and the relationship of substance to the finite.

still abstract, and in a natural mode, though it equally contains the spiritual determination within it. Accordingly ⁻the⁻⁵⁰ second shape of the objectification of the substantial consists in the fact that the concept of subjectivity or of the concrete, the development of the concrete and this development as totality, come to consciousness explicitly in the subject.

These are the four forms of the religion of nature. As noted, these configurations or determinations are existing configurations of | religion; so the course of these forms or determinations of spirit is at the same time the foundation of the history of religion.⁵¹   433

1. The Religion of Magic⁵²

a. The Concept of Magic

⁵³We shall discuss now the first stage of nature religion, the religion of magic, which we may deem unworthy of the name "religion." In order to grasp this standpoint of religion we must forget all the representations and thoughts that we are perhaps so familiar with and that themselves belong to the most superficial habits of our culture.⁵⁴ We must consider human beings all by themselves | upon   434

50. L (Var) reads: this

51. L (1827?) adds: Beyond nature religion and in the religion of beauty and sublimity God for the first time emerges—partly in thought, partly in phantasy—in distinctive independence as free vis-à-vis the immediate individual.

52. [Ed.] The treatment of the religion of magic is briefer in 1827 than in 1824 since Buddhism/Lamaism is no longer considered under this category. The section is also organized differently since now the phenomenology of primitive religious consciousness is concentrated in subsection a and examples of the religion of magic are in subsection b. While the latter are taken almost verbatim from 1824, the former differs considerably from the earlier lectures. Now all the "less developed" forms of magic involve a direct exercise of power over nature, from which is distinguished only a "more developed" form of magic—the religion of ancient China, the treatment of which is also revised considerably (see below, n. 96).

53. W₁ (Ed) adds: It has to be regarded from both sides, as the religion of magical power and as that of being-within-self.
   1. The Religion of Magical Power.

54. W₂ (1831) adds: For natural consciousness, which is what we here have before us, the prosaic categories such as cause and effect are not yet valid, and natural things are not yet degraded into external things.
   Religion has its soil only in spirit. The spiritual knows itself as the power over the natural, it knows that nature is not what has being in and for itself. This

the earth, the tent of the heavens above them and nature round about them, and so, to begin with, without any reflective thought,[55] altogether devoid of consciousness of anything universal; only on this basis do more worthy concepts of God emerge.

It is difficult to get the sense of an alien religion from within. ⁻To put oneself in the place of a dog requires the sensibilities of a dog.⁻[56] We are cognizant of the nature of such living objects, but we cannot possibly know what it would mean to transpose ourselves into their place, so that we could sense their determinate limits; for that would mean filling the totality of one's subjectivity wholly with ⁻⁻these characteristics. They remain always objects of our thought, not of our subjectivity, of our feeling; we can grasp such religions, but we cannot get the sense of them from within. We ⁻can grasp the Greek divinities, but we cannot get the inner sense of genuine adoration toward a divine image of that kind.⁻[57]

But the first nature religion is much more remote from the totality of our consciousness than this.⁻⁻[58] Human beings in that situation

---

[knowledge] constitutes the categories of the understanding, in which nature is grasped as the other of spirit and spirit is grasped as what is genuine. This basic determination is the starting point for religion.

Immediate religion, in contrast, is that in which spirit is still natural, and where the distinction between spirit as absolute power and spirit as what is single, contingent, transient, and accidental has not yet been drawn. This distinction, the antithesis between universal spirit (as universal power and essence) and subjective existence (with its contingency), has not yet entered into play. It forms the second stage within nature religion.

In the primal, immediate religion, here in this immediacy, humanity still knows no higher power than itself. There is, to be sure, a power over contingent life, over its purposes and interests, but this is still no essential power, as a universal in and for itself, but falls within the compass of humanity itself. The spiritual subsists in a singular, immediate mode.

55. W (Var) adds: or elevation to thinking,

56. An reads: We have the representational image of the elephant, but to think ourselves completely into its nature is beyond our capability; to do so we would have to have an elephant's nature.

57. An reads: have a representation of the Greek religion of beauty. We can understand it, and its gods, and grasp them in thought, but we cannot bend the knee to them.

58. W_2 (Var) reads: a singular determination of this kind, so that it would become our determinateness. We cannot enter experientially in this way even into religions that approach more nearly to our [own] consciousness; they cannot for a single moment become our determinateness to the point that we would, for example, worship the

still exist in a state of immediate desire, force, and action, behaving in accord with their immediate will. They do not yet pose any theoretical questions such as: "Where does this come from?" "Who made it?" and "Must it have a cause?" This inward divorce of objects into a contingent and an essential | aspect, into a causative aspect 435 and the aspect of something merely posited, or of an effect, does not yet occur for them. Similarly, even the will in them is not yet theoretical; there is not yet this rupture in them, nor any inhibition toward themselves. The theoretical element in willing is what we call the universal, right, duty—i.e., laws, firm specifications, limits for the subjective will. These are thoughts, universal forms that belong to the thought of freedom. They are distinct from subjective arbitrariness, desire, and inclination; all of the latter are restrained and controlled by the universal, or are conformed to this universal; the natural willing of desire is transformed into willing and acting in accord with such universal viewpoints.

But here human beings are still undivided with regard to willing; desire[59] is the governing factor here. Similarly in their representations, in the imagination of these human beings, they ˉcarry onˉ[60] in this undivided state, this benighted condition, a stupor in the theoretical domain and a wildness of will. This is just spirit's primitive and wild reliance upon itself. There is indeed a fear present here, a consciousness of negation, though not yet the fear of the Lord; it is instead the fear of contingency, of the forces of nature, which display themselves as mighty powers over against humanity.[61] The fear of the Lord, which is the beginning of wisdom,[62] is fear before a spiritually self-sufficient being opposed to arbitrariness. This fear

---

Greek statue of a god, however beautiful it might be. And the stage of immediate religion is still further off—as remote from us as it can be. L (Var) adds: In this case one must forget just those views that are most commonly accepted. W₂ (Var) continues: since in order to make it intelligible to ourselves we have to forget all the forms current in our culture.

59. W₂ (Var) adds: and wildness of will

60. Thus W; L reads: maintain themselves An reads: hold themselves Hu reads: relate themselves

61. W₁ (Ed) adds: We have here to deal (a) with magic in general, (b) with the characteristics of the religion of magic, and (c) with the cultus.

62. [Ed.] See Ps. 111:10; Prov. 1:7; Job 28:28.

first enters human experience when in one's singularity one knows oneself to be powerless, when one's singularity is inwardly shaken. The beginning of wisdom is when singular privateness and subjectivity senses itself as not being what is true, and, in the consciousness of its singularization and impotence, by way of negation, it passes over to knowledge, to universal being-in-and-for-self.

This earliest form of religion—although one may well refuse to call it religion—is that for which we have the name "magic." To be precise, it is the claim that the spiritual aspect is the power over

436 nature; | but this spiritual aspect is not yet present as spirit, is not yet present in its universality. Instead the spiritual is at first just the singular and contingent human self-consciousness which, in spite of being only sheer desire, self-consciously knows itself to be nobler than nature, and knows that self-consciousness is a power transcending nature.[63]

Two different points are to be noted here. First, insofar as immediate self-consciousness knows that this power lies within it, that it is the locus of this power, in the state where it is such a power it certainly distinguishes itself altogether from its ordinary state. When human beings do ordinary things, such as eating, drinking, sleeping, and the like, when they go about their simple occupations, they are concerned with particular objects; in these pursuits they know that they are dealing just with these things, for instance in fishing or hunting.[64] Consciousness of this ordinary existence ˉwith its instinctsˉ[65] and its activity is one thing, whereas the consciousness of oneself as having power over the general ˉvicissitudeˉ[66] of nature is another matter altogether. In the latter case individuals do not know themselves [to be engaged] in ordinary activities and instincts; rather one knows that, insofar as one is a higher power,

63. L (1827?) adds: So the main characteristic of this sphere is the direct mastery of nature by the will, by self-consciousness, the fact that spirit is something higher than nature. However bad this appears in one perspective, it is nonetheless higher than the situation where humanity is dependent on nature, and afraid of it.

64. W_2 (Var) adds: and they confine their energy to that activity alone.

65. W (Var) reads: and instincts Cf. An: where human beings are only conscious of the existence of nature and make use of natural objects, in pursuit of their desires

66. W_2 (Var) reads: power of nature, and over the vicissitudes

one must transport oneself into a higher state, distinct from ordinary consciousness. This higher state is the state and gift of particular human beings—ˉand these are the magiciansˉ[67]—who transport themselves into it in order to be this power.[68] | 437

The second point is that this power is a direct power over nature generally, one not to be compared with the indirect power that we exercise upon natural objects in their singularity. Such power of trained persons over single natural and perceptible things presupposes that they have already stepped back from the world, that the world has acquired externality in their eyes, that they have accorded to it over against them an autonomy, specific qualitative characteristics and laws, that these perceptible things are also relative to one another in their qualitative determinacy and stand in a web of connections with one another. ˉThe specially trained person exercises a powerˉ[69] through familiarity with the qualities of perceptible things, i.e., ˉofˉ[70] things as they are relative to other things; that is where something else has an impact upon them and their vulnerability is manifest. One learns to know this susceptibility, and through it acts upon things by equipping oneself with a means through which one lays hold of[71] this weakness. One brings external things into such a connection that they act upon one another according to one's purpose. Thus it is the one trained [in traditional lore] who freely releases [the power of] the world in its quality and qualitative connections. This really entails that human beings are free—inwardly free. For only free persons can allow the external world, other human beings, and natural things to confront them freely. But for the one who is not free, others are not free either. Only from the standpoint where human beings are inwardly free, and set the world free to confront them, does *indirect influence* upon natural things, a mediating dominion over nature, fall within their

67. *Thus Hu, similar in B; An reads:* not of races and strict castes
68. *L (1827?) adds, similar in W:* and who have to learn by tradition the ways of utilizing this state. There is a select group of individuals who go to the elders for instruction, and who sense within themselves this obscure inwardness.
69. *W (Var) reads:* This power, which freely releases [the power of] the world in its qualitative aspect, is exercised by the specially trained person
70. *W (Var) reads:* with
71. *W (Var) adds:* and capitalizes on

227

power and range of vision. In contrast, a *direct efficacy* of human beings by means of representation and will presupposes a corresponding absence of freedom, in which power over external things is indeed vested in human beings as the spiritual factor, but not as a power that behaves in a free manner. For this reason it does not behave in a mediating fashion, over against what is free; instead the power over nature has in this case a direct relationship—and | that is magic. ˉNow, in the self-consciousness of these peoples this is the noblest feature;ˉ[72] and it continues to insinuate itself deeply into other, higher religions in a secondary way, for instance the practice of witchcraft in Christendom, and of invoking devils. But, on the one hand, it is there known to be unavailing, and on the other hand it is regarded as something unfitting and godless.

Prayer has been regarded (even in the Kantian philosophy, for example) as if it were a kind of magic, because human beings want to effect and bring forth something not by means of natural mediation but directly from the spirit.[73] But the distinction is that, in turning to God in prayer, one is turning to an absolute will for which even the single individual is the object of care, which can grant the petition or not, and which in so doing is altogether determined by the furtherance of the good. ˉBut it is black magic when, at their own subjective caprice, human beings have the spirits or the devil under their control and compel them to do whatever they wish.ˉ[74] There is a mediation in this case, too, but one where the human will conjures and commands them, and those powers of nature obey it. From the standpoint of magic the human will is the authority and the higher powers are at its disposal.

This is the general characterization of this first and wholly immediate standpoint, i.e., that ˉhumanˉ[75] consciousness, this

72. *W (Var) reads:* As far as the outward existence of this view is concerned, it is found in a form that implies that this magic is what is highest in the self-consciousness of [these] peoples;

73. [*Ed.*] See Kant, *Religion within the Limits of Reason Alone,* trans. T. M. Greene and H. H. Hudson (New York, 1960), pp. 182–183 (on prayer as an illusion), 165–166 (on the illusion of thinking one can conjure up divine assistance by magic).

74. *Thus An; L (Var) reads, similar in W:* But magic consists precisely in the fact that, in their own natural state of desire, human beings have [*L:* nature *W:* it] in their power.

75. *Thus W; Hu reads:* the first human *L reads:* natural

human being in his own will, is known as power over the natural. But what is meant by "natural" here has by no means any wider scope; ¯the natural objects [controlled] are the things that immediately surround one. The | universal form that nature possesses for the will is: "That is just how it is"—without the application of any meditative thought. Human beings are at first insensible toward the environment, toward the stirring of nature. The sun rises and sets, and they observe it daily but remain unmoved; it becomes for them something they are used to. What is on the whole stable—day and night, the seasons—is just what *is;* that is what they are accustomed to. What touches or awakens interest in them is a disruption of the stable, i.e., such unstable conditions as earthquakes, thunderstorms, protracted drought, flood, rapacious beasts or enemies.¯[76]

439

b. Less Developed Religions of Magic

[77]Now we are going to cite more detailed descriptions of how these types of magic have developed in human societies. The religion of magic is still found today among wholly crude and barbarous peoples such as the Eskimos. Thus Captain Ross—and others, such as Parry[78]—discovered Eskimos who knew no other world than their icy rocks. When interviewed, these people said that they had no representation of God, or of immortality and the like. They do hold the sun and moon in awe. But they have only magicians or conjurers, who claim the authority to produce rain and gales, or to cause a whale to approach them. They say that they have learned their art

---

76. W_2 *(MiscP/Var?) reads:* as in our view of it. For at this stage the greater part of nature is still indifferent to humans, or is just as they are accustomed to see it. Everything is stable. Earthquakes, thunderstorms, floods, menacing beasts, enemies, etc., are another matter. To defend themselves against these they have recourse to magic.

77. *In B's margin:* 21 June 1827

78. [Ed.] John Ross, *A Voyage of Discovery, Made under the Orders of the Admirality, in His Majesty's Ships Isabella and Alexander, for the Purpose of Exploring Baffin's Bay, and Enquiring into the Probability of a North-West Passage,* 2d ed., 2 vols. (London, 1819), 1:168–169, 175–178, 179–180; William Edward Parry, *Journal of a Voyage for the Discovery of a North-West Passage from the Atlantic to the Pacific* (London, 1821). We know that Hegel was familiar with Ross's account, but not necessarily Parry's.

from ancient magicians ("angekoks"). These magicians put themselves into a wild state; their gestures make no sense. One could hear them invoke the ocean, but their words were not directed to a higher essence; they only have to do with natural objects. They have no representation of a universal essence. For example, someone asked one of them where the Eskimos believed they go after death. He replied that they were buried. In ages past an old man had indeed said they might go into the moon, but no rational Eskimo believes that any longer.

We still find this form widespread in Africa, and it is developed more fully among the Mongols and the Chinese. Long ago Herodotus said that the Africans are all magicians.[79] In whatever historical period people became acquainted with them, they were invariably characterized in this way. So in Africa, too, there are particular individuals whom we would term priests, and who are called Singhili. As do the shamans among the Mongols, | these people also transport themselves into a state of ecstasy, a wild state of stupefaction. This state is the higher standpoint that they attain in contrast with ordinary consciousness and ordinary action. Among the populace there are particular individuals who dedicate themselves to this ecstatic state and are esteemed for that reason; or else there is a particular family that is highly respected alongside the king and that exercises particular power over the tribe.

Where their condition is more developed, so that they form a kind of state, an aristocracy or monarchy, these magicians do not constitute a particular priestly caste, but instead the king himself is at the head of these Singhili; he both participates in such activities himself and also delegates them to his ministers; he makes these individuals into persons whose task is to exercise such authority. In contrast, among tribes where this type of organization is not prevalent, the clan or tribe always retains power even over these magicians. But these magicians do not possess a secure worldly power. When the people need their help, they bring them gifts; if the magicians refuse, then even violence is used against them ⁻[and they are] terribly ill-treated. The special occasions for their recourse

440

79. [Ed.] Herodotus, *Histories* 2.33.

230

to the magicians are in storms that last a long time and against which they cannot protect themselves, during sickness, and when they are of a mind to wage war.⁻⁸⁰ Here therefore we have "immediate" human beings, who ascribe to themselves this [direct] dominion over nature, or to whom it is ascribed.

Regarding the Africans, who still stand essentially at the stage of direct magic, we can indeed say that they also progress a small step further through their veneration of the dead, in that they ascribe power over nature to the deceased, to their departed relatives. A dead person is already no longer a wholly sensible | immediacy and singularity, but is elevated into the form of representation and is not in the immediate present. If the representation is stressed, then the deceased has lost sensible singularity and already partakes in the character of something more universal, something elevated to thought. At this stage the dead, the departed ancestors or relatives, do not receive veneration in the strict sense; there is here no cult of the dead, but instead present [ill] effects are to some extent attributed to them, and a remedy for these ills is sought from them. The onset of this trouble is attributed to them, but people turn to them for averting it as well. What we call "natural" these people still do not yet know to be natural; they know nothing of natural causality. So they attribute sickness, for example, not just to a living enemy but more especially to a dead one who has projected hatred upon the diseased person. For they represent the departed not as transfigured, but as wholly subject to sensible passions and necessities like those that the living themselves have. In the same way, too, a calamity of a different kind, such as crop failure and the like, is attributed to them.

Some of the bones of the dead are carefully preserved, and when one wishes to make use of them or they are supposed to render a service, then service or reverence is shown to them, a procession is made to them, an adoration or ablution performed. People even carry

441

80. *Thus B, An, Hu; L (Var) reads:* For example, if there is no rain or persistent drought, the priest must help them and must undertake the requisite ceremony; if he does not come willingly, he is dragged along forcibly and is ill-treated. Thus it is the will of the king or of the ordinary people, the will of the tribe; they have in their hands someone to whom they ascribe direct power [over nature].

them along with them in valuable coffers, especially the skulls of slain enemies through which, they believe, they have at their disposal might against the tribes to which those enemies belonged.

[81]A missionary (Cavazzi)[82] tells of terrible phenomena concerning the Jaga—a tribe from the south of Africa, from the Congo, with which the Portuguese had extensive dealings. They had a queen who had given laws to them. All the wilder types of magic were present among them to the highest degree, and the queen is supposed to have introduced the veneration of the dead, or at least made it into the sole cultus. If their Singhili want to produce rain, then sacrifices are brought to the dead; | they make gestures toward the sky, they address, entreat, command, scold, and threaten the sky, they take rods in their hands and strike out against the sky and spit at it; and when a cloud makes an appearance they redouble their entreaties, and when the rain will not come they utter the greatest abuse at the sky, shoot arrows toward it, and swear that they will treat it badly.[83]

The missionaries describe in detail different scenes that they observed. When it is a matter of making the sick well, one goes to the magician, who then declares the reason for the sickness; it is some enmity, and the enemies, in particular those who are deceased, must be compelled to desist from their vengeance. The precise way of accomplishing this is frightful, and usually it is accompanied by murder. The Singhili and all about begin a fearsome shrieking that lasts for several hours. One of their views about this is that the magician compels a dead person to enter into him and to disclose what must occur in order to have power or in order to conciliate another dead person—murder, gruesome practices, or bloody sacrifices. Also, the Singhili then states that he needs two human beings who must be sacrificed, and designates them from the

81. *Precedes in L (1827?):* So the dead play here an especially large role.
82. [*Ed.*] J. A. Cavazzi, *Historische Beschreibung der in dem unteren occidentalischen Mohrenland ligenden drey Königreichen Congo, Matamba, und Angola* (Munich, 1694), p. 233 (*Istorica descrizione de' tre regni Congo, Matamba, et Angola situati nell'Etiopia inferiore occidentale* [Bologna, 1687], pp. 198–199). Since it is not certain whether Hegel used the German or the Italian edition, we give the Italian page references in parentheses. The Jaga were leaders of one of the fiercest of the Bantu tribes of the Congo basin, the Bangala of Kwango, who were cannibals.
83. [*Ed.*] Cavazzi, *Historische Beschreibung,* pp. 250–251 (p. 215).

bystanders, takes a knife, stabs them, drinks their blood, distributes their pieces among the bystanders, and the whole company devours their flesh. Such bloody sacrifices are very common.[84] It is recounted of that queen of the Jaga that, in order to be strong in war, she pounded her own son in a mortar and, in company with her female companions, devoured his flesh and drank his blood.[85] What is evident here is precisely the frightful means through which [natural] human beings seek to raise themselves above ordinary consciousness, to make themselves aware of something higher—an elevation that manifests itself here in that horrible expedient of murdering human persons according to chance.

It is told of another king that when war was imminent, he consulted with the Singhili and received from them the | instruction   443 that during the night he should sound his horn and so give his bodyguards the sign[-86] to murder all of those they might encounter on the street. Thirty years ago an English ambassador found himself in this capital and, together with his entourage, he escaped destruction only because that secret was made public and he was warned. The resolution was actually carried out, and although not very many succumbed, this nightly havoc nevertheless continued for seventeen days.[87]

In all these cases we see a uniquely special elevation above immediate consciousness, and one that involves representations of the deceased, who on the one hand are regarded as powers[88] and yet on the other are compelled to do whatever those still alive want them to do. This goes so far that the Negroes, who with their still wild sense have not yet attained to a universal rationality, encounter the deceased in dreams and are tormented by these dead persons;

84. [Ed.] Ibid., pp. 259–264 (pp. 223–227).

85. [Ed.] Ibid., pp. 218–219 (pp. 187–188).

86. *Thus An; Hu reads:* there was a great procession to the grave of the enemy king, and there they prayed; then a command was issued, on behalf of the king,

87. [Ed.] See T. E. Bowdich, *Mission from Cape Coast Castle to Ashantee* (London, 1819), pp. 419–421. Bowdich does not actually refer to the Singhili but only to "the officers whose duty it is to attend at sacrifices"; and according to him the sign was given by drum rather than horn. In other respects Hegel's account is accurate but condensed.

88. *In B's margin:* 22 June 1827

various magical means are adopted against this. When their bodies still exist they are disinterred, the head is struck off, and the fluid from it is given to the tormented persons to drink, in order to cause the deceased pain and to take power from them.[89] In this way the empirical self-consciousness remains very much the master and has no other dominion over against it.

On this account every illness is supposed to be the consequence of an enmity, and in this connection they think the same thing about death too. Therefore they do not want human beings to appear to die of natural causes. Sick people, especially kings, are killed by them. If a king grows ill or old, then they do not let things get to the point where he would be killed by a hostile nature, but instead they slay him themselves. Dissatisfied chiefs seek by that means to get rid of the king themselves. If a king rules too harshly, then they inform him that he must die—he is allowed to determine the ceremonies himself.[90] In other words, they find it fitting that a human being should die through human will. Natural causation or connection is not yet present to the spirit of this | people; they attribute everything evil to the ill will of human beings, living as well as dead, or to other nonnatural forces; everything is explained in an unnatural manner and attributed to something else. This representation further intensifies into what we call "the devil." Belzoni,[91] an Italian who brought great treasures with him from Egypt, also transported a colossal head of Memnon to England, a stupendous work. The Egyptians had always seen this head lying on the bank of the Nile; but when they were motivated by monetary payment to carry this great head into the ship, and had indeed handled it themselves, they were very frightened and—despite the fact that they had done it— attributed the movement to the power of the devil.

The Negroes have an endless multitude of ¯divine images¯[92]

89. [Ed.] Cavazzi, *Historische Beschreibung*, pp. 257–258 (pp. 221–223).

90. [Ed.] Hegel is possibly referring to the same report which he gives at much greater length in his philosophy-of-history lectures. See *Lectures on the Philosophy of World History*, Nisbet ed., p. 187; Hoffmeister ed., p. 230. The source of the report has not been identified.

91. [Ed.] G. B. Belzoni, *Narrative of the Operations and Recent Discoveries in Egypt and Nubia*, 3d ed. (London, 1822), 1:68–69.

92. W *(Var) reads:* idols, natural objects

which they make into their gods or their "fetishes" (a corrupted Portuguese term).[93] The nearest stone or butterfly, a grasshopper, a beetle, and the like—these are their Lares[94]—indeterminate, unknown powers that they have made themselves; ⁻and if something does not work out or some unhappiness befalls them, then they throw this fetish away and get themselves another.⁻[95]

The use of charms and fetishes among these peoples does, of course, lead to the representation of a power outside of empirical consciousness, or of the will and passion of the living and the dead; but this power is set forth only as something external and sensible, and remains completely within the caprice of those who have raised things of this sort to such power.

We have yet to mention a more developed form of this religion whose character we have outlined, where humanity has not yet emerged from its subjective particularity, not yet gone out into the separation of something universal in and for itself, as opposed to its own isolated being and to nature. | This more developed form   445
is the religion of the Chinese empire.

c. The State Religion of the Chinese Empire and the Dao[96]
⁻This religion still stands within the scope of this principle; it is a developed religion of magic.

93. [*Ed.*] Hegel may be referring to the Journal by Professor Smith appended to *Narrative of an Expedition to Explore the River Zaire, Usually Called the Congo, in South Africa, in 1816, under the Direction of Captain J. K. Tuckey, R.N.* (London, 1818), p. 375.

94. *W (Var) adds:* from whom they expect to derive good fortune

95. *W (Var) reads:* and, accordingly, if anything unpleasant befalls them, [*W₂*: and they do not find the fetish serivceable,] they do away with it [*W₂*: and choose another].

96. [*Ed.*] Hegel's treatment of ancient Chinese religion is considerably revised in 1827 as compared with the 1824 version. He recognizes more clearly that Tian symbolizes heaven, although in his view it represents physical power rather than a spiritual deity. He discusses at greater length the relationship between Tian and the emperor, although he continues to view them as more closely identified than they were in fact. And he introduces for the first time references to the Dao and Daoism, which have their roots in the Zhou traditions (see below, n. 115). Hegel's basic source remains the Jesuit *Mémoires concernant les Chinois,* 16 vols. (Paris, 1776–1814), and he draws upon them more fully although he makes use of other sources as well. See the subsequent annotations for details. In place of the chaotic romani-

446 In the Chinese empire there is a religion of Fo or Buddha, which was introduced in A.D. 50[97] Then there is the ancient Chinese religion of Dao—this is a distinctive god, | reason. But the state religion, the religion of the Chinese empire, is the religion of heaven, where heaven or Tian is acknowledged as the highest ruling power. What is called "heaven" here is not merely the power of nature, but the power of nature bound up together with moral characteristics, through which this power of nature dispenses or withholds its blessings according to moral deserts and conduct.[98]

We seem, therefore, to have entered a quite different and higher sphere. For us "heaven" signifies "God"—without the admixture of anything physical. With this Tian, which is first of all physical power, we seem, insofar as it also determines itself morally, to have left the sphere of nature religion and magic behind. But if we consider it more closely, we find that we are still standing wholly within this sphere where the single human being, the empirical consciousness, the will of the individual, is what is highest.

Tian means "heaven." There were many controversies over this, especially among the Catholic orders that had been sent to China as missionaries.[99] They were most welcome at the court; they were

---

zation of Chinese characters in the sources available to L and W, we have used the Pinyin system, officially adopted in 1958 and now the accepted scholarly norm.

97. [Ed.] The *Allgemeine Historie der Reisen* (Leipzig, 1750), 6:358 gives a date "some sixty-five years after the birth of our Lord," while the *Mémoires concernant les Chinois* 5:51, 58 give A.D. 63 or 64. See also Francis Buchanan, "On the Religion and Literature of the Burmas," *Asiatic Researches* 6:262. Present estimates are between A.D. 65 and 67.

98. L (1827?) *adds:* Consequently this physical power also determines itself in a moral way.

99. [Ed.] The controversies among the different Catholic orders began with the missions to China on the part of the Franciscans, Dominicans, and Augustinians, beginning in 1633. The Papal bull *Ex quo singulari* condemned the Jesuit mission in 1742. Reference to the Capuchins is found only in *An,* and could be due to an error in the source or a misunderstanding on Hegel's part. The controversy did not center principally on the designation of God but on the permissibility of combining Chinese rituals, especially those of Confucianism and the ancestor cult, with Christianity. Hegel, however, represents it as focusing on the question how the designation of God as "heaven" is to be properly understood. This may be regarded as an indication that his treatment is based primarily on the account in the *Allgemeine Historie* 6:386, where it is presented in this light.

occupied with the preparation of the calendar, which the Chinese were at one time unable to do. The Jesuit missionaries propagated the Christian religion there, but they allowed the Chinese to use the name "Tian" for God; for this they were harshly indicted before the Pope by other orders (the Capuchins and Franciscans), because "Tian" designates the physical power and not a spiritual deity.⁻[100] Tian is the highest, though not only in the spiritual and moral sense. This Tian designates wholly indeterminate and abstract universality; it is the wholly indeterminate sum of the physical and moral nexus as a whole. In this context it is the emperor and not heaven who is sovereign on earth; it is not heaven that has given or gives the ⁻laws⁻[101] of religion and ethical life, which human beings respect. It is not Tian that rules nature, for the emperor rules everything and only he is connected with this Tian. Only he brings offerings to Tian at the four main festivals of the year; | it is only the emperor who   447

100. W₂ *(1831) reads:* We have now to consider the more specific forms in which pantheism has defined itself as a religion.
1. The Chinese Religion, or the Religion of Measure
a. Its General Determinacy
   In the first place, substance continues to be thought of under that aspect of being which does indeed come nearest to essence, yet still pertains to the immediacy of being; and spirit, which is distinct from substance, is a particular, finite spirit, i.e., it is a human being. This spirit is on the one hand the wielder of authority, the one who carries the power into effect; while on the other hand, as subject to the power, it is something accidental. If a human being [such as the Chinese emperor] is represented as this power, so that it is regarded as operative in him or that it comes, through the cultus, to the point of positing itself as identical with him, then the power has the shape of spirit, but of finite, human spirit; and with this we have the [element of] separation from others, over whom the power is exercised.
b. The Historical Existence of this Religion
   It is true that we have gone beyond the immediate religion constituted by the standpoint of magic, inasmuch as the particular spirit now distinguishes itself from the substance and its relationship to the substance in that it regards it as the universal power. In the Chinese religion, which is the closest approximation, in historical form, to this relationship to substance, substance is known as the entire sphere of essential being, as measure; measure is regarded as what has being in and for itself, the unchangeable, and Tian, heaven, is the objective intuition of this sphere of being-in-and-for-self. However, the characteristic of magic-working also still intrudes into this sphere, insofar as in actuality the singular human being, with its will and empirical consciousness, is what is highest. The standpoint of magic has here broadened to yield an organized monarchy, whose intuition has something grandiose and majestic.
   101. W *(Var) reads:* divine laws, laws

converses with Tian, who directs his prayers to Tian. He alone stands in connection with Tian, and thus it is the emperor who rules the whole earth. Among us the prince rules, but God does, too; the prince is bound by the divine commandments. But here [it] is the emperor who has dominion even over nature and rules the powers themselves, and that is why all things on earth are the way they are.

We distinguish the world or worldly phenomena in such a way that God rules beyond this world too.[102] That is where heaven is, which is perhaps populated by the souls of the dead. The heaven of the Chinese or Tian, by contrast, is something totally empty.[103] The souls of the dead do indeed exist and survive their departure from the body, but they, too, belong to the world,[104] and the emperor rules over them as well, putting them in their appointed places and removing them from them.[105] It is this single self-consciousness that consciously carries out the perfect governance.[106] |

448

102. W_2 *(Var) adds:* But here it is only the emperor that rules.

103. *In Hu's margin:* It has no sway over higher spirits or the bodies of the deceased, as is sometimes imagined to be the case in other religions.

104. W_2 *(Var) adds:* since they are thought of as lords over the natural spheres,

105. W_2 *(MiscP/Var?) adds (cf. n. 103):* If the dead are represented as directors of the natural realms, it might be said that in this way they are exalted; but in fact they are demoted into genii of the natural world, and therefore it is right that the self-conscious will should direct them.

Hence the heaven of the Chinese is not a world that forms an independent realm above the earth (as we picture it with angels and the souls of the departed, or in the way the Greek Olympus is distinct from life on earth). On the contrary, everything is upon earth, and everything that has power is subject to the emperor.

106. *W (1831) adds:* [W_1: In this connection, what is noteworthy is how what has being in and for itself is known as order and determinate existence. In this form, substance is conceived as measure. But there is also the power over these measures, over this substance—this power is the emperor. Measure itself is an established categorial determination; it is called Dao, or reason. W_2: As regards measure, there are established categorial determinations which are called reason (Dao).] The laws of Dao, or the measures, are categorial determinations or figurations, [W_1: not of abstract being or of abstract substance, but established, universal determinations. These figurations can in turn be viewed more abstractly, in which case they characterize nature and human spirit, they are laws of human will and human reason. W_2: not abstract being or abstract substance but figurations of substance, which can be viewed in more abstract fashion but also characterize nature and human spirit, are laws of human will and human reason.] The detailed exposition and development of these measures would comprise the entire philosophy and science of the Chinese. Here we merely need to draw attention to the principal points.

The measures[a] in their abstract universality are quite simple categories: being and not-being, one and two (which is equivalent in general to the many). These universal categories were denoted by the Chinese with straight lines. The basic figure is the line; a simple line (–) signifies the one, an affirmation or "yes"; the broken line (– –) denotes two, cleavage, and negation or "no." These signs are called Gua, and the Chinese story is that they appeared upon the shell of the tortoise. There are many different combinations of these signs, which in turn give more concrete meanings of the original categorial determinations. In particular, these more concrete meanings include the four quarters of the world and the center; four mountains corresponding to these regions of the world, and one in the center; and five elements, earth, fire, water, wood, and metal. There are likewise five basic colors, each of which belongs to [W_1: one region of the world. W_2: one element.] Each ruling dynasty in China has a particular color, element, etc. There are also five key notes in music, and five basic ways of characterizing human actions in relation to others. The first and highest is the behavior of children toward their parents, the second is reverence for deceased ancestors and the dead, the third is obedience to the emperor, the fourth is the behavior of brothers and sisters toward one another, and the fifth is how one behaves toward other people.

These determinations of measure constitute the basis—reason. Human beings have to conform to them; and as regards the natural elements, their genii are to be venerated.

There are those who devote themselves exclusively to the study of this reason, who hold aloof from all practical life and live in solitude. Yet what is always the important thing is that these laws should be applied in practical life. If they are observed, if human beings perform their duties, then everything is in order in nature as well as in the empire; both the empire and the [dutiful] individuals prosper. There is a moral coherence here between human action and what happens in nature. If misfortune overtakes the empire, whether owing to floods or to earthquakes, conflagrations, drought, or the like, this arises entirely from the human failure to follow the laws of reason, from the fact that the determinations of measure have not been properly maintained in the kingdom. Because of this omission the universal measure is destroyed, and this kind of misfortune strikes. This measure is known here as what has being in and for itself. This is the general foundation.

The next step concerns the implementation of measure. Maintenance of the laws is the prerogative of the emperor, of the emperor as the son of heaven, which is the whole, the totality of measures. The sky [W_1: is on the one hand the visible firmament, but it is also W_2: as the visible firmament is at the same time] the power over the measures. The emperor is directly the son of heaven (Tian-zi); he has to honor the laws and secure recognition for them. By means of a careful education, the heir to the throne is made acquainted with all the sciences and with the laws. The emperor alone renders honor to the law; his subjects have only to give [W_1: honor to him, as the one who administers the laws. W_2: him the honor that he renders to the law.] The emperor brings offerings. This means nothing else than that the emperor prostrates himself and reverences the law. Among the few Chinese festivals one of the main ones is that of agriculture. The emperor presides over it; on the day of the festival he himself plows the field; the corn that grows upon this field is used as offerings. The empress has under her direction the production of silk; this supplies the material for clothing, just as agriculture is the source of all nourishment. When floods, plague, and the like lay waste and scourge the country, the emperor alone must deal with

From the Jesuit memoirs and from ancient history books there has come to us a quite unusual representation that has something magnificent about it, a representation of the events antecedent to a change of dynasty | —how the Zhou dynasty came to rule and

449

the situation; [W₂: he acknowledges his officials, and especially himself, to be the cause of the misfortune—] if he and his magistrates had maintained the law properly, the misfortune would not have occurred. The emperor therefore commands the officials to examine themselves and to see how they have failed in their duty; and he in like manner [W₁: spends time in W₂: devotes himself to] meditation and penitence because he has not acted rightly. Thus the prosperity of the empire and the individual depends on the fulfillment of duty. In this way the entire service of God reduces to a moral life for the subjects, and nothing more. So the Chinese religion can be termed a moral religion (and this is the sense in which it has been possible to ascribe atheism to the Chinese). For the most part these determinations of measure and specific rules of duty derive from Confucius; his works are principally concerned with moral questions of this kind.

This might of the laws and of the determinations of measure is an aggregate of many particular determinations and laws. These particular determinations must now be known as activities too; as something particular they are subject to the universal activity, namely the emperor, who has power over the whole range of activities. But the particular powers are also represented as human beings, and especially as the departed ancestors of existing persons. For people are especially known as power when they are [W₁: dead. But they are also equally this power when they segregate themselves from the world, i.e., when W₂: departed, in other words no longer entangled in the interests of everyday life. But people can also be regarded as departed if they segregate themselves from the world, in that] they sink deeper within themselves, direct their whole activity to the universal or to the cognition of these powers; when they renounce the associations of everyday life and hold themselves aloof from all enjoyments; in this way too they have departed from concrete human life, and consequently they also come to be known as particular powers. In addition to them, there are also creatures of phantasy that possess this power. Thus the realm of these particular powers is very extensive. They are all subject to the [W₁: power W₂: universal power, namely that] of the emperor, who installs them and gives them commands. The best way to gain a knowledge of this wide realm of representation is to study a section of Chinese history as we have it in the information given by the Jesuits in the learned work *Mémoires sur les Chinois*.[b]

[Ed.] [a]Hegel's references to the categories of measure (*das Mass*, the measures *die Masse*), and their signs, the Gua, as found in the 1831 lectures, are derived from Fr. Gaubil's annotated translation of the Shu-jing published in Paris in 1770 under the title *Le Chou-King, un des livres sacrés des Chinois*, as well as from other sources, such as the *Mémoires sur les Chinois*. For the specific information contained in this paragraph, see *Le Chou-King*, pp. 165, 169–170; and *Mémoires* 2:35–36, 167, 181, 186. The Gua are discussed primarily in the Yi-jing, but Hegel does not seem to have been familiar with it. The two universal categories are more commonly known as yang (one line) and yin (two lines). [b]See *Mémoires* 15:228–241.

expelled its predecessor.[107] The establishment of this dynasty is fully narrated there, how the new prince Wu-wang decreed the laws of his | dynasty and organized the realm. This dynasty came to rule   450
in 1122 B.C. ‾Chinese history contains documents from 2300 B.C.‾[108] Since this description is very characteristic, I will present an excerpt from it. This new prince came to the throne. The [imperial] residence was not yet Beijing. The last prince of the preceding dynasty had consumed himself in flames, together with all his wealth, his mandarins, etc., in his palace in the capital—a palace that was itself a city. When the flames were extinguished, the new prince made his entrance, but had it proclaimed that he would not solemnly take possession of the throne until everything was regulated between him and heaven, i.e., until the laws and the administration of the empire were brought into order. This regulation consisted of the emperor's publication of the two books that had been preserved up to that time by an old man on an ancient mountain. One book contained the new | laws, ‾though they were almost the same as the old ones;‾[109]   451
and they were promulgated. The other book contained the titles of officials of the realms; the mandarins constituted [one of] the two classes of officials; the other kind of official consisted of the dead, the Shen. These Shen were appointed by the emperor just as were the living officials of the new administration. From that day on the emperor still rules the genii of his realm, who are the dead, and the state calendar today still consists of these two divisions. Then the narrative tells how the emperor's general undertook the filling of the offices according to the emperor's will. The general, who obtained the books and was commissioned with the nomination of the Shen,

107. [Ed.] For the information contained in this and the next paragraph, see *Mémoires concernant les Chinois* 15:228–241.

108. *Thus Hu, who reads: 23,000*
[Ed.] It is now known that this computation is not based on historical evidence but on later cosmological speculation. Hegel disregards the statement in the *Allgemeine Historie* 6:408–409 that Chinese chronology can only be reliably extended back to 400 B.C., and instead follows Gaubil's translation of the Shu-jing, which begins its dating of events from 2357 B.C.; see *Le Chou-King*, pp. 1 ff.

109. *Thus Hu; in An's margin:* the content of which, however, was nothing new; they are entirely those that had been introduced previously;

then tells of his expedition on the occasion of his investiture of the genii[110] in their offices, which is the main point.

¬The recognition of the dead, the nobility of the [earlier] empire, simultaneously honored their [surviving] families and linked them to the new dynasty.¬[111] The general was sent to one of the holy mountains; there he built an altar, set himself upon a throne, laid his scepter of command [before him], and bade all the dead to come into his presence. After the sacrificial offering, the general made known the emperor's command:[112] they should respectfully accept the decrees of heaven that were to be proclaimed to them by the emperor and announced by the general. He made known what sort of offices these spirits were given by the emperor. He continued by reproaching in the strongest terms the assembled genii because of their negligence. The Shen, especially the more recently dead, were rebuked for the poor administration of the realm, | as a result of which the empire fell into ruin. Then he said, to those who were the cause of the state's disorder, that they were dismissed by heaven and could go wherever they wished—even to enter upon a new life in order to rectify their errors. Then the whole company of the Shen drew back; the general donned his cuirass and took the yellow flag in his left hand. ¬Thereupon, from the throne, he ordered a certain Bo-qian to read aloud the register of the imperial promotions. First stood the name of Bo-qian; he had therefore become the first Shen. The general congratulated him, who had averted so much misfortune from the state by his victories. The fallen ones from the preceding dynasty were brought forward.¬[113] Among these stood Wen-zong, the name of the uncle and field marshal of the previous

452

110. *An adds:* (in the register)

111. *L (1827?) reads:* The Shen are not immediate natural powers or natural phenomena, but are rather the form of powers, or of forces, that [are] not merely represented for the imagination but are deemed to belong to human beings who are deceased. What was interesting here was, first, that no power was independent of the emperor, and, second, that those men who had been esteemed in the previous dynasty were also honored, and a bond (therefore, a political tie) was established between their families and the new emperor.

112. *In B's margin:* 25 June 1827

113. W_2 *(Var) reads:* The delegated commander in chief named the new Shen and ordered one of those present to take the register and read it aloud. He obeyed, and found his name to be the first on the list. The commander in chief congratulated him that his virtues had been recognized in this way. He was an old general. Then

ruler; he was at first unwilling to appear; then he came, but was unwilling to kneel; he alone remained standing. The general spoke to him, saying: you are no longer the one you were during your lifetime; now you are nothing; you should therefore heed the commands of heaven with complete deference. Then this Wen-zong did fall to his knees, and he was appointed the chief inspector over clouds, storms, and rain. Then twenty-four other genii were appointed over fire, epidemic diseases, etc.—in short, over everything of which natural humanity stands in need.

That is the imperial organization with respect to the invisible powers. The emperor is lord over the visible world of the mandarins just as he is over the invisible Shen. The Shen of rain, of rivers, and the like, are the general overseers who have the particular local genii under them, those who watch over the rain, rivers, etc., in smaller regions. Almost every particular mountain, shrub, or village has its particular Shen. The Shen were indeed worshiped; but one did not hold them in particular esteem. They were subordinate to the mandarins, to whom the emperor gave his commands directly. The mandarins | must take care to rule well; if they do not, then both they and the Shen are removed from office. This is the form of this nature religion: the emperor alone knows the mandates of heaven, he alone stands in communication with heaven, and his lordship extends over both the visible and the invisible.

453

We have yet to mention a particular circumstance concerning the reported constitution of Wu-wang.[114] After the emperor had made known to his people the official charter that had previously been disclosed to the Shen, the emperor held his own grand inauguration, performed a sacrifice to Tian, and elevated his entire deceased family to imperial dignity, whereby they enjoyed particular honor. Then he rewarded all his generals and officers. He showered them all with benefits—only one class remained excluded from his rewards, namely those who professed the particular faith of the Dao, the followers of the sect of the Dao.

---

the others were summoned, some having been killed in the interests of the new dynasty, others having fought and sacrificed themselves on behalf of the former dynasty.

114. [Ed.] Hegel's source for the account in this and the following paragraph is *Mémoires concernant les Chinois* 15:249–252.

Dao generally means "the way," the right way of spirit, i.e., it means "reason." The sect of the Dao occurs already (as we see) in the twelfth century B.C.[115] It was a noteworthy event that the emperor passed over esteemed officers with his rewards; ˉhis intention was in a subtle way to put them to one side,ˉ[116] to separate them from his other retainers. These gallant officers included masters of the teaching as well as some who were only initiates at a lower level. Seven noble officers had distinguished themselves by particular deeds of valor; in the eyes of the mass of soldiers they were regarded as Shen who had only assumed human bodies, and they presented themselves in that light as well. On a ceremonial day the emperor addressed them, saying he had not forgotten them, that he recognized very well the value of their merits. "Even though you have bodies," he continued, "you are Shen, of that there is no doubt. The outstanding actions that you have performed under my eyes are sufficient proof of that to me. The intention, for the sake of which you returned to the earth, can only be to acquire for yourselves new merits, to disclose new virtues. I can do no better than to put you 454 in a position | to practice these virtues, by safeguarding you against the corruption of the times." He therefore determined the mountains to be their residence, where they could spend their remaining time in intimate association with the Shen who no longer have human shape. They were supposed to take with them all who belonged to

115. [*Ed.*] A similar date is given in Hegel's sources. While the idea of the Dao (the "way," the ultimate ordering principle of the world as evident in the regular patterns of nature) goes back to the Western Zhou period (1122–771 B.C.), Daoism as a movement did not appear until toward the end of the Eastern Zhou dynasty. According to legend, its founder was Lao-zi, an elder contemporary of Confucius (551–479 B.C.), to whom is attributed the *Dao De Jing* (Classic of the Way and Its Power), which scholars today believe was probably compiled in the third century B.C. The doctrines of Confucius and Lao-zi were opposed in fundamental respects—the one being ordered to social ritualization and the other to natural conformity. However, they both represent appropriations of the ancient concept of the Dao. See N. Nielsen, N. Hein, F. Reynolds, et al., *Religions of the World* (New York, 1983), pp. 264, 266–276. While Hegel's reference to "the sect of the Dao" seems to suggest Daoism as a movement, he may have the older, generic concept in mind here, since he identifies it with reason rather than with mystical experience (as was characteristic of Daoism), and since he refers below to a later "renewal or improvement of the Dao teaching, attributed especially to Lao-zi" (see n. 120).

116. *An reads:* he wanted to purge his state of these men without deeds of violence,

their sect, all who strove solely to attain immortal life. He made these seven into chiefs over all the mountains of the realm and gave them all rights of dominion over the initiates. Thus they were to apply themselves to the study of the Dao and to the effort to make themselves immortal; together with the other Shen, they were also supposed to acquire information about the secrets of nature that are impenetrable to other human beings. Thus they were separated from actual society.

From this account we see that at that time there was already a class of people who occupied themselves with the inner life, who did not belong to this universal state religion but built up a sect that devoted itself to thinking, withdrew within itself and in its thinking sought to bring to consciousness what the true might be.[117]

Therefore, the next stage of this initial configuration of nature religion—which was this very knowing by immediate self-consciousness of itself as the highest, as the ruling element, i.e., this immediacy of taking immediate willing to be what is highest—is the return of consciousness into itself, the demand that consciousness should be inwardly meditative—and that is the sect of the Dao. Linked with this, in any case, is the fact that human beings who recede into thought or into the inner domain, who ˉapplied themselves to the abstraction of thought,ˉ[118] have at the same time the intentionˉof being immortal, of being pure sages,ˉ[119] of whom some are newly initiated while others have attained the mastery or the goal and | already regard themselves as higher essences also with respect to their existence and actuality.   455

Therefore we already find among the Chinese in antiquity this orientation toward the inner, to the Dao, an orientation to abstractly pure thinking, which orientation constitutes the transition to the

117. [Ed.] See *Mémoires concernant les Chinois* 15:209–210, although the stress in this passage is on acquiring knowledge "of all the operations of nature," in its entirety and as a whole.

118. W *(Var) reads:* apply themselves to the abstraction of thought, B *reads:* applied themselves to thought, L *reads:* live in the abstraction of thought,

119. *Thus Hu;* B *reads:* of becoming immortal, L *(Var) reads:* of becoming in essence immortal on their own account, W *reads:* of becoming immortal essences, pure on their own account,

[Ed.] Where *Hu* reads *Weise* (sage), L and W read *Wesen* (essence).

second form of nature religion. There occurred in later times a renewal or improvement of the Dao teaching, attributed especially to Lao-zi,[120] a sage who was somewhat older than Confucius but who lived contemporaneously with Confucius and Pythagoras.[121] Confucius is thoroughly moralistic and no speculative philosopher. Tian, this universal power of nature, which by the emperor's authority is an actuality, is linked to the moral nexus, and Confucius chiefly developed this moral aspect. His teaching coalesced with the state religion. All the mandarins had to have studied Confucius. But the sect of the Dao based itself solely on abstract thinking.

[122]Dao is the universal. It is quite noteworthy that the determination "three" immediately comes into play[123] to the extent that Dao is something rational and concrete. Reason has produced one, one has produced two, two produced three, and three the universe—the same doctrine that we see in Pythagoras. The universe rests upon the dark principle and is at the same time embraced by the bright principle, by light. A spirit or breath unites them, and brings about their harmony and maintains it.[124] The initial determination of the triad is the One, and is called J; the second determination is the Chi or light breathing; the third is Wei, what is sent, the messenger. These three symbols are perhaps not Chinese; one sees in them the three letters J, H, W, and correlates this with the Hebraic tetragram Jehovah, and with the trigram Yao of the Gnostics.[125] [126]The One

120. [Ed.] This is probably based on Abel-Rémusat, *Mémoire sur la vie et les opinions de Lao-Tseu* (Paris, 1823), who states, p. 2, that Lao-zi "flourished at the beginning of the sixth century B.C." and "is still considered to be the patriarch and reformer of the sect of the Dao."

121. [Ed.] See ibid., pp. 36 ff. Hegel makes no mention of the later, legendary report of a visit of Confucius to Lao-zi (ibid., p. 4).

122. *In B's margin:* 26 June 1827

123. W₂ *(Var) adds:* in Dao—in the totality—

124. [Ed.] Hegel's source for the three preceding sentences is again Abel-Rémusat, *Mémoire*, p. 31, although Abel-Rémusat does not at this point draw a parallel with Pythagoras or refer to the "dark principle" and the "bright principle," but only to "matter" and "aether."

125. [Ed.] The preceding two sentences are drawn from a much longer passage in Abel-Rémusat, *Mémoire*, pp. 40–49. The identification of J with the life-giving energy of the One, of Chi with a light breath, and of Wei with the messenger is not accepted by Abel-Rémusat, who attributes it to Montucci and says that the three characters in fact have no meaning but are used simply to denote sounds that do not

is the indeterminate, that without characteristics, the impoverished initial abstraction, what is wholly empty. ˉIf it is to be internally concrete, | to be living, then it must be determinate, and thus it is 456 the Two, and the Third is the totality, the consummation of determinateness. Thus, even in the first efforts of humanity to think in the form of triunity or trinity, we can observe this necessity.ˉ127 Unless three determinations are recognized in God, "God" is an empty word. Right at the beginning of thinking we find the very simplest and most abstract determinations of thought. If, from this assertion that the absolute power is, there occurs the progression to the universal, then thinking begins, though the thinking itself is originally quite empty and abstract. Further developments of this relationship are found in Chinese literature. The symbol of the Dao is on the one hand a triangle, and on the other hand three horizontal lines one above the other, the middle one of which is shortest, with a vertical stroke through all three as a sign that these three are to be grasped essentially as one.[128] In China these symbols are called Gua.[129] The [eight] Gua embody the elements of the higher Chinese reflection.

Thus in the sect of the Dao the beginning consists in passing over

---

occur in Chinese. And his lengthy discussion of whether the Hebraic tetragram (JHWH) came to be expressed in three Chinese characters, and if so how, is not at all reflected in Hegel's flat statement that they were correlated. This view was reinforced by H. J. Klaproth in his review of G. Pauthier, *Mémoire sur l'origine et la propagation de la doctrine du Tao, fondée par Lao-tseu* (Paris, 1831), in *Nouveau Journal Asiatique* 7 (1831): 491–493— a view no longer regarded as correct. Hegel also quotes from this passage of Abel-Rémusat in the *Lectures on the History of Philosophy* 1:124–135 (cf. *Werke* 13:444), but adds: "If philosophizing has got no further than such expressions, it is still at the first stage."

126. *Precedes in L (1827?), similar in* W₂: As soon as we arrive at the element of thinking, the determination "three" makes its appearance at once.

127. W₂ *(Var) reads:* If it is to have the principle of organic life and spirituality, an advance must be made to determination. Unity is actual only insofar as it contains two within itself, and this yields the triad.

128. [*Ed.*] Hegel's source for this assertion has not been identified. In any case it seems to be erroneous. The Gua (see the following note) include neither a triangle nor the sign described by Hegel consisting of three horizontal lines intersected by a vertical stroke. The latter suggests the sign 玉 (*wang*² = king, prince); the character for the Dao is much more complex: 道 (*dao*⁴ = way, truth, reason).

129. [*Ed.*] In regard to the eight Gua, see above, n. 106, annotation a.

into thought, the pure element; but one should not believe that a higher, spiritual religion has established itself in this case. The determinations of the Dao remain complete abstractions, and vitality, consciousness, what is spiritual, do not, so to speak, fall within the Dao itself, but are still completely within the immediate human being. Thus Lao-zi is also a Shen, or he has appeared as Buddha.[130] [131]The actuality and vitality of the Dao is still the actual, immediate consciousness; in fact, it is even a deceased individual such as Lao-zi, although it transforms itself into other shapes, into another human being, and it is vitally and actually present in its priests. Just as Tian, this One, is the ruling element, though as this abstract foundation, whereas the emperor is the actuality of this foundation, the one who in fact rules; so the same is the case with the Dao, with the representation of reason. Reason is likewise the abstract foundation that |

457 has its actuality for the first time in existing human beings. [132]Since the universal, the higher, is only the abstract foundation, the human being thus abides in it without any properly immanent, fulfilled inner element; one has no inner hold on oneself. One has for the first time a footing within oneself when freedom and rationality emerge, when one has the consciousness of being free and when this freedom elaborates itself as reason. This developed reason provides absolute principles and duties; and people who are themselves conscious of these principles in their freedom and within their conscience—people in whom they are immanent characteristics—have for the first time a footing within themselves, in their conscience. But insofar as human beings find themselves in that preceding relationship, where

130. [Ed.] See *Mémoires concernant les Chinois* 15:255, 258, where, however, it is not claimed that Lao-zi had appeared as Buddha, only that he had himself claimed to have been a Shen.

131. *Precedes in L (1827?), similar in W:* God is for us the universal, but inwardly determined. God is spirit, his existence is spirituality. But here

132. *Precedes in W₂ (1831):* Cultus is, properly speaking, the whole existence of the religion of measure, the power of substance having not yet inwardly assumed the shape of firm objectivity; and even the realm of representation, to the extent that it has developed in the realm of the Shen, is subject to the power of the emperor, who is himself merely the one who implements the substantive in actuality.

If, then, we inquire into cultus in the narrower sense, there is only the relationship of the general determinateness of this religion to inner life and to self-consciousness left for us to investigate.

the absolute is only an abstract foundation, they⁻¹³³ have no footing within themselves, no immanent, determinate inwardness. For that reason everything external is for them something inward; everything external has significance for them, it has a relation to them, and indeed a practical relation. This relationship is in general the constitution of the state, the circumstances of being ruled from without.

No inherent morality is bound up with the Chinese religion, no immanent rationality through which human beings might have internal value and dignity¹³⁴; instead everything is external, everything that is connected with them is a power for them, because in their rationality and morality they have no power within themselves. The consequence is an indeterminable dependence on everything external, the highest | and most contingent kind of superstition.¹³⁵ The Chinese are the most superstitious people of the world;¹³⁶ they have a ceaseless fear and anxiety of everything, because everything external has a significance for them, is a power over them, is something that exerts authority over them, something that can affect them. Divination in particular makes its home there; anxiety in the face of every contingent situation impels them to it. In every locale there are many who occupy themselves with prophesying; the correct place for one's dwelling, for one's grave (both the

458

133. *Thus An, Hu; L (1827?) reads, similar in W:* Only insofar as human beings have knowledge of God as spirit and of the determinations of spirit—only then have these determinations of the divine become essential, absolute determinations, or, in a word, rationality; what is duty within them, what, as far as they are concerned, is immanent within them. But where the universal is merely this abstract foundation as such, they

134. *W₂ (Var) adds:* and protection against what is external

135. *W₂ (1831) adds:* Speaking generally, what lies at the foundation of this external dependence is the fact that nothing that is particular can be placed in an inner relationship with the universal that remains merely abstract. The interests of individuals lie outside the universal determinations put into effect by the emperor. With regard to particular interests, what we find is rather the representation of a power that exists on its own account. It is not the universal power of providence, which extends its sway even over particular destinies. Instead, the particular is made subject to a particular power. This power is that of the Shen, and with this an enormous realm of superstition comes into play.

136. *[Ed.]* Hegel's examples of Chinese superstition are taken from *Allgemeine Historie* 6:389–390.

locality and the spatial arrangement)—the Chinese engage in such things throughout their entire lives. In the building of a house, if another house flanks one's own, or if the front has an angle facing it, then ¯all possible ceremonies are performed with respect to it, and so on.¯[137]

2. The Religion of Being-Within-Self (Buddhism, Lamaism)[138]

[139]Thus the second form of nature religion, the more determinate and intensive being-within-self, which is coherent with the mode of

---

137. *Hu reads:* they have first to consider the location carefully and to think whether it might not give rise to some misfortune. W_2 *(1831) omits:* and so on *and adds:* and the particular powers are rendered propitious by means of gifts. The individual is wholly without the power of personal decision and without subjective freedom.

138. [*Ed.*] In the 1827 lectures, Buddhism/Lamaism is no longer considered under the category of magic, as in 1824, but as the second form of nature religion, in which the absolute is grasped as substance, as being-within-self. In this connection, Hegel introduces another discussion of pantheism, arguing (as he does characteristically in the 1827 lectures) that no true religion is pantheistic in the sense of claiming that "everything is God," and comparing Oriental consciousness with Spinozism. See above, pp. 123–126. In the 1824 lectures, the question of pantheism is considered more briefly in the introductory discussion of the metaphysical concept of God. On the whole, the 1827 treatment of Buddhism is more fully developed and balanced than in 1824, evidencing a better mastery of the available sources. Hegel sometimes refers to Buddhism as "the religion of Fo"; Fo is the Chinese name of Buddha.

139. *Precedes in W_2 (1831), following the treatment of Hinduism, as in the order of the 1831 lectures:* Since there has been no rational determination such as could achieve solidity, the condition of this people as a whole could never become one that is founded in right and inwardly justified; it was always merely a condition of sufferance, a contingent and confused one.
3. The Religion of Being-Within-Self
a. Its Concept
The general foundation here is still the same as that which is peculiar to the Hindu religion; what advance there is consists merely in the necessity of the categorial determinations of Hindu religion being brought together again out of their wild, unrestrained falling-apart into separateness; it consists in their being brought out of their natural segregation, and into an inner relationship with one another, so that their unchecked reveling is stilled. This religion of being-within-self is the concentration and tranquilization of spirit as it returns, out of the destructive disarray of Hindu religion, into itself and into essential unity.
The essential unity and the differences have so far been mutually exclusive to the point where the latter stood independently by themselves, and vanished in the unity only in order to emerge again at once in all their independence. The relationship between the unity and the differences was an infinite progression, a constantly

going-into-self that we have just considered—a going-into-self in the Dao, which is still wholly abstract and does not separate itself from the immediate personality—is as follows. | The highest power or the 459 absolute is grasped not in this immediacy of self-consciousness but as substance, as an essence which, however, at the same time still retains this immediacy, so that it exists in one or more individuals. This substance, with its existence in these individuals, is power or dominion; it is the creation and maintenance of the world, of nature and of all things—the absolute power over the world.

This form has a multitude of more detailed configurations whose distinctions we do not want to go into. ˉThe religion of Fo—or of Buddha in India—belongs here; this Buddha is also called | Gautama. 460 The religion of the Lamas belongs in the same context. In India Buddha is a historical person. These deceased persons are revered, but at the same time they are represented as being present in their images just as they are in their priests. In the religion of Lamaism the view is that definite individuals are God, that they are the divine substance as living, as sensibly present here.ˉ[140] This sensible presence in a human being is the abiding, principal feature [of this religion]. It is the most widespread religion on earth—in Burma and

---

alternating disappearance of differences in unity and their [reemergence] in self-subsistent independence. Now this alternation is cut short, because what is implicitly contained in it is actually posited, namely the coming together of the differences in the category of unity.

As this being-within-self for which all other-connectedness is now precluded, the essence is self-contained essentiality, the reflection of negativity into itself, and thus it is what rests and persists within itself.

Defective as this determination may be, since the being-within-self is not yet concrete and is only the disappearance of the independent differences—

140. W₁ (Var) reads: With the Hindus, too, Buddha is a divine incarnation, and also a historical person, as is Fo. These are deceased historical persons; [as such] they are venerated, but they are also represented as present and operative in their images as well as in their priests.

Lamaism holds that some of these human beings are the deity itself, that they are the [divine] substance as living, as here present. There is in itself nothing contradictory in the fact that an individual—in this case, the Dalai Lama—is known as the absolute power of substance; he is, of course, mortal, like the rest of us, but even so the deity is present within him. Beyond this no extraordinary power attaches to him, but the power of substance is within him, an immediate, unconscious power that is utterly permeating and directly present. This view coheres very closely with what we were considering previously.

251

China, in Mongolia, etc. The peoples adhering to this religion are more numerous than the Muslims, as the Muslims in turn are more numerous than the Christians.

Here we find the form of substantiality in which the absolute is a being-within-self, the one substance; but it is not grasped just as a substance for thought and in thought (as it is in Spinoza); instead it has at the same time existence in sensible presence, i.e., in singular human beings. ˉWith reference to the character of the people who adhere to this religion, this substantiality involves an elevation above the immediate, singular consciousness as it presents itself in magic, where it is just the singular consciousness that is the power, [natural] desire, or a yet untamed savagery.ˉ141 At the stage to be considered here, on the other hand, the highest is known as the One, the substantial, and it involves an elevation above desire and singular will; it involves the limitation of untamed desire and immersion | in this inwardness, [i.e., it involves] unity. The image of Buddha is in the thinking posture, with feet and arms intertwined so that a toe extends into the mouth—this [is] the withdrawal into self, this absorption in oneself.142 Hence the character of the peoples who adhere to this religion is one of tranquillity, gentleness, and obedience, a character that stands above the wildness of desire and is the cessation of desire. Great religious orders have been founded among these peoples; they share a common life in tranquillity of spirit, in quiet, ˉtranquil occupation of the spirit,ˉ143 as do the Bonze in China and ˉthe shamans in Mongolia.ˉ144 Attainment of this

461

141. W₂ (1831/Var?) reads: This religion of substantiality has particularly influenced the character of the peoples who adhere to it inasmuch as it has made the immediate, singular consciousness an omnipresent requirement.

142. [Ed.] The image is not a representation of the Buddha. Hegel is probably referring to fig. 2 in plate xxi of the volume of illustrations accompanying Friedrich Creuzer's *Symbolik und Mythologie der alten Völker* (Leipzig and Darmstadt, 1819). Creuzer identifies (p. 9) the subject as Brahmā Nārāyana, a Hindu figure from the cosmogony of the Code of Manu whom he elsewhere (1:597) associates explicitly with the posture described. See also below, annotation a to n. 217.

143. W₂ (1831) reads: contemplation of the eternal, without taking part in worldly interests and occupations,

144. Thus An; L (Var) reads: the Rabane in Burma.

[Ed.] "Rabane" is probably a misreading for "Rahāns" or "Rahāne." See Francis Buchanan, "On the Religion and Literature of the Burmas," *Asiatic Researches* 6:273–280.

pure, inward stillness is expressly declared to be the goal for human beings, to be the highest state.

ˉSo far as this stillness is also expressed as a principle, especially in the religion of Fo, the ultimate or highest [reality] is therefore nothing or not-being. They say that everything emerges from nothing, everything returns into nothing.[145] That is the absolute foundation, the indeterminate, the negated being of everything particular, so that all particular existences or actualities are only forms, and only the nothing has genuine independence, while in contrast all other actuality has none; it counts only as something accidental, an indifferent form.ˉ[146] | For a human being, ˉthis state of negation is the   462 highest state: one must immerse oneself in this nothing, in the eternal tranquillity of the nothing generally, in the substantial in which all determinations cease, where there is no virtue or intelligence, where all movement annuls itself. All characteristics of both natural life and spiritual life have vanished.ˉ[147] ˉTo be blissful, human beings

145. [Ed.] The remainder of this paragraph follows fairly closely a passage in the *Allgemeine Historie* 6:368–369, which describes the concept of "the empty" or "nothing" found in the "religion of Fo" as the source from which everything emerges and to which everything returns. In other words, it is described in Western ontological categories as the ground of being, and it is in these terms that Hegel attempts to make sense of it. Union with the nothing, or the state of nirvana, is achieved by stripping away all desire and all mental and physical activity. One thereby becomes "perfect as the God Fo." The depiction of nirvana found here—although the term is not used in this passage from the *Allgemeine Historie*—is oriented to Mahāyāna Buddhism.

146. W_2 *(MiscP) reads:* 1. The absolute foundation is the stillness of being-within-self, in which all differences cease, and all determinations characterizing the [merely] natural state of spirit, all particular powers, have disappeared. Hence the absolute, as being-within-self, is the undetermined, the annihilation of everything particular, so that all particular existences, all actual things, are only something accidental, or are merely indifferent form.

2. Since reflection into itself as the undetermined (according to the standpoint of nature religion, do not forget) is merely immediate reflection, it is expressed as a principle in this form: nothing and not-being is what is ultimate and supreme. It is nothing that alone has true independence; every other actuality and every particular thing has no independence at all. Everything has emerged out of nothing, and into nothing everything returns. The nothing is the One, the beginning and the end of everything. However diverse human beings and things may be, there is only the one principle, nothingness, from which they proceed, and it is form alone that constitutes quality and diversity.

147. W *(Var) reads:* [W_1: this state of negation is the highest: W_2: inasmuch as the stillness of being-within-self is the extinction of everything particular, is nothingness, this state of negation is also the highest human state, and one's vocation is] to im-

themselves must strive, through ceaseless internal mindfulness, to will nothing, to want [nothing], and to do nothing. When one attains this, there is no longer any question of something higher, of virtue and immortality. Human holiness consists in uniting oneself, by this negation, with nothingness, and so with God, with the absolute. A human being who has reached this holiness, this highest level, is indistinguishable from God, is eternally identical with God; and thus all change ceases. The soul no longer has to fear [trans]migration. Thus the theoretical moment finds expression here: that this pure nothing, this stillness and emptiness, is the absolutely highest state; that the individual is [something] formal.⁻¹⁴⁸ In the practical do-
463   main | human beings will ⁻and act where they [suppose that they]
     are the power.⁻¹⁴⁹ ¹⁵⁰[But here] one has to make nothingness of
464   oneself.¹⁵¹ ⁻Within one's being one has to behave in this negative |

---

merse oneself in this nothing, in the eternal tranquillity, the nothing as such—or in the substantial in which all determinations cease, and there is [W₁: no virtue,] no will, no intelligence [W₁: where all characteristics of the natural state and of spirit have vanished].

148. *W (Var) reads:* By persistent immersion and inward mindfulness every human should become like this principle, should be without passion, without inclination, without action, and should arrive at a condition of willing nothing and doing nothing.

There is no question here of virtue or vice, of reconciliation or immortality. Human holiness consists, in this negation and silence, of uniting oneself with God, with the nothing, the absolute. The highest state consists in the cessation of all bodily motion, all movement of the soul. Once this stage has been attained, [W₂: there is no descent to a lower stage, no further change, and] one does not have to fear [trans]migration after death, for then one is identical with God. Here the theoretical moment finds expression: that a human being is something substantive and self-subsistent.

149. *W (1831) reads:* and when they will, what is is an object for them, which they alter and upon which they imprint their form. The practical value of religious sensibility is determined in accordance with the content of what is regarded as the true. But in this religion [W₁: there is at least this value W₂: there is, however, first of all this theoretical element still] present: that this unity, this purity, this nothingness is absolutely independent vis-à-vis consciousness, i.e., that its characteristic is not to act in opposition to what is objective, to mold it, but [W1: that this stillness may be preserved and produced in it. W₂: to let it be preserved so that this stillness is produced in it.]

150. *Precedes in L (Var):* This stillness, or emptiness, is the absolute. *Precedes in W (Var):* This is the absolute.

151. *W (1831) adds:* The value of a human being consists in this, that one's self-consciousness is affirmatively related to that theoretical substantiality. This is the opposite of the [Buddhist] relationship which, since the object has no determination

way, to resist not what is external but only oneself. The state that is represented as a human being's goal, this state of unity and purity, the Buddhists call nirvana, and it is described in the following way. When one is no longer subjected to the burdens of stress, old age, sickness, and death, nirvana has been attained; one is then identical with God,[152] is regarded as God himself, has become Buddha.

[153]At first glance it must astonish us that humans think of God as nothing; that must be extremely strange. More closely considered, however, this characterization means nothing other than that God

for it, is of a merely negative nature, and which for that very reason is affirmative only as a relation of the subject to its own inwardness (which is the power to change all objectivity into a negative)—or in other words, it is affirmative in its vanity alone. In the first place, that still, gentle state of mind has, momentarily in the cultus, the consciousness of such eternal tranquillity as essential, divine being, and this gives the tone and character for the rest of life. But it is also open to self-consciousness to make its entire life a continuous state of that stillness and of that contemplation devoid of existence; and this actual withdrawal from the externality of needs and the actuality of life into the quiet inner region, and the consequent attainment of union with this theoretical substantiality, must be considered the supreme consummation.

W₁ *continues:* A more detailed view of these general determinations is offered by the reports available to us about the characteristics that the worshipers of Fo or Buddha—or perhaps rather of Fo and Buddha, both being in equal measure the supreme head of the religion of Lamaism—adduce as the essence of this God of theirs.

There are still two other determinations to be mentioned, which derive from what has been demonstrated; one of them relates to the shape of God, the other to the external nature of the subjective self-consciousness. But we must confine ourselves to the general basic determinations of both, since they follow quite simply from the definition of the divine nature that has been given. For the divine nature itself has not got beyond the undeveloped abstraction of tranquil being-within-itself that lacks all determinacy. Consequently any further shaping or representation [of it] is surrendered, partly to the contingency of empirical historical events, and partly to that of the imagination; these less structured details belong to a description of the countless, confused products of the imagination concerning the adventures and destinies of these deities, and of their friends and disciples, as well as the other ceremonies and practices of the external cultus—a mass of material which has but little interest or value of any other kind as far as its inner content is concerned, and which (as we have already indicated) has not the interest of the concept.

[Ed.] Cf. n. 186.

152. *Similar in* W₁; W₂ *(MiscP) reads:* If one assumes this negative mental attitude and resists not what is external but only oneself, and if one unites oneself with nothingness, rids oneself of all consciousness, of all passion, one is raised to the state that the Buddhists call nirvana. One is then unburdened, no longer subject to stress, to sickness, old age, or death; one

153. *In B's margin:* 28 June 1827

purely and simply is nothing determinate, is the indeterminate; there is no determinacy of any sort whatsoever that is applicable to God; God is the infinite. For when we say that God is the infinite, that means that God is the negation of everything particular. When we adopt the forms that are commonplace today, i.e., "God is the infinite, the essence, the pure and simple essence, the essence of essences and only the essence," then this sort of talk is necessarily either totally or tolerably synonymous with the claim that God is nothing. That does not mean, however, that God is not, but rather that God is the empty, and that this emptiness is God. When we say, "We can know nothing of God, can have no cognition, no representation of God," then this is⁻¹⁵⁴ a milder | expression for the fact that for us God is the nothing, that for us God is what is empty; that means that we must abstract from every determination of whatever sort. What remains left over then is the nothing and the essence; and the essence only, without any further determination, is surely the empty, the indeterminate. That is a definite and necessary stage of religious representation: God as the indeterminate, as indeterminacy, as this total void in which ˉthe initial mode of immediacyˉ¹⁵⁵ is superseded, has disappeared.

465

The principal cultus for human beings [in this religion] is the uniting of oneself with this nothing, divesting oneself of all consciousness, of all passions. This cultus consists of transposing oneself into this abstraction, into this complete solitude, this total emptiness, this renunciation, into the nothing. When one has attained this, one is then indistinguishable from God, eternally identical with God.

In the doctrine of Fo we find ˉthe dogma ofˉ¹⁵⁶ the transmigration of souls. This standpoint is [higher than] that according to which the followers of the Dao wish to make themselves Shen, wish to make themselves immortal. While Daoism presents the attaining of immortality through meditation and withdrawal into oneself as the highest destination of human beings, it does not in that connection declare that the soul persists intrinsically as such and essentially, that

154. W (Var/Ed?) reads: That modern way is therefore only
155. W₂ (Var) reads: immediate being and its seeming independence
156. W (Var) reads: the representation of [W₂ adds: immortality and]

the spirit is immortal, but only that human beings can make themselves immortal through the process of abstraction[157] and that they should do so. The thought of immortality lies precisely in the fact that, in thinking, human beings are present to themselves in their freedom. In thinking, one is utterly independent; nothing else can intrude upon one's freedom—one relates only to oneself, and nothing else can have a claim upon one. ˉThis equivalence with myself, the I, this subsisting with self,ˉ[158] is what is genuinely immortal | and subject to no alteration; it is itself the unchangeable, what has actual being only within itself and moves only within itself. The I is not *lifeless* tranquillity but movement, though a movement that is not change; instead it is *eternal* tranquillity, eternal clarity within itself. Inasmuch as it is first at this stage that God is known as the essential and is thought in his essentiality—that being-within-self or presence-to-self is the authentic determination—this being-within-self or this essentiality is therefore known in connection with the subject, is known as the nature of the subject, and the spiritual is self-contained. This essential character also pertains [directly] to the subject or the soul; it is known that the soul is immortal, that it has within itself this [power of] existing purely, or being purely inward, though not yet of existing properly as this purity, i.e., not yet as spirituality. But still bound up with this essentiality is the fact that the mode of existence is yet a sensible immediacy, though only an accidental one. This is immortality, that the soul subsisting in presence to self is both essential and existing at the same time. Essence without existence is a mere abstraction; essentiality or the concept *must* be thought as existing. Therefore realization also belongs to essentiality. But here the form of this realization is still sensible existence, sensible immediacy.

So there is therefore the representation that the soul is immortal and still persists after death; but it is always known in another sensible mode, and this is the transmigration of souls. Because it is grasped abstractly as a being-within-self similar to God, it is thus

466

157. W *(Var) adds:* and elevation

158. *An reads:* Freedom is the genuinely infinite, *Hu reads:* This universal I—I am free—is the infinite, W₁ *(Var) adds:* the genuinely infinite, W₂ *(Var) adds:* the genuinely infinite—this, it is then affirmed at this standpoint,

a matter of indifference into what sensible form the soul passes over after death, whether into a human or an animal form; spirit is not known as something concrete. Only the abstract essence is known, and the determinate being or the appearance is just the immediate, sensible shape.[159] But a human being who attains this self-negation, this abstraction, is thus exempted from transmigration of souls, is relieved from resumption of this [mode of] existence, i.e., from being tied to this external, sensible configuration.

467 God is grasped as nothing, as essence generally; this has to be explained more precisely, | and in particular the fact that this essential God is nevertheless known as a specific, immediate human being, as Fo, Buddha, or Dalai Lama. This may appear to us as the most repugnant, shocking, and unbelievable tenet, that a human being with all his deficiencies could be regarded by other human beings as God, as the one who eternally creates, preserves, and produces the world. ˉA Dalai Lama has this image of himself and is revered as such by others.ˉ[160] We must learn to understand this view, and in understanding it we shall see its justification. We shall show how it has its ground, its rational aspect, a place in [the evolution of] reason. But it is also pertinent for us to have insight into its defective and absurd aspect. ˉIt is easy to say that such a religion is just senseless and irrational. What is not easy is to recognize the necessity and truth of such religious forms,ˉ[161] their connection with reason; and seeing that is a more difficult task than declaring something to be senseless.

159. *L adds, similar in W (1827?):* The fact that a human being passes over into this [new sensible] shape is now combined with [the thought of] morality, or of merit.

160. *W₂ (1831) reads:* When God is worshiped in human shape in the Christian religion, that is something altogether different; for the divine essence is there envisaged in the man who has suffered, died, risen again, and ascended to heaven. This is not humanity in its sensuous, immediate existence but a humanity that bears upon its face the shape of spirit. But it appears as the most monstrous contrast when the absolute has to be worshiped in the immediate finitude of human being; the latter is an even more inflexible singularization than is [the finitude of] the animal. For the human shape embodies the further demand of self-transcendence [*Erhebung*], and hence it seems repugnant that this demand should be debased into a sheer persistence in ordinary finitude.

161. *W (Var) reads:* We must learn to see in [all] religions that our object is not merely something senseless and irrational, that what matters more is to recognize what is true [in them],

Being-within-self is the essential stage, consisting in the progression from immediate, empirical singularity to the determination of essence, of essentiality; or to the representation or consciousness of substance, i.e., of a substantial power that governs the world, that causes everything to come about and be produced according to a rationally coherent pattern. About this substantial power we know only that it is something operating unconsciously; but just for that reason it is undivided efficacy, it has in it the characteristic of universality, it is the universal | power. For this to be made clear 468 to us, we need to recall at this point the efficacy, spirit, and soul of nature; in speaking this way we do not mean that the spirit of nature is a conscious spirit; we are not thereby thinking of anything conscious. The natural laws of plants and animals, of their organization and activity, are something devoid of consciousness. These laws are the substantial aspect of living organisms; they are their nature and their concept. This is what they are implicitly, the reason immanent in them, the living soul; but it is unconscious.

The human being is spirit, and one's vitality consists in spirit determining itself as soul, as the unity of what is living—a vitality which, in the unfolding of [a person's] organization, is simply one, permeating and supporting everything. This efficacy is present in the person so long as one lives, without one's knowing it or willing it, and yet one's living soul is the cause, i.e., the original thing [Sache]¹⁶² that makes it actual. The human being who is this very living soul knows nothing of this, does not will the circulation of the blood nor prescribe it, and yet one does it and the doing is one's own deed: the human being is the motive power that actualizes what takes place within its organization. This unconsciously operative rationality or unconsciously rational efficacy, the efficacy of nature, the ancients called νοῦς. Anaxagoras says that νοῦς rules the world.¹⁶³ But this

162. W (Var) adds: the substance
163. [Ed.] In the Lectures on the History of Philosophy, Hegel relies principally on the accounts of the pre-Socratics found in Aristotle. In one passage of the Metaphysics (984b15–22), Aristotle does attribute to Anaxagoras the view that "reason is present in nature, as in animals, as the cause of order," although he also asserts (985a18–21) that Anaxagoras only drags "reason" in to explain the creation of the world in a mechanical manner, when he does not know why something is "necessarily" so. See Aristotle, Metaphysics, ed. W. D. Ross (Oxford, 1924), 1:125–126. See also Aristotle, De anima A 2, and Plato, Phaedo 97b–99d.

rationality [is] not conscious. In more recent philosophy this rational efficacy has even been called intuiting; Schelling in particular designated God as intuiting intelligence.[164] "God is intelligence,"[165] and reason, as intuiting, is the eternal creating of Nature—what is called preservation of nature, for creating and preserving are not to be separated. In finite intuition we are immersed in things; they occupy us fully. This immersion in objects prior to any representing, reflecting, and judging, is the lower level of consciousness. Reflecting upon them, arriving at representations, producing points of view from oneself and applying these to objects, judging—these things are no longer intuiting as such.

469   This, therefore, is the standpoint of substantiality or of intuiting—the very one that we presently have before us; it is just the one | that should be understood as the standpoint of "pantheism" in its proper sense—this Oriental knowing, consciousness, or thinking of this absolute unity, of the absolute substance and its internal efficacy, an efficacy in which everything particular or singular is only something transitory or ephemeral, and not genuine independence. This Oriental way of viewing things is opposed to that of the Occident: just as the sun sets in the west, so it is in the West that human being descends into itself, into its own subjectivity. In the West singularity is the main determination, so that the singular [consciousness] is what is independent. Whereas in Oriental consciousness the main determination is that the universal is what is genuinely independent, in Western consciousness the singularity of things and of human beings stands higher for us. The Occidental viewpoint can indeed go so far as to maintain that the finite and finite things are autonomous, i.e., absolute. The expression "pantheism" has the ambiguity that universality alway has. Ἓν καὶ πᾶν means the one

164. [Ed.] Hegel is probably referring to Schelling's concept of intellectual intuition; further evidence to this effect is provided by the Lectures on the History of Philosophy 3:520–521 (cf. Werke 15:655). See F. W. J. Schelling, System of Transcendental Idealism (1800), trans. Peter Heath (Charlottesville, 1978), pp. 27–28; and On University Studies, trans. E. S. Morgan (Athens, Ohio, 1966), p. 49 (cf. Schelling, Werke 3:369–370, 5:255–256)—although God is not explicitly designated in these works as intuitive intelligence.

165. W (Var) reads: God, intelligence,

All, the All that remains utterly one; but πᾶν also means "every-thing," and hence the phrase passes over into a thoughtless, shoddy, unphilosophical view. Then one understands "pantheism" to mean that everything is God—the doctrine that "everything is God" [*Allesgötterei*], not the doctrine that "the All is God" [*Allgötterei*]. For in the doctrine that "the All is God," if God were the All there would be only one God; in the All the singular things are absorbed, they are merely accidental, or are only shadows or phantoms.[166] But philosophy is presumed to be "pantheism" in that first sense.[167] That is precisely the ambiguity of universality. If one takes it in the sense of a universality of reflection, then it is "allness" [*Allheit*], and allness is initially represented in such a way that the singular things remain independent. But the universality of thinking, substantial universality, is a unity with itself in which everything singular or particular is only something ideal, and has no true being.

On the one hand, this substantiality begins here. It is the basic determination, but *only* the basic determination, of our knowledge of God. The basis or ground, however, is not yet what is true. We say, "God is the absolute power, all actual being is only ideal within the absolute | power of God." Everything that ventures to say of itself that it is, that it has actuality, is[168] only a moment in the absolute power of the absolute God. Only God is, only God is the one, genuine actuality. Even though it is not yet idea, this represen-tation of substantiality underlies the representation of God in our

470

166. W *(Var/1831?) adds:* They come and go, their being consists precisely in this, that it disappears.

167. [*Ed.*] It is not entirely clear to what "in that first sense" refers. In regard to the two senses of πᾶν, the first would in fact be the philosophical sense, namely, that the All "remains utterly one." But this conception is not for Hegel something which philosophy is "presumed" to hold; rather it is a necessary philosophical conclusion—even if not the highest conclusion. Consequently he would seem to be referring to the second of the two senses he distinguishes, the doctrine that "everything is God." It is doubtful that "more recent philosophy" could be accused of a literal deification of everything that is. Yet a consistent philosophy of the understanding (Enlightenment rationalism) is commonly reproached for identifying the cosmos—as the totality of nonsublated but subsisting finite things—with God; whereas for Hegel the quintessence of the concept of the All was just the *negativity* of the finite. On the charge of "cosmotheism," see below, nn. 172, 177.

168. W₂ *(Var) adds:* sublated, is

261

religion, too.[169] The "omnipresence of God" (to the extent that this is not an empty phrase) is just the way that this substantiality is expressed; substantiality is its ground. But these[170] expressions are babbled away senselessly or in mere rote memory; there is no seriousness about them, ⁻for one is serious only about what is in thought. When Spinoza grasped the omnipresence of God in thought, as substantiality, he was reproached with pantheism,[171] for one forgets straightway that when God is grasped as substance, as all-effective, i.e., as operative in everything, then precisely by this comprehension all things are annihilated inasmuch as God is verily what is operative in them.⁻[172] As soon as one ascribes true being to the finite, as soon as things are independent and God is excluded from them, then God is by no means omnipresent; for when one says God is omnipresent, then one is at the same time saying that God is actual.[173] But God is not alongside things, in the interstices, like the God of Epicurus;[174] instead God is actual in the things; but then the things are not actual. This is the ideality of things. But in

169. *L (1827?) adds:* But it is difficult to grasp this. Although the finite is said to have no authentic being, opponents of this way of thinking forget this and say, "Well then, everything is God"; the finite that has just been sublated they straightway take as authentic being.

170. *W (Var) adds:* profound

171. [*Ed.*] Hegel sees here as elsewhere a connection between the general Oriental principle of unity and Spinoza's concept of substance. See Spinoza, *Ethics* (1677), part I, esp. prop. 15.

172. *Thus An; L and W (Var) read, one page previously:* This is how theologians in particular speak; indeed they even censure Spinozism on these grounds, inasmuch as what is singular or particular has disappeared in the Spinozistic substance and no truth, no actuality, no being is attributed to it.

[*Ed.*] Hegel is probably referring especially to F. A. G. Tholuck, *Die Lehre von der Sünde und vom Versöhner; oder, Die wahre Weihe des Zweiflers,* 2d ed. (Hamburg, 1825), p. 231, where Hegel's name was linked with those of Spinoza, Fichte, and the Eleatics as exponents of "pantheism of the concept," as distinct from "pantheism of the imagination" (Schelling) and "pantheism of feeling" (the mystics). The problem of interpreting Spinoza to which Hegel refers is more clearly dealt with by Jacobi than by Tholuck. Jacobi regards the argument—advanced by Hegel among others—that Spinoza is not an atheist but an acosmist (because he does not deny the existence of God but of the world) to be a mere play on words, and himself terms Spinoza a cosmotheist. On Spinoza's acosmism see above, p. 125, n. 27.

173. *W₂ (Var) adds:* and things are not.

174. [*Ed.*] Hegel is referring to the Epicurean doctrine that the gods live in the *intermundia,* the spaces between the different worlds. See Cicero, *De divinatione* 2.17, and *De natura deorum* 1.18.

this feeble thinking, one concludes that therefore the things are God, i.e., they are and remain insurmountably preserved, as an insurmountable actuality. So if we are serious when we say "God is omnipresent," | then God must have a truth for spirit, for the mind, for thought, and spirit must have an interest in this issue.[175]

Jacobi said of Spinozism that it is atheism,[176] he attacked it most violently, and yet this very Jacobi himself said: "God is the being in all determinate being."[177] This being, however, is nothing else but substance. But by the very fact that God is the affirmative, the singular thing is not the affirmative but is only what is ideal, what is sublated. Spinozistic philosophy was the philosophy of substantiality, not of pantheism; "pantheism" is a poor expression, because in it there is the possible misunderstanding that πᾶν be taken as a collective totality [*Allesheit*], not as universality [*Allgemeinheit*].

In all higher religions, but particularly in the Christian religion, God is the one and absolute substance; but at the same time God is also subject, and that is something more. Just as the human being has personality, there enters into God the character of subjectivity, personality, spirit, absolute spirit. That is a higher determination, although spirit remains nevertheless substance, the one substance. This abstract substance, the ultimate element of Spinoza's philosophy, this substance that is thought, that only is for thinking, cannot be the content of a folk religion; it cannot be the belief of a concrete spirit.[178] Concrete spirit supplies what is lacking, and the deficiency is that subjectivity, i.e., spirituality, is lacking. But at this point, at the level of nature religion which we are now dealing with, this spirituality is not yet spirituality as such, it is not yet a spirituality that is thought or universal; instead it is sensible and immediate spirituality. Here it is a human being as a sensible, external, immediate spirituality: a [particular] human being.

471

175. L, W (Var/1831?) add: God is the persisting of all things.
176. [Ed.] See Jacobi, *Werke* 4/1:216, also his Preface to Vol. 4 (pp. xxxvi–vii), where he says cosmotheism is just the same thing as atheism, which he defines (pp. 216–219) as the belief in a supreme being but one that acts only according to necessity. Thus Hegel's and Jacobi's concepts of atheism are different.
177. [Ed.] Jacobi, *Briefe*, p. 61 (*Werke* 4/1:87). Jacobi, however, is not representing his own view here but that of Spinoza, which he criticizes.
178. L (1827?) adds, similar in W: Spirit is concrete. It is only abstract thinking that sticks to this one-sided determinateness of substance.

263

472 This substantiality known in its truth is subjectivity inwardly, and thereby this pure substantiality includes spirituality; at the standpoint of immediacy, however, there is not yet self-knowing spirituality, but instead spirituality in an immediate | mode, though in the shape of a particular human being.[179]   [180]And if this human being abides within itself (in contrast with this substance, the universal substance), then when the question arises how a human individual can be represented as universal substance, we must recall what was stated above:[181] that as living substantiality the human being is after all this inwardly substantial actuality, an actuality determined by one's corporeality. It must be possible to think that in this vitality life is substantially effective within one.

This standpoint contains the universal substantiality in an actual shape. Here therefore is found the view that it is in mediation, in preoccupation with self or deep absorption within self, that a person is the universal substance, not just (let us say) in terms of his vitality; instead,[182] the voῦς [is] then posited as center, but in such a way that the voῦς within does not become conscious of itself in that person's character or development. This substantiality of the voῦς, this deep absorption represented in one individual, is not the meditation of a king who has before him in his consciousness the administration of his realm; it is to be represented in such a way that this absorption within the self, this abstract thinking in itself, *is* the effective substantiality, is the creating and preserving of the world. This is the standpoint of the Buddhist and Lamaist religion.

There are three Dalai Lamas: in Lesser Tibet, in Greater Tibet, and in southeastern Siberia, in the mountain valleys of the Asian plateau from which Genghis Khan set out.[183] It makes no difference that there are multiple high lamas, and that they are also the superiors of religious orders that dedicate themselves to a life of withdrawal, and that others are held in honor comparable to that of the Dalai

179. W₂ (Var) adds: of an empirical, single consciousness.

180. *In B's margin:* 29 June 1827.

181. [Ed.] See above, pp. 219–220.

182. W (Var) reads: but rather in the immersion within self or in the center of voῦς;

183. [Ed.] Hegel here erroneously calls all the high lamas Dalai Lamas. By this he means the Dalai Lama from Lhasa (an incarnation of Avalokiteshvara), the Panchen Lama (an incarnation of Buddha Amitabha) in Tashilumpo and, presumably, the chief

Lama. Here the subjective shape is not yet exclusive; only with the penetration of spirituality, of subjectivity and of substance, is God essentially One. Thus here the substance is indeed one, but the subjectivity and the shapes are multiple, and | it is immediately   473 implicit in them that they are multiple. For in its relationship to substantiality this configuration itself is, to be sure, represented as something essential, but also at the same time as something accidental. Antithesis or contradiction first emerges in consciousness and volition, in particular insight; hence there cannot be multiple worldly sovereigns in one land, but there can well be multiple Dalai Lamas. But although this spiritual efficacy does indeed have a spiritual form for its existence and its shape, it is still only efficacy of substance, and not a conscious efficacy, a conscious will.

There is a distinction between Buddhism and Lamaism; but this account is common to both.[184] It is said of Fo[185] that eight thousand times he has incarnated himself ⌐in existence as a human being.¬[186] ⌐Europeans have hardly ever come to where the great

of the Khutuktus. For Hegel's knowledge of the Panchen Lama, see below, n. 188; the report by Samuel Turner referred to there also mentions a visit by the Dalai Lama to the Panchen Lama. On the chief of the Khutuktus (legates of the Dalai Lama) see *Allgemeine Historie* 7:219–220. In Hegel's day the terms Greater Tibet (*Gross-Tibet*) and Lesser Tibet (*Klein-Tibet*) were used with a variety of meanings; by "Greater Tibet" Hegel also understands the area surrounding Lhasa, whereas in the *Allgemeine Historie* the term "Greater Tibet" is equated with Bhutan.

184. *W (1831) adds:* and those who worship Fo and Buddha worship the Dalai Lama also. The latter is worshiped, however, more under the form of someone deceased, but one who is also present under [the form of] his successors.

185. [*Ed.*] According to the *Allgemeine Historie* 6:360, the disciples of Fo claimed that their teacher had been born eight thousand times, but in animal as well as in human form. Cf. *Mémoires concernant les Chinois* 5:59.

186. *W (Var) reads:* and been present in the actual existence of a human being.

W_2 *(1831) continues:* Such are the basic determinations that follow from what is here the divine nature, and which are all that follow from it, since the divine nature itself has not got beyond the undeveloped abstraction of the tranquil being-within-self that lacks all determinacy. Consequently any further shaping or representation [of it] is surrendered, partly to the contingency of empirical historical events and partly to that of the imagination; the details belong to a description of the countless, confused products of the imagination concerning the adventures and destinies of these deities, and of their friends and disciples, and yield material that has but little interest or value so far as its inner substance is concerned, and which (as we have already indicated) has not the interest of the concept.[a]

In regard to the cultus too, we are not concerned here with outward ceremonies

474   lama in China lives, | whereas (about 1770) Englishmen visited the one in Lesser Tibet.⁻¹⁸⁷ From the English emissary, Turner, we have an account[188] of the lama in Lesser Tibet; the lama was a child two or three years of age whose predecessor had died of smallpox on a journey to Beijing, where he had been summoned by the Chinese emperor; the lama was rediscovered in a two-year-old child. Acting on this child's behalf in matters of governance, there was a regent, the minister of the previous Dalai Lama, known as his cupbearer.[189] That child was indeed still nursing, but was a lively spirited child who conducted himself with all possible dignity and propriety, and seemed already to have a consciousness of his high office.[190] And the emissaries could not adequately praise the regent—and his associates—for the noble disposition, insight, dignity, and dispas-

---

and customs. All we have to describe is the essential element, namely, how being-within-self, the principle of this stage, appears in the actual self-consciousness [of the worshipers].

[Ed.] ªCf. n. 151.

187. *An reads (in place of first clause):* The Chinese keep Europeans away from their sovereign domain, and so from Greater Tibet. W₁ *(1831) reads, similar in* W₂: There are three principal lamas. The first, or Dalai Lama, is to be found in Lhasa, to the north of the Himalayas, where Europeans have not yet come, since this city is indeed within Chinese territory. Then there is another lama in Lesser Tibet, in Tashilumpo, in the neighborhood of Nepal. L *(1827?) adds:* From reports about the Dalai Lama, he could be regarded as in the main a charlatan, who takes advantage of these peoples. The English, however, found matters quite otherwise.

[Ed.] On the principal lamas and the geographical terms, see above, n. 183. The *Allgemeine Historie* 7:222 speaks of a Capuchin friar, Brother Horace, as having paid a number of visits to the Dalai Lama, but this seems to have escaped Hegel's attention.

188. [Ed.] See Samuel Turner, "Copy of an Account Given by Mr. Turner, of His Interview with Teeshoo Lama," *Asiatic Researches* 1:197–205. The "cupbearer" is referred to in another narrative by Turner, "An Account of a Journey to Tibet," *Asiatic Researches* 1:207–220, in which he describes a journey by Poorungeer to Tashilumpo, although it is clear that the cupbearer and the regent are two different persons. The information that the young lama's predecessor had died of smallpox on a journey to Beijing and that the young lama was still nursing cannot have come from these accounts, but rather from an edited version of Turner's accounts in Harnisch, *Die wichtigsten Reisen* 6:343–345, 358–359. Hegel may also have been familiar with Turner's monograph on his journeys published in London in 1800.

189. W₁ *(1831) adds:* Lastly there is yet a third lama living in Mongolia.

190. *In An's margin:* It is absurd to think that this is a case of priestly deception and to regard the Dalai Lamas as charlatans. As soon as a Dalai Lama dies, the world spirit passes into another human individual, and the only difficulty then is to locate

sionate tranquillity that the child possessed. The previous lama had also been an insightful, dignified, and noble man.[191]

We have indicated the relevance of the fact that the substance is, as it were, present in particular in one individual, that it has concentrated itself in him in order to show itself outwardly. This substantial efficacy is what is universally effective in the world, this substance is the universal νοῦς; and it is not such a very different matter to suppose that the latter has its existence in one human being | in particular, that it is present to and for other people in a sensible, external manner. Here we will let these determinations stand. We are still at the standpoint of the substantiality that is indeed necessarily bound up with subjectivity, with spirituality; but here what is spiritual is still in immediate, sensible existence, and this subjectivity is still an immediate subjectivity. The standpoint of substantiality also constitutes the foundation of what is to follow, and we are not yet ready to abandon it; but we can now pass over to the third form.

475

3. The Hindu Religion[192]

⌐This is the third form of religion.¬[193] It is defined in such a way that here the substantiality is found in the totality of its externality; it

---

and identify him; a few external traits serve this purpose.[a] *Cf. W₁ (Var):* For when a Dalai Lama dies, the god has for a moment withdrawn his personal presence from humanity; but then he immediately appears in another human shape, and he has only to be sought out again, as he can be known by certain signs.

[*Ed.*] [a]This reference was probably drawn from the *Allgemeine Historie* 7:217. In any event, the information transmitted by Strauss that the Lama is recognized by facial lines shows that Hegel was acquainted with other regulations governing the succession. See unabridged ed., Vol. 2:735.

191. *L, W₂ (1827/1831?) add:* There is, however, an inner consistency in the fact that an individual in whom the [divine] substance has become concentrated should outwardly display this worthy, noble demeanor.

192. [*Ed.*] In 1827 Hegel does not appear to have provided a philosophical designation for Hinduism; he simply refers to it as *die indische Religion,* rather than as *die Religion der Phantasie* as in 1824. This may be because he now views Hinduism as having two primary characteristics: the unity of substance and the multiplicity of powers—and it is only with reference to the latter that Hindu phantasy comes into play. In 1831 primary emphasis is placed on the first characteristic since Hinduism is defined as "the religion of abstract unity"; thus 1827 plays a transitional role between 1824 and 1831. However, 1827 follows 1824 in treating Hinduism after Buddhism, whereas in 1831 the sequence is reversed. The decisive advance of religious con-

sciousness to substantiality is still accredited to Buddhism. The German term *Phantasie* is translated by the English variant spelling "phantasy" in order to convey the sense of visionary, fanciful imagination, as distinguished from that of an unreal mental image or illusion. Hegel's *die indische Religion* is rendered as "Hinduism" or "Hindu religion." Whereas in the preceding section, on Buddhism, we have consistently translated *Insichsein* as "being-within-self," in the present section we have alternated between this rendering and "self-containment," which is more appropriate when the reference is to the Hindu concept of Brahman as impersonal metaphysical substance.

193. W_2 *(1831) reads:* The second main form of pantheism, when this latter actually appears as religion, is still within the sphere of this same principle of the one substantive power, in which all that we see around us, and even human freedom itself, is only something negative or accidental. We saw that the substantive power, in its first form, is known as the multitude and range of essential determinations, and not known as what is in its own self spiritual. The question immediately arises, therefore, how this power is determined in its own self, and what its content is. Self-consciousness cannot, like the abstractly thinking understanding, confine itself in religion to the representational image of the power that is known only as an aggregate of determinations that merely *are*. For then the power is not yet known as real unity, subsisting by itself, it is not yet known as principle. The opposite of this way of defining it is for the manifold determinateness to be taken back into the unity of self-determination. This concentration of self-determining contains the beginning of spirituality.

1. As self-determining, and not merely as a multitude of rules, the universal is thought, and exists as thought. It is in our thinking alone that nature, the power that brings forth everything, exists as the universal, as this one essence, as this one power that is for itself. What we have before us in nature is this universal, but not *as* universal. What is true in nature is brought into prominence on its own account in our thinking as idea or, more abstractly, as universal. In its own self, however, universality is thought; and, as self-determining, it is the source of all determining. But at the stage where we now are, the stage where the universal emerges for the first time as what is determinative (or as principle), the universal is not yet spirit but abstract universality generally. Being known as thought in this way, the universal remains as such shut up within itself. It is the source of all power, but it does not externalize or express itself as such.

2. The act of differentiating and fully developing the difference belongs to spirit. The system of this full development includes both the concrete unfolding of thought on its own account and the unfolding which, as appearance, is both nature and the spiritual world. But since the principle that comes on the scene at this stage has not yet reached the point where this unfolding could occur within the principle itself—since, on the contrary, it is held fast in a simple, abstract concentration—the unfolding and the richness of the actual idea falls outside the principle, and consequently differentiation and manifoldness are abandoned to the wildest externality of phantasy. The particularization of the universal appears in a plurality of independent powers.

3. This multiplicity or wild dispersal of powers is [finally] taken back again into the initial unity. In terms of the idea, this retrieval, this concentration of thought, would consummate the moment of spirituality if the initial, universal mode of thinking were to make itself inwardly accessible to differentiation and were known inwardly as the act of retrieval. On the foundation of abstract thought, however, the retrieval

is represented and known in and by this externality, by the totality of the world. The first thing that we find here, therefore, is this same substantiality in which everything | else, the determinate and particular, the subject, is only something accidental, is even mortal. But the second thing, the additional aspect, is the concrete, the richness of the world, the particularizing of that universal substance which, with reference to the substance | or the universal power, also represents itself for consciousness; i.e., it is both spiritual power and natural power. The result is that those distinctions are also known as belonging to the absolute, those powers appearing in one aspect as particular and independent, but at the same time vanishing, being consumed, and standing under that initial unity, under the universal being-within-self of the initial substantiality.

476

477

⌐Here, therefore, the horizon is enlarged; we have here the totality. The viewpoint is concrete; that is the necessary progress. | We still have substance as this one essential power; but the other aspect is the concrete, what previously was, in this way or that, nothing but a contingent element. What is more determinately concrete is in the first place this, that the idea is one, it is immediate and identical with self. But just as the One is God, the absolute power, so also in the second place the idea differentiates itself internally; it particularizes itself, and these particularizations yield distinct, particular configurations or powers. The third aspect is that these particular configurations, these spiritual powers of nature, are represented as returned into and contained by the One. We have here an intelligible realm that particularizes itself, arrives at subsistence,

478

---

itself remains devoid of spirit. Nothing is lacking here as far as the moments of the idea of spirit are concerned; the idea of rationality is present in this advance. But these moments do not constitute spirit; the unfolding is not so consummated as to yield spirit, because the determinations remain merely universal. There is merely a perpetual return to that universality which is self-active but which is held fast in the abstraction of self-determining. Thus we have the abstract One and the wildness of unrestrained phantasy, which is, of course, known to remain identical with the first [principle] but which does not expand into the concrete unity of the spiritual. The unity of the intelligible realm achieves its specific permanence; but this last does not become absolutely free, for it remains confined within the universal substance.

But just because the unfolding does not yet truly return to the concept and is not yet inwardly taken back by the concept, it still retains its immediacy along with its return into the substance.

269

but does not become absolutely free on its own account, being instead contained by the universal substance. The foundation for rational development is present here, but only in its most general characteristics.

a. The One Substance

A more precise cognition of this standpoint specifies it as the standpoint of the Hindu religion.⁻¹⁹⁴ In Hinduism there is just this one

194. W (1831) reads: Subjectivity is inward power, as the connection of infinite negativity with itself; it is not merely implicit power—on the contrary, in subjectivity God is for the first time posited as power. Of course, these ways of characterizing it have to be distinguished from one another, and are of particular importance in relation both to the ensuing concepts of God and also to an understanding of the preceding ones. We must therefore consider them more closely.

Both in religion generally and in the wholly immediate and crudest religion of nature, power in general is the fundamental determination, as the infinitude which the finite, as sublated, posits within itself. And insofar as this is represented as outside the finite, is represented as *existing,* it nevertheless comes to be posited only as something that has emerged from the finite as from its ground. The determination that is all-important here is that the power is posited to begin with simply as the ground of the particular configurations or existences, and the relationship of the self-contained essence to these existences is that of substantiality [to what is accidental]. Thus it is merely implicit power or power lying within the existences; and as self-contained essence or as substance, it is posited solely as the simple and abstract, so that the determinations or differentiae are represented as being configurations existing in their own right outside it. This self-contained essence may indeed also be represented as self-sufficient, in the way that Brahman is self-thinking. Brahman is the universal soul; in creating, it goes forth out of itself as a breath, it contemplates itself, and from then on it is for itself. But this does not at the same time eliminate its abstract simplicity, for the moments, i.e., the universality of Brahman as such and the "I" for which that universality is, are not reciprocally determined, and their relation itself is therefore simple. Thus, as having being abstractly for itself, Brahman is, of course, the power and the ground of existences, and everything has emerged from it, just as—in saying to themselves, "I am Brahman"—they are all returned to it and have disappeared in it. They are either outside it (exist independently) or within it (have disappeared); there is only the relationship of these two extremes. But being posited as differentiated determinations, they appear as independent entities outside Brahman, because it is at first abstract, not inwardly concrete.

Posited only implicitly in this way, power acts inwardly without appearing as [external] efficacy. I appear as power insofar as I am cause, and more specifically insofar as I am subject—whenever I throw a stone, etc. But power that has being implicitly operates in a universal manner, without this universality being a subject on its own account. The laws of nature, for instance, are this universal mode of operation, grasped in its true character.

W₁ (Ed) continues: We have already indicated how this standpoint is manifest, how it appears in its existence.

substantiality, and it is, of course, present as pure thinking, pure being-within-self, and this self-containment is distinguished from the multiplicity of things; it is external to particularization, so that it does not have its existence or its reality as such in the particular powers. This is not the way God has his existence or determinate being in the Son, for this being-within-self instead remains abstractly inward, purely by itself, as abstract power; but at the same time it is power over everything, and the particularization or distinction falls outside of this being-within-self. But because it is abstract in this way, the self-containment must in turn have an existence, and insofar as this existence itself is still immediate, still outside the distinction, it is not authentically divine existence, but is once more an immediate existence in the concretely existing, immediate human spirit. |

479

b. The Multiplicity of Powers

That is the first aspect; the second then is the distinction into many powers, and these many powers [depicted] as a plurality of deities— an unbridled polytheism that has not yet progressed to the beauty of figure. These are not yet the beautiful deities of Greek religion; ⁻⁻nor is the prose of our understanding present here to any great extent. In part the powers are objects such as sun, moon, mountains, or rivers; or they are greater abstractions such as generation, perishing, ˉchange of shape.ˉ¹⁹⁵ These are the particular powers that maintain themselves externally to self-contained being, so that they are not yet taken up into spirit, are not yet posited as truly ideal, but also are not yet distinct from spirit. The substance is not yet spiritual,ˉˉ¹⁹⁶ for the powers are not yet posited outside of spirit. They are not yet considered by understanding, but neither are they

195. W (Var) reads: change, taking shape.
196. W₂ (MiscP) reads: Only when the prose of thinking has permeated all relationships, so that we humans behave everywhere in an abstractly thoughtful fashion, do we speak of external things. At this stage, on the contrary, thinking is only this substance, only this presence to self; it is not yet applied and has not yet permeated humanity as a whole. The particular powers, which are partly objects such as sun, mountains, rivers, or else are greater abstractions such as generation, perishing, change, taking shape, etc., are not yet taken up into spirit, not yet genuinely posited as ideal. But they are also not yet distinguished from spirit by the understanding, for pure being is still concentrated in that self-containment of substance which is not yet spiritual substance,

images of a beautiful imagination [*schöne Phantasie*]; they are merely fanciful [*phantastisch*]. They are particular powers, although it is a wild particularity in which there is no system but only intimations of what is understandable and necessary, echoes of understood moments but still no understandable totality or systematization, much less a rational one; instead only a multiplicity in a colorful throng. The specification that the particular is grasped with understanding is not yet present.

480 ⁻We say of natural objects that they are things that have external being, such as sun, moon, ocean, and the like.⁻[197] But here pure | being is not concentrated in that self-contained being. At this stage thinking has not yet permeated ⁻thought as a whole,⁻[198] spirit as a whole. ⁻Only the prose in which thinking is universal speaks of universal things. When we consider the world, we think it; we say that the objects are; that is their category, that they are external things; hence they are grasped prosaically. But at this stage thinking is the substance, the in-itself. Thinking is not yet applied; the natural powers are not yet grasped in categories;⁻[199] categories such as "independence" and "thing" are not yet in command.[200]

Furthermore, the objective content is not grasped in the mode of beauty either; i.e., these powers, universal natural objects or the powers of the soul such as love, are not yet grasped as beautiful figures. Moreover, there belongs to beauty of figure that free sub-

---

197. W₁ (*Var*) *reads:* We say of a universal natural entity (and likewise of universal natural powers) that such a thing *is;* for example, the sun is. These are externally existent beings, are "things": to say something is a "thing" is to predicate this reflected being of it.

198. *Thus B;* W₁ (*Var*) *reads:* humanity as a whole

199. W₁ (*Var*) *reads:* The understanding says that they are, that we think them and we think them as distinct from ourselves; this is their predicate, their category, this is how they are comprehended in prosaic terms. Not until prose or thinking has permeated all relationships, so that human beings everywhere behave in an abstractly thinking fashion, do they speak of external things. Here, on the contrary, thinking is only this substance, this presence to self; thinking is not yet applied; objects are not yet regarded in the form of this category, as external, as cohering, as cause and effect;

200. *L (1827?) adds, similar in* W₁: Independence of the natural powers is spiritual personality; although spirit has not yet advanced to [the level of] the understanding, they are nonetheless independent, inasmuch as they are personified.

jectivity which, even in the sensible, in determinate being, both is free and knows itself freely. For the beautiful is essentially the spiritual that expresses itself sensibly, that shows itself in a sensible mode of determinate being, but in such a way that this being is thoroughly and totally permeated by the spiritual, in such a way that the sensible does not have being on its own account, but only has complete significance within the spiritual and through the spiritual, and is the *sign* of the spiritual. This is genuine beauty—that the sensible does not have being on its own account, does not exhibit its own self but rather directly represents as itself something other than it itself is. In the living human being, in the human countenance, there are many external influences that inhibit pure idealization, this subsumption of the corporeal and sensible under the spiritual. | This   481 relationship [i.e., the mode of beauty] is not yet present here, and so, because the spiritual is at first still present only in this abstract characteristic of substantiality, the relationship has also not developed into these particularizations or particular powers; for the substantiality is still by itself, and has not yet permeated or overcome this particularization, these its particularities, and the sensible, natural mode of being. The substance is, as it were, a universal space that has not yet organized what fills it, namely, the particularization that has proceeded from it, has not yet idealized this and subordinated it to itself. Because these powers are not at the same time represented in a universal way, because they are present as independent only for representation but are not thought, the independence attributed to them is one that human beings have in principle. The highest determination that has been grasped is spiritual determination; those powers are personified, but in a fanciful mode, not in a beautiful mode.

The substance is the foundation, so that the distinctions emerge or appear from the One as independent deities, as universal powers, but in such a way that, besides being independent, these deities also resolve themselves again into the unity. This shocking inconsistency is present here and permeates the entire world of images. On the one hand, the independence of the deities is represented; on the other it is shown that they are the One, through which their particular shape and nature, their particularity, once again vanishes. At the

273

same time this One or this substance is not just objectively known, and does not yet have this [abstract] objectivity for thinking; instead the One has essential existence[201] as the human being who elevates himself to this abstraction, i.e., it has existence as human consciousness.

[202]The next feature is the representation of the objective content of this standpoint. The basic content is the one, simple, absolute substance; this is what the Hindus call "Brahman" and "Brahmā"; "Brahman" [Brahm, Brahman] is neuter or is, as we say, "the divinity"; "Brahmā" [Brahma] expresses the universal essence more as a person or subject. Incidentally, this is a distinction that is not consistently observed, and indeed in the different grammatical cases it disappears | of its own accord, for masculine and neuter have many cases the same.[203] [204]

The distinctions also emerge with respect to this simple substance, and ˉthese distinctions occur in such a way ˉ[205] that they are determined according to the instinct of the concept, that precisely the basic determination and development of the concept is present. The first is the totality in general as One, taken quite abstractly; it emerges here as one of three, it is downgraded, and what embraces the three is represented as distinct from this initial One. The second is determinacy or distinction in general, and the third is in accord with genuine determination, so that the distinctions are led back into the unity, the concrete unity. ˉThis formless unity is Brahman;

482

201. W₁ (Var) adds: in human consciousness

202. In B's margin: 2 July 1827

203. L (1827?) adds, similar in W: Moreover, no great stress should be laid on the distinction in this regard either, since Brahmā is only superficially personified, and the content of Brahman remains, as we said, this simple substance.

204. [Ed.] Wilhelm von Humboldt drew attention to the distinction, and the fact that it is often obscured in Sanskrit grammar, in a paper read to the Berlin Academy of Sciences on 30 June 1825 and again on 15 June 1826. See Über die unter dem Namen Bhagavad-Gītā bekannte Episode des Mahā-Bhārata (Berlin, 1826), pp. 22, 40–41. The problem was also discussed by A. W. Schlegel in a letter reproduced in his journal Indische Bibliothek 2, no. 4 (Bonn, 1827): 420–424. See also Hegel's review of Humboldt's paper in Jahrbücher für wissenschaftliche Kritik, 1827, p. 1476 (Berliner Schriften, pp. 136 ff.).

205. W (Var) reads: it is noteworthy that the way in which these distinctions occur is

according to its determinacy it is three in unity.⁻²⁰⁶ ⁻When we express it more precisely, the second moment is one of distinct powers. This triad is only a unity; distinction has no | right as against   483
the absolute unity, and so it can be called the eternal goodness; rightness or justice [*Gerechtigkeit*] accrues to the distinction from the fact that [though] what subsists [initially] is not, it attains its right, it becomes changed, it becomes a particular determinacy.⁻²⁰⁷ ⁻The triad as totality, which is a whole and a unity, the Hindus call Trimurti. "Murti" means "soul," or in general every emanation, everything spiritual; the Trimurti is the three essences.⁻²⁰⁸

The first, which is ⁻the simple substance,⁻²⁰⁹ is what is called Brahmā or Brahman; but we also meet with Parabrahmā, that which

206. L (Var) reads (at the end of this paragraph), similar in W (at this point): This threefold nature of the absolute, grasped according to its abstract form or when it is merely formal, is sheer Brahman, the empty essence; in its determinateness it is three, but only within a unity, so that this triad is only a unity.

207. W (Var) reads: If we define this more closely and speak of it under another form, the second [point] means that there are distinctions, different powers; but the distinct power has no right as against the one substance, the absolute unity; and since it has no right, we can call it eternal goodness that what is determinate [is allowed to] exist, too—it is a manifestation of the divine that even what has been distinguished [i.e., set apart] should attain the state that it *is*. This is the goodness by virtue of which what the power posits as show or semblance obtains momentary being. It is absorbed in the power, but goodness allows it to subsist.

Upon this second [point] follows the third, namely the rightness or justice through which—[though] the subsistent determinate [initially] is not—the finite attains to its end, its destiny, its right, which is to be changed, to be transformed always into another determinateness; this is justice in general. Becoming, perishing, and generation all belong to it in abstract fashion; even nonbeing has no right, for it is an abstract determination over against being and is itself the passing over into unity.

208. W (1831) reads: This totality, which is unity or a whole, is what the Hindus call Trimurti (*murti* = shape, and all emanations of the absolute are called *murti*). This highest being [is] inwardly differentiated in such a way that it has these three determinations within it.

This trinity in unity is indisputably the most striking and greatest feature in Hindu mythology. We cannot call them persons, for they lack spiritual subjectivity as a fundamental determination. But to Europeans it must have been in the highest degree astonishing to encounter this lofty principle of the Christian religion here; we shall become acquainted with it in its truth later on, and we shall see that spirit as concrete must necessarily be grasped as triune.

[Ed.] The 1831 lectures give the correct definition of the Sanskrit term *murti*. Hegel's source or sources are not known.

209. W (Var) reads: the One, the one substance,

is above Brahmā—a complicated business! All sorts of stories are told of Brahmā insofar as he is subject; but thought or reflection once again goes beyond such a characterization as Brahmā in which something determinate is grasped[210]; it goes beyond what is just determined as one of these three and makes for itself that higher aspect which is determined by its contrast with what is other. Insofar as Brahmā or Brahman is utterly substance and in turn appears only as one alongside another, it is the requirement of thought to have yet a higher, Parabrahmā—but then one cannot say in what determinate relation such forms stand to one another.

Brahmā is what is grasped as the substance from which everything proceeds or is begotten; this is the power that has brought forth or created everything. But inasmuch as the one substance (or the One) 484 is thus the abstract power, | it also equally appears as what is inert, as formless, inactive matter. Here, then, we have in particular the formative activity, as we would express it. Because it is only the One, the one substance is the formless—and this is also one way in which it becomes apparent that substantiality is not satisfied—namely because form is not present. Thus Brahman, the One, the self-same essence, appears as something inert, indeed appears as begetter but at the same time behaves passively, as if it were the feminine principle. Vishnu says: Brahman is my uterus,[211] in which I sow my seed, so that everything is procreated. [212]Everything goes forth from Brahmā: gods, world, human beings; but it is at once apparent that this One is inactive, is what is inert.[213]

This distinction also carries over into the different cosmogonies or portrayals of the creation of the world. We should not suppose, by the way, that the Hindus have a definite story or a firmly established representation of creation such as we possess ˉfrom the Jewish books;ˉ[214] instead, everyone there—poet, seer, or prophet—

210. W_2 (Var) adds: as one of these three
211. W (Var) adds: the mere recipient
212. Precedes in L (1827?), similar in W: Even in the definition "God is essence," the principle of movement, of bringing forth, is not contained; it involves no activity.
213. [Ed.] See James Mill, The History of British India, 3 vols. (London, 1817), 1:232.
214. W_1 (Var) reads: in the Christian and Jewish religion;

constructs his own representation in personal fashion, by speculative immersion within himself. Hence there is nothing fixed, but instead everyone has a different viewpoint. This creation is [described] one way in the Code of Manu, but differently in the Vedas and other religious works[215]—each account has its own special version. In general, one cannot say that the Hindus maintain this or that about creation; for everything is always simply the view of one sage; the common element consists only in the basic features that we have presented. Thus in the Vedas a description of the world's creation is advanced in which Brahmā is alone in solitude, wholly by himself, and in which an essence that is then represented as something higher says to him that he should expand and beget himself. For a thousand years, however, Brahmā had been in no position to grasp his expansion; for he | had again receded into himself. Here Brahmā is indeed represented as world-creating, but because he is the One, because of being inactive and needing to be summoned by something other and higher, Brahmā is represented as what is formless.[216] Hence there is need for another. On the whole, Brahmā is this one, absolute substance.[217] |

485

486

Then the second [essence] is Vishnu or Krishna, i.e., the embodying of Brahman; this is the determinate being of preservation,

215. [Ed.] For the cosmogony of the Code of Manu and of the Vedas, see annotations a, e to n. 217; see also Alexander Dow, *The History of Hindostan, from the Earliest Accounts to the Death of Akbar,* 2 vols. (London, 1768), 1:xlvi–xlix.

216. [Ed.] See Francis Buchanan, "On the Religion and Literature of the Burmas," *Asiatic Researches* 6:273–280.

217. *W (1831) adds:* As this simple activity, power is thought. In Hinduism this characteristic is the most prominent of all; it is the absolute foundation and is the One, Brahman. This form is in accordance with the logical development: first came the multiplicity of determinations, and the advance consists in the resumption of the determining into unity. That is the foundation. What still remains to be added is partly just historical, but partly it is the necessary development that follows from that principle.

As the active element, the simple power created the world. This creation is essentially a relating of thought to itself, a self-referring activity and not a finite one. This too is expressed in the Hindu ways of viewing the matter. They have a great number of cosmogonies, which are all more or less barbarous, and out of which nothing of a fixed character can be derived; [W_1: as was the case with the Jewish myths. W_2: there is not just one representation of the creation of the world, as in the Jewish and Christian religion.] In the Code of Manu, in the Vedas and Puranas, the cosmogonies are continually comprehended and presented differently; but there is always one feature essentially present in them, namely that this thinking, which is at home with itself, is the begetting of itself.

This infinitely profound and true feature constantly recurs in the various portrayals of the creation of the world. The Code of Manu begins as follows: "The Eternal with a single thought created the waters," and so on.[a] We also find that this pure activity is called "the Word," just as God is in the New Testament.[b] With the Jews of later times, e.g., Philo, σοφία is the first-created [being] that goes forth from the One.[c] The "Word" is held in very high esteem by the Hindus, it is the image of pure activity, something that has external, physical, finite being, but which does not abide. Instead it is only ideal, and disappears immediately in its externality. The Eternal created the waters, the record then says,[d] and deposited fructifying seed in them; this seed became a resplendent egg, and in it the eternal itself was born again as Brahmā. Brahmā is the progenitor of all spirits, of what exists and what does not exist. In this egg, the story goes, the great power remained inactive for a year; at the end of that time it divided the egg by thought, and created one part masculine and the other feminine. The masculine force is itself [W₂: begotten, and becomes again a begetter and] effective only when it has practiced strict meditation, i.e., when it has attained to the concentration of abstraction. Thought therefore is what brings forth, and what is brought forth is just that which brings forth, namely the unity of thinking with itself. The return of thinking to itself is found in other accounts too. In one of the Vedas (from which some fragments have for the first time been translated by Colebrooke[e]), a similar description of the first act of creation is to be found: "There was neither being nor nothing, neither above nor below, [W₂: neither death nor immortality,] but only the One enshrouded and dark. Outside of this One there existed nothing, and the One brooded by itself in solitude; through the energy of contemplation it brought forth a world out of itself; desire or impulse first formed itself in this thinking, and this was the original seed of all things."

Here again thinking is presented in its self-enclosed activity. The thinking is, however, further known as thinking in the self-conscious essence, in the human being who constitutes its actual existence. The Hindus could be reproached with having attributed a contingent existence to the One, since it is left to chance whether or not the individual raises itself to the abstract universal [W₂: to abstract self-consciousness]. But [this is unfair because] Brahman is immediately present in the caste of Brāhmans; it is their duty to read the Vedas and to withdraw into themselves. Reading the Vedas is the divine element (is God's very self), and so is prayer. The Vedas can even be read without taking in the sense, or in complete stupefaction; this stupefaction itself is the abstract unity of thought; the I and its pure intuitive activity is what is perfectly empty. Thus it is the Brāhmans in whom Brahman exists; through the reading of the Vedas Brahman *is*, [W₂: and human self-consciousness in the state of abstraction is Brahman itself].[f]

[Ed.] [a]See *Institutes of Hindu Law* (Calcutta, 1794), chap. 1, On the Creation, esp. pp. 1–2. [b]A probable reference to the cosmogony described by Alexander Dow (see above, n. 215). Hindu cosmogonies had already been compared with the creation by the Word, by William Jones, "On the Gods of Greece, Italy, and India," *Asiatic Researches* 1:244, although as Jones pointed out, in the case of the Code of Manu the creative activity is attributed to thought rather than word. [c]A probable reference to August Neander's treatment of Philo in *Genetische Entwicklung der vornehmsten*

the manifestation or appearance on earth that is quite completely developed, the appearing one, humanity, particular human beings. The Hindus enumerate many different instances of this incarnation. The general point is that here Brahmā appears as a human being. Nevertheless we still cannot say that it is Brahmā who appears as a human being; for this becoming-human is not posited as the bare form of Brahman. The vast poetic creations of the Hindus are relevant here.[218] The representations of these incarnations seem in part to contain resonances of historical events; it seems that there are princes and mighty kings among them, that they include great conquerors | who have given a new shape to the conditions of life, 487 who are deities.[219] ⌐These deities are also the heroes of amorous tales.¬[220]

The third [essence] is Shiva, i.e., Mahadeva[221]; this is [the moment of] change in general; the basic character is on the one hand the vast energy of life, and on the other the destroyer, the devastator, the wild energy of natural life. His principal symbol is therefore the bull

gnostischen Systeme (Berlin, 1818), p. 10. ᵈSee above, annotation a. ᵉSee H. T. Colebrooke, "On the Vedas," Asiatic Researches 8:404–405, where Colebrooke gives a translation of the Nāsadiya hymn from the eleventh chapter of the Rig Veda. In the part played by "darkness"and "desire," as portrayed in the hymn, Colebrooke sees an analogy to Hesiod, Theogony 116. ᶠOn the divinity of reading the Vedas, see esp. J. A. Dubois, Moeurs, institutions, et cérémonies des peuples de l'Inde (Paris, 1825) 1:186–187, a passage to which specific reference was made by P. von Bohlen, Das alte Indien (Königsberg, 1830), 2:13. The Brāhmans' duty to read the Vedas was supposedly assigned to them by the Supreme Being at the time they and the other castes were created (see Institutes of Hindu Law, p. 12). On reading them in a dull, thoughtless manner see H. T. Colebrooke, "On the Vēdas, or Sacred Writings of the Hindus," Asiatic Researches 8:390. On the immediate presence of Brahman in Brāhmans see Institutes of Hindu Law, p. 286.

218. W (Var/1831?) adds: Krishna is also Brahmā, Vishnu.

219. L (1827?) adds, similar in W: [W: and are thus described as deities.] The deeds of Krishna are conquests, and the way they happen is quite ungodlike.

220. W (Var) reads: Generally speaking, conquest and amours are the two aspects or the principal acts of the incarnations.

221. W (1831) adds: the great god, or Rudra, who ought to be the return into self. The first stage, Brahman, is the remote, self-enclosed unity. The second, Vishnu, is manifestation, life in human shape. (The moments of spirit are up to this point unmistakable.) The third stage ought to be the return to the first, in order that the unity should be posited as returning within itself. But it is just this third stage that is devoid of spirit; it is merely the category of becoming generally, or of generation and perishing.

on account of its strength, the image of natural virility but at the same time also the destroyer; the most general representation for it, however, is the lingam (something revered among the Greeks as the phallus), this symbol that most temples have—the innermost sanctum contains this image. Hence, as we said, the third aspect here is only change in general, procreation and destruction. [222]The authentic third aspect in the profound concept is spirit, the return of the One to itself, its coming-to-self; not just change, but change through which the [moment of] distinction is brought to reconciliation with the first [moment], and the duality is sublated.

In this religion, which still belongs to nature, this process of becoming is still grasped as sheer becoming, sheer change.[223] This 488 | distinction is essential and is grounded upon the whole standpoint. From the very standpoint of nature religion it is even necessary.

As we said, the distinctions presented are finally grasped as unity, as the Trimurti; and the Trimurti, not Brahmā itself, is grasped as the highest. But ⁻equally⁻[224] each person of the triad is also in turn taken alone, by itself, so that it is itself the totality, is the entire god.

It is noteworthy that the older portions of the Vedas do not speak of Vishnu, even less of Shiva; there Brahmā, the One, is God altogether alone. The distinctions of the Trimurti are determinations that are introduced only later.[225] ⁻There are also castes; one reveres

222. *Precedes in W₂ (1831), similar in W₁ (at the end of this paragraph):* Such are the three fundamental determinations. The whole is portrayed by a figure with three heads, again in a symbolical manner, and not beautifully.

[*Ed.*] Again Hegel is probably referring to an illustration depicting the Trimurti, accompanying Creuzer's *Symbolik und Mythologie*, plate xxii, fig. 1. The Trimurti is also said to be represented by the image of three conjoined human heads, in the account of FitzClarence's journey in Harnisch, *Die wichtigsten Reisen,* vol. 7 (1825), pp. 60–61.

223. *L (1827?) adds, similar in W:* It is not a change in the differentia, through which unity produces itself as the sublation of the difference into unity. Consciousness or spirit is also a change in the first or immediate unity. The other element is the primal division or judgment, the having of an other over against one. I know that I exist in such a way that, inasmuch as the other is for me, I have returned to myself in that other, I am within myself. But here, instead of being what reconciles, the third moment is only this wild play of begetting and destroying. *W₂ (1831) continues:* So the unfolding ends in a wild, delirious whirl.

224. *W (Var) reads:* just as this is grasped as Trimurti, so

225. [*Ed.*] This is probably derived from Colebrooke's "On the Vedas," *Asiatic Researches* 8:377–497, esp. pp. 494–495.

only Krishna, the other Shiva, and great strife arises from this.⁻²²⁶

²²⁷The one called Vishnu says about himself in turn that he is everything, that he is the absolutely formative activity, that Brahman is the womb in which he engenders all. Indeed, he even goes on to state: "I am Brahman."²²⁸ Here the distinction is sublated. Likewise when Shiva ˉavows thatˉ²²⁹ he is the absolute totality, the fire in jewels, the luster in metal, the power in the male, the reason in the soul; he, too, is in turn Brahman.²³⁰

ˉApart from these distinctions, the particular phenomena | and powers are further represented as both free and having being on their own account; but they are personified. Hence sun, moon, the Himalayas, the Ganges and the other rivers, are represented as persons; and similarly, particular subjective sentiments such as vengeance, or powers such as evil, are personified; everything is in confusion. Their being is a personification even if they are represented as animals; they are spoken of in human terms, and always as alive.²³¹ | The first bird to alight on the branch is the god of love; the cow and the ape enjoy great reverence. They do not have hospitals

489

490

226. W (Var) reads: The Hindus, moreover, are divided into many sects. Among many other differences the principal one is this, that some worship Vishnu and others Shiva. This is often the occasion of bloody conflicts; at festivals and fairs especially, disputes arise which cost thousands their lives.

[Ed.] This may be based on W. C. Seybold, Ideen zur Theologie und Staatsverfassung des höhern Alterthums (Tübingen, 1820), p. 45; see also Mill, History of British India 1:226.

227. Precedes in W (Var): Generally speaking these distinctions are to be understood as meaning that

228. [Ed.] See Mill, History of British India 1:232.

229. W (Var) reads: is brought on the scene speaking,

230. [Ed.] Hegel is obviously referring again here to the Atharvasira Upanishad; but most of the comparisons he lists in fact belong to the self-avowal of Krishna in the Bhagavad-Gita. He probably includes them here because he has already mentioned them in Part I (p. 124 above). On "the luster in metal" and "the reason in the soul" see Bhagavad-Gita, ed. A. Schlegel (Bonn, 1823), pp. 162 ff. (10.36, 22). The comparison to "the fire in jewels" is found elsewhere, serving as a reference to the Mahābhārata in the Mārkandēya-Purana; it is not certain what Hegel's source is.

L (1827?) adds, similar in W: In this way everything dissolves into one person, into one of these [three] distinctions, even the other two persons, along with the other powers, nature deities, and genii.

231. L (1827?) adds, similar in W₁: That the [divine] substance should also have animal form is a commonplace for the Hindus.

for sick people, but they do for sick cattle.[232] Even the god of heaven, Indra, stands far below Brahmā, Shiva, and Vishnu;[233] he in turn has many deities beneath him, even the stars. All of the particular powers in their peculiar natures attain this independence, although it is a vanishing independence.‾[234]

232. [Ed.] See Mill, *History of British India* 1:281, where a footnote refers to a report by Dr. Tennant to this effect, except that Tennant does not say there were no hospitals for the sick generally, but none "for the sick poor."

233. [Ed.] Hegel does not refer to the fact that this subordination of the old Vedic god of thunderstorm and of war, Indra, reflects the replacement of the old religion of the Vedas by Brahmanism, despite the fact that elsewhere he shows that he has a rudimentary knowledge of this development in the history of Hindu religion.

234. *W (1831) reads:* Apart from this main foundation and fundamental determination in the Hindu mythology, everything else is personified superficially through phantasy. Great natural objects, such as the Ganges, the sun, the Himalayas (which are in particular the dwelling place of Shiva), are identified with Brahman itself. Everything—love, deceit, theft, cunning, as well as the sensuous powers of nature in plants and animals, [W₂: so that substance has animal form]—is comprehended by phantasy [W₂: and represented as free on its own account]. Thus there arises an infinite world of deities of the particular powers and phenomena, which is known nonetheless to be subordinate to something above it. At the head of this world stands Indra, the god of the visible heavens. These gods are mutable and perishable, and subject to the supreme One; abstraction absorbs them. The power which humankind acquires by means of abstraction strikes them with terror; indeed, Vishvamitra even creates another Indra and other gods.ᵃ

W₂: Thus at one moment these particular spiritual and natural powers are regarded as gods subsisting independently, and at another moment [they are regarded] as vanishing [beings] whose nature it is to be submerged in the absolute unity, in substance, and again to arise out of it.

So the Hindus say that there have already been many thousand Indras, and there will be still more; in the same way the incarnations are posited as transient too.ᵇ Since the particular powers return into the substantive unity, the unity does not become concrete but remains abstract; and it also does not become concrete inasmuch as these determinacies emerge from it—rather they are phenomena defined as having their independence outside it.

W: To form an estimate of the number and value of these deities is out of the question here. There is nothing that partakes of a fixed shape, since the phantasy we are dealing with is totally lacking in determinacy. These configurations disappear again in the same way as they are created. Phantasy passes over from an ordinary external mode of existence to divinity, and this in turn reverts in like manner to what was its basis. It is impossible to speak of miracles here, for everything is a miracle, everything is crazy and is not determined by a rational nexus of thought categories. In any event much of it is symbolical.

[Ed.] ᵃSee below, n. 244. ᵇSee below, n. 255.

c. The Cultus

‾Now we are going to speak of the cultus, of the relation of human beings to Brahman.‾[235] The absolute or highest cultus is that most complete emptying out of the human, the renunciation in which the Hindus relinquish all consciousness and willing, all passions and needs (nirvana), [or] this union with God in the mode of integral self-concentration (yoga). The sort of person who lives only in contemplation, who has renounced all worldly desires, is called a yogi. On the one hand the devotion of the Hindus, when concentrated within themselves, is a passing state like our devotion; ‾on the other hand, however, the Hindus make this abstraction into | the   491 character of their consciousness, and of their entire existence. [Their goal is] total indifference toward everything, and complete austerity. One essential determination is that, while it is the case for Hindus, as it is for us, that devotion is a momentary elevation after which one returns to one's former activity and interests, it is also the case that for them this abstraction also appears as something that persists for the whole of life, so that what prevails is total indifference toward everything ethical, toward all worthy human pursuits. In this state devoid of thought, in this pure egoism, the human being is Brahman itself. But when an Englishman[236] asked such a person: "What is Brahman, this meditation? Do you have a temple for Brahman?" the reply was: "We revere one Brahmā. We have no temple for Brahmā, but only for Vishnu and Krishna, just as the Catholics have no church for God, but always just for a saint." (Canova pledged his great artistry to his native city, in order to build a magnificent church to the honor of God; but the clergy would not allow it, for it must belong to a saint.[237]) When one asks the Hindu what this absorption is called, however, the reply is: "When I direct

235. W₁ (Var) reads: The relationship of the subject to the absolute and especially to Brahman (which relationship is the cultus) will show more precisely what this Brahman properly is.

236. [Ed.] Francis Wilford, "An Essay on the Sacred Isles in the West," Asiatic Researches 11:125–126.

237. [Ed.] Hegel makes the same comparison in his Humboldt review, p. 1484 (Berliner Schriften, pp. 145–146; cf. pp. 708–709), citing official reports as his source. It has not been possible to identify them more precisely.

my devotion to the honor of some god, when I concentrate totally within myself, then I say inwardly to myself that I am Brahman itself, that I am the highest essence."²³⁸ Pure being-with-myself is Brahman.⁻²³⁹

²⁴⁰The highest point in this cultus is the state of being dead to the world, the making of this inward immobility of self into one's character or one's fixed principle. ²⁴¹⁻⁻Those who have attained this are | called yogis. There are distinct levels of yogis. An Englishman²⁴²

492

238. [Ed.] See above, n. 236.

239. W₁ (Var) reads: but on the other hand, the fact is that humans make this abstractness (which they initially attain only momentarily) into their character, the character of their entire consciousness, of their entire existence. Hence they do not just elevate themselves momentarily, but remain at this level, completely indifferent to ethical concerns, to the ties that bind us together as human, to society, to what merits their attention and involvement. One who remains at this abstract level, who renounces everything and is dead to the world in general, is a yogi.

One who inwardly concentrates oneself in this thoughtlessness, this emptiness, this pure selfhood, this pure presence to self, is Brahman. And the highest mode of the cultus for Hindus is to make this abstractness something completely habitual.

W₂ (1831 with 1827?) reads: The highest point to which one attains in the cultus is that union with God which consists in the annihilation and stupefaction of self-consciousness. This is not affirmative liberation and reconciliation, but is rather a wholly negative liberation, complete abstraction. It is the complete emptying that renounces all consciousness, will, passions, needs. In the Hindu view, persistence within one's own consciousness is ungodly. Human freedom consists not in emptiness, but precisely in being at home with oneself in one's willing, knowing, and acting. To the Hindu, on the contrary, the complete submergence and stupefaction of consciousness is what is highest, and one who remains at this abstract level and is dead to the world is called a yogi.

240. In B's margin: 3 July 1827

241. W₁ (Var) reads (parallel in main text follows): Even nowadays there are still individual Hindus who inflict such exercises and torments on themselves in order to attain to the power of the Brāhmans, a power that is itself above the gods; for example, they spend ten years with their arms above their heads, they have themselves buried alive, have themselves swung through fire, etc.

One who has reached the highest rung on the ladder of penances (in other words, he has had himself buried alive) has attained consummation and is the actual Brahmā who has power over all gods; Indra and all the gods of nature are subject to him, so that he is accounted to be what we saw previously in the sorcerer (namely that this singular subject exercises all power over the violent forces of nature). The Brāhman is born with this merit of the yogi; he is twice-born, and hence he has universal power over nature.

242. [Ed.] Samuel Turner, An Account of an Embassy to the Court of the Teshoo Lama in Tibet, Containing a Narrative of a Journey through Bootan, and Part of Tibet (London, 1800), pp. 270–272.

who had journeyed to the Dalai Lama reported that he had known one who was at the first stage and who had slept in a standing position for twelve years. The second stage was going to be when he would keep his hands folded over his head for another twelve years. After one had accomplished this, other trials then ensued, such as sitting in the midst of five fires for three and three-quarter hours. One yogi got to the point where he wanted to hang suspended by one foot over a fire, also for three and three-quarter hours, but he was unable to endure it. The greatest test is to allow oneself to be buried alive and to continue in this situation for three and three-quarter hours. Having endured all this, one is then perfect and has absolute power over the whole of nature, over all deities; one is Brahmā himself, and is accorded the status that we saw previously in the case of the sorcerer, of having power over the forces of nature.[243] ¯From an epic we know that a certain Vishvamitra wanted to attain this status (cf. the poem "Rāmāyana").¯[244] | 493

243. [Ed.] It is clear from his Humboldt review, p. 1459 (Berliner Schriften, p. 117), that Hegel is again referring here to Humboldt's paper on the Bhagavad-Gita (see above, n. 204).

244. W (1831) reads: There is an episode in the Rāmāyana[a] that transposes us completely to this standpoint. The story of the life of Vishvamitra, the companion of Rama (an incarnation of Vishnu), is related as follows: There was a mighty king, and being so mighty, he demanded a cow (which in India is worshiped as the generative force of the earth) from the Brāhman Vasishta, after he had got to know of its marvelous energy. Vasishta refused to give it; thereupon the king seized it violently, but the cow escaped back to Vasishta and reproached him for having allowed it to be taken from him, [W₁: and promised him, as a Brāhman, all power, which would be greater than that of a Kshatriya, which the king was. W₂: since the power of a Kshatriya (which the king was) did not exceed that of a Brāhman.] Vasishta then charged the cow to raise up for him a power wherewith to resist the king, who then confronted this power with his whole army, and both armies struck repeatedly at one another. Finally, however, Vishvamitra was conquered, after his hundred sons too had been destroyed by means of a wind that Vasishta had caused to issue from his navel. Full of despair, he handed over the government to his sole remaining son and betook himself with his consort to the Himalaya Mountains in order to obtain the favor of Mahadeva (Shiva). Moved by the severity of his exercises, Mahadeva is prepared to fulfill his wishes. Vishvamitra asks to have complete knowledge of the science of archery, and this is granted him. Armed with this, Vishvamitra intends to coerce Vasishta; with his arrows he lays waste his forest. But Vasishta seizes his staff, the Brahmā weapon, and lifts it up; thereupon all the gods are filled with apprehension, for this violence threatened the entire world with destruction. They entreat the Brāhman to desist. Vishvamitra acknowledges the Brāhman's power and

now resolves to subject himself to the severest disciplines in order to attain that power. He retires into solitude and lives a thousand years in abstraction, alone with his consort. Brahmā comes to him and addresses him thus: "I recognize thee now as the first royal sage." Not content with this, Vishvamitra begins his penances anew. Meanwhile a Hindu king had applied to Vasishta with the request that he would raise him up to heaven in his bodily shape. The request was refused, however, on account of his being a Kshatriya; but as he haughtily persisted in it, Vasishta degraded him to the chandala caste. He then betook himself to Vishvamitra with the same request. Vishvamitra prepares a sacrifice, to which he invites the gods; however, they refuse to come to a sacrifice offered for a chandala. But Vishvamitra, through his strength, raises the king to heaven. At the command [W_1: of the gods W_2: of Indra] he falls down, but Vishvamitra sustains him between heaven and earth, and thereupon creates another heaven, another Pleiades, another Indra, and another circle of gods. The gods were filled with astonishment, repaired in humility to Vishvamitra, and agreed with him about a place to be assigned to that king in heaven. After the lapse of a thousand years, Vishvamitra [W_1: was called W_2: was rewarded, and Brahmā called him] chief of the sages. [W_2: But he did not yet declare him to be a Brāhman. Then Vishvamitra begins his penances all over again.] The gods in heaven become apprehensive; Indra attempts to excite his passions (for a perfect sage and Brāhman should have subjugated his passions). He sends him a very beautiful girl, with whom Vishvamitra lives for twenty-five years; but then he removes himself from her, having overcome his love. In vain, too, do the gods try to provoke his anger. Finally, his Brāhmā strength has to be conceded.

Precedes in W_1 *(1831):* It is only the Brāhmans who are privileged to read the Vedas, and this privilege belongs to them by right of birth. Their whole life expresses the existence of Brahman; they enter into all worldly affairs, to be sure, but they are regarded as already possessing the absolute power in themselves. All other castes stand far below the Brāhman caste. The highest point that can be attained in the cultus is stupefaction, the annihilation of self-consciousness; this is not affirmative liberation and reconciliation, but rather wholly negative liberation, complete abstraction. In the Hindu view, persistence within one's own consciousness is ungodly. But human freedom consists precisely in being free in willing, knowing, and acting. To the Hindu, on the contrary, the complete submergence and stupefaction of consciousness is what is highest.

The Brāhmans are the existence of Brahman.[b] According to the myth, they issued from its mouth. Those who are not Brāhmans can also raise themselves to this level, but only through ceaseless asceticism, by forcing themselves to mortify themselves for years at a time and so attaining what the Brāhman has immediately through birth. When the most ignorant Brāhman reads the Vedas, Brahman is within him. Other Hindus can raise themselves to this level, by bringing themselves to the point of being quite lifeless in the final stupefaction of consciousness. This is a basic trait in Hindu life. What the great epic poems of the Hindus principally express[c] is the Brāhman's loftiness, and they treat of the monstrous tasks and penances that the Kshatriyas have performed in order to attain this perfection of power. Hindu renunciation is the way of perfection that does not presuppose sin.[d]

[Ed.] [a]The account transmitted by W follows fairly closely *The Ramayuna of Valmeeki* in the translation by W. Carey and J. Marshman, vol. 1 (Serampore, 1806), secs. xli–lii, except that it is not Vasishta but Vishvamitra who terrifies the gods and

The Brāhmans enjoy from birth the status of the yogi; they are called twice-born‾ —first a natural birth, secondly one via the abstraction of spirit. This means that when a Brāhman is born, then a powerful god is born; the king should | beware of provoking such 494 a person to anger, for he could destroy the king's entire power. No king can call them to account. The other castes have boundless reverence for these Brāhmans. According to the Hindu law books the Brāhman holds this elevated status even though he is only human like everyone else. Nowadays the life of the Brāhmans has changed very much; they are employed by the English as scribes and in other activities. In the last insurrection of the Burmese, Brāhmans also were among the captives; | they were shot just like the others—though 495 according to the laws Brāhmans cannot be brought to justice by the king.[245]

worlds by use of "the Brahmā weapon." It is also not Vasishta himself but his sons who utter the curse whereby the king is made a chandala. The same error occurs in the extract Hegel made from the English translation in his Humboldt review, pp. 1460–1464 (Berliner Schriften, pp. 119–123), despite the fact that he was also familiar with a German translation of the same episode by Franz Bopp in Über das Conjugationssystem der Sanskritsprache (Frankfurt am Main, 1816), pp. 159–235. Thus we may assume that in lecturing, Hegel based himself on the text of his review or the materials he had assembled for it. The shifts between past and present tense occur in W_1 and W_2. [b]For the idea that Brāhmans are sprung from the mouth of Brahman, see Institutes of Hindu Law, p. 12. [c]This in fact applies only to the Rāmāyana. [d]This sentence indicates that the term "penances" (Büssungen) is an inappropriate expression for what the Hindus call "austerities" (Sanskrit tapas)—the term in fact used by Hegel's source, the Carey-Marshman translation. Without sin there can be no "penance." Hegel may have been unfamiliar with the English term "austerities." In the 1824 lectures, where his source was most likely Bopp's German translation, he uses the term Strengigkeiten instead of Büssungen and says specifically that such Strengigkeiten are not "penances" (Bussübungen) for offenses committed. The W text adds following Strengigkeiten the misspelled word "austereties"—probably the hand of the editor.

245. [Ed.] On the concept of the twice-born, see Institutes of Hindu Law, p. 38. The statement that Brāhmans cannot be "brought to justice [gerichtet]" by the king probably refers to pp. 237–238; the German verb can mean either "sentenced" or, sometimes, "executed" (more properly, hingerichtet), and it is clear from the source that the latter is intended here. On the power and elevated social status of the Brāhmans, p. 224; on their divine dignity, pp. 13, 286. The source of Hegel's remark concerning changes in the status of Brāhmans has not been positively identified, although it is possible he is again referring to an incident in Mill's History of British India 2:129–130, 134, where the author describes how the French governor of

[246]Thus the highest point is this detached contemplation as Brahman wholly for itself, which comes into existence in this deep absorption in nothing, in this wholly empty consciousness and intuition. The remaining content of spirit and nature, however, is allowed to run wild in all directions. The [contemplative] unity that stands uppermost is, to be sure, the power from which everything proceeds and into which everything returns; but it does not become concrete as the bond of the manifold powers of nature, nor does it become concrete in spirit as the bond of the many and varied spiritual activities and sensibilities. In the first instance, when the unity becomes the bond of natural things we call it necessity; this is the bond of natural forces and phenomena. This is how we consider natural properties and things, as being in their independence essentially conjoined to one another. Laws and understanding are in nature, in the fact that phenomena cohere in this way. But the unity of Brahman remains solitary, by itself; hence its fulfillment is here a wild and unruly one. Similarly in the spiritual domain, we do not have the concrete here; the universal or thinking does not become something concrete in the spirit, something internally self-determining. When thinking determines itself internally and the determinate is sublated within this universality, when pure thinking is concrete, that is what we call reason. There is duty and right only in thinking. These determinations, posited in the form of universality, are rational with regard to conscious truth and insight, and likewise with regard to the will. But such concrete unity, reason, and rationality does not also become that One of Brahman, that solitary unity. On this account there is no right or duty present here either. For freedom of will and of spirit is precisely a being present to oneself

---

Pondicherry exacted forced labor from all the inhabitants, regardless of caste, and later had six Brāhmans shot from the muzzles of guns as spies. In his Humboldt review, p. 1490 (*Berliner Schriften*, pp. 152–153), Hegel also referred to FitzClarence's report that any Brāhman who held a subordinate post with the English was treated with scant respect.

246. *Precedes in L (1827?):* No reverence is shown to Brahman; it is not worshiped or venerated, has no temple or altars; its unity is not related to what is real, to actually effective self-consciousness. From the fact that consciousness of the One is isolated in this way, it follows that at this level nothing in the relationship to the divine is defined by reason.

in determinacy; but this presence to self or this unity is here abstract
and lacks determination. | 496

In one respect this is the source of the fanciful polytheism of the
Hindus. We have noted that there is here no category of being. They
have no category for what we call the independence of things, for
what we articulate by the phrase "there are" or "there is"; rather,
in the first instance, human beings know themselves alone as independent. For this reason an independent element in nature is represented
as endowed with our own human type of independence, the kind
we carry in our own being—in our human shape and consciousness.
Hence the imagination here makes everything into deities. This is
what we see in its own way among the Greeks, too, where every
tree is made into a dryad, every spring into a nymph. There we say
that the beautiful imagination of human beings animates everything,
ensouls everything, represents everything as inspirited; that human
beings walk among their own kind, anthropomorphize everything,
and through their beautiful fellow-feeling give to everything the
beautiful mode [of life] that they themselves have.[247] Among the
Hindus, on the contrary, it is a wild and unruly mode. We duly note
that they are so generous as to share their mode of being; but we
must state that this liberality has its ground in an impoverished image
of themselves and, to be precise, in the fact that their humanity does
not yet have in it the content of freedom, of the eternal, of actual
being truly in and for itself, and they do not yet know that their own
content or specification is nobler than the content of a spring or a
tree.[248] Among the Greeks there is more a play of imagination, while
among the Hindus there is no higher self-feeling or self-awareness
present. The view that they have of being is simply the one they have
of themselves; they set themselves on the same plane with all their
images of nature. This is the case because thinking has slipped back
so wholly into abstraction.

Furthermore the powers of nature, whose being is known and
represented anthropomorphically, transcend concrete human beings
who, as physical beings, are dependent on them and have not yet

247. W₂ (Var/1831?) adds: and so embrace everything as ensouled.
248. W₂ (Var/1831?) adds: Everything is squandered on the imagination, and
nothing is kept back for living.

distinguished their freedom from their natural aspect. Coherent with this is the fact that human life has no higher worth than the being 497 | of natural objects or the life of a natural being. Human life has worth only when humanity itself is inwardly nobler; but for the Hindus human life is something contemptible and despicable—it has no more value than a sip of water. Here one cannot ascribe worth to self in an affirmative way, but only negatively: life gains worth only through negation of self. Everything concrete is only negative when measured against this abstraction. Every aspect of the Hindu cultus follows from this, such as the fact that human beings sacrifice themselves and their parents and children; widow-burning after the death of the husband fits in here too.[249] This sacrifice [of self] has a higher value when it is done expressly with regard to Brahman or some god; for the god is also Brahman. It counts as a higher sacrifice when they climb up to the snowy crags of the Himalayas where the sources of the Ganges are, and cast themselves into these streams.[250] Those are not penances for transgressions, not offerings in recompense for some evil, but rather a sacrifice merely to gain worth for oneself. This worth is just what can only be attained in a negative manner.[251]

Bound up with the fact that the human being is in this way without freedom and has no inner self-worth, there is a concrete expansion of this unspeakable and endlessly variable superstition, these tremendous fetters and limitations. The relationship of dependence

249. [Ed.] See H. T. Colebrooke, "On the Duties of a Faithful Hindu Widow," *Asiatic Researches* 4:205–215.

250. [Ed.] Hegel is referring to an anonymous review of Alexander von Humboldt's *Sur l'élévation des montagnes de l'Inde,* in *The Quarterly Review* (London), 22, no. 44 (1820): 415–430. See also his reference to a report of Turner on the practices of a yogi, above, n. 242; and to the mortification of Vishvamitra, above, n. 244.

251. *W₂ (1831) adds:* The Hindu's animal-worship is also closely connected with the position that is here given to humanity. An animal is not a conscious spirit, but precisely in this concentration of unconsciousness, human being is not far removed from the beasts. Among the Hindus efficacy is not viewed as a specific activity but as simple force that operates through everything. Particular activity is held of little account; only stupefaction is valued, and all we are then left with is the organic life of the animal. When no freedom, no morality, no ethical life is present, then power is known only as internal, obscure power, such as pertains both to animals and to those people in the most complete torpor.

upon outward and natural things that is insignificant to the European is made into something fixed and abiding. For this is precisely where superstition has its ground: in the fact that human beings are not indifferent to external things—and they are not indifferent when they have no inward freedom, when they do not | have true independence of spirit.[252] Thus it is prescribed with what foot one should stand up, and how one should pass water, whether to the north or to the south. This is where the prescriptions that Brāhmans have to observe fit in (see also the tale of Nala in the Mahābhārata).[253] And just as the superstition arising from this lack of freedom is unbounded, so it also follows that there is no ethics to be found, no determinate form of rational freedom, no right, no duty. The Hindu people are utterly sunk in the depths of an unethical life.

[254]The essence is absolute unity, inward self-absorption of the subject. This self-absorption has its existence in the finite subject, in the particular spirit. To the idea of the true there belongs the universal, the substantial unity with self, and self-equivalence; but this belongs to the true in such a way that it is not only indeterminate, not only substantial unity, but is determinate within itself. What is called Brahman has determinacy external to it. The supreme determinacy of Brahman is, and can only be, the consciousness and knowledge of its real existence; and this determinacy or this subjectivity of the unity is here the subjective self-consciousness as such. In another form the determinacy is the particularization of the

498

252. W_2 (1831) adds: All that is indifferent is fixed, while all that is not indifferent, all that belongs to right and morality, is jettisoned and given over to caprice.

253. [Ed.] Hegel is referring to the extremely detailed prescriptions in the Institutes of Hindu Law, chap. 4 ("On Economics and Private Morals"). The prescription "with what foot one should stand up" is not, however, found in this chapter. The phrase "to the north or to the south" reads in Hu (our only source at this point) gegen Winter oder gegen Süden. Sec. 4.50 instructs a Brāhman to void feces or urine "to the north" by day and "to the south" by night; however, 4.48 instructs him never to do so "facing the wind." Hegel probably cited both passages, while Hube conflated them, mishearing Wind as Winter. For the tale of Nala, see Franz Bopp, ed. and trans., Nalus: Carmen Sanscritum e Mahābhārato (London, 1819).

254. [Ed.] The next thirteen paragraphs (ending on p. 300) are derived almost exclusively from L; they are not substantiated by B and only in a very fragmentary fashion by An and Hu. However, it is clear from the dates given by B that the text delivered was more or less of a length that would include them.

universal, the particular spiritual and natural powers. This particular aspect also steps outside the unity, and as a result there is only a fluctuation, so that the particular powers that have the value of deities are at one time independent and at another vanishing; they are what perishes in abstract unity or in substance, and then emerges from it once more. Thus the Hindus say: "There have indeed been many thousand Indras and there will be still more."[255] In the same vein, incarnations are posited as something transitory. Although the particular powers return into the substantial unity, it does not become concrete; rather it remains an abstractly substantial unity; and

499 although these determinacies emerge out of it, | the unity does not become concrete even on that account, for they are outside it, they are phenomena posited with the characteristic of independence.

d. Transition to the Next Stage

[256]¯¯The transition at which we stand is this [state of] being distinct; this existence or subjectivity collapses into a category where we are

255. [Ed.] See H. T. Colebrooke, "On the Philosophy of the Hindus," *Transactions of the Royal Asiatic Society* 1 (1824): 27, although the statement was originally intended in a historical sense, meaning that the Vedic world of gods would give way to later philosophical conceptions, rather than in the futuristic sense that Hegel gives it.

256. W₂ (MiscP) reads (parallel in main text follows): In respect of its necessity, this transition is based upon the fact that the truth which in the preceding stages is present implicitly, as the foundation, is here actually drawn forth and posited. In the religion of phantasy, and [that] of being-within-self, this subject, this subjective self-consciousness, is identical, but immediately identical, with the substantive unity that is called Brahman or that is indeterminate nothingness. This One is now grasped as unity determined within itself, as implicitly subjective unity, and consequently this unity is grasped as implicit totality. If the unity is defined as implicitly subjective, it contains the principle of spirituality; and it is this principle that unfolds in the religions that stand at this transitional point.

In Hinduism, moreover, the One (or the unity of Brahman) and determinateness (or the many powers of the particular, and the emergence of differences) stood in the relationship that the differentiae were at one moment held to be independent while at another they had disappeared and were submerged in the unity. The dominant and universal feature was the alternation between origination and perishing, between the particular powers' being annulled in the unity and their emerging from it. It is true that in the religion of being-within-self this alternation was brought to rest insofar as the particular differentiae fell back into the unity of nothingness; but this unity was empty and abstract, while the truth, by contrast, is the inwardly concrete within the universal. Subjectivity is a determinate being, is being for another, manifestation, appearance. The transition is that this subject, this subjective self-consciousness, is posited as identical with the substantial unity that is called Brahman, that this One is now | grasped as determinate unity within itself, as subjective unity intrinsically, and so this unity is grasped as totality in itself. In accord with the initial element in which this unity is implicitly determined, is grasped as subjective, the unity therefore has implicit in it what makes it into spiritual unity, what belongs to it because its being is spiritual; because it is subjectively determined implicitly, it has the principle of spirituality in itself. ¯This unity is spiritual, although it is not yet absolute spirit. But since it is also concrete totality, it no longer requires the self-conscious subject. For the Hindus it is not separated, and is inseparable, from them; insofar as it is still what is incomplete—not being the subjective unity implicitly—the unity still has the subject outside it. As complete totality it no longer needs the subject. At this point, however, begins genuine independence, and with it this separation of consciousness from ob-

500

---

unity and totality. In this way even that abstract unity, together with diversity, enters into the genuine unity in which the differentiae are sublated, are ideal, are posited negatively as dependent but are at the same time preserved.

W₂ (1831) continues: Up to this point, therefore, the unfolding of the moments of the idea, the self-differentiation of the thought of absolute substance, was defective, because on the one hand the shapes lost themselves in rigid fixity, while on the other hand it was only the flight that achieved unity (or to put it another way, the unity was merely the disappearance of the differences). But now the reflection of manifoldness into itself comes into play—or the fact that thought itself contains determination within itself, in such a way that it is self-determining; and determining has worth and inner content only to the extent that it is reflected into this unity. With this the concept of freedom, of objectivity, is posited, and as a result the divine concept becomes a unity of the finite and the infinite. The infinite is the thought that is only self-contained, the pure substance; the finite (according to this thought-category) consists of the many gods; the unity is negative unity, the abstraction that submerges the many in this One. But the One has not gained anything through this submergence; it is as undetermined as before. The finite is affirmative only outside the infinite, not within it; and hence, as affirmative, it is finitude without any rationality. But at this next stage the finite, or the determinate in general, is taken up into infinitude, the form is commensurate with the substance, infinite form is identical with the substance that determines itself inwardly and is not merely abstract power.

ject or content, the objectivity of the absolute, consciousness of its self-made independence.‾[257]

Up to this point we had this unseparated unity. Heretofore the highest aspect in this form of religion was still not separated from the subjective, empirical self-consciousness—it was just this unseparated unity. Now | the split occurs, and it does so precisely to the extent that this content becomes known in itself as concrete totality.

Implicit in this transition are two noteworthy definitions that have to be relegated to the science of logic for their development, and that emerge here more as subsidiary propositions to which we will appeal further.

[258]One of these lemmas is that this unity that we saw as Brahman, and then these determinacies—these many powers, the empirical subject, this emergence or emerged being of the distinctions which at one time count as independent but at another time have vanished and hence have perished—are not mutually external, that that unity and these distinctions revert to the concrete unity. Their truth is the internally concrete totality or unity, such that what is present is no longer an alternation between particular powers being annulled in the unity and their emerging from it—an alternation of origination and perishing as for the Hindus. Instead, the idea or the true is this, that the distinctions are sublated in the unity; they are ideally or negatively posited on the one hand as without independence, but equally on the other hand they are preserved. The fact that this concrete unity is what the true is gets developed in logic, and here we can only refer to it.‾‾

The other, equally essential definition is that at this point there occurs for the first time the separation of empirical self-consciousness from ‾absolute self-consciousness,‾[259] from the content of the

257. W₂ (Ed?) reads, in a later passage: So substantive unity is still inseparable from the subject, and insofar as it is still what is incomplete, and is not yet in itself subjective unity, it still has the subject outside it. We do not yet have the objectivity of the absolute, the consciousness of its independence on its own account.

258. In B's margin: 5 July 1827

259. W (Var) reads: the absolute,

highest, so that here God attains proper objectivity for the first time. On the preceding levels it is the inwardly absorbed empirical self-consciousness that is Brahman, this inward abstraction; or the highest is present as a human being. Only now does the break between objectivity and subjectivity begin, and only here does the objectivity properly merit the name "God," even though this object is still incomplete. And we have this objectivity of God at this point, because this content has determined itself implicitly as being concrete totality in itself. This means that God is spirit, that God is spirit in all religions.

Nowadays when one says especially of religion that subjective consciousness belongs to it, that is a correct | view. This is the instinct   502
that subjectivity belongs to religion. But we see what the [prevalent] view is, namely that the spiritual can occur as an empirical subject; ⌐we see that people take a natural thing as their god,¬²⁶⁰ with the result that spirituality is able to fall only within consciousness, and God, too, as natural essence, is able to be the object of this consciousness. Thus on the one side there is God as a natural essence. But God is essentially spirit—this is the absolute determination of religion and accordingly the fundamental determination, the substantial foundation in every form of religion. The natural thing is represented in a human guise, even as personality, or as spirit or consciousness; but the gods of the Hindus are only superficial personifications. Personification still does not produce the result that²⁶¹ God is known as spirit. There are these particular objects, such as sun and tree, that are personified (even in the incarnation [of God]); but the particular objects have no independence, because they are particular²⁶²; they have only an imputed independence. What is highest, however, is the spirit, whereas this ⌐characterization derives¬²⁶³ from empirical, subjective spirit, from subjective self-

260. W₂ (Var) reads: which can then as empirical consciousness have a natural thing for its God,
261. W₂ (Var) adds: the object or
262. W₂ (Var) adds: and natural objects
263. W₁ (Var) reads: spiritual characterization derives W₂ (Var) reads: spiritual characterization and independence derives in the first instance

consciousness, and applies to it either to the extent that it is developed, or because Brahman has its existence in and through absorption of the subject into itself.

But now it is no longer the case that the human being is simply God, and God simply the human being, that God is only in an empirically human mode; instead God is truly and intrinsically objective, God is [264] essentially object and is altogether in opposition to human beings. We will take up later their reconciliation and return, the fact that God even appears as a human being, as the God-man.[265] But it is from this point onward that God's objectivity begins. As this concrete totality, God is in a twofold way. That is the

503 fourth mode of this wild totality. |

This new form is the incipient separation from the immediate individual, the incipient severance and objectification of what is known as the highest.[266] ‾This resumption, differentiation, or

504 objectification has two forms. It is first portrayed in a pure | and

264. W₂ *(Var) adds:* in himself totality, concretely determined within himself, i.e., is known as being in himself subjective; as a result he is for the first time

265. *[Ed.]* See Hegel's portrayal of the Christian religion, below, pp. 432 ff.

266. W₂ *(1831) reads:* But if the universal is grasped as inwardly self-determining, then it comes into opposition with what is other, and is in strife with this its other. In the religion of power there is no opposition, no strife, for the accidental has no value for substance.

Since it determines itself by its own act, power does not now, to be sure, have these characteristics as something finite. On the contrary, what is determined subsists in its implicit and explicit truth. Thereby God is defined as the good; and "good" is not here posited as a predicate—on the contrary, God is *the* good. In what is indeterminate there is neither good nor evil. Here, on the other hand, the good is the universal, but it has a purpose, a determinacy concordant with the universality in which it subsists.

To begin with, however, self-determining at this transitional stage is exclusive. Thus good comes into relation with what is other, with evil, and this relation is strife—a dualism. Reconciliation (here only as becoming or as what is to be) is not yet thought of as within and implicit to the good itself.

A necessary consequence of this is that the strife comes to be known as a characteristic of substance itself. The negative is posited in spirit itself, and this is compared with its affirmation, so that this comparison is present in sensation and constitutes pain and death. The strife that resolves itself at this stage is, in the last analysis, spirit's struggle to come to itself, to attain to freedom.

From these fundamental determinations there results the following division of this transitional stage.

1. The first determination is that of Persian religion. Here the being-for-self of

simple way, but then in a seething manner, as a unity that is at the same time struggle, the fermenting of these distinct elements into a unity—an impure subjectivity that is the striving toward pure unity itself. The first of these modes is for us the fourth form.‾267

4. The Religions of Transition268

a. The Religion of Light (Persian Religion)269

The first form is thus the pure, simple totality, though for that very reason still the abstract totality. It is the form in which God is known as what truly has being in and for itself, and known truly as this;

---

the good is still superficial, so that the good has a natural shape, but as a natural being that is shapeless: light.

2. The form in which strife, pain, or death itself becomes part of the essence: the Syrian religion.

3. The struggling out of strife, the advance to the determination of free spirituality in the proper sense, the overcoming of evil, the consummated transition to the religion of free spirituality: the Egyptian religion.

Generally speaking, however, what is common to these three forms of religion is the resumption of the wild, unrestrained totality into concrete unity. That giddy whirl [Taumel] in which the determinations of unity are precipitated into externality and contingency, where this wild world of gods, without any concept, proceeds out of unity, as it did out of Brahman, and where development breaks up into confusion because it is not concordant with the unity—this state devoid of anything to give it steadfastness has now passed away.

267. W₂ (Var, possibly with editorial additions) reads: This resumption into the substantive unity, which is in itself subjective, has two forms, however. The first resumption is that seen in Parseeism; here it occurs in a pure, simple fashion. The second is that which ferments in the Syrian and Egyptian religions, where the fermentation of totality mediates itself into unity, and unity comes into being in the strife of its elements.

268. [Ed.] In the 1824 lectures, the transition from nature religion to spiritual religion is provided by Egyptian religion; in 1827 Persian religion is also included among the transitional forms. God is now known as that which is self-determining within itself, and hence as good, but this goodness is still represented in natural images such as light. The interpretation of Persian religion is essentially similar to what is already found in 1824, but its reclassification reflects a general upgrading of the Near Eastern religions, a process that is carried even further in 1831.

269. [Ed.] The historical name used by Hegel is die Religion der Parsen, "the religion of the Parsees" or "Parseeism." Today Parseeism usually refers to the Zoroastrian sect in India descended from a group of Persian refugees who fled from the Muslim persecutions of the seventh and eighth centuries A.D. However, Hegel intends by this term the religion of ancient Persia, whose classic text was the Zend-

so God is in truth what is independent, what is inwardly determinate, and hence God is the good. But for that reason God is the good that itself still has its existence in a natural mode. In general, this form is what is called the religion of light; and in it the concept of subjectivity, or of what is concrete, the development of the concrete and its demonstration as totality, come directly to consciousness for the subject. We have to consider the determinations in it more closely, and to exhibit their necessity, which is a necessity arising from the concept or from thought. We shall on the one hand presuppose the logical element, but on the other hand only hint at the sort of necessity this is.

The first point is that the resumption is what is true. It is a substantial unity that is inwardly subjective, and hence it is altogether self-determining; in other words, this unity determines itself, but not in such a way that its determinations once more attain externality or contingency. That wild, nonconceptual world of deities emerges from Brahmā; the development is not compatible with the unity, but falls outside it and is fragmented. But here, in contrast, the unity

505 is inwardly self-determining. So the determinateness is not an | empirical or manifold determinateness, but is itself what is pure, universal, and self-identical; it is a determining of substance whereby it ceases to be substance—the unity that defines itself as subject. It[270] has a content, and the fact that this content is what is determined by it and in conformity with it (or that it is the universal content) is what is called the good or the true. For goodness and truth are only forms that pertain to the subsequent distinctions of knowing and willing, though in the supreme subjectivity they are only one truth, i.e., they are particularizations of this one truth. The fact that this universal is through the self-determining of spirit, that

---

Avesta, and which today is known as Zoroastrianism. Hegel is aware that in modern times the old religion survives in India and in Iran only in small sects (see n. 284), and at one point he specifically distinguishes between "Parsees" (*Parsen,* the people of the religion) and "Persians" (*Persern,* the people of the land) (see n. 286). Since "Parsee" simply means "Persian," and since Zoroastrianism was the state religion of the ancient Persian Empire, we can refer to it as "Persian religion," which is the term used in the editorial section headings, but in the text we usually follow Hegel's practice and translate as "religion of the Parsees."

270. W_2 *(Var) reads:* and begins to be subject. This unity, as self-determining,

it is determined by spirit and for spirit, is the aspect according to which it is truth. It is the good inasmuch as it is posited through spirit, and is a self-determining in conformity with its unity; i.e., it is its own self-determining whereby in its universality it remains true to itself, and no other determinations than that unity itself emerge. It is therefore the true content that has objectivity, the good that is the same thing as the true; this good is at the same time the self-determining of the One, of the absolute substance, and hence it remains immediately the absolute power. The good as absolute power: that is the definition of the content.

The second point is that precisely in this determining of the absolute lies the connection with the concrete, with the world, with concretely empirical life in general. All things proceed from this power. This fact, that all things proceed from it, is only a subordinate moment of what we saw previously,[271] that this mode of self-determination has abstract significance as a mode of determination; it is not a self-determining that has gone back into self and remains identical, [as what is] universally true and good, but is just a general determining instead.[272] This moment is present here too, but as subordinate. It is[273] the world in its manifold | existence; but the   506 important point is that the connection of the good with the concrete world is contained in the good, inasmuch as the good is self-determining and this absolute determination lies within the good itself.

There is subjectivity or particularity in general within this substance, within the One itself, the absolute subject. This element that pertains to particular life, this determinacy, is at the same time posited within the absolute itself and is, accordingly, an affirmative coherence of the absolute, the good and true, the infinite, with what is called the finite. In the previous forms of religion the affirmative

271. [Ed.] See the discussion of Hinduism, above, pp. 267 ff.

272. W₂ (1831) adds: Power as such is neither good nor wise; it has no purpose, but is determined merely as being and nonbeing; it is characterized by wildness, by a general disorderliness [Aussersichkommen] of action. For this reason power is intrinsically what lacks determination.

273. W₂ (Var) adds: therefore concrete life, cf. Ho: The good is that in which concrete life too can intuit its affirmation,

coherence is found in part only in that pure absorption in which the subject says, "I am Brahman"; but that is an absolute, abstract coherence, which subsists only through this obscuring or abandoning of all concrete actuality of spirit, that is, only through negation. This affirmative coherence is, as it were, a pure strand; moreover, it is the abstractly negative—those acts of sacrifice and self-mortification. In the affirmative coherence at this present stage, however, it is said that [finite] things are altogether good. Because of it, the stones, animals, and human beings are altogether good; the good is a present substance in them, and what is good is their life, their affirmative being. So far as they remain good, they belong to the realm of the good; they are received into grace from the outset: it is not the case that only a subset of them are twice-born, as in India, but rather the finite is created from the good and is good.

The third point to note is that although this good is, of course, internally subjective, although it is internally determined and determines itself as good, although it is in conformity with the substantial unity, with the universal itself, in this definition it is still abstract. The good is internally concrete, yet this determinateness of being concrete is itself still abstract.[274] The good [thing] can be employed 507 this way or that, or the | human agent has good intentions; but the question is, "What is good?" A further development or determination of the good is required. Because we still have the good in such an abstract way, it is still one-sided for us, still burdened with an antithesis. It is the absolute antithesis to another, and this other or opposite is evil.

In this simplicity of the good the negative is not yet accorded its rightful place. Hence we have two principles, the realm of the good and that of evil, this Oriental dualism. It is this great antithesis that has here arrived at its universal abstraction.[275] The good is indeed

274. W₂ (1831) adds: For the good not to be abstract, the form must be developed, the moments making up the concept must be posited. In order to be the rational idea, in order to be known as spirit, its determinations, the negative element, the differentiae as constituting its powers, must be posited in it through thought, and so known.

275. L (1827?) adds, similar in W: There is manifoldness and differentiation, to be sure, in the multitude of previous gods; but for this duality to have become the universal principle, for the differentiated elements to stand confronting each other as this duality—that is another matter altogether.

the true and the powerful, but it is in conflict with evil, so that evil stands over against it and persists as an absolute principle. [276]Evil ought surely to be overcome, to be counterbalanced; but what ought to be is not. "Ought" is a force that cannot make itself effective, it is this weakness or impotence.[277]

Religion and philosophy as a whole turn upon this dualism. This is the concern of religion and of philosophy—the distinction grasped in its complete universality. In the mode of thought this antithesis attains the universality that is proper to it. Dualism is a form [of thought] even today; but when we speak of it today, it is in meager and delicate forms. Whenever we take the finite to be autonomous, so that the infinite and the finite stand opposed to one another, so that the infinite has no part in the finite and the latter cannot cross over to the infinite,[278] we have the same dualism as the antithesis of Ahriman and Ormazd, or that of Manichaeism—except that we lack the thought or the heart to represent these antitheses to ourselves [honestly]. The finite, in its broadest sense maintaining itself as finite and autonomous, over against and thereby in conflict with the infinite or the universal, is what is evil. But all the same, we stick with this thoughtlessness in which both are accorded value, finite as well as infinite. God, however, is only *one* | principle, *one* power, and therefore the finite, and evil as well, have no true independence.

508

276. *In B's margin:* 6 July 1827
277. [*Ed.*] Hegel implicitly relates Persian religion to the philosophy of Kant and Fichte, according to which, in Hegel's view, the good is to be realized only in a progression that extends to infinity, and thus is not recognized as something already present at all times. See Kant, *Critique of Practial Reason,* esp. pp. 126–127 (Kant, *Werke* 5:122); and Fichte, *Science of Knowledge,* p. 231 (Fichte, *Gesamtausgabe* 2:397).
278. [*Ed.*] Hegel is criticizing contemporary attempts, beginning with Jacobi, to reemphasize the gulf between finite and infinite in contrast to Spinoza's attempt to replace this type of transition from the one to the other by the principle of an immanent cause. In Hegel's view, the consequence of present-day criticism of the pantheistic concept of immanence is that the transition from finite to infinite becomes unintelligible, and this in turn has the result that the infinite, placed in isolation on the other side, likewise becomes something finite too. See in this connection Jacobi, *Briefe,* p. 24 (*Werke* 4/1:56); also Schelling, "Philosophische Briefe über Dogmatismus und Kriticismus," letters 6 and 7, in *Philosophisches Journal einer Gesellschaft teutscher Gelehrter* 3 (1795): 190–191, 196 ff.; and Schelling, *Abhandlungen zur Erläuterung des Idealismus der Wissenschaftslehre,* in *Sämmtliche Werke* 1:367–368.

⁻The third determination is that the good in its universality has at the same time a natural mode, a pure manifestation, a natural being, the simple manifestation—light. Light is this abstract subjectivity within the sensible. Space and time is the abstract; the concrete, [not in particular] but in its physical universality, is light.⁻²⁷⁹ ⁻From this [naturalistic] viewpoint, Brahmā would only be space that does not yet have the inner strength to be represented as internally independent; Brahmā requires the empirical self-consciousness of the human being.⁻²⁸⁰

²⁸¹⁻⁻There is perhaps a difficulty, in that the good to which we have come is also still supposed to have in itself essentially the aspect of natural being, | although it is of course the pure natural being

509

279. W (Var) reads: But furthermore, good, [W₁: in its W₂: by virtue of its] universality, has at the same time a natural mode of existence, of being for other— [W₁: a form of W₂: light, which is] pure manifestation. In the same way that the good is what is self-identical or is subjectivity in its pure identity with [W₁: itself, so the manifestation is what is pure and simple, namely light. Light is this abstract subjectivity in the sensuous realm—pure physical intuition—as the good is in the realm of the spiritual. Space and time are the primary abstractions in the sphere of mutual exclusion, but the concrete physical element in its universality is light as the good. W₂: itself in the spiritual realm, so light is this abstract subjectivity in the sensuous realm; space and time are the primary abstractions in the sphere of mutual exclusion, but the concrete physical element in its universality is light.] W₂ (1831) continues: If therefore the inwardly good, because of its abstractness, comes to have the form of immediacy and therefore of naturalness (for immediacy is what is natural), then this immediate good, which has not yet purified itself and raised itself to the form of absolute spirituality, is light. For in the natural world light is pure manifestation, the act of self-determining, but in a wholly simple, universal manner.

280. W (Var) reads: If Brahman had to be represented in a sensuous fashion, it could only be represented as abstract space. But Brahman still does not have the inner strength to be represented independently; instead it has the empirical self-consciousness of the human being as its reality.

281. W₁ (1831) reads (parallel in main text follows): In the Hindu religion, Brahman was what is highest—the One as unconsciousness and indeterminateness; at this stage, substance is not yet determined in itself. What comes next is the self-determining One; and the inward determination of the One, in its highest form, is what is good. The true and the good are one and the same; the former [is expressed] in knowing, the latter in willing. That is what power advances to. Power is neither wise nor good; it has no purpose, but is determined merely as being and nonbeing. It is characterized by wildness, by a general disorderliness. For this reason power is intrinsically what lacks determination. (It is then a logical progression that the indeterminate passes over to the determinate, and we adopt this point as a lemma

of light. But nature cannot be altogether omitted from spirit; it belongs to spirit. Even when God is grasped as internally concrete and as pure spirit, God is at the same time essentially creator and lord of nature. Therefore the idea in its concept, God in his inward essence, must posit reality or this externality that we call nature. The moment of natural being cannot be lacking; but here it is abstract, it is still in immediate unity with | the spiritual, with the good,   510 because the good itself is still this abstraction. The good contains determinateness within itself, and in the determinateness is the root of all natural being. We say, "God creates the world." "Creating" is the subjectivity to which the determinateness in general belongs. The determination of nature lies within this activity or subjectivity, and indeed the more precise relation is that it is something created. But here this further precision is not yet present; what we have instead is abstract determinateness. This determinacy has essentially the form of nature generally, the form of light and of immediate unity

---

[to our argument]; but this progression must also be one accessible to the imagination.) What lacks determination passes over to a purpose, and to one that is concordant with universality too; it passes over to the absolutely final end (which is the good in general), and this is the final end that has to be realized. Brahman, we can say, is what is inwardly good; and this is itself still abstract to begin with; because of its abstractness this self-contained good is posited in the form of immediacy, but of pure immediacy. Immediacy, however, is what is natural, or the purely physical, which is light, the manifestation that is only determined in a quite simple and universal manner. It is not the good that has purified itself, but is to begin with the immediate good. There is a logical or conceptual linkage here, so it is not to be taken as contingent that light has been intuited as the good.

But in the next step, the good passes over directly into its antithesis, into evil and darkness. W: Light is an infinite expansion, it is as rapid as thought; but in order for its manifestation to be real, it must strike upon [W_1: a dark object, a solid body. W_2: something dark.] Nothing is made manifest by pure light [W_1: as such]; it is only by means of this other that determinate manifestation enters on the scene and good accordingly emerges in opposition to evil. This manifestation is a determining, but it is not yet the [W_2: concrete] development of the determining; hence the concreteness of the determining lies outside it; owing to its abstractness it [W_1: is related to an other. This antithesis belongs to the concept of spirit, and the question is what position it occupies vis-à-vis the unity. W_2: has its determination in the other. Without the antithesis there is no spirit, and it is only in the development of spirit that the question arises as to what stance the antithesis occupies toward the mediation and toward the original unity.]

with the good; for the immediate, just as it stands, is the ⁻absolute,⁻²⁸² because the determinateness [we are dealing with] is only this universal, undeveloped one. Hence the light has darkness over against it. In nature these determinations are external to one another. This is the impotence of nature, that light and its negation are side by side, although light is the power of banishing darkness. Therefore the ⁻idea of⁻²⁸³ God that we have here is itself still something powerless. Because of its abstraction, it is unable to embrace the antithesis or contradiction within itself and to endure it, so it has evil alongside it instead. Light is the good and the good is light—this inseparable unity is the basic idea.⁻⁻

²⁸⁴⁻⁻Historically this is the religion of the Parsees. Ormazd and Ahriman are superficial personifications. When the content | is still

282. *W (Var/Ed?) reads:* abstract,
283. *W (Var) reads:* determination in
284. *W (1831) reads (parallel in main text follows):* [W_1: This W_2: This religion of light—or of what is immediately good—] is the religion of the ancient Parsees, founded by Zoroaster. There are still some communities that belong to this religion, in Bombay and on the shores of the Black Sea, in the neighborhood of Baku, where naphtha springs are particularly numerous; and some have imagined they could find an explanation for the fact that the Parsees have made fire the object of their worship in this accident of geography.[a] We get some information about this religion from Herodotus and other Greek writers,[b] but it is only in later times that a more accurate knowledge of it has been achieved, through the discovery of this people's principal and fundamental books (the Zend-Avesta) by the Frenchman Anquetil du Perron;[c] these books are written in the ancient Zend language, a sister language to Sanskrit.

The light that is worshiped in this religion is not like a symbol of the good, an image under which the good can be represented; on the contrary, it might just as well be said that the good is the symbol of light. Neither of them is the meaning or the symbol, but they are directly identical. [W_1: What is substantive here confronts the subject in its particularity; W_2: At this stage—among the Parsees—worship enters on the scene, and substantiality is here objectified for the subject in its particularity;] humanity as a particular kind of good confronts the universal good, [W_1: and also] light in its pure, as yet undisturbed, manifestation [W_2: i.e., the good as natural existence].

The Parsees have also been called fire-worshipers.[d] This is incorrect inasmuch as the Parsees do not direct their reverence toward consuming, material fire, but only to fire as [W_1: light. And this light is personified too, but only superficially, for substance is not yet known as subject. W_2: light, which comes into appearance as the truth of what is material.] . . .

[W_1: It has been claimed that the first syllable "Or-" has affinities with the Hebrew אוֹר.[e]] The stars are lights appearing singly. [W_2: Since what appears is something particular, natural,] there arises a distinction between what appears and what is implicit; [W_1: the stars are W_2: and what has implicit being is then also something particular, a genius. Just as the universal light is personified, so too are the particular lights. Thus the stars are] personified as genii. On the one hand they are appearance, but on the other they are personified as well. They are not differentiated into light and good, however; instead it is the whole unity that is personified; the stars are spirits of Ormazd, i.e., of the universal light, and of what is good in and for itself.

These stars are called the Amshaspands,[f] and Ormazd, who is the universal light, is also one of the Amshaspands. The realm of Ormazd is the realm of light, and in it there are seven Amshaspands. One might think of the planets in this connection, but they are not more precisely characterized either in the Zend-Avesta or in any of the prayers, not even in those that are addressed to them individually. The lights are the companions of Ormazd, and reign with him. Like this realm of light, the Persian state is portrayed as the realm of righteousness and good. The king was surrounded by seven magnates, too, who formed his council, and were regarded as representatives of the Amshaspands, just as the king was thought of as the deputy of Ormazd. Taking turns day by day, the Amshaspands govern with Ormazd in the realm of light; so what is posited here is merely a superficial distinction of time.

To the good or to the realm of light belongs all that has life. What is good in all beings is Ormazd; by thought, word, and deed he is the life-giving element. So we still have pantheism here, to the extent that the good or light is the substance informing everything; all happiness, blessing, and felicity flow together in it; whatever exists as loving, happy, strong, etc., that is Ormazd. He bestows the radiance of light on all beings, upon trees as well as upon noble humans, upon beasts as well as upon the Amshaspands.

[*Ed.*] [a]Hegel is probably referring to J. G. Rhode, *Die heilige Sage und das gesammte Religionssystem der alten Baktrer, Meder und Perser oder des Zendvolks* (Frankfurt am Main, 1820), p. 111, where the author speaks of the continuous petroleum (naphtha) flares emitted from holes in the ground in the neighborhood of present-day Baku (which is on the Caspian Sea, not the Black Sea). In regard to Hegel's knowledge of the Parsees in Bombay, see Carsten Niebuhr, *Voyage de M. Niebuhr en Arabie et en d'autres pays de l'orient*, 2 vols. (Switzerland, 1780), 2:460–464. [b]See Herodotus, *Histories* 1.131–140. Of the other classical writers who gave an account of Zoroastrianism, Hegel was familiar in particular with Plutarch, *De Iside et Osiride* 46–47, and with those whose references to the subject were included in *Zend-Avesta, Zoroasters lebendiges Wort*, trans. and ed. J. F. Kleuker from the French ed. of Anquetil du Perron, 5 vols. (Riga, 1776–1783), supp., vol. 2, pt. 3. [c]Hegel was familiar with the Zend-Avesta through Kleuker's translation (see annotation b). It is uncertain whether or not he also knew the original French text of Anquetil du Perron (Paris, 1769–1771). [d]See *Zend-Avesta*, ed. Kleuker, 1:149–150 (cf. *Zend-Avesta* [SBE], 2:357–361). On how and why the Parsees first became known as "fire worshipers," see Joseph Görres, *Das Heldenbuch von Iran aus dem Schah Nameh des Firdussi*, 2 vols. (Berlin, 1820), 1:8. [e]It has not been possible to identify Hegel's source positively. He is probably referring to Kleuker's linguistic parallels in his edition of the *Zend-Avesta*, supp., vol. 2, pt. 2, p. 14; but similar parallels were to be found in several other authors of the period. For example, Friedrich Sickler drew a parallel between אור and the Greek ΩP, but only as an ending; see *Kadmus; oder, Forschungen in den Dialekten des semitischen Sprachstammes* (Hildburghausen, 1818),

not an inwardly developed subjectivity, the personification is only formal. The deities were represented as subjects or persons among the Hindus, too; but how the person is determined in its substance or its essence depends solely on the content. If the substance | is not yet determined as developed subjectivity, then the subjectivity, which appears as personality, is only a superficial mode; that is again the case here.

512

Everything belongs to the light, everything living, all essence, all spirituality. The entire world in all its levels and kinds is Ormazd, and in this realm of light everything is good. Distinction belongs to subjectivity. Everything hinges on the way in which the distinctions are brought to unity, whether they are mutually external or are posited in a truly ideal fashion. Thus even light differentiates itself, and sun, stars, and planets are also personified. The sun is the power of vitality, upon which the cycle of vitality depends and with which it therefore coheres. Hence the sun and the planets are represented as the first principal spirits, as deities presiding over the world of light by turns, a heavenly people pure and great, each protecting, benefiting, and blessing [the world]. By the same token the act, the growth of finite things, everything energetic, everything spiritual— all is light, is Ormazd. Light is not simply the universal, sensible life, but is the energy, spirit, soul, love and bliss therein; all this belongs

---

p. xxii. Schelling established a similar connection, to which he traces the name of the deity Chrysor, and with which he associates the meaning of the German prefix *Ur-*, the inner, essential fire; see *The Deities of Samothrace*, n. 64 (p. 34) (*Sämmtliche Werke* 8:388). ^fEvidence for Ormazd himself being an Amshaspand (Amesha Spenta) could be found in the *Zend-Avesta*, ed. Kleuker, 1:81 (cf. *Zend-Avesta* [SBE], 3:196); see also A. H. L. Heeren, *Ideen über die Politik, den Verkehr und den Handel der vornehmsten Völker der alten Welt*, 2 vols. (Göttingen, 1804–1805), 1:509; and J. G. Rhode, *Die heilige Sage und das gesammte Religionssystem der alten Baktrer* (Frankfurt am Main, 1820), pp. 316–317, 365. Regarding the organizational similarity between the kingdom of light and the Persian state, see below, n. 286. It is in the 1831 lectures that Hegel first deals in any detail with the Amshaspands. They are not referred to in the Zoroaster Gāthās but only in the later parts of the Avesta. The Amesha Spentas are glorious immortal beings who possess saving powers. As their names indicate, they are personifications of certain qualities; the six usually mentioned in addition to Ormazd are Good Thinking, Truth, Mastery, Submissiveness, Wholeness, Not Dying. They are regarded as protective spirits for the realm of the ethical as well as for that of the natural.

to the realm of Ormazd. He is the substance, and all the particular things contain this substantial element; for that reason they are good, and belong to the realm of light, as good actions do also. In their particular existence, however, things are distinguished from the universal as well. Everything living—sun, star, tree—is revered as something good, but only the good or the light in it, not its particular shape, its finite, transitory mode.[285] |

513

The state, too, is represented in this way. The prince of the Parsees[286] is regarded as deputy of the highest light [i.e., the sun], but not of the pure Ormazd himself; his officials are regarded as deputies of the planets and stars, the ministers and aides of Ormazd.¨ One among them is Mithra, whom Herodotus already knows, the μεσίτης or mediator.[287] It is peculiar that Herodotus already singles him out; for in the religion of the Parsees the determination of mediation or reconciliation seems not yet to have been dominant. The worship of Mithra was developed generally only later

285. L (1827?) adds (following a sentence from the 1824 lectures), similar in W: There is a separation between the substantial and what belongs to transience. But that is a minor difference; the absolute distinction is between good and evil.

286. L (1827?) adds, similar in W₁: —and it was reputedly the same with the Persians—

[Ed.] This organizational similarity between the kingdom of light and the Persian state is emphasized in the introduction to Zend-Avesta, ed. Kleuker, 1:57–72. Rhode, Heilige Sage, pp. 536 ff., is very reticent in this regard; but Heeren states categorically, Ideen über die Politik 1:513, that the form of government is modeled on the hierarchy in the kingdom of Ormazd, though subsequently, pp. 527 ff., he also mentions the differences and concludes from them that Zoroaster cannot have been a contemporary of the Persian state as we know it.

287. [Ed.] Hegel is referring to Herodotus, Histories 1.131, where, however, the reference is to Mitra, who seems to be a Persian love-goddess quite distinct from Mithra—Herodotus says that Mitra is the Persian name for Aphrodite. Moreover, it is not, as Hegel seems to think, Herodotus who calls Mithra the "mediator" but Plutarch, De Iside et Osiride 46. Creuzer also, though he distinguishes between the Mithra mentioned in Plutarch and the Mitra mentioned in Herodotus, proceeds to combine them as a single androgynous deity; see Symbolik und Mythologie 1:728–738. The situation is further confused by the fact that the Persian Mithra does correspond to an Indian god of light, Mitra, who is obviously distinct from Herodotus's love-goddess. In any event it is important to distinguish between the Persian Mithra and the later Roman cult of Mithra(s), which the Romans imported into northern and western Europe.

on, when the need for reconciliation became stronger and more conscious, more vital and determinate in the human spirit. Herr Rhode[288] in Breslau disagrees about this with Creuzer, who exalts Mithra a great deal; [Rhode] maintains that in the Zend writings Mithra does not yet have his complete development; that is quite true. He gained a particular development among the Romans in the Christian era (and even in the Middle Ages we still find a secret worship of Mithra, ostensibly connected with the Order of Knights Templar). One essential image belonging to the Mithra cult is that of Mithra thrusting the knife into the neck of the bull; it has been found frequently in Europe.

ˉOne kind of genii in this religion are the so-called Fravashis. Here we find the representation that the water of immortality springs from a tree—a striking agreement with the tree of knowledge.ˉ[289]

Light is the highest element in everything that the Parsees revere. The Parsee cultus follows immediately from this determination of their religion.[290] | The entire life of the Parsee should be this cultus, one should carry out the good in words, deeds ˉand thoughts,ˉ[291]

514

288. [*Ed.*] Rhode's repeated criticisms of Creuzer's *Symbolik und Mythologie* on this score relate to the first edition (1810–1812). In the second edition (1819–1821) Creuzer replied very sharply (1:783) to Rhode's criticisms, without really entering into their substance. The criticisms were directed not only against Creuzer's fusion of later, Hellenistic ideas with the Mithra of the Zend-Avesta but in general against Creuzer's tendency to interpret Oriental mythology in the light of Greek antiquity and then to readmit the ideas thus retrojected into earlier times, in other words to derive Greek mythology from the East.

289. W_1 *(Var) reads, similar in* W_2 *(at the end of next to last paragraph):* A distinction is posited in humanity too; something higher is distinguished from our immediate corporeality, naturalness, and temporality, from the insignificance of our external being or finite existence. This higher aspect is represented by the genii, the Fravashis. One among the trees is singled out; from the tree called Hom springs the water of immortality; Hom is to be compared with the tree of the knowledge of good and evil. These are parallels that should be noted, but no great weight should be attached to them.

290. W_2 *(1831) adds:* Its purpose is to glorify Ormazd in his creation, and the adoration of the good in everything is its beginning and end. The prayers are simple and uniform, without any distinctive nuances. The main characteristic of the cultus is that humans should keep themselves pure inwardly and outwardly and should maintain and disseminate this purity everywhere.

291. W *(Var) reads:* everywhere, should foster all that is good among humans, as well as human beings themselves, [W_1: should foster all life,]

should dig ˉwells,ˉ[292] plant trees, make life fruitful, be lively and cheerful, and promote all good, so that good and light may flourish everywhere.[293] [294]

Transition to the Next Stage[295]

The religion of light was the first form in this transition, this resumption of the manifold, the natural, into concrete unity; the second form, which contains concrete subjectivity within itself, is the abandonment to externality of that simple subjectivity; the subjectivity is developed, but in a way that is at the same time still wild and has not yet attained the composure of the spirituality that actually is inwardly free. Just as this development was fragmented for the Hindus—with alternating generation and perishing, but no return into itself—so here we have determinateness in its untrammeled state, but in such a way that these elementary powers of the spiritual and the natural are essentially tied to subjectivity, so that it is *one* subject that traverses these moments, ˉone subject that keeps distinction enclosed within itself and overpowers it.ˉ[296]

The onesidedness of this form consists in the fact that this pure unity of the good—this reversion to self and presence to self—is lacking; here freedom | merely arises, thrusts itself outward, and brings itself forth, but does not yet attain completion. It is not yet the beginning whereby the end or result is produced. So we have

515

292. W *(Var) reads:* canals,

293. W *(1827?) adds, following a sentence from 1824:* Such is this one-sidedness of abstraction.

294. [*Ed.*] On the Parsee cultus, see *Zend-Avesta,* ed. Kleuker, esp. 2:114, 118 (SBE 3:390).

295. [*Ed.*] This transitional section anticipates in certain respects the separate discussion in the 1831 lectures of "Phoenician" or "Syrian" religion as the "religion of anguish." See the reference in the concluding paragraph to the dying and rising of God, as well as the allusion to "other diverse configurations" of the type from which Egyptian religion has been singled out at the beginning of the next section (below, n. 317).

296. W *(1831) reads:* We had generation and perishing in Hinduism too, but not subjectivity or the return into the One, not a One that passes through these forms or these differences itself, and in and from them returns to itself. It is this higher power of subjectivity which, when it is developed, lets the distinction go out of itself, yet keeps it enclosed within itself, or rather overpowers it.

here subjectivity in its reality, though not yet in truly actual freedom but only seething in and out of this reality.

Here the dualism of light and darkness that we had before us at first begins to unify itself, so that the dark or negative aspect occurs within subjectivity itself, an aspect that in its intensification becomes evil. The unifying within self of opposed principles is what subjectivity is—it is the might to endure and resolve this contradiction within itself. Ormazd always has Ahriman opposed to him. To be sure, the representation that in the end Ahriman will be overcome and Ormazd alone will rule is maintained too, but it is not expressed as a present state, it is only something future. God, the essence or the spirit, must be present and contemporary, not relegated to the domain of imagination, into the past or the future.[297]

This standpoint is the unity, the drama of the subjectivity that itself traverses these different moments—it is the affirmation that itself passes through negation and reconciles negation with itself, concluding with the return into self, with reconciliation. But it does this in such a way that the deed of subjectivity is found only in its ferment, rather than its being the subjectivity that actually has fully attained and consummated itself. These are the moments of this stage.

A subject is this distinction, something inwardly concrete, a development in which subjectivity introduces itself into the developed powers and unites them in such a way that[298] this subject has a history, the history of life and of spirit. It is inner movement, in which it fragments into the distinction of these powers and inverts itself into something strange to itself. The light does not perish; but here it is a subject that estranges itself from itself and is held fast in its own negativity, yet within and out of this estrangement it restores itself. | The result is the representation of free spirit, though at first only the drive to bring forth its emergence.[299]

516

297. W₂ (Var?) adds: The next requirement is that the good must also be posited in actual fact as real power within itself, and must be grasped not only as universal subjectivity but also as real subjectivity.

298. W (Var) adds: they are set free,

299. L (1827?) adds, similar in W: Here we have God as subjectivity generally, and the principal moment in it is that negation does not fall outside, but within, the

[300]It is this moment of negation that we have to make some further remarks about. ̃The moment of negation, ̃[301] insofar as it is posited as natural, and is a determinate aspect of natural being, is death. Hence the determination that makes its entry here is the death of God. The negative as an abstract expression has very many determinacies, it is change in general. Even change involves partial death. On the natural level negation appears as death; in this guise negation itself is still within natural being, is still not purely in spirit, or the spiritual subject as such. On the spiritual level negation appears within human life, within spirit itself, as the characteristic that one's natural will is something other for one, that essentially and spiritually one distinguishes oneself from one's natural will. Here this natural will is the negation, and the human being comes to itself and is free spirit in overcoming this naturalness; one has reconciled one's heart or natural individuality—which is other than rationality or the rational—with the rational, and so one is present to oneself. This being at home with self, this reconciling, is present only through the movement or through this process. The natural will appears as evil; thus negation (as natural will) appears as something already there. In raising themselves up to their truth, human beings find this natural determination already there in opposition to the rational.

We shall discuss negation in a still higher and more spiritual form later on.[302] For in another perspective, negation is something posited by spirit. Thus God is spirit in that God begets his Son or his own other, | posits what is other than himself; ̃but in this other, God is present to himself. ̃[303] There the negation is something vanishing as well, and therefore negation in God is this determinate, essential moment.

517

---

subject itself; and the subject is essentially a return into itself, i.e., it is self-communion. This being at home with itself includes the difference that consists in positing or having an other than itself. It includes negation, but it also includes the return into itself, and being at home or identical with itself in this return—i.e., it includes affirmation.

300. *In B's margin:* 9 July 1827

301. *W (Var) reads:* There is *one* subject; the moment of the negative,

302. [*Ed.*] See below, pp. 417–432.

303. *Thus also W; W (Var) adds:* [W₂: and beholds himself and is eternal love.] Here the negation is likewise the vanishing element. *In An's margin:* a negation that immediately vanishes again, however, since God beholds himself in the Son himself.

But here we have at first only the representation of subjectivity in general. The subject itself goes through these distinct conditions as its own, so that this negation is immanent in it. Insofar as this negation therefore appears as a natural determination, the determination of death makes its entrance too, and God with the characteristic of subjectivity appears here ̄as the eternal history, ̄[304] as being the absolutely affirmative, which itself dies,[305] becoming estranged from itself and losing itself; but through this loss of self it rediscovers itself and returns to itself. It is[306] one and the same subject that traverses these[307] determinations. The negative that we had [in Persian religion] in the form of evil as Ahriman, so that the negation did not belong to the ̄being ̄[308] of Ormazd, here belongs to the self of God.

[309]In Hindu mythology there are many incarnations; for instance, Vishnu is the history of the world and is now in the eleventh or twelfth incarnation;[310] similarly, in that religion it is the case that the Dalai Lama and Buddha, likewise Indra, the god of natural life, die, and other gods also die and come back again. But this dying is different from the negativity we are discussing here,[311] for the latter pertains especially to the subject. In making this distinction everything depends on logical determinations. Analogies and similitudes can be found in all religions, for example God's becoming human [in Christianity] and | the incarnations [in Hinduism]. Volney[312] even linked

518

304. *W (Var) reads:* in his eternal history, and shows himself
305. *W (Var) adds:* —the moment of negation—
306. *W (Var) adds:* in this religion, then,
307. *W (Var) adds:* different
308. *W (Var) reads:* self
309. *Precedes in L (1827?), similar in W:* We have already had negation in the form of death too.
310. [*Ed.*] It has not been possible to identify Hegel's source. Since reference to an "eleventh or twelfth" incarnation occurs only in *L* and *W* (11:433) and is not corroborated by *An, Bo,* or *Hu,* it is probable that we have here an erroneous transmission by the transcript upon which both *L* and *W* may have relied. Buddha is reckoned as the ninth incarnation of Vishnu (see Creuzer, *Symbolik und Mythologie* 1:578, citing an Iranian source); the tenth incarnation—Kalki—has not yet occurred.
311. *W (Var) adds:* namely death,
312. [*Ed.*] See C. F. C. de Volney, *Les ruines; ou, Meditations sur les revolutions des empires,* 2d ed. (Paris, 1798), pp. 275, 386.

Krishna and Christ by virtue of their names.[313] But correlations of this kind are extremely superficial even though they embody a common element, a similar characteristic. The essential thing, the thing that matters, is precisely a further determination that is overlooked. The thousandfold dying of Indra or the rising again of Krishna is of a different kind than the death of the subject: the substance remains one and the same. At the death of the lama the negation does not apply to the substance; the substance just vacates ˉtheˉ[314] body of one lama, but has immediately selected another. The substance is not concerned with this dying, this negation; here the negation is not posited in the [divine] self or in the subject as such; it is not a proper, inner moment or immanent determination of the substance, and the latter has not the anguish of death. Thus it is only now that for the first time we have the dying of God as internal to God himself, the determination that the negation is immanent in God's essence[315]; and it is essentially through this that this God is verily characterized as subject. This is what the subject is—bringing itself forth by giving to itself inwardly this otherness, and returning to itself through the negation of itself. For this reason the third determination in regard to this anguish and death is rising again from the dead and being restored [to life].

b. Egyptian Religion[316]

ˉReligion exists in this mode of determinacy as the religion of the Egyptians. What I have stated is its soul or principal determination; it is on this account that Egyptian religion has been singled out from

313. *In An's margin:* in his *Ruins*
314. *W (Var) reads:* this individual
315. *W (Var) adds:* is within himself.
316. [*Ed.*] In 1827 as in 1824, Hegel describes Egyptian religion as the religion of the enigma or riddle (*Rätsel*) because everything in it symbolically denoted something that remained unexpressed, and it did so in ways that were enigmatic and obscure. The primary instance of this, he says, is the image of the sphinx, half human and half animal, in which we see the artistic shape forcing its way out of the animal form into the human; it has not yet arrived at the shape of beauty, which was the shape of Greek religion; it remains enigmatic, lacking Greek clarity. Hegel's source of information remained primarily the classical authors (Herodotus and Plutarch), but he was increasingly familiar with recent archaeological expeditions (see ensuing notes).

other diverse configurations[317] as the principal figure [of this
519   type].⌐[318] |

When we consider it in detail, the image of this standpoint is that
the principal figure, called Osiris, has opposed to him (as his enemy)
the negation as external or other, as Typhon.[319] But the negation
does not remain thus external to him, so that he would only abide
in struggle, as in the case of Ormazd; instead, the negation enters
into the subject itself. The subject is killed, Osiris dies; but he is
perpetually restored, and thus—posited as one born a second time,
as a representation—he is not something natural but something set
apart from the natural and the sensible. Thereby he is defined and
posited as belonging not to the natural as such but to the realm of
representing, to the soil of the spiritual, which endures beyond the
finite. According to his own inner definition, Osiris is the god of
representation, the represented god. The fact that he dies, but is also
restored to life, expresses explicitly the point that he is present in
the realm of representation as opposed to sheerly natural being. But
he is not merely represented in this way, for he is also known as
such; it is two different things, whether he simply is as a represented
being, or is also known as a represented being.

In his role as a represented being, then, Osiris is the ruler in the

317. [Ed.] Hegel probably has in mind here the so-called Phoenician or Syrian
religion, to which he devotes a separate section in the 1831 lectures.

318. W₂ (Var) reads: In this religion, as it actually exists in the religion of the
Egyptians, we encounter an endless multiplicity of images. But the soul [or living
principle] of the whole is what constitutes the chief characteristic, and it is emphasized
in the principal figure.

W₁ (1831) has the following transition to the Eygptian religion at another place:
If we express the idea as meaning that spirit is what coalesces with itself through the
negation of the other, and stress this moment of negation of the other on its own
account and in isolation, then we are beginning from the other of spirit, and not from
spirit, not from the fact that spirit is the setting of something against itself; but the
other of spirit as such is nature generally, so that the transition then appears as the
moment that has been stressed. The next step, then, is where the passing-over is not
yet grasped as reconciliation in love, but as strife and struggle. God is intuited in
this struggle itself; what is to be attained by it is the elevation of spirit out of the
natural state. We find this struggle most notably in the Egyptian religion; this is the
religion of ferment, in which everything is mixed together.

319. [Ed.] On the opposition of Osiris and Typhon, see Plutarch, De Iside et
Osiride, esp. chap. 13; also Diodorus Siculus, Bibliotheca historica 1.21.

realm of the dead, of Amenti;[320] just as he is lord of the living, so also he is lord of what no longer exists sensibly, of the soul that continues to exist divorced from the body, from the sensible and the transitory.[321] | Typhon, the evil one, is overcome, and pain with   520
him, and Osiris is the judge over right and justice. Inasmuch as evil is overcome and condemned, judging enters for the first time at this point in such a way that this judging is the decisive thing, i.e., the good has the might to enforce its authority.[322]

If we say then that Osiris is a ruler of the dead, this means that the dead are precisely those who are not posited in the sensible or the natural realm, but endure by themselves on a higher plane. Linked to this is the fact that the singular subject is known as something that endures; it is withdrawn from the transitory and is secure by itself, is distinct from the sensible. For this reason it is a most important saying of Herodotus about immortality, that the Egyptians were the first to declare that the human soul is immortal.[323] We find survival and metamorphosis in China and India, but—like the perpetuation of the individual—in Hinduism immortality itself is only something subordinate and nonessential. The highest state there is not an affirmation or perpetuation, but rather nirvana, a state of annihilation of the affirmative, one that only seems to be affirmative, that of being ˉsimilarˉ[324] to Brahman. This identity with Brahman, however, is at the same time dissolution into that unity which does indeed seem to be affirmative but is totally devoid of determination or internal distinction. In Egyptian religion, then, the following is logically involved: the highest element of consciousness is subjectivity as such; this is totality and is capable of being inwardly

320. [Ed.] Plutarch, De Iside et Osiride 27, 29; also Herodotus, Histories 2.123.
321. W₁ (Var/1831?) adds: This involves the higher vocation of humanity. W₂ (Var/1831?) adds: The realm of the dead is the one where natural being is overcome; it is the realm of representation where precisely what does not have natural existence is preserved.
322. W (Var) adds: and to destroy what is null, what is evil.
323. [Ed.] Herodotus, Histories 2.123. Hegel also refers to this report by Herodotus on a separate sheet (Berliner Schriften, pp. 706–707), but there observes that belief in immortality rests on the feeling of the inner infinitude of spirit and that this was not yet present in Egyptian religion.
324. W (Var) reads: identical

independent—it is the representation of true independence. The independent is what is not in antithesis but overcomes it. It does not ˉsetˉ[325] something finite over against itself but has the antitheses within itself and by the same token has overcome them. This characteristic of subjectivity, which is objective and befits the objective, befits God, is also the characteristic of subjective self-consciousness in the mode of immortality. It | knows itself as subject, as totality and true independence and thus as immortal.[326]

521

This is the universal. Around this universal plays an endless throng of representations and deities. Osiris is but one of them, and according to Herodotus[327] he is even one of the later deities; but he has elevated himself above all the deities, most notably[328] as ruler of the dead or as Serapis (which is the focus of greatest interest).[329]

325. *W (Var) reads:* retain

326. W_2 *(Var/1831?) adds:* With this knowledge the higher vocation of humanity has dawned upon consciousness.

327. [*Ed.*] Herodotus, *Histories* 2.144–145. Hegel's account is a condensation and to some extent an inference from Herodotus's actual words. Hegel also misrepresents the relationship between Osiris and Serapis: Serapis is not a particular incarnation of Osiris but a Hellenistic amalgam incorporating, it is true, many features of the earlier Osiris. Hegel probably has in mind Plutarch's statement, *De Iside et Osiride* 27, that Osiris received the name of Serapis "after he had changed his nature." Hegel's knowledge of the Serapis cult also came from J. D. Guigniaut, *Sérapis et son origine: Commentaire sur les chapitres 83–84 du livre IV des Histoires de Tacite* (Paris, 1828).

328. *W (Var) adds:* in the kingdom of Amenti,

329. *W (1831) adds:* [W_1: But the principal figure is Osiris.] Herodotus, following the statements of the priests, gives a sequence of the Egyptian gods, and Osiris is here to be found among the later ones. [W_2: But] the further development of the religious consciousness also takes place within a religion itself, and we have already seen in the case of the Hindu religion that the cultus of Vishnu and Shiva is of later date. In the sacred books of the Parsees, Mithra is listed among the other Amshaspands and stands on the same level with them; but Herodotus already gives prominence to Mithra,[a] and by Roman times, when all religions were brought to Rome, the worship of Mithra was one of the principal religions, [W_1: not the worship of Osiris. W_2: while the worship of Ormazd did not have the same importance.]

Among the Egyptians too, Osiris is said to be a deity of later date. We know that in the time of the Romans Serapis, a special shape of Osiris, was the main deity of the Egyptians; yet [W_2: even though he emerged for spirit at a later stage] Osiris is nonetheless the [Egyptian] deity in which [W_1: the higher consciousness W_2: the totality of consciousness] disclosed itself. [W_1: Just as the Parsees have the antithesis of light and darkness, so the Egyptians have that between Osiris, who portrays light or the sun, and Typhon or evil generally. But this antithesis W_2: The antithesis contained

As with | Mithra, so also here: the [logical] determination that lies   522
within him has been lifted out as the most interesting one, and just
as the Parsee religion became the worship of Mithra, so the Eygptian
religion became that of Osiris. Osiris, however, became the focus
not of the immediate world but of the spiritual, intellectual world.

From what we have said, we can see that here for the first time
we have subjectivity in the form of representation. We are dealing
with a subject, with something spiritual that is represented in a
human fashion. But it is not an immediate human being that is
revered by the Egyptians—its existence is not posited in immediacy,
in the realm of immediately determinate being, but in the realm of
representation. It is a content that in its movement is subjectivity,
one that has within it the moments and movement through which
it is subjectivity; but even in its form, on the soil of spirituality, it
is exalted above the natural. Thus the idea is posited on this soil
of representation, and its deficiency is that it is only the representation

---

in the Egyptian way of viewing the matter] for its part loses its profundity and becomes
a superficial one. Typhon is physical evil and Osiris is the vitalizing principle; the
barren desert belongs to the former, and he is represented as the burning wind, the
scorching heat of the sun. Another antithesis is the natural one between Osiris and
Isis, the sun and the earth, which is regarded as the principle of procreation generally.
Thus even Osiris dies, vanquished by Typhon, and Isis seeks everywhere for his bones;
the god dies, which is again this negation. The bones of Osiris are then buried, but
he himself has now become the ruler of the realm of the dead. Here we have the course
of living nature, a necessary cycle returning into itself. The same cycle also belongs
to the nature of spirit, and this is expressed in the fate of Osiris. Here again the one
signifies the other.

The other deities are [logically] tied to Osiris; [W_1: They are, as it were, only
singularized moments of Osiris, who unites the whole within him. One of the principal
deities is Amon (Jupiter Ammon), who especially represents the sun, W_2: for he is
their point of union, and they are only singularized moments of the totality that he
represents. Amon for instance is the moment of the sun,] a characteristic which also
pertains to Osiris. There are, in addition, a great number of deities who have been
called calendrical deities because they relate to the natural revolutions of the year.
Particular periods of the year, such as the spring equinox, the early summer, and
the like, are singled out and personified in the calendrical deities.

Osiris, however, signifies not only what is natural but what is spiritual. He is a
lawgiver, he instituted marriage, he taught agriculture and the arts. These figurative
accounts contain historical allusions to ancient kings; and thus Osiris contains historical
features too. In the same way the incarnations of Vishnu and the [legendary] conquest
of Ceylon [by Rama] seem to allude to the history of India.

[Ed.] ªSee above, n. 287.

of subjectivity, that subjectivity is only abstractly there in its foundation, that it is still present only in its abstract foundation. The depth of the universality of the antithesis is not yet in it, subjectivity

523 | is not yet present in its absolute universality, absolute spirituality. Because it is not yet known in the depth of universality, but only in representation, it is thus a contingent, superficial, external universality.

The content that is in the representation is not bound to time; on the contrary, it is universality.¯³³⁰ That something is in this time, in this space, that it is this sensible singularity, is stripped away. Through representation, in that it is on the soil of spirit, everything already has a universality even though but little of the sensible is stripped away (as, for instance, in the representation of a house). Thus the universality is only an external universality, what is common to many instances. ³³¹This coheres with the fact that the foundation, this representation of subjectivity, has not yet gone down absolutely into its inward depth, it is not yet the internally fulfilled foundation, so that the world would be posited in it ideally, and all natural things would be absorbed in it.

To the extent that this subjectivity is the essence, it is the universal foundation, and the history that the subject is, is known at the same time as the movement, life, and history of everything in the immediate world. As a result, we have the distinction that this universal subjectivity is also the foundation of the natural, that it is the inner universal, or that which is the substance of the natural. We have therefore two determinations here, the natural and the inner substance, and that gives us the definition of the symbolic. Another foundation is ascribed to natural being, the immediately sensible receives another substance: it is no longer immediately itself, for it represents something else that is its substance and its significance (and that is what a symbol is). The story of Osiris is³³² also the inner, essential story of the natural, of the order of nature in Egypt. To

330. W₁ *(Var) reads:* it is universality. W₂ *(Var) reads:* it is planted in the soil of universality.

331. *Precedes in* W₂ *(Var):* The fact that external universality is still the dominant feature here,

332. W₂ *(Var) adds:* in this abstract connection

this story belong the sun and its path, and the Nile with its fecundating and changing stages. | 524

The story of Osiris therefore is the story of the sun. The sun climbs to its zénith and then recedes. Its rays and its strength grow more feeble [up to] December 21; but after this period of growing feeble and weak, it begins again to rise higher in the sky; it is reborn with new strength. In this way Osiris signifies the sun and the sun Osiris.[333] The sun, the year, and the Nile are grasped as this cycle turning back upon itself.

The particular aspects in a cycle of this kind are momentarily represented as independent, as particular deities each of which designates a single aspect, a moment of this cycle. If we say the Nile is the inner, that the sun and the Nile are the significance of Osiris, that other deities are calendrical deities, all this is correct.[334] One is the inner element and the other is the portrayer, the sign or signifier by which the inner discloses itself outwardly; here there is changeableness, this being the case at one time, the reverse at another. The natural cycle of plants, of seeds, and of the Nile occurs in this manner, for its life is the same universal story. One can take them reciprocally, one as the inner, and the other as the form of its presentation or the form for grasping it. But what is in fact the inner is Osiris, subjectivity as such, this cycle going back into itself.

This is how the symbol is the ruling element, something inner and on its own account that has an outward mode of determinate being. The two are distinct from each other. It is the inner, the subject,

333. L (1827?) adds, similar in W: The sun is comprehended as this cycle, and the year regarded as the one subject that of its own accord traverses these various states. The natural realm is grasped in Osiris in the sense that it is a symbol of Osiris. Thus Osiris is the Nile, which rises, making everything fruitful, overflows its banks, and then becomes small and impotent during the hot season—here the evil principle comes into play—but eventually recovers its strength.

334. [Ed.] Hegel is probably referring to Creuzer, Symbolik und Mythologie 1:279, 289–290, where Creuzer argues that the Osiris myth as a whole and in its details is an allegorical portrayal of the solar and lunar years. Regarding the identification of Osiris and the Nile, see Plutarch, De Iside et Osiride 36, although he merely says that the Nile is an "emanation" of Osiris; and neither he nor Creuzer speaks in this connection of "the inner element" as opposed to a sign. See also C. F. Dupuis, Origine de tous les cultes; ou, Religion universelle, 4 vols. (Paris, 1795), esp. 1:366–395.

that has here become free and independent, so that the inner is the substance of the outer, not in a contradiction or dualism with it but as the significance, the representation on its own account, as against the sensible mode of determinate being. The final aspect in this sphere is that, inasmuch as the significance constitutes the focus over against the sensible aspect, ¨there lies in it the impulse¨[335] | to bring the representation to an intuited state. [336]The representation as such must express itself, and it is human beings who must bring this significance forth from themselves to intuitable visibility. The immediate has disappeared. If it is to be brought to intuition, to the mode of immediacy—and representation has the need to complete itself in this manner—if the representation so integrates itself, then this immediacy must be ¨a mediating,¨[337] a human product. Previously we had the intuitable aspect—the immediacy as natural thing—in a natural mode that is quite unmediated. In India, for instance, Brahman has its existence, the mode of its immediacy, in thinking, in the sinking of the human being into self. Or in Persia, ¨light is¨[338] the form of immediacy, which is in an immediate way. But here, since representation is the starting point, it must bring itself to intuition, to immediacy; and therefore immediacy is here mediated and posited by human beings. It is the inner that has to be brought to immediacy. The Nile and the course of the year are immediate existences, but they are symbols of what is inner; their natural history is comprehended in representation as the subject. This comprehended being, both this process as a subject and the subject itself, is inwardly this returning movement; this cycle is the subject, it is this comprehended whole that is the representation, and as subject it should be made intuitable.

Generally speaking, this impulse toward intuition can be regarded as the cultus of the Egyptians, the infinite impulse to labor, to construct outwardly what is to begin with still inward, what is

335. W (Var) reads: [W₁: subjectivity in this determinacy, subjectivity as represented, W₂: the fact that subjectivity is represented in this determinacy as the focus] is closely connected with the impulse

336. In B's margin: 10 July 1827

337. W (Var) reads: something mediated,

338. W₂ (Var) reads: the good is light, and therefore in

contained in representation, and for that reason has not yet become clear to itself. The Egyptians toiled for millennia, above all to prepare and preserve their soil; their labor in its connection with their religion, however, is the most astonishing thing ever brought forth either upon the earth's surface or beneath it: works of art that are extant now only in dilapidated ruins | (as compared with what they once were)   526 but which have amazed everyone on account of their beauty and of the effort involved in their construction. This was the occupation and the deed of this people, to keep on bringing forth such works. The entire people was involved in this endeavor, driving on beyond all measure. There was no pause in this production; the toiling spirit did not rest from making its representation visible to itself, from bringing to clarity and consciousness what it inwardly is. These works are grounded immediately in the definition that God has in this religion.[339] | 527

339. W (1831) adds: [W_1: Thus in Osiris we see spiritual moments also revered, W_2: First of all we may recall how, in Osiris, spiritual moments are also revered,] such as right, morality, the institution of marriage, art, and so forth. But Osiris is especially the lord of the realm of the dead, the judge of the dead. We find countless pictures in which Osiris is portrayed as the judge, with a scribe before him who is enumerating for him the deeds of the soul that has been brought into his presence.[a] This realm of the dead, the kingdom of Amenti, constitutes one of the main features in the religious representations of the Egyptians. Just as Osiris and Typhon were opposed as the life-giving and the destructive principles, and the sun was opposed to the earth, so here the antithesis of the living and the dead now comes on the scene. The realm of the dead is just as fixed a representational image as the realm of the living. It discloses itself when natural being is overcome; it is there, in the realm of the dead, that what no longer has natural existence persists.

The enormous works of the Egyptians, which have come down to us today, are almost entirely works that were destined for the dead. The famous labyrinth had as many chambers above as beneath the ground.[b] The palaces of the kings and priests have been transformed into heaps of rubble, while their graves have defied time. We have found deep grottoes extending for quite some distance that were hewn in the rock for the mummies, and all their walls are covered with hieroglyphics. But what excites the greatest admiration are in particular the pyramids, temples for the dead [that were built] not so much in their memory as in order to serve them as burial places and as dwellings. Herodotus says that the Egyptians were the first who taught that souls are immortal.[c] It may occasion surprise that, although the Egyptians believed in the immortality of the soul, they nonetheless devoted so much care to their dead; one might think that people who deem their souls immortal should no longer have particular regard for their bodily side. Yet it is precisely the peoples who do not believe in immortality who deem the body to be of little account after its death

This colossal diligence of an entire people was not yet in and for itself pure fine art; rather it was the impulsion toward fine art. Fine art involves the characteristic of free subjectivity; spirit must have

528 become free from desire, | free from natural life generally, from subjugation by inner and outer nature; it must have become inwardly

---

[W_2: and do not provide for its preservation]. The honor that is shown to the dead is in every way dependent upon the way immortality is represented. [W_1: Humans do not want nature to exert its power directly W_2: Even if the body must fall into the grip of a natural power that is no longer under the control of the soul, then at least we humans do not want nature as such to be what exerts its power and physical necessity] over the inanimate body, this noble casket of the soul. [W_2: It must be we humans, rather, who bring this about—at least in some degree.] So we seek to protect the body against nature as such or we return it (of its own free will, so to speak) to the earth or destroy it by fire. In the Egyptian mode of honoring the dead and preserving the body, there is no mistaking the fact that they knew human beings to be exalted above the power of nature, and hence they sought to preserve the human body from that natural power in order to exalt the body (as well as the soul) above nature. The ways that different peoples deal with the dead are altogether bound up with their religious principles, and the different burial customs always have significant connections [with those principles].

[W_2: Well then, in order to grasp the particular standpoint of art at this stage, we have to recollect that although subjectivity does, of course, emerge here, it only emerges in a basic way, and the picturing of it still passes over into that of substantiality. Consequently the essential differences have not yet mediated and spiritually permeated one another but are still only mixed together instead.] [W_1: There are a few other W_2: There are several] noteworthy features that can be listed to elucidate the way that what is present and living is intermixed and combined with the idea of the divine— so that on the one hand the divine is made into something present, or on the other hand human, and in fact even animal, figures are elevated into a divine and spiritual moment. Herodotus refers us to the Egyptian myth that the Egyptians had been ruled by a succession of kings who were gods.[d] Here we have the mixture already, in that the god is known as the king, and the king in turn as the god. There are also countless artistic portrayals representing the consecration of kings, in which the god appears as the consecrator and the king as the son of this god; and then, too, the king himself is represented as Amon. It is related of Alexander the Great that the oracle of Jupiter Ammon declared him to be the son of that god.[e] This is quite in accordance with the Egyptian character, for the Egyptians said the same thing about their own kings. And the priests too are regarded on the one hand as priests of the god, but also as the god himself. We have many monuments and inscriptions from the later Ptolemaic age, where King Ptolemy is always just called the son of God or God himself; and the Roman emperors are treated in the same way.

[W_1: Particularly astonishing in the case of the Egyptians W_2: Astonishing to be sure—although in the light of the intermingling of the representation of substantiality with that of subjectivity, no longer inexplicable—] is the animal worship that was practiced [W_2: by the Egyptians] with extreme crudity. The different districts of Egypt

free, it must have the need to know itself as free, and to be free, as the object of its own consciousness. Inasmuch as spirit has not yet arrived at the stage | of freely thinking itself, it must freely intuit   529 itself, it must have itself before its eye intuitively as free spirit. The fact that it becomes an object for intuition in the mode of immediacy

---

worshiped particular animals, such as cats, dogs, monkeys, and so on, and even went to war with one another on their account. The life of these animals was held absolutely sacred, and their killing was severely punished. Dwellings and possessions were allotted to them, moreover; and provisions were collected for them. Yes, and even in time of famine, starving human beings were left to die, rather than their drawing upon these stores.[f] Apis was most revered, for they believed that this bull represented the soul of Osiris. In the coffins in some of the pyramids, Apis-bones have been found carefully preserved.[g] [W_1: It has been said that all forms of religion were to be found in Egypt, including animal worship; to be sure, W_2: All the forms and shapes of this religion were mingled in with animal worship. To be sure,] this worship of animals belongs to the most offensive and odious aspect of it. But we have already shown, in connection with the religion of the Hindus, how human beings could come to the point of worshiping animals. If God is known [W_2: not as spirit but] as power in general, then this power is an unconscious working—perhaps a universal life. Hence when this unconscious power emerges into outward shape, it is initially the shape of an animal. For the animal is itself something unconscious, it bears within it a dull, still life (as compared with human free will) such that it may seem as if it had within itself that unconscious power [W_2: which works in the whole]. One especially typical [W_2: and characteristic] configuration [W_2: however,] is that the priests or scribes frequently appear in sculptures and paintings wearing animal masks—as also do the embalmers of mummies. This duplication—an external mask concealing another figure beneath it—conveys the awareness that consciousness is not just submerged in dull, animal vitality, but knows itself also to be separated from that animal state, and recognizes a further meaning in this fact.

[W_1: Regarding the political state of Egypt, W_2: We find the struggle of spirit seeking to extricate itself from immediacy in the political state of Egypt too;] our histories often speak of the battles of the kings with the priestly class, and Herodotus mentions them as dating from the earliest times, saying that King Cheops caused the temples of the priests to be closed, while other kings reduced the priestly caste to complete subjection and wholly excluded them [from politics].[h] [W_2: This antithesis is no longer [typically] Oriental.] Here we see human free will rebelling against religion. This emergence from dependence is a trait which it is essential to take into account.

[W_1: There are some naive and highly intuitive portrayals of spirit's struggle to escape from the natural state. This emergence and struggle is expressed in many shapes. W_2: This struggle of the spirit to escape from the natural state and its emergence from it is, however, expressed in particular in naive and highly intuitive portrayals in the visual arts. We need only to remember the image of the Sphinx as one example.] In Egyptian works of art everything is symbolical; significance attaches even to their smallest detail; even the number of pillars and of steps is not calculated to serve ordinary external purposes, but instead signifies such things as the months [of the year]

(which is a product) implies that this, its determinate being or immediacy, is wholly determined by spirit, and has through and through the character of dwelling here as a free spirit. But this is just what we call the beautiful, where all externality is completely characteristic and significant, is determined from within as from what is free. It is a natural material such that its features are only witnesses to the spirit that is internally free. The natural moment must be mastered everywhere in such a way that it serves only for the expression and revelation of spirit. And since the content in the

---

or the number of feet that the Nile has to rise in order to overflow the land. The spirit of the Egyptian people is, in fact, an enigma. In Greek works of art everything is clear, everything is set forth; in Egyptian art we are everywhere presented with a problem—the work of art is an external object that hints at something [else] not yet expressed.

[W_2: But even though at this stage spirit is still in a state of fermentation and still entangled in obscurity, and even though the essential moments of the religious consciousness partly are just mixed together and partly are in a state of mutual strife in terms of, or rather because of, this mixing: in any case, what is emerging here is free subjectivity.]

[Ed.] [a]Hegel's knowledge of portrayals of this kind probably comes in particular from the collection of the Prussian general and Egyptologist J. H. C. von Minutoli, which he saw in Berlin in April 1823; see Hegel's letter to Creuzer, 6 May 1823, Hegel: The Letters, trans. Clark Butler and Christiane Seiler (Bloomington, 1984), p. 370 (no. 450a). See also the list of items in J. Passalacqua, Catalogue raisonné et historique des antiquités découvertes en Égypte (Paris, 1826). [b]See Herodotus, Histories 2.148. Herodotus says that the labyrinth, which he claims to have seen himself, was built slightly above the lake of Moirios, near the so-called "city of crocodiles"; he gives a detailed description of it and says it was even more grandiose than the pyramids. [c]See above, n. 323. [d]Herodotus, Histories 2.144. In the Temple of Zeus there were 345 statues representing 345 generations of high priests. Herodotus says he was told that before the line of high priests, Egypt had been ruled by gods, the last of whom was Horus, the son of Osiris, whom the Greeks called Apollo. [e]Hegel is referring to Alexander's visit to the oracle of Ammon in the Libyan oasis of Siwa; see Plutarch, Life of Alexander 27. The story recounted by Plutarch was that the prophet who gave utterance to the oracle intended to address Alexander as "my son" (paidion) but through unfamiliarity with Greek said paidios instead, which Alexander interpreted to mean "son of Zeus." [f]See Diodorus Siculus, Bibliotheca historica 1.84, though what Diodorus says is that many actually resorted to cannibalism but no one was ever accused of eating one of the sacred animals. [g]This is based on G. B. Belzoni, Narrative of the Operations and Recent Discoveries within the Pyramids, Temples, Tombs, and Excavations, in Egypt and Nubia (London, 1822), 1:425–426; see also Belzoni's description of the mummified remains of cattle, sheep, monkeys, foxes, cats, crocodiles, fish, and birds, pp. 261 ff. [h]See Herodotus, Histories 2.124, 127.

Egyptian determination is this subjectivity, there is present here that | impulsion or craving for fine art which operated especially in the 530 domain of architecture and at the same time sought to pass over to beauty of figure. Insofar as this was only craving, however, beauty itself has not yet emerged here as such.

This craving or impulsion involves the struggle of meaning with material, with external shape generally; it is only the attempt or the striving to place the stamp of inner spirit on outer configuration.[340] Here it is only craving because meaning and its portrayal, representation and determinate being, are still separated; as distinction they are in principle mutually opposed. The distinction subsists because the subjectivity is to begin with only general and abstract; it is not yet fulfilled and concrete.[341] ⌐The figure has not yet risen to be a

340. *L (1827?) adds, similar in W:* The pyramid is a self-sufficient crystal [*ein Kristall für sich*], in which a dead person is preserved; but in the work of art, which is reaching out for beauty, the externality of the configuration is imbued with the inner soul, with the beauty of what is within.

341. *W (1831) adds:* Thus the Egyptian religion actually exists for us in the works of Egyptian art, in what they tell us when they are combined with the historical record that has been preserved for us by ancient historians. In recent times in particular, the ruins of Egypt have been examined by many investigators; the mute language of the statues has been studied, and the enigmatic hieroglyphs as well. [*W₁*: Above all, therefore, we must *W₂*: We must] recognize the superiority of a people that has consigned its spirit to works of language over one that has only left mute works of art behind it for posterity. [*W₂*: But we must at the same time bear in mind that no written [religious] documents were yet in existence among the Egyptians because spirit had not yet clarified itself but had consumed all its energy[a] in what was indeed an external strife, as is apparent in the works of art.] By dint of prolonged study, progress has been made in deciphering the hieroglyphic language, to be sure; but in some ways the goal has still not quite been achieved, and the hieroglyphs will always be hieroglyphs.[b] Numerous rolls of papyri have been found alongside the mummies, and it was believed that these constituted a real treasure-trove that would yield important conclusions. They are nothing but a kind of archive, however, and for the most part they contain deeds of purchase regarding pieces of land or objects that the deceased had acquired. So it is therefore principally the extant works of art whose language we have to decipher, [*W₁*: and apart from that we can only hold fast to the information handed down by the Greeks. *W₂*: and from which a cognitive grasp of this religion is to be derived.]
Now if we contemplate these works of art, we find that everything in them is wonderful and fanciful, but always with a definite meaning, which was not the case among the Hindus. Thus we have here the immediacy of externality along with the meaning, or thought. We find both together in the monstrous conflict of the inner

531 free and beautiful one, | it is not yet spiritualized to clarity; what is sensible and natural has not yet been completely transfigured into the spiritual so that it would be only an expression of the spiritual; and this organization and its features are only signs, only signifiers of the spiritual.⁻³⁴²

The Egyptian principle therefore still lacks clarity and transparency on the part of the natural or external features of the configuration; what abides is just the task of becoming clear to itself. ⁻ ⁻The stage this principle exhibits can be grasped quite generally as that of the *enigma:* the meaning is something inner that impels itself to make itself outwardly visible; but it has not yet arrived at the consummation of its portrayal in externality.⁻³⁴³ The inscription of the

---

with the outer; there is a monstrous urge on the part of what is inner to work itself free, and the outer aspect portrays this struggle of spirit for us.

[Ed.] ᵃ*sich abarbeiten.* This verb has the double meaning of "wearing oneself out" and "working oneself clear." The contrast between *sich noch nicht abgeklären* and *sich abarbeiten* in this sentence suggests the former meaning, but Hegel may have intended both, especially in light of what he says at the end of the variant about the "urge on the part of what is inner to work itself free." ᵇA reference to the success achieved over preceding years in deciphering hieroglyphic script thanks to the Rosetta Stone. See J. F. Champollion, *Lettre à M. Dacier relative à l'alphabet des hiéroglyphes phonétiques* (Paris, 1822); and *Précis du système hiéroglyphique* (Paris, 1824). Hegel speaks of numerous investigations of Egyptian ruins and writings, but we do not know to what extent he was informed of the attempts made by Silvestre de Sacy and Johann Akerblad to decipher the hieroglyphs. Hegel's daybook indicates that already in Jena he had become acquainted with earlier efforts through reports in the *Allgemeine Litteratur-Zeitung,* vol. 4 (October–December 1802). In the *Philosophy of World History,* Sibree ed., p. 200 (Lasson ed., p. 463), Hegel deals at greater length with the deciphering work of Thomas Young and J. F. Champollion. He also owned a copy of the French translation of Brown's *Aperçu sur les hiéroglyphes d'Égypte* (Paris, 1827), which discusses the problems in detail. Brown (p. 34), however, contests Champollion's claim to be the first to decipher the hieroglyphs and contends that the credit belongs to Young's article on Egypt in a supplementary volume to the *Encyclopaedia Britannica.*

342. *Similar in W; An reads:* The spiritual [content] and the form are not yet in free unity.

343. *W₁ (1831) reads:* Hence we can intuit the Egyptian spirit only as still caught up in a state of fermentation. This obscurity toils, so to speak, in the field of outward expression; in these works of art we find the moments mixed together, especially the moments of strife. We have already considered the antithesis of good and evil, or of light and darkness, in the religion of the Parsees; and we find these antitheses again here.

temple of the goddess Neith in Sais is given in full as follows: "I am what was, what is, and what will be; | no mortal has yet lifted my veil.¯¯³⁴⁴ The fruit of my body is Helios, etc."³⁴⁵ This still hidden essence expresses clarity or the sun, that which is itself becoming clear or the spiritual sun, as the son who is born from it.

532

This clarity is what is attained in the forms of religion that we now have to consider, in the religion of beauty, or that of the Greeks, and in the religion of sublimity, or the Jewish religion.³⁴⁶ In Greek religion the riddle is solved; according to one very significant and admirable myth the Sphinx is slain by a Greek and the riddle is resolved in this way: the content is the human being, the free, self-knowing spirit. So much, then, for the first form, the religion of nature, with which we have tarried so long because it is the more remote from us, and because nature is burdened precisely with the fragmentation [of the religions] into their proper independence.

We proceed now to the second stage of ethnic religion, which we have to consider next.

344. W₂ (MiscP) reads: It is now that the spiritual consciousness seeks for the first time—as what is *inward*—to struggle free from the natural state.

The most important presentation, the one in which the essence of this struggle is rendered completely visible to intuition, is to be found in the image of the goddess at Sais, who was portrayed as veiled. What is symbolized in this image, and is explicitly expressed in the superscription in her temple—"I am what was, what is, and what will be; no mortal has yet lifted my veil"—is that nature is something inwardly differentiated, namely, something other than the appearance that presents itself immediately—it is an enigma, it has an inner [content], something hidden.

But this inscription continues as follows.

345. [Ed.] Hegel quotes this inscription not in the form handed down by Plutarch, *De Iside et Osiride* 9, but in the form found in Proclus, *In Platonis Timaeon* 1.30 (except for the final sentence). Hegel's statement that the inscription stood in the temple of the goddess is a further reference to Proclus; according to Plutarch it was on the goddess's throne at Sais. Drawing on Schiller, "Das verschleierte Bild zu Sais," *Die Horen*, vol. 1, no. 9 (1795) (cf. Schiller, *Nationalausgabe* 1:254–256), Hegel understands the veil as a shroud for the statue of Neith, not as an allusion to the goddess's virginity. Elsewhere he criticizes the customary reference to a "veil" of the goddess, citing from Aloys Hirt, *Ueber die Bildung der aegyptischen Gottheiten* (Berlin, 1821), p. 7, the formula, "No one raised my tunic," noting that there was no mention of a veil in the description, nor was one to be seen in the pictorial representations. See "Hegel und die ägyptischen Götter: Ein Exzerpt," ed. Helmut Schneider, *Hegel-Studien* 16 (1981): 65.

346. W₂ (Var) adds: i.e., in art and in the beautiful human shape on the one hand, and in objective thought on the other.

B. THE ELEVATION OF THE SPIRITUAL
ABOVE THE NATURAL:
THE RELIGION OF THE GREEKS AND THE JEWS[347]

This is the stage where the spiritual elevates itself above the natural, to a freedom that is partly beyond natural life, and partly within it, so that the [simple] blending of the spiritual and the natural ceases. It is the second stage of the ethnic religions.

The first stage was the religion of nature. It comprises much within it. On the one hand it is the most difficult to grasp because it is the farthest removed from our imagination, and because it is the crudest and most incomplete stage. On the other hand the natural thus has diverse configurations within it because in this form of naturalness and immediacy [the moments of] the universal, absolute content fall apart from one another. What is higher is also deeper, for there these different moments are comprehended in the ideality of subjective

---

347. [*Ed.*] Our title for Sec. B is adopted from the heading found in the Königsberg anonymous transcript used as the basis for Lasson's edition. According to Lasson (2/1:249–250), the heading was quite lengthy and consisted of a phrase, "The Elevation of the Spiritual above Nature," followed by the words making up the first sentence of the preface to the section, and ending with a second heading, "Religion of the Greeks and the Jews." The first phrase corresponds to the language used in the summary of the whole of *Determinate Religion* at the beginning of Part II: "The second stage of religion is the elevation of the spiritual above the natural." The second phrase is supported by the Hube transcript. Thus we have combined the two phrases. This is apropos because the problematic of "elevation" pervades Hegel's entire discussion of Greek and Jewish religion. It should be noted, however, that the German edition uses as a heading for Sec. B: "The Religion of Beauty and Sublimity: The Religion of the Greeks and the Jews."

The 1827 lectures restore the basic structural arrangement of the *Ms.* in the sense that Roman religion is considered under a third separate category, that of "expediency," which is not a subcategory of Sec. B as in 1824. Far from representing the "elevation of the spiritual above the natural," the purposiveness of Roman religion is not yet (or no longer) a free and purely spiritual purposiveness. It is rather an external, utilitarian, totalitarian purpose, although universal in a political sense. While it may combine elements from the religions of beauty and sublimity, it also destroys them; their true fulfillment is found only in the Christian religion.

The most significant organizational innovation of the 1827 lectures, however, is the reversal of the order in which the religions of sublimity and beauty were treated in the first two series, so that now Greek religion is considered first and Jewish religion second. The reasons for this change and its implications are discussed in the Editorial Introduction.

unity, and this fragmenting of immediacy | is sublated, is brought   533
back into subjective unity. That is the reason why whatever falls
under the determination of natural life exhibits such a multiplicity
of configurations, which present themselves as indifferently external
to one another, as properly independent.

The universal characteristic of this [second] stage is the free
subjectivity that has satisfied its [definitive] craving or impulse. It
is the free subjectivity that has attained lordship over the finite
generally, over the natural and finite aspects of consciousness, over
the finite whether it be physical or spiritual, so that now the subject
is spirit and the spirit is known as spiritual subject. [The subject is]
related to the natural and the finite in such a way that the natural
is ⌐only instrumental;⌐[348] it has only the characteristic of glorifying,
manifesting, and revealing the spirit; [what it reveals is] that in this
freedom and power, in this reconciliation with itself within the
natural and the finite, the spirit is on its own account and is free.
It has come forth and is distinguished from this finite natural-spiritual
[world]; it is distinct from the situation of empirical, changeable
consciousness, as well as from that of external being. That is the
characteristic determination of this sphere. Because spirit is free and
the finite is only an ideal moment in it, spirit is posited as inwardly
concrete, and because we consider it as inwardly concrete (i.e.,
consider spirit's freedom as inwardly concrete), it is rational spirit;
the content constitutes the rational aspect of spirit. According to the
relationship of the content, this determinacy formally is just the one
that we stated above: that the natural and finite is only a ⌐sign⌐[349]
of spirit, and is only instrumental to its manifestation. Hence we
have here the religion within which rational spirit is the content.

This free subjectivity has at once a double determination, one we
have to distinguish. In the first place, the natural and finite is
transfigured in the spirit, in the freedom of spirit. Its transfiguration
consists in the fact that it is a sign of spirit, in which connection the
natural itself constitutes in its finitude the other side to that [spiritual]
substance; or, in this transfiguration of the physically or spiritually

348. *W (Var) reads:* partly just instrumental, but partly the garment of the spirit
[that is] present concretely within it, as representing that spirit;
349. W_2 *(Var) reads:* witness

natural element, it stands over against that essentiality, the substan-
534 tiality, or the god. The god is the free subjectivity of which the |
finite is posited only as a sign, ˉwithin whichˉ³⁵⁰ the god, the spirit,
appears. That is the mode of present individuality, or of beauty—
Greek religion. The other form is the religion of sublimity, namely
that in which the sensible, the finite, the spiritually and physically
natural element, is not taken up and transfigured in free subjectivity.
For when it is transfigured in free subjectivity, the finite element still
has at the same time a natural and external aspect: although it is
elevated into a sign of spirit, it is nevertheless not purified of
externality and sensibility. The other determination, therefore, is that
free subjectivity is raised up into the purity of thinking, this other
extreme. We have this in the religion of sublimity—ˉin theˉ³⁵¹ form
that is more in keeping with the content than the sensible aspect is.
Here [however] the sensible is ruled by this free subjectivity, which
is in itself a power and within which the other is only an ideal element
and has no genuine subsistence as opposed to free subjectivity.³⁵²

In the first form the reconciliation of the spiritual and the natural
has occurred, so to speak, in such a way that the natural is only a
sign or moment of the spiritual. But the spiritual continues to be
afflicted with this externality. It is in the second form that the finite
is first ruled by spirit, with spirit elevating itself [so that it is] raised
up beyond naturalness and finitude, and is no longer afflicted with
and clouded by the external (as is still the case with the form of
beauty). The first form yields the religion of beauty, the second the
religion of sublimity.

1. The Religion of Beauty, or Greek Religion

We could directly call this the religion of the Greeks, which is an
infinite, inexhaustible theme. The content that especially interests
us is that this religion is a religion of humanity. Humanity comes
535 to its right, to its affirmation, | in which what the human being
concretely is, is portrayed as the divine. There is no content in the

---

350. *Thus also* W₂; W₁ *(Var) reads:* inasmuch as
351. *W (Var) reads:* a
352. *W (Var) adds:* Spirit is what raises itself, what is raised above the natural,
above finitude. This is the religion of sublimity.

Greek divinities that was not essentially familiar to humans. Here we have to consider first the objective, God in his objectivity; and secondly the cultus.

a. The Divine Content[353]

There are three aspects to distinguish in the content, namely (1) what is full of import as such, the divine in its essentiality, (2) what stands over this divine aspect as the higher [power], i.e., fate, and (3) what stands beneath this divine aspect as the subordinate [level], i.e., the external individualities.

As for the import as such or the pure content, the substantial foundation is, as we showed in the transitional remarks, rationality in general, the freedom of spirit or essential freedom. This freedom is not caprice; it must certainly be distinguished from that. It is essential freedom by definition, the freedom that determines itself. Because the freedom that determines itself is the foundation of this relationship, it is rationality or, more precisely, ethical life. The way this follows here is to be assumed as a lemma: freedom is the self-determining, what is formal; it first appears as something formal. That this formal element turns over into the content that we call ethical life is something we presuppose. Concrete rationality is essentially what we call ethical principles. The point that freedom is a willing of nothing else than itself, i.e., freedom, and that this is ethical life and that ethical determinations result from it, cannot be developed further here.

Because ethical life constitutes the essential foundation here, what we are dealing with is the initial [mode of] ethical life so to speak, ethical life in its immediacy. There [simply] is this [social] rationality, the rationality or ethical life being wholly universal, being therefore in its substantial form. The rationality does not yet subsist as a subject, it has not yet raised itself up out of this unalloyed unity in which it is ethical life, into the unity of the subject, nor has it deepened itself inwardly. For this reason | the spiritual and essentially 536 ethical characteristics appear as a mutually external [complex]. It is a content most full of import, but [its elements are] mutually external.

353. *Text reads:* 1. The Content. *In B's margin:* 12 July 1827

Ethical life has to be distinguished altogether from morality; the latter is the subjectivity of the ethical, what knows itself as inwardly accountable—having premeditation, intention, ethical purpose, and also knowing the substantial being that the ethical realm is. Ethical life is just the substantial being, the true being of the ethical, but it is not yet the knowing of this ethical domain. The ethical is an objective content such that a subjectivity or this internal reflection is not yet present.

Because it has this character, the ethical content fragments. Its foundation is constituted by the πάθη,[354] the essential spiritual powers, the universal powers of ethical life—especially political life, life in the state, and also justice, valor, family, oaths, agriculture, science, and the like. Bound up with the fact that the ethical fragments into these, its particular determinations, ˉis the factˉ[355] that the ˉcreaturelyˉ[356] domain also comes forward against these spiritual powers. The character of immediacy that has this fragmentation as its consequence involves the characteristic that natural powers [such as] heaven and earth, mountains and streams, day and night, emerge over against [the spiritual]. These are the general foundations.

But however much this fragmentation obtains, in which the natural powers appear as by themselves, as autonomous, the unity of the spiritual and the natural likewise emerges more and more, and this is the essential thing; it is not, however, the neutralization of the two, but instead the spiritual is not only the preponderant aspect in it but also the ruling and determining one; while the natural on the contrary is idealized and subjugated.

The relationship appears on the one hand in the fact that there are nature deities: Cronus, Time (in this mode, an abstraction), Uranus, Oceanus, Hyperion, Helios, Selene. In the cosmogonies, which are at the same time theogonies, we encounter these nature deities—universal powers of nature, formations and configurations

---

354. [Ed.] See Clement of Alexandria, *Exhortation to the Heathen* 2: "And some even of the philosophers, after the poets, make idols of forms of your passions [πάθη], such as fear, and love, and joy, and hope" (*Ante-Nicene Fathers* 2:178).

355. W₂ *(Var) reads:* is the other fragmentation, namely,

356. W *(Var) reads:* natural

of nature, which we number together among the Titans.[357] They, too, are personified; but in their case the personification is superficial; | it is only personification, for the content of Helios, for example, is something natural and not something spiritual, it is no spiritual power. That Helios is represented in a human fashion or is active in human fashion is an empty form of personification. Helios is not the god of the sun—the Greeks never express themselves this way; one nowhere finds ὁ θεὸς τοῦ ἡλίου; there is not a natural sun and then also a Helios as god of the sun, but rather Helios, the sun, is the god. ˉOceanus is likewise the god itself. These are theˉ[358] powers of nature.

The second point, therefore, is that these powers of nature are subordinated to the spiritual ones, and this is not merely our view of the Greek gods, for the Greeks have expressed it themselves; they are conscious of it themselves. About this aspect we need only say what the Greeks themselves have said about their gods; for the concept, the essential, is contained in what they said. A major point of their mythology is that the gods, with Zeus at their head, have gained the mastery for themselves by a war, by violence. The spiritual power has cast down the giants, the Titans, from the throne; the sheer power of nature has been overcome by the spiritual, the spiritual has elevated itself above it and now rules over the world. Thus this war with the Titans is not a mere fairy tale but is the essence of Greek religion. The entire concept of the Greek gods lies in this war of the gods.[359] ˉThat the spiritual principle elevated itself, that it subordinated the natural to itself, is the gods' own proper deed and history.ˉ[360] | The Greek gods have indeed done none other than

357. [Ed.] See Hesiod, *Theogony* 133–134, 168 ff., 371.

358. W_1 *(Var) reads:* Oceanus is not god of the sea and such like; he is the god [itself]. . . . What we have here are these W_2 *(Var) reads:* Oceanus is not god of the sea in such a way that the god and what he rules over are distinguished from each other; on the contrary, these powers are

359. *L (1827?) adds, similar in W:* When they take up the cause of an individual, of Troy, this is not something that gods do to one another. W_2 *(Var) continues:* So it is no longer *their* history and is not the historical development of their nature.

360. W_2 *(Var/1831?) reads:* But the fact that, as the spiritual principle, they have attained the mastery and have overcome the natural realm is what constitutes their essential act; and this is the essential consciousness that the Greeks have of them.

this. ˉThe Titans were banished to the edge of the earth; therefore they still exist. But, in their being posited as subordinate to the spiritual, not only are they external with respect to the spiritual, but they also constitute an intrinsic determination with respect to the spiritual gods. The victory over them is of the kind in which they nevertheless still retain their rights and their honor. They are powers of nature, but they are not the higher, ethical, and true power, the spiritually essential forces. Nevertheless there is still a natural moment contained in those forces themselves.ˉ361 But it is only a trace of the natural element, and hence it is only one aspect in them.

But there are still two varieties to be distinguished among the ancient gods themselves. For it is not only the nature powers, which are sheer power, that belong among them; Dike, the Eumenides, the Erinyes, the Oath, the Styx, νέμεσις, and φθόνος are counted among them too. Although they are of a spiritual type, these deities distinguish themselves from the newer ones in that they are the aspect of the spiritual as a power that has being only inwardly; they are the powers that merely subsist within themselves but that are also spiritual. Yet because the spirituality that subsists only inwardly is only an abstractly crude spirituality and is not yet true spirituality, they are for this reason counted among the ancient gods; they are the universals that are to be feared: the Erinyes are just the internal judges, the Oath is this certainty in my inmost self—whether or not I declare it externally, its truth resides within me; we can compare the Oath with conscience. In contrast, Zeus is the political god, the god of laws and of lordship, but of laws that are well known. What is valid here is not the laws of conscience but right according to public laws. In the state it is not conscience but rather the laws (what is established) that have the right. What conscience, if it is of the correct

361. W (1831) reads: Thus the natural gods are subdued, and driven from their throne; the spiritual principle is victorious over the religion of nature, and the natural forces are banished to the borders of the world, beyond the world of self-consciousness, though they have also retained their rights. Though they are the powers of nature, they are posited also as ideal, as subject to the spiritual; so that they constitute one determination with respect to what is spiritual or to the spiritual gods themselves, and the natural moment is still contained in the gods themselves.

334

sort, ought to know as the right must also | be objective.[362] Alongside   539
Dike, Nemesis is also an ancient deity; she is [found] together with
φθόνος [and] with love and consists in bringing down the stiff-
necked, the proud, the self-exalting ones whose wrong consists only
in being someone exalted, and is not an ethical wrong. It is a justice
that is of the superficial sort, consisting only in equalization and in
leveling; it is envy, a dragging down of what is superior so that it
stands on the same level with the rest. Only strict, abstract right is
contained in Dike. Orestes is pursued by the Eumenides, therefore
by gods of strict right; he is acquitted by Athena, by ethical right,
the visible, ethical power of the state.[363]

Here we want to give a few examples of how the natural is mingled
with the spiritual. Zeus is the firmament generally, atmospheric
change (*sub Jove frigido*);[364] he is the thunderer; but, apart from
this natural principle, he is not merely the father of gods and human
beings but also the political god, the god of the state, and the right
and ethical life of the state, the highest power on earth, [and also]
the power of hospitality.[365] Phoebus is sometimes the knowing god.
But obviously, according to the analogy of the substantial logical
determination, knowing corresponds to light and [Apollo] is the
aftereffect of the sun's power; he is Helios, the sun that shines upon
everything. Indeed, light and knowing correspond implicitly and
explicitly, and the logical determination is just that of making

362. *L (1827?) adds, similar in W:* What is genuine is not hidden but manifest.
If human beings appeal to their conscience, one may have one conscience and another
another; in order that one's conscience may be of the correct sort, what one knows
to be right must be in conformity with objective right, it must not merely dwell within
one. If conscience is right, then it is a conscience recognized by the state, once the
state is ethically constituted.

363. *L (1827?) adds, similar in W:* Ethical right is something other than merely
strict right; the new gods are the gods of ethical right.
[*Ed.*] See Aeschylus, *Eumenides,* esp. 734–741.

364. [*Ed.*] Horace, *Carmina* 1.1.25.

365. *Thus Hu; L (1827?) adds (after an insertion from 1824), similar in W:* with
reference to the old customs at a time when the relationship of the different [city-]
states was not yet defined, and hospitality was the essential sphere of the ethical
relationship of citizens belonging to different states. *Precedes in W:* He is, moreover,
a many-sided ethical power, the god of hospitality

335

540   manifest | whether in the natural or in the spiritual [realm]. So
Phoebus is not only the knowing one, the revealing one, the oracle;
he is also called the Lycian Apollo, and λύκειος has an immediate
connection with light. That comes from Asia Minor; the natural
aspect, the light, is more prominent to the East. In his work on the
Dorians, to be sure, Müller[366] denied this affinity of Phoebus with
the sun, but right at the beginning of the *Iliad* Phoebus sends
pestilence over the Greek camp near Troy;[367] this connects directly
with the sun, this effect of the hot summer, the sun's heat, and in
a hundred other portrayals we find this same point echoed.[368]

Pindar and Aeschylus too (in the *Eumenides*) speak of a succession
of oracles of the ancient gods right up to the new god Phoebus.[369]
In the *Eumenides* of Aeschylus the initial scenes take place before
the temple of Apollo. There Pythia states that the first to be
worshiped are Gaia and Themis, and then the other or new gods.[370]

---

366. [*Ed.*] See Karl Otfried Müller, *Geschichten hellenischer Stämme und Städte*,
vol. 2 (Breslau, 1824), pp. 284, 287–288. Müller's conclusion was that the
identification of Apollo and the sun was a late development, after the old gods had
been turned into predicates of νοῦς or interpreted as material forces and objects.
Müller himself also established a link between Apollo's epithet λύκειος and the adjective
λευκός ("light"), without however attaching weight to it as an argument for identifying Apollo and the sun. In opposing Müller, Hegel also implicitly took up a position
against J. H. Voss and in support of Friedrich Creuzer, according to whose interpretation, based ultimately on Herodotus, "two Egyptian sun-gods contributed to
the genesis of a twofold Hellenic Apollo" (Creuzer, *Symbolik und Mythologie* 2:158;
cf. also pp. 132 ff. for the interpretation of λύκειος). On other matters, such as the
assessment of the symbolic character of the Greek gods, belief in the mysteries, and
Mithra, Hegel is not so close to Creuzer's viewpoint (see above, n. 288).

367. [*Ed.*] Homer, *Iliad*, bk. 1, esp. vv. 9–10 concerning Apollo's anger against
Agamemnon.

368. *L (1827?) adds, similar in W:* Even the pictures of Phoebus have attributes
and symbols that are closely connected with the sun. *W (1831) continues:* The same
divinities that were Titanic and natural in the earlier phase appear later with a spiritual
basic character, and this is the predominant one; it has been disputed, indeed, that
there was any natural element still in Apollo. In Homer at all events, Helios is the
sun, but at the same time he is immediately brightness, the spiritual moment that
shines upon and illuminates everything. But even at a later period Apollo still retained
something of his natural element, for he was portrayed with a nimbus around his head.

369. [*Ed.*] This succession does not occur in Pindar himself but in a general
scholium to the Pythian hymns.

Thus we see what follows: that the natural gods are the lowest and the spiritual gods are higher. This is not to be taken historically, but in a spiritual way.⁻³⁷¹ |

541

³⁷²Thus the first mode of giving oracles, the noise and rustling of leaves and suspended cymbals, as in Dodona, is by mere natural sounds. Only later appears [the figure of] the priestess who gives the oracle in human tones (although in keeping with the oracle's mode she does not do so in clear speech).³⁷³ Similarly, the Muses are at first nymphs, i.e., springs, the rippling, murmuring, and burbling of brooks; everywhere the beginning arises from the natural mode, from powers of nature that are transformed into a god of spiritual content.³⁷⁴

370. [Ed.] Aeschylus, *Eumenides* 1–8.

371. *W (1831) reads:* Here we have the summons to worship. The first to be worshiped is the giver of oracles (Γαῖα), the nature-principle, then Θέμις, who was already a spiritual power, though, like Dike, she belongs to the ancient gods; next comes night, and then Phoebus—the oracle has passed over to the new gods. Pindar also speaks of a similar succession [W₁: of the gods W₂: in connection with the oracle]. He makes night [W₁: first among the gods W₂: the first oracle-giver], then comes Themis and next Phoebus. Thus we have here the transition from natural figures to the new gods. In the sphere of poetry, where these doctrines originate, this [sequence] is not to be taken historically [W₂: is not so hard-and-fast as to preclude any deviation from it].

372. *Precedes in L (1827?):* This is the universal, even though it was not particularly noticeable in the gods taken one by one.

373. [Ed.] See Etienne Clavier, *Mémoire sur les oracles des anciens* (Paris, 1818), pp. 72–75.

374. *W₂ (1831) adds:* A similar transformation can be seen in Diana. The Diana of Ephesus is still Asiatic and is represented with many breasts and bedecked with images of animals. Her foundation is natural life in general, the procreative and sustaining force of nature. The Diana of the Greeks, on the other hand, is the huntress who slays animals; she has not the sense and meaning of hunting generally, but of the hunt directed at wild animals. And these animals are indeed subdued and killed through the bravery of spiritual subjectivity, whereas in the earlier spheres of the religious spirit they were regarded as absolutely inviolate.

[Ed.] This portrayal of Diana of Ephesus is found in Minucius Felix, *Octavius* 22.5 in terms similar to those used by Hegel. However, Hegel probably has in mind not this text but the illustration in Creuzer's *Symbolik und Mythologie*, plate 3, no. 4. In his *Handbuch der Archäologie der Kunst* (Breslau, 1830), pp. 472–478, K. O. Müller also discusses the difference between the modes of portrayal prevalent in Greece and those in Asia Minor.

[375]Prometheus gave fire to humanity and taught people to sacrifice.[376] This means that the animals had belonged not to humanity but to a spiritual power, i.e., human beings had [previously] eaten no meat. Then Prometheus took the entire offering to Zeus; he had made two constructs, one wholly of bones and entrails with the skin drawn over it, and the other entirely of meat; but Zeus seized the first one. So to sacrifice means to hold a feast, with the gods receiving the entrails and the bones. Zeus was deceived when the bones wrapped in fat were offered up to him while human beings themselves enjoyed the meat. This [Titan] Prometheus taught human beings to lay hold of animals | and make them their food.[377] [378]So it was Prometheus who taught human beings to eat meat, and imparted to them other skills as well; he is recalled with gratitude as the one who made human life easier. ¬But notwithstanding the fact that human powers of understanding are displayed here, he still belongs among the Titans for the very reason that these skills are only to satisfy human needs—they have no ethical authority, they are not laws.¬[379] A passage in Plato,[380] where he speaks of Prometheus, contends that Prometheus indeed fetched fire from the

542

375. *Precedes in W (1831):* Prometheus, who is also reckoned among the Titans, is an important, interesting figure. Prometheus is a natural power; but he is also a benefactor of human beings, in that he taught them the first arts. He brought fire down from heaven for them; the power to kindle fire already presupposes a certain level of civilization; humanity has already emerged out of its primitive barbarism. The first beginnings of culture have thus been preserved in grateful remembrance in the myths.

376. [*Ed.*] Hesiod, *Theogony* 510–615, and *Works and Days* 48–58.

377. *L (1827?) adds, similar in W:* Among the Hindus and Egyptians, on the other hand, it is forbidden to slaughter animals.

378. *Precedes in L (1827?):* Artemis is the human power to hunt animals. In this connection there are various myths that refer to this new departure in the matter of the relationship of human beings to animals.

379. *W (1831) reads:* But Prometheus is a Titan. He is chained to the Caucasus and a vulture constantly gnaws at his liver, which always grows again—a pain that never ceases. What Prometheus taught human beings was only the skills that pertain to the satisfaction of natural needs. In the simple satisfaction of these needs there is never any [final] satiety; instead the need comes back again, and always has to be ministered to afresh. That is what is signified by this myth.

[*Ed.*] See in particular Hesiod, *Theogony* 520 ff., and Aeschylus, *Prometheus Bound.*

380. [*Ed.*] Plato, *Protagoras* 321c–d.

Acropolis but that he was unable to bring the πολιτεία or ethical life down to human beings; that was kept in the citadel of Zeus, ⁻Zeus withheld it for himself.⁻[381] In Aeschylus[382] Prometheus says that in his defiance he takes solace and satisfaction in the fact that to Zeus will be born a son who will cast him down from his throne: Heracles, the only god who was first a human being and then was placed among the gods. What is asserted here is that Heracles will attain the lordship of Zeus; that can be viewed as a prophecy that has come to pass.

[383]⁻Up to this point we have considered concrete characteristics of the Greek gods; now we want to indicate the abstract ones.⁻[384] The | gods are scattered; Zeus rules them as a family. The higher power, absolute unity, stands above the gods as a pure power. This power is what is called destiny, fate, or simple necessity. It is without content, is empty necessity, an empty, unintelligible power that is devoid of the concept. It is not wise, for wisdom falls within the circle of the gods and includes concrete characteristics that belong in the sphere of the particular, and pertain to single gods. Destiny is devoid of purpose and wisdom, it is a blind necessity that stands above all, even above the gods, uncomprehended and desolate. The abstract cannot be comprehended. Comprehending means knowing something in its truth. What is debased and abstract is incomprehensible; what is rational is comprehensible because it is inwardly concrete.

As far as the disposition of finite self-consciousness [toward this

543

---

381. W (1831) reads: and this expresses the fact that it belonged to Zeus personally.

382. [Ed.] Aeschylus, Prometheus Bound 755–768.

383. In B's and Hu's margin: 13 July 1827

384. Thus Hu; L reads: The two moments that have still to be considered are the extremes. The midpoint of this religion is the thought of God in his concrete determination. . . . The other two moments are the abstract determinations as opposed to the concrete ones. . . . There is a plurality of gods; in and for itself, of course, the content is the genuine, spiritual, ethical substance; but it is still fragmented, it is still divided into many particularities. W₁ (Var) reads: 1. There is a plurality of gods—[though] the content is in and for itself the genuine, spiritual, ethical substance. But it is still fragmented, [there are] still many particularities, and together they make a unity. W₂ (1831/Var?) reads: The unity that binds the plurality of the particular gods together is still at first a superficial unity.

necessity] is concerned, and its relationship to it, this necessity [is viewed as] underlying everything, gods and human beings alike; on the one side there is an iron power, on the other a blind obedience without freedom. But there is still one form of freedom that is at least present, and that is on the side of [finite] disposition. In having this conviction regarding necessity, the Greek achieves inner peace in saying: It is this way and there is nothing to be done about it; I must be content with it. This implies that I *am* content with it and thus that freedom is present after all, in that it is my own state. This conviction implies that human beings are confronted by this simple necessity. In adopting this standpoint and saying, "It is this way," one has set aside everything particular, one has renounced it and abstracted from all particular goals and interests. Dissatisfaction occurs when human beings hold fast to a goal ˉand there is no harmony or agreement | between what they want and what is.ˉ385 But from this standpoint [of fate] all dissatisfaction and vexation are removed, because human beings have withdrawn into this pure rest, this pure being, this "it is." In that abstract freedom there is on the one hand in fact no solace for human beings.386 One needs solace [only] insofar as one demands a compensation for a loss; but here ˉno compensation is needed, for one has given up the inner root of what one lost. One has wholly surrendered what has been given up.ˉ387 That is the aspect of freedom, but it is abstract and not concrete freedom, the freedom that only stands above the concrete but is not posited in essential harmony with what is determinate,

544

---

385. *W (1831) reads:* and will not give this up; and if things do not match this end or are even in conflict with it, they are dissatisfied. There is no harmony then between what is actually present and what they want, because they have within themselves the ought: "That ought to be."

Thus discontent and inward cleavage are present; but from this standpoint one does not hold firmly to any purpose or interest in the face of actually existing circumstances. Misfortune, discontent, is nothing but the contradiction, [W_1: that there is opposition to what I want to be. W_2: the fact that something is contrary to my will.]

386. W_2 *(Var) adds:* but solace is also unnecessary.

387. W_2 *(Var) reads:* one has renounced the inner root of racking worry and discontent and has wholly surrendered what is lost, because one has the strength to look necessity in the face.

the freedom that is pure thinking and being, or being-within-self, the annulment of the particular.[388]

⌐The opposite extreme to that universality is external singularity, and this likewise is not yet taken up into the middle term; it also stands on its own account, as does that abstraction of thinking, of retreat into self.⌐[389] Both extremes emerge from the same ground, from the same general determinacy, viz., that rationality, the rational content and ethical import, is still immediately present, is still | in   545
the form of immediacy— ⌐⌐this is the logical determination from which the further characteristics proceed. Singular selfhood is subjectivity, but only in an external way. It is still not the one infinite subjectivity that is posited; for in that the external singularity is superseded. ⌐Here on the contrary⌐[390] the singularity is an external one just because it is not yet infinite subjectivity;⌐⌐[391] and the manifold content that plays about the gods falls on the side of externality. ⌐Hence contingency of content enters into this sphere.⌐[392] ⌐⌐So we should not believe, for instance, that the twelve main gods of Olympus are ordered and arrayed in correspondence with the concept. ⌐They are not sheer allegories but are | concrete   546
(though not infinite) spirituality instead. They are also individual figures, and as concrete essences they have diverse properties; [but]

388. W₂ (MiscP/1831?) adds: In contrast, there is in the higher forms of religion the consolation that the absolutely final end will be attained despite misfortune, so that the negative changes around into the affirmative. "The sufferings of this present time are the path to blessedness [die Leiden dieser Zeit sind der Weg zur Seligkeit]."
[Ed.] The rhyming of the German suggests that the source may be a Lutheran hymn, but there is also an allusion to Rom. 8:18: "I consider that the sufferings of this present time are not worth comparing with the glory [Herrlichkeit] that is to be revealed to us."

389. Precedes in W₁ (MiscP/Var?): Necessity is the one extreme. W₂ (MiscP/Var?) reads: Abstract necessity as this abstraction of thought and of the retreat into self is the one extreme; the other extreme is the singularity of the particular divine powers.

390. W₁ (Var) reads: External singularity is one thing, while subjectivity as inwardly infinite is something different. Here

391. W₂ (MiscP/Var?) reads: in other words, subjectivity is not posited as infinite subjectivity, and hence singularity comes on the scene in its external guise;

392. W₂ (MiscP/Var?) reads: But since particularity is not yet tempered by the idea, and necessity is not a meaningful measure of wisdom, an unlimited contingency on the part of the content enters into the sphere of the particular gods.

they are only imagined as concrete in such a way that what is inward is only one property. They are, however, still no universals.⁻³⁹³ ⁻⁻³⁹⁴

The natural element is still a factor in these determinations of the concrete and constitutes one side of the contrast. For instance, the sun rises and sets; the year, the appearance of the months, plays a part here, and for that reason the Greek gods have been made into calendar gods.³⁹⁵

One moment that we have to hold on to [firmly] is the so-called philosophical meaning [*Philosopheme*]; this is a moment that has its seat originally in the mystery rites. The mysteries are related to the manifest religion of the Greeks in the way that natural elements are related to the spiritual import: ⁻They are the most ancient cultus, the crude, natural cultus.⁻³⁹⁶ Just as the ancient gods are in the main only natural elements, so the content of the mysteries is the sort of crude content that spirit has not yet permeated. This is the relationship that both is necessary in and for itself and also at the same time is historical. But just as it was believed that ⁻particular depths of

393. W₂ (1831) reads: Finally, the free individuality of the gods is the main source of the manifold contingent content that is ascribed to them. Even though they are not yet infinite, absolute spirituality, they are at least concrete, subjective spirituality. As such they do not have an abstract content, and there is not just one property in them, but they unite several characteristics within them. If they possessed only *one* property, it would be only an abstract inner [content], or one simple meaning, and they themselves would merely be allegories, i.e., only *imagined* to be concrete. But in the concrete richness of their individuality they are not tied to the limited direction and kind of efficacy of one single exclusive property. Instead they can let themselves go freely in any direction they choose, including arbitrary, contingent ones.

394. W₁ (Var) reads: The twelve principal gods of Olympus, for example, are not ordered by means of the concept, they do not constitute a system. Moreover, they are concrete spirituality but not yet absolute subjectivity, and hence they are individual figures.

As concrete spirituality they do not have abstract content; what they have in them is not one distinctive property but several (as concrete). Were there only one property they would be allegories, they would only be *imagined* as concrete, with the result that the inward [content] or the meaning would be just the one distinctive property. But here we have subjective spirituality, though not yet infinite subjectivity.

395. W₁ (Var?) adds: as Dupuis does.

[Ed.] Dupuis, *Origine de tous les cultes* 1:317 ff. Dupuis identified Heracles in particular as a calendrical deity.

396. W₁ (Var) reads: This is either ancient religion or a more recent, imported cult.

religion were at home in India,¯³⁹⁷ so it is believed here.³⁹⁸ From all of this [the mystery rites],¯³⁹⁹ some elements also find their way into the concrete representation of the spiritual gods who are raised above this level. Inasmuch as the representations of origination and perishing are carried over into the spiritual circle, there are echoes of that transference here too. This is the case when an endless number of amours is acribed to Zeus, occasioned by the sort | of myths re- 547 ferring to natural relationships and natural powers.⁴⁰⁰

The other aspect of the content is that of appearance or of its shape.⁴⁰¹ At this stage beauty is everywhere the dominant factor. The god appears. These powers, these absolutely ethical and spiritual determinations, are known, they exist for the empirical self-consciousness. Thus they exist for an other, and what must concern us now is the precise manner in which they exist for their other, for the [worshiper's] subjective self-consciousness.

The first point is therefore that this content reveals itself in the innermost [being], comes into prominence within the spirit; but this

397. *Thus L; An reads:* great and ancient wisdom belonged to the Hindus and Chinese,
   [*Ed.*] Hegel is probably referring in particular to Friedrich Schlegel, *Ueber die Sprache und Weisheit der Indier* (Heidelberg, 1808), pp. 90, 103 (cf. *Kritische Friedrich-Schlegel-Ausgabe* 8:193, 205). See above, n. 22.
398. *L (1827?) adds, similar in W₁:* Origination and perishing was comprehended in Hinduism as a content and was known in particular as a universal power. The mysteries contain premonitions in which an attempt was made to see the natural forces grasped in a universal way.
399. *W₁ (Var) reads:* this epoch,
400. *L (1827?) adds, similar in W:* Another relevant feature is the locality in which the consciousness of a god first began; in this regard the cheerfulness of the Greeks, the element of production, gave rise to a number of delightful stories. To investigate these different aspects, to decide where this or that single detail originated, is the task of scholarship.
401. *L, W (1831) add:* So far we have considered the way that the configuration of the divine is grounded in the implicit potential of these divinities, i.e., in their individual natures, their subjective spirituality, their geographically and temporally contingent emergence, or as it occurs in the involuntary transformation of natural determinations into the expression of free subjectivity. The configuration that we have now to consider is the one that is accomplished with consciousness. This is the appearing of the divine powers that occurs for "another," i.e., for subjective self-consciousness, and is known and shaped within the latter's own comprehension.

ethical and true content can reveal itself only within a spirit that itself is in itself and has been elevated to this spiritual freedom. These universal determinations come to consciousness for it, they manifest and reveal themselves inwardly. Contrariwise the other aspect is that, inasmuch as this level is only one of initial freedom and rationality, that which is a power within the spirit appears as an outward mode [of intuition]. That is the natural aspect with which this standpoint is still afflicted.⁴⁰² This whole external aspect is the rustling of the trees at Dodona, the silence of the wood where Pan is, falling stones, thunder and lightning—in short, the external phenomena in nature

548 that are taken to be something higher. | These phenomena occasion only the initial manifestation, so to speak, for the consciousness for which these determinations exist.⁴⁰³

¨So the other to that immediacy or being, whether internal or external, is the grasping of that initially abstract [freedom], and is the real stuff of self-consciousness. ¨¨But the organ by which self-consciousness grasps this subsisting thing, this substantial and essential [being], is phantasy, which images what is initially abstract, the inwardly or outwardly subsisting [essence], and produces it as

549 what is first deemed to be a god.¨⁴⁰⁴ | Explanation here consists in

402. W₂ (Var) adds (cf. the following footnote): If the authorities and laws that announce themselves to the inward [thought] are spiritual and ethical, still they are [such] initially just *because* they are, and it is not known whence they come.

[Ed.] Hegel is referring to Antigone's defense of her behavior vis-à-vis Creon; see Sophocles, *Antigone*, vv. 453–457.

403. L (1827?) adds, similar in W₁ (cf. the preceding footnote): These shapes [W₁: authorities] and these laws simply *are*, the ethical *is*, and no one knows whence it came; it is eternal, or it is something external, thunder and lightning.

404. W₂ (Var/1831?) reads: It is self-consciousness that grasps, clarifies, or images what was initially abstract (whether inwardly or outwardly so) and produces it as what is deemed to be God.

W₂ (1831) continues: Natural phenomena or this immediate, external [mode of appearing], however, are not appearance in the sense that the essence would be only a thought within us—as when we speak of the forces of nature and their expressions. Here it does not lie in the natural objects themselves, does not lie objectively in them as such, that they exist as appearances of what is inward; as natural objects they exist only for our sense perception, for which they are not an appearance of the universal. Thus it is not in light as such, for example, that thought, the universal, announces its presence; on the contrary, in the case of natural essence we must first break through the outer shell behind which thought, or the inwardness of things, is hidden.

making it representational, in enabling consciousness to represent to itself something divine. We have already seen what the definition of this phantasy is: because this content still has in it this finitude of being immediate rationality, so that it presents itself as a particular, as a content that is not yet within infinite subjectivity, it involves finitude as such and is afflicted with the natural aspect. Phantasy is the activity of giving shape either to what is inwardly abstract or to what is external, what is initially an immediate being (for example, thunder or the ocean's roar); it shapes both of these aspects and posits them as something concrete, one of which is the spiritual and the other the natural; the result is that the external being is no longer independent but is downgraded into being just a sign of the indwelling spirit, into serving just to make the implicit spirit apparent.⁻⁻⁴⁰⁵

Hence the gods of the Greeks are products of human imagination or sculptured [*plastisch*] deities formed by human hands. They originate therefore in a finite manner, one produced by poets, by the Muse. The gods have this finitude because they have finitude within them in accord with their own import; that is, they have particularity, or the falling asunder of the spiritual power and the natural

---

But the natural, the external, at the same time must be posited in itself, it must in its externality be posited as sublated and in itself be posited as appearance, with the result that it has meaning and significance only as the outward expression and organ of thought and of the universal. Thought must be for intuition; in other words, what is revealed is on the one hand the sensuous mode, while what is perceived is at the same time thought, the universal. It is the necessity that has to appear in a godlike way, i.e., it has to appear within [finite] being as necessity in immediate unity with finitude. This is posited necessity, i.e., the necessity that has being and exists as simple reflection into itself.

405. W₂ (MiscP/1831?) reads: Phantasy is now the organ with which self-consciousness gives shape either to what is inwardly abstract or to what is external, what is initially an immediate being, and posits it as concrete. In this process what is natural loses its independence and is downgraded into the sign of the indwelling spirit, so that it just lets the implicit spirit be apparent.

W₂ (1831) continues: The freedom of spirit here is not yet the infinite freedom of thought; the spiritual essentialities are not yet [subjected to] thought. If human beings were thoughtful in such a way that pure thinking constituted the foundation, there would be for them only one God. But here they do not come upon their essentialities as present and unmediated natural shapes; to the contrary, they bring them forth for the imagination. As the midpoint between pure thought and immediately natural intuition, this bringing forth is phantasy.

550   aspect. ``This finitude of content is why they | originate in a finite manner as human products.⁴⁰⁶ At this stage the divine is grasped neither by pure thinking nor in pure spirit. ``God is not yet worshiped in spirit and in truth [John 4:24].``⁴⁰⁷ The divine is not yet [present] as absolute truth, it is not even grasped by the external understanding, in the abstract categories of the understanding; for these categories are what constitute prose. For this reason these gods are humanly made—not [with respect to] their rational content but [in their appearing] as gods. Every priest was, so to speak, such a maker of gods. Herodotus says that Homer and Hesiod made the Greeks' gods for them.⁴⁰⁸ ``⁴⁰⁹ ⁴¹⁰This interpretation of an external [phenomenon] just means shaping it, giving it the shape of the activity

551   of a god. ``The explanation | here is not for the understanding but``⁴¹¹ is produced by phantasy for phantasy.

406. *L (1827?) adds:* The gods' shape is one that is posited by the subjective side and by finite spirit, and human beings themselves are conscious that they are the ones who have brought forth this shape.

407. *Thus An, similar in Hu; L (Var) reads, similar in W₁:* There is truth in this rationality, the truth that this is only something manifesting the spiritual.

408. *W₁ (Var/1831?) adds:* i.e., every priest or experienced old man.

[*Ed.*] Herodotus, *Histories* 2.53. What Herodotus actually said was that Homer and Hesiod "established the genealogy of the gods in Greece and gave them their eponyms, apportioned offices and honors among them, and revealed their form."

409. *W₂ (1831) reads:* They are discovered by the human spirit, not as they are in their implicitly and explicitly rational content, but in such a way that they are *gods*. They are made or poetically created [*gedichtet*], but they are not fictitious [*erdichtet*]. To be sure, they emerge from human phantasy in contrast with what is already at hand, but they emerge as *essential* shapes, and the product is at the same time known as what is essential.

It is in this sense that we have to understand Herodotus when he says that Homer and Hesiod made the Greeks' gods for them. The same could be said of every priest or experienced old graybeard who was capable of understanding and expounding the appearance of the divine and of the essential powers in the natural.

410. *Precedes in L (1827?), similar in W:* When the Greeks heard the roaring of the sea at the funeral of Achilles, Nestor came forward and said that Thetis was taking part in the mourning.ᵃ And during the plague Calchas said that it was sent by Apollo because he was angry with the Greeks.ᵇ

[*Ed.*] ᵃHomer, *Odyssey* 24.47–56. ᵇHomer, *Iliad* 1.92–96.

411. *Thus Hu; L (1827?) reads, in part similar in W:* In the same way they give a shape to the inward element. Achilles restrains his anger; the poet expresses this inner prudence, the restraining of anger, as the doing of Pallas: Achilles has been restrained by Pallas. We explain things quite differently in physics and psychology. Here explaining consists in making the matter visualizable by consciousness. It becomes

[412]Insofar as spirit has natural and sensible existence, the human figure is the only way in which it can be intuited. | That does not 552 mean, however, that spirit is something sensible or material, but rather that the mode of its immediacy and reality, its being for an other, is its being intuited in human shape. That is why the Greeks

---

so because it is given shape that is an image, W₂ *(1831) continues:* Those innumerable charming tales and the endless quantity of Greek myths originated in this kind of interpreting.

From whatever side we are able to consider the Greek principle, we see the sensuous and the natural permeating it. In the way that they issue from necessity, the gods are limited, and also for that reason they have the resonance of the natural in them, since they betray their own origin from the struggle with the powers of nature. The appearance with which they announce themselves to self-consciousness is still external, and even the phantasy that gives form and shape to this appearance still does not elevate their starting point into pure thought. We have now to see how this natural moment is wholly transfigured into beautiful shape.

412. *Precedes in* W₁ *(1831) (in* W₂ *partly shortened, partly MiscP?):* These gods are spiritual powers, but spirit is fragmented into its particularities, there are many of these spiritual powers, and hence we have polytheism here; this is the side of finitude. One side of this finitude is that freedom still bears the resonance of the natural state, while the other moment of it has just been noted.

The many powers are [there] for humanity. They are the absolute essentialities of human spirit, and in this way they are distinct from the changeable individuality of humans; but they are *represented;* and for that reason another form of finitude comes into play, one pertaining to the imaginative mode. What we have here is not yet the infinite freedom of thought, the spiritual essentialities are not yet [subjected to] thought; if these humans were thoughtful, there would be for them only one God. But divinity here falls entirely within [the range of] representation, which is not the foundation of pure thinking. It is only the religion of absolute truth that has thinking as its pure foundation. The Greek gods subsist for phantasy. Human beings do not come upon these essentialities as natural shapes ready to hand; they bring them forth for the imagination instead; and this bringing forth *is* phantasy. The shapes of the gods emerge from human phantasy in contrast with what is already there for the finding, but they emerge as *essential* shapes; there is a sensuous element involved in this, but it is raised through beauty into conformity with the spiritual. The Greek religion is the religion of beauty. There is a spiritual foundation in the Greek gods, but inasmuch as they are represented objectively, a natural element enters into them. They have the natural [side] in their manifestation: they are made or poetically created [*gedichtet*] (thinking and poetizing are linked), but they are not fictitious [*erdichtet*]. And this [poetic] product is known to be what is essential; it is something spiritual, not burdened by the natural. Instead, nature itself has only the meaning of the spiritual, because it is beautiful. [W₁: Manifestation here falls on the subjective side, it is finite. Thus God is something made by human beings. Poets, sculptors, and painters taught the Greeks what their gods were; they beheld their god in the Zeus of Phidias. What is manifested and exhibited for phantasy [however] is the representational shape of a thought. For this reason the Greek religion is the religion of beauty. The consciousness of free spirituality pertains to beauty even though the content is limited and finite. But if it is to be manifested in sensous form, free spirituality can be manifested only in human shape. This is the shape of spirit that has existent being. W_2: If manifestation falls on the subjective side in this process, so that God appears as something made by human beings, that is only *one* moment. For this positedness of God is mediated rather by the sublation of the singular self; that is why it was possible for the Greeks to intuit their god in the Zeus of Phidias. The artist did not give them his own work (in some abstract sense); he gave them the proper appearance of the essential, the shape of necessity in existent being.]

W continues: Thus [W_1: this shape W_2: the shape of the god] is the ideal shape. Before the time of the Greeks there was no genuine ideality, [W_1: neither with the Hindus nor in the Near East nor with the Egyptians. Moreover, this Greek ideality could not W_2: nor could it] occur at any subsequent time. Certainly the art of the Christian religion is beautiful, but ideality is not its ultimate principle. [W_1: The Greek gods are anthropopathic, i.e., they involve the determinations of finitude generally, even as something immoral, which may perhaps originate in higher myths. But the main defect is not that there is too much of the anthropopathic in the Greek gods; not at all, for there is still too little humanity in them for one thing. There is still too little that is human in God. W_2: We cannot get at what is lacking in the Greek gods by saying that they are anthropopathic, a category of finitude to which we can then also impute the immoral element, for example the amours of Zeus, which may have their origin in older myths based on a [mode of] intuiting that is still natural. The main defect is not that there is too much of the anthropopathic in these gods, but that there is too little.] [W_1: Humanity must be grasped in the divine or in God as *this* human being; but only as a moment, as one of the persons of God, in such a way that this actually existing human being is posited in God, but as taken up into infinitude—and this only by means of a process, in that he, as this single, sensibly existing human being, is sublated. The Jewish commandment, "Thou shalt not make unto thyself any image of God,"[a] refers to the fact that God is essentially for thought; but the other moment of divine life is its externalization in human shape, so that this shape is involved in it as [its] manifestation. The manifestation, however, is only one side and is essentially taken back into the One, who thus is [present] for the first time as spirit for thought. Spiritual freedom has not yet come to consciousness in infinitude. W_2: In this inversion, however, it also becomes clear that the externalization of God in human shape is only one side of the divine life; for this externalization and manifestation is taken back again into the One, who thus for the first time is [present] as spirit for thought and for the community; the single, actually existing human is sublated and is posited in God as a moment, as one of the persons of God. In this way humanity, as this human being, is for the first time truly within God, the appearance of the divine is thus absolute, and its element is spirit itself. The Jewish view that God is essentially for thought alone, and the sensuousness of the Hellenic beauty of shape, are equally contained in this process of the divine life and, being sublated, they are freed from their limitedness.]

[*Ed.*] [a]See Deut. 27:15. This original form of the prohibition comes closest to Hegel's interpretation since here the stress lies on not worshiping God in an image made by human hands. The later, better-known formula of Exod. 20:4 relates rather to the ban on worshiping foreign gods.

represented the gods as human beings. | People have taken amiss   553
this practice of the Greeks as also that of [other] peoples. [413]It must
not be said that human beings do it because it is their own shape,
as if that were all it amounted to; but in fact they are right to do
it because this is the only shape in which spirit exists;[414] ⌐the
spiritual surely cannot come forth, for example, in the shape of a
lion.⌐[415] [416]⌐The organization of the human body is, however, only
the [phenomenal] shape of the | spiritual; the necessity of this linkage   554
belongs to the realm of physiology or of the philosophy of nature
and is a difficult point, in fact one still too little discussed.⌐[417]

These are the principal moments on which the knowledge of God
in his determinacy depends.

413. *Precedes in L (1827?):* Xenophanes said that if lions had gods, they would
picture them as lions. But it is just this point that lions never get to. *Cf.* W₁ *(Var):*
A philosopher of ancient times says that if lions had gods, they would picture them
as lions.

[*Ed.*] Hegel is referring to a fragment of Xenophanes contained in C. A. Brandis,
*Xenophanis Parmenidis et Melissi doctrina e propriis philosophorum reliquiis
veterumque auctorum testimoniis exposita* (Altona, 1813), p. 68. See Xenophanes,
frag. 15, in G. S. Kirk, J. E. Raven, and M. Schofield, *The Presocratic Philosophers,*
2d ed. (Cambridge, 1983), p. 169: "But if cattle and horses or lions had hands, or
were able to draw with their hands and do the works that men can do, horses would
draw the forms of the gods like horses, and cattle like cattle, and they would make
their bodies such as they each had themselves."

414. *L (Var) adds:* That is not a matter of chance, but the physiological link with
the shape assumed by spirit. W₁ *(Var) adds:* That is not a matter of chance. On the
contrary, the linkage is a necessary one.

415. W₁ *(Var) reads:* in animal shapes spirit does not give itself its *own* existence.

416. *Precedes in L (1827?):* As Aristotle pointed out, in the transmigration of
souls it is assumed that the soul and the corporeal organization of a human being
are only accidentally connected. W₁ *(Var) reads:* As Aristotle noted, in the transmigration of souls it is assumed that the soul and the corporeal organization of a human
being are only contingently posited. The human organism is only the shape of the
spiritual. W₂ *(Var) reads:* That only the human organization can be the shape of the
spiritual was stated long ago by Aristotle, when he marked it as a defect of the [doc-
trine of the] transmigration of souls that on that view the corporeal organization of
a human being would be merely contingent.

[*Ed.*] Aristotle, *De anima* 407b13–26.

417. W *(Var) reads:* The proper task of physiology is to discern the human
organism, the human shape, as [W₁: the one authentic shape for spirit W₂: the only
one that is authentically adequate for spirit]; but it has so far done little in this respect.

b. The Cultus

Now we shall discuss the cultus. The cultus of the Greek religion covers a wide scope; we can draw attention only to the main points. [418]The character of [any] cultus is this, that empirical consciousness raises itself up, giving itself the consciousness or feeling of the indwelling of the divine within it, of its unity with the divine. The general character of this [Greek] cultus is that the subject has an essentially affirmative relationship to its god. Here the cultus involves the recognition and reverence of these ˉabsolute powers, of this essential inner substance that is removed from contingency.ˉ[419] ˉBut at the same time these powers are the ethical aspect that is proper to humanity, the rational aspect of [human] freedom, the ethical vocations of human beings, their extant and valid | rights, their own spirit, not an external substantiality and essentiality. This implies that, with respect to the content, one has this affirmative relationship to one's gods; this substantial element that is revered as God is at the same time the proper essentiality of the human being.ˉ[420] ˉThus, for example, Pallas Athena is not the goddess of the city.ˉ[421] What is represented in Pallas Athena is the living, actual spirit of the Athenian people according to its essentiality. The Erinyes are

555

418. *In B's margin:* 16 July 1827

419. W₁ *(Var) reads:* substantial powers, of the essential inner substance of the natural and spiritual universe (which is removed from contingency), in the way that these essentially valid spiritual powers are present in the empirical consciousness.

420. W *(1831) reads:* [W₂: The Greeks are therefore the most *human* people. They affirmatively endorse and develop all that is human; for them the human is the norm.]

This religion is, in general, a religion of humanness. In other words, concrete humanity is present to itself in its gods—concrete humanity in its being, in all its needs, inclinations, passions, and habits, in its ethical and political determinations, or with respect to everything that is of value and essential in all this. The gods have this content of the noble and the true which is at the same time the content of concrete humanity. This human quality of the gods is what is defective, but at the same time what is attractive in Greek religion. There is nothing unintelligible, nothing incomprehensible, in it; the god has no content that is not known to us humans and which we do not find or do not know within ourselves. [W₂: Human confidence in the gods is at the same time human confidence in humanity itself.]

L *(1827?) adds, similar in W:* The Pallas who restrains the outbreak of Achilles' wrath is Achilles' own prudence.

421. *Thus Hu; An reads:* Athena is the city of Athens, the goddess [is] Athens.

the presentation of the [guilty] human's own deed, and the consciousness that plagues and torments one (insofar as one knows that deed as evil *within* one). They are the just ones, and for this very reason the well-disposed ones, the Eumenides.[422] Eros is the power, but precisely the subjective sensibility, of the human [lover]. In the recognition of this objective [power] the human [worshipers] are at the same time in communion with themselves, and for this reason in the cultus they are free. Here there is not only the negative relationship as with the Hindus, where the relationship of the subjects—even when of the highest sort—is only the sacrifice or negation of their consciousness.

¯Freedom constitutes the cheerfulness or serenity of this cultus.¯[423] In the cultus, honor is bestowed upon the god, but revering God turns into the reverence proper to humanity itself, the reverence that makes the consciousness of one's affirmative relationship and unity with the gods valid in one's own self. In this worship, human beings celebrate their own ¯honor.¯[424] But inasmuch as the god still has an external, natural aspect, this unification has further modifications. Bacchus and Demeter, wine and bread, are external [goods] for the human being. The way to make oneself identical | with them is to consume them, to assimilate them into oneself. The singular [natural product], the gift of the gods, still remains external to the [divine] power of nature. But the natural forces or productive

556

---

422. *L (1827?) adds, similar in W:* This is not a euphemism; on the contrary, it is the Eumenides who desire right, and those who infringe it have the Eumenides within themselves.

423. *Thus B, similar in Hu, An; L, W₂ (1827/1831?) read:* Speaking generally, this religion has the character of absolute cheerfulness or serenity[a]; self-consciousness is free in its relationship to its own essentialities, because they *are* its own; and at the same time it is not fettered to them because absolute necessity floats above the essentialities themselves and they return into it too, just as consciousness with its particular ends and requirements sinks back into it.

[*Ed.*] [a]"Cheerfulness or serenity" renders *Heiterkeit*. If Hegel meant to depict the Greeks as serene, this may be an attitude toward them influenced by Schiller or Hölderlin. The typical Greek disposition, however, was more an active, energetic happiness than a calm, passive composure (especially by contrast with the meditative disciplines of the Oriental religions).¯

424. *W₁ (Var) reads:* subjectivity.

powers are spiritual essences as well; Bacchus and Demeter are the mystical divinities.[425]

In the festivals where the god is worshiped, it is humanity that shows itself forth; the worshipers let the divine be seen in themselves, in their joyfulness and cheerfulness, in the display of their bodily dexterity.[426] Their artistic productions have a place in these festivals too, ˉand human artists are honored in the festivals at the same time (in dramas etc.).ˉ[427] At the festival of Pallas there was a great procession. Pallas is the people or nation itself; but the nation is the god imbued with life, it is this Athena who delights in herself.

Besides the content of the gods we must recall the two previously mentioned relationships, i.e., those of necessity and contingency. The dispositon corresponding to necessity is the restfulness that holds itself in stillness, or in the freedom that is still an abstract freedom. To this extent it is a flight; but at the same time it is freedom insofar as the human being is not vanquished or bowed down by fate as something external. Whoever has this consciousness of independence, should he die, is indeed outwardly defeated but not conquered, not vanquished.

In addition to this relationship to simple necessity within the consciousness of the divine and its relation to human beings, there is also, conversely, another aspect to mention briefly, namely that the divine is also known to share in the lot of the finite and in the abstract necessity of the finite. To the abstract necessity of the finite there belongs death someday, the natural negation of the finite. But in the way it appears in the divine, finitude is the subordination of the ethical powers | themselves. Because they are particular, they have to experience transitoriness in themselves, one-sided being and the lot of one-sidedness. This is the consciousness that the ancients have represented and brought to view most notably in the tragedies— necessity as something that fulfills itself, something that has import

557

---

425. L (1827?) adds, similar in W₁: Demeter, or Ceres, is the founder of agriculture, of property, of marriage. In general, both [Bacchus and Demeter] are in charge of the mysteries.

426. W₁ (Var) adds: and beauty.

427. W₁ (Var/1831?) reads: so that they regard them as having divine content, but at the same time as [displaying] their own expertise and skill.

and content. The chorus is withdrawn from natural destiny, it abides in the peaceful course of the ethical order and arouses no hostile power. The heroes, however, stand above the chorus, above the peaceful, static, uncleft ethical process; they are the ones who properly will and act. They bring forth order, and because of their action, changes are effected; in further development a cleavage comes about. The higher cleavage, the cleavage that is properly of interest for spirit, is that in which the ethical powers themselves appear as severed and as coming into collision. The resolution of the collision is when the ethical powers that are in collision (due to their one-sidedness) themselves renounce the one-sidedness of independent validity; and the way that this renunciation of one-sidedness appears is that the individuals who have committed themselves to the realization of the singular, one-sided, ethical power perish. ¯For example,¯⁴²⁸ in the *Antigone* the love of family, the holy, the inner, what is also called the law of the lower deities because it belongs to sentiment, comes into collision with the right of the state. Creon is not a tyrant, but rather the champion of something that is also an ethical power. Creon is not in the wrong; he maintains that the law of the state, the | authority of the government, must be preserved   558 and punishment meted out for its violation.⁴²⁹ Each of these two sides actualizes only one of the two, has only one side as its content. That is the one-sidedness, and the meaning of eternal justice is that both are in the wrong because they are one-sided, but both are also in the right. In the unclouded course of ethical life, both are acknowledged; here each has its validity, but one counterbalanced

428. *L reads:* I regard it as the absolute example of tragedy when *W (1831/Var?)* reads: Fate [*Fatum*] is what cannot be conceptualized; it is where justice and injustice disappear in abstraction; in contrast, in tragedy destiny [*Schicksal*] falls within the sphere of ethical justice. We find the most sublime [expressions] of this in the tragedies of Sophocles. Both destiny and necessity are spoken of in them; the destiny of the [tragic] individuals is portrayed as something incomprehensible, but the necessity is not blind; on the contrary, it is recognized as authentic justice. This is what makes these tragedies such immortal spiritual products of ethical understanding and comprehension [*W₂:* or such eternal models of the ethical concept]. Blind destiny is an unsatisfying thing. In these tragedies, justice is *comprehended*. The collision between [*W₁:* ethical *W₂:* the two highest ethical] powers is portrayed in a plastic fashion in the absolute example furnished by tragedy when
429. [*Ed.*] See Sophocles, *Antigone,* esp. 480–485, 659–675.

by the other's validity.[430] In this way the conclusion of the tragedy is reconciliation, not blind necessity but rational necessity, the necessity that here begins to be [rationally] fulfilled.

[431]This is the clarity of insight and of artistic presentation that Greece reached at its highest stage of culture; but there still remains something unresolved, to be sure, in that the higher element does not emerge as the infinitely spiritual power; there remains an unhealed sorrow here because an individual perishes. The higher reconciliation would consist in the subject's disposition of one-sidedness being overcome, in its dawning consciousness that it is in the wrong, and its divesting itself of its unrighteousness in its own heart. But to recognize its guilt and one-sidedness, and to divest itself of it, does not come naturally in this domain. This higher [reconciliation] would make external punishment and natural death superfluous.

The first signs and anticipations of this reconciliation do indeed
559 emerge here too; | but the inner conversion still appears more as an external purification.[432] In the *Eumenides* Orestes is acquitted by

430. *W (Var/1831?) adds:* It is only the one-sidedness [in their claims] that justice comes forward to oppose.

W₂ (1831) continues: We have another example of collision portrayed in Oedipus. He has slain his father, and is seemingly guilty, but he is guilty because his ethical power is one-sided; that is to say, he falls unconsciously into this horrible deed.[a] Yet he is the one who excels in knowing, the one who solved the riddle of the Sphinx.[b] Hence a counterweight is set up as [his] Nemesis. The one who knew so much stands in the power of the unconscious, so that he falls as deeply into guilt as the height on which he stood. Here, then, there is the antithesis of the two powers, that of consciousness and that of unconsciousness.

[*Ed.*] [a]See Sophocles, *Oedipus Rex*, esp. 800–819, 1183–1185. [b]A reference to the Theban sphinx legend, as distinguished from the Egyptian sphinx.

431. *Precedes in L, W (1831):* It is justice that is in this way satisfied with the maxim, "There is nothing that is not Zeus,"[a] i.e., eternal justice. Here we have an active necessity, but one which is completely ethical; the misfortune suffered is perfectly clear. There is nothing blind or unconscious here.

[*Ed.*] [a]See Sophocles, *Trachiniae* 1277–1278.

432. *L (1827?) adds, similar in W:* A son of Minos had been slain in Athens; for this reason a purification was carried out, and the deed was declared to be undone. It is spirit that wants to make what has been done undone.

[*Ed.*] See Diodorus Siculus, *Bibliotheca historica* 4.60–61. See 1824 lectures, n. 691.

the Areopagus.[433] In that instance, too, there is a collision. He has murdered his mother—on the one hand here is the greatest crime against piety; on the other hand he has gained justice for his father. He was head of the family and also of the state. In one and the same action he committed an outrage and at the same time carried out complete and essential necessity. "The acquittal is a uniting of these one-sided stances."[434] *Oedipus at Colonus* hints at reconciliation, and more precisely at the Christian representation of reconciliation: [Oedipus] comes to honor among the gods, the gods call him to them.[435] Today we require more, because for us the representation of reconciliation is higher: [we have] the consciousness that this reversal (whereby what has been done is made undone) can occur within the inner self. Human beings who turn over a new leaf, who surrender their one-sidedness, have purged it from within themselves, from within their wills where the enduring abode or place of the deed would be, i.e., they have negated the deed at its root. But this kind of reconciliation is not pervasive among the ancients. It is more in accord with our feelings that the tragedies have denouements that are reconciling.

This is the relationship of necessity.

The other is the relation to the other extreme, to the singularity that we see playing about these divine essences themselves, the singularity that is present in the human [agent] and comes in question here. This singular aspect is the contingent aspect, and at this level of religion human beings are not yet free, not yet universal self-consciousness; they are indeed the self-consciousness of ethical life, but [only] of its substance generally, and the ethical substance is not yet the subjectivity that is inwardly universal.

In the sphere of the contingent, therefore, what a human being has to do falls outside of ethical duty. Since God | is not yet determined as absolute subjectivity, this contingent element is not yet placed in the hands of a providence, but instead in those of destiny.   560

433. [*Ed.*] Aeschylus, *Eumenides,* esp. 734–741.
434. *Thus Hu; L, W (Var/1831?) read:* Acquittal [*Lossprechen*] means precisely this, making something undone.
435. [*Ed.*] Sophocles, *Oedipus at Colonus,* esp. 1623–1628, 1658–1664.

This means that human beings do not know themselves as free; they are not the decisive subjectivity. Connected with this is the fact that they allow the decision to be given from without; here occurs the aspect of religion that we call oracles. These oracles have a natural origin, for ⁻here no articulated answer was given.[436] Their manifestation is some sort of external transformation, metallic forms, the rustling of trees, the blowing of the wind, visions, examination of sacrificial animals, and contingencies of that sort. People needed such things in order to reach decisions. The Greeks are not free in the sense that we are free, i.e., in their self-consciousness; they let themselves be determined from without.⁻[437]

These are the principal moments of the religion of beauty. Spirit or reason is the content, but reason is still substantial in its content, so that it falls asunder into its particular [shapes]. In its form, the spiritual shape, the human shape, has the natural in it, [but] as ideal,

---

436. [Ed.] In the Ms. Hegel refers to them as "very naive oracles," alluding to the Greek motto (Αἱ τῶν δαιμόνων φωναὶ ἄναρθροι εἰσίν) found on the back of the title page of Goethe's Zur Morphologie (1823), which is vol. 2 of his Zur Naturwissenschaft überhaupt.

437. W₁ (Var) reads: they are external in character for human beings, and the manifestation is some sort of external, natural change—sounds from the rustling of leaves or ringing tones.

No articulated answers are given by oracles. In Delphi it was the wind that blew out of the gorge and produced a rushing noise. Elsewhere it is visions, or the examination of sacrificial animals, chance externalities that have a natural origin or are externalities as such—these it is that humans use in order to make their resolve.

The free Greek is not free in self-consciousness as we are free. The commander who wishes to engage in battle, or the state that is about to establish a colony, consults the oracle;[a] this democracy still did not have the force or energy of self-consciousness that [enables] the people to determine itself, to form its own resolve.

Socrates was the first to recognize that one's own resolve is what counts. His δαιμόνιον is nothing else but this.[b] He says of it that it only told him what was good, and then only about completely external, contingent circumstances. It did not reveal any truths to him, but only gave him the decision in singular cases of action. Here fate [Fatum] is the subjective will, the resolve.

[Ed.] [a]The Lectures on the History of Philosophy 1:423 (cf. Werke 14:97) shows that Hegel is here thinking in particular of Xenophon, Anabasis, and Herodotus, Histories 9.33 ff. [b]In Xenophon, Memorabilia 1.1.1–9, esp. 1.1.4, Socrates is said to have spoken in such and such a way, or advised his friends to do thus and so, because his daimonion (divine sign) had so indicated. See also Plato, Apology, esp. 24b–c, 26b–e.

so that it is only an expression of the spiritual and is no longer something independent. The finitude of this religion has been made plain from every aspect. | 561

2. The Religion of Sublimity, or Jewish Religion[438]

What is common to the religions of this sphere is this ideality of the natural, the fact that it is subordinated to the spiritual, that God, who is spirit, is known as spirit. To begin with, then, God is known as spirit whose determinations are rational and ethical. But this God still has a particular content, i.e., is still only his ethical power. God's appearance is that of beauty; but this appearance is a natural material and a soil of sensible, external stuff or of sensible representation. The soil of that religion is not yet pure thought. The necessity of the elevation of the religion of beauty into the religion of sublimity lies in what we have discussed already, i.e., in the need that the particular spiritual powers, the ethical powers, should be embraced within a spiritual unity. The truth of the particular [moment] is the universal unity, ˉwhich is subjectivity and is inwardly concrete,ˉ[439] inasmuch as it has the particular within it but at the same time subsists essentially as subjectivity. But for this rationality that subsists as subjectivity—indeed, it even subsists as universal subjectivity with respect to its content and is free with respect to its form—for this pure subjectivity the soil is pure thought; it is withdrawn from the natural and so from the sensible [realm], withdrawn both from external sensibility and from sensible representation. It is the spiritually subjective unity—and for us this is what first merits the name of God.

438. [*Ed.*] As noted earlier (n. 347), in the 1827 lectures the treatment of the religion of sublimity follows that of the religion of beauty; the reasons for this reversal are discussed in the Editorial Introduction. The 1827 interpretation of Judaism carries further the favorable reassessment initiated in 1824. Almost the entire section is devoted to an analysis of the representation of God as creator and the implications of this for understanding the relationship between God and the world. While this material is already present in 1824, it is expanded and systematically ordered, becoming the focus of the whole section.

439. *W₁ (Var) reads:* and subjectivity is inwardly concrete *W₂ (Var) reads:* which is inwardly concrete

a. The Unity of God

This subjective unity is not substance, ˉfor it is subjective,ˉ[440] but it is indeed absolute power; the natural is only something that is posited by it, is only ideal and not something that is independent. The unity does not appear or reveal [itself] in natural material, but instead does so essentially in thought: thought is the mode of its determinate being or appearing. Absolute power ˉwe have seen often enough already;ˉ[441] but the main point is that here it is concrete and inwardly determinate—hence it is absolute wisdom. |

562

Also, the rational determinations of freedom, the ethical determinations ˉunited in one purpose and one determination of this subjectivity, areˉ[442] holiness. In this way ˉdivinityˉ[443] determines itself as holiness. The higher truth of God's subjectivity is not just a beautiful subjectivity where the import or the absolute content is still separated out into particularities[444]—a relationship like that of animals to human beings. Animals do in fact have particular characters; the character of universality belongs to humans. The ethical rationality of freedom and the explicitly self-subsistent unity of this rationality is what authentic, inwardly self-determining subjectivity is. This is wisdom and holiness. [445]The contents of the Greek deities are the ethical powers; they are not holy, because they are still particular and limited.

Here the absolute, or God, subsists as the One, as subjectivity, as universal and pure subjectivity, or conversely this subjectivity that is the universal inwardly is precisely the one inwardly determined unity of God.[446] It is not a matter of the unity being exhibited implicitly, of the unity of God being the underlying ground, being implicit: that is the case in the Hindu and Chinese religion. For there,

440. W (Var) reads: but rather subjective unity,
441. Thus Hu; L (Var) reads: is also in the earthly realm; W (Var) reads: is also in Hinduism;
442. W (Var) reads: are united in one determination, one purpose, and thus the defining characteristic of this subjectivity is
443. W (Var) reads: ethical life
444. W₂ (Var) adds: but is the characteristic of holiness; and the relationship between these two determinations is
445. In B's margin: 17 July 1827
446. W (Var/1831?) adds: so that there is a consciousness of God as One.

when God's unity is only implicit, God is not posited as infinite subjectivity and the unity is not known, it is not [present] as subjectivity for consciousness.[447]

Thus the unity of God contains one power within it, which is accordingly the absolute power. Every externality,[448] every sensible configuration | and sensible image, is sublated in it. For this reason   563
God here subsists without shape[449]—he subsists not for sensible representation but only for thought. The inwardly infinite, pure subjectivity is the subjectivity that is essentially thinking. As thinking it subsists only for thinking, and therefore subsists in its [activity of] judgment. Thinking is the essential soil for this object. Here we must now mention the characteristic of divine particularization, of divine judgment.

b. Divine Self-Determination and Representation

God is wisdom; what this involves is God's self-determining, God's judging, and hence (more precisely) what is called God's creating.[450] God's wisdom consists in being purposive, or determinative. But this wisdom is at first still abstract, being still the initial subjectivity, ˉthe initial wisdom,ˉ[451] and therefore God's ˉjudgmentˉ[452] is not yet

447. W (1831) adds: God is now known as a personal One [Einer] rather than as a neuter One [Eines] as in pantheism. Thus the immediately natural mode [of representing God] disappears, for instance the mode that is still posited in the Parsee religion as light. Religion is posited as the religion of spirit, but only in its foundation, only upon the soil that is proper to it, the soil of thought.

448. W (Var/1831?) adds: and consequently all that belongs to sensible nature,

449. W (Var/1831?) adds: without any externally sensible shape; having no image,

450. W (1831) adds: Spirit is what is utterly self-mediating inwardly, or what is active. This activity is a distinguishing from self, a judging (or primal division). The world is what is posited by spirit; the world is made out of its nothing. But the negative of the world is the affirmative, the Creator, in whom the nothing is what is natural. Within its nothing, therefore, the world has arisen out of the absolute fullness of the power of the good. It has been created from its own "nothing," which (its other) is God.

451. W (Var) reads: and that is why it is abstract to begin with,

452. W (Var) reads: particularization

[Ed.] The interchange between "judgment" (Urteil) and "particularization" (Besonderung) is not surprising since etymologically the two terms have a similar sense, that of "sundering" (sondern), "division" or "parting" (teilen). Hegel intends to connect them through their root meanings: the divine particularization is a judging, a primal division (see n. 450 and the last sentence of the preceding paragraph of the main text).

posited as internal to itself. Instead what is assumed is that God decrees, and what is posited or determined by God subsists at once in the form of an unmediated other.[453] Were God's wisdom concrete, then God would be his own self-determining in such a way that God himself would produce within himself what is created and sustain it internally, so that it would be[454] known as sustained within him as his Son; God so defined would be known as ˉtruly concreteˉ[455] spirit. But since the wisdom is here abstract, the judgment or what is posited is thus something subsisting although only as a form: it is the subsisting world. |

564

Thus God is creator of the world. The world is something immediate, but in such a way that the immediacy is only something mediated: the world is only a created product.[456]   [457]God's creating is very different from procession, wherein the world goes forth from God. ˉˉFor the Hindus, the ˉworlds goˉ[458] forth from Brahmā.ˉˉ[459] In the Greek cosmogonies the highest or spiritual gods finally go

453. *W (1831) adds:* The higher view is certainly that of God's creation within himself, that he is in himself beginning and end, and hence he has the moment of movement (which still falls outside him at this present stage) within himself, in his inner nature.

454. *W (Var) adds:* created and

455. *W (Var) reads:* the concrete God, genuinely known as

456. *L (1827?) adds (cf. n. 461):* The creature is something that is not inwardly independent; it may *be* (or it has being), but it does not have independence. This distinction is essential.

457. *Precedes in* W_2 *(1831):* Since power is represented as absolute negativity, so its essence (i.e., what is identical with itself) is to begin with in a state of repose, of eternal calm and seclusion. But just this self-contained solitude is merely a moment of power, not the whole. Power is also negative relation to self, inner mediation, and since it refers negatively to itself, this sublation of abstract identity is the positing of difference, of determination, i.e., it is the creation of the world. But the nothing from which the world is created is the absence of all difference, the very category in which power or essence was first thought of. So if it is asked where God got matter from, the answer is, just that simple reference to self. Matter is what is formless, what is identical with itself; this is only one moment of the essence, and as such it is something other than absolute power, and hence it is what we call matter. The creation of the world, therefore, means the negative reference of power to itself, insofar as it is initially defined as what is only identical with itself.

458. *Thus B; An reads:* world goes *Hu, L, W read:* gods go

459. *W (1831) reads:* All peoples have theogonies or, what comes to the same thing, cosmogonies, in which the fundamental category is always going-forth, not being-created. *W (Var):* The gods go forth from Brahmā.

forth; they are the last to emerge. [460]What has gone forth is what exists, what is actual, so that the ground from which it has gone forth is posited as sublated, as nonessential, and what has gone forth ˉcounts as independent.ˉ[461] Here, in contrast, the subjectivity of the One is what is absolutely first, the initiating factor, and the conditioned state | is sublated. Over against this posited [being], over against the world, which is God's creation, over against the totality of its determinate being, of its negation, over against the totality of immediate being, God is what is presupposed; God is the absolute subject, which remains the absolutely first. Here the fundamental definition of God is this: subjectivity that relates itself to itself. As abiding subjectivity that has being within itself, it is what is first. But for the Greek gods—and precisely for the highest or spiritual gods—the status of having gone forth belongs directly to their finitude. It is the condition of their being, the presupposition upon which their nature rests, just as in the case of finite spirit [its] nature is presupposed.

565

Thus over against the determination of the One as the subject is the particular, what comes forth in this producing, in nature, externality and dependence; in general, what is created in the posited [world]. Only the divine subjectivity that is abiding within itself is self-relation and accordingly is the first.

But although subjectivity is here what makes the absolute beginning, it is the initiating factor only, and it is not the case that this subjectivity could be determined also as the result.[462] God is the first; God's creation is an eternal creation; but God is the initiator of creation, not the result. If the divine subjectivity were determined as result, as self-creating, then it would be grasped as concrete spirit.[463]

460. *Precedes in W (1831):* At this point the inadequate category of going-forth disappears, since the good, or the absolute power, is a subject. This going-forth is not the relationship of what is created [to its creator].

461. *W (Var/1831?) reads (cf. n. 456):* is posited not as a creature but as something independent, not as the sort of thing that lacks inward independence. *W₁ adds:* It may *be,* it has being, but not independence.

462. *W (Var) adds:* and as concrete spirit.

463. *L (1827?) adds:* For at the higher stage, when God is defined as spirit, he is the one who does not step outside himself, and so he is also the result, or that which is self-creating.

If what is created from the absolute subject were this subject itself, then in this distinction the distinction would likewise be superseded, the last subject would be⁻⁴⁶⁴ that which results from itself. We do not yet have that determination here, but only the one where the absolute subject is what is utterly initiating, is the first.⁴⁶⁵ |

566

The second aspect is God's relation to what is created. What we call God's attributes—these characteristics of God in relation to the world and to the creatures—are God's determinacies. Or in other words, since we already saw God's particularizing or self-determining, and saw this as the creation of the world, saw the determinate as a subsisting world, then the attributes of God are God's relation to the world. That is to say, the attributes are the determinate [result] itself but as known in the concept of God. One aspect [the world] is the determinate known as what has being, not as reverting into God or belonging to God, and the other [the attributes] is the state of determinateness as God's own determinacy. This is what is called God's relations to the world, and it is a misguided expression if it means that we only know about this relation of God to the world but know nothing about God. Instead that relation is God's very own determinateness, and hence God's own attributes.

⁴⁶⁶The way in which one human being is related to another— that is just what is human, that is human nature itself.⁴⁶⁷ When we are cognizant of how an object is related [to everything else], then we are cognizant of its very nature. To distinguish between the two [i.e., relation and nature] is to make misguided distinctions that collapse straightaway because they are the productions of an understanding that does not know what it is doing—an understand-

464. W₁ (Var) reads: last subject would be the first, W₂ (Var/Ed?) reads: first subject would be the last,

465. L (1827?) adds: God is not yet grasped here as spirit, as what first returns into itself through its particularization. But since God is what is utterly first, his creating must not be thought of under the guise of human producing.

466. Precedes in L (1827?), similar in W: Even from the sensual point of view something is, and that something is on its own account. Its properties, its relation to another, are distinct from it; yet these are what constitute its peculiar nature.

467. L (1827?) adds, similar in W: The acid is nothing else than the specific mode of its relation to the base—that is the nature of the acid itself.

ing unfamiliar with them, one that does not know what it is dealing with in these distinctions.

As something external and unmediated, [but] as the determinacy of God himself, this determinacy is God's absolute power; as we have seen, however, this power is wisdom.

The specific moments of wisdom are goodness and justice. Goodness consists in the fact that the world is. The world does not attain being [proper].[468] Being, the truly actual, *is* only in God. The being of what is | mutually external, outside of God—that being has 567 no claims; it is only the self-externalization of God, the fact that God releases himself from himself, and sets his content (which is the determinacy of absolute subjectivity) free even from his absolute unity—that is God's goodness, and only here can God be the creator in the true sense as infinite subjectivity. In that role God is free, and so his determinateness or self-determining can be set free. Only what is free can have its determinations over against it as free, or can let them go as free. This release that lets them go their separate ways so as to yield the totality of finitude, or the world—this [mode of] being is goodness. Justice in turn is the manifestation of the nullity or ideality of this finite [being], it is the fact that this [finite] being is not genuine independence—this manifestation [of God] as power is what endows finite things with their right.

This goodness and justice must not be regarded merely as moments of substance but as moments of the one subject; in substance these determinations are found to be subsisting just as immediately as not subsisting but as coming into being. But here the One subsists not as substance but as the personal One, as subject. The being of things is posited herein as purpose; it is the specification of purpose, the proper determinacy of the concept. The world ought to be, and likewise it ought to transform itself and pass away. This is justice as the specification of purpose, justice as the subject

---

468. W (1831) *adds:* for being is here downgraded to a moment, and is only a createdness or positedness. This judgment or primary division [*Ur-teilen*] is the eternal goodness of God. What has been differentiated has no right to be, it is outside the One, it is a manifold and therefore a limited, finite [thing] whose destination is *not* to be; that it nonetheless *is,* is the goodness of God. But as something posited, it also passes away, it is only appearance.

that distinguishes itself from its own determinations, or from its world.

The third aspect is the form of the world, the character that things in general obtain, the reality that they receive. Or, the world is now prosaic, it confronts us essentially as a collection of things, it is rendered profane. Now nature is divested of divinity. In the Orient and especially with regard to the Greek god, people delight in friendliness and cheerfulness, and in the relationship to nature and to the divine, in the fact that inasmuch as human beings relate themselves to nature they relate themselves to the divine.[469] This unity

568 of the divine | and the natural—we call it the identity of the ideal and the real—is an abstract and wholly formal determination, an identity that is cheaply obtained. In fact it is everywhere. What matters most would be the authentic specification of this identity; and the authentic identity is the one found within infinite subjectivity, that which is grasped not as neutralization or reciprocal blunting [of differences], but just as infinite subjectivity. Since infinite subjectivity determines itself as such, and lets its determinations go free as the world, these determinations are things without any independence as they truly are. They are not deities but merely natural objects. The particular ethical powers, which are in essence the supreme deities for the Greeks, have independence only according to their form, because the content as particular is dependent and finite. That is a false form. For the situation with dependent things that are immediate is this: we are only aware of their being as something formal, something without independence. The only being that pertains to them, therefore, is not absolute or divine but is an abstract, one-sided being. Since abstract being is their lot, they stand under the categories of being; and since finitude is their lot, they are subject to the categories of the understanding.

At this stage, therefore, there are prosaic things, just as the world contains prosaic things for us also, as understanding beings—external things in the manifold nexus of understanding, of ground and consequent, of quality and quantity, subject to all these categories of the understanding. Here then is what we call natural or necessary connection; and for that reason the category of "miracle" emerges

469. L (1827?) adds, similar in W: Their liberality spiritualizes what is natural, makes it something divine, gives it a soul.

here for the first time too, as opposed to the natural connection of things. In Hindu religion, for instance, there is no miracle; everything is jumbled together there from the outset. Only in contrast with order, with the lawfulness of nature, with natural laws—even though these laws are not recognized and one finds only a consciousness of a natural nexus—only in that context does the category of "miracle" arise; then miracle is represented as God being sporadically manifest in singular events.[470] The true miracle is the appearance | of spirit in nature, and the authentic appearance of spirit is, in its fundamental aspect, the spirit of humanity and the human consciousness of the world.[471]   569

In this religion, therefore, the world appears as finite things that act upon one another in a natural way, things that stand within an intelligible nexus. The relationship therefore is: God, world, creation of the world, the fundamental categories of worldly things. Miracle is grasped as a contingent manifestation of God; the genuine manifestation of God in the world, however, is the absolute or eternal manifestation, and the mode or manner of this manifestation, its form, appears as what we call "sublimity," and for that reason we call this religion the religion of sublimity. The infinite subject in its self-containment one cannot call sublime; it is the absolute in and for itself, [i.e.,] it is holy. Sublimity emerges as the appearance or relation of this infinite subject to the world. The world is grasped as a manifestation of this subject, but as a manifestation that is not affirmative; or one that, to the extent that it is indeed affirmative, still has the primary character that the natural or worldly is negated as unbefitting ˉthe subjective,ˉ[472] ˉso that God's appearing is at once grasped as sublimity that is superior to appearance in [ordinary] reality.ˉ[473]

470. W_2 (Var) adds: and at the same time in opposition to their [natural] outcomes.
471. L (1827?) adds, similar in W: For what we know of the world is that in all this confusion and manifold contingency it still maintains regularity and reason everywhere—relatively speaking, this is a miracle.
472. W (Var) reads: and is known as such,
473. W (Var) reads: [W_1: It is the appearance and manifestation of God in the world in such a way that this appearing W_2: Sublimity is therefore the mode of God's appearance and manifestation in the world, and it may be defined as follows: this appearing] does at the same time show itself as sublime, as superior to appearance within [ordinary] reality.

In the religion of beauty we have a reconciliation of the meaning with the material, with the sensible mode, with being for another; the spiritual reveals itself wholly in this outward manner. The outward mode is a sign of the inner, and this inner is completely recognized in the shape of its externality. ˉSublimity, by contrast, simultaneously annihilates | the matter or the material in which the sublime appears. The material is directly and expressly known as inadequate; it is not an inadequacy that is unconsciously overlooked. For it does not suffice for sublimity that the substantial is in and for itself something higher than its shape; instead the primary point is that the inadequacy is directly posited in the shape. For the Hindus there is only wildness and grotesqueness, but no sublimity.

570

God is explicitly the One, the one power as inwardly determined. God is the wise one, i.e., he manifests himself in nature but in a sublime manner. The natural world is only something posited and limited, only a manifestation of the One in such a way that God is at the same time superior to this manifestation; God at once distinguishes himself from the manifestation even within it, and does not get his being-for-self, his essential presence [*Dasein*] from this externality, as in the religion of beauty.ˉ474 Nature is submissive and manifests only God, but in such a way that God subsists at the same time outside this manifestation.

Theˉfourth aspectˉ475 is God's purpose. Here we are concerned with the category of *essential* purpose, namely that above all God is wise—wise in nature generally. Nature is God's creation and God makes his power recognized in it, though not only his power but also his wisdom. This is evident in its products, from their purposeful

---

474. W₂ *(Var/MiscP?) reads:* The sublimity of the appearance, by contrast, simultaneously annihilates its reality, its matter and material. In his appearance God also distinguishes himself from it, in such a way that it is expressly known as inadequate. The One does not therefore have his being-for-self and his essential presence [*Dasein*] in the externality of the appearance, as do the gods of the religion of beauty; and the inadequacy of the appearance is not something that is unconsciously overlooked, but is expressly and consciously posited as such.

475. *Hu reads, similar in An:* third aspect

[*Ed.*] The three preceding aspects are: (1) creation, (2) the attributes of God, (3) the form of the world. If this is an error of Hegel, it is explicable from the fact that he was using the Griesheim transcript of the 1824 lectures as the basis of the 1827 presentation, and in G the theme of purpose is the "third point."

orientation. But this purpose is only something undetermined and superficial, it is more ˉexternal.ˉ[476] The true purpose and its realization do not fall within nature as such, but essentially within consciousness instead. Purpose manifests itself in nature, but its essential appearance is its appearing within consciousness as in its reflection [*Widerschein*]; it appears reflectedly in self-consciousness in such a way that its purpose is to become known by consciousness, and for consciousness the purpose is to acknowledge it. Acknowledgment and | praise of God is the determination that emerges here: the whole world should proclaim the glory of God, and indeed God's universal glory. Not merely the Jewish people but the whole earth, all peoples, all the Gentiles should praise the Lord.[477] This purpose of becoming known by consciousness can above all be called God's theoretical purpose; the more determinate sort is the practical purpose that is realized in the spirit of the world as such.

571

So this essential purpose is in the first place ethical life or uprightness, namely, that all human beings should keep legality or right in mind in whatever they do; this legality or right is precisely what is divine, and insofar as it is something worldly within finite consciousness, it is something decreed by God. God is the universal; the human being, in determining itself or its own will,[478] is free and therefore universal will. It is not one's own particular ethical life or right conduct that is the basic determination here, but rather walking before God, a freedom from self-seeking aims, the righteousness that has value before God. The human being does what is right in relation to God, to the glory of God; so this righteousness has its seat principally in the will, in the inner self.

The natural state of existence, of human beings and their action, stands opposed therefore to this willing, to this inwardness with regard to God. This broken state is posited in humanity: God *is* on his own account, while nature has a sort of being [*ein Seiendes*], but

476. *Thus Hu; L (1827?) reads, similar in W:* an external purposiveness: "Thou givest to the beast its fodder" [Ps. 147:9].

In B's margin: 19 July 1827

477. [*Ed.*] See Ps. 117:1: "Praise the Lord all ye nations, praise him all ye peoples." See the quotation of this Psalm in the 1831 text contained in n. 492 below.

478. W_2 *(Var) adds:* in terms of this universal

under [the Lord's] dominion. This same distinction is found within the human spirit, namely, the distinction between right conduct as such and humanity's natural existence. But the latter is determined by the spiritual relationship of the will, just as nature in general is something posited by absolute spirit. Humanity's natural mode of being, our external, worldly existence, is posited in connection with the inner aspect. If one's will is an essential will and one's action is right conduct, then the outward existence of the human agent should also be in agreement with this inner aspect or right; a human being should ˉprosper, but should prosper only according to his

572 works.ˉ[479] One should ˉin general | not only behave ethically,ˉ[480] observe the laws of one's country, and sacrifice oneself for one's country, no matter how one fares as a consequence; but also there crops up the definite requirement that prosperity should come to the one who does right. We have here the relationship that real existence or outwardly determinate being is conformed and subordinated to the inner aspect, to the right, and is determined by it; and this relationship comes into play here in consequence of, and on the ground of, the fundamental relationship of God to the natural and finite world. Here there is a purpose, and this purpose shall be carried out—a distinction, however, that should at the same time be in harmony, so that natural existence shows itself to be ruled by the essential, by the spiritual. The natural existence of human beings is likewise supposed to be determined and ruled by the truly inward, by ˉwhat is upright.ˉ[481] In this way human well-being is affirmatively and divinely legitimated; but it has this legitimation only to the extent that it is conformed to the divine, to the ethically divine law.

This is the bond of necessity, but it is no longer blind as in Greek religion, no longer just an empty, indeterminate necessity devoid of concept, so that the concrete is outside it.[482] Now, on the contrary, the necessity is concrete; what is actual being in and for itself is what

479. W (Var) reads: prosper only according to his works.
480. W₂ (Var/Ed?) reads: not only behave ethically in general,
481. W₂ (Var) reads: right-doing.
482. L (1827?) adds, similar in W: Among the Greeks the gods, the ethical powers, stand apart from necessity and are under it; necessity does not have what is ethical and right in its definition.

gives the laws—it wills the right, the ˉlaw.ˉ483 In consequence, this being has conformed to it a determinate mode of being that is affirmative, an existence that is well-being, prosperity. In this sphere, human beings know this unity and harmony. That prosperity is permitted or indeed owed to one, is something conditional; the human being taken as a whole is an end for God. But the human being as a whole is itself something inwardly differentiated, for it involves both will and external existence. Such a [divided] person knows then that God is the bond of this necessity, is this unity that produces well-being commensurate with the inner will, makes it correspond to right conduct; one knows that this connection ˉis the divine, universal | will (and the divine is the power), but moreover that it is also the inwardly determined will of the finite spirit.ˉ484   573

The consciousness that this linkage obtains is the faith and confidence that is a fundamental feature of the Jewish people; and indeed it constitutes one of their remarkable features. The Old Testament scriptures are full of this confidence.485 It is this pattern of events too that is presented in the Book of Job, ˉa book whose connection with the Jewish tradition is not precisely known.ˉ486 487 Job is guiltless; he finds his misfortune unjustifiable and so is dissatisfied. This means there is an antithesis within him, the con-

483. *W (Var) reads:* good.

484. W_1 *(Var) reads:* exists—the divine universal will (and the divine is the power to achieve this), but also this inwardly determined will. W_2 *(Var) reads:* exists, for the divine, universal will is at the same time the inwardly determined will, and hence it is the power to bring about this connection.

485. *W (Var) adds:* especially the Psalms.

486. *Thus B; W (Var) reads:* the only book whose connection with the soil of the Jewish people is not precisely known.

487. [*Ed.*] The origin and date of compilation of the Book of Job were at that time highly controversial matters. J. D. Michaelis, whose translation of the Old Testament into German was published in 1769, regarded it as the oldest book in the Bible, possibly written by Moses to comfort the Israelites in Egypt. This view is reflected in the prominence Hegel accords to it, especially in the first two lecture series. J. G. Herder, by contrast, in *The Spirit of Hebrew Poetry* (1787), trans. James Marsh, 2 vols. (Burlington, Vt., 1833), vol. 1, dialogue 5 (esp. pp. 103–111), expressed the view that the author was not an Israelite at all. In his translation and commentary, *Das Buch Hiob* (Heidelberg, 1824), F. W. C. Umbreit discussed the opposing standpoints and concluded that the book is purely Hebraic in origin, but of post-Mosaic date.

sciousness of the justice or righteousness that is absolute and of the incongruity between his fate and this righteousness. He is dissatisfied precisely because he does not regard necessity as blind fate; it is known to be God's purpose to bring about good things for those who are good. The critical point, then, occurs when this dissatisfaction and despondency has to submit to absolute, pure confidence. This submission is the end point. On the one side there stands the requirement that the righteous should prosper, and ˉon the other side is a submission, a renunciation, an acknowledgment of God's power; upon that submission there follows the restoration of good fortune by God, precisely as the consequence of this acknowledgment.ˉ488 This trust in God, this unity and the consciousness of this harmony of the power of God with the ˉtruthˉ489 and righteousness of God, the consciousness that God is inwardly characterized as purpose and that God has purposes, is the first step, and God's blessings are what follow from it. That trust in God is none other than the consciousness of this harmony between power and wisdom. |

574

We have still to draw attention here to this inwardizing of spirit, its own movement within itself. A human being is supposed to do right; that is the absolute commandment, and this right conduct has its seat in one's will. As a result one is directed to one's inner being, and one must be occupied with consideration of one's inwardness, with whether it is in the right, whether one's will is good. The inner inquiry about this and the grief when it is not so, the crying of the soul for God, this descent into the depths of spirit, this longing of spirit for the right, for conformity to the will of God, is a particular characteristic that is dominant in the Psalms and the Prophets.

In addition, however, this [divine] purpose appears at the same time as a limited one. It is indeed the aim that human beings should know and acknowledge God, that they should do whatever they do for God's glory, that what they will should be conformed to God's

488. W (1827 with 1831?) reads: on the other side even this discontent must give way. This renunciation, this acknowledgment of God's power, restores Job to his property and his former happiness; this acknowledgment is followed by the restoration of his good fortune. At the same time this good fortune must not be expressed by the finite [creature] as a right vis-à-vis the power of God.

489. W (Var) reads: wisdom

will, that their will should be true will. [But] this aim has also a limitation, and we will now indicate to what extent this limitation lies in the definition of God, how far the concept or representation of God still contains a limitation. If the representation of God is limited, then these further realizations of the divine concept within human consciousness will also be limited.[490]

God is what is self-determining in its freedom and according to its freedom, ˜God is the spiritual, free being˜[491]—this is wisdom. But this wisdom, this purpose, is only an initial purpose, wisdom in general. The wisdom and self-determining of God does not yet include God's development. This development in the idea of God is first found in the religion where the nature of God is open and manifest. The defect of this idea at the present stage is that God is indeed the One, but yet is within himself only in the *determinacy* of this unity; he is not what is eternally self-developing within itself. This is still not a developed determination; | to this extent what we call wisdom is an abstraction, it is abstract universality.   575

[492] ˜Hence a limitation is present in [this] religion, insofar as it is consciousness of God, a limitation understood partly in terms of

490. *L (1827?) adds, similar in W:* This is always the essential but also the most difficult point, to recognize limitation in the One as also a limitation of the idea, so that the idea is not yet the absolute idea.

491. *W (Var) reads:* in such a way that the spiritual is the free

492. *W (1831) reads (parallel in main text follows):* (2) God is the exclusive Lord and God of the Jewish people. It need not surprise us that a [W₂: an Oriental] nation should limit religion to itself, and that its religion should appear as wholly tied to its nationality, for we see this in Eastern lands quite generally. The Greeks and the Romans were the first to adopt foreign forms of worship; all types of religion infiltrate Roman culture, but they do not have the status of a national religion there. But in the Eastern lands, religion is completely tied to nationality. The Chinese and the Persians both have their state religions, which are just for them. Among the Hindus, birth already indicates each individual's social status and relationship to Brahman; hence they do not in any way demand that others should adopt their religion. For the Hindus such a demand makes absolutely no sense because, on their view, all the peoples of the earth belong to their religion, and the foreign peoples are reckoned collectively as one particular caste. All the same, this exclusiveness rightly astonishes us more in the case of the Jewish people, for the binding of religion to nationality completely contradicts the view that God is grasped only in universal thought and not in a partial [*partikular*] definition. For the Persians God is the good; that too is a universal way of characterizing him, but it is itself still in the sphere of immediacy, so that God is identical with light, and that is a partial view. The Jewish God is only

576 the fact that the Jewish God is only a national God, has restricted himself to this nation. | Certainly this is the case, but such is true of other religions as well; the God of the Christians is restricted too. We may well be aware of a [universal] Christendom, but we also represent it as one [particular] family, one nation, or one people;

for thought, and that stands in contrast with his limitation to the nation. It is true that consciousness rises to universality among the Jewish people too, and this is expressed in several passages. Psalm 117:1[–2]: "Praise the Lord all ye nations, praise him all ye peoples. For his grace and truth are great toward us to all eternity." The glory of God is to be made manifest among all peoples; it is in the later prophets especially that this universality emerges as a higher demand. Isaiah makes God even say: "Of the heathen who shall honor Jehovah will I make priests and Levites,"[a] and a similar thought is expressed in the words, "In every nation anyone who fears God and does what is right is acceptable to him."[b] This, however, comes later. According to the dominant basic idea, the Jewish people is the chosen people, and universality is thus reduced to partiality [*Partikularität*]. [W_1: But this partiality derives from the subjective side. What is proper to the Jews is their worship and acknowledgment of Jehovah; W_2: But we have already seen above, in the development of the divine purpose, how its limitation is grounded in the limitation that is still involved in the definition of God, and we have shown that this limitation in turn stems from the nature of the servile consciousness; and we can now see also how this partiality derives from the subjective side too. What is proper to the Jews, as his servants, is this worship and acknowledgment of Jehovah;] and they are quite conscious that it is peculiar to them. It is also linked to the history of the Jewish people: the Jewish God is the God of Abraham, of Isaac, and of Jacob, the God who brought the Jews out of Egypt. [W_1: etc. W_2: and there is not the slightest reflection that God also may have done other things, that he also may have dealt affirmatively with other peoples.] So partiality here enters on the scene from the subjective side, [W_2: from the side of the cultus,] and in any case it can be said that God is the God of those who worship him, for God is the one who is known in the subjective spirit, and knows himself in it. This moment belongs essentially to the idea of God; and knowing and acknowledging belong essentially to this definition of him. It often appears in what is for us a distorted guise, as when, for instance, God is said to be mightier and stronger than the other gods, as if there were other gods in addition to him.[c] But for the Jews, these are the false gods. [W_1: This partiality pertains therefore to the side of subjective worship.]

It is this people that worships him, and so he is the God of this people, he is its Lord in fact. He it is who is known as the creator of heaven and earth, he has established for everything its purpose and measure, bestowed on everything its distinctive nature, and even given to humanity its measure, its goal, and its right. This is the definition under which he (as the Lord) gives his people their laws, laws of every kind, both the universal laws, the Ten Commandments, which are the universal basic ethical and rightful foundations of lawgiving and morality and are not regarded [by them] as rationally based but as [simply] prescribed by the Lord, and also all the other political ordinances and regulations. Moses is called the lawgiver of the Jews, but he was not to the Jews what Solon and Lycurgus were to the Greeks (for these two legislated

thus this consciousness of God is also consciousness of a national God. When we represent ourselves thus as a family, then God is | 577 restricted to this family. In the consciousness of the family that knows such a God there is, however, not only the element that God is the universal creator and lord of the world; in addition, God should also

---

simply as human beings). Moses just made known the laws of Jehovah; according to the story, it was Jehovah himself who engraved them on the stone.[d] Attached to the most trifling regulations, e.g., to those concerning the arrangement of the tabernacle, or to the usages in connection with sacrifices and all other ceremonial matters, we find in the Bible the formula "Jehovah says." All law is given by the Lord, and hence it is positive commandment throughout. There is in it a formal, absolute authority. The particular aspects of the political constitution are not developed out of the universal purpose at all, nor are they left to human beings to determine, for the unity [of the absolute] does not permit human caprice, human reason, to persist alongside it, and every political change is called a falling away from God. But as something given by God, the particular is [valid] as established forever. And the eternal laws of right and morality are here placed in the same rank and stated in equally positive form with the most trifling regulations. This forms a marked contrast with our concept of God. Their cultus is then the service of God; the good or righteous person is one who performs this service by keeping and observing both the moral commandments and the ceremonial laws. That is the service of the Lord.

That the Jewish people gave itself up wholly to this service is connected with their representation of God as the Lord. This explains also their admirable steadfastness, which was not a fanaticism of conversion, as exists in Islam, [W_2: a religion that is already purged of nationality and recognizes believers only,] but a fanaticism of stubbornness. It rests entirely on the abstraction of the one Lord. Vacillation of spirit occurs only when various interests and points of view come to stand beside one another; in a combat between them, one can take one side or the other, but in this concentration on the one Lord, the spirit is completely held fast. It follows that there is no freedom vis-à-vis this firm bond; thought is tied utterly to this unity, which is the absolute authority. Many consequences follow from this. Certain institutions were regarded as divine among the Greeks too, but these had been established by human beings; the Jews, however, drew no distinction between the divine and the human in this way. [W_1: And for this reason W_2: And on account of their lack of freedom] they did not believe in immortality either; for although one might, if one wished, point to a few traces of it, these passages always remain very general in character and do not exert the least influence on religious and moral points of view. The immortality of the soul is not yet recognized; hence there is no higher purpose than the service of Jehovah, and the purpose of humanity with reference to itself is to preserve life for oneself and one's family as long as possible. According to the law, each family received a plot of land, which could not be transferred to the ownership of someone else; and this was to provide for the family. The main purpose of life was consequently the preservation of it.

[*Ed.*] [a]See Isa. 66:21. [b]See Acts 10:35. Hegel seemingly regards this verse as an Old Testament text, somewhat similar to Ps. 146:18–20 or 147:11 and Isa. 56:6–7,

578 be universally honored, all peoples should attain a cognition [of him] | such that they do not hold the knowledge of God to be something particular just for themselves. In accord with the nature of this unity, the proclaimed purpose is that all peoples should come to cognition of the true God, that this knowledge should spread throughout the whole earth. It is only a limitation in this respect and not a limitation of the religion [as such].

But at this stage the limitation is present in yet another way. Because the purpose is still in fact abstract, the consequence is that the commandments, both those in force as properly religious and those of the cultus, appear only as something given by God, as something prescribed and immutable, something eternally and firmly posited. The purpose is still abstract; and when we speak of "abstraction" in the purpose, we are referring to something immediate in its determinate being or existence—something subsisting in just this one way, something immutable.

c. The Cultus

The cultus is what is called ceremonial service, an action done because it is so commanded, so prescribed, a carrying out of [a law] that is abstract, wise indeed, and universal; but for the very reason that what is done in this way is [also] the carrying out of something particular, it therefore involves the requirement that these activities be understood, that their wisdom be known; it demands the insight that these activities are rational, that they have a connection with the particularity of human life and sensibilities (indeed, with its *legitimate* particularity). But here wisdom is not a developed wisdom. Here there are particularities in which the wisdom is not recognized; it is undeveloped and does not penetrate into feeling. To that extent the divine commandment is only an abstract precept of wisdom; in

---

although he judges correctly that it cannot date from before the Exile or post-Exilic period. ᶜSee, e.g., Jethro's avowal in Exod. 18:11: "Now I know that the Lord is greater than all gods." Hegel is referring to the widespread evidence for a period of Old Testament henotheism, to which one of the sources available to him, C. P. W. Gramberg's *Kritische Geschichte der Religionsideen des Alten Testaments,* 2 vols. (Berlin, 1829–1830), devoted an entire chapter (chap. 6). ᵈThis is in accord with one tradition: Exod. 31:18, 32:16, 34:1; Deut. 4:13, 9:10, 10:1–4; but cf. Exod. 24:4, 34:27–28.

this mode it is not understood, it is done as something external. Because God is absolute power, the activities are intrinsically indeterminate, and for that reason they are external, being determined quite arbitrarily.

The same pattern holds for other commandments beyond the scope of the cultus itself. Details of the political constitution and other institutions are likewise given as something prescribed by God only abstractly, something simply to be obeyed and forever immutable. As worldly, the political domain and statutory institutions are inherently changeable; but here they are taken to be something that is immutable. Part of this same pattern is the fact that the territory that this people has in its possession likewise counts as an immutable possession. | 579

There is one family; the condition is wholly patriarchal, the political constitution imperfect. The people possesses a land; the particular family has its particular lot, share, and family goods. This is an inalienable possession which forever belongs to the family, and the individual cannot freely dispose of it. If it was sold or obligated for debts, it reverted to the family in the Jubilee Year.[493] This is not a rising above, not an indifference to, worldly existence or property. Property in the legal sense is not yet present. These features constitute the limitation in the idea and in the realization of the idea in self-consciousness.¯

C. THE RELIGION OF EXPEDIENCY: ROMAN RELIGION[494]

[495]The religion of nature was the first form. The second, that of spiritual being-for-self, comprised the religion of beauty and the religion of sublimity. The third form of the determinate religions is that of purposiveness, the totality in this domain [of determinate religion], being primarily the unification of the religions of beauty and of sublimity.

493. [Ed.] See Lev. 25.
494. [Ed.] The treatment of Roman religion in 1827 is quite similar to that of 1824 and is of comparable length. Only the transitions are different—the transitions from Greek and Jewish to Roman religion, and from Roman to Christian—and these are analyzed in the Editorial Introduction.
495. In B's margin: 20 July 1827

1. The Concept of Purposiveness

[496]It is the next requirement of thinking that abstract necessity should be filled by particularity, by inward purpose. We had that already in the religion of sublimity; but there the purpose partly is an abstract wisdom, and partly (in its reality) is only an isolated purpose expressed in a single family that is restricted to a natural territory. The higher stage now is that this purpose is enlarged to embrace ⁻particularity in general. | This developed, extensive, ⁻[497] manifold particularity we had in the religion of beauty; the fact that it is now also posited in unity cannot furnish that truly spiritual unity, the pure spirit of thinking as in the religion of sublimity.

580

⁻First of all it [the religion of expediency] is the one relative totality,⁻[498] a totality in which those two religions do indeed lose their one-sidedness, but the two principles perish conjointly, each by means of assimilation into its opposite; still, it is this very homogeneity that interests us in them. The religion of beauty loses the concrete individuality of its gods and hence also their ethical, independent content; the gods are reduced to means. The religion of sublimity loses the orientation toward the One, the eternal, the transcendent. ⁻In their combination the two religions turn into a primarily empirical universal purpose, into a fully developed, externally universal aim. In the religion of expediency the purpose is this comprehensive [universal], but one that is external and therefore falls within the human sphere.⁻[499] [500] This [human]

496. *Precedes in L (1827?), similar in W:* In the religion of beauty we have empty necessity, and in the religion of sublimity we have unity as subjective. To the former there pertains ethical substantiality, what is right, what is present and actual in empirical self-consciousness—outside of necessity. In it we have the ethical powers represented as individuals, as spiritual, concrete subjects (particular folk-spirits, living spirits). This particularity, when reduced to a single theme, is the next determinacy.

497. W_1 *(Var) reads:* particularity, and develops it. The extensive, W_2 *(Var/Ed?) reads:* power, and power itself is developed in consequence. The extensively developed,

498. W_2 *(Var) reads:* Instead the characteristics of the earlier stages are merely taken back into a relative totality, into

499. W_2 *(Var) reads:* But their union results in progress, in that the singular purpose and the particular purposes are broadened into one universal purpose.

500. W_1 *(Var?) adds:* Thus it is the religion of the understanding.

[*Ed.*] In the *Ms.*, Hegel describes Roman religion as, among other things, the religion of the "understanding" (*Verstand*), because it is the understanding that holds fast to finite, external purposes.

purpose is to be realized, and the deity is the power for realizing it.[501]

This is the relationship of purposiveness; it has this defect, that the purpose is one posited by human beings, it is an external and empirical purpose. But this defect has its ground in a yet higher defect—in the fact that God has *this* purpose. This purpose is to be realized. According to its content it is an external purpose; so its realization is external too—within the finite, out in the world. ‾‾The | true ‾realization‾[502] would be that the purpose or the concept is   581 realized, and through this realization is posited the unity of the concept, God or the divine subject, with that in which it is realized, i.e., with objectivity.[503] This latter is then God's nature itself, it is the inner purposiveness in which the aspect of reality itself in the concept is identical with the concept; it is this process, this movement, in which the concept itself objectifies itself and posits this objective aspect as identical with itself‾‾[504]—in which it is the absolute purpose, the absolutely final purpose. But at the present stage the absolute idea is not yet present as this circle, as this self-relation; and for this reason the concept ‾that is to be realized‾[505] is something external, and the content that is to be realized is the sort that occurs within the world, in human consciousness, insofar as it is to be realized.

What the purpose here consists in is, more precisely, as follows. In the religion of sublimity the purpose, albeit a limited one, is an essential purpose as well, though one that is as yet undeveloped. Thus its inner [being] is the family, or natural ethical life as such. Now this purpose gets enlarged; the comprehensive, essential end is in general the state. This state is an external, worldly end, so that the ‾content‾[506] does not yet properly fall within God himself; it does

501. W_1 *(Var) adds:* There is an affirmative unity of God and humanity, and God is the power to realize that purpose.

502. *Thus B, Hu, similar in An;* W_1 *(Var) reads:* purposiveness

503. W_1 *(Var) adds:* with its realization.

504. W_2 *(MiscP/1831?) reads:* Genuine purposiveness is where the unity of the concept, the unity of God, the divine subject, with that in which the concept realizes itself, with objectivity and realization, is posited. It is the very nature of God that accomplishes itself in objectivity, so that it is identical with itself under the aspect of reality.

505. W_1 *(Var) reads:* the substantial, what is to be objectified,

506. W_1 *(Var) reads:* purpose

of course fall within God, but is not God's own proper nature. Also, this state is, to begin with, only the abstract state; it is the unification of human beings under one bond but in such a way that the unity is not yet a rational organization internally, and the state is not yet a rational organization internally because, so to speak, God is not yet rational organization within himself, God is not yet concrete spirit. The purposiveness is external; if it were grasped as internal, it would be God's own proper nature. Because God is not yet this 582 concrete idea, not yet his true fulfillment through himself, this | purpose or the state is not yet this rational organization or rational totality internally; hence also it does not merit the name "state." Instead it is dominion, the uniting of individuals and peoples within one bond, under one power. And since we have here the distinction between purpose and realization, this purpose is initially present as subjective only and not as developed, while the realization is conquest, acquisition of dominion, the realization of a purpose that is a priori, that takes priority over the peoples and simply fulfills itself. That is what the specification of the purpose involves; this distinction is quite essential.

We pointed out earlier that Athena is the spirit of the people. There [in Greek religion] the well-being of the city of Athens and its fortune is not the purpose of Athena; in that instance there is no relationship of a purpose that ought to be realized. On the contrary, Athena is the substantial unity, the spirit of the people, and Athens is the outward existence of this spirit, is immediately identical with it. ˉPallas is not the goddess of Athens, who has Athens for her purpose.ˉ[507] But now this category of external purposiveness is the main point upon which everything hinges.[508]

2. The Configuration of the Gods

Our second task is to describe the external appearance of this religion or the soil on which it came to be, and the type of configuration of its god or gods. As an external phenomenon, this religion is the religion of the Romans. We always introduce the external appearance

507. W_1 (Var) reads: This is not the relationship of purpose to the realization of purpose.
508. W_1 (Var) adds: That is the general characteristic of this sphere.

in order first to show that the religion accords with the determinacy of the concept; and this provides the opportunity to develop concretely the more detailed characteristics that are contained in the concept. On a superficial view, Roman religion is lumped together with Greek religion; but the spirit in the one is essentially quite different from that in the other. Even though they have configurations [of the gods] in common, these nevertheless have a quite different standing in Roman religion from what they had in Greece. The whole religion and the religious disposition is essentially distinct in each case, as is quite evident even from an external and superficial consideration. | For it is generally granted that the state or the constitution and the political fate of a people depend upon its religion, that religion is the basis and susbstance of politics, its foundation. But the spirit, culture, and ˉhistoryˉ[509] of the Greeks and the Romans are essentially distinct from one another; ˉtherefore the two religions also must be distinct.ˉ[510]

Moreover, with regard to the abstract disposition or the orientation of spirit, the first thing to note is the seriousness of the Romans. Where there is a purpose that is to be realized, an essentially firm purpose, the understanding comes into play and with it the seriousness that holds firmly to this purpose as against the variety of other impulses in the mind or in the external environment.

The cheerfulness or serenity of Greek religion, its basic dispositional feature, has its ground in the fact that there is, to be sure, a purpose in Greek religion too, something revered and holy. But at the same time the freedom from purpose is immediately present in it, in that the Greek gods are many. Each Greek god has a more or less substantial trait of its own, an ethical essentiality; but just because there are so many particularities, the consciousness or spirit also simultaneously stands above this multiplicity or manifold and is withdrawn from its particularity. Consciousness lays aside what is determined as essential and can even be treated as an end; consciousness is itself this mode of treating things ironically. In contrast, wherever there is a highest principle or highest purpose,

583

509. W (Var) reads: character
510. W₂ (Var) reads: and this in itself must lead to the distinction in religious substance.

this cheerfulness cannot occur. Moreover, the Greek god is a concrete individuality; each of these many particular individuals in turn has within it many different characteristics: it is an opulent individuality which must necessarily have contradiction in it and must exhibit it simply because the antithesis [of one and many] is not yet absolutely reconciled. Because the gods have this abundance of outward characteristics in themselves, indifference toward these particularities is also present, and frivolity can have fun with them. The contingency that we observe in the divine stories about these gods falls under
584   this heading. |

⌐The definite⌐[511] purpose is precisely the purpose of dominion, and the god is the power of realizing this purpose, the highest or universal power, this dominion over the world. We can see this god in the figure of Fortuna Publica, for example. ⌐This Fortuna Publica is the inherent⌐[512] necessity, the necessity that embodies the Roman purpose itself; it is just Rome itself. Rome is the dominant lord and, as such, is exalted as a holy, divine essence. This dominant Rome in the form of a ruling god is Jupiter Capitolinus.[513] He is the principal god who makes Rome dominant—the Jupiter who has the meaning of ruling and has a purpose within the world, and it is the Roman people through whom and for whom he accomplishes this purpose.[514]

The second point is that this God of real [world] dominion is not the genuine One, the spiritual One; and just for that reason the particular falls outside this unity of dominion. The power is only

511. W_1 (Var) reads: The character of the Roman disposition is this seriousness on the part of the understanding, a seriousness that has a definite purpose; this
512. W (Var) reads: It is the necessity that is for others a cold, unsympathetic necessity; it is the inherent
513. W (Var?) adds: a particular Jupiter—for there are many Jupiters, maybe three hundred Joves in all.
[Ed.] Hegel is probably relying on a faulty recollection of a reference in Tertullian's Apology 14.9. Tertullian quotes the figure of three hundred Joves from a satire by Varro, no longer extant, in order to pour scorn on Roman religion. A similar criticism is found in Minucius Felix, Octavius 22.6.
514. W_2 (MiscP/1831?) adds: The Roman people is the universal family, whereas in the religion of beauty many families were the divine purpose, and in the religion of the One, by contrast, one family only.

abstract, it is only power; it is not a rational organization, or a self-contained totality. For that very reason the particular makes its appearance as something that falls outside the One, the ruler. And so we have here the appearances of gods of the sort that, as indicated, may also in fact be Greek gods or else ones equated with them—for one nation sometimes does equate its gods with those of other nations. Thus the Greeks [sometimes] find their gods in Persia, Syria, and Babylon, [a discovery] which was after all at the same time something different from the distinctive way in which their own gods were intuited and characterized; only at a level of superficial generality are they to be viewed as similar. ˉBut they [the Roman gods] have no free individuality | as in Greece. Theyˉ515 appear to be old and gray, so to speak; we know not where they came from, but only that they have been introduced from elsewhere. These Roman gods have then no true meaning; in the poets they are only a lifeless imitation of the Greek gods. There is not to be found in them that consciousness or feeling of humanity and subjectivity which is the substantial element in gods as it is in humans, and in humans as in gods. They show themselves to be derivative; they appear to be machinery devoid of sense. (Mechanical gods of this kind were introduced in France also.516) They show themselves to be really gods of the understanding who have no place in ˉa beautifulˉ517 imagination.

585

Apart from these particular gods that appear to be common to both Romans and Greeks, the Romans have many of their own typical gods and forms of worship. Dominion is the goal of the citizen; but the individual is not wholly taken up with that. The

515. W₁ (Var) reads: Generally speaking, these [Roman gods]—or many of them—are the same [as the Greek gods]. But these [Roman] gods, who do not have that beautiful, free individuality [of the Greek gods], W₂ (Var) reads: Generally speaking, the particular Roman deities—or many of them—are the same as the Greek gods. However, they do not have that beautiful, free individuality, for they

516. [Ed.] Hegel criticizes French dramatists in almost identical terms in the *Lectures on Aesthetics*, without however citing the names of authors or works there either. In the *Ms.* he does specifically criticize Racine's *Phèdre* for making Hippolytus fall in love with Aricia, thus robbing the drama of ethical content.

517. W (Var) reads: a beautiful, free spirit, within a beautiful, free

individual has also a particular purpose, and these private purposes fall outside of that abstract purpose.[518] But these particular purposes become wholly and prosaically private matters; what emerges here is the shared private concerns [*Partikularität*] of human beings according to the multiple aspects of their need, or of their ties with and dependence upon nature. The god is not the concrete individuality.[519] Private life [*Partikularität*] by itself in this way, forsaken by that universality, is just the wholly common and prosaic private concerns | of human beings. But that is their human goal; one needs this thing and that, and whatever is a human goal then becomes in this sphere a determination of the divine. Thus human purposes count as divine purposes and accordingly as divine powers. Human purpose and divine purpose are one and the same; but the goal is one that is external to the idea. In this way the goal is first of all the universal goal; dominion over the world is one aspect. This is the abstract power that is oppressive and burdensome for individuals, the power that consumes and sacrifices them. The second aspect is the goal as private; for that reason private aims, needs, and powers also appear as gods, because [fulfillment in] the human sphere is the fulfillment of God.

586

This is the basic feature of Roman religion. It is the common needs that furnish the content for the gods here. So we have many highly prosaic deities. The content of these gods is practical utility; [520]they serve ordinary, practical functions. The Lares and Penates belong to the private citizen, to be sure, though they are connected with natural ethical life and piety, i.e., with the ethical unity of the family. But most [of the religion] has a content that pertains to merely private utility.

518. *L (1827?) adds, similar in* W: As against the universal of dominion there is something particular present, human purposes and interests, these private purposes, human life and human needs. Thus on one side we see this universal power that is sovereignty; in it individuals are sacrificed, having no value as such. The other side, the determinate element, falls outside the divine unity just because God is what is abstract, and the human element is essentially purpose. The filling of God with a content is the human aspect.

519. *W (Var) adds:* Jupiter is merely sovereignty, while the particular gods are dead, devoid of life and spirit, or, what is worse, they are borrowed.

520. *In B's margin:* 23 July 1827

Since this human life and activity also takes on a form that is at all events lacking the negative [moment] of evil, the satisfaction of these needs is thus a simple, peaceful, uncultured, natural state. The satisfaction of the needs appropriate to it appears as a host of gods. A state of innocence hovers before the Roman mind as the Age of Saturn. They have many festivals[521] connected with the benefit of the earth's fruitfulness and the human ability to utilize the gifts of nature. Furthermore, these are gods of the skills and types of activity that are wholly concerned with immediate needs and their satisfaction: for example, Jupiter Pistor, the baker or the skill of baking[522]; Fornax, the oven in which the grain was dried | ⁻and the oven for baking, is the oven goddess.⁻[523] Vesta [is at first] the fire for baking bread (⁻and later has a higher significance⁻[524] relating to family piety); the festival of Pales, the goddess of livestock fodder; Juno Moneta [the mint]. ⁻And [there are gods] for all sorts of human conditions [and concerns]: the goddesses Pax, Tranquillitas, Vacuna [leisure], Febris [fever], Pestis [plague], Robigo or wheat rust, and Aerumna, the goddess of trouble and care—all these relate to quite prosaic needs. Nothing could be so devoid of imagination as a circle of such gods!⁻[525] [526]

⁻This multitude of gods constitutes a very wide-ranging circle of divinities, to be sure; but it is the immediate character of the universality of Roman destiny, or of the ruling Jupiter—it lies in the very

587

521. *W (Var) adds:* and a host of gods
522. *W (Var) adds:* ranks as something divine, and the power to exercise it counts as something essential
523. *W (Var) reads:* is a goddess by herself.
524. *W (Var) reads:* for as Ἑστία she has acquired a higher significance
525. W_1 *(Var) reads:* Certain special human conditions [and concerns] are also regarded as divine power, insofar as they are injurious or useful, or insofar as they appear friendly or inimical: the goddesses Pax and Tranquillitas, Vacuna, the goddess of leisure, also Febris, Fames [famine], Robigo or wheat rust, Aerumna and Angerona (i.e., care and woe), etc. They also dedicated altars to the plague.
  Furthermore, these are gods of the skills and types of activity that are wholly concerned with immediate needs and their satisfaction—highly prosaic deities, devoid of phantasy: there is nothing more devoid of imagination than a circle of such gods. Here spirit is more perfectly at home in the finite and in what is immediately useful.
526. [*Ed.*] For this description of Roman festivals and divinities, Hegel is relying on the detailed account provided by K. P. Moritz, *Anthousa; oder, Roms Alterthümer* (Berlin, 1791).

definition of this foundation—that all these gods together, the individual gods, are gathered into one.[527] The extension of the Romans' worldly dominion consisted in this: that individuals and peoples were brought under one power and rule, and likewise their ethical powers, the divine national spirits, were ‾compressed into one pantheon,[528] assembled under one destiny, subordinated to the one Jupiter Capitolinus. Whole cargoes of gods were hauled to Rome from | Egypt, Greece, Persia (the Mithra worship), etc. Rome ‾is a potpourri of all sorts of religions;[529] the total condition is one of confusion.[530]

588

3. The Cultus

Our third topic is the character of the cultus. Its specification lies in what has already been said: God is served for the sake of a purpose, and this is a human purpose. The content does not begin, so to speak, with God—it is not the content of God's nature—but instead it begins with humans, with what human purpose is. The Romans were praised by Cicero[531] for being the most pious nation, one that[532] associates religion with everything it does.[533] This, we can say, is in fact the case. What is present [in this piety] is precisely the abstract inwardness of the Roman principle, the universality of the purpose that is the destiny in which particular individuals with their ethical life and humanity are suppressed and not permitted to have concrete presence or self-development. This universality[534] is the foundation for the way that everything is connected with the universal, and because everything is connected with this inwardness, there is religion

527. W₂ *(Var) reads:* Viewed from another aspect, however, there was also a more general religious requirement (together with the oppressive power of Roman destiny) that assembled the individual gods into a unity.

528. W₁ *(Var) reads:* suppressed by one power and sovereignty,

529. W *(Var) reads:* thus became the assembly of all religions, of the Greek, Persian, Egyptian, and Christian religions, and of the worship of Mithra;

530. W *(Var) adds:* in which every kind of cultus is jumbled together.

531. [*Ed.*] Although this does not appear to be an actual citation from Cicero, he did express himself more or less to this effect on several occasions, e.g., in *De natura deorum* 2.8.

532. W *(Var) adds:* thinks on the gods in all aspects of life, one that

533. W *(Var) adds:* and thanks the gods for everything.

534. W *(Var) adds:* and inwardness

in everything.[535] But at the same time this inwardness, this higher or universal element, is only the form; the content or purpose of this power is human, it is given by human beings, and the gods as powers are supposed to carry it out. More specifically, we see that the Romans worship the gods because they need them and when they need them, especially in ̄times of particular exigency. ̄[536] [537]For the Romans, such need is the | general theogony from which their gods arise. The oracles and the Sibylline Books are the higher means for informing the people what ̄ought to be done. ̄[538] But they are in the hands of the state, of the magistrates. Thus on the one hand the individual perishes in the universal, in the sovereign authority, in the Fortuna Publica; but on the other hand human purposes hold sway and the human subject has an independent, essential value. These extremes and their contradiction are the whirlpool in which Roman life tosses and turns.

589

Roman virtue or *virtus* is that cold patriotism [which dictates] that the individual must serve the interest of the state or the sovereign authority completely. The Romans themselves even made this negativity, this submergence of the individual in the universal, into a spectacle; it is what constitutes an essential feature in their religious plays. The religious dramas of the Romans consist of the shedding of torrents of blood. There is no ethical interest, no tragic reversal and upheaval that would have for its content an ethical interest or a misfortune that might be connected with ethical characteristics; instead the picture is that of the dry, cold conversion of death. Hundreds and thousands had to slay one another. This cold-blooded murder was a delight to their eyes; in it they beheld the nullity of

535. *W₂ (1831/MiscP?) adds:* Thus, in complete accord with the Roman spirit, Cicero derives religion from *religare,* for in fact religion in all its relationships was for the Roman spirit something that binds and commands.
[*Ed.*] This etymology of "religion" is not as unambiguous as Hegel makes out. The derivation from *religare,* which he accepts as correct, is in any event not to be found in Cicero but in Lactantius, *Divinae institutiones* 4.28.2, who there opposes Cicero's derivation from *relegendo (De natura deorum* 2.72).
536. *W (Var) reads:* the exigency of war.
537. *Precedes in W (Var):* The introduction of new gods happens at times of exigency and fear or because of vows.
538. *W (Var) reads:* is to be done or is to happen in order to obtain a benefit.

human individuality, the worthlessness of the individual (because individuality has no ethical life within it). It was the spectacle of the hollow, empty destiny that relates to human beings as a contingency, as blind caprice.

There is a further characteristic that can be linked to this, one that draws together all that we have said; despite the fact that it is not an integral part of religion, it can become caught up in it. ¨¨Since cold, irrational destiny or sheer dominion is in fact what 590 predominates, in the viewpoint prevalent in the Roman | Empire there appears, transcending individuals, the all-pervasive power, the power of arbitrariness [that is vested in] the emperor—a power that can rage wildly and without restraint, beyond all legal or ethical bounds. It was in fact quite consistent for the emperor, this supreme power, to receive divine honors; for he is purely and simply this ungrounded power over individuals and their circumstances.

This, therefore, is one aspect, the perishing of ¨the individuals;¨[539] and the other extreme stands opposed to it.¨¨[540] Namely, a goal for the power is present at the same time too. In one respect it is blind, and spirit is not yet reconciled and brought into harmony; for that reason the two sides stand one-sidedly opposed to each other. This power is a purpose, and the purpose is the human, finite purpose. This [divine] purpose is dominion over the world, and its realization is the dominion of human beings—of the Romans. In the real sense this universal purpose has its ground or seat in self-consciousness. ¨So the independence of this self-consciousness is thereby posited.¨[541] On the one side there stands an indifference to concrete life, on the other the reserve or inwardness that is equally the inwardness of the divine and that of the individual, though it is a wholly abstract inwardness on the part of the individual. This involves what constitutes for the Romans the basic feature, the fact that the abstract person as such has attained this visible status. The

539. W₁ *(Var) reads:* the individual in general;
540. W₂ *(MiscP/1831?) reads:* In contrast with this extreme of empty destiny in which the individual perishes, the destiny that finally found its personal portrayal in the power of the emperor, an arbitrary power that rages wildly regardless of ethical considerations, the other extreme is the worth of the pure singularity of subjectivity.
541. W *(Var) reads:* So this self-consciousness is independent, since the purpose pertains to it.

abstract person is the person with rights. Hence the elaboration of right[542] is an important feature of Roman culture; but right is restricted to juridical right, to the right of property. There are higher rights than this: human conscience has its right,[543] and a right much higher still is that of ethics, of morality. But these higher rights are no longer present here in their concrete and proper sense, for the abstract right of the person prevails here instead, a right that consists in the determination of property alone. It is personality, to be sure, that maintains this exalted position, but only abstract personality, only subjectivity in this abstract sense. |

591

These are the basic features of the religion of expediency.[544] Contained in it are the moments whose unification constitutes the definition of the next and final stage of religion. The moments that in the religion of expediency are individuated though they subsist in relationship and for that very reason in contradiction—when these moments (present here in a spiritless way) are united in accord with their *truth*, they give form to the determinate shape of spirit and of the religion of spirit.

542. W *(Var) adds:* or the category of property
543. W *(Var) adds:* (for it is equally a right)
544. W *(1831) adds:* [W_1: In this religion God was known as what is purposive too; but here the purpose W_2: In this religion of purposiveness the purpose] is none other than the Roman state, so that the Roman state is the abstract power over all other national spirits. In the Roman pantheon the gods of all the peoples are assembled and cancel out one another through the very fact of their union. The Roman spirit [W_1: brings to pass this misfortune of the destruction of the beautiful life and consciousness. It was fate [*Fatum*] as the Roman spirit that destroyed this happiness and serenity of the preceding religion. W_2: as this fate destroyed the happiness and serenity of the beautiful life and consciousness of the preceding religions, and compressed all their shapes into unity and uniformity.] This abstract power it was which produced this monstrous misery and a universal sorrow, a sorrow that served to prepare the birth pangs of the religion of truth. [W_1: By it the limitation and finitude in the religion of the beautiful spirit was negated too.] Repenting of the world, laying aside finitude, and [W_1: renouncing all hope of finding satisfaction in this world W_2: despairing of finding satisfaction in temporality and finitude, a despair that gained the upper hand in the spirit of the world]—all of this served to prepare the soil for the genuine, spiritual religion. This preparation had to be carried out on the part of humanity [W_1: —"When the time was fulfilled," we are told, "God sent his Son"; the time was fulfilled when this despair of finding satisfaction in temporality and finitude had gained the upper hand in the spirit. W_2: in order that "the time might be fulfilled."]

[*Ed.*] A reference to the New Testament concept of the fullness of time; cf. Mark 1:15; Gal. 4:4; Eph. 1:10.

PART III
THE CONSUMMATE RELIGION

THE LECTURES OF 1827

Introduction

1. Definition of This Religion²

ˉThe first [division] was the *concept of religion* in general; the second, religion in its particularity or *determinate religion,* the last of these being the religion of expediency. The third is the *consummate religion,* the religion that is for itself, that is objective to itself.

This is always the pattern in scientific knowledge: first the concept; then the particularity of the concept—reality, objectivity; and finally the stage in which the original concept is an object to itself, is for itself, becomes objective to itself, is related to itself. So this is the pattern in philosophy: first the concept of the conceptualizing science—the concept that *we* have. But at the end science itself grasps its concept, so that this concept is for itself.ˉ³

---

1. [*Ed.*] The title found in the Königsberg Anonymous, used by Lasson, is: "Part III. The Revelatory Religion." Erdmann offers as a title the words used by Hegel in the second sentence: "Part III. The Consummate Religion, the Religion That Is For Itself, or the Religion That Is Objective to Itself." The titles in the extant transcripts are as follows: *An:* "III. The Revealed Religion"; *Hu:* "Part III. The Christian Religion"; *B:* "III. The Revelatory Religion, or the Religion That Is Objective to Itself."

2. [*Ed.*] In this section, Hegel briefly summarizes the substance of the introductory remarks found in the *Ms.* and (in considerably expanded form) in the 1824 lectures. The agenda of the 1827 introduction is different, as we shall see below in Secs. 2–3. The polemic against the subjectivism of present-day theology is past, and Hegel now faces a different challenge.

3. *W (1831) reads:* We have now arrived at the realized concept of religion, the *consummate religion,* in which it is the concept itself that is its own object. We have defined religion more precisely as the *self-consciousness of God.* Self-consciousness

And therefore the sphere into which we are now entering is the concept of religion that is for itself, i.e., the *revelatory religion*. Religion is for the first time what is revelatory, is manifested, when the concept of religion is for itself, i.e., when religion or its concept has become objective to itself—not in limited, finite objectivity, but such that it is objective to itself in accord with its concept. |

178

This can be defined more precisely as follows. Religion, in accord with its general concept, is the consciousness of God as such, consciousness of absolute essence. Consciousness, however, is a differentiating, a division within itself. Thus we have already two moments: consciousness and absolute essence. These two are, first of all, externalized forms in a finite nexus and relationship—empirical consciousness on the one hand, and essence in the abstract sense on the other. They stand in a finite relationship to each other, and to this extent they are both finite; in consciousness we accord-

---

in its character as consciousness has an object, and it is conscious of itself in this object; this object is also consciousness, but it is consciousness as an object, and consequently it is finite consciousness, a consciousness that is distinct from God, from the absolute. Determinateness and consequently finitude are present in this form of consciousness. God is self-consciousness; he knows himself in a consciousness that is distinct from him, which is implicitly the consciousness of God, but is also the divine consciousness explicitly since it knows its identity with God, an identity that is mediated, however, by the negation of finitude. It is this concept that constitutes the content of religion. We define God when we say that he distinguishes himself from himself and is an object for himself but that in this distinction he is purely identical with himself—that he is *spirit*. This concept is now realized; consciousness knows this content and knows that it is utterly interwoven with this content: in the concept that is the process of God, consciousness is itself a moment. Finite consciousness knows God only to the extent that God knows himself in it; thus God is spirit, indeed the Spirit of his community, i.e., of those who worship him. This is the consummate religion, the concept that has become objective to itself. Here it is manifest what God is: he is no longer a "beyond," an unknown, for he has made known to human beings what he is, and has done so not merely in an external history but in consciousness. We have here, therefore, the religion of the manifestation of God, since God knows himself in finite spirit. God is utterly revelatory: this is the [essential] circumstance here. The transition was our having seen that the knowledge of God as free spirit is still burdened with finitude and immediacy so far as its content is concerned. This finitude had yet to be done away with by the labor of spirit; it is nothingness, and we have seen how this nothingness has been made manifest to consciousness. The unhappiness, the anguish of the world was the condition, the preparation on the subjective side for the consciousness of free spirit as absolutely free and consequently infinite spirit.

We dwell initially on (A) the universal features of this sphere.

ingly have two elements that are related to each other in a finite, external way. Thus consciousness knows even the absolute essence only as something finite, not as what is true. God, however, is himself consciousness, differentiating himself within himself. Since God, as this differentiating of himself within himself, is consciousness, so is he, as consciousness, such that he gives himself as object for what we call the side of consciousness.

But when religion grasps itself,[4] its content and | object is this whole—*consciousness relating itself to its essence,* knowing itself as its essence and knowing its essence as its own—and that is spiritual religion.

This means that *spirit* is the object of religion,[5] and the object of the latter—essence knowing itself—is spirit. Here for the first time, spirit is as such the object, the content of religion, and spirit *is* only *for* spirit. Since it is content or object, it is, as spirit, this self-knowing or self-differentiating, and it itself furnishes the other side, that of subjective consciousness, which appears as finite. It is the religion whose fulfillment is itself.

2. The Positivity and Spirituality of This Religion[6]

This is the abstract determination of this idea or the sphere where religion is in fact idea. This is because an idea in the philosophical

179

4. *Thus also W; L (1827?) adds:* the other determination in it emerges. The consciousness of God means that finite consciousness has this God, who is its essence, as an object—it knows him as its essence, sets him over against itself. Thus

5. *Thus L, similar in B, Hu, An; W (1831) adds:* Thus we have two elements, consciousness and object; but in the religion that has itself as its fulfillment, that is revelatory, that has comprehended itself, religion or the content itself is the object.

6. [Ed.] This section is new in the 1827 lectures, although it incorporates some materials used elsewhere in the earlier lectures. Against the charges of his critics, Hegel insists that Christianity is a *positive* religion, whose truth is mediated to consciousness in sensible historical fashion, and which has a necessary element of external authority. Yet the essential, rational truth revealed by this religion, while mediated positively, derives solely from its *spirituality* and can be verified only by the witness of spirit (see n. 16), not by historical proofs. Here materials from the Ms.'s treatment of the cultus in Part III and from the 1824 lectures' treatment of the cultus in Part I are incorporated into the 1827 introduction to the revelatory religion. In contrast with the whole debate in late Enlightenment thought over reason versus revelation, Hegel claimed that the *revealed* (positive) religion is also one in which reason and truth are made open, manifest (*offenbar*). The term "revelatory" gathers up both the positivity and the spirituality of this religion.

sense[7] is the concept that has an object, has determinate being, reality, objectivity; it objectifies itself, and is no longer merely inner and subjective, but its objectivity is at the same time a return to itself.[8]

The consummate religion is the idea and has as its object what it [actually] is, namely, the consciousness of essence; thereby it is objectified.[9] This absolute religion is the *revelatory* [*offenbar*] religion, the religion that has itself as its content and fulfillment. But it is also called the *revealed* [*geoffenbart*] religion—which means, on the one hand, that it is revealed by God, that God has given himself for human beings to know what he is; and on the other hand, that it is a revealed, *positive* religion in the sense that it has come to humanity from without, has been given to it. In view of the peculiar meaning that attaches to the positive, it is interesting to see what positivity is.

In the first place, the absolute religion is, of course, a positive
180 religion in the | sense that everything that is *for* consciousness is *objective* to consciousness. *Everything must come to us from outside.* The sensible is thus something positive. Initially there is nothing positive other than what we have before us in immediate intuition. Everything spiritual also comes to us in this fashion, whether it be the spiritual in general or the spiritual in finite or historical form. This mode of external spirituality, and spirit expressing itself outwardly, are likewise positive. The ethical realm, the laws of freedom, entail a higher, purer spirituality; the ethical by nature has nothing *externally* spiritual about it; it is not something external and contingent but is the nature of rational spirit itself. But even the ethical comes to us in an external mode, chiefly in the form of education, instruction, doctrine: it is simply given to us as something valid as it stands. Laws—e.g., civil laws, laws of the state—are likewise something positive: they come to us and are there for us as valid. They are not merely something external

7. [*Ed.*] See esp. *Science of Logic*, pp. 755 ff. (*GW* 12:173 ff.).

8. *Thus B, Hu, An; L, W (1827?) add:* or—to the extent that we speak of the concept as a goal—is the fulfilled, accomplished goal, which precisely as such is objective.

9. *Thus B; L (1827?) adds, similar in W:* [now] exists in a fashion similar to how at first it was the concept—or *our* concept—and the concept alone.

for us, as are sensible objects, so that we can leave them behind or pass them by; rather, in their externality, they also ought to have, for us subjectively, an essential, subjectively binding power. When we grasp or recognize the law, when we find it rational that crime should be punished, this is not because law is positive but rather because it has an essential status for us. It is not simply valid for us externally because it *is* so; rather it is also valid for us internally, it is rationally valid as something essential, because it also is itself internal and rational. Positivity does not in any way detract from its character as rational and therefore as something that is our own. The laws of freedom always have a positive aspect, an aspect marked by reality, externality, contingency in their appearance. Laws must be determinate. Externality already enters into the determination or the quality of punishment, and even more into its quantity. Positivity simply cannot be removed from punishment but is wholly necessary to it. ˉThis final determination of the immediate, this immediate [factor],ˉ10 is something positive, i.e., not at all rational in and for itself. For example, in the case of punishment, round numbers determine the amount of the penalty; | it is not possible to determine by reason what the absolutely just penalty is. Whatever is positive *according to its nature* is also irrational. It must be determinate, and is so in such a way that it has or contains ˉnothing rationalˉ11 in it.

This aspect is also necessary in the case of the revelatory religion. Since historical, externally appearing elements are found in it, there is also present a positive and contingent [feature], which can just as well take one form as another.12 Because of the externality and appearance that are posited along with it [i.e., revelation], this positive [feature] is always present. However, we must distinguish between the positive as such, the abstract positive, and ˉ[the positive in the form of] rational law.ˉ13 The law of freedom is not valid simply because it is there, but rather because it is the determination

181

10. *L reads:* —this final determination of the immediate. This immediate [factor] *W (Var) reads:* This final determinacy of the immediate

11. *Thus Hu, W; L reads:* a rational element

12. *Thus L, Hu, An; W (Var) adds:* This occurs also in the case of religion.

13. *Thus L; W₁ (Var) reads:* law, the rational law. *W₂ (Var) reads:* the positive in the form of and as the law of freedom.

of our rationality itself. When it is known in this way, then it is not something that is merely positive or externally valid. Religion also appears as positive in the entire content of its doctrines. But it should not remain in this form; it should not be a matter of mere representation or of bare remembrance.

The second aspect of positivity is connected with the verification of religion, namely, that this external [feature] should bear witness to the truth of a religion, and should be regarded as the ground of its truth. Verification may sometimes take the form of the positive as such—namely, *miracles* and *testimonies,* ˉwhich are supposed to verify the fact that this individual has done this or that,ˉ[14] has given this or that doctrine. Miracles are positive occurrences, sensible givens, perceptible alterations in the sensible world, and this perception itself is sensible because it consists in a sensible alteration. In regard to this form of positivity, it has already been remarked[15]ˑ that it certainly | can bring about a kind of verification for human beings as sentient beings. But that is only the beginning of verification, it is the sensible or as it were unspiritual verification, by which precisely what is spiritual cannot be verified. The spiritual as such cannot be directly verified by the unspiritual, the sensible. The chief thing about this aspect of miracles is that in this way they are actually put aside. For, on the one hand, the understanding can attempt to explain the miracles naturally, it can advance many probabilities against them; but this involves confining one's attention to the external, eventlike character of miracles and directing one's arguments against this aspect. What matters most to reason with respect to miracles, on the other hand, is that what is spiritual cannot be verified externally. For the spiritual is higher than the external; it can be verified only from within and through itself; it is confirmed only in and through itself. This is what can be called "the witness of spirit."[16]

182

14. L *reads:* which are supposed to verify the fact that this individual *Hu reads:* that this individual has done this or that, *An reads:* that this individual W_1 *(Var) reads:* the verification that this individual W_2 *(Var) reads:* which are supposed to prove the divinity of the revealing individual, and that this individual

15. [*Ed.*] See above, pp. 159–161.

16. [*Ed.*] The expression *Zeugnis des Geistes* contains an ambivalence or double meaning for Hegel. On the one hand, it can refer to the witness of the Holy Spirit or the Spirit of God, by which authentic faith is awakened in human subjects; on

This very point has found expression in religious narratives. Moses performs miracles before Pharaoh, and the Egyptian magicians imitate him;[17] which is to say that no great value is placed on miracles. The main point, however, is that Christ indeed says, "You demand signs and wonders," and so reviles the Pharisees, who demand from him attestations of this sort;[18] he himself also says, "After ˉmy deathˉ[19] many will come who perform miracles in my name, but I have not recognized them."[20] Here Christ himself rejects miracles as a genuine criterion of truth. This is the essential point, and we must hold fast to it. Verification by miracles, as well as the attack upon miracles, belong to a lower sphere that concerns us not at all.

The witness of spirit is the authentic witness. It can be of diverse sorts. ˉIn an indeterminate, more general way,ˉ[21] it can be whatever accords with spirit, whatever awakens in it, or produces in its inwardness, a deeper resonance. In history, all that is noble, lofty, and divine speaks to us internally; to it our spirit bears witness. This witness may remain nothing more than this general resonance, this inner agreement, | this empathy and sympathy. But beyond this, 183 the witness of spirit may also be connected with insight and thought. Insofar as this insight is not sensible in character, it belongs directly to thought; it appears in the form of reasons, distinctions, etc., in the form of mental activity, exercised along with and according to the specific forms of thought, the categories. This thinking may

the other hand, it can refer to the witness of *our* spirit to spiritual truth. The two meanings are in fact two aspects of a single truth, since the Spirit of God witnesses only in and through our spirits: there is no divine witness apart from the activity of human spirit; however, the latter is not an autonomous, singular activity but the inner working of the one holy and universal Spirit. In some contexts, especially those concerned with the formation of the community of the Spirit, Hegel intends the former meaning, while in others (such as the paragraphs immediately following) the stress falls on the latter. In accord with our principle of capitalizing "spirit" when it has the representational-religious function of referring to the Holy Spirit, we translate as either "the witness of the Spirit" or "the witness of spirit," depending on how we construe the primary intention of specific passages.

17. [*Ed.*] See Exod. 7:9–12, 22; 8:3.
18. [*Ed.*] A conflation of John 4:48 and Matt. 12:38–39.
19. *Thus An; L reads:* my resurrection
20. [*Ed.*] A paraphrase of Matt. 7:22–23.
21. *Thus L; W (Var) reads:* indeterminately and generally,

appear in more or less mature forms; it may serve as the presupposition of one's heart or of one's spiritual life in general—the presupposition of universal principles, which are acknowledged to be valid and which direct the life of a human being, serving as one's maxims. These need not be conscious maxims, but they are the means by which the character of a human being is formed, the universal that has obtained a firm foothold in one's spirit. This is a permanent, governing element in one's spirit. It is upon firm foundations of this kind, on presuppositions like this, on ethical principles of this type, that the powers of reasoning and defining can begin. In this respect the levels of development and ways of life of human beings vary considerably, just as do their needs. The highest need of the human spirit, however, is so to think that the witness of spirit is present [for it] not merely in that first resonating mode of sympathy, nor in the second way of providing firm foundations[22] upon which views may be established and firm presuppositions from which conclusions can be drawn and deductions made. The witness of spirit in its highest form is that of philosophy, according to which the concept develops the truth purely as such from itself without presuppositions. As it develops, it cognizes—in and through its development it has insight into—the necessity of the truth.

Faith and thought have often been opposed in such a way that we say: one can ˜be convinced˜[23] of God, of the truths of religion, in no other way than by thinking.[24] But the witness of spirit can be present in manifold and various ways; it is not required that for
184 all of | humanity the truth be brought forth in a philosophical way. The needs of human beings are different in accord with their cultivation and their free spiritual development; and this diversity in accord with the stage of development also encompasses that standpoint [we call] trust or belief on the basis of *authority*. Miracles

22. *Thus L; W (Var) adds:* and principles
23. *Thus B; L, W₁ (Var) read:* have an awareness   W₂ *(Var) reads:* have a genuine conviction
24. *Thus B, An, similar in Hu; L, W (Var) add:* Hence the proofs of the existence of God have been declared the sole means of knowing the truth and of being convinced.

also have their place here, but it is interesting to note that miracles have been reduced to a minimum—namely, to those recounted in the Bible.

[25]That sympathy of which we have spoken earlier, where the spirit or the soul cries out, "Yes, that is the truth"—that sympathy is so immediate a form of certainty that it can be as secure for one person as thinking is for another. [It is] something so immediate that just for this reason it is something posited, given, or positive; [it is so immediate] that precisely this immediacy has the form of positivity and is not brought forth by means of the concept.[26] We ought to bear in mind, however, that only human beings have religion. Religion has its seat and soil in the activity of thinking. The heart and feeling that directly sense the truth of religion are not the heart and feeling of an animal but of a thinking human being; they are a thinking heart and a thinking feeling, and whatever [measure] of religion is in this heart and feeling is a thought of this heart and feeling. [27]But to be sure, insofar as we begin to draw conclusions, to reason, to give grounds, to advance to the categories of thought, this is invariably thinking.

Since the doctrines of the Christian religion are present in the Bible, they are thereby given in a positive fashion; and if they are subjectively | appropriated, if spirit gives witness to them, this can happen in an entirely immediate fashion, with one's innermost being, one's spirit, one's thought, one's reason, being touched by them and assenting to them. Thus the Bible is for Christians the basis, the fundamental basis, which has this effect on them, which strikes a chord within them, and gives firmness to their convictions.

185

---

25. *Precedes in L (1827?), similar in* W₂: In general, however, there is still something positive in these different forms of the witness of spirit.

26. *Thus L with Hu, An;* W₂ *(Var) reads:* Because of its immediacy, sympathy—this immediate certainty—is itself something positive, and the reasoning that proceeds from something posited or given has just such a foundation.

[*Ed.*] Cf. the following footnote.

27. *Precedes in L (1827?):* Likewise, as we have noted in the second instance, in any process of reasoning that has a firm foundation and presupposition, the foundation is something positive, posited, given. Reasoning has a foundation that has not investigated itself, that has not been produced by the concept.

[*Ed.*] Cf. the preceding footnote.

Beyond this, however, human beings, because they are able to think, do not remain in the immediacy of assent and testimony, but also indulge in thoughts, in deliberation, in considerations concerning this immediate witness. These thoughts and considerations result in ˉa developedˉ28 religion; in its most highly developed form it is *theology* or scientific religion, whose content, as the witness of spirit, is [also] known in scientific fashion.

But here the opposing thesis perhaps comes in, for the theologians say that we ought to hold exclusively to the Bible. In one respect, this is an entirely valid principle. For there are in fact many people who are very religious and hold exclusively to the Bible, who do nothing but read the Bible, cite passages from it, and in this way lead a very pious, religious life. Theologians, however, they are not; such an attitude has nothing of a scientific, theological character.29 But just as soon as religion is no longer simply the reading and repetition of passages, as soon as what is called explanation or interpretation begins, as soon as an attempt is made by inference and exegesis to find out the *meaning* of the words in the Bible, then we embark upon the process of reasoning, reflection, thinking; and the question then becomes how we should exercise this process of thinking, and whether our thinking is correct or not. It helps not at all to say that one's thoughts are based on the Bible. As soon as these thoughts are no longer simply the words of the Bible, their content is given a form, more specifically, a logical form. Or certain presuppositions are made with regard to this content, and with these one enters into the process of interpretation. These

---

28. *Thus L, B, An; W (Var) reads:* still further development in

29. *Thus L, An, W₁, similar in Hu; W₂ (MiscP) adds:* Goeze, the Lutheran zealot, had a celebrated collection of Bibles; the Devil quotes the Bible too, but that by no means makes the theologian.

[Ed.] The Hamburg Hauptpastor Johann Melchior Goeze was Lessing's chief opponent in the controversy surrounding Reimarus's *Fragments*. It began with the publication of Goeze's book, *Versuch einer Historie der gedruckten niedersächsischen Bibeln vom Jahr 1470 bis 1621* (Halle, 1775), with which it is unlikely that Hegel was familiar. But Lessing alluded many times to Goeze's Bible collection; see his *Anti-Goeze, d.i. Notgedrungene Beiträge zu den freiwilligen Beiträgen des Herrn Pastor Goeze* (Braunschweig, 1778), nos. 1, 9, in Lessing, *Vermischte Schriften*, vol. 6 (Leipzig, 1791), pp. 159, 275 (Lessing, *Sämtliche Schriften* 13:142, 195).

presuppositions are the permanent element in interpretation; one brings along representations and principles, which guide the interpretation. | ⎜186

The interpretation of the Bible exhibits its content, however, in the form of a particular age; ˉthe interpretation of a thousand years ago ˉ[30] was wholly different from that of today. Among the presuppositions that one brings to the Bible today belong, for example, the views that humanity is good by nature, or that we cannot cognize God.[31] Thus here the positive can enter again in another form: we bring with us certain propositions such as that human beings have these feelings, are constituted in this or that particular way. So everything then depends on whether this content, these views and propositions, are true; and this is no longer the Bible, but instead words that spirit comprehends internally. If spirit expresses in a different way what is expressed in the Bible, then this is already a form that spirit gives [the content], the form of thinking. The form that one gives to this content has to be investigated. Here again the positive enters, in the sense that, for example, the formal logic of inference has been presupposed, namely, finite relations of thought. In terms of the ordinary relations of inference, only the finite can be grasped and cognized, only the understandable, but not the divine. This way of thinking is not adequate to the divine content; the latter is ruined by it. Insofar as theology is not a mere rehearsal of the Bible but goes beyond the words of the Bible and concerns itself with what kinds of feelings exist internally, it utilizes forms of thinking, it engages in thinking. If it uses these forms haphazardly, ˉbecause one ˉ[32] has presuppositions and prejudices, the result is something contingent and arbitrary. [What is pertinent here] can only be forms that are genuine and logically developed in terms of

30. *Thus Hu; An reads:* indeed a thousand years ago [it] *L reads:* the first interpretation in the early period of the church *W (Var) reads:* the first interpretation

31. *L (1827?) adds, similar in W:* Imagine how someone with these prejudices in mind must distort the Bible! People bring these prejudices to the Bible, although the meaning of the Christian religion is precisely the cognition of God; it is indeed the religion in which God has revealed himself, has said what he is.

[*Ed.*] The allusions are to Kant and Jacobi.

32. *Thus L; W (Var) reads:* because it

necessity. But the investigation of these forms of thought falls to philosophy alone. Thus theology itself does not know what it wants when it turns against philosophy. Either it carries on unaware of the fact that it needs these forms, that it itself | thinks, and that it is a question of proceeding in accord with thought; or ˉit fostersˉ[33] a deception, by reserving for itself the option to think as it chooses, in contingent fashion, when it knows that the cognition of the true nature of spirit is damaging to this arbitrary sort of cognition. This contingent, arbitrary way of thinking is the positive element that enters in here. Only the *concept* on its own account liberates itself truly and thoroughly from the positive. For in philosophy and in religion there is found this highest freedom, which is thinking itself as such.

187

Doctrine itself, the content, also takes on the form of the positive, as noted above; it is valid, it is firmly established, it is ˉan entity that has to be reckoned with in actual society.ˉ[34] Everything rational, every law, has this form.[35] But only its *form* is positive; its *content* must be that of spirit. The Bible has this form of positivity, yet according to one of its own sayings,[36] "The letter kills, but the Spirit gives life" [2 Cor. 3:6]. It is a question, then, as to which spirit we bring in, which spirit gives life to the positive. We must know that we bring with us a concrete spirit, a thinking, reflecting, sensing spirit; we must be aware of this spirit, which is at work, comprehending the content. This comprehension is not a passive acceptance, but since it is spirit that comprehends, it is at the same time its activity. Only in the mechanical sphere does one of the sides remain passive in the process of reception. Spirit, therefore, reaches out to, attains the positive realm; it has its representations

33. *Thus L; W₁ (Var) reads:* it is   *W₂ (Var) reads:* it is not serious about it but rather is

34. *L (Var) reads:* an entity reckoned with by everyone.   *Hu reads:* a thing to be reckoned with in actual society.   *W (Var) reads:* something binding, to be reckoned with in society.

[*Ed.*] Cf. the following footnote.

35. *Thus L; W (Var) adds:* namely, that it is an entity and, as such, is what is essential and binding for everyone.

[*Ed.*] Cf. the preceding footnote.

36. *In B's margin:* 26 July 1827

and concepts, it is logical in essence, it is a thinking activity. This, its [own] activity, spirit must know.

This thinking can proceed in one or another of the categories of finitude. It is, however, spirit that begins in this way from the positive but is itself there essentially alongside it. It is to become the true and proper Spirit, the Holy Spirit, which comprehends the divine and knows its content to be divine. This is the witness of spirit, | which, as we have shown above,[37] may be more or less 188 developed. In regard to positivity, the main point is that spirit conducts itself in a thinking fashion and its activity occurs within the categories or determinations of thought; here ˉspirit is purely active, sentient, or rational.ˉ[38] But most people are not conscious of the fact that they are active in this reception. Theologians are like the Englishman who didn't know that he was speaking prose;[39] because they work exegetically and (so they believe) in a passively receptive way, [they] have no inkling of the fact that they are thereby active and reflective. But if thinking is merely contingent, it abandons itself to the categories of finite content, of finitude, of finite thinking, and is incapable of comprehending the divine in the content; it is not the divine but the finite spirit that moves in such categories. As a result of such a finite thinking and comprehending of the divine, or of what is in and for itself, as a result of this finite thinking of the absolute content, the fundamental doctrines of

37. [Ed.] See above, pp. 397–399.

38. *Thus L; W (Var) reads:* spirit is active, whether it be in sentient or rational fashion, etc.

39. [Ed.] Hegel is alluding here to the dialogue between M. Jourdain and the teacher of philosophy in Molière's *Le Bourgeois Gentilhomme,* act 2, scene 4, where the philosopher assures M. Jourdain that he is indeed speaking prose (and that one must really speak either prose or verse). Hegel erroneously ascribes M. Jourdain's lack of culture to an Englishman. That this is actually an error of Hegel and not of Hube's transcription (our only source for this passage) is confirmed by the following comment about Newton's lack of awareness of the conceptual presuppositions of the physical sciences, found in the *Lectures on the History of Philosophy* 3:323 (*Werke* 15:447): "Newton is so complete a barbarian as regards his conceptions that his case is like that of another of his countrymen who was surprised and rejoiced to learn that he had talked prose all his life, not having had any idea that he was so accomplished." It was probably because of this association with Newton that the erroneous ascription of M. Jourdain's naïveté to an Englishman came about. Cf. Hegel, *Briefe* 2:251.

Christianity have for the most part disappeared from dogmatics. Philosophy ¯is preeminently, though not exclusively,¯⁴⁰ what is at present essentially orthodox; the propositions that have always been valid, the basic truths of Christianity, are maintained and preserved by it.

In our present consideration of this religion, we shall not set to work in *merely historical* fashion, which would entail starting with external matters, but rather we shall proceed *conceptually.*⁴¹ The form of activity that begins with externals appears to be [capable of] comprehension only on one side, while on the other it is ¯independent.¯⁴² Our attitude here essentially takes the form of an activity such that thinking is conscious of itself, of the process involved in the categories of thought—a thinking that has tested and recognized itself, that knows how it thinks and which are the finite and which the true categories of thought. The fact that we began from the other side, from the positive side, ¯from the individual | development of the subject, from education in faith—[this has]¯⁴³ to be put aside insofar as we proceed *scientifically.*

189

3. Survey of Previous Developments⁴⁴

This is the point at which to survey our previous course and to discuss the relation of this course to the final stage of religion; here

40. *Thus L, similar in W; An (Var) reads:* alone is

41. [*Ed.*] In the *Philosophy of Religion* as a whole, Hegel offers a speculative transfiguration of religion, not a merely historical (*historisch*) description of it. This is true also of the Christian religion, to which he now turns; it is already being viewed and interpreted from the standpoint of the absolute philosophy. Hegel does not intend to deny the positive, historical (*geschichtlich*) character of religion, and of the Christian religion especially; but since his intention is to proceed *scientifically* in this work, as he says in the last sentence of the paragraph, and since scientific cognition entails the speculative grasp of what is true, actual, rational, and spiritual, merely historical details are deemphasized.

42. *Thus Hu; L, W (Var) read:* [merely] activity.

43. *Thus An with Hu; L (Var) reads:* occurs in education etc., and has   *W (Var) reads:* occurs in education and is necessary there, but here it has

44. [*Ed.*] This section expands considerably the brief concluding section to the 1824 introduction (Sec. 4), where Hegel discussed the relation of the consummate religion to the preceding religions. The present survey is developed in rather strictly logical categories and describes the process by which finite spirit "rises" to the absolute through the various forms of religious consciousness, which, when taken together, constitute the history of religion. The survey reflects Hegel's penchant for

for the first time we are able to comprehend the course as a whole and its meaning. We refer back to what has already been said.[45] Religion is spirit as consciousness of its essence. On the one hand, there is a spirit that is the spirit of distinction; the other spirit is spirit as essence, as true, nonfinite spirit. This separation or diremption, this distinguishing, which resides in the concept of spirit, is what we have called the elevation of spirit from finite to infinite.[46] This elevation appears metaphysically in the proofs for the existence of God. Finite spirit makes infinite spirit its object, knows it as its own essence. If we allow ourselves to speak this way, the word "finite" becomes an indefinite, abstract word, in turn making the word "infinite" also indefinite; and spirit, defined as infinite, is designated only in an indeterminate way—indeed, not only indeterminately but also one-sidedly.

One must be clear about these logical definitions of "finite" and "infinite."[47] When we keep them apart, we are in the realm of finite thinking. When we say "infinite spirit," the word "infinite" is itself understood in a one-sided way because it has the finite over against it. In order not to be one-sided, spirit must encompass finitude within itself, and finitude in general means nothing more than a process of self-distinguishing. Consciousness is precisely the mode of finitude of spirit: distinction is present here. One thing is on one side, another on the other side; something has its limit or end in something else, and in this way they are limited. Finitude is this distinguishing, which in spirit takes the form of consciousness. Spirit must have consciousness, distinction, otherwise it is not spirit; accordingly, this is the moment of finitude in it. It must have this character of finitude within itself—that may seem blasphemous. But if it did not have it within itself, and thus if it confronted finitude

---

summing up previous stages of the discussion, but it may also reflect the closer association with the *Logic* that is characteristic of the 1827 lectures as a whole. Hegel is at pains to show in these lectures that the concept of religion and the various historical forms that it assumes correspond strictly to logical moments of the concept itself.

45. [*Ed.*] See above, pp. 128 ff., 391.

46. *L (1827?) adds:* Just as spirit defines itself as finite, it [also] defines itself vis-à-vis spirit as infinite.

47. [*Ed.*] For this and what follows, see *Science of Logic*, pp. 137–156 (cf. *GW* 11:78–85).

190   from the other | side, then its infinitude would be a spurious infinitude. When we view the characteristic of finitude as something contradictory to God, then we take the finite as something fixed, independent—not as something transitional, but rather as something essentially independent, a limitation that remains utterly such—and then we have not properly recognized the nature of the finite and the infinite. The finite is not, however, the absolute. Neither are finite things absolute, nor is the absolute the definition of finitude logically or in thought; rather the definition of the latter is precisely to be not true in itself. If God has the finite only over against himself, then he himself is finite and limited. Finitude must be posited in God himself, not as something insurmountable, absolute, independent, but above all as this process of distinguishing that we have seen in spirit and in consciousness—a distinguishing that, because it is a transitory moment and because finitude is no truth, is also eternally self-sublating. Infinite spirit is posited in a one-sided abstraction when we say that the finite elevates itself to the infinite. The finite is here taken just as indefinitely as infinitude. This is the deficiency; this abstraction of the infinite has to be sublated, and likewise the abstraction of the finite, in which we initially perceive the finitude. The *consideration* of finitude is what gives us development and progressive determination.

We began with the *concept of religion*.[48] Religion is the spirit that relates itself to itself and thus to its essence, to true spirit; it is reconciled with true spirit and finds itself in it. Because this concept of religion is *only* a concept, it is finite; it is not yet the *idea,* the realization, the actualization of the concept. It is *in* itself the true, but it is not yet *for* itself; but the essence of spirit is to be for itself what it is in itself or what its concept is. Since, therefore, finitude is so defined that this being-in-itself is only spirit in its concept or religion in its concept, any advance appears to sublate the concept, i.e., the one-sidedness, deficiency, or mere abstraction of the concept, whether it be grasped now as finitude or as abstract infinitude. Our advance had, therefore, the signification or character of sublating this abstraction. The second point is this: whatever is

48. [*Ed.*] As treated in Part I of the lectures.

conceptual to begin with | —i.e., merely conceptual or subjective   191
in the sense that it has the content only in itself—is at the same
time the first or immediate. Whatever is only in itself or in accord
with its concept—such as the human being as a child—is, in its
existence as a determinate being, at first only something immediate;
and immediacy, therefore, is the finitude that we have to deal with
first.

So this is the course we have taken. First we have considered the
concept of spirit or of religion. But this in-itself, or the concept
merely as such, is nothing but the immediate modality of the concept, immediate being, and this we have in *the natural*.[49] The natural
is whatever is *immediately;* finitude is immediate being. In its immediate being, spirit is empirical consciousness, immediate self-
consciousness, which views itself as essence, knows itself as the
power of nature. This immediate spirit is indeed fulfilled, determinate in itself, concrete, but it is only empirically concrete. For
the content by which it is filled is the content of inclinations and
desires, instincts and passions; and this first fulfillment is the fulfillment of spirit's merely natural state. This constitutes the finitude
of spirit, its natural, empirical self-consciousness. Spirit is fulfilled,
but empirically, not by its concept; but what is needful is that it
must become *for* itself what it is *in* itself, it must arrive at its concept.
This progression is logical: it lies in the nature of the determining
process itself to determine itself further in this way—this is logical
necessity.

The further form of this finitude we have also seen. This finitude,
which is unmediated being, can also be defined as the unitary being
of immediate, finite spirit with itself, or as spirit that has not yet
arrived at the separation through which it distinguishes this natural
state and desire from itself, and therefore it is not yet self-contained,
it has not yet attained the determination of freedom. In order to
be free, spirit must remove this immediate, natural, empirical state,
withdrawing from it. The next step, therefore, is the withdrawal-

49. [*Ed.*] "Nature Religion" constitutes the first of the three main divisions of
Part II, *Determinate Religion,* in the 1827 lectures. The religion of natural immediacy,
or magic, represents the first and most primitive form of nature religion.

into-self of spirit from its submersion in the natural. We have seen various forms of this.[50] The outstanding example is the religion of India—this being-within-self, Brahman, pure self-consciousness, the severance by means of which the being-within-self of pure self-consciousness is posited in abstraction from everything concrete and natural | and from all worldly delight and imagery. But this separation is at the same time abstract: this way of thinking is on the one hand still empty; on the other hand it is an immediate self-consciousness that has not yet distinguished itself from itself, has no object, and is nothing other than subjective, abstract knowledge. From this sort of cognition, then, there emerges a first form of unity or reconciliation,[51] namely, that this inwardness fills itself with externality, that it shows itself no longer as an abstraction but as something concrete, that it takes this externality into itself, showing itself above all as *power*. This is the unrefined condition in which the inward has only the signification of something external, an external that still remains only in its natural state.

The second stage was the beginning of *spiritual religion*,[52] namely, a religion of being-withdrawn-into-self,[53] a religion of the freedom of spirit, for which the natural (which was the previous fulfillment) is not an independent content, constituting a fulfillment in an immediate way, but is only the appearance of something inward instead, the appearance of the ethical, which has rational inwardness as its defining character. This inwardness is so concrete

---

50. [*Ed.*] Hegel here turns to the second form of nature religion, the religion of being-within-self (*Insichsein*), which in this summary he identifies with Buddhism and Hinduism, but which in his actual treatment he distinguishes, regarding Buddhism (the religion of being-within-self in the strict sense) as the earlier form, and Hinduism (the religion of phantasy) as the later form.

51. [*Ed.*] This is an apparent reference to what are described in the 1827 lectures as "the religions of transition" from nature religion to spiritual religion, namely, the religion of light (Persian religion) and Egyptian religion, and in particular to the connection in these religions between the pure (spiritual) inwardness of the good and the pure (natural) externality of light.

52. [*Ed.*] "Spiritual religion" (or the religion of spiritual individuality, in which "spirit" is still construed as *finite*) is the second main division of *Determinate Religion*. In this paragraph Hegel describes Greek religion as the religion of ethical inwardness.

53. [*Ed.*] *Insichgegangensein*, literally, "being-gone-within-self."

within itself, therefore, that concreteness belongs to it and constitutes the definition or nature of inwardness: the concrete is the ethical as such. But it does indeed have the natural as its manifestation, its appearance; this concrete inwardness—the ethical—is, however, not yet posited within itself as subjectivity. Thus a condition of finitude comes about in which the ethical distinguishes itself into particular ethical powers; it is only a collection of these powers with a particular content—an encompassing totality, to be sure, though only a wholeness and not subjectivity—˜for the appearance still occurs in sensible fashion.˜[54]

The other mode of finitude is that the external still is [has the character of] sensible being. In this second sphere of withdrawal-into-self, over against the *religion of beauty* we have seen the *religion of sublimity*[55]—that is, spirituality fulfilled within itself in such a way that these particularities, these ethical powers, are brought together in a single purpose by means of which the One, the spirit, is defined as having being within itself, | as wise. Here, therefore, we have spirit in its freedom, at once inwardly concrete and inwardly determinate, which is to say that it exists as the Wise One. This spirit first merits for us the name of God, while the previous one did not. It is no longer substance but subject. Thus spirit has a purpose within itself; it is inwardly determinate. But the content of its subjectivity, its infinite determination, its inner content that we call purpose, is still abstract.

193

The third stage is the one where *purpose*[56] receives a comprehensive, universal content, although chiefly within the world in external fashion—[specifically] among the Romans. Wisdom is a

54. *L (1827?) reads:* One can make light of the fact that particularity has not been taken up into absolute harmony or unity.

55. [*Ed.*] The religion of beauty (Greek religion) and the religion of sublimity (Jewish religion) together constitute spiritual religion (the religion of spiritual individuality). In the 1827 lectures, Hegel treats Greek religion first, followed by Jewish religion—just the reverse of the order in which he discusses these religions in the other lecture series. In Jewish religion, what is "external" over against the ethical inwardness of the Greeks—namely, the one good, wise, all-powerful God—is still construed as a finite, sensible being.

56. [*Ed.*] The "religion of purposiveness" (*Zweckmässigkeit*) or koman religion constitutes the third and final division of *Determinate Religion*.

purpose [of this kind], but in the form of an abstraction. Once this purpose is developed, its mode is externality. It is a worldly purpose, a unity, but still an abstract unity, which even in this reality is only abstract and consequently [mere] domination as such. The purpose, therefore, takes the form of subjectivity possessing comprehensive reality, but in such fashion that the subject, while comprehensive, comprehends only what is finite.

The transition [to the consummate religion] is the spirit that has entered into itself: it is the concept that has only *itself* as its purpose—this inwardly subsisting mode [of being] whose purpose is only itself, is God himself. The idea has only itself as purpose; and now this concept is purified in order to have a more comprehensive purpose, but one that is also taken back into subjectivity. Spirit now has as its final purpose its concept, its concrete essence itself; it eternally realizes and objectifies its purpose, and is free in it— indeed it is freedom itself because this purpose is its own nature. Thereby finitude is sublated. This progression has the more specific character of containing that which is inwardly self-determining, the determinateness of spirit. It involves the fact that spirit shows itself in this sphere as inwardly posited. Spirit is precisely that which determines itself infinitely. To be sure, the series of forms that we have passed through is a succession of stages that follow upon one another; but these forms are encompassed within the infinite, ab- solute form, in absolute subjectivity, and only the spirit so defined as absolute subjectivity *is* spirit.

On the one hand we have seen a stripping away of these deter- minacies, these modes of finitude and of finite forms. On the other hand it is the nature of spirit, of the concept itself, to determine 194 itself in this way; | in order to be spirit, the concept must first traverse these forms. Only when this content has traversed these determinations is it spirit. Spirit is essence—but only insofar as it has returned to itself from out of itself, only insofar as it is that actual being which returns and is at home with itself, that being which posits itself from itself as at home with itself. This positing produces the distinctive determinations of its activity, and these distinctive determinations are the forms through which spirit has to move.

We have said that spirit is immediate. This is a mode of finitude. All the same, it is spirit, the concept, that determines itself. The first of its determinate forms is that of inward self-diremption and of being immediately, in accordance with this form of finitude. The concept determines itself, posits itself as immediate; that concept for which spirit so determines itself, posits itself as immediate, we ourselves still are. The last stage, however, is that this concept, this subjectivity for which spirit is, is not to remain something external to spirit, but rather is itself to be absolute and infinite subjectivity, infinite form. The infinite form is the circuit of this determining process; the concept is spirit only because it has achieved determinacy through this circuit, has moved through it. This is how it first becomes concrete. [57]This means on the one hand a stripping away of the mode of finitude, and on the other hand a self-diremption and a return to self from diremption; only so is it posited as spirit. At first, spirit is only a presupposition; that it *is* as spirit and comes to be comprehended as spirit is nothing immediate, and cannot happen in an immediate fashion. It is spirit only as that which dirempts itself and returns into itself again—i.e., only after traversing this circuit. What we have traversed in our treatment is the becoming, the bringing forth of spirit by itself, and ˉonly as such, or as eternally bringing itself forth, is it spirit.ˉ[58] This course is, therefore, the grasping or comprehension of spirit. It is the concept that determines itself, and takes these determinations back into itself, as the concept; in this way the concept is | infinite subjectivity.   195 [59]What results is the concept that posits itself, and has itself as its content. This, then, is the absolute idea. The idea is the unity of concept and reality; it is concept *and* objectivity. Truth consists in objectivity being adequate to the concept; but what is adequate to the concept is only the concept itself insofar as it has itself as its counterpart or object. The content as idea is the truth.

57. *In B's margin:* 27 July 1827
58. *Hu reads:* that which it now traverses, it is as such, namely, spirit.
59. *Precedes in L (1827?):* In this way, the absolute objectification of spirit consists precisely in the fact that the concept determines itself, fulfills itself with its own concept, with itself. The circuit of these forms is the process of self-positing by the concept. These forms, comprehended together in their unity, are the concept.

Freedom is the following aspect of the idea: the concept, because it is conceptually at home with itself, is free. The idea alone is what is true, but equally so it is freedom. The idea is what is true, and the true is thus absolute spirit. This is the true definition of spirit. The concept that has determined itself, that has made itself into its own object, has thereby posited finitude in itself, but posited *itself* as the content of this finitude and in so doing sublated it—that is spirit.

[60]We are accustomed to say of God that he is the creator of the world, that God is wholly just, all-knowing, totally wise. But this is not the authentic way of cognizing what the truth is, what God is; it is the way of representation, of understanding. It is necessary, of course, to define the concept by predicates too, but this is an incomplete, reflective way of thinking; it is not thinking by means of the concept, thinking the concept of God, the idea. Predicates signify particular determinations; attributes, as particular determinations of this kind, are distinguished from one another. If one thinks of these differences determinately, they fall into contradiction with each other, and this contradiction is not resolved, or is resolved only in an abstract, superficial manner. We resolve it merely in an abstraction, by allowing the | attributes to temper each other mutually or by abstracting from their particularity.[61] The outcome is that in this way God, because he is thus defined by predicates, is not grasped as living. This amounts to the same thing we have just stated, namely, that the contradictions are not resolved, or they are only abstractly resolved. The vitality of God or of spirit is nothing other than a self-determining (which can also appear as a predicate), a self-positing in finitude, [which involves] distinction and contradiction, but [is] at the same time an eternal sublating of this con-

60. *Precedes in L (1827?):* The task of philosophy is to cognize what God, the absolute truth, is. The customary, usual procedure (apart from proofs for the existence of God) is to assert this or that about God and to define him by means of predicates. His attributes tell us what he is, render him determinate.

61. [*Ed.*] Hegel is criticizing the procedure of the *theologia naturalis*, which appends to the proofs a derivation of the divine attributes and seeks to overcome the contradictions between them by arguing for their compossibility. See Wolff, *Theologia naturalis*, Pars prior, §§ 1067, 1070; and Baumgarten, *Metaphysica*, § 807.

tradiction. This is the life, the deed, the activity of God; he is absolute activity, creative energy [*Aktuosität*], and his activity is to posit himself in contradiction, but eternally to resolve and reconcile this contradiction: God himself is the resolving of these contradictions. From this point of view, definition by predicates is incomplete, since they are only particular determinations whose contradiction is not resolved. They represent God as though he were not himself the resolution of these contradictions, as though he were not himself the one who resolves them. It would seem, then, that it is only our human particularity that comprehends specific, distinguishable aspects in God, and that these characteristics are rather just our own. But the particularity does not merely belong to our reflection; rather it is the nature of God, of spirit, it is his concept itself. In the same way, however, God is the one who resolves the contradiction—not by abstraction but in concrete fashion. This, then, is the living God.[62]

4. Division of the Subject[63]

Since we have now indicated the position of our earlier discussion in relation to the idea of God itself—namely, that it is the concept itself that sets up these distinctions and attains to itself through them, becoming for the first time idea in this way—we are now able to view the idea in its development and completion. We turn first to the division of the subject. In its outward aspect, | we can   197 say that this idea is for us. We now have the following distinctions regarding God as the absolute idea.

(1) First, God is the absolute idea for [us in the mode of] *thought* or *thinking*. Insofar as the content is [present] for thought, for the

---

62. L (1827?) adds: That God is living, the vitality of God, signifies that the particularities in him and their resolution are not merely an external aspect and are not grasped merely from our side.

63. [Ed.] In the Ms. and in the 1824 lectures, the "division of the subject" is found at the beginning of the second main section ("Concrete Representation" in the Ms., "The Development of the Idea of God" in the 1824 lectures). Since the 1827 lectures lack a first section, containing the ontological proof of the existence of God—which in 1827 has been moved to *The Concept of Religion*—the "division" falls logically into the introduction, followed by the three main sections in which the three "elements" of the consummate religion are explicated.

soil of thinking, it can and must be grasped also in the mode of representation. Since indeed the eternal idea is for the thinking of humanity as a whole, and the thinking of humanity as a whole is extraneous to philosophical thinking, which transposes itself into the form of thinking itself, this thinking must also occur in the mode of representation. The idea of God is first to be considered as it is for thinking or in itself. This is *the eternal idea of God for itself,* what God is for himself, i.e., the eternal idea in the soil of thinking as such.

(2) Second, God is the eternal idea, not for us in the mode of thinking, but rather for finite, external, empirical spirit, for *sensible intuition,* for *representation.* The determinate being that God gives himself for the sake of representation is, in the first instance, *nature;* and therefore one of the ways God is there for representation is that finite, empirical spirit recognizes God from [the evidence of] nature. The other way, however, is that God is [present] for finite spirit *as finite spirit.* Thus, finite, concrete spirit is itself necessarily involved in the way that God is for it, the way God is manifest for it. To be more precise, God as such cannot properly *be* for spirit as finite; rather the basis of his being for finite spirit lies in the fact that the latter does not hold fast to its finitude as a subsisting being or something fixed, but is instead precisely the process of reconciling itself with God. As finite spirit, it is placed in a condition of separation; it has fallen away from God, it is apart from God. Since it is still related to God in this state of being apart from God, the contradiction consists in its cleavage and separation from God. The concrete spirit, the finite spirit defined as finite, is therefore in contradiction to its object or content, and this gives rise above all to the need to sublate this contradiction and separation that appear in finite spirit as such—in other words, the need for *reconciliation.* This need is the starting point; the next step is that God comes into being for finite spirit, that the latter should arrive at a knowledge and certainty of the divine content, and that the divine content should represent *itself* to that finite spirit which is at the same time the *representing* spirit, spirit in finite, | empirical form. This can happen only insofar as spirit does indeed appear to it, but in an external fashion, and insofar as it is able to bring to consciousness (in this external fashion) what God is.

(3) [64]Third, God comes to be, one may say, for *sensibility*, for *subjectivity* and in the subjectivity of spirit, in the innermost being of subjective spirit. Here reconciliation, the sublation of that separation, is made actual; here *God as spirit is [present] in his community,* and the community is liberated from that antithesis and has the consciousness or certainty of its freedom in God.

These are the three ways by which the subject is related to God, the three modes of God's determinate being for subjective spirit. Since it is *we* who have made this distinction, this trichotomy, we have arrived at it more or less empirically, from our own standpoint. We know, in terms of our own spirit, that first of all we are able to think without this antithesis or cleavage within us, that secondly we are finite spirit, spirit in its cleavage and separation, and that thirdly we are spirit in the state of sensibility and subjectivity, of return to self—[which is] reconciliation, innermost feeling. Of these three, the first is the realm of *universality;* the second, the realm of *particularity;* the third, that of *singularity.*[65] These three realms are a presupposition that we have taken up as our definition. They are not to be regarded, however, as realms that are externally distinct, or as externally subsisting modes vis-à-vis God; rather it is the idea itself that makes these distinctions. The absolute, eternal idea is:

(1) First, in and for itself, God in his eternity before the creation of the world and outside the world.

(2) Second, God creates the world and posits the separation. He creates both nature and finite spirit. [66]What is thus created is at first an other, posited outside of God. But God is | essentially the   199
reconciling to himself of what is alien, what is particular, what is posited in separation from him. He must restore to freedom and

64. *Precedes in L (1827?):* Thus we have God in the first sphere of thinking in general; second, we have him in the form of representation.

65. *[Ed.]* The moments of universality (*Allgemeinheit*), particularity (*Besonderheit*), and singularity (*Einzelheit*) are the constitutive moments in the dialectic of the concept. See *Science of Logic,* pp. 600–621 (*GW* 12:32–52); *Encyclopedia,* §§ 183–187. The logical idea is the principle of universality; nature, the principle of particularity; and finite spirit, the principle of singularity. Each of these, in turn, mediates between the other two; together they constitute the structure of Hegel's entire philosophical system. The unity of all three is the infinite subjectivity of absolute spirit.

66. *Precedes in L (1827?), similar in W:* This creation [W: What is created], this other-being, divides of itself into two sides—physical nature and finite spirit.

to his truth what is alien, what has fallen away in the idea's self-diremption, in its falling away from itself. This is the path and the process of reconciliation.

(3) In the third place, through this process of reconciliation, spirit has reconciled with itself what it distinguished from itself in its act of diremption, of primal division, and thus it is the Holy Spirit, the Spirit [present] in its community.

These are not external distinctions, which *we* have made merely in accord with what we are; rather they are the activity, the developed vitality, of absolute spirit itself. It is itself its eternal life, which is a development and a return of this development into itself; this vitality in development, this actualization of the concept, is what we have now to consider.[67]

---

67. W *adds the "Division of the Subject" contained in the 1831 lectures; the fuller version of W$_2$ reads:* We have, speaking generally, to consider the idea as divine self-revelation, and this revelation is to be taken in the sense indicated by the three determinations just mentioned.

According to the first of these, God is [present] for finite spirit purely and solely as thinking. This is the theoretical consciousness in which the thinking subject has an attitude of full composure and is not yet posited in this relationship itself, is not yet posited in the process [of reconciliation], but remains in the wholly undisturbed calm of thinking spirit. Here God is thought for thinking spirit, the latter's thought consisting in the simple conclusion that God brings himself into harmony with himself, is immediately present to himself, by means of his differentiation—which, however, is still [found] here in the form of pure ideality and has not yet reached the form of externality. This is the first relationship, which is only for the thinking subject, and is occupied only with the pure content. This is *the kingdom of the Father.*

The second determination is *the kingdom of the Son,* in which God is [present] for representation in the element of representing as such. This is the moment of particularization as such. In this second standpoint, that which was God's "other" in the first moment, though without being defined as such, now obtains the *determination* of the other. Considered from the first standpoint, God as the Son is not distinguished from the Father, but is merely expressed in the mode of sensibility. In the second element, however, the Son obtains the determination as other, and thus we pass out of the pure ideality of thinking and into representation. If, according to the first determination, God begets only a son, here he brings forth nature. Here the other is nature, and distinction comes into its own. What is distinguished is nature, the world as a whole, and the spirit that is related to it, the natural spirit. What we have earlier designated as "subject" comes into play as itself the content; human being is involved in this content. Since human beings are here related to nature and are themselves natural, they have the character of subjects only within the sphere of religion, and consequently we have here to consider nature and humanity from the point of view of religion. The Son comes into the world, and this

A. THE FIRST ELEMENT:
THE IDEA OF GOD IN AND FOR ITSELF[68]

In accord with the first element, then, we consider God in his eternal idea, as he is in and for himself, prior to or apart from the creation | of the world, so to speak.[69] Insofar as he is thus within himself, it is a matter of the eternal idea, which is not yet posited in its reality but is itself still only the abstract idea. But God is the creator of the world; it belongs to his being, his essence, to be the creator; insofar as he is not the creator, he is grasped inadequately. His creative role is not an *actus* that ˉhappenedˉ[70] once; [rather,] what takes place in the idea is an *eternal* moment, an eternal determination of the idea. |

Thus God in his eternal idea is still within the abstract element of thinking in general—the abstract idea of thinking, not of conceiving. We already know this pure idea, and therefore we need only dwell on it briefly.

Specifically, the eternal idea is expressed in terms of the holy

200

201

---

is the beginning of faith. When we speak of the coming of the Son into the world, we are already using the language of faith. God cannot properly *be* for finite spirit as such because, to the extent that God is for it, it follows immediately that finite spirit does not hold fast to its finitude as a subsisting being, but rather is in a relation to spirit, reconciles itself with God. As finite spirit its stance is one of falling away, of separation from God; thus it is in contradiction to its object, its content, and this contradiction constitutes, in the first instance, the need for the sublation of the contradiction. This need is the first step, and the next one is that God should come to be for spirit, that the divine content should represent itself to spirit—though at the same time this spirit exists in an empirical, finite fashion. Hence what God is appears to it in empirical fashion. But since in this history the divine steps into view for spirit, the history loses the character of external history. It becomes divine history, the history of the manifestation of God himself.

This constitutes the transition to *the kingdom of the Spirit*, which comprises the awareness that human beings are implicitly reconciled with God and that reconciliation exists for humanity. The process of reconciliation itself is comprised in the cultus.

68. [*Ed.*] "The First Element," like that of the 1824 lectures, and like Sec. B.a of the *Ms.*, "The Idea In and For Itself," concerns the immanent or logical Trinity. It is given an especially full treatment in the 1827 lectures, perhaps in response to recent attacks on the doctrine of the Trinity by F. A. G. Tholuck and others (see 1827 *Intro.*, nn. 17, 18).

69. [*Ed.*] See *Science of Logic*, p. 50 (GW 11:21).

70. *Thus L; W₁ (Var) reads:* was undertaken

417

Trinity: it is God himself, eternally triune. Spirit is this process, movement, life. This life is self-differentiation, self-determination, and the first differentiation is that spirit *is* as this universal idea itself. The universal contains the entire idea, although it only contains it, it is only implicitly the idea. In this primal division is found the other, the particular, what stands over against the universal— that which stands over against God as distinguished from him, but in such a way that this distinguished aspect is God's entire idea in and for itself, so that these two determinations are also one and the same for each other, an identity, the One. Not only is this distinction implicitly sublated, and not only do we know that, but also it is established that the two distinguished moments are the same, that this distinction is sublated insofar as it is precisely what posits itself as no distinction at all; hence the one remains present to itself in the other.

That this is so is the Holy Spirit itself, or, expressed in the mode of sensibility, it is eternal love: *the Holy Spirit is eternal love.*

When we say, "God is love," we are saying something very great and true. But it would be senseless to grasp this saying in a simple-minded way as a simple definition, without analyzing what love is. For love is a distinguishing of two, who nevertheless are absolutely not distinguished for each other. The consciousness or feeling of the identity of the two—to be outside of myself and in the other— this is love. I have my self-consciousness not in myself but in the other. I am satisfied and have peace with myself only in this other— and I *am* only because I have peace with myself; if I did not have it, then I would be a contradiction that falls to pieces. This other, because it likewise exists outside itself, has its self-consciousness only in me, and both the other and I are only this consciousness of being-outside-ourselves and of our identity; we are only this intuition, feeling, and knowledge of our unity. This is love, and 202 without knowing that love is both a | distinguishing and the sublation of the distinction, one speaks emptily of it. ˉThis is the simple, eternal idea.ˉ[71]

71. *Thus Hu; L (1827?) reads, similar in* W₁, *first and last sentence similar in* W₂: God is love: he is this distinguishing and the nullity of the distinction, a play of distinctions in which there is nothing serious, distinction precisely as sublated, i.e., the simple, eternal idea. We deal with the simple idea of God—the fact that

[72]When we speak of God in order to say what he is, it is customary to make use of attributes: God is thus and so; he is defined by predicates. This is the method of representation and understanding. Predicates are determinate, particular qualities: justice, goodness, omnipotence, etc. Because they have the feeling that this is not the authentic way to express the nature of God, the Orientals say that God is πολυώνυμος [worshiped under many names] and does not admit of exhaustion by predicates[73]—for names are in this sense the same as predicates. The real deficiency in this way of defining by predicates consists in the very fact that gives rise to this endless number of predicates, namely, that they designate only particular characteristics, of which there are many, and all of them are borne by the subject.[74] Because there are particular characteristics, and because one views these particularities in their determinateness, one thinks and develops them, they fall into opposition and contradiction with each other as a result, since they are not only distinct but opposed, and these contradictions remain unresolved.

This is also evident when these predicates are taken as expressing God's relation to the world.[75] The world is something other than God. Predicates as particular characteristics are not appropriate to the nature of God. Here, then, is the occasion for the other method, which regards them as relations of God to the world: e.g., the omnipresence and omniscience of God in the world. Accordingly, the predicates do not comprise the true relation of God to himself, but rather his relation | to an other, the world. So they are limited and thereby come into contradiction with each other.   203

We are conscious of the fact that God is not represented in living fashion when so many particular characteristics are enumerated alongside one another. Put in another way, this is the same point

---

[W₁ reads: as] it is in the simple element of thinking and is the idea in its universality; this is the essential determination of the idea, the determination by which it has truth. We make the following remarks about this idea, its content and form.

72. In B's margin: 30 July 1827

73. [Ed.] Hegel may be referring here to Philo, to whom Neander attributes just this expression (Gnostische Systeme, p. 12).

74. Thus L, B, Hu, W₁; W₂ (Var) adds: which is inwardly without distinction.

75. [Ed.] Most likely an allusion to Schleiermacher's derivation of the divine attributes, namely, as modifications of the feeling of absolute dependence, or of God's relation to self and world. See Der christliche Glaube, 1st ed., § 64.

that was stated earlier: the contradictions among the different predicates are not resolved. The resolution of the contradiction is contained in the idea, i.e., in God's determining of himself to distinguish himself from himself while [remaining] at the same time the eternal sublation of the distinction. The distinction left as is would be a contradiction.[76]

If we assign predicates to God in such a way as to make them particular, then we are immediately at pains to resolve their contradiction. This is an external action, a product of our reflection, and the fact that it is external and falls to us, and is not the content of the divine idea, implies that the contradictions cannot in fact be resolved. But the idea is itself the resolution of the contradictions posited by it. Its proper content, its determination, is to posit this distinction and then absolutely to sublate it; this is the vitality of the idea itself.

At the point where we now stand, our interest is in passing over from concept to being. We should also recall our characterization of the metaphysical proofs of God,[77] which serve as the route for going from the concept to being.[78] The divine idea is the pure concept, without any limitation. The idea includes the fact that the concept determines itself and thereby posits itself as what is self-differentiated. This is a moment of the divine idea itself, and because the thinking, reflecting spirit has this content before it, the need

204 arises for this transition and progression. |

We observed the logical aspect of this transition earlier.[79] It is contained in those so-called proofs by means of which the transition ought to be made, in, from, and through the concept, into objectivity

76. *Hu adds:* This resolution is forever and always sublated, not left standing on its own account. *L (1827?) adds, similar in W:* If the distinction were permanent, then finitude would persist. The two sides confront each other independently, yet remain in relation; hence an unresolvable contradiction emerges. The idea does not involve leaving the difference alone, but rather resolving it. God posits himself in this distinction and likewise sublates it.

77. [Ed.] In the 1827 lectures, all the proofs for the existence of God are treated in Part I, *The Concept of Religion*, Sec. B.4.c. In this paragraph and the next, Hegel provides a brief summary of the ontological proof.

78. *Thus B; W₂ (Var) adds, similar in W₁:* so that the concept is not merely concept but also *is*, has reality.

79. [Ed.] See above, pp. 180–189.

and being (all within the element of thought). What appears as a subjective need and demand is the content, is one moment of the divine idea itself. When we say, "God has created the world," this also entails a transition from concept to reality; but the world is there defined as the essentially other of God, as the negation of God, it is what has being outside God, without God, godlessly. Insofar as the world is defined as the other, we do not have the distinction as a distinction within the concept itself; it is not contained in the concept before us. But now being and objectivity are to be exhibited *in* the concept as its activity and consequence, as a determination of the concept. This shows, therefore, that what we have here, within the idea, is the same content and exigency that is found in the form of those proofs of the existence of God. In the absolute idea, in the element of thinking, God is this utterly concrete universal, the positing of self as other, but in such a way that the other is immediately defined to be himself, and the distinction is only ideal, it is immediately sublated, and does not take on the shape of externality. This means precisely that what is distinguished ought to be exhibited in and within the concept.[80] It is the logical aspect in which it becomes clear that every determinate concept is self-sublating, it occurs as the contradiction of itself, and ⁻is a positing of what is distinguished from it.⁻[81] Thus the concept itself is still burdened with one-sidedness and finitude, as indicated by the fact that it is something subjective, posited as subjective; the characteristics of the concept and its distinctions are posited only as ideal and not as distinctions in fact. This is the concept that objectifies itself.[82]

When we say "God," we speak of him merely as abstract; or if we say, "God the Father," we speak of him as the universal, | only abstractly, in accord with his finitude. His infinitude means precisely that he sublates this form of abstract universality and immediacy, and in this way distinction is posited; but he is precisely the sublating

205

80. *Thus also W; L (1827?) adds:* What this transition itself concerns we have considered at the appropriate time.

81. *Thus L, An; W (Var) reads:* is thus a coming to be of what is distinguished from it and a positing of itself as such.

82. *Thus also W; L (1827?) adds:* This is the logical aspect, which is presupposed.

of the distinction. Thereby he is for the first time true actuality, the truth, infinitude.

This is the speculative idea, i.e., the rational element, insofar as it is thought, the thinking of what is rational. For the nonspeculative thinking of the understanding, distinction remains as distinction, e.g., the antithesis of finite and infinite. Absoluteness is ascribed to both terms, yet each also has a relation to the other, and in this respect they are in unity; in this way contradiction is posited.

The speculative idea is opposed not merely to the sensible but also to what is understandable; for both, therefore, it is a secret or mystery. It is a μυστήριον for the sensible mode of consideration as well as for the understanding. ‾In other words, μυστήριον is what the rational is; among the Neoplatonists, this expression already means simply speculative philosophy.‾[83] The nature of God is not a secret in the ordinary sense, least of all in the Christian religion. In it God has made known what he is; there he is manifest. But he is a secret or mystery for external sense perception and representation, for the sensible mode of consideration and likewise for the understanding.

The sensible in general has as its fundamental characteristic externality, the being of things outside each other. Space-time is the externality in which objects are side by side, mutually external, and successive. The sensible mode of consideration is thus accustomed to have before it distinct things that are outside one another. Its basis is that distinctions remain explicit and external. In reason this is not the case. Therefore, what is in the idea is a mystery for sensible consideration. For in [the region of] the idea, the way [things are looked at], the relations [ascribed to things], and the categories [employed] are entirely different from those found in sense experience. The idea is just this distinguishing which | at the same time is no distinction, and does not persist in its distinction. God intuits

206

83. *Thus L; Hu reads:* The speculative is accordingly [*canceled:* reason] the mysteries, and nothing else—simply reason. In the pagan religions God is no secret. *W (Var) reads:* For both it is a μυστήριον, with respect, that is, to what is rational in it.

[*Ed.*] Hegel attributes the connection between mystery and speculation to Proclus in particular; see above, p. 130 n. 44.

himself in what is distinguished, he is united with himself only in his other, and is only present to himself in it; only there does God close with himself and behold himself in the other. This is wholly repugnant to sense experience, since for it one thing is here and another there. Everything counts as independent; what counts for it is not to be the sort of thing that subsists because it possesses itself in another. For sense experience, two things cannot be in one and the same place; they exclude each other. But in the idea, distinctions are not posited as exclusive of each other; rather they are found only in this mutual inclusion of the one with the other. This is the *truly supersensible* [realm], not ˉthat of the understanding,ˉ[84] which is supposed to be above and beyond; for the latter is just as much a sensible [realm] where things are outside one another and indifferently self-contained.[85]

In the same way this idea is a mystery for the understanding and beyond its ken. For the understanding holds fast to the categories of thought, persisting with them as utterly independent of each other, remaining distinct, external to each other, and fixed. The positive is not the same as the negative, the cause is not the effect, etc. But for the concept it is equally true that these distinctions are sublated. Precisely because they are distinctions, they remain finite, and the understanding persists in finitude. Indeed, even in the case of the infinite, it has the infinite on one side and finitude on the other. But the truth of the matter is that neither the finite nor the infinite standing over against it has any truth; rather both are merely transitional. To that extent this is a mystery for sensible representation and for the understanding, and both resist the rationality of the idea.[86]

[87]What has life *is*, and it has drives and needs; accordingly, it

---

84. *Thus L; W (Var) reads:* the ordinary supersensible,

85. *Thus L; W (Var) omits:* self-contained *and adds:* To the extent that God is defined as spirit, externality is sublated; accordingly, this is a mystery to the senses.

86. *Thus L; W (Var) adds:* The opponents of the doctrine of the Trinity are merely the partisans of sensibility and understanding.

87. *Precedes in L (1827?), similar in W:* Moreover, the understanding is equally powerless to grasp anything else whatever, to grasp the truth of anything at all. Animal life, for example, also exists as idea, as the unity of the concept, as the unity

207   has | distinction within itself, the latter arises within it. Thus life itself is a contradiction, and the way the understanding comprehends such distinctions is that the contradiction remains unresolved; when the distinctions are brought into relation with each other, only the contradiction remains, which is not to be resolved.[88] Life has certain needs and thus is in contradiction, but the satisfaction of the need annuls the contradiction. I myself am distinguished ˉfor myselfˉ[89] from myself in my drives and needs. But life is the resolving of the contradiction, the satisfying of the need, giving it peace, though in such a way that the contradiction emerges once more. The distinction, the contradiction, and its annulment alternate back and forth.[90] When considering drive and satisfaction on their own account, the understanding does not grasp the fact that even in the act of affirmation and self-feeling, the negation of self-feeling, limitation, and lack are simultaneously found, yet at the same time, as self-feeling, I reach beyond this lack. This is the determinate representation of the μυστήριον; a mystery is called inconceivable, but what appears inconceivable is precisely the concept itself, the speculative element or the fact that the rational is thought. It is precisely through thinking that the distinction comes out specifically.[91] Now when the understanding comes to this point, it says, "This is a contradiction," and it stands still at this point; it stands by the contradiction in the face of the experience that it

208   is life itself which sublates the contradiction. | When [for example] drive is analyzed, the contradiction appears, and then the understanding can say, "This is inconceivable."

---

of soul and body. For the understanding, by contrast, each is on its own. To be sure, they are distinct, but equally it is their nature to sublate the distinction. Life or vitality is simply this perennial process.

88. *L (1827?) adds, similar in W:* This is the case; the contradiction cannot cease when the distinctions are maintained to be perennial in character, just because the fact of this distinction is insisted upon.

89. *Thus L; W (Var) reads:* in myself

90. *L (1827?) adds, similar in W:* They do not occur simultaneously but succeed each other in temporal progression, and accordingly the entire process is finite.

91. *L (1827?) adds, similar in W:* The thinking of the drive is only the analysis of what the drive is; as soon as I think "drive," I have the affirmation and therein the negation, the self-feeling, the satisfaction, and the drive. Thinking it means recognizing what is distinguished, what is within it.

Thus the nature of God is inconceivable; but, as we already said, this is just the concept itself, which contains the act of distinguishing within itself. The understanding does not get beyond the fact of the distinction, so it says, "This can't be grasped." For the principle of understanding is abstract identity with itself, not concrete identity, in accord with which these distinctions are [present] within a single [concept or reality]. According to the abstract identity, the one and the other are independent, each for itself, yet at the same time are related to each other.[92] This is what is called inconceivable. The resolution of the contradiction is the concept, a resolution which the understanding does not attain because it starts from the presupposition that the two [distinguished moments] both are and remain utterly independent of each other.

ˉOne of the circumstances contributing to the assertion that the divine idea is inconceivable is the fact that, | in religion, the content of the idea appears in forms accessible to sense experience or understanding, because religion is the truth for everyone. Hence we have the expressions "Father" and "Son"—a designation taken from a sentient aspect of life, from a relationship that has its place in life. In religion the truth has been revealed as far as its *content* is concerned; but it is another matter for this content to be present in the *form* of the concept, of thinking, of the concept in speculative form.ˉ[93]

209

92. *Thus L; W (Var) adds:* therefore the contradiction is present.
93. *Cf. the amplification of this theme by the 1831 lectures, inserted by W₁ in the context of the 1824 lectures, and by W₂ in the context of the 1827 lectures at p. 418; W₂ reads, similar in W₁:* This eternal idea, accordingly, finds expression in the Christian religion under the name of the Holy Trinity, which is God himself, the eternally triune God.

Here God is present only for the person who thinks, who remains silently within himself. The ancients called this "enthusiasm";ª it is a purely theoretical contemplation, the supreme repose of thought, but at the same time its highest activity, namely, to grasp the pure idea of God and to become conscious of that idea. The mystery of the dogma of what God is, is imparted to human beings; they believe in it, and already have the highest truth vouchsafed to them, although they apprehend it only in the form of representation, without being conscious of the necessity of this truth, without conceiving it. Truth is the disclosure of what spirit is in and for itself; human beings are themselves spirit, and therefore the truth is for them. Initially, however, the truth that comes to them does not yet possess for them the form of freedom; it is for them merely something given and received, though they can receive it only because they are spirit. This truth, this idea, has been called the *dogma of*

Yet another form of understandability is the following: When we say, "God in his eternal universality is the one who distinguishes himself, determines himself, posits an other to himself, and likewise

---

the Trinity—God is spirit, the activity of pure knowing, the activity that is present to itself. It was chiefly Aristotle who comprehended God under the abstract determination of activity.[b] Pure activity is knowing (in the Scholastic age, *actus purus*), but in order to be posited as activity, it must be posited in its moments: knowing requires an other, which is known, and since it is knowing that knows it, it is appropriated to it. This explains why God, the actual being that is eternally in and for itself, eternally begets himself as his Son, distinguishes himself from himself— the absolute primal division. What God thus distinguishes from himself does not take on the shape of an other-being, but rather what is thus distinguished is immediately only that from which it has been distinguished. God is spirit, and no darkness, no coloring or mixture enters into this pure light. The relationship of father and son is drawn from organic life and is used in representational fashion. This natural relationship is only figurative and accordingly never wholly corresponds to what should be expressed. We say that God eternally begets his Son, that God distinguishes himself from himself, and thus we begin to speak of God in this way: God does this, and is utterly present to himself in the other whom he has posited (the form of love); but at the same time we must know very well that God is himself this entire activity. God is the beginning, he acts in this way; but he is likewise simply the end, the totality, and it is as totality that God is the Spirit. Merely as the Father, God is not yet the truth (he is known in this way, without the Son, in the Jewish religion). Rather he is both beginning and end; he is his own presupposition, he constitutes himself as presupposition (this is simply another form of differentiation); he is the eternal process. The fact that this is the truth, and the absolute truth, may have the form of something given. But that this should be *known* as the truth in and for itself is the task of philosophy and the entire content of philosophy. In it is seen how all the content of nature and spirit presses forward dialectically to this central point as its absolute truth. Here we are not concerned to prove that this dogma, this tranquil mystery, is the eternal truth; this comes to pass, as has been said, in the whole of philosophy.

In W$_1$ *there follows a further passage from the 1831 lectures, which in* W$_2$ *is transmitted at a later point (p. 425, 1st par.), in part more fully, in part abridged;* W$_1$ *reads:* Against this truth the understanding adduces its categories of finitude. But there is no reference at all here to the notion of three as a number; it would be the most thoughtless and unconceptual procedure to introduce this form here. Principally, the understanding sets up its notion of identity against it [the truth of divine self-differentiation]: God is the One, the essence of essences, it says. But this is only an untrue abstraction, a product of the understanding without truth, empty identity as an absolute moment. God is spirit, making himself objective and knowing himself in this objectivity: this is concrete identity [W$_2$ *continues:* and thus the idea is also an essential moment], whereas identity without distinction is the false product of the understanding and of modern theology; identity by itself is a false, one-sided characteristic. The understanding, however, believes that it has done everything when it detects a contradiction; it believes that it has prevailed over everything since

sublates the distinction, thereby remaining present to himself, and is spirit only through this process of being brought forth," then the understanding enters in | ˜and counts one, two, three.˜[94] Oneness is to begin with wholly abstract. But the three ones are expressed more profoundly when they are defined as persons. Personality is what is based upon freedom—the first, deepest, innermost ˜mode,˜[95] but it is also the most abstract mode in which freedom announces its presence in the subject. "I am a person, I stand on my own"—this is an utterly unyielding position. So when these distinctions are defined in such a way that each of us [is taken] as one or indeed as a person, then through ˜this definition of the person˜[96] what the idea demands appears to be made even more unattainable, namely, to regard these distinctions as distinctions which are not distinct but remain absolutely one, [and so to attain] the sublating of this distinction. Two cannot be one; each is a rigid, unyielding, independent being-for-self. Logic shows that the category of "the one" is a poor category, the wholly abstract unit.[97] If I say "one" [of God], I [must also] say this of everything else. | But as far as personality is concerned, it is the character of the person, the subject, to surrender its isolation and separateness. Ethical life,

210

211

---

identity is supposed to be the foundation [of everything]. But [even] if there were a contradiction, it is the nature of spirit to sublate it eternally. Here, however, opposition and contradiction are not yet found in the first element, but only in the second.

[Ed.] ᵃIn referring to "enthusiasm" as a "purely theoretical contemplation," Hegel apparently has in mind Plato: "The love for ideas is what Plato calls enthusiasm" (Lectures on the History of Philosophy 2:30 [Werke 14:199]). He is thinking especially of the description of the contemplation of the ideas in The Republic 475e–477b, although Plato does not speak there of "enthusiasm." In any case, both Hegel and Plato distinguish enthusiasm in this sense from any sort of suprarational ecstasy, which would be the opposite of presence of mind; cf. Plato, Timaeus 71e–72a. ᵇSee Aristotle, Metaphysics 1072b18–30.

94. Thus L, similar in B, Hu, An; W (1831) reads: and brings its categories of finitude to bear, counts one, two, three, mixing in the unfortunate form of number. But there is no reference to number here; counting betokens a complete lack of thought. Thus by introducing this form, one introduces a complete absence of concept.

95. Thus B; L, W (Var) read: freedom

96. Thus L, similar in W₁; W₂ (Var) reads: this infinite form, namely, that each moment should be as a subject,

97. [Ed.] See Science of Logic, pp. 164–170 (cf. GW 11:91–97).

love, means precisely the giving up of particularity, of particular personality, and its extension to universality—so, too, with ˜friend-ship.˜⁹⁸ In friendship and love I give up my abstract personality and thereby win it back as concrete. The truth of personality is found precisely in winning it back through this immersion, this being immersed in the other.⁹⁹

¹⁰⁰But, even though representation grasps the content in its own forms, the content still belongs to thinking. We are considering the idea in its universality, as it is defined in and through pure thinking. This idea is the one truth and the whole truth; therefore everything particular that is comprehended as true must be comprehended according to the form of this idea. Nature and finite spirit are products of God; therefore rationality is found within them. That something is made by God involves its having the truth within it, the divine truth as a whole, i.e., the determinateness of this idea in general. The form of this idea is only in God as spirit; if the divine idea is grasped in the forms of finitude, then it is not posited as it is in and for itself—only in spirit is it so posited. In the finite forms it exists in a finite way; but, as we have stated, the world is some-thing produced by God, and therefore the divine idea always forms the foundation of what the world as a whole is. To cognize the truth of something means to know and define it according to the truth, in the form of this idea in general.

In the earlier religions, particularly in Hinduism, we ˜have had˜¹⁰¹ anticipations of the triad as the true category.¹⁰² | This idea of threefoldness indeed came to expression with the recognition that the One cannot remain as one, that it is what it ought to be not as one¹⁰³ but rather as movement and distinction in general, and as the relation of these distinctions to each other. Nevertheless,

212

98. *L (1827?) adds:* Inasmuch as I act rightly toward another, I consider the other as identical with myself.   *W (Var) reads:* family, friendship; here this identity of one with another is present. Inasmuch . . . [*continues with L*]

99. *L (1827?) adds, similar in W:* Such forms of the understanding show them-selves immediately in experience as the sort that annul themselves.

100. *In B's margin:* 31 July 1827

101. *Thus B, similar in Hu, An; L, W₂ read:* have

102. *W₁ (Var) adds:* and we see that the category of the triad is the true category.

103. *Thus L; W (Var) adds:* —the One is not what is true—

the third element here—ˉin the Trimurtiˉ[104]—is not the Spirit, not genuine reconciliation, but rather origin and passing away, or the category of change, which is indeed the unity of the distinctions, but a very inferior union—a reconciliation that is still abstract. Even in the Christian religion the Holy Trinity does not appear in the immediate appearance [itself]; rather the idea is first completed only when the Spirit has entered into the community and when the immediate, believing spirit has raised itself to the level of thinking.[105]

It is also well known that the Trinity played an essential role for the Pythagoreans[106] and Plato, but its determinate characteristics are left entirely in a state of abstraction: partly in the abstraction of numerical units (one, two, three); partly (and specifically for Plato) in somewhat more concrete fashion, the nature of the one, then the nature of the other (that which is distinct within itself, θάτερον); and finally the third, which is the unity of the two.[107] Here the triad is found not in the Hindu mode of fanciful imagination but in mere abstraction. These are categories of thought that are better than numbers, better than the category of number, but they are still wholly abstract categories of thought. They are found, most surprisingly, in Philo, who carefully studied Pythagorean and Platonic philosophy, among the Alexandrian Jews and in Syria. Consciousness of this truth, this triune idea, arose especially among the heretics, indeed primarily among the Gnostics,[108] although they brought this content to expression in obscure and fanciful notions.[109] |

213

104. *Thus Hu; W (Var), preceding this sentence, reads:* The Trimurti is the most uncontrolled form of this [triadic] category.
    [*Ed.*] The Trimurti is later Hinduism's divine triad: Brahmā, Vishnu, Siva.
    105. *L (1827?) adds, similar in W:* It is of interest to consider these fermentations of an idea and to learn to recognize their ground in the marvelous appearances that manifest themselves.
    106. [*Ed.*] See Proclus, *Platonic Theology* 3.9–14.
    107. [*Ed.*] See Plato, *Timaeus* 34c–35b.
    108. [*Ed.*] Hegel's information on Philo and the Gnostics in this paragraph and the next derives primarily from Neander's *Gnostische Systeme.* See esp. pp. 8, 10, 12–15, 34, 94–95, 98.
    109. *Thus L; W (Var) adds:* We see here, however, at least the struggle of spirit for the truth, and that merits recognition.

Apart from those already mentioned above, one can point to a countless number of forms in which the content of the Trinity appeared distinctly and in various religions. But this properly belongs to church history. The main features are as follows: First, the Father, the One, the ὄν, is the abstract element that is expressed as the abyss, the depth (i.e., precisely what is still empty), the inexpressible, the inconceivable, that which is beyond all concepts. For in any case what is empty and indeterminate is inconceivable; it is the negative of the concept, and its conceptual character is to be this negative, since it is only a one-sided abstraction which makes up only one moment of the concept.[110] The second moment, other being, the action of determining, self-determining activity as a whole, is, according to the broadest designation, λόγος—rationally determinative activity, or precisely the word. The word is this simple act of letting itself be heard that neither makes nor becomes a hard-and-fast distinction, but rather is immediately heard, and that, because it is so immediate, is likewise taken up into interiority and is returned to its origin. This second moment is also defined as σοφία, wisdom, the original and wholly pure human being, ˉan existing otherˉ[111] or as that initial universality, something particular and determinate.[112] For this reason it has been defined as the archetype of humanity, Adam Kadmon, the only-begotten. This is not something contingent but rather an eternal activity, which does not happen merely at one time. In God there is only one birth, the act as eternal activity, a determination that itself belongs essentially to the universal.[113] The essential point is that this σοφία, the only-begotten, remains likewise in the bosom of God; so that the distinction is no distinction. |

214   tinction is no distinction. |

These are the forms in which this truth, this idea, has fermented. The main point is to know that these appearances, wild as they are,

110. *L, W (1827?) add:* The One for itself is not yet the concept, the true.

111. *Thus L; W (Var) reads:* something existing, something other,

112. *Thus L; W (1831) adds:* God is the creator, and is such indeed in the specification of the Logos as the self-externalizing, self-expressing word, as the ὅρασις, God's vision.

113. *Thus L; W (1831) adds:* This is a genuine differentiation, which affects the quality of both; however, it is only one and the same substance, and thus the distinction here is still constituted only superficially, indeed as a person.

are rational—to know that they have their ground in reason, and to know what sort of reason is in them. But at the same time one must know how to distinguish the form of rationality that is present and not yet adequate to the content. For this idea has ˉin factˉ[114] been placed beyond human beings, beyond the world, beyond thought and reason; indeed, it has been placed over against them, so that this determinate quality, though it is the sole truth and the whole truth, has been regarded as something peculiar to God, something that remains permanently above and beyond, and does not reflect itself in the other (in what appears as the world, nature, humanity). But to this extent, this fundamental idea has not been treated as the universal idea.

Jacob Boehme was the first to recognize the Trinity in another manner, as universal. His way of representing and thinking is rather wild and fanciful; he has not yet risen to the pure forms of thinking. But the ruling foundation of the ferment [in his mind], and of his struggles [to reach the truth], was the recognition of the presence of the Trinity in everything and everywhere. He said, for example, that it must be born in the hearts of human beings.[115] The Trinity is the universal foundation of everything considered from the point of view of truth, albeit as finite, but in its finitude as the truth that lies in it. Thus Jacob Boehme sought to make nature and the heart or spirit of humanity representable—in his own way, to be sure, but according to the [logical] determinations of the Trinity.

In more recent times, especially through the influence of the Kantian philosophy, the triad has been put to use again as a type or a schema for thought, so to speak—not in any extensive way, certainly, though indeed in quite specific categorial forms.[116] But this is the one aspect, namely, that when this idea is known as the essential and sole nature of God, it must not be regarded as something above and beyond, as it was formerly; rather it is the goal of cognition to know the truth in particular things as well. If it is thus cognized, then whatever in such particular things is the true

114. *Thus L; W (Var) reads:* frequently
115. [*Ed.*] See Jacob Boehme, *Aurora, oder Morgenröhte im Aufgang,* in *Theosophia revelata* (1715), 10.116.
116. [*Ed.*] See Kant, *Critique of Pure Reason,* B 110.

215 contains the form of this idea. For cognition in fact means knowing something in its | determinateness; but its nature is that of determinateness itself, and the nature of determinateness is what has been expounded in the idea. ˜[To show] that this idea is what is true as such, and that all categories of thought are this movement of determining, is the [task of] logical exposition.˜[117]

B. THE SECOND ELEMENT: REPRESENTATION, APPEARANCE[118]

1. Differentiation

a. Differentiation within the Divine Life and in the World

We now consider, therefore, the eternal idea in the second element, in the form of *consciousness* or of *representation* in general; in other words, we consider this idea insofar as it emerges out of universality and infinitude into the determinacy of finitude.

Once again, the first aspect or form is that of the universality of the idea with respect to content—but precisely in this sense: that God is everywhere. He is everywhere present; the presence of God is just the element of truth that is in everything. We can comment further here: [119]what is universal or abstract must precede everything else in scientific knowledge; scientifically, one must start with it. But in existence it is in fact what comes later. It is the in-itself, which nevertheless appears subsequently, specifically in knowledge—the in-itself that comes to consciousness and knowledge later.

117. *Thus L, similar in* W₁; *Hu reads:* To show that the Trinity is what is true is the task of logic. *W (Var) adds:* and is logical necessity.
[*Ed.*] Cf. Hegel's formulation of the result of this logical exposition at the beginning of the section on the absolute idea in *Science of Logic,* pp. 824–825 (*GW* 12:236–237).

118. [*Ed.*] The structure of "The Second Element" in the 1827 lectures is almost identical with that of 1824, and we have adopted the same section headings. The only structural variation in 1827 is that the treatment of the story of the fall precedes the discussion of the knowledge of evil and estrangement. There are, however, differences of content and emphasis between 1827 and 1824.

119. *Precedes in L (1827?), similar in* W: At first the idea was found in the element of thinking; this is the foundation, and we began with it.

The form of the idea comes to appearance as a result, even though this result is essentially the in-itself, the beginning. Just as the content of the idea is such that the last is first and the first last, so it is that what appears as a result is at the same time the presupposition, the in-itself, the foundation. And now we have to consider this idea in the second element, the element of *appearance* in general.

We can comprehend this progression from two sides.

First of all, the subject for which this idea is [present] is the thinking subject. Even the forms of representation take | nothing 216 away from the nature of the fundamental form, namely, that this latter is [available] for human being only as a thinking being. The subject behaves in general as a thinking subject, thinking this idea; yet the subject is also concrete consciousness. The idea must therefore be [present] for this subject as concrete self-consciousness, as an actual subject.

Or one might say that this idea is the absolute truth. Absolute truth is for thinking. But the idea must not only be the truth for the subject; the subject must also have the [sort of] certainty about the idea that belongs to the subject as such, as a finite, empirically concrete, sentient subject. The idea possesses certainty for the subject only insofar as it is a perceptible idea, insofar as it exists for the subject. If I can say of anything, "it is so" [*das ist*], then it possesses certainty for me; this is immediate knowledge, this is certainty. To prove that "what is so" is also *necessary,* that it is what is true that is certain for me—that is the further process of mediation and is no longer something immediately apprehended; so this mediation is the transition into the universal.[120]

The other side of this progression starts from the idea. Eternal being-in-and-for-itself is what discloses itself, determines itself, divides itself, posits itself as what is differentiated from itself, but the difference is at the same time constantly sublated. Thereby actual being in and for itself constantly returns into itself—only in this way is it spirit. What is distinguished is defined in such a way that

---

120. *L adds (1827?), similar in* W: Having started with the form of truth, we now proceed to the fact that the truth obtains the form of certainty, that it exists for me.

the distinction immediately disappears, and we have a relationship of God, of the idea, merely to himself. The act of differentiation is only a movement, a play of love with itself, which does not arrive at the seriousness of other-being, of separation and rupture. The other is to this extent defined as "Son"; in terms of sensibility, what-has-being-in-and-for-itself is defined as love, while in a higher mode of determinacy, it is defined as spirit that is present to itself and free. In the idea as thus specified, the determination of the distinction is not yet complete, since it is only abstract distinction in general. We have not yet arrived at distinction in its own proper form; [here] it is just one | determinate characteristic. [121]The distinguished elements are posited as the same; they have not yet come to be defined so that they are distinctly determined.

From this side the primal division of the idea is to be conceived in such a way that the other, which we have also called "Son," obtains the determination of the other as such—that this other exists as a free being for itself, and that it appears as something actual, as something that exists outside of and apart from God. Its ideality, its eternal return into actual being in and for itself, is posited in the first form of identity, the idea, in an immediate and identical way. Otherness is requisite in order that there may be difference;[122] it is necessary that what is distinguished should be the otherness as an entity. Only the absolute idea determines itself and is certain of itself as absolutely free within itself because of this self-determination. For this reason its self-determination involves letting this determinate [entity] exist as something free, something independent, or as an independent object. It is only for the being that is free that freedom *is;* it is only for the free human being that an other has freedom too.[123] It belongs to the absolute freedom of the idea that, in its act of determining and dividing, it releases the other to exist as a free and independent being. This other, released as something free and independent, is *the world* as such.

121. *Thus L, W₁; precedes in W₂ (Var):* To that extent we can say that we have not yet arrived at distinction.

122. *Thus L, W₁; W₂ (Var) adds:* and that it may come into its own,

123. *Thus L, W; Hu adds:* As free, human beings do not comport themselves according to desires; they leave them aside.

The truth of the world is only its *ideality*—for it is not true that it possesses genuine actuality. Its nature is to *be*, but only in an *ideal* sense; it is not something eternal in itself but rather something created, whose being is only posited. For the world, to be means to have ¯being only for an instant,¯[124] so to speak, but also to sublate this its separation or estrangement from God. It means to return to its origin, to enter into the relationship of spirit, of love—to *be* this relationship of spirit, of love, which is the third element. The second element is, therefore, the process of the world in love by which it passes over from fall and separation into reconciliation. | 218

This is the second element—the creation of the world. The first element, within the idea, is only the relationship of the Father to the Son in eternal reconciliation, or, alternatively, nonreconciledness, because no fall is present yet. But the *other* also obtains the determinacy of other-*being*, of an actual entity. It is in the Son, in the determination of distinction, that the advance to further distinction occurs, that distinction comes into its own as [true] diversity.

As we have already said,[125] Jacob Boehme expressed this transition inherent in the moment of the Son as follows: the first only-begotten one was Lucifer, the light-bearer, brilliance and clarity, but he inwardly fancied himself, i.e., he posited himself for himself, he strove to be, and thereby he fell. But the eternal only-begotten One appeared immediately in his place. Looked at from this standpoint, that [first] other is not the Son but rather the external world, the finite world, which is outside the truth—the world of finitude, where the other has the form of being, and yet by its nature is only the ἕτερον,[126] the determinate, what is distinct, limited, negative. The finite world is the side of distinction as opposed to the side that remains in unity; hence it divides into the *natural world* and

124. *Thus B, An; L, W (Var) read:* only an instant of being,
125. [*Ed.*] This cross-reference was probably introduced into the text by Lasson in order to camouflage the repetition relating to the 1824 lectures, but possibly Hegel is referring to p. 431 above.
126. [*Ed.*] From Hegel's *Lectures on the History of Philosophy* 2:64 (*Werke* 14:233), we may assume that he is here alluding to Plato (see *Sophist* 254e–259d and *Parmenides* 143a–c).

the world of *finite spirit*. On its own account, nature ~enters into relationship~ [127] only with humanity, not with God, for nature is not knowledge. God is spirit; nature knows nothing of spirit. It is created by God, but of itself it does not enter into relationship with him—in the sense that it is not possessed of knowledge. It stands in relation only to humanity, and in this relationship it provides what is called the dependent side of humanity. But to the extent that thinking recognizes that nature is created by God, that understanding and reason are within it, nature is known by thinking human beings. To that extent it is posited in relation to the divine, 219   because its truth is recognized.[128] |

127. *Thus L, Hu, W₁, similar in An; B, W₂ (Var) read:* appears in relationship

128. *W₂ (1831) adds, located elsewhere in W₁:* The manifold forms of relationship of finite spirit to nature do not belong here [in the philosophy of religion]. Their scientific treatment forms part of the phenomenology of spirit or the doctrine of spirit.[a] Here this relationship has to be considered within the sphere of religion, so as to show that nature is for human beings not only the immediate, external world but rather a world in which humanity knows God; in this way nature is for humanity a revelation of God. We have already seen[b] how this relationship of spirit to nature is present in the ethnic religions where we encountered those forms that belong to the advance of spirit from immediacy, in which nature is taken as contingent, to necessity and to a wise and purposeful mode of activity. Thus the consciousness of God on the part of finite spirit is mediated by nature. Humanity sees God by means of nature; thus far nature is only the veil and the untrue configuration [of God].

What is distinguished from God now is actually an other, and has the form of an other: it is nature, which is for spirit and for humanity. Through it unity is to be accomplished and the consciousness attained that the goal and destination of religion is reconciliation. The first step is the abstract consciousness of God, the fact that humanity raises itself in nature to God: this we have seen in the proofs for the existence of God; and here too belong those pious reflections as to how gloriously God has made everything and how wisely he has arranged all things. These elevated thoughts go straight to God and may start from any set of facts. Piety makes edifying observations of this kind, it starts with the most particular and insignificant things, recognizing in them something that is higher in principle. Mixed in with these observations there is often the distorted notion that what goes on in the world of nature is to be regarded as something higher than what is found in the human sphere. This way of looking at things, however, is inappropriate because it starts from singulars. Another form of observation can be opposed to it, namely, that the cause should be appropriate to the appearance and should itself contain the element of limitation that belongs to the appearance; we require a particular ground on which this particular effect is based. The observation of a particular appearance always has this inappropriate aspect. Further, these particular appearances belong to the realm of the natural. God, however, must be conceived as spirit, and the

b. Natural Humanity

[129]~The truth is [now to be] considered as posited in the second element, in the finite element.~[130] The first thing we have now to consider is the *need* for truth; the second is the *mode* and *manner* of its appearance. |

220

Regarding the first point, the need for truth, it is presupposed that there is present within subjective spirit the demand to know the absolute truth. This need directly implies that the subject exists in a state of untruth. As spirit, however, the subject implicitly surmounts its untruth at the same time, and consequently the latter is for it something that *ought* to be overcome. More strictly defined, untruth means that the subject exists in a state of cleavage from itself; hence the need [for truth] expresses itself in this way: that the cleavage within the subject and its attendant cleavage from the truth should be annulled, that the subject should be reconciled, and that this reconciliation can in itself be only a reconciliation with the truth. This is the more precise form of the need. The way it is defined is that the cleavage is all within the subject, that the subject is evil, that it *is* the split and the contradiction—yet not a contra-

---

element in which we cognize him must likewise be spiritual [cf. John 4:24]. "God thunders with his thundering voice," it is said, "and yet is not recognized" [cf. Job 37:5]; the spiritual person, however, demands something loftier than what is merely natural. In order to be recognized as spirit, God must do more than thunder [W₁ reads: God is more than a mere thunderer].

Follows additionally in W₂ (MiscP): The higher mode of viewing nature, and the deeper relation in which it is to be placed to God, is that in which nature itself is conceived as something spiritual, i.e., as the natural aspect of humanity. It is only when the subject ceases to be classed as belonging to the immediate being of the natural and is posited as what it intrinsically is, namely, as *movement,* and when it has gone into itself, that finitude as such is posited, and indeed as finitude in the process of the relationship in which the need for the absolute idea and its appearance come to exist for it.

[Ed.] ᵃIt is not clear from this reference whether Hegel has in mind the *Phenomenology of Spirit* of 1807 or the chapter by the same title in the *Encyclopedia of the Philosophical Sciences* (1830), §§ 413–439. It is probably the latter since the "doctrine of spirit" could refer to the "Psychology" of the *Encyclopedia,* §§ 440–482. ᵇThis is a reference to the cosmological and physicotheological proofs of the existence of God found in Part II; see the teleological proof according to the lectures of 1831 in the Appendix to Vol. 2 of the unabridged ed.

129. *In B's margin:* 2 August 1827

130. *Thus Hu; L (1827?) reads, similar in W₁:* The absolute idea must come to be *for* consciousness and *in* it; it must become the *truth* for the subject and in it.

diction that simply falls apart, but rather one that simultaneously holds itself together. It is only through its holding together that it is split and has the contradiction within itself.

Consequently, it is requisite that we recall to mind and define the nature or character of humanity on its own account—how it is to be regarded, how human beings should regard ˉthemselves,ˉ[131] what they should know about themselves. At this point we encounter two opposed definitions, both at once. The first is that *humanity is by nature good*. Its universal, substantial essence is good; far from being split within itself, its essence or concept is that it is by nature what is harmonious and at peace with itself. Opposed to this is the second characterization: *humanity is by nature evil*—that is, its natural, substantial aspect is evil. These are the antitheses that are present for us at the outset for | external consideration: sometimes one view has been in vogue, and sometimes the other. It should be added, moreover, that this is not just the way that *we* view the situation; it is human beings [generally] who have this knowledge of themselves, of how they are constituted and what their definition is.

221

Humanity is by nature good:[132] This is the more or less predominant notion of our time.[133] If only this proposition is valid, that humanity by nature is good, is not cloven, then it has no need of reconciliation; and if reconciliation is unnecessary, then the entire process we are here considering is superfluous.

It is [indeed] essential to say that humanity is good: human beings are implicitly spirit and rationality, created in and after the image of God [Gen. 1:26–27]. God is the good, and human beings as ˋspirit are the mirror of God; they, too, are *implicitly* good. This is a correct statement. Precisely on this proposition, and on it alone, the possibility of their reconciliation rests. The difficulty and ambiguity of the proposition, however, reside in the definition of the "implicitly" [*an sich*]. Humanity is "implicitly" good: this seems

131. *Thus L, Hu; B, W read:* it *An reads:* it (themselves)

132. [*Ed.*] Hegel attributed this view primarily to Kant, although it is properly traced to Rousseau, esp. to his *Émile.* See unabridged ed., Vol. 3:100.

133. *L adds (Var/Ed?):* In treating the community, a topic for consideration will be how religious intuition and the religious relationship are developed and determined within it.

to say it all, but the "implicitly" designates precisely a one-sidedness which implies that everything has *not* been said. Humanity is "implicitly" good: this means that human beings are good only in an inner way, or according to the concept, and not according to their actuality. But insofar as they are spirit, they must be in actuality, i.e., *explicitly,* what they are in truth. Physical nature remains in the condition of implicitness [*Ansich*]; it is "implicitly" the concept.[134] Precisely this word "implicitly"—the notion that humanity is "implicitly" good—contains the deficiency. The implicitness of nature consists in the laws of nature; it remains true to its laws and does not go beyond them. It is this that constitutes its substantiality, and hence it is within the sphere of necessity. The other side, however, is that human beings ought to be explicitly what they are implicitly—they ought to become this explicitly. "Good by nature" means "immediately good," and spirit is precisely something that is not natural and immediate. On the contrary, humanity as spirit is what steps forth out of natural life | and passes over   222
into a separation between its concept and its immediate existence. But in the case of nature the concept of nature does not arrive at its being-for-self; this separation of an individual from its law, from its substantial essence, does not occur in nature just because [in it] the individual is not free. But human being is what sets its implicit being, its universal nature, over against itself and enters into this separation.

The other characterization derives immediately from what has just been said, namely, that human being ought not to remain as it is immediately, but should pass beyond its immediacy: this is the concept of spirit. It is correct that human beings are good by nature; but with that, one has only said something one-sided. It is this passing beyond the natural state of humanity, beyond its implicit being, that for the first time constitutes the cleavage within humanity; it is what posits the cleavage. Thus the cleavage is a stepping forth out of natural life and immediacy. But this is not to be construed to mean that there would be no evil until the stepping forth;

134. L (1827?) adds, similar in W: But in it the concept does not arrive at its being-for-itself [*Fürsichsein*].

rather this stepping forth is already contained in the natural state itself. ˉThe implicit constitutesˉ[135] the immediate; but because the implicit being of human being is spirit, humanity in its immediacy is already involved in stepping forth from immediacy, in falling away from it, from its implicit being. Here lies the basis for the second proposition: *humanity is by nature evil;* its implicit being, its natural being, is what is evil. In the natural being of humanity, the deficiency is directly present. Because human being is spirit, it is distinguished from its implicit being and *is* the cleavage.[136] When humanity exists only according to nature [*nur nach der Natur ist*], it is evil. The way humanity is implicitly, or according to its concept, is of course what we refer to abstractly as humanity "according to nature"; but concretely the person who follows passions and instincts, and remains within the sphere of desire, the one whose law is that of natural immediacy, is the natural human being. At the same time, a human being in the natural state is one who wills, and since the content of the natural will is only instinct and inclination, this person is evil. From the formal point of view, since the natural human being has volition and will, | it is not an animal any more; but the content and purposes of its volition are still natural. It is from this standpoint—obviously the higher standpoint—that humanity is evil by nature; and it is evil just because it is a natural thing.

What we vacuously represent to ourselves, in taking the original condition of the human being to have been the state of innocence, is the state of nature, the animal state. Humanity ought not to be innocent [in this sense], it ought not to be brutish; insofar as human being is good, it ought not to be so in the sense that a natural thing is good. Rather it is up to its responsibility [*Schuld*], its will, to be good—it ought to be *imputable*. Responsibility means, in a general sense, the possibility of imputation. The good person is good by and through his will, and hence in virtue of his responsibility. Innocence [*Unschuld*] means to be without a will—without indeed being evil, but also at the same time without being good. Natural

223

135. *Thus L, W₁; W₂ reads:* The implicit and the natural state constitute
136. *L (1827?) adds, similar in W:* In the natural state, one-sidedness is directly present.

things and animals are all good, but this kind of goodness cannot be attributed to humanity.[137]

What is absolutely required is that human being should not persist as a natural will, a natural essence. It is simultaneously possessed of consciousness, to be sure, but as human being it can still be essentially natural inasmuch as the natural constitutes the purpose, content, and definition of its volition. We must look at this definition more closely: the human being is human as a subject, and as a natural subject it is *this* single individual; the will involved is this singular will, and it is fulfilled with the content of its singularity. This means that natural humanity is selfish. But we demand of one who is called good that he should at least be guided by general principles and laws. Strictly speaking, the naturalness of the will is the selfishness of the will; in its naturalness, the will is private, distinguished from the universality of willing and opposed to the rationality of the will that has been cultivated into universality.

So whenever we consider what humanity is implicitly, the deficiency of implicit being is directly involved. But the fact that, insofar as its will is natural, humanity is evil, does not annul the other side, the fact that it is implicitly good, which always remains part of its concept. Humanity, however, is reflection and consciousness, | and therefore it engages in the process of distinguishing; for this reason it is something actual, a "this," a subject, distinct from its concept. And since this subject exists to begin with *only* in a state of distinction and has not yet returned to unity, to the identity of subjectivity and the concept, to rationality, the actuality that it has is the natural actuality that is selfishness. The condition of evil directly presupposes the relation of actuality to the concept; this simply posits the contradiction between implicit being or the concept and singularity, the contradiction between good and evil. This is the antithesis that is our first topic of inquiry. It is false to ask whether humanity is only good by nature or only evil. That is a false way of posing the question. In the same way, it is superficial to say that

224

137. L (1827?) adds, similar in W: Insofar as one is good, one should be so by means of one's will.

humanity is both good and evil equally. Implicitly, according to its concept, human being is good; but this implicitness is a one-sidedness, and the one-sidedness is marked by the fact that the actual subject, the "this," is only a natural will. Thus both of them, both good and evil, are posited, but essentially in contradiction, in such a way that each of them presupposes the other. It is not that only one of them is [there], but instead we have both of them in this relation of being opposed to each other.

This is the first fundamental definition, the essential determination of the concept [of natural humanity].

c. *The Story of the Fall*[138]

This accordingly is the mode and manner of the shape in which this conceptual determination appears representationally as a story and is represented for consciousness in an intuitable or sensible mode, so that it is regarded as something that *happened*. It is the familiar story in Genesis. The gist of it is that God created human beings in his own image: this is the concept of the human being.[139] Humankind lived in Paradise; we can call it a zoological garden. This life is called the state of innocence. The story says, too, that

---

138. [*Ed.*] In the 1827 lectures, the discussion of the story of the fall (Gen. 3) is not simply appended at the end of the treatment of differentiation and natural humanity, as in the *Ms.* and the 1824 lectures. Rather it is integrated as the representational, storylike version of what has just been treated conceptually. This then enables Hegel to conclude the entire discussion of differentiation with the conceptual insight that it is humanity's cognitive capacity—specifically the knowledge of good and evil—that gives rise to estrangement (or cleavage) and hence to evil (Sec. d). A smooth transition is then provided from the fact of estrangement to the need for reconciliation, which is taken up in Sec. B.2.

In this section and the next, the term *Erkenntnis* is translated as "knowledge" rather than as "cognition" when the reference is to such familiar expressions as "the tree of knowledge" or "the knowledge of good and evil." Also in these sections Hegel customarily uses the term *Entzweiung* ("cleavage," "rupture," etc.) instead of *Entfremdung* ("estrangement," "alienation"). The terms are virtually synonymous since to be "split" or "cloven" within oneself is to exist in a state of estrangement or self-alienation. We have maintained the terminological distinction, although in the present context "estrangement" could be a more idiomatic rendering of *Entzweiung*.

139. *L (1827?) adds:* This concept is now represented as something that also has being.

the tree of the knowledge of good and evil stood in Paradise, and that human beings disobeyed God's command by eating of it. On the one hand, it is formally set down that this eating was the transgression of a commandment. The content, however, is the essential thing, namely, that the sin consisted in having eaten of the tree of knowledge of good and evil, and | in this connection there   225
comes about the pretense of the serpent that humanity will be like God when it has the knowledge of good and evil.

It is said, then, that human beings have eaten of this tree. It is clear, as far as the content is concerned, that the fruit is an outward image—it belongs only to the sensible portrayal. What it really means is that humanity has elevated itself to the knowledge of good and evil; and this cognition, this distinction, is the source of evil, is evil itself. Being evil is located in the act of cognition, in consciousness. And certainly, as we already said earlier,[140] being evil resides in cognitive knowledge; cognition is the source of evil. For cognition or consciousness means in general a judging or dividing, a self-distinguishing within oneself. Animals have no consciousness, they are unable to make distinctions within themselves, they have no free being-for-self in the face of objectivity generally. The cleavage,[141] however, is what is evil; it is the contradiction. It contains the two sides: good and evil. Only in this cleavage is evil contained, and hence it is itself evil. Therefore it is entirely correct to say that good and evil are first to be found in consciousness.

The first human being is represented as having brought about this fall. Here again we have this sensible mode of expression. From the point of view of thought, the expression "the first human being" signifies "humanity in itself" or "humanity as such"—not some single, contingent individual, not one among many, but the absolutely first one, humanity according to its concept. Human being

140. [Ed.] This cross-reference has probably been inserted into the text by Lasson in order to camouflage the repetition of the corresponding passage in the Ms.

141. [Ed.] Hegel here draws upon the etymological similarity between the terms Entzweiung ("cleavage," "division into two" [Ent-zwei-ung]) and Urteil ("judgment," "primal division" [Ur-teil]). Because knowledge or cognition (Erkenntnis) entails an act of judgment, it issues in division, cleavage, and estrangement; and because evil is "contained" in the cleavage, knowledge is the source of evil.

as such is conscious being; it is precisely for that reason that humanity enters into this cleavage, into the consciousness that, when it is further specified, is cognition. But inasmuch as universal humanity is represented as a first man, he is represented as distinguished from others. Hence the question arises: if there is only one who has done this, how is that deed transmitted to others? Here the notion of an inheritance of sin that is passed on to all others comes into play. By this means the deficiency involved in viewing humanity as such representationally as a first man is corrected. The one-sidedness involved in representing the cleavage belonging to the concept of human being generally as the act of a single individual is absorbed by this notion of a communicated or inherited sin. 226 Neither the original representation | nor the correction are really necessary; for it is humanity as a whole that, as consciousness, enters into this cleavage.

But in the same way as this cleavage is the source of evil, it is also the midpoint of the conversion that consciousness contains within itself whereby this cleavage is also sublated.[142] The story reports that an alien creature, the serpent, seduced humanity by the pretense that, if one knows how to distinguish good and evil, one will become like God. In this way the story represents the fact that humanity's deed springs from the evil principle. However, the confirmation of the fact that the knowledge of good and evil belongs to the divinity of humanity is placed on the lips of God himself. [143]God himself says: "Behold, Adam has become like one of us" [Gen. 3:22]. So the words of the serpent were no deception. This is customarily overlooked along the lines of the ingrained prejudice to the effect that this is an irony of God,[144] that God has made a joke.[145]

---

142. *L (1827?) adds:* The highest cleavage, the distinction between good and evil (good as such by definition exists only in contrast with evil, and evil only in contrast with good), is certainly cognitive knowledge; and human being as such, as spirit, eats of the tree of the knowledge of good and evil.

143. *In B's margin:* 6 August 1827

144. [*Ed.*] See J. G. Herder, *Aelteste Urkunde des Menschengeschlechts,* vol. 2 (Riga, 1776), pp. 108–109.

145. *L (1827?) adds:* However, what distinguishes human being as human, as spirit, is precisely cognition and cleavage.

Labor and the childbearing of woman are then declared to be the punishment for sin [Gen. 3:16–19]. In general, this is a necessary consequence. The animal does not labor, or it does so only when compelled, and not by nature; it does not eat its bread in the sweat of its brow or produce its own bread, but rather finds the satisfaction of all its needs directly in nature. Human beings, too, find the material for their satisfaction in nature, but this material is, so to speak, the least important element for them; the infinite provision for the satisfaction of their needs occurs only through labor. Labor done in the sweat of one's brow, or bodily work, and the labor of the spirit, which is the harder of the two, are immediately connected with the knowledge of good and evil. That | humanity must make   227 itself what it is, that it must produce and eat bread in the sweat of its brow, belongs to what is most essential and distinctive about it and coheres necessarily with the knowledge of good and evil.

The story further depicts a second tree, a tree of life, that stood in Paradise. God wanted to drive Adam out [of Paradise (Gen. 3:22–23)], so that he would not be immortal. This, too, is expressed in a simple, childlike image. For the wishes of human beings, there are two ˜directions.˜[146] One line is directed toward living in undisturbed happiness, in harmony with oneself and external nature; it is the animals that remain in this unity, while humanity has to pass beyond it. The other line answers rather to the wish to live eternally. And the representation of the tree of life is formed in accord with ˜this latter wish.˜[147] When we consider it more closely, it is directly evident that this is only a childlike representation. Human being as a single living thing, its singular life, its natural life, must die.[148] So on the one hand, it is said that human beings in Paradise and without sin would be immortal; they would be able to live forever.[149] For, if outward death were only a consequence

146. *Thus L; W₁ (Var) reads:* branches. *W₂ (Var) reads:* types of good.

147. *Thus An; B reads:* the wish. *L reads:* these two wishes. *W reads:* these wishes.

148. *L (1827?) adds, similar in W:* But when the story is viewed more closely, this is seen to be the wondrous aspect of it, the self-contradictory aspect.

149. *L (1827?) adds, similar in W:* (In this story, immortality on earth and immortality of the soul are not separate.)

of sin, then humanity in Paradise would be implicitly immortal. On the other hand, however, it is also said that human beings will become immortal for the first time when they have eaten of the tree of life—but it cannot be assumed that they would have eaten of the tree of life without sin, for this was forbidden them.

The fact of the matter is that humanity is immortal only through cognitive knowledge,[150] for only in the activity of thinking is its soul pure and free rather than mortal and animallike. Cognition and thought are the root of human life, of human immortality as a totality within | itself. The animal soul is submerged in corporeality, while spirit is a totality within itself. This is the first point that is represented.

d. Knowledge, Estrangement, and Evil

The second point is that the view we have grasped as essential in [the realm of] thought should become actual in humanity as such— i.e., that human beings should realize the infinity of this antithesis between good and evil within themselves, and that as natural beings they should *know* themselves to be evil in their naturalness. They should become conscious of this antithesis[151] within themselves and know that they are the ones who are evil. But it also pertains to this that evil at the same time refers to the good, that there is present [along with evil] the demand of the good, of being good, and that one becomes aware of this contradiction, undergoing anguish because of it, because of this cleavage. We have encountered the form of this antithesis in all religions. But the antithesis to the power of nature, to the ethical law, the ethical will, and ethical life, or to fate—these are all subordinate antitheses that contain only ˜something˜[152] particular. The person who violates a commandment is evil, but only in this particular case; he stands in opposition to this particular commandment. In the Parsee religion,[153] we saw that

---

150. [*Ed.*] See Fragment 3 from Michelet, unabridged ed., Vol. 3:387.
151. *Thus L; W₂ adds:* not only in general but of it
152. *Thus L, W₁; W₂ (Var) reads:* the antithesis to something
153. [*Ed.*] The religion of Persia, or Zoroastrianism.

good and evil, light and darkness, stand in universal antithesis to each other. There, however, the antithesis is *external* to human beings, and they themselves are outside it. This abstract antithesis is not present within them.

It is therefore required that ⌐humanity should comprehend this abstract antithesis *within* itself.¬ [154] It is not that one has transgressed this or that commandment, but rather that one is intrinsically evil—universally evil, purely and simply evil in one's innermost being. [155] This evil character is the essential definition of one's concept: this is what one must bring to consciousness. It is with this depth that we are concerned. Depth means abstraction | —the pure universalization of the antithesis so that its two sides attain this wholly universal specification vis-à-vis each other.

Speaking generally, this antithesis has now two forms. On the one hand, it is the antithesis of evil as such, the fact that it is humanity itself that is evil: this is the *antithesis vis-à-vis* God. On the other hand, it is the *antithesis vis-à-vis the world,* the fact that humanity exists in a state of rupture from the world: this is unhapppiness or misery, the cleavage viewed from the other side.

We have first to consider the relation of the cleavage to one of the extremes, namely, to God. It is an aspect of there being the need for universal reconciliation in humanity—and this means divine, absolute reconciliation—that the antithesis has attained this infinite degree, that this universality [of evil] encompasses the innermost being, that nothing remains outside this antithesis, and that therefore the antithesis is not something particular. This is the deepest depth. Human beings are inwardly conscious that in their innermost being they are a contradiction, and have therefore an infinite *anguish* concerning themselves. Anguish is present only where there is opposition to what ought to be, to an affirmative. What is no longer in itself an affirmative also has no contradiction, no anguish.

229

---

154. *Thus L; W*₁ *(Var) reads:* humanity should overcome this abstract antithesis. W₂ *(Var) reads:* humanity should have this abstract antithesis within itself and should overcome it.

155. *Thus L; W (Var) adds:* evil in one's core.

447

Anguish is precisely the element of negativity in the affirmative, meaning that within itself the affirmative is self-contradictory and wounded. This anguish is thus one moment of evil. Evil merely on its own account is an abstraction; it *is* only in antithesis to the good, and since it is present in the unity of the subject, the latter is split, and this cleavage is infinite anguish. If the consciousness of the good, the infinite demand of the good, is not likewise present in the subject itself, in its innermost being, then no anguish is present and evil itself is only an empty nothingness, for it *is* only in this antithesis.

Evil and anguish can be infinite only when the good or God is known as *one* God, as a pure, spiritual God. It is only when the good is this pure unity, only when we have faith in *one* God, and only in connection with such a faith, that the negative can and must advance to this determination of evil and negation can advance to this universality. One side of this cleavage becomes apparent in this way, through the elevation of humanity to the pure, spiritual unity of God. This anguish and this consciousness are the condition of the absorption [*Vertiefung*] of humanity into itself, | and likewise into the negative moment of cleavage, of evil. This is ˜an objective,˜[156] inward absorption into evil; inward absorption of an affirmative kind is absorption into the pure unity of God.

At this point it is evident that humanity, I as a natural human being, ˜do not correspond to˜[157] what the truth is, but likewise the truth of the one good remains firmly fixed within me. This lack of correspondence is characterized as what ought not to be. The task and demand are infinite. One can say: Since I am a natural human being, I have, on the one hand, consciousness of myself, but on the other hand my natural being [*Natürlichkeit*] consists rather in a lack of consciousness with regard to myself, in being without a will. I am the sort of being that acts according to nature, and in this respect I am innocent, it is often said, having no consciousness

156. *Thus L, W₁; W₂ reads:* a negative,
157. *L, W₁ read:* does not correspond to   *Hu reads:* am unsuitable to   W₂ *reads:* do not correspond to, and am caught in the many natural particularities [vis-à-vis]

of what I do, being without a will of my own, acting without inclination, allowing myself to be surprised by instinct. But *here,* in the antithesis that we have observed, the innocence disappears, for precisely the natural being of humanity, lacking in consciousness and will, is what ought not to be. In the face of the pure unity and perfect purity that I know as absolute truth, this natural being is declared to be evil. What has been said implies that[158] the absence of consciousness and will is to be considered as itself essentially evil. And thus the contradiction remains, no matter how one twists ˉoneselfˉ[159] about. Since this so-called innocence is defined as evil, my lack of correspondence to my essence and to the absolute remains; and from one side or the other I know myself always as what ought not to be.

This is the relation to the one extreme, and the result, the more determinate mode of this anguish, is my humiliation, my remorse; I experience anguish because I as a natural being do not correspond to what at the same time I *know* to be my own essence, to what I should be in my own knowing and willing. | 231

Concerning the relation to the other extreme, the world, the separation appears as *unhappiness* [*Unglück*]—the fact that humanity is not satisfied in the world.[160] As natural beings, human beings are related to other natural beings, and others are related to them as powers [*Mächte*], and to this extent each is as contingent as the other. However, the higher requirements of humanity, those having to do with ethical life, are requirements and determinations of freedom. Insofar as these requirements, which are implicitly justified in the concept of humanity—for human beings know what is good, and the good is in them—do not find satisfaction in existence, in the external world, humanity is in a state of unhappiness.

It is this unhappiness that drives and presses human beings back into themselves; and since the fixed demand that the world should be rational is present within them but does not find fulfillment, they

158. *Thus L; W (Var) adds:* when we arrive at this point
159. *Thus L; W (Var) reads:* it
160. *L (1827?) adds, similar in W:* Its natural needs have no further right or claim to satisfaction.

renounce the world, seeking happiness and satisfaction in the harmony of the self with itself. [The demand becomes] that they renounce the world and achieve the satisfaction of their happiness [in this inner harmony]. In order to achieve the harmony of their affimative side with their determinate being, they give up the external world, transfer their happiness into themselves, and seek satisfaction within themselves.

˘This element˘[161]—the anguish that comes from universality, from above—we saw in the Jewish people; it does not release me in my natural existence, in my empirical willing and knowing, from the infinite demands of absolute purity. The other form [of cleavage or estrangement], the being driven back into oneself by unhappiness, is the standpoint at which the Roman world arrived—the universal unhappiness of the world. We saw the formal inwardness that satisfies itself in the world ˘as the dominion of God's purpose,˘[162] which is represented, intended, and known as a worldly dominion.

Each of these sides has its one-sidedness. The first may be described as the sensation | of ˘humiliation;˘[163] the other is the abstract elevation of human being inwardly—the human being who is concentrated within himself—and hence it is Stoicism and Skepticism. The Stoic or Skeptic sage was directed back to himself and was supposed to be satisfied within himself. Through independence and rigid self-containment, he was supposed to find happiness and be in harmony with himself; in this abstract self-absorption, in the presence of [his own] self-conscious interiority, he was supposed to be at rest.

These are the highest, most abstract moments of all; here the antithesis is at its height, and both sides embrace the antithesis in its most complete universality—in the universal itself—and in its innermost essence, its greatest depth. But, as we have said, both

232

161. *Thus Hu, similar in An; L reads:* We already found these two forms of cleavage in the particular religions. W_1 *(Var) reads:* We found these two forms: W_2 *(Var) reads:* With respect to this demand and this unhappiness, we found these two forms:

162. *Thus L; W (Var) reads:* [we saw] this dominion, the purpose of God,

163. *Thus Hu, W; L (Var) reads:* humility;

forms are one-sided. The first contains that anguish and abstract humiliation the crowning feature of which is the utter lack of correspondence between the subject and the universal, the cleavage or rupture that is not bridged, is not healed. This is the standpoint of the most abstract antithesis between the infinite on the one side and a fixed finitude on the other—and this finitude is abstract finitude. Here everything that is reckoned as belonging to me is simply evil. This abstraction finds its complement on the other side, namely in the process of internal thought; here we have the correspondence of self with self, [the claim] that I am satisfied, and can be satisfied within myself. This second form, however, is just as one-sided on its own account, because it comprises only the affirmative side, and indeed the one-sided affirmation of myself within myself. The contrition of the first side is only negative, lacking in self-affirmation; the second side is now supposed to be this pure affirmation, this self-satisfaction. But this satisfaction of myself within myself is only an abstract satisfaction; it occurs only by means of flight from the world and from actuality—by means of this inactivity. Since this is a flight from actuality, it is also a flight from *my* actuality—and indeed not from my external actuality, but from that of my own volition. The *actuality* of my volition—I as a specific subject, as a will filled with content—is no longer mine, but what remains for me is the *immediacy* of my self-consciousness. To be sure, the latter is completely | abstract, but the final extremity of depth is contained therein, and ˉI have preserved it therein.ˉ[164] It is not an abstraction from the abstract actuality within me or from my immediate self-consciousness, from the immediacy of my self-consciousness. On this side, therefore, affirmation is the predominant factor, but it does not include the negation of the one-sidedness of immediate being found on the other side; while on that side the negation is [itself] the one-sided factor. These two moments contain within themselves the need for a transition.

The concept of the preceding religions has refined itself into this

<hr/>

164. *Thus L; B reads:* and that which I have preserved for myself therein. *W (Var) reads:* I have preserved myself therein.

antithesis; and the fact that the antithesis has disclosed and presented itself as an actually existing need is expressed by the words,
"When the time had fully come, God sent forth his Son" [Gal. 4:4].
This means: the Spirit is at hand, the need for the Spirit that points
the way to reconciliation.

2. Reconciliation

a. The Idea of Reconciliation and Its Appearance in a Single Individual

[165]The deepest need of spirit is that the antithesis within the subject
itself should be intensified to its universal, i.e., its most abstract,
extreme. This is the cleavage, the anguish that we have considered.
That these two sides do not fall completely apart, but rather constitute a contradiction within the unity of the subject, demonstrates
at the same time that the subject is the infinite power of unity: it
can bear this contradiction. This is the formal, abstract, yet infinite
energy of unity that it possesses. What satisfies this need is the
consciousness of atonement, of the sublation, the nullification of
the antithesis, so that the latter is not the truth. Rather, the truth
is the attainment of unity through the negation of the antithesis;
this is the peace, the reconciliation, that the need demands. Reconciliation is what is demanded by the need of the subject, and this
exigency resides in the subject as infinite unity or as self-identity.

The sublation of the antithesis has two sides. First, the subject
must become conscious of the fact that the antithetic opposites are
not [things] in themselves, but that instead the truth, the inner
nature [of spirit], consists in the sublatedness of the antithesis.
Second, because the antithesis is implicitly and truthfully sublated,
234 | the subject as such, in its being-for-itself, can reach and attain
peace and reconciliation through the sublation of the antithesis.

That the antithesis is *implicitly* sublated constitutes the condition,
the presupposition, the possibility that the subject should also sublate this antithesis *explicitly*. In this respect it may be said that the
subject does not attain reconciliation on its own account, i.e., as
this [single] subject and in virtue of its [own] activity or conduct;

165. *In B's margin:* 7 August 1827

reconciliation is not brought about, nor can it be brought about, by the subject in its way of conducting itself. The subject's activity consists only in positing, in doing, the one side. The other side is what is substantial and foundational, that without which there is no possibility of resolving the antithesis—namely, that implicitly this antithesis is not present. Put more precisely, the antithesis arises eternally and just as eternally sublates itself; there is at the same time eternal reconciliation. That this is the truth may be seen in the eternal, divine idea: God is the one who as living spirit distinguishes himself from himself, posits an other and in this other remains identical with himself, has in this other his identity with himself. This is the truth.

It is this truth that constitutes one side of what must come to consciousness in humanity, namely, the side that has substantial being in itself. This can be expressed more precisely as follows: the antithesis is incongruous in principle. The antithesis (or evil) is the natural state of human being and willing; it is human immediacy, which is precisely the modality of natural life. Along with immediacy, finitude is likewise posited, and this finitude or naturalness is incongruous with the universality of God, with the infinite, eternal idea, which is utterly free within itself and present to itself. This incongruity is the point of departure that constitutes the need [for reconciliation]. But the more precise determinacy [of it] is not that this incongruity of the two sides disappears for consciousness. The incongruity is [there], it resides in spirituality. Spirit is the process of self-differentiating, the positing of distinctions. If the distinctions are made, then in the respect that they are distinct they are not equal; they are distinct, not congruous with one another. *This* incongruity cannot disappear, for otherwise the judgment of spirit, its | vitality, would disappear, and it would cease to be spirit. It is   235
rather the case that the two sides are not merely incongruous and that the identity of the two persists in spite of their incongruity. The other-being, the finitude, the weakness, the frailty of human nature is not to do any harm to that divine unity which forms the substance of reconciliation. That no harm is done has been seen in the divine idea. For the Son is other than the Father, and this otherness is difference—otherwise it would not be spirit. But the

other is [also] God and has the entire fullness of the divine nature within itself. The character of otherness in no way detracts from the fact that this other is the Son of God and therefore God.[166] This otherness is what eternally posits and eternally sublates itself; the self-positing and sublating of otherness is love or spirit.

Evil, the one side, has been abstractly defined as only the other, the finite, the negative, and God is placed on the other side as the good, the positive, the true. But this is not a true representation. For that which is negative and other also contains affirmation within itself. It must be brought to consciousness[167] that the principle of affirmation is contained within that negative, and that in the affirmative principle there lies the principle of identity with the other side—even as God, as truth, is not just abstract identity with himself, but on the contrary the other, negation, the positing of oneself otherwise, is God's own essential determination, and the proper determination of spirit. ⁓⁓Hence this need could come to consciousness. This implicit being, this implicitly subsisting unity | of divine and human nature, must come to consciousness in infinite anguish—but only in accord with implicit being, with substantiality, so that finitude, weakness, and otherness can do no harm to the substantial unity of the two. Or expressed differently, the substantiality of the unity of divine | and human nature comes to consciousness for humanity in such a way that a human being[168] appears to consciousness as God, and God appears to it as a human being. This is ⁓the necessity and need⁓[169] for such an appearance.

Furthermore, the consciousness of the absolute idea that we have in philosophy in the form of thinking[170] is to be brought forth not for the standpoint of philosophical speculation or speculative thinking but in the form of *certainty*. The necessity [that the divine-human unity shall appear] is not first apprehended by means of thinking; rather it is a certainty for humanity. In other words, this content—the unity of divine and human nature—achieves certainty,

236

237

---

166. *Thus L; W (Var) adds:* nor does it detract from this other in human nature.
167. *Thus L, W₁; W₂ (Var) adds:* within finite being
168. *Thus L, Hu; An adds:* (but not every human being)
169. *Thus L; W₁ (Var) reads:* the necessity of this need
170. *[Ed.]* See *Science of Logic*, pp. 824–844 (GW 12:236–253).

obtaining the form of immediate sensible intuition and external existence for humankind, so that it appears as something that has been seen in the world, something that has been | experienced. It   238
is essential to this form of nonspeculative consciousness that it must be *before* us; it must essentially be *before* me—it must become a certainty for humanity. For it is only what exists in an immediate way, in inner or outer intuition, that is certain. In order for it [this divine-human unity] to become a certainty for humanity, *God had to appear in the world in the flesh* [cf. John 1:14]. The necessity that God [has] appeared in the world in the flesh is an essential characteristic—a necessary deduction from what has been said previously, demonstrated by it—for only in this way can it become a certainty for humanity; only in this way is it the truth in the form of certainty.

⌐At the same time there is this more precise specification to be added, namely, that the unity of divine and human nature must appear in *just one human being*. Humanity in itself as such is the universal, or the thought of humanity.⌐[171] From the present standpoint, however, it is not a question of the thought of humanity but of sensible certainty; thus it is just one human being in whom this unity is envisaged—humanity as singular, or in the determinacy of singularity and particularity. Moreover, it is not just a matter of singularity *in general,* for singularity in general is something universal once more. But from the present standpoint, singularity is not something universal; universal singularity is found in abstract thinking as such. Here, however, it is a question of the certainty of intuiting and sensing. The substantial unity [of God and humanity] is what humanity implicitly is; hence it is something that lies beyond immediate consciousness, beyond ordinary consciousness and knowledge. Hence it must stand over against subjective consciousness, which relates to itself as ordinary consciousness and is defined as such. That is exactly why the unity in question must appear for others as a singular human being set apart; it is not present in the others, but only in one from whom all the others are excluded.

171. *Thus L; W (Var) reads:* The unity of divine and human nature, humanity in its universality, is the thought of humanity. W_2 *(Var) adds:* and the idea of absolute spirit, which has being in and for itself.

¨Thus this one stands over against the others as what humanity implicitly is—a single individual [who is there] as the soil of

239 certainty.¨ [172] |

Thus there are two conditions for this appearance. The first is that consciousness can achieve this content, this substantial unity, the consciousness of which is given and which is its reconciliation. The second condition is the consciousness of the determinate form of this exclusive singularity.¨¨ [173]

172. *Thus L, which reads in German: So ist er ihnen drüben als das Ansich und ein Einzelner als Boden der Gewissheit. W₁ (Var) reads:* Thus it [es (the unity?))] stands over against the others as what humanity implicitly is—singularity on the soil of certainty. *Hu reads:* For only in this way does this one become what stands over there [*das Drüben*] for the intuition of human beings. *W₂ (Var) reads:* —but no longer as what implicitly is [*das Ansich*], which is over there [*das drüben ist*], but as singularity on the soil of certainty.

173. *W₁, and in part also W₂, transmit a parallel to this passage from the 1831 lectures. The text below follows W₁, but the passages contained in W₂ in somewhat fuller form are also given. W₁ (1831) reads:* The one mode of revelation that leads as a whole to the elevation [of spirit], whose general characteristics we have considered earlier, is revelation by way of nature and the world. The other mode is the higher one and occurs through finite spirit. This is what first displays the interest of the standpoint at which we now find ourselves. Divinity is recognized by finite human beings in what is objectively available to intuition, sensibility, and immediate consciousness.

This is the appearance of God in the flesh. God should be known as being for other, for humanity, and the human is an intuiting and sensing being—this singular human being. The possibility of reconciliation is present only when the implicitly subsisting unity of divine and human nature is known. Human beings can know themselves to be taken up into God only when God is not something alien to them, only when they are not merely an extrinsic accident upon God's nature, but rather when they are taken up into God in accordance with their essence and freedom. The implicitly subsisting unity of divine and human nature must be revealed to humanity in an objective way; this is what happened through the incarnation of God.

W₂ reads: The possibility of reconciliation resides only in the fact that the implicitly subsisting unity of divine and human nature is known; this is the necessary foundation. Human beings can know themselves to be taken up into God inasmuch as God is not something alien to them and they are not related to him as an extrinsic accident [*W₁ reads:* as something extrinsic]—[i.e.,] when they are taken up into God in accordance with their essence, their freedom and subjectivity [*W₁ reads:* when they are subjects in God in accordance with their essence and freedom]. But this is possible only in virtue of the fact that this subjectivity of human nature is [present] within God himself. *W₁ continues:* and the implicitly subsisting unity of divine and human nature is [there] for them when God appears as human. Similarly, in a quite inferior form we have seen the incarnations of the Hindu deities, the Dalai Lama, and Buddha—[these are] human beings revered as deities. Among the Greeks there

In the church Christ has been called the "God-man." This is a monstrous compound, which directly contradicts both representation and understanding. But what has thereby been brought into human consciousness and made a certainty for it is the unity of divine and human nature, implying that the otherness, or, as we also say, the finitude, weakness, and frailty of human nature, does not damage this unity, just as otherness does not impair the unity

---

is even a human being, Heracles, who swings himself up into heaven through his bravery and his deeds, and is received among the gods. All this is quite different from what we have before us at this point; but all the same the impulsion toward this way of determining the implicitly subsisting unity is unmistakable. The form is still quite inferior, to be sure: in Hindu pantheism, substance dons only the mask of subjectivity, for it does not attain to actual, free subjectivity.

W₂ *reads:* This determination, namely, that God becomes human [*dass Gott Mensch wird*], and consequently that finite spirit has the consciousness of God within the finite itself, is the most difficult moment of religion. According to a common representation, which we find among the ancients especially,ᵃ the spirit or soul has been relegated to this world as something alien; this indwelling [of the soul] in the body, and this singularization to [the limit of] individuality, are held to be a degradation of spirit. This is what characterizes the purely material side, or immediate existence, as untrue. But on the other hand immediate existence is at the same time an essential determination; it is where spirit is sharpened to a final point in its subjectivity. Human beings have spiritual interests and are spiritually active; they can feel that they are hindered in exercising these interests and activities because they feel that they are physically dependent and must make provision for their sustenance etc. Thus they fall away from their spiritual interests because of their bondage to nature. But the moment of immediate existence is contained within spirit itself; it is [logically] characteristic of spirit to advance to this moment. Natural life is not merely an external necessity; on the contrary, spirit as subject, in its infinite relatedness to itself, has the [logical] character of immediacy in it. Now, inasmuch as it is to be revealed to humanity what the nature of spirit is, and the nature of God is to become manifest in the entire development of the idea, this form [of immediacy] must also be present here, and this is precisely the form of finitude. The divine must appear in the form of immediacy. This immediate presence is only the presence of the spiritual in its spiritual shape, i.e., in the human shape. In no other way is this appearance genuine—not, for instance, the appearance of God in the burning bush [Exod. 3:2 ff.], and the like. God appears as a single person to whose immediacy all [the usual] physical needs are attached. In Hindu pantheism a countless number of incarnations occur; but there subjectivity, the human being, is only an accidental form in God; it is only a mask that substance adopts and exchanges in contingent fashion. As spirit, on the other hand, God contains the moment of subjectivity and uniqueness in himself; his appearance, therefore, can only be a single one, it can take place only once.

[*Ed.*] ᵃHegel is referring to Gnostic representations of the imprisonment of the spirit and soul in matter, with which he was familiar through Neander's *Gnostische Systeme* (on Basilides, see pp. 36–37; on Valentinus, pp. 106–107).

that God is in the eternal idea. It is the appearance of a human being in sensible presence; God in sensible presence can take no other shape than that of human being. In the sensible and mundane order, only the human is spiritual; so if the spiritual is to have a sensible shape, it must be a human shape.

b. The Historical, Sensible Presence of Christ

This ˜appearance of the God-man˜[174] has to be viewed from two different perspectives at once. First, he is a human being in accord with his external circumstances. This is the nonreligious perspective [die irreligiöse Betrachtung] in which he appears as an ordinary human being. Second, there is the perspective that occurs in the Spirit or with the Spirit. Spirit presses toward its truth because it has an infinite cleavage and anguish within itself. It wills the truth; the need of the truth and the certainty thereof it will have, and must have. Here for the first time we have ˜the religious view [das Religiöse].˜[175] |

240

When Christ is viewed in the same light as Socrates, then he is regarded as an ordinary human being, just as in Islam he is regarded as a messenger of God in the general sense that all great men are messengers of God.[176] If one says no more of Christ than that he is a teacher of humanity, a martyr to the truth, one is not adopting ˜the religious standpoint;˜[177] one ˜says˜[178] no more of him than of Socrates. But there is this human side of Christ too—his appearance as a living human being—and we shall mention briefly its moments.

The first moment is that he is *immediately a human being* in all the external contingencies, in all the temporal exigencies and conditions, that this entails. He is born like every other human being,

---

174. *Thus L; Hu, An reads:* appearance *W (Var) reads:* historical appearance

175. *Thus L, Hu; An reads:* the religious perspective [*religiöse Betrachtung*]. *W (1831) reads:* the genuine perspective in religion. These two sides are to be distinguished here—the immediate perspective and that of faith. Through faith we know that this individual has a divine nature, and in that way the "beyondness" of God is superseded.

176. [*Ed.*] Hegel was critical of the comparison of Socrates and Christ frequently found in the Enlightenment; see unabridged ed., Vol. 3:244n. 215.

177. *Thus L, Hu; W (Var) reads:* the Christian standpoint, that of the true religion;

178. *Hu reads:* speaks

and as a human he has the needs of other human beings; only he does not share the corruption, the passions, and the evil inclinations of the others, nor is he involved in particular worldly interests, along with which integrity and teaching may also find a place. Rather he lives only for the truth, only for its proclamation; his activity consists solely in completing the higher consciousness of humanity.[179]

˜Thus the second moment is that of his teaching office.˜[180] The question now is this: "How can, how must this teaching be constituted?" This original teaching cannot be constituted in a manner similar to the later doctrine of the church; it must have its own distinctive aspects, which in the church[181] partly take on another character and are partly set aside.[182] Once the community is established, once the kingdom of God has attained its determinate being and its actuality, these teachings are either interpreted in other ways or else they fall by the wayside.[183] |

241

Since what is at issue is the consciousness of absolute reconciliation, we are here in the presence of a new consciousness of humanity, or a new religion. Through it a new world is constituted, a new actuality, a different world-condition, because [humanity's] outward determinate being, [its] natural existence, now has religion as its substantiality. This is the aspect that is negative and polemical, being opposed to the subsistence of externality in the consciousness[184] of humanity. The new religion expresses itself precisely as a new consciousness, the consciousness of a reconciliation of

179. *Thus L, similar in An; W₁ (1831) adds:* This affords an intuition of what is available for the community. It is available at the same time in a sensuous way, and to this extent it is an emptying out [*Entäusserung*] of the divine, of the idea, which has to annul itself.

180. *Thus L, similar in An; W (1831) reads:* The teaching of Christ also belongs on this human side.

181. *Thus L; W (Var) adds:* in necessary fashion

182. *Thus L; W (1831) adds:* As this immediate teaching, Christ's teaching cannot be Christian dogmatics, cannot be the doctrine of the church.

183. *Thus L; W₁ (1831) adds:* The primitive [*unmittelbare*] Christian teaching arouses sensibilities by means of representation. Its content, which at the highest level is explication of the nature of God, is [directed] precisely at sensible consciousness and comes to the latter as intuition, not doctrine, which has the concept as its form—this only became necessary in the church later on when science began.

184. *Thus Hu; W (Var) adds:* and faith

humanity with God. This reconciliation, expressed as a state of affairs, is the kingdom of God, an actuality.[185] The souls and hearts [of individuals] are reconciled with God, and thus it is God who rules in the heart and has attained dominion.

This kingdom of God, the new religion, thus contains implicitly the characteristic of negating the present world. This is its polemical aspect, its revolutionary attitude toward all the determinate aspects of that outer world, [all the settled attitudes] of human consciousness and belief. [186]So what is at issue is the drawing of those who are to achieve the consciousness of reconciliation away from present actuality, requiring of them an abstraction from it. The new religion is itself still concentrated and does not actually exist as a community, but has its vitality rather in that energy which constitutes the sole, eternal interest of its adherents who have to fight and struggle in order to achieve this for themselves, because it is not yet coherent with the world consciousness and is not yet in harmony with the condition of the world.

Hence the first emergence of this religion directly contains this polemical aspect. It poses the demand that one should remove oneself ˉfrom finite thingsˉ[187] | and elevate oneself to an infinite energy for which all other bonds are to become matters of indifference, for which all other bonds—indeed, all things hitherto regarded as ethical and right—are to be set aside. Thus Christ says: "Who is my mother, who are my brothers? Whoever does the will of God is my mother, [my] sister, and [my] brother." Or: "Follow me! Leave the dead to bury the dead. Go forth and proclaim the kingdom of God." "I have not come to bring peace on earth, but rather children will leave their parents and follow me."[188]

185. *Thus L; W (Var) adds:* in which God rules.

186. *Precedes in L (1827?), similar in W:* The previous [state of things] is now altered; the way things used to be, the previous condition of religion and the world, cannot continue as before.

187. *Thus L, W; An reads:* from worldliness *Hu reads:* from the world *B reads:* from worldly, earthly thought

188. [*Ed.*] Here Hegel conflates and quotes loosely from Matt. 12:48, 50; Mark 3:33–34; Luke 9:59–60; Matt. 8:21–22; and Matt. 10:34–38. The last clause ("but rather children will leave . . .") is not found in any of the Gospels but may be inferred from Matt. 10:35–38. These quotations are found in the extant sources rather than *L*, which at this point interpolates 1824 text in place of 1827.

We see here a polemical attitude expressed against the ethical relationships that have hitherto prevailed. These are all teachings and characteristics that belong to its first appearance, when the new religion constitutes the sole interest [of its adherents], which they were bound to believe they were still in danger of losing. This is the one side.

This renunciation, surrender, and setting aside of all vital interests and moral bonds is an essential characteristic of the concentrated manifestation of the truth, a characteristic that subsequently loses its importance when the truth has achieved a secure existence. ˉBeyond thatˉ[189] is the proclamation of the kingdom of God. Humanity must transpose itself into this kingdom[190] in such a way as to cast itself immediately upon this truth. This is expressed with the purest, most colossal boldness, as, for example, at the beginning of the Sermon on the Mount: "Blessed are the [poor] in spirit, for theirs is the kingdom of God. Blessed are the pure in heart, [for] they shall see God" [Matt. 5:3, 8].[191] |

243

[192]Nothing is said about any mediation through which this elevation [of soul] may come to pass for humanity; rather what is spoken of is this immediate being, this immediate self-transposition into the truth, into the kingdom of God. It is to this kingdom, to this intellectual, spiritual world, that humanity ought to belong.

With respect to details, there are more specific teachings, among which the teaching about love constitutes a focal point: ˉ"Love your neighbor as yourself" [Matt. 22:39].ˉ[193] But these teachings are already found in the Old Testament [cf. Deut. 6:5; Lev. 19:18].[194]

---

189. *Thus Hu; L, W₁ read:* It *W₂ (Var) reads:* Beyond that, in the affirmative sphere,

190. *Thus L; W (Var) adds:* as the kingdom of love for God

191. *W (1831) adds:* Words like these are among the greatest that have ever been uttered; they are an ultimate focus that annuls every superstition, every bondage on the part of human beings. It is of the highest importance that, by means of Luther's translation of the Bible, a folk-book has been placed in the hands of the people, a book in which the heart, the spirit, can find itself at home in the highest, infinite fashion; in Catholic lands there is in this respect a great lack. There [in Protestant regions?] the Bible is the means of deliverance from all servitude of spirit.

192. *In B's margin:* 8 August 1827

193. *Thus Hu; W₁ (Var) reads:* "Love God above all and your neighbor as yourself" [cf. Matt. 22:37–39].

194. *Thus Hu, similar in B; W₁ (1831/Var?) adds:* What can be regarded as

Thus the following [distinctive] moment or determinate aspect enters into these teachings. Because the demand, "Seek first . . . "[195]—[i.e.,] cast yourself upon the truth—is expressed so directly, it emerges almost as a subjective declaration, and to this extent the person of the teacher comes into view. Christ speaks not merely as a teacher, who expounds on the basis of his own subjective insight and who is aware of what he is saying and doing, but rather as a prophet. He is the one who, because his demand is immediate, expresses it immediately from God, and God speaks it through him. His having this life of the Spirit in the truth, so that it is simply there without mediation, expresses itself prophetically in such a way that it is God who says it. It is a matter of the absolute, divine truth that has being in and for itself, and of its expression and intention; and the confirmation of this expression is envisaged as God's doing. It is the consciousness of the real unity of the divine will and of his harmony with it. In the form of this expression, however, the accent is laid upon the fact that the one who says this is at the same time essentially human. It is the Son of Man who speaks thus, in whom this expression, this activity of what subsists in and for itself, is essentially the work of God—not as something suprahuman that appears in the shape of an external revelation, but rather as [God's] working in a human being, so that the divine presence is essentially identical with this human being. |

244   We still have to consider the fate of this individual, namely, that he became, humanly speaking, a martyr to the truth in a way that coheres closely with his earlier role, because the establishment of the kingdom of God stands in stark contradiction to the worldly

moral commandments are [found] partly in other religions and partly in the Jewish religion.

195. [*Ed.*] See Matt. 6:33: "Seek first his kingdom and his righteousness, and all these things shall be yours as well." The phrase that follows ("Cast yourself upon the truth"), while appearing to be a saying of Jesus, is in fact found nowhere in the Gospels. Hegel may have had in mind a saying such as that found in Luke 16:16 ("The law and the prophets were until John; since then the good news of the kingdom of God is preached, and everyone enters it violently"), or John 16:13 ("When the Spirit of truth comes, he will guide you into all the truth"); but more likely it is intended as Hegel's interpretation of what it *means* to seek and to enter the kingdom of God (see the preceding two paragraphs).

authority [*vorhandenen Staate*], which is grounded upon another mode, a different determinate form, of religion.

These are the principal moments in the ˉappearance of this man, upon the human view of it. But this is only one side, and it is not a religious view.ˉ[196] |

245

196. *Thus L; W (1831) reads:* human appearance [W₁ *reads:* teaching] of Christ. This teacher gathered friends about him. Inasmuch as his teachings were revolutionary, Christ was accused and executed, and thus he sealed the truth of his teaching by his death. Even unbelief can go this far in [the view it takes of] this story: it is quite similar to that of Socrates, only on a different soil. Socrates, too, brought inwardness to consciousness; his δαιμόνιον is nothing other than this. He also taught that humanity must not stop short at obedience to ordinary authority but must form convictions for itself and act according to them. Here we have two similar individualities with similar fates. The inwardness of Socrates was contrary to the religious beliefs of his people as well as to their form of government, and hence he was put to death: he, too, died for the truth.

Christ happened to live among another people, and to this extent his teaching has a different hue. But the kingdom of heaven and the purity of heart contain, nonetheless, an infinitely greater depth than the inwardness of Socrates. This is the outward history of Christ, which is for unbelief just what the history of Socrates is for us.

With the death of Christ, however, the reversal of consciousness begins. The death of Christ is the midpoint upon which consciousness turns; and in the comprehension of it lies the difference between outward comprehension and that of faith, which entails contemplation with the Spirit, from the Spirit of truth, the Holy Spirit. According to the comparison made earlier, Christ is a human being like Socrates, a teacher who lived his life virtuously, and who brought humanity to the awareness of what the truth really is and of what must constitute the basis of human consciousness. But the higher view is that the divine nature has been revealed in Christ. This consciousness is reflected in those often-quoted passages which state that the Son knows the Father, etc.—sayings which of themselves have at the outset a certain generality about them and which exegesis can draw out into the arena of universal views, but which faith comprehends in their truth through an interpretation of the death of Christ. For faith is essentially the consciousness of absolute truth, of what God is in and for himself. But we have already seen what God is in and for himself: he is this life-process, the Trinity, in which the universal places itself over against itself and therein remains identical with itself. God, in this element of eternity, is the conjoining of himself with himself, the closure of himself with himself. Only faith comprehends and is conscious of the fact that in Christ this truth, which has being in and for itself, is envisaged in its process, and that through him this truth has been revealed for the first time.

[*Ed.*] On the *daimonion* ("genius" or "demon") of Socrates, see esp. Xenophon, *Memorabilia* 1.1.7–9; Plato, *Apology* 10–14; also Hegel, *History of Philosophy*, pp. 421–425 (cf. *Werke* 14:94–101). On the comparison of Socrates and Christ, see above, n. 176.

c. The Death of Christ and the Transition to Spiritual Presence

It is this second view that leads us for the first time into the religious sphere as such, where the divine itself is an essential moment. Among those friends and acquaintances who were taught by Christ, there was present this presentiment, this representation, this desire for a new kingdom, a new heaven and a new earth, a new world. This hope and certainty penetrated the actuality of their hearts and became entrenched there. But the suffering and death of Christ superseded his human relationships, and it is precisely in his death that the transition into the religious sphere occurs.[197] On the one hand it is a natural death, brought about by injustice, hatred, and violence.

But in the hearts and souls [of believers] is the firm [belief] that the issue is not a moral teaching, nor in general the thinking and willing of the subject within itself and from itself; rather what is of interest is an infinite relationship to God, to the present God, the certainty of the kingdom of God—finding satisfaction not in morality, ethics, or conscience, but rather in that than which nothing is higher, ˜the relationship˜[198] to God himself. All other modes of satisfaction involve the fact that they are still qualities of a subordinate kind, and thus the relationship to God remains a relationship to something above and beyond, which in no sense lies present at hand.

The defining characteristic of this kingdom of God is the *presence of God*, which means that the members of this kingdom are expected to have not only a love for humanity but also the consciousness that God | is love. This is precisely to say that God is present, that his presence must exist as one's own feeling, as self-feeling. The kingdom of God, God's presentness, *is* this determination [of one's feeling]; so the certainty of God's presentness belongs to it. But since the kingdom is on the one hand [present] in need or feeling [on the part of the subject], the latter must, on the other hand, distinguish itself from it, must establish a distinction between this

246

197. *L adds:* it is the meaning of or the way of comprehending this death. *W (Var) adds:* It is a question of the meaning of, of the way of comprehending, this death.

198. *Thus L; W₁ (Var) reads:* relationship *W₂ (Var) reads:* absolute relationship

presence of God and itself, but in such a way that this presence remains certain to it, and this certainty can here occur only in the mode of sensible appearance. [199] Because this is how the content

199. W_1 here contains a lengthy passage from the 1831 lectures, which is also found in W_2, although dispersed into several disconnected segments. Our text follows the order of W_1, which is also confirmed by Strauss, but the wording is that of W_2. The parallel in the main text follows, ending with the penultimate paragraph of this section. W_2 (1831) reads:

We have seen God as the God of free humanity, though still at first in the subjective, limited forms of the folk-spirits and in the contingent shapes of phantasy; next we saw the anguish of the world following upon the suppression of the folk-spirits. This anguish was the birthplace for the impulse of spirit [W_1 reads: the birthplace of a new spirit, the impulse] to know God as spiritual, in universal form and stripped of finitude. This need was engendered by the progress of history and the progressive formation of the world-spirit. This immediate impulse, this longing, which wants and desires something determinate—this instinct, as it were, of spirit, which is impelled to seek for this [W_1 reads: —this is the witness of the Spirit and the subjective side of faith. This need and this longing]—demanded such an appearance, the manifestation of God as infinite spirit in the shape of an actual human being. [W_1 reads: The faith that rests upon the witness of the Spirit then makes the life of Christ explicit for itself. Instead of this sentence, W_2 gives as a transition: The eternal idea itself means that the characteristic of subjectivity as actual, as distinguished from mere thought, is allowed to appear immediately. On the other hand, it is faith, begotten by the anguish of the world and resting on the testimony of the Spirit, which explicates the life of Christ.] The teaching and the miracles of Christ are grasped and understood in this witness of faith. [W_1 reads: The words of Christ are truly grasped and understood only by faith.] The history of Christ is also narrated by those upon whom the Spirit has already been poured out. The miracles are grasped and narrated in this Spirit, and the death of Christ has been truly understood through the Spirit to mean that in Christ God is revealed together with the unity of divine and human nature. Thus the death of Christ is the touchstone, so to speak, by which faith is verified, since it is here, essentially, that its understanding of the appearance of Christ is set forth. This death means principally that Christ was the God-man, the God who at the same time had human nature, even unto death. It is the lot of human finitude to die. Death is the most complete proof of humanity, of absolute finitude; and indeed Christ has died the aggravated death of the evildoer: not merely a natural death, but rather a death of shame and humiliation on the cross. In him, humanity was carried to its furthest point.

Now, however, a further determination comes into play. God has died, God is dead—this is the most frightful of all thoughts, that everything eternal and true is not, that negation itself is found in God. The deepest anguish, the feeling of complete irretrievability, the annulling of everything that is elevated, are bound up with this thought. However, the process does not come to a halt at this point; rather, a reversal takes place: God, that is to say, maintains himself in this process, and the latter is only the death of death. God rises again to life, and thus things are reversed. The resurrection is something that belongs just as essentially to faith [as the crucifixion].

247   behaves, | we have here the religious aspect, and the formation of the community begins here. This content is the same as what is called the outpouring of the Holy Spirit: it is the Spirit that has

---

After his resurrection, Christ appeared only to his friends.ᵃ This is not an external history for unbelievers; on the contrary, this appearance occurs only for faith. The resurrection is followed by the glorification of Christ, and the triumph of his ascension to the right hand of God concludes this history, which, as understood by [believing] consciousness, is the explication of the divine nature itself. [W₁ reads: of God. This history is the explication of the divine nature itself.] If in the first sphere we grasped God in pure thought, then in this second sphere we start from the immediacy appropriate to intuition and sensible representation. The process is now such that immediate singularity is sublated: just as in the first sphere the seclusion of God came to an end, and his original immediacy as abstract universality, according to which he is the essence of essences, has been sublated, so here the abstraction of humanity, the immediacy of subsisting singularity, is sublated, and this is brought about by death. But the death of Christ is the death of this death itself, the negation of negation. We have had the same course and process of the explication of God in the kingdom of the Father, but this is where it occurs insofar as it is an object of consciousness. For at this point the urge to *see* the divine nature was present.

Concerning Christ's death, we have still finally [W₁ reads: particularly] to emphasize the aspect that it is God who has put death to death, since he comes out of the state of death. In this way, finitude, human nature, and humiliation are posited of Christ—as of him who is strictly God—as something alien. It is evident that finitude is alien to him and has been taken over from an other; this other is the human beings who stand over against the divine process. It is their finitude that Christ has taken [upon himself], this finitude in all its forms, which at its furthest extreme is evil. This humanity, which is itself a moment in the divine life, is now characterized as something alien, not belonging to God. This finitude, however, on its own account (as against God), is evil, it is something alien to God. But he has taken it [upon himself] in order to put it to death by his death. As the monstrous unification of these absolute extremes, this shameful death is at the same time infinite love.

It is out of infinite love that God has made himself identical with what is alien to him in order to put it to death. This is the meaning of the death of Christ. It means that Christ has borne the sins of the world and has reconciled God [with the world (2 Cor. 5:18–19)].

Suffering and death interpreted in this way are opposed to the doctrine of moral imputation, according to which all individuals are accountable only for themselves, and all are agents of their own actions. The fate of Christ seems to contradict this imputation, but the latter only applies in the region of finitude, where the subject stands as a single person, not in the region of free spirit. It is characteristic of the region of finitude that all individuals remain what they are. If they have done evil, then they *are* evil: evil is in them as their quality. But already in the sphere of morality, and still more in that of religion, spirit is known to be free, to be affirmative within itself, so that its limitation, which extends to evil, is a nullity for the infinitude

revealed this. The relationship [of believers] to a mere human being is changed into a relationship | that is completely altered and trans- 248 figured by the Spirit, so that the nature of God discloses itself therein, and so that this truth obtains immediate certainty in its manner of appearance.

In this experience, then, Christ, who at first was regarded as a teacher, friend, and martyr to the truth, assumes quite a different posture.[200] | On the one hand, the death of Christ is still the death 249 of a human being, a friend, who has been killed by violent means; but when it is comprehended spiritually, this very death becomes the means of salvation, the focal point of reconciliation. To have before oneself the intuition of the nature of spirit and of the satisfaction of its needs in a sensible fashion is, therefore, what ˉhas been ˉ[201] disclosed to the friends of Christ only after his death.[202] [203]The authentic disclosure was given to them by the Spirit, of whom Christ had said, "He will guide you into all truth" [John 16:13]. By this he means: only that into which the Spirit will lead you will be the truth. Regarded in this respect, Christ's death assumes the character of a death that constitutes the transition to glory, but to a glorification that is only a restoration of the original glory. Death,

---

of spirit. Spirit can undo what has been done. The action certainly remains in the memory, but spirit strips it away. Imputation, therefore, does not attain to this sphere.

For the true consciousness of spirit, the finitude of humanity has been put to death in the death of Christ. This death of the natural has in this way a universal significance: finitude and evil are altogether destroyed. Thus the world has been reconciled; by this death it has been implicitly delivered from its evil. In the true understanding [Verstehen] of death, the relation of the subject as such [to death] comes into view in this way. Here any merely historical view comes to an end; the subject itself is drawn into the process. The subject feels the anguish of evil and of its own estrangement, which Christ has taken upon himself by putting on humanity, while at the same time destroying it by his death.

[Ed.] ᵃSee Matt. 28:9–10, 17–20; Mark 16:9 ff.; Luke 24:13 ff.; John 20–21.

200. L (1827?) adds, similar in W: Up to this point only the beginning has been posited, which is now carried forward by the Spirit to an end, a result, the truth.

201. Thus B, Hu; L reads: was

202. W (Var) adds: Thus the conviction that they were able to derive from his life was not yet the proper truth; rather first the Spirit [had to be sent].

203. Precedes in L (1827?), similar in W: Prior to his death he was to them an outwardly sensible individual.

the negative, is the mediating term through which the original majesty is posited as now achieved. The history of the resurrection and ascension of Christ to the right hand of God begins at the point where this history receives a spiritual interpretation.[204] That is when it came about that the little community achieved the certainty that God has appeared as a human being.

But this humanity in God—and indeed the most abstract form of humanity, the greatest dependence, the ultimate weakness, the utmost fragility—is natural death. "God himself is dead," it says in a Lutheran hymn,[205] expressing an awareness that the human, the finite, the fragile, the weak, the negative are themselves a moment of the divine, that they are within God himself, that finitude, negativity, otherness are not outside of God and do not, as otherness, hinder unity with God. | Otherness, the negative, is known to be a moment of the divine nature itself. This involves the highest ˉideaˉ[206] of spirit. In this way what is external and negative is converted into the internal. On the one hand, the meaning attached to death is that through death the human element is stripped away and the divine glory comes into view once more—death is a stripping away of the human, the negative. But at the same time death itself is this negative, the furthest extreme to which humanity as natural existence ˉis exposed; God himself is [involved in] this.ˉ[207]

250

The truth to which human beings have attained by means of this history, what they have become conscious of in this entire history, is the following: that the idea of God has certainty for them, that humanity has attained the certainty of unity with God, that the human is the immediately present God. Indeed, within this history as spirit comprehends it, there is the very presentation of the process of what humanity, what spirit is—implicitly both God and dead.

204. *Thus also W; L (1827?) adds:* Religious history is [found] where a spiritual interpretation of the history of Christ before his death prevails; for, of course, even the Gospels were written only after the outpouring of the Spirit. *In An's margin:* The overstepping of sensible verification: the church cannot undertake an investigation of it [the history of Christ] in a sensible manner.

205. [*Ed.*] Johannes Rist, "O Traurigkeit, O Herzeleid" (1641).

206. *Thus L, W₁; W₂ (Var) reads:* cognition of the nature of the idea

207. *Thus L with Hu; W (Var) reads:* and just for that reason, God himself, is exposed.

This [is] the mediation whereby the human is stripped away and, on the other hand, what-subsists-in-itself returns to itself, first coming to be spirit thereby.

It is with the *consciousness* of the community—which thus makes the transition from mere humanity to the God-man, to the intuition, consciousness, and certainty of the union and unity of divine and human nature—that the community begins; this consciousness constitutes the truth upon which the community is founded. This is the explication of reconciliation: that God is reconciled with the world, or rather that God has shown himself to be reconciled with the world, that even the human is not something alien to him, but rather that this otherness, this self-distinguishing, finitude as it is expressed, is a moment in God himself, although, to be sure, it is a disappearing moment.[208]

For the community, this is the history of the appearance of God. | This history is a divine history, whereby the community has come to the certainty of truth. From it develops the consciousness that knows that God is triune. The reconciliation in Christ, in which one believes, makes no sense if God is not known as the triune God, [if it is not recognized] that God *is,* but also is as the other, as self-distinguishing, so that this other is God himself, having implicitly the divine nature in it, and that the sublation of this difference, this otherness, and the return of love, are the Spirit.[209]

These are the moments with which we are here concerned and which establish that humanity has become conscious of the eternal history, the eternal movement, which God himself is. Other forms such as that of sacrificial death reduce automatically to what has been said here. "To sacrifice" means to sublate the natural, to sublate otherness. It is said: "Christ has died for all."[210] This is not

251

208. *L (1827?) adds, similar in* W: But in this moment he has shown himself to the community.

209. *L (1827?) adds, similar in* W: This consciousness involves the fact that faith is not a relationship to something subordinate but to God himself.

210. [*Ed.*] See 2 Cor. 5:14–15: "For the love of Christ controls us, because we are convinced that one has died for all; therefore all have died. And he died for all, that those who live might live no longer for themselves but for him who for their sake died and was raised."

a single act but the eternal divine history: it is a moment in the nature of God himself; it has taken place in God himself.[211~~]

This is the presentation of the second [element of] the idea, the idea in appearance, the eternal idea as it has become [present] for the immediate certainty of humanity, i.e., as it has appeared. In order that it should become a certainty for humanity, it had to be a sensible certainty, which, however, at the same time passes over into spiritual consciousness, and likewise is converted into the immediately sensible—in such a way that the movement and history of God is seen in it, the life that God himself is.

C. THE THIRD ELEMENT: COMMUNITY, SPIRIT[212]

252

The third element is the element of the community. The first [moment of this element] is, then, the immediate origin of the community—this we have | already observed. It is the outpouring of the Holy Spirit [Acts 2]. [It is] spirit that comprehends this history

211. L (1827?) adds, first sentence similar in W: It is also said that in Christ all have died [cf. 2 Cor. 5:14]. In Christ this reconciliation has been represented [as being] for all, just as the Apostle compares faith in the crucified with viewing the bronze serpent.

[Ed.] From the context it must be assumed that Hegel is referring to the Apostle Paul, in which case it is likely that he has conflated two texts: 1 Cor. 10:9 and John 3:14. Paul alludes to the first part of the story concerning the setting up of a bronze serpent on a pole (Num. 21:5–9), but the comparison with faith in Christ is not found in Paul, as claimed by Hegel; see 1 Cor. 10:9: "We must not put the Lord to the test, as some of them did and were destroyed by serpents." Therefore it is probable that Hegel has in mind not the words of the Apostle but rather those of Jesus in conversation with Nicodemus in John 3:14–15: "And as Moses lifted up the serpent in the wilderness, so must the Son of Man be lifted up, that whoever believes in him may have eternal life." (According to the story in Numbers, anyone bitten by a serpent would save him- or herself from death, by viewing the bronze serpent set up on a pole.)

212. [Ed.] The treatment of the "third element" is relatively brief in the 1827 lectures as compared with 1824 and 1821. The semester ended on Friday, 10 August, in 1827, and Hegel had already nearly completed the lecture on Wednesday, 8 August, before reaching the "third element" (see n. 192). The Wednesday lecture was an addition to the regular schedule, and during the last week of the course Hegel lectured five straight days, Monday through Friday. Fortunately, several of the themes treated in the final section of the lectures in 1824 and 1821 had already

spiritually as it is enacted in [the sphere of] appearance, and recognizes the idea of God in it, his life, his movement. The community
is made up of those single, empirical subjects who are in the Spirit
of God. But at the same time this content, the history and truth of
the community, is distinguished from them and stands over against
them. On the one hand, faith in this history, in reconciliation, is
an immediate knowledge, an act of faith; on the other hand, the
nature of spirit in itself is this process, which has been viewed both
in the universal idea and in the idea as [it occurs] in appearance;
and this means that the subject itself becomes spirit, and thus a
citizen of the kingdom of God, by virtue of the fact that the subject
traverses this process in itself. ¯It has been set forth above²¹³ that
the human subject—the one in whom is revealed what is through
the Spirit the certainty of reconciliation for humanity—has been
marked out as singular, exclusive, and distinct from others.¯²¹⁴ Thus
for the other subjects the presentation of the divine history is something that is objective for them, and they must now traverse this
history, this process, in themselves. In order to do this, however,
they must first presuppose that reconciliation is possible, or more
precisely, that this reconciliation has happened in and for itself, that
it is the truth in and for itself, and that reconciliation is certain.²¹⁵
In and for itself, this is the universal idea of God; but the other
side of the presupposition is that this is certain for humanity, and
that this truth is not [valid] for it [simply] through speculative
thinking. This presupposition implies the certainty that reconciliation has been accomplished, i.e., it must be represented as some-

---

been discussed in 1827, such as the transition from sensible to spiritual presence,
and the question of the verification of faith (whether by miracles or the witness of
the Spirit). Thus Hegel could cover "the origin of the community" rather briefly.

213. [Ed.] See above, pp. 455–456,

214. *Thus L (the cross-reference is not found in B, Hu, or An); W₂ (MiscP)
reads:* Thus in this divine drama the other that is for [human] subjects is objective
to them in the same way that in the [Greek] chorus the audience finds itself objectified.
W (Var) continues: Initially, of course, the subject, the human subject—the one in
whom is revealed what becomes through the Spirit the certainty of reconciliation
for humanity—has been defined as singular, exclusive, and distinct from others.

215. *Thus also W; L (1827?) adds:* The perishing of sin and the negation of
immediacy are indicated by the bodily, sensible death [of Christ].

253   thing historical, as something that has been accomplished on earth, in [the sphere of] appearance.[216] | This is the presupposition in which we must first of all believe.

1. The Origin of the Community

~For the origin of faith there is necessary~[217] first a human being, a sensible human appearance, and second, spiritual comprehension, consciousness of the spiritual. The content is spiritual, involving the transformation of immediacy into what has spiritual character. Verification is spiritual, it does not lie in the sensible, and cannot be accomplished in an immediate, sensible fashion.[218] The transformation of something immediate into a spiritual content is a transition that we have seen in the form of the proofs for the existence of God[219]—namely, that there is also a sensible world, although the truth is not the sensible, not the immediate world of finitude, but is rather the infinite.

[220]As to the empirical mode of the appearance, and investigations concerning the conditions surrounding the appearance of Christ after his death, the church is right insofar as it refuses to acknowledge such investigations; for the latter proceed from a point of view implying that the real question concerns the sensible and historical elements in the appearance [of Christ], as though the confirmation of the Spirit[221] depended on narratives of this kind about something

216. L (1827?) adds, similar in W: For there is no other mode of what is called certainty.

217. Thus L; W (Var/1831?) reads: 1. The origin of the community is what occurs as the outpouring of the Holy Spirit. The origin of faith is

218. L (1827?) adds: Accordingly, objections can always be raised against the sensible facts.

219. [Ed.] See above, pp. 162–189.

220. Precedes in L (1827?), similar in W₁: This conversion, which already begins with the resurrection and ascension, is what we call the origin of the community.

[Ed.] This sentence, if authentic, indicates that the resurrection belongs as much to the history of the community as it does to the history of Christ. It constitutes the point of transition from the Son to the Spirit, from the second to the third element. In nonrepresentational language, the resurrection means for Hegel the spiritual presence of Christ in the community, Christ's presence as spirit. However, he uses resurrection language with reference to this actuality only infrequently.

221. Thus L; W (Var) adds: and its truth

represented as [merely] historical [*historisch*], in historical [*ge-schichtlich*] fashion. It is said that the Holy Scriptures should be treated like the writings of profane authors. One can do this with regard to what concerns the merely historical, the finite and external. But for the rest, | it is a matter of comprehension by the Spirit;   254
the profane [aspect] is not the attestation of the Spirit.

[222]Thus the community itself is the existing Spirit, the Spirit in its existence [*Existenz*], God existing as community.

The first moment is the idea in its simple universality for itself, self-enclosed, having not yet progressed to the primal division, to otherness—the Father. The second is the particular, the idea in appearance—the Son.[223] It is the idea in its externality, such that the external appearance is converted back to the first [moment] and is known as the divine idea, the identity of the divine and the human. The third element, then, is ˜this consciousness—God as the Spirit.˜[224] This Spirit as existing and realizing itself is the community.

The community begins with the fact that the truth is at hand; it is known, extant truth. And this truth is what God is: he is the triune God; he is life, this process of himself within himself, the determining of himself within himself. The second aspect of this truth, then, is that it has also appeared, it has a relation to the subject, and is [present] for the subject; moreover, the subject is essentially related to it, and is meant to be a citizen of the kingdom of God. That the human subject ought to be a child of God implies that reconciliation is accomplished in and for itself within the divine idea, and secondly that it has appeared too, and hence the truth is certain for humankind. The appearing is precisely this certainty, the idea as it comes to consciousness in the modality of appearance. The third aspect is the relationship of the subject to this truth, the fact that the subject, to the extent that it is related to this truth,

222. *In B's margin:* 9 August 1827
223. *L (1827?) adds, similar in* W₁: Insofar as the first element is concrete, otherness is indeed already contained in it; the idea is eternal life, eternal bringing forth.
224. *Thus B, Hu,* W₁; *An reads:* God as the Spirit within consciousness. *L (Var) reads:* this consciousness of God as the Spirit.

arrives precisely at this conscious unity, deems itself worthy of this known unity, brings this unity forth within itself, and is fulfilled by the divine Spirit.

The fact that the single subject is now filled by the divine Spirit is brought about by mediation in the subject itself, and the mediating
255 factor is | that the subject has this faith. For faith is the truth, the presupposition, that reconciliation is accomplished with certainty in and for itself. Only by means of this faith that reconciliation is accomplished with certainty and in and for itself is the subject able and indeed in a position to posit itself in this unity. This mediation is absolutely necessary.

In this blessedness mediated through the laying hold of the truth, the difficulty that is immediately involved in the grasping of the truth is overcome. This difficulty is that the relationship of the community to this idea is a relationship of the single, particular subject; it is removed in the truth itself. It consists in the fact that the subject is different from absolute spirit.[225] This difference is removed, and its removal happens because God looks into the human heart, he regards the substantial will, the innermost, all-encompassing subjectivity of the human being, one's inner, true, and earnest willing. But apart from this inner will, and distinct from this inner, substantial actuality, there is still the external and deficient side of humanity: we commit errors; we can exist in a way that is not appropriate to this inward, substantial essentiality, this substantial, essential inwardness. ˜The difficulty is removed by the fact that God looks into the heart and sees what is substantial, so that externality—otherness, finitude, and imperfection in general, or however else it may be defined—does no damage to the absolute unity; finitude is˜[226] reduced to an inessential status, and is known as inessential. For in the idea, the otherness of the Son is a transitory, disappearing moment, not a true, essentially enduring, absolute moment.

This is the concept of the community in general, the idea which, to this extent, is the process of the subject within and upon itself,

225. *Thus L, W₁; W₂ (Var) adds:* it is what appears as its finitude.
226. *Thus L, similar in An; W (Var) reads:* But externality—otherness in general, finitude, imperfection, or however else it may be defined—is

the process of the subject that is taken up into the Spirit, is spiritual, so that the Spirit of God dwells within it. This process, which is its pure self-consciousness, is at the same time the consciousness of | truth, and the pure self-consciousness that knows and wills the   256 truth is precisely the divine Spirit within it.

2. The Subsistence of the Community

The community, whose concept we have just seen, also *realizes* itself. The real community is what we generally call the *church*. This is no longer the *emerging* [*entstehende*] but rather the *subsisting* [*bestehende*] community, which maintains itself. In the subsisting community the church is, by and large, the institution whereby [its] subjects come to the truth, appropriate the truth to themselves, so that the Holy Spirit becomes real, actual, and present within them and has its abode in them, whereby the truth can be within them and they can enjoy and give active expression to the ˜truth of˜[227] the Spirit; it is the means whereby they as subjects *are* the active expression of the Spirit.

The first thing that is present in the church is its universality, which consists in the fact that the truth is here presupposed, that it exists as truth already present—not, as in the case of the emerging church, that the Holy Spirit is poured out and engendered for the first time. This is a changed relationship to the beginning [of their religion] for [its] subjects, and for the subjects in their beginnings. The presupposed, extant truth is the *doctrine* of the church, its doctrine of faith. We know the content of this doctrine: it is[228] the doctrine of reconciliation. It is no longer the case that a person is elevated to [the sphere of] absolute meaning by the outpouring and ordaining of the Spirit, but rather that this meaning is something that is known and acknowledged. It is the absolute capability of the subject, both within itself and objectively, to share in the truth, to come to the truth, to abide in the truth, to attain to the consciousness of truth. This consciousness of doctrine is here present and presupposed.

227. *Thus L; W (Var) reads:* truth, of
228. *Thus L; W (Var) adds:* in one word

Thus it is that doctrine is elaborated within the community itself only as something presupposed and finished. The Spirit that was shed abroad is the beginning, that which makes the beginning, which raises up. The community is the consciousness of this Spirit, 257 the expression of what | spirit has discovered and what it has been touched by, namely, that Christ is for spirit. Hence doctrine has been essentially brought forth and developed in the church. First it is [present] as intuition, faith, feeling—as the felt witness of the Spirit like a flame of fire. ¯But it is supposed to be present and presupposed; thus it must be developed from the concentration and interiority of feeling into representation as something immediately present.¯[229] Accordingly, the doctrine of faith is essentially constituted in the church first of all, and then later it is thinking, developed consciousness, which also asserts its rights in the matter, adducing the other [forms of truth] to which it has attained by way of the cultivation of thought, by way of philosophy. For these thoughts, on behalf of these thoughts, and on behalf of this otherwise known truth, thinking first develops a consciousness that is only intermixed with other, impure thoughts. Thus doctrine is developed out of other concrete contents that are intermixed with impurities. This doctrine is present to hand and must then be preserved too. This happens in the church. There, that which is doctrine must also be taught. It *is*, it exists, it is valid, it is acknowledged and immediately presupposed. But it is not present in a sensible manner, such that the comprehension of the doctrine can take place through the senses—in the way that the world, for example, is of course presupposed as a sensible entity, to which we are related externally and sensibly. Instead, spiritual truth exists only as known, and the fact that it also appears, and the mode of its appearance, is precisely this, that it is taught. The church is essentially a teaching church, by virtue of which there is a teaching office whose function is to expound doctrine.

Human beings are already born into this doctrine; they have their beginnings in this context of valid truth, already present, and

229. *Thus L with B and Hu, similar in* W₁; W₂ *(MiscP) reads:* But this characteristic of bringing forth is itself merely a one-sided one because the truth is at the same time implicitly present and presupposed; the subject is already taken up into the content.

in the consciousness of it. The relationship of single members to this presupposed truth that subsists in and for itself has yet a second aspect. Since individuals are born into the church, they are destined ˉstraightaway, while they are still unconscious,ˉ[230] to participate in this truth, | to become partakers of it; their vocation is for the truth.   258 The church expresses this too, in the sacrament of *baptism,* which says that the human being, the individual, is in the fellowship of the church, where evil has been overcome, implicitly and explicitly, and God is reconciled, implicitly and explicitly. [231]Initially, doctrine is related to this individual as something external. The child is at first spirit only implicitly, it is not yet realized spirit, is not yet actual as spirit; it has only the capability, the potentiality, to be spirit, to become actual as spirit. Thus the truth is something external to it, and comes to the subject initially as something presupposed, acknowledged, and valid. This means that the truth necessarily comes to humanity at first as *authority.*

All truth, even sensible truth—although it is not truth in the proper sense—comes to people initially in the form of authority; i.e., it is something present that possesses validity and exists on its own account. That is how it comes to me—as something distinct from me. Similarly, the world comes to us in sense perception as an authority confronting us: it *is,* we find it so, we accept it as something that is really there and relate ourselves to it as such. That is how it is, and it is valid just the way it is. Doctrine, which is spiritual, is not present as a sensible authority of that kind; it must be *taught,* and it is taught as valid truth. Custom is something that is valid, an established conviction. But because it is something spiritual, we do not say, "It is," but rather, "It is right." However, because it confronts us as what is real, we also say, "It is." And because it presents itself to us as something valid, we call its way of being "authority."

Just as people have to learn sensible content from authority, and to be content with the way things are just because they are so—

230. *Thus L; W (Var) reads:* although still unconsciously, nonetheless

231. *Thus L; precedes in* W₁ *(1831), similar in* W₂: Even though the individual is not spared the real, infinite anguish of being unfit in its relationship to God, it is nonetheless eased; but this is no longer the real struggle from which the community arose.

the sun is there, and because it is there I must put up with it—so also they have to learn doctrine, the truth.[232] What is learned in this way must | be taken up by individuals into themselves in order to assimilate it, to appropriate it. As we have already said,[233] the inner spirit is the absolute possibility of this knowledge; it conforms to this content that is itself spirit. What is there in human inwardness, i.e., in one's rational spirit, is therefore brought to consciousness for the individual as something objective; or what is found within the individual is developed so that one knows it as the truth in which one abides. This is the concern of education, practice, cultivation. With such education and appropriation it is a question merely of becoming habituated to the good and ˉthe true [Wahrhafte].ˉ[234] To this extent it is not a matter of overcoming evil because evil has been overcome in and for itself.[235] The child, inasmuch as it is born into the church, has been born in freedom and to freedom. For one who has been so born, there is no longer an absolute otherness; this otherness is posited as something overcome, as already conquered. The sole concern of such cultivation is to prevent evil from emerging, and the possibility of this does in general reside in humanity. But insofar as evil does emerge among human beings when they do evil, at the same time it is present as something implicitly null, over which spirit has power: spirit has the power to undo evil.

Repentance or *penitence* signifies that, through the elevation of human beings to the truth, which they now will, their transgression

232. L (1827?) adds, similar in W: The latter, however, arises not through sensible perception, through the activity of the senses on us, but rather through doctrine as what is really there, or through authority.

233. [Ed.] See above, p. 474.

234. B reads: truths [Wahrhaften]. L reads: the rational [Vernünftige]. W (Var) reads: the true [Wahre].

235. Thus L; W (1831) adds: It is a question only of contingent subjectivity. Linked with that element of faith consisting in the determination that the subject is not as it ought to be, there is simultaneously the absolute possibility that the subject can fulfill its destiny, can be received into the grace of God. This is the concern of faith. The individual must lay hold of the implicitly subsisting unity of divine and human nature; this truth is laid hold of through faith in Christ. Thus God is no longer a beyond for the individual; and the laying hold of this truth is opposed to the basic determination referred to above, namely, that the subject is not as it ought to be.

is wiped out. Because they acknowledge the truth over against their evil and will the good—through repentance, that is to say—their evil comes to naught. Thus evil is known as something that has been overcome in and for itself, having no power of its own. The undoing of what has been done cannot take place in a sensible manner; but in a spiritual | manner or inwardly, what has been done can be undone.[236] Therefore it is the concern of the church that this habituating and educating of spirit should become ever more inward, that this truth should become ever more identical with the self, with the human will, and that this truth should become one's volition, one's object, one's spirit. The battle is now over, and the consciousness arises that there is no longer a struggle, as in the Parsee religion or the Kantian philosophy,[237] where evil is always sure to be overcome, yet it stands in and for itself over against ¯the supreme good, so that in these views there is nothing but¯[238] an unending progression.[239]

¯The subsistence of the community is completed by sharing in the appropriation of God's presence [i.e., the *communion*]. It is a question precisely of the conscious presence of God, of unity with God, the *unio mystica,* [one's] self-feeling of God, the feeling of God's immediate presence within the subject. This self-feeling, however, since it exists, is also a movement, it presupposes a movement,

260

236. *L (1827?) adds, similar in W:* The sinner is forgiven; he is reckoned as one accepted by the Father among human beings.

237. [*Ed.*] On Hegel's criticism of the Kantian idea of an unending improvement in ethical conditions, see his *Lectures on the History of Philosophy* 3:461, 498 (*Werke* 15:593, 633); and on the comparison of Persian religion and Kantian philosophy, above, *Determinate Religion,* n. 277. On the concept of an unending progression, see Hegel's *Science of Logic,* pp. 227–228 (cf. *GW* 11:140–142).

238. *Thus L; W (Var) reads:* the good, and the highest thing is

239. *L (1827?) adds, similar in W:* Here, by contrast, evil is known in the Spirit to be overcome in and for itself, and because it is overcome in and for itself, the subject has only to make its own will good in order for evil, the evil deed, to disappear. *After an insertion from the 1824 lectures, W (1831) continues:* Acting in the belief that reconciliation has been implicitly achieved is, on the one hand, the act of the subject, but on the other hand it is the act of the divine Spirit. Faith itself is the divine Spirit that works in the subject. But the subject is not a passive receptacle; rather the Holy Spirit is equally [*ebenso*] the subject's spirit to the extent that the subject has faith. In such faith the latter acts in opposition to its natural life, sets it aside, puts it away.

a sublation of difference, so that a negative unity issues forth.[240]
This unity begins with the host.ˉ[241] [242]Concerning the latter, three
kinds of view are now prevalent. According to the first, the host—
261 this external, sensible thing | —becomes by consecration the present
God, God as a thing in the manner of an empirical ˉthing.ˉ[243] The
second view is the Lutheran one, according to which the movement
does indeed begin with something external, which is an ordinary,
common thing, but the communion, the self-feeling of the presence
of God, comes about only insofar as the external thing is consumed—not merely physically but in spirit and in faith. God is
present only in spirit and in faith.[244] Here there is no transubstan-

240. W (1831) adds: Thus the Lord's Supper is also the midpoint of Christian
doctrine, and from this point all the differences within the Christian church receive
their coloration and definition.
241. Thus L; among the extant sources only the following is found in Hu
(probably added later): Communion [Genuss] is the consciousness of God's immediate presence in the subject's heart: unio mystica. W (Var) reads: The ultimate
in this sphere is sharing in this appropriation, in this presence of God [der Genuss
dieser Aneignung, der Gegenwärtigkeit Gottes]. It is precisely a matter of the conscious presence of God, of unity with God, the unio mystica, [one's] self-feeling of
God.
242. In B's margin: 10 August 1827
[Ed.] Since B lacks the preceding passage, it is obvious that Hegel's final lecture
began with the topic of this paragraph, the sacrament of communion, for which he
uses the difficult-to-translate term Genuss.
243. Thus Hu; L reads: existence. W (1831) reads: thing [possibly from 1824
(G): —likewise partaken of empirically by human beings]. Since God is thus known
as something external in the Lord's Supper—this midpoint of doctrine—this externality is the foundation of the whole Catholic religion.ᵃ Thus arises the servitude
of knowledge and activity [in this religion]; this externality pervades all further
characteristics [of it] since the true is represented as something fixed and external.
As something existing outside the subject, it can pass into the control of others; the
church is in possession of it as well as of all the means of grace. In every respect
the subject is a passive, receptive subject that knows not what is true, right, and
good, but has only to accept the standard from others.
[Ed.] ᵃSee Hegel's defense against the reproach of his having defamed the Catholic
religion in Berliner Schriften, pp. 572–575.
244. Thus L; W (1831) adds: Sensible presence is nothing on its own account,
nor does consecration make the host into an object of veneration; rather the object
exists in faith alone, and thus it is in the consuming and destroying of the sensible
that we have union with God and the consciousness of this union of the subject
with God. Here the grand awareness has arisen that, apart from communion and
faith, the host is a common, sensible thing: the process is genuine only within the
subject's spirit.

tiation, or at any rate only one by which externality is annulled, so that the presence of God is utterly a spiritual presence—the consecration takes place in the faith of the subject. The third view is that the present God exists only in representation, in memory, and to this extent he does not have this immediate subjective presence.[245]

˜The subject is expected to *appropriate* doctrine, the truth, and hence | the third aspect of the community's self-maintenance is the partaking of the presence of God.˜[246]   262

3. The Realization of the Spirituality of the Community

The third [aspect] is the *realization* of the spirituality of the community in universal actuality. This involves the *transformation* of the community at the same time. The standpoint is this: in religion the *heart* is reconciled. This reconciliation is thus in the heart; it is spiritual. It is the pure heart that attains to this partaking [*Genuss*] of God's presence within it, and consequently reconciliation, the enjoyment [*Genuss*] of being reconciled. At the same time, however, this reconciliation is abstract and has the world as such over against it. The self that exists in this reconciliation, in this religious communion, is the pure heart, the heart as such, universal spirituality; but at the same time the self or subject constitutes that aspect of spiritual presence in accord with which there is a developed worldliness present in it, and thus the kingdom of God, the community, has a relationship to the worldly. In order that reconciliation may be real, it is required that it should be known in this development, in this totality; it should be present and brought forth [into actuality]. The principles for this worldly realm are ready to hand in the spirituality of the community; the principle, the truth, of the worldly *is* the spiritual.

The spiritual is the truth of the worldly realm in the more prox-

---

245. *Thus L; W (1831) adds (adopting a statement from the 1824 lectures and the Ms.):* [it is] a merely moral relationship.

[*Ed.*] The reference here, of course, is to the Reformed view, but it applies properly only to Zwingli, not to Calvin.

246. *Thus L; Hu reads:* These are the three modes of the community.

[*Ed.*] The three are doctrine, repentance, and communion.

imate sense that the subject, as an object of divine grace and as one who is reconciled with God, already has infinite value in virtue of its vocation; and this is made effective in the community. On the basis of this vocation, the subject is known as spirit's certainty of itself, as the eternity of spirit. The vocation to infinitude of the subject that is inwardly infinite is its *freedom*. The substantial aspect of the subject is that it is a free person, and as a free person it relates itself to the worldly and the actual as a being that is at home with itself, reconciled within itself, an utterly secure and infinite subjectivity. This vocation of the subject ought to be foundational in its relation with what is worldly. This freedom of the subject is its rationality—the fact that as subject it is thus liberated and has attained this liberation through religion, that in accord with its religious vocation it | is essentially free. This freedom, which has the impulse and determinacy to realize itself, is rationality. ˜Slavery contradicts Christianity because it is contrary to reason.˜[247] What is required, therefore, is that this reconciliation should also be accomplished in the worldly realm.

The first form of this reconciliation with worldliness is the immediate one, and just for this reason it is not the genuine mode of reconciliation. It appears as follows: at first the community contains the element of spirituality, of being reconciled with God, within itself, in abstraction from the world, so that spirituality renounces the worldly realm, placing itself in a negative relation to the world and also to itself. For the world is in the subject; it is there as the impulse toward nature, toward social life, toward art and science. What is concrete in the self, its passions etc., certainly cannot be justified vis-à-vis the religious aspect just because they are natural impulses; but on the other hand, monkish withdrawal means that the heart is not concretely developed, that it exists as something undeveloped, or that spirituality, the state of being reconciled, and the life of reconciliation are and ought to remain concentrated within themselves and undeveloped. But the very nature of spirit is to develop itself, to differentiate itself even unto worldliness.

The second way of defining this reconciliation is that worldliness and religiosity do indeed remain external to each other, but they

247. *Thus An*

have to enter into relation all the same. Hence the relation in which they stand can itself only be an external one, or more precisely, a relation in which one prevails over the other, and thus there is no reconciliation at all. The religious, it is felt, should be the dominant element; what is reconciled, the *church,* ought to prevail over what is unreconciled, the worldly realm. Accordingly, this is a uniting with a worldly realm that remains unreconciled. In itself, the worldly sphere is uncultured, and as such it ought only to be dominated. But the dominating power takes this same worldliness up into itself, ˜including all of its passions; as a result of its dominion, there emerges in the church itself a worldliness devoid of spirit˜[248] 264
| just because the worldly realm is not in itself reconciled. A dominion predicated on the lack of spirit is posited, in terms of which externality is the principle and humanity in its relatedness exists at the same time outside itself—this is the relationship of *unfreedom* in general. In everything that can be called human, in all impulses, in all attitudes that have reference to the family and to activity in public life, a cleavage enters into play. The ruling principle is that humanity is not at home with itself. In all these forms, it exists in a general condition of servitude, and all these forms count for nothing, they are unholy. Inasmuch as human being subsists in them, it is essentially a finite and ruptured being which has in that form no validity; what is valid is something else. This reconciliation with the worldly realm, and with the human heart, comes about in such a way that it is precisely the opposite of [genuine] reconciliation. The further development of this condition of rupture within reconciliation itself is what appears as the corruption of the church, the absolute contradiction of the spiritual within itself.

The third way is that this contradiction is resolved in the *ethical realm,*[249] or that the principle of freedom has penetrated into the

---

248. *Thus An:* including . . . passions; *and L:* as . . . spirit W₁ *is similar to L;* W₂ *(Var) reads:* all inclinations, all passions, whatever is worldliness devoid of spirit emerges in the church as a result of this very dominion

249. [*Ed.*] This theme is explicitly developed by Hegel under the category of "objective spirit" in the *Encyclopedia* (1830), §§ 483 ff., and in the whole of the *Philosophy of Right.* The terms used here are *Sittlichkeit* (ethical realm, ethical life, social ethics) and *Sittliche* (ethics, the ethical), not *Moralität,* which refers to the subjective morality of conscience.

worldly realm itself, and that the worldly, because it has been thus conformed to the concept, reason, and eternal truth, is freedom that has become concrete and will that is rational.[250] The institutions of ethical life are divine institutions—not holy in the sense[251] that celibacy is supposed to be holy by contrast with marriage or familial love, or that voluntary poverty is supposed to be holy by contrast with active self-enrichment, or what is lawful and proper. Similarly, blind obedience is regarded as holy, whereas the ethical is an obedience in freedom, a free and | rational will, an obedience of the subject toward the ethical. Thus it is in the ethical realm that the reconciliation of religion with worldliness and actuality comes about and is accomplished.

265

Thus reconciliation has three *real* stages: the stage of immediacy [or of the heart], which is more an abstraction than it is reconciliation; the stage in which the church is dominant, a church that is outside itself; and the stage of ethical life.

The second [moment] is that the *ideal* side emerges explicitly in religious consciousness. Inwardness knows itself as subsisting with itself[252] precisely in this reconciliation of spirit with itself; and this knowledge of being at home with itself is precisely thinking. Thinking means reconciledness, being at home or at peace with oneself, even though the peace is a wholly abstract, undeveloped one.[253]

---

250. *Thus L; W (1831) adds:* It is in the organization of the state that the divine has broken through [*eingeschlagen*] into the sphere of actuality; the latter is permeated by the former, and the worldly realm is now justified in and for itself, for its foundation is the divine will, the law of right and freedom. The true reconciliation, whereby the divine realizes itself in the domain of actuality, consists in the ethical and juridical life of the state: this is the authentic discipline [*Subaktion*] of worldliness.

[Ed.] See *Philosophy of Right,* trans. T. M. Knox (Oxford, 1952), §§ 257–258, 260, 270 remark.

251. *Thus L, W₁; W₂ (Var) adds:* according to which the holy is opposed to the ethical

252. *Thus L; W (Var) adds:* and being at home with itself

[Ed.] The distinction is between *bei sich selbst seiend* in the main text and *bei sich selbst zu sein* in the footnote. The latter phrase occurs subsequently in the main text.

253. *Thus L; W (1831) adds:* Thus arises the infinite demand that the content of religion should be confirmed by thought, and this requirement should not be turned aside.

Thinking is the universal, the activity of the universal, and it stands generally in contrast with the concrete, as it does with the external. It is the freedom of reason that has been acquired in religion and now knows itself to be for itself in spirit. This freedom now turns against merely spiritless externality and servitude, for the latter is utterly opposed to the concepts of reconciliation and liberation. Thus thinking enters in, defying and destroying externality in whatever form it appears. This is the negative and formal mode of acting which, in its concrete shape, has been called the *Enlightenment*.[254]

This thinking first emerges as abstract universality as such, and is directed not merely against the external but also against the concrete in general. For this reason, it is also directed against the idea of God, against the idea that God as triune is not a dead abstraction but rather relates himself to himself, is at home with himself, and returns to himself. In concreteness there are of course determinations and distinctions. Since abstract thinking turns against | externality in general, it also is opposed to distinction as such because in distinction a reciprocally opposed externality is indeed present—but in the idea of God, in the *concrete* truth, this externality is likewise resolved.[255] Abstract identity prevails as the rule for this abstract thinking, for understanding. Genuine identity is the truth of the concrete. When everything concrete in God has been thus eradicated, this is expressed by saying: "We cannot know God"—i.e., know something specific about God.[256] For to know God cognitively means to know him according to his attributes; but [on this view] he is to remain a pure abstraction. The principle of freedom, inwardness, and religion itself is grasped by this formal perspective, but at first only abstractly.

266

But then the other way in which determination enters into universality, according to this abstraction, is the characteristics that reside in the natural impulses and inclinations of the subject. From

254. *L (1827?) adds, similar in W:* It consists in this: that thinking has turned against externality, and that the freedom of spirit that resides in reconciliation is maintained.

255. *L (1827?) adds, similar in W:* This thinking therefore proceeds to annul everything that is concrete and determinate in God.

256. [*Ed.*] A reference to the Kantian view, popularized by Jacobi, that theoretical knowledge of God is not possible, only the practical faith that God exists.

this standpoint it is said that human being by nature is good.[257] This pure subjectivity indeed clings to the category of the good, since the latter coincides with this identity and pure freedom; but the good itself must by the same token remain for it an abstraction. Here the category of the good is nothing other than the caprice and contingency of the subject as such. This is the extreme of this form of subjectivity and freedom, which renounces the truth and its development and moves within itself, knowing that what it regards as valid is only its own definitions, and that it is the master of what is good and evil. This is an inward weaving of spirit within itself, which can just as readily assume the form of hypocrisy and extreme vanity as it can peaceful, noble, pious aspirations. This is what is called the pious life of feeling, to which *Pietism* also restricts itself.

267 Pietism acknowledges no objective | truth and opposes itself to dogmas and the content of religion, while still preserving an element of mediation, a connection with Christ, but this is a connection that is supposed to remain one of mere feeling and inner sensibility.[258] Such piety, together with the vanity of subjectivity and feeling, is then turned polemically against the philosophy that wants cognition. The result of this subjectivity is that everything fades away in the subject, without objectivity, without firm determinacy, without any development on the part of God, who in the end no longer has any content at all.

~The mode [of thought] first designated [i.e., the Enlightenment] is the ultimate pinnacle of the formal culture of our time.~[259] But the two extremes opposing each other in the further development of the community are, first, this unfreedom and servitude of spirit in the absolute region of freedom, and second, abstract subjectivity or ~subjectivity~[260] devoid of content.[261]

257. [*Ed.*] See above, n. 132.
258. *Thus L; W (1831) adds:* For such piety, everyone has his own God, his own Christ, etc. This privatism [*Partikularität*], in which everyone has his own individual religion, worldview, etc., is certainly present among humanity. But in [true] religion, by means of life in the community, this privatism is consumed, it no longer has validity for truly pious people, it is set to one side.
259. *Thus L; W (Var) reads:* This ultimate pinnacle of the formal culture of our time is simultaneously the greatest crudity since it possesses only the *form* of culture.
260. *Thus L; W (Var) reads:* subjective freedom
261. *This paragraph is found only in L; among the extant sources, only the*

The third [moment], then, consists in the fact that subjectivity develops the content from itself, to be sure, but in accord with necessity. It knows and acknowledges that a content is necessary, and that this necessary content is objective, having being in and for itself. This is the standpoint of *philosophy*, according to which the content takes refuge in the concept[262] and obtains its justification by thinking. This thinking is not merely the process of abstraction and definition according to the law of identity; it does not have the concrete "over there," but rather is itself essentially concrete, and thus it is comprehension, meaning that the concept determines itself in its totality and as idea. It is free reason, which has being on its own account, that develops the content in accord with its necessity, and justifies the content of truth. This is the standpoint of a knowledge that recognizes and cognizes a truth. ⌐The Enlightenment of the understanding and Pietism volatilize all content. The purely subjective | standpoint⌐[263] recognizes no content and hence no truth. 268
The concept indeed produces the truth—this is subjective freedom—but it recognizes this truth as at the same time not produced, as the truth that subsists in and for itself. This objective standpoint is alone capable of bearing witness to, and thus of expressing the witness of, spirit in a developed, thoughtful fashion.[264] Therefore, it is the justification of religion, especially of the Christian religion, the true religion; it knows the *content* [of religion] in accord with its necessity and reason. Likewise it knows the *forms* in the devel-

---

following is found in Hu: These are the two extremes in the life of the community.

[*Ed.*] The two extremes are, in other words, the religion of the Enlightenment (the "servitude of spirit in the absolute region of freedom") and of Pietism ("subjectivity devoid of content"). Between these two extremes, speculative philosophy will find the mean.

262. [*Ed.*] *in den Begriff flüchtet.* This famous metaphor inspired the title of a recent collection of essays on Hegel's philosophy of religion, *Die Flucht in den Begriff* ("The Flight into the Concept"), ed. F. W. Graf and F. Wagner (Stuttgart, 1982); to which W. Jaeschke has offered the appropriate rejoinder, "Die Flucht vor dem Begriff: Ein Jahrzehnt Literatur zur Religionsphilosophie (1971–1981)" ("The Flight from the Concept . . ."), in *Hegel-Studien* 18 (1983), 295–354.

263. *Thus An with L; W reads, similar in L:* The purely subjective standpoint, the volatilization of all content, the Enlightenment of the understanding, W_2 *(Var) adds:* as well as Pietism,

264. *Thus L; W (Var) adds:* and it is contained in the better dogmatic theology of our time.

opment of this content. The two belong together: form and content. We have seen these forms: the modes of the appearance of God, the ways in which it is represented for the sensible consciousness and for the spiritual consciousness that has arrived at universality and thought, this whole development of spirit we have seen. The content is justified by the witness of spirit, insofar as it is thinking spirit. The witness of spirit is thought. Thought knows the form and determinacy of the appearance, and hence also the limits of the form. The Enlightenment knows only of negation, of limit, of determinacy as such, and therefore does an absolute injustice to the content. Form and determinacy entail not only finitude and limit; rather, as totality of form, determinacy is itself the concept, and these various forms are themselves necessary and essential. In the appearance of God, God determines himself. Sustained by philosophy, religion receives its justification from thinking consciousness.

Ingenuous piety has no need of [justification]; the heart gives the witness of spirit and receives the truth that comes to it through authority; it has a sense of satisfaction and reconciliation through this truth.[265] But insofar as thinking begins | to posit an antithesis to the concrete and places itself in opposition to the concrete, the

269

265. *Thus L; W (1831) adds:* In faith the true *content* is certainly already found, but it still lacks the *form* of thinking. All the forms that we have considered earlier*—feeling, representation, etc.—are indeed capable of having the content of truth, but they themselves are not the true form, which makes the true content necessary. Thinking is the absolute judge, before which the content must verify and attest its claims.

Philosophy has been reproached for placing itself above religion. But as a matter of fact this is surely false because philosophy has only this and no other content, although it gives it in the form of thinking; it places itself only above the *form* of faith, while the *content* is the same in both cases.

The form of the subject as one who feels, etc., concerns the subject as a single individual; but feeling as such is not eliminated by philosophy. The question is only whether the *content* of feeling is the truth and can prove itself to be true in thought. Philosophy *thinks* what the subject as such *feels,* and leaves it to the latter to come to terms with its feeling. Thus feeling is not rejected by philosophy but rather receives its true content through philosophy.

[*Ed.*] *See above, pp. 138–151. Not much material on this topic has been preserved from the 1831 lectures.

process of thinking consists in carrying through this opposition until it arrives at reconciliation.

This reconciliation is philosophy. Philosophy is to this extent theology. It presents the reconciliation of God with himself and with nature, showing that nature, otherness, is implicitly divine, and that the raising of itself to reconciliation is on the one hand what finite spirit implicitly is, while on the other hand it arrives at this reconciliation, or brings it forth, in world history. This reconciliation is the peace of God, which does not "surpass all reason,"[266] but is rather the peace that *through* reason is first known and thought and is recognized as what is true.[267]

Two positions are opposed to philosophy. First there is the vanity of the understanding, which is displeased by the fact that philosophy still exhibits the truth in religion and demonstrates that reason resides within it. This Enlightenment wants to have nothing further to do with the content, and therefore is highly displeased that philosophy, as conscious, methodical thinking, curbs the fancies, the caprice, and the contingency of thinking. In the second place, ingenuous religiosity [is opposed to philosophy]. The different positions are as follows: | (a) immediate religion; (b) the Enlightenment of the understanding; and (c) the rational cognition of religion. ˉIt is this last that I have sought to exhibit in these lectures.ˉ[268] [269]

270

266. [*Ed.*] An allusion to the German translation of Phil. 4:7, which uses *Vernunft* ("reason") rather than *Verstand* ("understanding"): "And the peace of God, which surpasses all reason, will keep your hearts and minds in Christ Jesus."

267. *L (1827?) adds:* This reconciliation by means of the concept is also the goal of these lectures.

268. *Thus Hu, similar in B; L (1827?) reads:* It is my hope that these lectures have afforded a guide and contributed to this rational cognition of religion as well as to the general advancement of [genuine?] religious piety [*Religiosität*].

269. *Follows below in B, similar in Hu:* Concluded 10 August 1827.

APPENDIXES

SYSTEMATIC STRUCTURE OF
THE PHILOSOPHY OF RELIGION

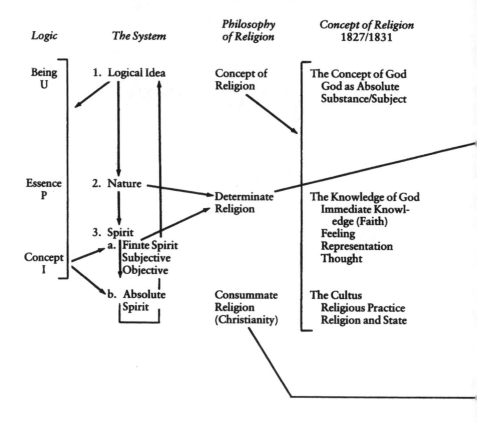

Logic	The System	Philosophy of Religion	Concept of Religion 1827/1831
Being U	1. Logical Idea	Concept of Religion	The Concept of God God as Absolute Substance/Subject
Essence P	2. Nature	Determinate Religion	The Knowledge of God Immediate Knowledge (Faith) Feeling Representation Thought
Concept I	3. Spirit a. Finite Spirit Subjective Objective b. Absolute Spirit	Consummate Religion (Christianity)	The Cultus Religious Practice Religion and State

The Deep Structure

Logic	*Consciousness*
U = Universality (*Allgemeinheit*)	Immediacy, Identity
P = Particularity (*Besonderheit*)	Differentiation, Cleavage
I = Individuality or Singularity (*Einzelheit*) – Subjectivity	Return, Reunification

See the Editorial Introduction, p. 13

Determinate Religion		_Consummate Religion_
1827	1831	1824/1827/1831

Immediate or Nature Religion
  Religion of Magic
  Chinese Religion
  Buddhism
  Hinduism
  Persian Religion
  Egyptian Religion
	Immediate or Nature Religion
	  Primitive Religion
	  Religion of Magic
		Idea of God In and For Itself—Kingdom of the Father
		  (Immediate Unity)

Elevation of the Spiritual above the Natural
  Greek Religion
  Jewish Religion
	Internal Rupture of Religious Consciousness
	  Chinese Religion
	  Hinduism
	  Buddhism
		Representation, Appearance—Kingdom of the Son
		  (Differentiation and Reconciliation)

Religion of Expediency (Universal and purposive, but finite and unspiritual—the absolute state religion)
  Roman Religion
	Religion of (Finite) Freedom and Reconciliation
	  Persian Religion
	  Jewish Religion
	  Egyptian Religion
	  Greek Religion
	  Roman Religion
		Community, Spirit—Kingdom of the Spirit
		  (Consummation and Return)

COMPARATIVE STRUCTURE OF
HEGEL'S INTRODUCTION

Manuscript	*1824 Lectures*
Preface (2a–b)	Preface
1. On the Purpose of the Philosophy of Religion (3a–b)	1. The Relation of the Philosophy of Religion to the Whole of Philosophy (cf. *Ms. Concept*, Sec. A)
2. The Relation of the Philosophy of Religion to Religion (2b, 4a–b)	
3. Opposition between Religious Consciousness and the Rest of Consciousness (4b–8a)	2. The Position of the Philosophy of Religion vis-à-vis the Needs of Our Time ————
4. Need for the Reconciliation of Religion and Cognition (8a–9b)	3. The Relationship of the Philosophy of Religion to Positive Religion
	4. Preliminary Questions
5. Division of the Subject (10a–b)	5. Survey of the Stages of Our Discussion

a. Concept of Religion	a. Concept of Religion
	      Universal Substance
	      Differentiation: Consciousness
	      Sublation of Difference: Cultus

b. Development of the Concept	b. Determinate Religion
c. Consummation of the Concept	c. Revelatory Religion

1827 Lectures	*1831 Lectures*
Preface	Preface
1. Comparison of Philosophy and Religion with Regard to Their Object	
	1. The Relationship of Philosophy, Religion, and Theology
2. The Relationship of the Science of Religion to the Needs of Our Time	
3. Survey of the Treatment of Our Subject	2. Division of the Subject
Moments of the Concept	Moments of the Concept
a. Concept of Religion Universality Relationship: Consciousness Reunification: Cultus	a. Concept of Religion Abstract Concept Feeling, Representation, Faith Community and Cultus Religion and Worldly Life
b. Determinate Religion	b. Determinate Religion
c. Consummate or Absolute Religion	c. Revelatory Religion

COMPARATIVE STRUCTURE OF
THE CONCEPT OF RELIGION

Manuscript	1824 Lectures
A. The Concept of Religion in — — — — → General (10a–15b)	(to B.3.a,b and Intro.) — — — — — — — —
	A. Empirical Observation ———————
	1. Immediate Knowledge
B. Scientific Conception of the Religious Standpoint	2. Feeling
	3. Consciousness in More Determinate Form
1. Distinction between External and Internal Necessity (16a–18a)	4. Relationship of Finite and Infinite
	5. Transition to Speculative Concept
2. Speculative Definition of — ⌐ the Concept of Religion (14a–b)	B. Speculative Concept of Religion 1. Definition of the Concept of Religion
3. Religious Relationship as Unity of Absolute Universality and Absolute Singularity (18a–22b)	
C. Necessity of This Standpoint (22b–25a)	2. Necessity of the Religious Standpoint
D. Relationship of Religion to Art and Philosophy (25b–30b)	3. Realization of the Concept of Religion
1. Intuition (Art)	a. Theoretical Relationship: the Representation
2. Representation (Religion)	of God
3. Thought (Philosophy)	(cf. *Ms.* Sec. A)
	b. Practical Relationship: the Cultus (cf. *Ms.* Sec. A)

1827 Lectures	*1831 Lectures*
- - - - - - - - - → (to C)	

(The Problem of the Beginning)

A. The Concept of God	A. General Concept

B. The Knowledge of God
  1. Immediate Knowledge (Faith)
  2. Feeling
  3. Representation
  4. Thought
    a. Thought and Represen-
       tation
    b. Immediate and Mediated
       Knowledge
    c. Religious Knowledge as
       Elevation to God
       (Proofs)
	B. The Single Forms of
	     Religion
	  1. Feeling
	  2. Representation
	  3. Faith

C. The Cultus (cf. *Ms.* Sec. A)	C. The Cultus
	D. Relationship of Religion to the State

DETERMINATE RELIGION

Manuscript	1824 Lectures
Introduction (31a)	Introduction
A. Immediate Religion (32a) ⟶	A. Immediate Religion, or ⟶
	Nature Religion
	Introduction
	a. The Original Condition
	b. Immediate Religion in General
a. The Metaphysical Concept of God	(α) The Metaphysical Concept of God:
(32b) [The Cosmological Proof] ⟶	⟶ The Cosmological Proof ⟶
b. Concrete Representation (34a)	(β) The Representation of God
c. The Side of Self-Consciousness:	(γ) The Forms of Nature Religion
Subjectivity, Cultus (37a)	1. The Religion of Magic
Brief Reflection on the State,	a. Singular Self-Consciousness as
Freedom, Reason (39a)	Power over Nature
	b. Formal Objectification of the
	Divine Object
	c. The Religion of Ancient China
	d. The Religion of Being-Within-
	Self (Buddhism, Lamaism)
	2. The Religion of Phantasy (Hinduism)
	a. The Representation of God
	b. The Cultus
	3. The Religion of the Good or of
	Light (Persian Religion)
	4. Transition from Nature Religion to
	Spiritual Religion: The Religion
	of the Enigma (Egyptian Religion)
	a. The Representation of God
	b. Cultus in the Form of Art
B. The Religion of Sublimity and Beauty ⟶	B. The Religions of Spiritual ⟶
(39a)	Individuality
	Introduction
	a. Division of the Subject
a. Metaphysical Concept (41a)	b. The Metaphysical Concept of God:
[The Cosmological Proof] ⟶	⟶ Cosmological & Teleological Proofs ⟶
	c. The More Concrete Definition of
	God
b. Concrete Representation,	1. The Religion of Sublimity
Form of the Idea (43a)	(Jewish Religion)
α. The Religion of Sublimity (43a)	a. God as the One
β. The Religion of Necessity (44b)	b. The Form of Divine Self-
c. Cultus (47a)	Determination
α. The Religion of Sublimity (47a)	c. The Cultus
β. The Religion of Beauty (49a)	2. The Religion of Beauty
α. Spirit of the Cultus; Religious	(Greek Religion)
Self-Consciousness (49a)	a. The Concept in General
β. The Cultus Itself (51a)	b. The Content and Shape of
	Divine Representation
	c. The Cultus
C. The Religion of Expediency or ⟶	3. The Religion of Expediency ⟶
Understanding (59a)	(Roman Religion)
a. Abstract Concept (61a)	a. The Concept of Necessity and
The Teleological Proof (62b)	External Purpose
b. Configuration or Representation of	b. The Configuration of the Gods
the Divine Essence (64b)	c. The Cultus
c. The More Specific Nature of these	
Powers and Deities in General (66b)	

1827 Lectures

Introduction
A. Immediate Religion, or Nature Religion
   Introduction
     a. The Original Condition
     b. The Forms of Nature Religion

  1. The Religion of Magic
     a. The Concept of Magic
     b. Less Developed Religions of Magic
     c. The State Religion of the Chinese Empire and the Dao
  2. The Religion of Being-Within-Self (Buddhism, Lamaism)
  3. The Hindu Religion
     a. The One Substance
     b. The Multiplicity of Powers
     c. The Cultus
     d. Transition to the Next Stage
  4. The Religions of Transition
     a. The Religion of Light (Persian Religion)
        Transition to the Next Stage
     b. Egyptian Religion
B. The Elevation of the Spiritual Above the Natural: The Religion of the Greeks and the Jews

  1. The Religion of Beauty, or Greek Religion
     a. The Divine Content
     b. The Cultus

  2. The Religion of Sublimity, or Jewish Religion
     a. The Unity of God
     b. Divine Self-Determination and Representation
     c. The Cultus
C. The Religion of Expediency: Roman Religion
   1. The Concept of Purposiveness
   2. The Configuration of the Gods
   3. The Cultus

1831 Lectures

Introduction
   Division of the Subject
A. Natural Religion
   1. Rational Religion: Deism
   2. Primitive Religion

3. The Religion of Magic
B. The Internal Rupture of Religious Consciousness
   Introduction
   [Cosmological Proof, Pantheism]
   1. Chinese Religion: The Religion of Measure
   2. Hindu Religion: The Religion of Abstract Unity
   3. Buddhism and Lamaism: The Religion of Annihilation

C. The Religion of Freedom
   1. Transitional Forms
      a. The Religion of the Good
         (1) Persian Religion
         (2) Jewish Religion
      b. The Religion of Anguish
      c. Egyptian Religion: The Religion of Ferment

2. Greek Religion
   a. Summary
   b. The Teleological Proof
   c. The Religion of Freedom and Beauty
3. Roman Religion: The Religion of Expediency

499

COMPARATIVE STRUCTURE OF
THE CONSUMMATE RELIGION

Manuscript	*1824 Lectures*
Introduction (73a)	Introduction
1. Definition of This Religion (73a)	1. The Consummate Religion
2. Characteristics of This Religion (73a)	2. The Revelatory Religion
	3. The Religion of Truth and Freedom
	4. Relation to Preceding Religions
A. Abstract Concept (74a)	I. The Metaphysical Concept of God
B. Concrete Representation (76a)	II. The Development of the Idea of God
[Division of the Subject]	[Division of the Subject]
a. The Idea In and For Itself: The Triune God (77a)	A. The First Element: The Idea of God In and For Itself
b. The Idea in Diremption: Creation and Preservation of the Natural World (80a)	B. The Second Element: Representation, Appearance
c. Appearance of the Idea in Finite Spirit: Estrangement, Redemption, and Reconciliation (82a)	1. Differentiation a. Differentiation within the Divine Life and in the World
α. Estrangement: Natural Humanity (82b)	b. Natural Humanity
(α) The Original Condition (83b)	c. Knowledge, Estrangement, and Evil
(β) The Fall (85b)	d. The Story of the Fall
β. Redemption and Reconciliation: Christ (88a)	2. Reconciliation
(α) Idea of Divine-Human Unity (88a)	a. The Idea of Reconciliation and Its Appearance in a Single Individual
(β) Appearance of the Idea in a Single Individual (88b)	
(γ) The Teaching of Christ (89b)	b. The Historical, Sensible Presence of Christ
(δ) The Life and Death of Christ (91b)	c. The Death of Christ and the Transition to Spiritual Presence
(ε) Resurrection and Ascension of Christ (94a)	
C. Community, Cultus (95b) Standpoint of the Community in General (95b)	C. The Third Element: Community, Spirit
α. The Origin of the Community (98a)	1. The Origin of the Community
β. The Being of the Community; the Cultus (101b)	2. The Subsistence of the Community
γ. The Passing Away of the Community (104a)	3. The Realization of Faith

1827 Lectures	1831 Lectures
Introduction	Introduction
(Ms.) ──▶ 1. Definition of This Religion	1. Definition of This Religion
2. The Positivity and Spirituality of This Religion	
3. Survey of Previous Developments	2. Transition to This Religion
(*Concept of Religion*, Sec. B.e)	I. The Abstract Concept of God
	II. The Idea of God in Representational Form [Division of the Subject]
4. Division of the Subject	
A. The First Element: The Idea of God In and For Itself	A. The Kingdom of the Father
B. The Second Element: Representation, Appearance	B. The Kingdom of the Son
1. Differentiation	
a. Differentiation within the Divine Life and in the World	1. Differentiation
b. Natural Humanity	
c. The Story of the Fall	
d. Knowledge, Estrangement, and Evil	
2. Reconciliation	2. Reconciliation
a. The Idea of Reconciliation and Its Appearance in a Single Individual	a. The Idea of Reconciliation and Its Appearance in a Single Individual
b. The Historical, Sensible Presence of Christ	b. The Historical, Sensible Presence of Christ
c. The Death of Christ and the Transition to Spiritual Presence	c. The Death of Christ and the Transition to Spiritual Presence
C. The Third Element: Community, Spirit	C. The Kingdom of the Spirit
1. The Origin of the Community	
2. The Subsistence of the Community	1. The Self-Consciousness of the Community
3. The Realization of the Spirituality of the Community	2. The Realization of Religion

501

BIBLIOGRAPHY OF SOURCES
FOR HEGEL'S PHILOSOPHY
OF RELIGION

This bibliography includes all of the sources to which Hegel explicitly makes reference in the *Lectures on the Philosophy of Religion* or which can be inferred with reasonable certainty from his formulations. Works cited in the footnotes as evidence for ideas contained in the lectures, but which cannot be established as sources upon which Hegel himself drew, are not included in the bibliography.

In the footnotes, works are frequently cited in abbreviated form, without full bibliographical information. In cases where a short title is not immediately recognizable from this bibliography, it is so designated in parentheses following the full title. Frequently cited works by Hegel are listed at the beginning of this volume.

With respect to classical authors, the bibliography does not list specific works—e.g., individual tragedies of Aeschylus or dialogues of Plato—but rather editions with which Hegel is likely to have been familiar. In the footnotes, classical works are cited in the abbreviated short form customary today, followed by book, chapter, and section references, but without indicating the editions that Hegel himself used or modern editions. Works with both Greek and Latin titles are cited only with the Latin title.

The sources given in this bibliography fall into four groups:
- Works listed in the Auction Catalogue of Hegel's Library are designated by an asterisk (*).
- Works to which Hegel refers in these lectures or elsewhere, and which he almost certainly made use of, are designated by a dagger (†).

503

– Works probably used by Hegel, but for which there are no explicit references, are listed without a sign.
– Modern editions or English translations to which reference is made in the footnotes are indented following the original entries. Otherwise modern editions are not included.

Abel-Rémusat, Jean Pierre. *Mémoires sur la vie et les opinions de Lao-Tseu*. Paris, 1823.

* ———. *Observations sur quelques points de la doctrine samanéenne, et en particulier sur les noms de la triade suprême chez les différens peuples buddhistes*. Paris, 1831.

Aeschylus. *Tragoediae*. Edited in accordance with the Glasgow transcript. Leipzig, 1812.

Allgemeine Historie der Reisen zu Wasser und zu Lande; oder, Sammlung aller Reisebeschreibungen. Vols. 6 and 7. Leipzig, 1750.

Amherst. "Gesandschaftsreise nach und durch China." In Harnisch, *Die wichtigsten Reisen 5* (Leipzig, 1824). See Harnisch.

Ammianus Marcellinus. *Rerum gestarum qui de XXXI supersunt libri XVIII ad optimas editiones collati*. With introduction and appendixes prepared under the auspices of the Zweibrücken Society. Zweibrücken, 1786.

Anakreons und Sapphos Lieder nebst andern lyrischen Gedichten. Edited and translated by J. F. Degen. 2d ed. Leipzig, 1821.

Anselm of Canterbury. *Opera*. 2d ed. Paris, 1721.

———. *Proslogium; Monologium; An Appendix, In Behalf of the Fool, by Gaunilon; and Cur Deus Homo*. Translated by S. N. Deane. Chicago, 1903.

* Aristophanes. *Comoediae undecim*. Basel, 1532.

* Aristotle. *Opera quaecunque hactenus extiterunt omnia*. Edited by Desiderius Erasmus. 2 vols. in 1. Basel, 1550. (Hegel owned the edition of 1531.)

* ———. *Metaphysik*. Translated by E. W. Hengstenberg. Edited by C. A. Brandis. Vol. 1. Bonn, 1824.

* ———. *Physik*. Translated and edited by C. H. Weisse. Leipzig, 1829.

* ———. *Von der Seele und von der Welt.* Edited and translated by C. H. Weisse. Leipzig, 1829.

* Arrian. *Expeditio Alexandris.* Stereotype ed. Edited in accordance with the best manuscripts. Leipzig, 1818.

Asiatic Researches; or, Transactions of the Society Instituted in Bengal for Inquiring into the History and Antiquities, the Arts, Sciences, and Literature, of Asia. Vols. 1–11. London, 1806–1812. (Reprint of the Calcutta edition, 1788 ff.)

Bailly, Jean Sylvain. *Histoire de l'astronomie ancienne, depuis son origine jusqu'à l'établissement de l'école d'Alexandrie.* 2d ed. Paris, 1781.

* Baumgarten, Alexander Gottlieb. *Metaphysik.* 2d ed. Halle, 1783.

* Bekker, Georgius Josephus. *Specimen variarum lectionum et observationum in Philostrati vitae Apollonii librum primum.* Additional notes by F. Creuzer. Heidelberg, 1818.

Belzoni, Giovanni Battista. *Narrative of the Operations and Recent Discoveries within the Pyramids, Temples, Tombs, and Excavations, in Egypt and Nubia; and of a Journey to the Coast of the Red Sea, in Search of the Ancient Berenice; and Another to the Oasis of Jupiter Ammon.* 3d ed. 2 vols. London, 1822.

† *The Bhagavat-Geeta; or, Dialogues of Kreeshna and Arjoon, in Eighteen Lectures, with Notes: Translated from the Original, in the Sanskreet, or Ancient Language of the Brahmans.* London, 1785.

† *Bhagavad-Gita, id est* Θεσπέσιον Μέλος; *sive, Almi Krishnae et Arjunae colloquium de rebus divinis, Bharateae episodium.* Edited, with critical commentary and Latin translation, by A. W. von Schlegel. Bonn, 1823.

* Boehme, Jacob. *Theosophia revelata; Das ist, Alle göttliche Schriften des gottseligen and hocherleuchteten deutschen Theosophi.* 1715.

* Bohlen, P. von. *Das alte Indien mit besonderer Rücksicht auf Aegypten.* 2 vols. Königsberg, 1830.

† Bopp, Franz. *Ueber das Conjugationssystem der Sanskritsprache in Vergleichung mit jenem der griechischen, lateinischen, persischen und germanischen Sprache.* Together with episodes of the Rāmāyana and the Mahābhārata in exact metrical translations from the original text and selections from the Vedas. Edited by K. J. Windischmann. Frankfurt am Main, 1816.

* ———, ed. and trans. *Ardschuna's Reise zu Indra's Himmel, nebst anderen Episoden des Mahā-Bhārata.* Edited for the first time in the original language, translated metrically, and provided with critical notes. Berlin, 1824.

———, ed. and trans. *Nalus: Carmen Sanscritum e Mahābhārato.* With Latin translation and annotations. London, Paris, Strasbourg, 1819.

* ———, trans. *Die Sündflut nebst drei anderen der wichtigsten Episoden des Mahā-Bhārata.* Translated from the original. Berlin, 1829.

† Bouterwek, Friedrich. *Idee einer Apodiktik: Ein Beytrag zur menschlichen Selbstverständigung und zur Entscheidung des Streites über Metaphysik, kritische Philosophie und Skepticismus.* 2 vols. Halle, 1799.

Bowdich, T. Edward. *Mission from Cape Coast Castle to Ashantee, with a Statistical Account of That Kingdom, and Geographical Notices of Other Parts of the Interior of Africa.* London, 1819.

† Brandis, Christian August. *Xenophanis Parmenidis et Melissi doctrina e propriis philosophorum reliquiis veterumque auctorum testimoniis exposita.* Altona, 1813.

* Brown[e], [James]. *Aperçu sur les hiéroglyphes d'Égypte et les progrès faits jusqu'à présent dans leur déchiffrement.* Translated from English. With a plate illustrating the Egyptian alphabets. Paris, 1827.

Brown, John. *Elementa medicinae.* Preface by P. Moscati. Hildburghausen, 1794.

———. *Sämmtliche Werke.* Edited by Andreas Röschlaub. Vols. 1–2, *Anfangsgründe der Medizin.* Frankfurt am Main, 1806.

Bruce, James. *Reisen zur Entdeckung der Quellen des Nils in den Jahren 1768, 1769, 1770, 1771, 1772 und 1773.* Translated by J. J. Volkmann. Preface and notes by J. F. Blumenbach. Vol. 4. Leipzig, 1791.

Brucker, Jacob. *Historia critica philosophiae.* Vol. 3. Leipzig, 1743. Vol. 4, Part 2. Leipzig, 1744.

Buchanan, Francis. "On the Religion and Literature of the Burmas." *Asiatic Researches* 6:163–308.

Buhle, Johann Gottlieb. *Geschichte der neuern Philosophie seit der Epoche der Wiederherstellung der Wissenschaften.* 6 vols. Göttingen, 1800–1804.

* Buttman, Philipp. *Ueber den Mythos des Herakles.* A lecture presented 25 January 1810 at the commemoration of Frederick II in the Royal Academy of Sciences. Berlin, 1810.

Cavazzi, Joannes Antonius. *Historische Beschreibung der in dem unteren occidentalischen Mohrenland ligenden drey Königreichen Congo, Matamba, und Angola, und derjenigen Apostolischen Missionen so von denen P. P. Capucinern daselbst verrichtet worden.* Edited and translated by Fr. Fortunato Alamandini. Munich, 1694.

Cavazzi da Montecuccolo, Giovanni Antonio. *Istorica descrizione de' tre regni Congo, Matamba, et Angola situati nell'Etiopia inferiore occidentale e delle missioni apostoliche esercitatevi da religiosi Capuccini.* Bologna, 1687.

† *Le Chou-king, un des livres sacrés des Chinois, qui renferme les fondements de leur ancienne histoire, les principes de leur gouvernement & de leur morale: Ouvrage recueilli par Confucius.* Translated with notes by Fr. Antoine Gaubil. Revised by Joseph de Guignes. Paris, 1770.

* Cicero. *De natura deorum.* Based on the J. A. Ernesti edition, including the variorum notes from the J. Davis edition, with a critical apparatus and notes by G. H. Moser and additional notes by F. Creuzer. Leipzig, 1818.

————. *Opera.* 5 vols. Leipzig, 1737.

* Clavier, Etienne. *Mémoire sur les oracles des anciens.* Paris, 1818.

* Clement of Alexandria. *Opera omnia graece et latine quae extant.* Based on the edition by Daniel Heinsius. Cologne, 1688.

————. *Exhortation to the Heathen* and *The Stromata.* In *The Ante-Nicene Fathers,* edited by Alexander Roberts and James Donaldson, 2:163–206, 299–568. New York, 1885.

Colebrooke, Henry Thomas. "On the Duties of a Faithful Hindu Widow." *Asiatic Researches* 4:205–215.

————. "On the Philosophy of the Hindus." *Transactions of the Royal Asiatic Society* (London) 1 (1824): 19–43, 92–118, 439–466, 549–579.

————. "On the Religious Ceremonies of the Hindus, and of the Brāhmans Especially." *Asiatic Researches* 5:345–368; 7:232–287, 288–311.

————. "On the Vēdas, or Sacred Writings of the Hindus." *Asiatic Researches* 8:377–497.

† *Confucius Sinarum philosophus; sive, Scientia Sinensis, latine exposita.* Compiled by Frs. P. Intorcetta, C. Herdtrich, F. Rougemont, and P. Couplet, S.J. Paris, 1687.

† *The Works of Confucius, Containing the Original Text, with a Translation.* Vol. 1, *To Which is Prefixed a Dissertation on the Chinese Language and Character,* by Joshua Marshman. Serampore, 1809.

* Creuzer, Friedrich. *Abriss der römischen Antiquitäten zum Gebrauch bei Vorlesungen.* Leipzig and Darmstadt, 1824.

* ————. *Briefe über Homer.* See Herrmann, Martin Gottfried.

* ————. *Commentationes Herodoteae: Aegyptiaca et Hellenica.* Part I. With summaries, scholia, and variant readings of the Palatine Codex. Leipzig, 1819.

* ————. *Symbolik und Mythologie der alten Völker, besonders der Griechen.* 2d ed. 4 vols., plates. Leipzig and Darmstadt, 1819–1821.

† Delambre, Jean Joseph. *Histoire de l'astronomie ancienne.* 2 vols. Paris, 1817.

* Descartes, René. *Specimina philosophiae; seu, Dissertatio de methodo.* Translated from the French; complete text checked and in places emended by the author. New ed., carefully reviewed and corrected. Amsterdam, 1656.

———. *Meditationes de prima philosophia, in quibus Dei existentia, & animae humanae a corpore distinctio, demonstrantur: His adjunctae sunt variae objectiones doctorum virorum in istas de Deo & anima demonstrationes; cum responsionibus auctoris.* Latest ed., including additions and emendations. Amsterdam, 1663.

* ———. *Principia philosophiae.* New ed., carefully reviewed and corrected. Amsterdam, 1656.

———. *A Discourse on Method and Selected Writings.* Translated by John Veitch. New York and London, 1951. Contains: *Discourse on the Method of Rightly Conducting the Reason and Seeking Truth in the Sciences* (1637); *Meditations on the First Philosophy* (1641); *The Principles of Philosophy* (1644).

* Devīmāhātmyam. *Mārkandeyi Purāni sectio.* Edited by L. Poley, with Latin translation and annotations. Berlin, 1831.

* Dio Cassius. *Historiae Romanae quae supersunt.* Stereotype ed. Edited in accordance with the best manuscripts. 4 vols. Leipzig, 1818.

* Diodorus Siculus. *Bibliothecae historicae libri XVII.* Lyons, 1552.

* Diogenes Laertius. *De vitis, dogmatibus et apophthegmatibus clarorum philosophorum libri decem.* In Greek and Latin. Leipzig, 1759.

† Dow, Alexander. *The History of Hindostan, from the Earliest Account of Time to the Death of Akbar; Translated from the Persian of Mahummud Casim Ferishta of Delhi, Together with a Dissertation Concerning the Religion and Philosophy of the Brahmins; with an Appendix, Containing the History of the Mogul Empire, from Its Decline in the Reign of Mahummud Shaw, to the Present Times.* 2 vols. London, 1768.

Dubois, Abbé Jean Antoine. *Moeurs, institutions et cérémonies des peuples de l'Inde.* 2 vols. Paris, 1825.

Dupuis, Charles François. *Origine de tous les cultes; ou, Religion universelle.* 4 vols. Paris, 1795.

* Eichhorn, Johann Gottfried. *Einleitung in das Alte Testament.* 2d ed. Reutlingen, 1790.

* Euripides. *Hippolytus.* In Greek and Latin. Edited by G. H. Martin, from the text established by Brunk, with notes. Leipzig, 1788.

* ———. *Tragoediae octodecim.* Edited by J. Oporinus. Basel, 1544.

* Fichte, Johann Gottlieb. *Appellation an das Publikum über die durch ein Kurf. Sächs. Confiscationsrescript ihm beigemessenen atheistischen Aeusserungen: Eine Schrift, die man erst zu lesen bittet, ehe man sie konfiscirt.* Jena, Leipzig, Tübingen, 1799.

* ———. *Gerichtliche Verantwortungsschrift gegen die Anklage des Atheismus.* Jena, 1799.

* ———. *Grundlage der gesammten Wissenschaftslehre als Handschrift für seine Zuhörer.* Leipzig, 1794.

———. *Science of Knowledge (Wissenschaftslehre).* Translated by P. Heath and J. Lachs. New York, 1970.

* ———. *Das System der Sittenlehre nach den Principien der Wissenschaftslehre.* Jena and Leipzig, 1798.

* ———. "Ueber den Grund unsers Glaubens an eine göttliche Weltregierung." *Philosophisches Journal einer Gesellschaft teutscher Gelehrten* (Jena and Leipzig), edited by J. G. Fichte and I. Niethammer, vol. 8, no. 1 (1798).

———. "On the Foundation of Our Belief in a Divine Government of the Universe." In *Nineteenth-Century Philosophy*, edited by P. L. Gardiner, pp. 19–26. New York, 1969.

† ———. *Versuch einer Critik aller Offenbarung.* Königsberg, 1792.

———. *Attempt at a Critique of All Revelation.* Translated by Garrett Green. Cambridge, 1978.

————. *Gesamtausgabe.* Published by the Bavarian Academy of Sciences. Edited by R. Lauth, H. Jacob, and H. Gliwitzky. Division I. Stuttgart–Bad Cannstatt, 1964 ff.

† Forster, George. *Johann Reinhold Forster's Reise um die Welt, während den Jahren 1772 bis 1775 in dem von Seiner itztregierenden Grossbrittanischen Majestät auf Entdeckungen ausgeschickten und durch den Capitain Cook geführten Schiffe the Resolution unternommen.* Written and edited by his son and travel companion, George Forster. Translated from English by the author, with excerpts from Captain Cook's diary and other additions for the German reader, and illustrated with prints. Vol. 1. Berlin, 1778.

* Frandsen, Petrus. *Haruspices.* Berlin, 1823.

* Frank, Othmar. *De Persidis lingua et genio: Commentationes Phaosophico-Persicae.* Nuremburg, 1809.

† Fries, Jakob Friedrich. *Wissen, Glaube und Ahndung.* Jena, 1805.

* Gibbon, Edward. *The History of the Decline and Fall of the Roman Empire.* New ed. 12 vols. Leipzig, 1821.

* Görres, Joseph. *Das Heldenbuch von Iran aus dem Schah Nameh des Firdussi.* 2 vols. Berlin, 1820.

* Goethe, Johann Wolfgang von. *West-östlicher Divan.* Stuttgart, 1819.

† ————. *Wilhelm Meisters Wanderjahre; oder, Die Entsagenden: Ein Roman.* Part I. Stuttgart and Tübingen, 1821.

————. *Wilhelm Meister's Travels; or, The Renunciants: A Novel.* Translated by Thomas Carlyle. 2 vols. New York, 1901.

* ————. *Zur Farbenlehre: Des ersten Bandes erster, didaktischer Theil: Entwurf einer Farbenlehre.* Tübingen, 1810.

————. *Theory of Colours.* Translated by C. L. Eastlake. 1st ed. 1840. Reprint. Cambridge, Mass., 1970.

† ————. *Zur Naturwissenschaft überhaupt, besonders zur Morphologie: Erfahrung, Betrachtung, Folgerung, durch Lebensereignisse verbunden.* Vol. 2, Part 1, *Zur Morphologie.* Stuttgart and Tübingen, 1823.

————. *Werke.* Commissioned by Grand Duchess Sophie of Saxony. Divisions 1–2. Weimar, 1887 ff.

* Gramberg, C. P. W. *Kritische Geschichte der Religionsideen des Alten Testaments.* Preface by W. Gesenius. Vol. 1, *Hierarchie und Kultus.* Berlin, 1829. Vol. 2, *Theokratie und Prophetismus.* Berlin, 1830.

Grotius, Hugo. *De veritate religionis Christianae.* New ed. In *Operum theologicorum tomus tertius, continens opuscula diversa.* Amsterdam, 1679.

* Guigniaut, Joseph Daniel. *Sérapis et son origine: Commentaire sur les chapitres 83–84 du livre IV des Histoires de Tacite.* Paris, 1828.

* Guilhem de Clermont-Lodève, Guillaume-Emmanuel-Joseph, Baron de Saint-Croix. *Recherches historiques et critiques sur les mystères du paganisme.* 2d ed. Revised by Baron Silvestre de Sacy. 2 vols. Paris, 1817.

Haller, Albrecht von. *Versuch schweizerischer Gedichte.* 6th ed. Göttingen, 1751.

Hammer-Purgstall, Joseph von. *Geschichte der schönen Redekünste Persiens, mit einer Blüthenlese aus zweyhundert persischen Dichtern.* Vienna, 1818.

Harnisch, Wilhelm, comp. *Die wichtigsten neuern Land- und Seereisen: Für die Jugend und andere Leser bearbeitet.* 16 parts. Leipzig, 1821–1832. (= *Die wichtigsten Reisen*)

† Heeren, A. H. L. *Ideen über die Politik, den Verkehr und den Handel der vornehmsten Völker der alten Welt.* 2 vols. Göttingen, 1804–1805.

Herder, Johann Gottfried. *Aelteste Urkunde des Menschengeschlechts.* Vol. 2, containing Part 4. In *Herder's Sämmtliche Werke: Zur Religion und Theologie.* Vol. 6. Tübingen, 1806.

————. *Vom Geist der ebräischen Poesie: Eine Anleitung für die Liebhaber derselben und der ältesten Geschichte des menschlichen Geistes.* Vol. 1. Leipzig, 1787.

————. *The Spirit of Hebrew Poetry.* Translated by James Marsh. 2 vols. Burlington, Vt., 1833.

* ———. *Gott: Einige Gespräche.* Gotha, 1787. 2d ed.: *Gott: Einige Gespräche über Spinoza's System; nebst Shaftesburi's Naturhymnus.* Gotha, 1800
———. *God: Some Conversations.* Translated by F. H. Burkhardt. Indianapolis and New York, 1940.

* Herodotus. *Historiarum libri XI; Narratio de vita Homeri.* With Valla's Latin versions. Edited by H. Stephanus. Also contains Ctesias's *De rebus Persis et Indis.* 2d ed. Paris, 1592. Hegel's other edition of Herodotus lacks a Greek text: Herodotus. *Libri novem, Musarum nominibus inscripti,* trans. Lorenzo Valla. Cologne, 1562.

* Herrmann, Martin Gottfried. *Die Feste von Hellas historisch-philosophisch bearbeitet and zum erstenmal nach ihrem Sinn und Zweck erläutert.* 2 vols. Berlin, 1803.

* Herrmann, Martin Gottfried, and Friedrich Creuzer. *Briefe über Homer und Hesiodus vorzüglich über die Theogonie von Gottfried Herrmann und Friedrich Creuzer: Mit besonderer Hinsicht auf des Ersteren Dissertatio de Mythologia Graecorum antiquissima und auf des Letzteren Symbolik und Mythologie der Griechen.* Heidelberg, 1818.

* Hesiod. *Opera et dies, et Theogonia, et Clypeus. Theognidis sententiae. Sybillae carmina de Christo, quorum mentionem facit Eusebius & Augustinus. Musaei opusculum de Herone & Leandro. Orphei Argonautica, Hymni, & de Lapidibus. Phoclydis Paraenesis.* Venice, 1543.

† Hirt, Aloys. *Ueber die Bildung der aegyptischen Gottheiten.* 11 tables. Special edition published by the Royal Academy of Sciences. Berlin, 1821.

d'Holbach, Paul Henri Thiry [Boulanger, pseud.]. *Le christianisme dévoilé; ou, Examen des principes et des effets de la religion chrétienne.* London, 1756.

* ——— [Mirabaud, pseud.]. *Système de la nature ou des loix du monde physique & du monde moral.* 2d ed. 2 vols. London, 1771.

——— [Abbé Bernier, pseud.]. *Théologie portative; ou, Dictionnaire abrégé de la religion chrétienne.* London, 1768.

* Homer. *Ilias.* Stereotype ed. Edited in accordance with the best manuscripts. 2 vols. Leipzig, 1819–1821.

———. *Odyssea.* New ed. 2 vols. Leipzig and Leiden, 1820.

* Horace. *Eclogae.* Corrected and annotated by W. Baxter. Additional variant readings and notes by J. M. Gesner. 2d ed. Leipzig, 1772.

* [Hülsemann.] *Ueber die Hegelsche Lehre; oder, Absolutes Wissen und moderner Pantheismus.* Leipzig, 1829.

* Humboldt, Wilhelm. *Über die unter dem Namen Bhagavad-Gītā bekannte Episode des Mahā-Bhārata.* Paper read to the Academy of Sciences, 30 June 1825 and 15 June 1826. Berlin, 1826.

Hume, David. *Geschichte von Grossbritannien.* Translated from English. Vols. 18–20. Frankenthal, 1788.

† *Institutes of Hindu Law; or, The Ordinances of Menu, According to the Gloss of Cullūca, Comprising the Indian System of Duties, Religious and Civil, Verbally Translated from the Original Sanscrit.* Calcutta, 1794.

* Jacobi, Friedrich Heinrich. *Jacobi an Fichte.* Hamburg, 1799.

———. *Auserlesener Briefwechsel.* 2 vols. Edited by Friedrich Roth. Leipzig, 1827.

† ———. *David Hume über den Glauben; oder, Idealismus und Realismus: Ein Gespräch.* Breslau, 1787.

† ———. *Ueber die Lehre des Spinoza in Briefen an den Herrn Moses Mendelssohn.* New, enlarged ed. Breslau, 1789.

* ———. *Von den Göttlichen Dingen und ihrer Offenbarung.* Leipzig, 1811.

* ———. *Werke.* 6 vols. Leipzig, 1812–1825.

* Jäsche, Gottlob Benjamin. "Ansichten des Pantheismus nach seinen verschiedenen Hauptformen: Eine Parallele zwischen dem Alten und dem Neuen in der antidualistischen Philosophie des Ἕν τὸ Πᾶν. *Dörptische Beyträge für Freunde der Philosophie, Litteratur und Kunst* (Dorpat and Leipzig), edited by Karl Morgenstern, 1814, no. 1 (published in 1815).

Jones, William. "On the Chronology of the Hindus." *Asiatic Researches* 2:111–147.

———. "On the Gods of Greece, Italy, and India." *Asiatic Researches* 1:221–275.

Josephus. *Des fürtrefflichen jüdischen Geschicht-Schreibers Flavii Josephi Sämmtliche Wercke.* Edited by J. F. Cotta. Tübingen, 1735.

* Kant, Immanuel. *Critik der practischen Vernunft.* Riga, 1788.

———. *Critique of Practical Reason.* Translated by L. W. Beck. New York, 1956.

† ———. *Critik der reinen Vernunft.* 2d ed. Riga, 1787.

———. *Critique of Pure Reason.* Translated from R. Schmidt's collation of the 1st (A) and 2d (B) editions by N. Kemp Smith. London, 1930.

* ———. *Critik der Urtheilskraft.* Berlin and Libau, 1790.

———. *Critique of Judgement.* Translated by J. C. Meredith. Oxford, 1952.

———. *Grundlegung zur Metaphysik der Sitten.* Riga, 1785.

———. *The Fundamental Principles of the Metaphysics of Ethics.* Translated by O. Manthey-Zorn. New York, 1938.

* ———. *Die Religion innerhalb der Grenzen der blossen Vernunft.* Königsberg, 1793.

———. *Religion within the Limits of Reason Alone.* Translated by T. M. Greene and H. H. Hudson. La Salle, Ill., 1934.

———. *Gesammelte Schriften.* Edited by the Royal Prussian Academy of Sciences. Berlin, 1900 ff.

* Klaproth, Heinrich Julius. Review of *Mémoire sur l'origine et la propagation de la doctrine du Tao, fondée par Lao-tseu,* by G. Pauthier. *Nouveau Journal Asiatique; ou, Recueil de mémoires, d'extraits et de notices relatifs à l'histoire, à la philosophie, aux langues et à la littérature des peuples orientaux* (Paris) 7 (1831): 465–493.

Köppen, Friedrich. *Ueber Offenbarung, in Beziehung auf Kantische und Fichtische Philosophie.* 2d ed. Lübeck and Leipzig, 1802.

* Lactantius. *Divinarum institutionum libri VII; De ira Dei, lib. I; De opificio Dei, lib. I; Epitome in libros suos, liber acephalos.* Edited by M. Thomasius, with notes, a comprehensive index, and Latin equivalents for Greek terms. Antwerp, 1570.

* LaPlace, Pierre Simon. *Darstellung des Weltsystems.* Translated from French by J. K. F. Hauff. 2 vols. Frankfurt am Main, 1797.

* Leibniz, Gottfried Wilhelm. *Essais de theodicée sur la bonté de Dieu, la liberté de l'homme, et l'origine du mal.* New ed., augmented by a history of the life and works of the author, by M. L. de Neufville. Amsterdam, 1734.

————. *Theodicy: Essays on the Goodness of God, the Freedom of Man, and the Origin of Evil.* Edited by Austin Farrer. Translated by E. M. Huggard from the Gerhardt edition. New Haven, 1952.

† ————. *Opera omnia.* Edited by L. Dutens. Geneva, 1768.

————. *Die philosophischen Schriften.* Edited by C. J. Gerhardt. 7 vols. Berlin, 1875–1890.

————. *Selections.* Edited by Philip P. Wiener. New York, 1951.

Lessing, Gotthold Ephraim. *Anti-Goeze; D. i. Nothgedrungene Beyträge zu den freywilligen Beyträgen des Hrn. Past. Goeze.* Braunschweig, 1778.

————. *Axiomata, wenn es deren in dergleichen Dingen gibt: Wider den Herrn Pastor Goeze, in Hamburg.* Braunschweig, 1778,

————. *Briefe, die neueste Litteratur betreffend: Geschrieben in den Jahren 1759 bis 1763.* 24 parts, index. Berlin and Stettin, 1776.

————. *Eine Duplik.* Braunschweig, 1778.

† ————. *Nathan der Weise.* Drama in five acts. 1779.

————, ed. *Zur Geschichte und Litteratur: Aus den Schätzen der Herzoglichen Bibliothek zu Wolfenbüttel.* Fourth contribution by G. E. Lessing. Braunschweig, 1777. (The author is Hermann Samuel Reimarus.)

————. *Sämtliche Schriften.* Edited by K. Lachmann. 3d ed. Revised by F. Muncker. Leipzig, 1886–1924.

* Lobeck, Christianus Augustus. *Aglaophamus; sive, De theologiae mysticae Graecorum causis libri tres.* With various fragments from the Orphic poets. 2 vols. Königsberg, 1829.

* Longinus, Dionysius. *De sublimitate.* Edited by S. F. N. More from the text established by Z. Pearce, with the editor's selection from previous commentaries and additional comments of his own. Leipzig, 1769.

* Lucian of Samosata. *Opera.* Greek and Latin. Edited in accordance with the edition of T. Hemsterhus and J. F. Reitz; with variant readings and annotations. 9 vols. Zweibrücken, 1789.

[Luther, Martin.] *Die gantze Heilige Schrift Deudsch.* Wittenberg, 1545.

† [Macartney.] *Reise der englischen Gesandtschaft an den Kaiser von China, in den Jahren 1792 und 1793: Aus den Papieren des Grafen von Macartney, des Ritters Gower and andrer Herren zusammengetragen von Sir George Staunton.* Translated from English by J. C. Hüttner. 2 vols. Zürich, 1798–1799.

† de Mailla, Joseph-Anne-Marie de Moyriac. *Histoire générale de la Chine; ou, Annales de cet empire, traduits du Tong-Kien-Kang-Mou.* 13 vols. Paris, 1777–1785.

* Maimon, Salomon. *Lebensgeschichte.* Edited by K. P. Moritz. 2 vols. Berlin, 1792.

† [Masson, Charles-François Philibert.] *Mémoires secrets sur la Russie, et particulièrement sur la fin du règne de Catherine II. et le commencement de celui de Paul I.: Formant un tableau des moeurs de St. Pétersburg à la fin du XVIIIe siècle.* 3 vols. Paris, 1800–1802.

† *Mémoires concernant l'histoire, les sciences, les moeurs, les usages, etc. des Chinois par les missionaires de Pekin.* 16 vols. Paris, 1776–1814.

* Mendelssohn, Moses. *Jerusalem; oder, Über religiöse Macht und Judentum.* Berlin, 1783.

* ———. *Morgenstunden; oder, Vorlesungen über das Daseyn Gottes.* Berlin, 1786.

† [Meyer, Johann Friedrich von.] *Die Heilige Schrift in berichtigter Uebersetzung mit kurzen Anmerkungen.* 3 vols. Frankfurt am Main, 1819.

Michaelis, Johann David. *Deutsche Uebersetzung des Alten Testaments, mit Anmerkungen für Ungelehrte.* 13 vols. 1769–1783. Part I, containing the Book of Job. Göttingen and Gotha, 1769. Part II, containing the Book of Genesis. Göttingen and Gotha, 1770.

Mill, James. *The History of British India.* 3 vols. London, 1817.

Milton, John. *Das Verlohrne Paradies.* Translated from English in free verse, with annotations, by F. W. Zacharias. 2 vols. Altona, 1760–1763.

Molière, Jean-Baptiste. *Le Bourgeois Gentil-Homme: Comédie-Ballet.* In *Les œuvres de Monsieur de Molière.* New ed. Vol. 4. Paris, 1733.

* Moritz, Karl Philipp. *Anthousa; oder, Roms Alterthümer. Ein Buch für die Menschheit. Die heiligen Gebräuche der Römer.* Berlin, 1791.

† Müller, Karl Otfried. *Geschichten hellenischer Stämme und Städte.* Vols. 2–3, *Die Dorier.* Breslau, 1824.

* ———. *Handbuch der Archäologie der Kunst.* Breslau, 1830.

† Neander, August. *Genetische Entwickelung der vornehmsten gnostischen Systeme.* Berlin, 1818.

Niebuhr, Carsten. *Voyage de M. Niebuhr en Arabie et en d'autres pays de l'orient: Avec l'extrait de sa description de l'Arabie & des observations de Mr. Forskal.* 2 vols. Switzerland, 1780. (In the Catalogue of the Hegel Library this work is cited as: Niebuhr. *Reisen durch Aegypten and Arabien, mit Karten.* 2 pts. Bern, 1779).

* Niethammer, Friedrich Immanuel. *Der Streit des Philanthropinismus und Humanismus in der Theorie des Erziehungs-Unterrichts unsrer Zeit.* Jena, 1808.

Parmenides. *See* Simplicius.

* Passalacqua, Joseph. *Catalogue raisonné et historique des antiquités découvertes en Égypte.* Paris, 1826.

Paterson, J. D. "Of the Origin of the Hindu Religion." *Asiatic Researches* 8:44–87.

* Pausanias. *Graeciae descriptio.* Edited in accordance with the best manuscripts. 3 vols. Leipzig, 1818.

† Philo. *Opera omnia graece et latine.* Edited by A. F. Pfeiffer from the text established by T. Mangey. 5 vols. 2d ed. Erlangen, 1820.

* Philostratus. *Historiae de vita Apollonii libri VIII.* Eusebius of Caesarea. *Adversus Hieroclem, qui ex Philostrati historia Apollonium Tyaneum salutori nostro Jesu Christo aequiparare contendebat, confutatio, sive apologia.* Latin translations carefully corrected against the Greek, and editorial annotations added by Gybertus Longolius [i.e., Gilbert de Longueil]. Cologne, 1532.

* Pindar. *Carmina.* Revised and edited by C. G. Heyne, with variant readings and annotations. 5 vols. Göttingen, 1798–1799. Vol 3. *Scholia in Pindari Carmina, Volumen II, Pars II: Scholia in Pythia Nemea et Isthmia.* Göttingen, 1798.

* Plato. *Opera quae extant omnia.* Latin translation by Joannes Serranus [i.e., Jean de Serres]. Edited by H. Stephanus. 3 vols. [Geneva], 1578.

* Plutarch. *Quae supersunt omnia.* Edited by J. G. Hutten, with annotations and variant readings. 14 vols. Tübingen, 1791–1804.

* Proclus. *In Platonis theologiam libri sex.* Edited by Aemilius Portus, with a short life of Proclus by Marinus Neapolitanus. Hamburg and Frankfurt am Main, 1618. Also contains *Institutio theologica.*

———. *In Platonis Timaeon commentariorum libri quinque, totius veteris philosophiae thesaurus. Et in eiusdem politices difficiliorum quaestionum omnium enarratio.* Cologne, 1534.

* Quatremère, Etienne. *Mémoires géographiques et historiques sur l'Egypte, et sur quelques contrées voisines, recueillis et extraits des manuscripts coptes, arabes, etc. de la Bibliothèque Impériale.* 2 vols. Paris, 1811.

* Racine, Jean. *Œuvres*. Vol. 3. Paris, 1817.

† *The Ramayuna of Valmeeki, in the Original Sungskrit*. Translated and annotated by William Carey and Joshua Marshman. Vol. 1. Serampore, 1806.

* *Ramayana; id est, Carmen epicum de Ramae rebus gestis*. A work of the ancient Hindu poet Valmiki. Edited by A. W. von Schlegel on the basis of a collation of manuscript codices, with a Latin translation and critical notes. Vol. 1, pt. 1. Bonn, 1829.

† Review of *Sur l'élévation des montagnes de l'Inde*, by Alexander von Humboldt. *The Quarterly Review* (London) 22, no. 44 (1820): 415–430.

† Rhode, J. G. *Die heilige Sage und das gesammte Religionssystem der alten Baktrer, Meder und Perser oder des Zendvolks*. Frankfurt am Main, 1820.

* ———. *Über Alter und Werth einiger morgenländischen Urkunden*. Breslau, 1817.

Rixner, Thaddae Anselm. *Handbuch der Geschichte der Philosophie zum Gebrauche seiner Vorlesungen*. 3 vols. Sulzbach, 1822–1823.

Robinet, Jean-Baptiste. *De la nature*. New ed. Amsterdam, 1763.

* Rosen, Fridericus. *Corporis radicum sanscritarum prolusio*. Berlin, 1826.

† ———. *Radices Sanscritae, illustratas edidit*. Berlin, 1827.

† Rosenmüller, Er. Fr. Karl. *Das alte und neue Morgenland; oder, Erläuterungen der heiligen Schrift aus der natürlichen Beschaffenheit, den Sagen, Sitten und Gebräuchen des Morgenlandes*. 6 vols. Leipzig, 1817–1820.

Ross, John. *A Voyage of Discovery, Made under the Order of the Admirality, in His Majesty's Ships Isabella and Alexander, for the Purpose of Exploring Baffin's Bay, and Enquiring into the Probability of a North-West Passage*. 2d ed. 2 vols. London, 1819.

Rousseau, Jean-Jacques. *Discours sur l'origine et les fondemens de l'inégalité parmi les hommes*. Amsterdam, 1755.

———. *Aemil; oder, Von der Erziehung*. Translated from French, with annotations. Berlin, Frankfurt am Main, Leipzig, 1762.

* Roy, Remmohon (Bramin). *Auflösung des Wedant; oder, Auflösung aller Wed's des berühmtesten Werkes braminischer Gottegelahrtheit, worin die Einheit des höchsten Wesens dargethan wird, so wie auch, dass Gott allein der Gegenstand der Versöhnung und Verehrung sein könne.* Jena, 1817.

† Rückert, Friedrich. "Mewlana Dschelaleddin Rumi." In *Taschenbuch für Damen auf das Jahr 1821*, pp. 211–248. Tübingen, 1821.

Sailer, Sebastian. *Schriften im schwäbischen Dialekte.* Edited by Sixt Bachmann. Buchau, 1819.

Saint-Croix, Baron de. *See* Guilhem de Clermont-Lodève, Guillaume-Emmanuel-Joseph, Baron de Saint-Croix.

* Schelling, Friedrich Wilhelm Joseph. "Darstellung meines Systems der Philosophie." *Zeitschrift für spekulative Physik* (Jena and Leipzig), edited by Schelling, vol. 2, no. 2 (1801).

* ————. "Philosophische Briefe über Dogmatismus und Kriticismus." *Philosophisches Journal einer Gesellschaft teutscher Gelehrter* (Neu-Strelitz), edited by F. I. Niethammer, 2, no. 3 (1795): 177–203; 3, no. 3 (1795): 173–239.

* ————. *System des transscendentalen Idealismus.* Stuttgart, 1800.

————. *System of Transcendental Idealism* (1800). Translated by Peter Heath. Introduction by Michael Vater. Charlottesville, 1978.

* ————. *Ueber die Gottheiten von Samothrace.* Lecture presented to the Bavarian Academy of Sciences, 12 October 1815, as a supplement to the *Weltalter.* Stuttgart and Tübingen, 1815.

————. *Schelling's Treatise on "The Deities of Samothrace."* Translated by R. F. Brown. American Academy of Religion Studies in Religion, vol. 12. Missoula, Mont., 1977.

* ————. *Von der Weltseele: Eine Hypothese der höhern Physik zur Erklärung des allgemeinen Organismus.* Hamburg, 1798.

† ———. *Vorlesungen über die Methode des academischen Studium*. Tübingen, 1803.

———. *On University Studies*. Translated by E. S. Morgan. Edited by Norbert Guterman. Athens, Ohio, 1966.

———. *Sämmtliche Werke*. Edited by K. F. A. Schelling. 1st Div. 10 vols. Stuttgart and Augsburg, 1856–1861.

* Schiller, Friedrich, ed. *Die Horen: Eine Monatsschrift*. Tübingen, 1795.

———. *Nationalausgabe*. Vols. 1 and 10. Weimar, 1943, 1980.

* Schlegel, August Wilhelm. *Comparaison entre la Phèdre de Racine et celle d'Euripide*. Paris, 1807.

* ———, ed. *Indische Bibliothek*. Vol. 2, no. 4. Bonn, 1827.

Schlegel, August Wilhelm, and Friedrich Schlegel, eds. *Athenäum: Eine Zeitschrift*. Vol. 1, no. 2. Berlin, 1798.

† Schlegel, Friedrich. *Über die neuere Geschichte*. Lectures presented in Vienna, 1810. Vienna, 1811.

* ———. *Ueber die Sprache und Weisheit der Indier: Ein Beitrag zur Begründung der Alterthumskunde: Nebst metrischen Uebersetzungen indischer Gedichte*. Heidelberg, 1808.

———. *Kritische Friedrich-Schlegel-Ausgabe*. Edited by Ernst Behler, with Jean-Jacques Anstett and Hans Eichner. Paderborn, Munich, Vienna, 1958 ff.

———, ed. *Lyceum der schönen Künste*. Vol. 1, pt. 2. Berlin, 1797.

† Schleiermacher, Friedrich Daniel Ernst. *Der christliche Glaube nach den Grundsätzen der evangelischen Kirche im Zusammenhange dargestellt*. 1st ed. 2 vols. Berlin, 1821–1822.

———. *Kritische Gesamtausgabe*. Div. 1, vol. 7/1-2, *Der christliche Glaube*. 1st ed. Edited by Hermann Peiter. Berlin and New York, 1980.

———. *The Christian Faith*. Translated from the 2d German ed. of 1830 by H. R. Mackintosh, J. S. Stewart, et al. Edinburgh, 1928. (= *The Christian Faith* or *Glaubenslehre*)

† [Schleiermacher, Friedrich.] *Über die Religion: Reden an die Gebildeten unter ihren Verächtern*. Berlin, 1799.

* Seneca. *Opera Philosophica*. Halle, 1762.

* ———. *Opera, quae extant omnia.* Lyons, 1555.

Sextus Empiricus. *Opera.* In Greek and Latin. *Pyrrhoniarum institutionum libri III.* Edited and translated into Latin by H. Stephanus. *Contra mathematicos, sive disciplinarum professores, libri VI. Contra philosophos libri V.* Translated by G. Hervetus. Greek texts checked against manuscript codices, Latin versions revised, and the whole annotated by J. A. Fabricius. Leipzig, 1718.

* Seybold, W. C. *Ideen zur Theologie und Staatsverfassung des höhern Alterthums.* Tübingen, 1820.

Shakespeare, William. *Schauspiele.* New ed. Translated by J. J. Eschenburg. Vol. 12. Strasbourg, 1779.

Simplicius. *Commentarii in octo Aristotelis physicae auscultationis libros cum ipso Aristotelis textu.* Venice, 1526.

* Sophocles. *Tragoediae septem.* Emended in accordance with the best available copies. Translated and annotated by R. F. P. Brunck. 2 vols. Strasbourg, 1786.

* Spinoza, Benedictus de. *Opera quae supersunt omnia.* New ed. Edited by H. E. G. Paulus, with a life of the author and some notes on the history of the writings. 2 vols. Jena, 1802–1803.

† ———. *Adnotationes ad Tractatum theologico-politicum.* Edited from the author's original manuscript by C. T. de Murr, with a preface and notes on Spinoza's writings. The Hague, 1802.

———. *Chief Works.* Translated by R. H. M. Elwes. London, 1883. Contains: *Theologico-Political Treatise* (1670); *The Ethics* (1677); *On the Improvement of the Understanding* (1677); *Correspondence.*

Stobaeus, Joannes. *Eclogarum physicarum et ethicarum libri duo.* Supplemented and corrected from manuscript codices and furnished with annotations and a Latin version by A. H. L. Heeren. Göttingen, 1792.

Suetonius. *Opera.* New edition with commentary and key to names referred to by the author, by D. K. W. Baumgarten-Crusius. 3 vols. Leipzig, 1816–1818.

* *Sybillae carmina. See* Hesiod.

Tacitus. *Opera.* New ed. by J. J. Oberlin, based on the text established by J. A. Ernesti. 2 vols. Leipzig, 1801.

* Tennemann, Wilhelm Gottlieb. *Geschichte der Philosophie.* 11 vols. Leipzig, 1798–1819.

* Terence. *Comoediae sex.* New annotated ed. by Christopherus Colerus. Frankfurt am Main, 1594.

† Tholuck, Friedrich August Gotttreu. *Blüthensammlung aus der morgenländischen Mystik nebst einer Einleitung über Mystik überhaupt und morgenländische insbesondere.* Berlin, 1825.

† [Tholuck, Friedrich August Gotttreu.] *Die Lehre von der Sünde und vom Versöhner; oder, Die wahre Weihe des Zweiflers.* Hamburg, 1823. 2d ed. 1825.

* Tholuck, Friedrich August Gotttreu. *Die speculative Trinitätslehre des späteren Orients: Eine religionsphilosophische Monographie aus handschriftlichen Quellen der Leydener, Oxforder und Berliner Bibliothek.* Berlin, 1826.

* Thucydides. *De bello Peloponnesiaco libri VIII.* Edited by H. Stephanus. Latin version based on the translation by Lorenzo Valla. Frankfurt am Main, 1594.

† Tiedemann, Dieterich. *Geist der spekulativen Philosophie.* 6 vols. Marburg, 1791–1797.

† Tuckey, J. K. *Narrative of an Expedition to Explore the River Zaire Usually Called the Congo, in South Africa, in 1816, under the Direction of Captain J. K. Tuckey, R.N.: To Which Is Added the Journal of Professor Smith.* London, 1818.

Turner, Samuel. "An Account of a Journey to Tibet." *Asiatic Researches* 1:207–220.

———. "Copy of an Account Given by Mr. Turner, of His Interview with Teeshoo Lama at the Monastery of Terpaling, Enclosed in Mr. Turner's Letter to the Honourable the Governor General, Dated Patna, 2d March, 1784." *Asiatic Researches* 1:197–205.

———. "Des Hauptmann Samuel Turner's Reise in Bhutan und Tibet." In Harnisch, *Die wichtigsten Reisen* 6 (Leipzig, 1824): 287–362. *See* Harnisch.

————. *An Account of an Embassy to the Court of the Teshoo Lama, in Tibet: Containing a Narrative of a Journey through Bootan, and Part of Tibet.* London, 1800.

* Volney, Constantin François de Chasseboeuf. *Les ruines; ou, Meditations sur les revolutions des empires.* 2d ed. Paris, 1798.

Voltaire. *La Bible enfin expliquée.* London, 1776.

————. *Dictionnaire philosophique.* 7 vols. In *Œuvres complètes* (1784), vols. 37–43.

————. *Examen important de Milord Bolingbroke.* In *Œuvres complètes* (1784).

* Weisse, Christian Hermann. *Darstellung der griechischen Mythologie.* Part I, *Ueber den Begriff, die Behandlung und die Quellen der Mythologie: Als Einleitung in die Darstellung der griechischen Mythologie.* Leipzig, 1828.

* ————. *Ueber das Studium des Homer und seine Bedeutung für unser Zeitalter: Nebst einem Anhange mythologischen Inhalts und einer Rede über das Verhältniss des Studiums der Geschichte zu der allgemeinen Nationalbildung.* Leipzig, 1826.

† Wilford, Francis. "An Essay on the Sacred Isles in the West, with Other Essays. III. Sweta Devi; or the White Goddess." *Asiatic Researches* 8:245–376; 9:32–243.

* Windischmann, Carl Joseph Hieronymus. *Die Philosophie im Fortgang der Weltgeschichte.* Part I: *Die Grundlagen der Philosophie im Morgenland.* Bonn, 1827–1829.

Wolff, Christian. *Philosophia moralis sive ethica, methodo scientifica pertractata.* Part 3. Halle, 1751.

————. *Philosophia prima sive ontologia methodo scientifica pertractata, qua omnis cognitionis humanae principia continentur.* New ed. Frankfurt am Main and Leipzig, 1736.

————. *Theologia naturalis methodo scientifica pertractata. Pars prior, integrum systema complectens qua existentia et attributa Dei a posteriori demonstrantur.* New ed. Frankfurt am Main and Leipzig, 1739. *Pars posterior, qua existentia et attributa Dei ex notionis entis perfectissimi et naturae animae demonstrantur.* 2d ed. Frankfurt am Main and Leipzig, 1741.

* Xenophon. *Quae extant opera.* Edited by H. Stephanus. 2d ed. [Geneva], 1581.
* ———. *Anabasis: De expeditione Cyri minoris: Feldzug nach Oberasien.* Edited by F. H. Bothe with a Greek-German index. 2d ed. Leipzig, 1818.

† *Zend-Avesta, Zoroasters lebendiges Wort, worin die Lehren und Meinungen dieses Gesetzgebers von Gott, Welt, Natur, Menschen; ingleichen Ceremonien des heiligen Dienstes der Parsen usf. aufbehalten sind.* [Translated and edited by J. F. Kleuker] from the French edition of Anquetil du Perron. 5 vols. Riga, 1776–1783. (= *Zend-Avesta,* ed. Kleuker)

The Zend-Avesta. Sacred Books of the East, 3 vols. Oxford, 1880, 1883, 1887. [= *Zend-Avesta* (SBE)]

GLOSSARY

The glossary contains a selection of frequently used and/or technical terms, especially those posing problems in translation. In its successively amended versions, it has served only as a guide, to which the translators have not felt obliged to adhere when context or English idiom have required different renderings. When more than one English word is given, the generally preferred terms are listed first, while terms following a semicolon may be suitable in less technical contexts. "Cf." indicates related but distinguished German terms, which generally are translated by different English equivalents. Adjectives are listed without endings. This glossary is indexed only on German terms; the index serves partially as an English-German glossary.

German	*English*
absolut	absolute
Absolute	the absolute
allgemein	universal, general
Allgemeine	the universal
Andacht	devotion, worship
Anderssein	other-being, otherness
anerkennen	recognize, acknowledge (cf. "erkennen")
Anerkenntnis	recognition (cf. "Erkenntnis")

angemessen	suitable, appropriate, commensurate, fitting
anschauen	intuit, envisage
Anschauung	intuition, envisagement (cf. "Wahrnehmung")
an sich	in itself, implicit (cf. "in sich")
Ansich	in-itself, implicit being
Ansichsein	being-in-self
Anundfürsichsein	being-in-and-for-self
Arbeit	labor (cf. "Werk")
auffassen	comprehend, grasp (cf. "begreifen," "fassen")
Auffassung	comprehension
aufheben	sublate; transcend, supersede, annul
Aufhebung	sublation; transcendence, supersession, annulment
auflösen	resolve, dissolve
Auflösung	resolution
Bedeutung	meaning, significance (cf. "Sinn")
Begierde	desire, appetite
beglaubigen	verify, attest, confirm
Beglaubigung	verification, attestation
begreifen	conceive
Begreifen	conception, conceiving
Begriff	concept
bei sich	with self, present to self, at home
Beisichsein	presence with (to) self, self-communion, at home with self
beobachten	observe
Beobachtung	observation (cf. "Betrachtung")
Beschäftigung	occupation, concern
besonder	particular
Besonderheit	particularity
bestehen	subsist
Bestehen	subsistence

bestimmen	determine, define, characterize
bestimmt	determinate, definite
Bestimmtheit	determinateness, determinacy
Bestimmung	determination, definition; character(-istic, -ization), destination, vocation, specification
betrachten	consider, treat, deal with
Betrachtung	consideration, treatment (cf. "Beobachtung")
Bewusstsein	consciousness
beziehen	relate, connect
Beziehung	relation, connection, reference (cf. "Verhältnis," "Zusammenhang")
Bild	image
bildlich	imaginative, figurative
Bildung	culture, formation, cultivation
bloss	mere, simple, sheer
Boden	soil, ground, territory
Brahm	Brahman (ultimate reality)
Brahma	Brahmā (first member of the Hindu triad)
Brahman, Brahmine	Brāhman (member of the priestly caste)
darstellen	present, portray, set forth
Darstellung	presentation, portrayal, exposition (cf. "Vorstellung")
Dasein	determinate being, existence (cf. "Existenz," "Sein")
Denkbestimmung	category, thought-determination
denken	think
Denken	thinking, thought (cf. "Gedanke")
denkend	thinking, thoughtful
Einbildung	imagination (cf. "Phantasie")
Eine (der, das)	the (personal) One, the (neuter) One
einfach	simple

529

Einzelheit	singularity, single (or singular) individual (cf. "Individuum")
einzeln	single, singular
Einzelne	single individual (cf. "Individuum")
Element	element (cf. "Moment")
empfinden	sense
Empfindung	sensibility, sensation (cf. "Gefühl")
entäussern	divest, externalize
Entäusserung	divestment, externalization
Entfremdung	estrangement
entgegensetzen	oppose
Entgegensetzung	opposition
Entzweiung	cleavage, rupture, severance; cleaving, split
erheben	elevate, raise up
Erhebung	elevation, rising above
Erinnerung	recollection (cf. "Gedächtnis")
erkennen	cognize; recognize (cf. "anerkennen," "kennen")
Erkenntnis	cognition (cf. "Anerkenntnis," "Kenntnis," "Wissen")
erscheinen	appear (cf. "scheinen")
Erscheinung	appearance, phenomenon (cf. "Manifestation")
Erziehung	education
Existenz	existence (cf. "Dasein"—when the distinction is important, "Existenz" is given in square brackets)
existieren	exist (cf. "sein")
fassen, erfassen	grasp (cf. "auffassen," "begreifen")
Form	form (cf. "Gestalt")
für sich	for (by, of) itself, on its own account, explicit
Fürsich	for-itself
Fürsichsein	being-for-self, explicit being

Gebiet	field, realm
Gedächtnis	memory (cf. "Erinnerung")
Gedanke	thought, thoughts (cf. "Denken")
Gefühl	feeling (cf. "Empfindung")
Gegensatz	antithesis, contrast; antipathy, opposition (cf. "Entgegensetzung")
Gegenstand	object
gegenständlich	objective
Gegenwart	presence, present
Geist	spirit
Gemeinde	community
Gemüt	disposition; mind, soul, heart (cf. "Gesinnung")
Genuss	enjoyment, partaking, communion
geoffenbart	revealed (cf. "offenbar")
Geschichte	history; story (cf. "Historie")
geschichtlich	historical (often used as synonymous with "historisch")
Gesinnung	conviction, disposition
Gestalt	figure, shape
Gestaltung	configuration
Glaube	faith, belief
glauben	believe
Gleichgültigkeit	indifference
Gleichheit	equivalence
Glück	fortune
Glückseligkeit	bliss, happiness
Grund	ground, reasons
Grundlage	foundation
herabsetzen	degrade, reduce
hinausgehen	overpass, go beyond
Historie	history (cf. "Geschichte")
historisch	historical (often used as synonymous with "geschichtlich")
ideal, ideell	ideal

Idee	idea
Individuum	individual (cf. "Einzelne")
in sich	within itself, into self, inward, internal, self-contained (cf. "an sich")
jenseitig	otherworldly
Jenseits	the beyond, the other world
kennen	know (cf. "wissen")
Kenntnis	information, acquaintance (cf. "Erkenntnis," "Wissen")
Kraft	force, strength, energy (cf. "Macht")
Kultus	cultus
Lehre	teaching, doctrine
lehren	teach
Leidenschaft	passion
Macht	power (cf. "Kraft")
Manifestation	manifestation (cf. "Erscheinung")
Mannigfaltigkeit	manifold(ness)
Mensch	human being
Menschheit	humanity
mit sich	with self; integral
Moment	moment (cf. "Element")
Moral	morals
Moralität	morality (cf. "Sittlichkeit")
nachdenken	deliberate, meditate, ponder
Nachdenken	deliberation, meditation, meditative thought
Natur	nature
natürlich	natural
Natürliche	the natural
Natürlichkeit	natural life, natural state, naturalness; simplicity, unaffectedness
offenbar	revelatory, manifest (cf. "geoffenbart")
Offenbaren	revealing
Offenbarung	revelation
partikulär	private (cf. "besonder")

Phantasie	phantasy; fanciful imagination (cf. "Einbildung")
Positive	the positive, positivity
Räsonnement	argumentation, reasoning
realisieren	realize (cf. "verwirklichen")
Realität	reality (cf. "Wirklichkeit")
Recht	right
reflektiv	reflective
Reflexion	reflection
rein	pure
Sache	matter, subject matter; thing, fact, cause
Schein	semblance, show
scheinbar	seeming
scheinen	seem
schlechthinnig	utter, simple (cf. "absolut")
schliessen	conclude, infer
Schluss	syllogism, conclusion
Schmerz	anguish, sorrow; pain
seiend (part. and adj.)	having being, subsisting
Seiende(s)	actual being (God and cognates); a being, entity, subsisting being (finite objects)
sein (verb)	be: is (God and cognates); is, exists, occurs, etc. (finite objects)
Sein (noun)	being
setzen	posit
Setzen	positing
Sinn	sense, meaning (cf. "Bedeutung")
sinnlich	sensible, sentient, sensuous
Sinnlichkeit	sensuousness, sensible nature
sittlich	ethical
Sittlichkeit	ethics, ethical life, ethical realm (cf. "Moralität")
spekulativ	speculative
Spekulative	the speculative, speculation

533

Subjekt	subject
Subjektivität	subjectivity
substantiell	substantive, substantial
teilen	divide
Teilung	division, separation (cf. "Urteil")
trennen	separate
Trennung	separation
Trieb	drive, impulse, instinct
Übergang	transition, passing over
übergehen	pass over
übergreifen	overreach
überhaupt	generally, on the whole; altogether, after all, in fact, etc.
Überzeugung	conviction
umfassen	embrace, contain
unangemessen	incongruous, unsuitable, inadequate, incommensurate
Unglück	misery, unhappiness
unmittelbar	immediate (cf. "unvermittelt")
Unmittelbarkeit	immediacy
unterscheiden (verb)	distinguish, differentiate
Unterscheidung	differentiation, distinction (cf. "Unterschied")
Unterschied	distinction (cf. "Unterscheidung")
unterschieden (past part. and adj.)	distinguished, differentiated (part.); distinct, different (adj., cf. "verschieden")
unvermittelt	unmediated (cf. "unmittelbar")
Urteil	judgment, primal division (cf. "Teilung")
urteilen	judge, divide
Vereinzelung	singularization
sich verhalten	comport oneself, relate oneself
Verhalten	attitude, comportment
Verhältnis	relationship, relation (cf. "Beziehung," "Zusammenhang")

Verhältnisse (pl.)	conditions, circumstances, state of affairs
vermitteln	mediate
Vermittlung	mediation
Vernunft	reason
vernünftig	rational
verschieden (adj.)	different, distinct (cf. "unterschieden")
Verschiedenheit	difference, diversity
versöhnen	reconcile
Versöhnung	reconciliation
Verstand	understanding
verwirklichen	actualize (cf. "realisieren")
Verwirklichung	actualization (cf. "Wirklichkeit")
vollendet	consummate; perfect, complete, final
Vollendung	consummation
vorhanden	present, at hand, extant
vorhanden sein	be present, be at hand, exist (cf. "sein")
vorstellen	represent; imagine
vorstellend	representational, representative
Vorstellung	representation; image, imagination, view, notion
wahr	true
Wahre	the true
wahrhaft(ig)	true, genuine, authentic
Wahrheit	truth
Wahrnehmung	(sense) perception (cf. "Anschauung")
Werk	work (cf. "Arbeit")
Wesen	essence; being
Widerspruch	contradiction
Willkür	caprice, arbitrariness; free choice, free will
wirklich	actual
Wirklichkeit	actuality (cf. "Realität")

wissen	know (cf. "kennen")
Wissen	knowledge, knowing (cf. "Erkenntnis," "Kenntnis")
Wissenschaft	science, scientific knowledge
Zeugnis	witness, testimony
Zufall	chance
Zufälligkeit	contingency
Zusammenhang	connection, connectedness, nexus, coherence (cf. "Beziehung," "Verhältnis")
Zweck	purpose; end, goal, aim
zweckmässig	purposeful, expedient
Zweckmässigkeit	purposiveness, expediency

INDEX

BIBLICAL REFERENCES

The following index includes not only texts cited by Hegel himself but also those to which he alludes, directly or indirectly. Synoptic parallels are generally not given but only the passages cited by Hegel or closest to his formulation.

INDEX